Comparative Economics

Jahangir Amuzegar (Ph.D., Economics, University of California, Los Angeles) has been Executive Director of the International Monetary Fund since 1973. For the past five years, he has also been Distinguished Adjunct Professor at the American University and is now a Professorial Lecturer at the School of Advanced International Studies, Johns Hopkins University. The author's extensive writing in the field of economics includes several books and numerous articles on foreign trade and foreign aid, North–South relations, OPEC, and economic development.

Comparative Economics
National Priorities, Policies, and Performance

Jahangir Amuzegar

Little, Brown and Company
Boston   *Toronto*

Library of Congress Cataloging in Publication Data

Amuzegar, Jahangir.
  Comparative economics.

  Includes bibliographies and index.
  1. Comparative economics. 2. Economic policy.
I. Title.
HB90.A48   338.9   80-21976
ISBN 0-316-038016

Production Editor: Clive Martin

Cover design: Dianne Schaefer

Library of Congress Catalog Card No. 80-21976

ISBN 0-316-038016

9 8 7 6 5 4 3 2

HAL
Published simultaneously in Canada
by Little, Brown & Company (Canada) Limited

Printed in the United States of America

Contents

PART FIVE: THE TASK OF COMPARISON

Preface

HOW HUMAN SOCIETIES fulfill the thousand-and-one desires of their members has long intrigued prophets, philosophers, political revolutionaries, social reformers, and political economists. Their findings are the story of economic systems in theory and practice—comparative economics. Some knowledge of world economic systems is vital for a better understanding of behavior, organization, and decisions of nations in an interdependent world, decisions that increasingly affect global peace, prosperity, and progress.

The study of comparative economics is useful and essential for several reasons. First, since economics as a social discipline has to do with national, political, and social considerations, a study of different economies can explain how noneconomic factors determine or influence each society's collective solutions to basic economic problems. Second, by relating the main body of abstract economic principles to the realities of world politics and world business, comparative economic analysis can broaden one's mind toward major international economic issues of the day and modify attitudes toward economic approaches different from one's own. Third, the study of various decision making mechanisms in different countries provides a rational basis for measuring and evaluating economic performance in each country. Finally, it is partly through the comparative examination of various national organizations that the essentially relevant, empirical, and humanistic aspects of international economic relations can be understood and appreciated.

This text is written primarily for university students and readers interested in the nature of economic problem solving in the modern world. The structure and methodology of this text differ somewhat from others in the field. Some texts select the structure and performance of a few major countries in order to illustrate the traditional capitalist, socialist, and communist trilogy. Others focus their major attention on the theoretical and ideological aspects of rival "systems" with scant regard to their application in actual world economies. Still others tend to describe the functioning of certain select countries at the expense of a generalized analytical framework. This book attempts to combine these different traditional treatments

xi

into an integral approach by providing the reader with certain basic tools to analyze the principles of economic problem solving in the real world, and to apply these principles to real world economies.

The focal point of this approach is that an economic organization or system consists of two basic elements: a set of goals that determines its political or ideological direction, and a combination of means designed to obtain these goals. The logical basis for comparing national economies or "economic systems" would thus relate to the kind of national agenda, its qualities and priorities, and the type of processes and mechanisms employed to achieve those objectives.

The conceptual part of this book deals with five principal mechanisms of decision making. The descriptive segment takes up the application of these mechanisms in relation to a select number of countries. The choice of mechanisms and the selection of countries is made solely for their comparative significance: no mechanism and no country is favored or disfavored. The evaluation of each mechanism's strengths and weaknesses, and the appraisal of each country's performance, too, are made from a position of political neutrality: no attempt is made to show that a given national response to certain economic problems is intrinsically better or worse than another.

Comparative Economics is not a book on *economic geography*, dealing with population, natural resources, and physical characteristics of different economies. Nor is it a text on *economic history*, concerned with the historical dynamics of economic institutions in each country. The descriptive materials drawn from the experiences of selected countries are meant merely to show comparable *examples* of decision making techniques, and not a comprehensive account of each country's political, economic, and social institutions. Readers interested in a more detailed picture will find ample references to original source materials in the footnotes and suggested additional readings.

Much of the factual and descriptive materials in the country chapters, while presently up-to-date, should be regarded as only analytically illustrative and not necessarily permanent features of the economy under discussion. National agencies, statutes, and conditions are changing all the time, and specific descriptions are bound to be quickly outdated. The factual materials are included in the text chiefly for their relevance in inter-country comparisons, and not for their own exclusive significance. The reader's attention should thus focus on the essential differences or similarities in national response to economic problems, rather than on institutional details which are not crucial to a comparison.

The text is divided into five parts. Part One presents the political and ideological bases of economic organizations, the nature of basic economic problems, and the need for organization. Part Two deals with economic issues and social values, providing the framework of national economic objectives, and the similarities and differences of such national agenda. Part Three discusses socioeconomic strategies and tactics used in the management of a modern economy, emphasizing the relevant assumptions, institutions, and techniques of decision making. Part Four is devoted to an examination of the relative significance of each decision making process in a number of contemporary nation-states in the Western democracies, the Eastern bloc, and the Third World. Part Five takes on the task of evaluation, offering some glimpses into the performance of various economies within the context of certain common objectives.

Part One

THE TASK OF IDENTIFICATION

AN ECONOMIC SYSTEM is essentially a social organization or scheme for solving society's basic economic problems. In a nation composed of myriad individuals, each with his own needs, wishes, skills, and motivations, the production and exchange of goods and services require a social *organization* to ensure the provision of the right goods at the right time in the right place for the right people. The predominant tasks of such an organization are to determine society's economic goals, establish priorities among these goals, and devise appropriate strategies for achieving them.

A human society may consist of castaways on a tropical island, a small city-state, a viable nation, or the entire world community. The content and character of human societies may be influenced by material resources, methods of production and exchange, religious customs, business laws, socioeconomic institutions, and political ideologies. Yet the *basic* economic challenge faced by all communities, regardless of their sociopolitical order, is essentially the same: how to satisfy too many mouths chasing after too few mouthfuls.

Some societies may give top priority to maximum individual freedoms in the choice of employment and the disposition of income and savings. Others may emphasize social welfare programs, such as universal education, guaranteed health care, and security of income and employment. Still others may place high priority on military and political strength. Yet the basic necessity of a social *organization* remains the same for all: how to take stock of the nation's choices and goals, and how to mobilize the country's available resources in the service of achieving those goals.

Throughout history, the structure and functions of the social organization or system have been the subject of erudite treatises, as well as rabble-rousing tracts, but all observers remain committed to a single underlying issue: how to cope with dynamic socioeconomic relationships between a nation's priorities and the requirements for satisfying those objectives.

Chapter 1 attempts to show that the classification of economic systems on the basis of ideological labels oversimplifies comparative analysis and fails to identify real-world cases. Chapter 2 tries to buttress this argument by showing that the nature of *basic* economic problems and the necessity for economic organization largely defy political and ideological categorization.

1

Rhetoric and Reality
in
Comparative Analysis

CAPITALISM, SOCIALISM, COMMUNISM, and the myriad other isms that have filled man's history have all claimed to hold the key to a more rational social order and a better future for mankind. These secular religions, with their own deities, hierarchies, and rituals, have been both blindly accepted by the true believer and sacrilegiously attacked by the infidel. Depending on the preconceptions, prejudices, and passions of their advocates or opponents, these ideologies have been regarded as the repository of good, if not absolute truth, or the embodiment of evil, if not patent falsehood.[1]

While traditional doctrines still evoke strong emotional responses among the faithful and the unsophisticated, they have lost much of their force with political leaders and social reformers. Isms are now usually used to mobilize national and patriotic support for pragmatic political programs or as expedient party platforms for expelling in-groups.

Postwar literature on comparative economic systems has sufficiently exposed the abstract, conceptual, and normative nature of traditional isms, the models to which no real-life economy can be expected to correspond completely. The possibility of numerous combinations among distinctive features of alternative, supposedly rival, isms also has been amply demonstrated.[2] And while the debate on the virtues of capitalism, socialism, and communism still goes on in the popular press,[3] ideological passions in these debates are much more subdued, mostly because none of the traditional ideologies offers a monopoly on basic national objectives: economic growth, efficiency, or equity; none holds the key to full

1. Ideology is defined as a coordinated set of ideas or a form of sociopolitical philosophy that aspires both to explain social order and to change it. An ideology that ignores objective reality is a dogma; one that distorts reality is a fairy tale. Some ideologies do both.

2. In this extensive literature, the pioneering interdisciplinary work of Robert Dahl and Charles Lindblom, *Politics, Economics and Welfare,* (New York, Harper, 1953) deserves special mention. Our general approach takes its major cue from them.

3. See, for example, "Can Capitalism Survive", Time, July 14 1975, and "Social-ism's Trials and Errors," *Time*, March 13 1978.

3

employment, price stability, or environmental safety. All systems and isms are still groping for the hidden path to prosperity and progress.

The Polemic in Microcosm

To the eighteenth-century French Physiocrats,[4] to Adam Smith, and even to Karl Marx, a laissez-faire regime was the source of expending wealth and the backbone of technological progress. To Smith, who never used the term capitalism, it was a system of natural order and harmony under which society's progress toward real wealth and greatness could be accelerated, and the real value of the annual produce of its land and labor increased. It was a system of no preferences and no restraints, a system under which the people's industry was directed toward employment most suitable to the interest of society.

Marx, too, admitted that pre-Marxian capitalism, the first economic system to harness man's activity, had played a most revolutionary role in history, accomplishing wonders far surpassing those of Egypt and Rome. It had given a cosmopolitan character to production and consumption in every country, drawn all nations into civilization, rescued a considerable part of the population from the idiocy of rural life, and, in a hundred years, created more massive and more colossal productive forces than all preceding generations together.

To the present-day economic conservative, capitalism still is all these things and much more: it is a *natural* order, a system based on individual rights, self-reliance, and private initiative blessed by efficiency and good service under which economic justice can be won by free men and women through free enterprise. To these contemporary advocates, capitalism is a system of order without stability, and security without status.

To the ideologues of the Soviet Union, Communist China, and Eastern Europe, the capitalist image is not so haloed, nor do modern-day "liberals" regard capitalism as the best of all possible worlds. Among the two-thirds of the world population who comprise the bulk of the less-developed nations, *capitalism* is often a nasty word, epitomizing unjust exploitation of the poor by the rich, unfair distribution of income and opportunity, prolonged and wasteful unemployment, lack of economic security, internal strife, alienation, and wars.

Pope Paul VI's celebrated encyclical of April 1967, *Populorum Progressio,* "On People's Development," referred to capitalism as a "woeful system" that "considers profit as the key motive for economic progress, competition as the supreme law of economics, and private ownership of the means of production as an

---

4. A group of political economists who believed in the supremacy of natural order and the necessity for the state not to interfere with the natural laws that affect social and economic relationships.

absolute right that has no limits and carries no corresponding social obligations." This brand of capitalism, in the pope's view, had been "the source of excessive sufferings, injustices, and fratricidal conflicts."

The polemic, to be sure, is not limited to capitalism. Other doctrines share a similar fate. The early utopian socialists advocated a system of voluntary communal ownership of productive means, fraternal cooperation in productive enterprise, and unselfish income sharing among co-workers. The latter-day British Fabians regarded socialism as symbolizing social justice, political freedom, and democratic process.[5] To some of the emerging peoples of the less-developed world, socialism is equated with social equality, peaceful coexistence, and the possibility of planning and ensuring higher rates of growth.[6] The West's conservatives, however, equate socialism with paternalism, big government, welfare handouts, deficit spending, negative income tax, and the absence of work ethics.

Even in its simplest and purely formalistic definition—public ownership and operation of major means of production—the term *socialism* is today an ambiguous concept. In its broader and more philosophical sense of equality, love, brotherhood, and cooperation, it is even vaguer. Marx derided pre-Marxian socialism as utopian and nonsensical in order to claim "scientific" respectability for his own. Post-Marxian socialists, on the other hand, came to the conclusion that their only means of success, if not survival, was to abandon Marxist dogma once and for all. Vilfredo Pareto and Enrico Barone, Italian political economists who were by no means socialist sympathizers, are now considered the first ideological thinkers to put forth a "pure theory" of a socialist economy. Joseph Schumpeter, a highly respected champion of economic liberalism with the highest regard for capitalistic achievements, argued that capitalism was faltering and socialism was on the march.

A similar controversy surrounds communism. To its admirers, communism still means a nirvana where all production is concentrated in the hands of the whole nation, thus putting an end to class antagonism and making the state (as the protector of the interests of the propertied class) totally unnecessary.[7] In such a society, each man is presumed voluntarily to forego the fruits of his ability in order to meet the needs of others, so that the free development of each becomes the condition for the free development of all.

To its detractors, including an articulate group of disenchanted ex-followers (France's "New Philosophers"), communism symbolizes the evils of one-party rule, a censored press, and limits on political association. It reflects thought controls,

5. A British Labour prime minister called it "a society based on cooperation instead of competition."

6. Senegal's President Senghor defines socialism as "the rational organization of human society according to the most scientific, the most modern, and the most efficient methods."

7. Jean Paul Sartre, the prince of existentialism, has called Marxism, "the unsurpassable philosophy of our time."

dogmatic conformity, subordination of individuals to the state—in short, a monstrous "reactionary machine," an inherently evil ideology.

Evolution of a System: A Related Controversy

Adam Smith was essentially interested in the evolution of human societies through the interactions of men and social institutions. At the root of Smith's analysis lies the fundamental relationships between individual human behavior and the national interest. To Smith and his disciples, economic relations are essentially *natural* and harmonious; they are led by an "invisible hand" toward a state of equilibrium. If only the incompetence of the government and the "clamorous importunity of vested interests" could be kept in check—and people allowed to pursue their own selfish interests—the inexorable logic of the system would see to it that the search for personal satisfaction would benefit society as a whole. (See chapter 2.)

Marx and his followers saw economic relations as essentially conflicting: capitalists exploiting workers; propertyless masses opposed to the propertied class; rulers against rank and file. In the Marxist view, economic actions have a tendency toward disequilibrium, with periodic crises of booms and depressions, inflation and unemployment. Marxists also see the prevailing nature of an economic system not as a matter of natural creation or of choice, but rather as a reflection of the stage of economic development. In Marxian thought, a country's economic system at any juncture in history is determined by its position in the process of evolution from a primitive to a mature society. To Marx, economic systems—like other national, political, social, and cultural organizations—follow the existing processes of production and exchange. These processes, in turn, are supposed to follow the dictates of "dialectic materialism," according to which each stage of economic development gives rise to a newer and better system until perfection is reached.

This "inexorable" social-historical process of evolution presumably started with *primitive communism*, an essentially classless society, poor and stagnant, with no legally protected property ownership and with production based on individual or family self-sufficiency at or near a subsistence level. Lured by the possibilities of increased production through specialization and exchange, self-sufficiency gradually gave way to slavery and *feudalism*, where the predominant means of production (land and human labor) became the legal property of a privileged class and the masses of slaves or serfs were without both freedom and property. The rising significance of machinery and equipment as major instruments of modern agriculture and industrial production, and the use of capital in commercial and financial transactions, led to *capitalism*. The capitalist stage of development, in Marx's historical perspective, is characterized by an uneasy coexistence of two groups with opposing economic interests: a propertied class of owner-employers and a propertyless class of free but still dispossessed workers.

This fundamental class conflict would, in Marx's view, eventually lead to revolution by the desperate workers and to the establishment of socialism. Under socialism, private ownership of productive factors ceases to exist, and class conflicts begin to fade away. In this stage of economic development, the "dictatorship of the proletariat" has the difficult task of eradicating all economic and behavioral vestiges of capitalism, changing socioeconomic institutions from a superfluous pursuit of profit to an essential search for real prosperity, and altering man's inner motive from competitive acquisition to cooperation.

Full communism is the final stage of Marx's dialectics. To him, it is the final, the most perfect, the most moral, and the most aesthetic economic system, for there are no antagonistic classes, no oppressive state, no exploitation of man by man. Instead, there is material plenty, harmonious social relationships, and opportunity for self-expression, creativity, and cooperation.[8]

In between Smith's naturalism and Marx's determinism are the rationalists, who consider the adoption of socioeconomic objectives and the processes of resource allocation and income distribution a matter of *rational* choice. Economic organizations are selected, modified, combined, and changed not according to any predetermined natural law or historical sequence, but as a consequence of convergence or divergence of political and economic realities at any juncture in history. In this rationalist view, the choice of an economic system is, in most instances, a matter of pragmatism and convenience. Thus, an economic system consists of a set of basic goals, institutions, and policies that govern the production, distribution, and use of goods and services. These arrangements cut across stages of economic growth: different countries at a similar stage of economic development may show substantial variance in the choice of their economic organization. The rationalists admit that every economic system is invariably *influenced* by the physical environment: size, population, topography, location, and resource endowment. They agree that sociocultural forces, such as traditions, religion, and ideology, play important parts. They also believe that the level of economic development (industrialism, urbanization, and technological progress) are influencing factors. But these forces, they maintain, do not *determine* the character and content of an economic system in the sense that a direct causal relationship can be established between them. In other words, no immutable relationship can be found between, say, physical environment and economic institutions. The nature of the organizational mix is, for all practical purposes, a question of actions, reactions, and interactions by individuals and groups in a society.

8. Dialectic materialism, holding the view that all mental processes evolve from material ones, is thus directly opposed also to "idealism," which asserts that reality exists only through ideas and only as spirit or consciousness.

Liberalism vs. Conservatism:
The Democratic Squabble

Within the countries that reject both communism and socialism as an ideological label, philosophical divergence revolves around the choice bewteen *liberalism* and *conservatism*. Conservatives, generically and historically speaking, favor the status quo, while liberals, by implication, are for change and innovation. The eighteenth century liberals viewed the largely oligarchic government of their time as a threat to the freedom and innovative spirit of the people; they abhorred state shackles on the movement of goods and people, and resented government intrusion in the economy; they were the original anti-establishmentarians, emphasizing diffusion of power and greater individual freedom through less government. The opposing conservatives, on the other hand, regarded the state as a source of affirmative action not only in the area of national progress and prosperity but also as a protector of the interests of the poor and the powerless.

With the passage of time, the coming of universal suffrage and of popular participation in the democratic process, the rise of private industrial interests, and the spread of a propertyless urban working class, the old positions reversed themselves. As the goals of individual assertiveness, self-improvement, self-expression and economic security became increasingly dependent on the decision and actions of many "towering centers of power," the government became called upon to protect the individual against the injustice and excesses of private interest groups. Thus those who regarded the state as stifling individual ingenuity and imaginative capacity formulated the demand that government work on behalf of the individual in order to automatically assure him of his rights. So while the common goal still remained that of individual freedom, happiness and prosperity, the image of government drastically changed. The focus changed, from the issue of change against the *status quo*, to that of the relationship between the state and the individual.

Contemporary liberals insist that they are as committed to individual freedom, to the rule of law, and even to the free market, as any staunch conservative. But they do not see the contemporary market as perfect, nor even as efficient or self-equilibrating. They are ready to invoke the power of government to redress the market's rigidities, distortions and failures. They do not feel that an enhancement of the state's role in society necessarily comes at the expense of individual freedom or dignity, but often that it guarantees and complements individual liberty and equality of opportunity. They consider the government as a bulwark against unjust discrimination, private greed, concentration of industrial power, infringements on workers' rights and impositions on farmers' security. The freedoms that are supposedly abridged by the state are in their views the freedoms to exploit workers, to cheat customers and investors, to squeeze suppliers, to waste natural resources. They look to the government as a valuable instrument of democracy, a vehicle for public idealism, a functional necessity for meeting public demands.

Contemporary conservatives, as the liberals see them, are almost instinctively against government. They regard any government beyond the function of police as a major constraint on individual liberty and a destroyer of self-reliance; they believe that government is beset by inefficiency, waste, and corruption; is entangled in an abominable bureaucracy; stifles free enterprise with excessive regulation; becomes a burden and a menace to society; and is devoid of creativity for advancing the quality of life.[9]

Profound as the philosophical gulf between liberals and conservatives may seem in principle, the difference between their practical policies and programs are often a matter of degree rather than of kind. No contemporary liberal is indifferent to the need for basic human rights and individual liberties to be kept immune from state intrusion. And no contemporary conservative condones or supports unchecked abuses of economic power in a totally laissez-faire environment. The differences are frequently over the means to secure the same objectives. Curiously enough, government itself is not as much a center of controversy as are government beneficiaries and government benefactors. "Free-spirited" farmers in all Western democracies, for example, love government price supports, subsidies and low-cost credits; but they abhor government acreage allotment and export embargoes. Free enterprise businessmen everywhere detest government restrictions and regulations of their own activities, but do not object to stiffer measures on their rivals. Even conservative intellectuals do not seem to mind using public funds and public facilities. So the basic liberal-conservative disagreement is not over the fact of government *per se*, but over *which* government, on *whose* side, and in *what* direction.

Theoretical Systems and Traditional Features

Leading texts on comparative economic systems commonly identify capitalism with private property, the profit motive, private enterprise, and private direction of the economy. Socialism is defined in terms of social ownership of means of production, centralization of decision making and authority, and a substantial amount of public enterprise. Communism is viewed as a system of communal ownership, cooperative production, distribution according to need, and the absence of state as a coercive power. A closer look at these characteristics and their theoretical underpinnings show that each ism is based on certain *assumptions* regarding human nature, a set of politicoethical relationships between individuals and society, and a number of somewhat exclusive socioeconomic *institutions* and problem-solving *techniques*.

Capitalist ideology, for example, considers human nature individualistic;

9. For a succinct and lucid discussion of these issues see Arthur Schlesinger Jr., "Is Liberalism Dead?", *The New York Times Magazine*, March 30 1980.

self-centered, competitive, rational, and acquisitive men and women work to serve their own interests, and in the process, they serve the common interests. Under Marx's full communism, by contrast, people are regarded as essentially community oriented, unselfish, collaborative, and naturally productive regardless of material rewards. Democratic socialism (and particularly its Christian varieties), assumes that humankind is inherently egalitarian, cooperative, peace-loving, and good.[10]

In terms of individual-state relationships, classical capitalism idealizes consumers' sovereignty, diffusion of power, individual moral responsibility, and an intellectual capacity to provide for one's own economic livelihood, security, and self-development. Noncapitalist ideologies, such as post-medieval British mercantilism, place the power and the glory of the state over and above the freedom and welfare of individuals. Communism, in its transition to a programmatic, stateless, classless society, gives different priorities to private consumption and other consumer-oriented sectors. Democratic socialism recognizes the vitality of individual liberty and dignity, but harbors an ideological bias in favor of economic rights, balanced economic opportunity, and guaranteed economic security.

With respect to socioeconomic *institutions*, capitalism emphasizes the sanctity of private property rights, inviolability of profit motive in the benign pursuit of individual self-interest, and impersonal forces of the free market. Full communism renounces such institutions as private ownership, material incentives, and markets; it attempts to replace them with a situation where, in Marx's terminology, income is distributed "from each according to his ability, to each according to his need." Socialism is generally exemplified by the institutions of collective ownership, a mixture of pecuniary and nonmaterial incentives ("to each according to his labor"), and various degrees of reliance on the market.

In the choice of *techniques* of economic decision making, capitalism is synonymous with free private enterprise, absence of central direction, and a minimum of interference with the impersonal dicta of market forces. Full communism is identified with the free association of a classless work force in cooperative enterprise with no "exploitation" and therefore no need for the state to protect one class against the other. Socialism is pictured as leaning toward various degrees of state enterprise, central planning, and public regulations.

Comparison of Real-World Economies

The stark anachronism of these exclusive characteristics for classifying modern nation-states hardly needs elaboration. There is no country in the world today which, by virtue of certain exclusive tenets, can stand out as a representative of

---

10. Fascism and naziism regard people not as isolated, independent, individuals but as ethnocentric members of a social organism.

classical capitalism, democratic socialism, utopian communism, or other isms. The bases upon which world political economies have been traditionally identified with these isms (United States with capitalism, Soviet Union with communism, Scandinavian countries with socialism) are becoming increasingly nebulous.

In the real world, no national economy can now be classified as typically capitalist, that is, with no restriction on individual initiative, private property, profit motive, or market prices. Nor can any country be characterized as typically socialist or communist on the basis of state enterprise, national planning, or ownership of means of production. Becoming increasingly murky are also such ideological polarizations as the dignity of individual versus the glory of the state; the virtue of freedoms and initiative versus the safety and security of government paternalism; the precedence of unmet needs versus the claims of ability and luck; the right to private gains versus the obligation to share; the wisdom of the overseer versus the judgment of the overseen; the primacy of private gain versus public welfare.

The traits traditionally identified with one ism or another (individual freedoms with capitalism, security with socialism) are now professed by avowedly competing nations. In the race for political and economic survival and supremacy, the means historically associated with one ism or another (profit motive with capitalism, planning with communism) are now pragmatically combined in various measures by avowedly rival economies.

Several more realistic and meaningful substitutes to this ideological taxonomy exist. One approach focuses on the mechanism of economic coordination, on the characteristic aspects of decision making by tradition, by the market, or by central planning. It seeks to identify world economies by the overriding significance of a given decision-making mechanism in the system. The United States, for example, is identified as the prototype of an "imperfectly competitive market system." France, Sweden, and Japan are classified as "planned market economies." The Soviet Union and China are categorized as "centralized command systems."[11] The difficulty with this essentially realistic approach is somewhat similar to that of classification by ideologies: it tries to fit large amorphous objects into small square boxes. The need still is for comparisons in terms of various *mixtures* of decision-making mechanisms, instead of one single important one.

The approach adopted in this book is to compare world economies on the basis of national priorities, the mechanisms they use to achieve these objectives, and their success in this endeavor. In each of these areas, similarities and differences may be found to transcend ideological or systemic identifications. Capitalist and noncapitalist countries may, for example, share many common objectives, such as faster growth and higher standard of living. Communist and noncommunist countries may have many similar institutions, such as private markets, modern management techniques, and monetary incentives, as well as planning and public

11. See Egon Neuberger and William Duffy, *Comparative Economic Systems: A Decision-Making Approach* (Boston: Allyn and Bacon, 1976), chapters 9 and 11.

enterprise. Success in achieving specific goals may relate to no specific ideology or choice of policy instrument; the goals of full employment, growth, or equitable income distribution may be attainable by a combination of techniques that are a monopoly of no ideology or ism. Above all, countries with similar goals and similar means may end up having different rates of performance, unrelated to their choice of ideology.

To set the stage for a comparison of contemporary nation-states in terms of national economic goals, the mechanisms chosen for attaining these goals, and the extent of success in matching means and ends, a brief digression on the nature of basic economic problems and the requirements of their solution will be helpful.

Suggestions for Additional Readings

ARON, R. *The Opium of the Intellectuals*. New York: Greenwood House, 1977.

BELL, D. *The Cultural Contradiction of Capitalism*. New York: Basic Books, 1976.

CROSLAND, A. *The Future of Socialism*. Westport: Greenwood Press, 1977.

CUTLER, A. ET AL. *Marx's Capital and Capitalism Today, Parts 1 and 2*. London: Routledge, 1977 and 1978.

DESAI, M. *Marxian Economics*. Totowa: Rowman, 1979.

FREEDMAN, R., ED. *Marx on Economics*. New York: Harcourt Brace, 1961.

FRIEDMAN, M. *Capitalism and Freedom*. Chicago: Chicago University Press, 1962.

HALM, G. N. *Economic Systems: A Comparative Analysis*. New York: Holt, 1968.

HEILBRONER, R. L. *Marxism: For and Against*. New York: Norton, 1980.

KRISTOL, I. *Two Cheers for Capitalism*. New York: Basic Books, 1978.

LENIN, V. I. *State and Revolution*. New York: International Publishers, 1932.

LEVY, B. H. *Barbarism with a Human Face*. New York: Harper, 1979.

LINDBECK, A. *The Political Economy of the New Left*. New York: Harper, 1977.

LUARD, E. *Socialism without the State*. New York: St. Martin's, 1979.

MANDEL, E. *Marxist Economic Theory*. New York: Monthly Review, 1969.

NOZICK, R. *Anarchy, State and Utopia*. New York: Basic Books, 1974.

O'BRIEN, D. P. *The Classical Economists*. New York: Oxford University Press, 1979.

PRYBYLA, J. S., ED. *Comparative Economic Systems*. New York: Irvington, 1969.

ROBINSON, J. *An Essay on Marxian Economics*. New York: St. Martin's, 1966.

SCHUMPETER, J. A. *Capitalism, Socialism and Democracy*. London, Allen & Unwin, 1972.

SHONFIELD, A. *Modern Capitalism: The Changing Balance of Public and Private Power*. New York: Oxford University Press, 1969.

SILK, L. *Capitalism: The Moving Target*. New York: New York Times Book Co., 1974.

SIMON. W. E. *A Time for Truth*. New York: McGraw-Hill, 1978.

STEINFELS, P. *Neoconservatism*. New York: Simon and Schuster, 1979.

WARD, B. N. *The Socialist Economy: A Study of Organizational Alternatives*. New York: Random House, 1967.

WILES, P. J. D. *The Political Economy of Communism*. Oxford: Basil Blackwell, 1962.

WOLFSON, M. *A Reappraisal of Marxian Economics*. New York: Columbia University Press, 1966.

2

Economic Problems and Social Organization

ECONOMICS CAN BE DEFINED as the study of how a human society manages to satisfy its various needs out of resources at its disposal.[1] As a social science dealing with people and society, economics is related to other social disciplines. Psychology gives economics its assumptions regarding human motivation, attitudes, and behavior. Political science and ethics underline the climate in which national economic goals are established and altered. Sociology explains the social environment in which changes in political and moral values affect socioeconomic institutions and administrative techniques. And so forth.

The subject matter of economics is the satisfaction of human wants (food, clothing, shelter, recreation, leisure, or time for meditation). Wants may be biological or psychological, real or fancied. Economists usually try to keep clear of philosophical distinctions between wants, needs, wishes, or whims; they are concerned simply with the things people are after. Whether or not people should be after these things is not their concern.[2]

The task of satisfying human wants is restrained by nature's niggardliness. Economists call this *scarcity*. Scarcity means there is not enough of everything to go around for everyone to have as much as one wishes to have without somehow paying for it. In shorthand, there is no such thing as a free lunch. The almost limitless scope of human imagination in the face of scarce resources and limited technological knowledge introduces the essential core of economics: the necessity of *choice*. People seldom have everything they want. They have to give up something in order to get other things. What is true of an individual or a household is equally true of a community or a nation. The quantity of goods and services that a society can

---

1. The reader who is too familiar with the discussion in this chapter can skip it and go directly to chapter 3.
2. This description of economics as a "value-free" science is not unanimously accepted. Many dissenters, economists and noneconomists, argue that any attempt to avoid moral judgment in social analyses is erroneous and impractical. They believe that economists do and should make value judgments; that in fact it is their professional duty to recommend specific policies. But this itself is perhaps also a value judgment.

produce at any given time depends on the quantity and quality of its resources, its capacity for resource mobilization, and the prevailing technology. No society can totally satisfy its members out of the limited resources at its disposal.

Economic principles or laws (diminishing returns, opportunity costs, diminishing marginal utility, supply and demand, comparative advantage, and so on) try to relate scarce economic resources to the seemingly limitless human expectations. These laws are partly formalized truisms, partly statements of empirical real-life phenomena, and partly general propositions based on observed human choice. Since human choice cannot always or precisely be controlled by social forces, economic principles on the whole lack the relatively high precision of more exact sciences such as astronomy or physics. But they are nevertheless useful tools to interrelate economic variables and to determine the cause-and-effect links among those variables. Any discussion of an economic system must, therefore, begin with a review of these variables and their relationships.

Basic Economic Problems

Economic problems, based on the imperatives of scarcity and the necessity of choice, can be conveniently divided into two categories: satisfaction of current wants and provision for the future.

The satisfaction of current wants generally involves three distinct, but interrelated decisions. First, the decision as to *what* to produce, for it is not possible to produce everything. Among the items selected to be produced, how much of one should be sacrificed for the attainment of others (how much bread and how many circuses—since neither can be produced *ad infinitum*).

Once this is decided upon, the second decision would be *how* to produce? By what processes or techniques? By which combination of available factors? This problem arises because most people's wants or needs can be produced in a number of different ways by different *combinations* of resources. Bread can be baked in brick or cast-iron ovens; circuses can offer a variety of animals, midgets, and clowns; steel can be produced by electric or coal furnaces. The four traditional (and generalized) factors of production—natural resources, human labor, capital, and entrepreneurship—can be combined in different proportions in order to produce the same quantity of a product or service. Production techniques rationally follow the dictates of domestic resources endowment: in the capital-intensive economy of California, rice fields are planted from the air by low-flying planes; in the labor-intensive economies of Southeast Asia, rice grains are sown on the ground by hand.[3]

The third decision relates to income distribution: *for whom* to produce? How to divide the national product? An aristocratic or a feudal society would naturally

3. Resource allocation does not always follow the rationality or efficiency criterion. Military, political, or prestige considerations, for example, may override efficiency considera-

have a different distribution pattern than an egalitarian or a rural community. A developing country bent on rapid economic development would have a different distribution scheme than a developed, mature, affluent nation. The choice of alternative distribution patterns depends upon the nature of national objectives and social-welfare considerations.

Provision for future wants is the second basic economic problem. Every society is interested in survival, if not growth. Both of these goals require setting aside part of current production for future use—for two reasons. First, resources, no matter how abundant, are eventually exhaustible. Iron and coal and oil and watersheds do not last forever; they have to be replaced and renewed. Machines, equipment, buildings, and facilities also wear out; they have to be repaired, renovated, or changed. The second imperative is population growth. Unless resources are increased or better used, national standards of living will decline even with a stable population. And for the maintenance of the same standard of living, most societies must provide for their future needs if their population happens to be on the rise.

A society interested in progress and growth has a much stronger reason to make special provision for its future. Such provision requires diverting resources from the production of consumer goods to capital investment and expanding productive capacity. In other words, some current consumption must be sacrificed in favor of increased future production. This sacrifice may take the simple form of "conservation" (abstaining from wasteful use), or it may involve more sophisticated acts of saving and investment.

At the core of economic growth lies an increase in productive investment. Gross investment is simply the maintenance of society's stock, taking care of the wear and tear. Net investment may be defined as an increase in a nation's wealth or an increase in the nation's physical or technological capacity for producing wealth. An expansion of wealth-producing facilities—bigger plants, more sophisticated equipment, more skilled workers, better-trained managers—is necessary for greater production. Productive capacity expansion requires investment. Such investment requires savings, and saving is refraining from present consumption.

Economic Interdependence and the Need for Organization

In a one-man economy (Robinson Crusoe's, for example), all economic decisions are made by one individual for his own well-being. There can be no conflicts of

---

tions on the choice of production techniques. Wheat is produced in Western Europe at much higher cost than that of imports from abroad. Beet sugar production in the United States costs American consumers much more than would cane sugar imports. The money-losing intercontinental airlines of many countries are another example of noneconomic resource allocation. In all these cases, other considerations take precedence over efficiency.

goals and no need for a decision-making *mechanism*. In larger communities where there are differences in personal talent, motivation, taste, and temperament, there is need for an arrangement to satisfy different individual wishes and to coordinate different individual efforts for that purpose. As the size of a society expands and its problems grow more complicated, the need for more sophisticated arrangements becomes more acute.

In an advanced society—characterized by specialization and division of labor—the daily convenience, improved livelihood, and indeed the very survival of individuals depend on the decisions and actions of millions of others. A scientist, for example, can spend his entire day in his laboratory without worrying about cooking his meals, making his own suits, fixing his house, or straightening his car's fender, because others will eagerly provide these goods and services for him as long as he is willing to pay for them. In such a society, every individual's satisfaction depends on the cooperation of others. Each individual's decisions, in turn, have repercussions on other individuals' moves and actions. Consequently, in order for the right goods to be produced by the right methods for the right people in the right time and place, there is need for a social *organization*. The main task of such an organization is to allocate scarce resources among competing uses and users within the framework of society's political, social, and other objectives.

How an economy is organized influences the solution of the basic economic problems of *what*, *how* and *for whom* to produce. A society where the ownership and control of means of production are diffused among a vast number of individuals, as in the United States, would obviously have a different production and distribution pattern than the one where major ownership and control of real capital are concentrated in the state's hands, as in the Soviet Union or China. Similarly, a society immersed in tradition, such as the South Pacific islands, and one that is essentially organized around vested interest groups under the state's aegis, as was pre-war Italy, would show a different development direction than those of present-day Cuba or modern Japan.

Social organization for rational allocation of factors of production requires three subordinate tasks: calculation, motivation, and coordination. Calculation involves analysis of costs and benefits of alternative goods and services through a comparison of foregone values (opportunity costs) and expected returns. Such a stock taking of values "used up" and values "created" involves the collection of cost-price data on the sources and uses of productive factors, the sorting and interpretation of data collected on the aggregate supply and demand, and a determination of the most profitable methods of obtaining an optimum gross national product (GNP) within the available technology.

Once such a cost-benefit determination is made, the second task of the social organization is the mobilization of resources for producing desired goods and services. Mobilization of resources requires motivation or incentives offered to resource owners in order to steer them toward the desired composition of GNP.

The third task, coordination, consists of the control of individual actions in such a way as to avoid duplication, friction, or waste. Every society must have a way of bringing together the economic activities of its economic actors—in such a manner that consumers meet their needs, workers find suitable jobs, resource owners receive appropriate incomes, business firms succeed in realizing expected returns, and entrepreneurs get access to investment outlets.

The achievement of these three tasks, in turn, necessitates the use of certain economic tools. Some of these tools, like money, prices, and markets, are not "system-oriented"; they are universally used in all social organizations regardless of national, political, or ideological orientation. Others, such as private enterprise, price control, central planning, or collective bargaining, have been traditionally identified as hallmarks of competing ideologies and systems.

The Nature and Role of Economic Tools

In all social organizations, the objective utility, or want-satisfying quality, of scarce goods and services must be quantified by a common denominator (price) so that people can make a subjective but rational choice among alternatives. In all modern systems, there must be a medium of exchange (money) to facilitate the myriad transactions among economic units. In all societies, there must be a legal framework within which the rights to property are defined. Every economic system needs enterprises or business firms (with entrepreneurs and business managers) to combine materials, labor, machines, and know-how to produce desired goods or services. Every economy must also possess an incentive structure to induce workers, resource owners, and production organizers to cooperate in productive business activity.

Prices, Money, and Markets

The exercise of choice, particularly a rational choice,[4] by any economic decision maker—an individual, a corporate entrepreneur, or a state planning commission—requires prior knowledge of the relative scarcity of goods, services, and productive factors. Relative scarcities are measured by values attached to available supplies. Prices are monetary coefficients of scarcity; they serve as a common denominator for economic choice making.

    4. An economic choice may be considered rational if its given objective (or output) is obtained by a *minimum* of efforts, time, or similar resource inputs. Rationality is often synonymously used for efficiency. The analogy is basically correct in a static situation, but in a dynamic world, the design of an economic action may be rational, but its outcome may fall short of maximum efficiency owing to unforeseen changes in the process of goal achievement. A nonrational design also may end up in windfall efficiency because of sheer luck. Rationality may be considered *ex ante* or planned efficiency. Efficiency, is, in a sense, *realized* rationality.

In a "market economy" (chapter 5), scarcities are as a rule reflected in relative price ratios, which are freely determined by the forces of supply and demand. In a "command economy" (chapter 8), relative prices are centrally determined; their main function is to ration goods and services among consumers and provide weights for aggregating enterprise output. Their allocative function is limited. Mixed economies, too, need to have relative values assigned to the means of production as well as to consumer items in order to regulate orderly distribution and use.

The necessity of pricing as a rationing device is one thing; the method of establishing prices is another. Pricing itself is ideologically neutral; it applies to all forms of a modern social organization. The "price mechanism" (which presupposes price ratios) refers to a particular method of price determination. Price ratios may be determined in a number of different ways: by tradition or by a central authority; through corporate administration or by collective bargaining; in a competitive or regulated market. The price (or market) mechanism, however, is a process by which prices are determined by the impersonal forces of the market—Adam Smith's "invisible hand." No advanced economy can do away with prices, but most countries may decide to downgrade, neglect, or altogether dispense with the *price mechanism*. By the same token, no exchange economy can function without money as a method of reflecting values, but each nation may choose different financial institutions or different monetary policies.

The *market* is basically a communicating device, a clearinghouse of information and actions for economic actors and units. It is an indispensable part of economic decision making. In a modern economy, organized around specialization and division of labor, a way must be found for facilitating exchange of goods and services among individuals—buying, selling, investing, or whatever. The need is for both a marketplace where actual transactions can take place, and an economic registry where changes in resource availability, consumer tastes, and technology can be recorded. The market as an institution meets both of these needs.

Physical markets are places where goods, services, commodities, or shares of stocks can actually be bought and sold. Markets may be free or controlled. Free markets are characterized by interplay of supply and demand; controlled markets may be identified by a variety of restrictions and regulations imposed on movements of goods and services, on prices charged, or on terms and conditions of market transactions. Depending on the extent of physical, economic, and political barriers to the movements of resources, markets may be purely local, regional, or national. There are also worldwide markets, as in the case of precious metals, basic commodities, some manufactured products, certain types of skilled labor, and currencies.

The market as a physical place for trade and barter should be distinguished from the *market system*. Markets for facilitating exchange between buyers and sellers are as old as human specialization and division of labor; they are universal. The *market system*, on the other hand, is of relatively recent origin, a subject of study and analysis by the classical economists of the eighteenth and nineteenth centuries.

It is a process by which the basic economic problems are solved by the free play of private decisions and actors (chapter 5).

Enterprise and Ownership

Economic activity for the solution of basic economic problems requires business *enterprise*. An enterprise is a systematic and purposeful undertaking that involves both management decisions and risk taking. The purpose of an enterprise may be to make profits, to fulfill prescribed production quotas, or to supply community needs in accordance with other objectives. The driving force may come from a shrewd investor or a lackluster bureaucrat, an intrepid gambler or a lucky dowager. The direction and management may be centralized or decentralized; it may be in the hands of the owner, a director, a private business committee, or a public commission.

The enterprise itself, depending on its nature, may be completely owned and run by private individuals or private groups; it may be totally owned and operated by the community; or it may present one of a hundred different mixtures of private and public ownership and operation. From a legal standpoint, an enterprise may take the form of a proprietorship; it may be one of various kinds of partnership; or it may be instituted in a host of different corporate forms or cooperatives.[5]

It should also be noted that in spite of significant theoretical distinctions between private and public enterprises, the practical differences between large private firms and public agencies in a modern economy are often not very substantial. In both cases, the internal organization is largely bureaucratic, and the objectives are often diversified. Major operational decisions or innovative actions are often made by committees. Management is rewarded by contractual salaries and not by residual profit. And survival often depends on external maneuvers as much as internal efficiency. On the whole, the larger the organization and the wider the gap between ownership and management, the greater are the similarities between the two categories.

Economic enterpise, in turn, is inescapably linked with ownership, a temporary or permanent claim on resources. Property ownership is one of mankind's oldest institutions. Property, in the broad economic sense, is an abstract sum of income-producing assets. Ownership consists of a bundle of legal claims on the lawful use and disposal of property. Property in this broad sense can be owned privately, jointly, communally, or by the whole nation. To understand the social

---

5. For these and other reasons, it would be futile to divide economic enterprise into such mutually exclusive designations as free and controlled, private and public, capitalist and noncapitalist. The true distinction between private and public enterprise should be sought not necessarily in their legal ownership but in their basic objectives, type of service, method of receiving appropriations, incentives for cost reduction, and so on.

significance of property, an important distinction must be made between the ownership rights attached to it and its allocative role in the exercise of that ownership.

In the legal and moral sense, property consists of the asset holder's ability to dispose of his possession in any way he wishes. This ownership ability can be infringed upon, drastically curtailed, or even totally abolished by the community. Private versus public ownership of property in this sense is a distribution issue, which indicates who benefits from the returns on assets. As a dynamic social lever, however, property plays a far more important role: it stimulates, directs, and coordinates economic enterprise. Return on property is an incentive for its creation and maintenance. Property's allocation function cannot be easily tampered with without far-reaching effects on the size of production.[6]

Entrepreneurs, Managers, and Bureaucrats

At the heart of individual or private enterprise stands the *entrepreneur*, the man with an original pioneering idea, an enterprising spirit, a risk-taking courage—in short, someone who often knows better than others what the market will bear.

In the postwar literature, sophisticated distinctions are made between entrepreneurs, managers, and bureaucrats. The *manager* is defined as an individual who oversees the operation of a going concern and tries to increase the firm's efficiency within the limits of known technology. The *entrepreneur*, on the other hand, has the task of locating new ideas and putting them into effect; he is never satisfied with routine practice, but must lead, inspire, and innovate. A *bureaucrat* is defined as an individual who tries to serve his bureau's intent and to maximize his own personal satisfaction (whether for more money or for public service) by following a routine and safe course of action to justify the bureau's existence and increased budget.

In reality, the distinctions between modern entrepreneurs, managers, and bureaucrats are not clear cut. In most cases, and at different times, one person may play a combined role. A modern corporate executive, for example, is usually expected to be an entrepreneur-manager; he often also finds it expedient to act as a fail-safe bureaucrat. In most cases, the prerequisites of survival and success in a business enterprise and a government bureau are the same: stamina, ambition, political skill, zeal to win, and a knack for turning defeat into triumph.

6. The ownership of property has in the past been used as a distinguishing feature of traditional isms, with private holdings characterizing capitalism, and public ownership symbolizing socialism and communism. One major reason for this categorization has been the tendency to regard the claim function of property as inseparable from its control function. Today, however, not only are these two functions often separated, but property ownership itself is subject to so many restrictions as to make the dichotomy between private and public increasingly less meaningful.

Incentives and Rewards

Underlying the success of business enterprise is its system of incentives, its rewards and penalties. It is the system that provides monetary and nonmonetary incentives and punishments, thereby affecting the actions and reactions of decision makers in their collaboration to produce desired goods and services. While the economic debate on what makes people work has not yet been settled, all agree on the necessity of human motivation and incentives for economic action. Thus, *wages* are commonly considered the monetary rewards for human effort; *rent*, a payment for the use of income-producing fixed assets; *interest*, a price for the use of capital; and (pure) *profit*, a prize for risks of entrepreneurship.

Of the four incentives mentioned above, wages paid for human labor are the most widely accepted as a reward for useful economic activity; as an incentive, they are the least controversial. The explanation is simple. If people are to submit to irksome taks or to a long and difficult process of learning, training, and preparation in order to perform certain functions, they ought to be motivated (compensated) somehow. Wages and salaries thus affect human decisions to work or not to work, how diligently to work, and how long.

Pure rent, payment for the use of land (unrelated to the investment, improvement, or upkeep of the land), is regarded as either a *profit* or *interest*. The similarity with profit is based on the belief that land is a gift of nature and in need of no economic reward, for its supply cannot be increased; the return to land is thus regarded as a monopoly profit based on legal ownership. The analogy with interest is rooted in the contention that land ownership is but one form of capital ownership. If capital itself should require an incentive for its accumulation and supply, so should land. Some economists regard pure rent as a surplus return to any factor that is fixed in supply; it is considered a return over and above what is necessary to keep a factor of production in its present use.

Disagreements concerning the nature and function of economic incentives arise with some intensity and frequency in regard to the payment of *interest* on capital. Economists (and noneconomists) still have not settled the issue of exactly why individuals must be paid a price for the use of their money. In capitalist societies the question seems easily answerable: savers expect to receive interest on their "abstinence." Banks pay interest to savers because they can lend these assets to prospective investors at still higher rates, making something extra for themselves. And investors are willing to pay interest on borrowed funds because they can put these assets to profitable uses. This money game explains the distributive and allocative functions of interest. Interest plays the double role of inducing individuals to refrain from consuming all of their income and allowing others to use their savings in exchange for a reward. It also helps allocate available savings (investable funds) among the most productive projects. If no interest were charged on borrowed capital, there would be no way of knowing *how long* a project should be allowed to go on before producing any return or where the cutoff should be in separating highly productive projects from white elephants. In noncapitalist societies, both roles of interest are somewhat muted, because scarcity of consumer goods may create a good deal of forced savings; the allocative function may or may not be allowed full sway.

The most complex and most controversial of the four income categories is *profit*. To its capitalist devotees, profit is both the kingpin and the backbone of investment, innovation, and economic progress. To its detractors, it is a symbol of exploitation, injustice, and business mischief. Is profit really an incentive, and if so, for what? The answers depend on what one means by profit. Profit is generally defined as total revenue minus total costs. Total costs, in turn, refer not only to the out-of-pocket outlays and business overheads, but to the opportunity cost, the values foregone. Normal profit is thus the opportunity cost of capital invested. Anything that exceeds normal profit is identified as pure or excess profit. Excess profit may arise from pure rent, a monopoly position, or sheer luck.

Much of the hostility toward profit making as an antisocial behavior stems from the misconception that profit is excessive, unnecessary, and unearned income. In reality, profit may be much more than a mere monopoly income. Economists generally define "economic," or "pure," profit in such a way as to exclude all implicit or imputed returns to productive resources. In economic terminology, pure profit excludes management salaries, interest paid or payable to owner-managers, and implicit returns to machinery or equipment. The term *profit* also theoretically excludes monopoly incomes or monopoly revenues attributable to market imperfections of one sort or another.

Economic, or pure, profit is thus a *residual* income under conditions of dynamic competition; it is what is left of the enterprise's revenue after total costs of production are taken into account. In the dynamic world, pure profit is generally attributed to *uncertainty*, defined as uninsurable risks. Some risks (fire, thefts, storms, or other acts of God) are actuarially insurable, and insurance premiums are part of the costs of production. Pure profit exists only because the outcome of a business venture is unpredictable and because there is no objective measure of the probability of gains or losses. Many economists and most businessmen argue that unless there is an adequate reward, people will not be sufficiently motivated to go into risky business ventures. Profit is the incentive that leads people to take such risks.[7]

Since there seems to be an observable link in Western free enterprise economies between the rate of profit and the businessman's willingness to invest in productive capacity, one must assume that the existence of alternative investment

---

7. There is, however, much debate as to whether risk taking needs to be rewarded at all, and if so, what the "adequate" rate of return should be. We know that people like to gamble, knowing full well that *as a group* they will come out losers. Thus, it is argued that if people are willing to bear gambling risks even when their final gains and losses will show a new negative balance, why should they have to ask for a positive reward in business risks where the balance is often positive?

opportunities promises different rates of return and that businessmen would not volunteer for any given risk-bearing prospect unless they were given a net positive incentive.

Assuming this to be true, the question remains: Who should get this net premium or surplus? The obvious answer is: Those who assume business risks. But who are these risk bearers? Stockholders? Managers? Suppliers of factors of production? Consumers? No simple answers are available. Everyone connected with a modern business enterprise seems to bear a part of its risks. Whether or not everyone also receives a commensurate share of *profit*, however, is not certain.

Pure profit is a phenomenon of a dynamic and/or imperfectly competitive world; it does not and cannot exist under conditons of static or perfectly competitive equilibrium (chapter 5). In a dynamic situation, the main function of profit is to serve as a guide to profitable investment in accord with social objectives. A related function of profit is to act as a controlling device for continuous adaptations of production to changing socioeconomic conditions. It works through reallocation of productive factors, adjustment to new processes, and meeting new demands. A third role, closely related to the two others, is to provide sufficient incentive for entrepreneurs to reduce costs, improve product, and introduce more efficient operational techniques. The level of profit serves as success indicator among alternative investment decisions. And its realization—when it is not the result of artificial scarcity or monopoly—can be presumed to increase real GNP. On the other hand, the absence of profit (loss) serves as a check or penalty on bad investment, inefficiency, and waste.

Economic Problems, Organization, and Decision Making Mechanisms

Earlier in this chapter, it was showed why a rational mobilization of resources in the service of desired production, distribution, and consumption requires an organization. Organization is considered necessary for the collection of information on factors of availability and scarcity, the provision of incentives for obtaining rational economic decisions; and the coordination of economic activities and enterprise so as to ensure efficiency and avoid resources waste.

The last section examined the economic tools commonly used to fulfill these tasks. The main functions of these elements, as was indicated, were to supply pertinent data to economic agents in order for them to make the right decisions, to offer incentives through which such decisions can mobilize resources for the production and distribution of the right goods and services, and to ensure appropriate changes in the decisions of various independent agents as times and conditions change so as to avoid prolonged shortages of wanted goods or surpluses of unwanted items.

We are now ready to discuss the alternative organizations or systems that are adopted by contemporary nations to handle the tasks of calculation, motivation, and coordination. Most economic analysts refer to three basic organizations or systems: tradition, the market, and command—corresponding to the prevailing situation in primitive societies, the Western industrialized nations, and the centrally directed economies. These categories are still rather restrictive and exclusionist. As later chapters will show, no country today relies exclusively on either tradition, the market, or command. As there are certain universal economic tools (money, price, enterprise, and incentives), so too are there certain common decision-making processes that defy ideological orientations.

In our analysis, all modern economies utilize some combinations of different economic organizations or systems. In all societies, traditions and customs play some role in the people's behavior and actions. In the so-called market-directed Western industrialized countries, selective public ownership and operation, government regulation, and various other state controls are used to counterbalance the deficiencies of the market. The centrally directed economies, too, in addition to allowing for a small interplay of market forces, make extensive use of other processes besides command.

From a wider angle, the processes and mechanisms of decision making may be regarded as ranging from the decentralized and market-directed process at the one end of a spectrum to the centralized and leaders-directed mechanism at the opposite end. The common denominator and the shared distinguishing feature of all these mechanisms is their loci of decision-making power. In other words, who is calling the shots and from what position? In this way of thinking, economic activity can be organized (and economic decisions can be made) by a *single* line of command, by a *few* chosen negotiators, by *many* elected representatives, or by *all* the economically active people through referenda or other means. There are many variations within each category.

Our study identifies and examines five alternative processes or mechanisms of decision making along the organizational spectrum: the market, democratic representation, group bargaining, command, and international cooperation. As later chapters detail, the market mechanism refers to a management process under which an "infinite" number of agents make independent, individual decisions on their own behalf. Decision making by democratic representation (or proxy) refers to a mechanism where a relatively large number of delegates try to reach considered, rational decisions through a majority vote on behalf of their constituents. Bargaining represents the case of negotiations among a few organized groups toward a compromise. The command process points to a mechanism where power is concentrated in a centralized, hierarchical line of authority. And the cooperation process relates to decision making by international agreements extending beyond national frontiers.[8]

---

8. A national economy can theoretically be organized by three other processes: anarchy, full communism, or tradition. However, as no contemporary nation-state is making use of these processes, they will not be discussed here.

The market mechanism is variously called the price system, free enterprise, or capitalism—all symbolizing *individual sovereignty*. Under this mechanism, the consumer is king, and his market-related demands are the system's overriding considerations. In parallel with this terminology, we can identify our own selected mechanisms also in terms of *sovereignty*. Decision making by proxy thus becomes *delegated sovereignty*. Bargaining may be referred to as *multilateral sovereignty*. The command mechanism would relate to *unilateral sovereignty*. And the international cooperation process would be described as *supranational sovereignty*.

As indicated before, no contemporary society is organized by any one of these processes alone. Modern countries make use of all of them in varying mixtures.

In discussing the five selected mechanisms of decision making in the forthcoming chapters, each mechanism will be examined for its essential features, its basic structure, its specific method of operation, and, finally, its comparative strengths and weaknesses.

Suggestions for Additional Readings

ALLEN, G. C. *Monopoly and Restrictive Practices*. London: Allen & Unwin, 1968.

BARAN, P. A., AND P. M. SWEEZY. *Monopoly Capital*. New York: Monthly Review, 1968.

BAUMOL, W. J. "Entrepreneurship in Economic Theory." *American Economic Review*, May 1968.

BORNSTEIN, M., ED. *Comparative Economic Systems: Models and Cases*. Homewood: Irwin, 1979.

BOULDING, K. E. *Economics as a Science*. New York: McGraw-Hill, 1970.

BROWN, A. A. ET AL. *Perspectives in Economics*. New York: McGraw-Hill, 1971.

CARSON, R. L. *Comparative Economic Systems*. New York: Macmillan, 1973.

ECKSTEIN, A., ED. *Comparison of Economic Systems*. Berkeley: University of California Press, 1971.

GALBRAITH, J. K., AND N. SALINGER. *Almost Everyone's Guide to Economics*. Boston: Houghton Mifflin, 1978.

GROSSMAN, G., ED. *Economic Systems*. Englewood Cliffs: Prentice-Hall, 1974.

HAYEK, F. A., *Individualism and Economic Order*. Chicago: University of Chicago Press, 1948.

HOUGH, R. R. *What Economists Do*. New York: Harper, 1972.

KNIGHT, F. H. *Economic Organization*. New York: Harper, 1962.

MUNDELL, R. A. *Man and Economics*. New York: McGraw-Hill, 1968.

MURPHY, R. E. *Adaptive Processes in Economic Systems.* New York: Academic Press, 1965.

PRYOR, F. L. *Property and Industrial Organization in Communist and Capitalist Nations.* Bloomington: University of Indiana Press, 1973.

Part Two

THE TASK OF DIRECTION

PART ONE QUESTIONED the myths of capitalism, socialism, and communism as applied to modern politicoeconomic organizations. It also outlined the basic economic problems shared by all economic entities, as well as the necessity for an organization (or system) to solve these problems.

The solution of basic economic problems in each country naturally follows the dictates of national aspirations and priorities. National objectives are, in turn, a reflection of a people's value system or philosophy of life—its outlook, expectations, ideals, and "ideology." These goals are not all or always economic goals. In addition to their search for economic prosperity and material welfare, individuals seek such noneconomic goals as power, status, prestige, and popularity. So do nations. But instinctively and otherwise, a good portion of individual and national energies are directed to *economic* well-being. And these are the focus of our study and the content of Part Two.

The task of direction discussed in this part involves the establishment of national goals, sorting out priorities among these goals, and providing the necessary machinery for adjustments to changing conditions. Chapters 3 and 4 present an overview of major national economic objectives that contemporary nations are trying to reach or maintain. A brief analysis of the inherent conflicts and harmonies among these objectives will provide the backdrop against which various countries' economic goals can be compared and the direction of their economies examined.

3

National Economic Goals

NATIONAL GOALS have throughout history differed from time to time and from country to country. They have ranged from warfare to welfare. A *national* goal, by definition, means a course of action that serves the common wishes and aspirations of the whole nation. National objectives must, in other words, be in the *public interest*. The public interest, however, is ambiguous; there is no universal concept of the public interest or of national purpose. Those who have a "holistic" view of society, who argue that society is a unitary organism by itself, above or beyond its individual members, regard national goals as a single set of objectives that apply to the public as a whole and may be different from those held by individual members. Many who reject this conception and consider society a mere aggregate of its membership argue that national goals must be those commonly shared by members of the public. According to this individualistic view, national goals can be regarded as only those that may enhance the community's "total ability" or satisfaction—as measured by the sum of individual pleasures and gratifications, resulting in the greatest happiness of the greatest number. In between these two concepts of the community is another view that treats national goals as basically the aggregate of ends sought by individuals, but excludes selfish or antisocial motives.

There are other intricacies in the concept of national goals. First, the selection of objectives is essentially a political and ethical choice, not an economic one; as such, it can only have political relevance and moral validity. Second, national economic objectives are subservient to broad political and philosophical considerations and are determined within the confines of a prevailing political "ideology." Third, the criteria for distinguishing purely political-moral considerations from basically economic goals are not adequately developed, and their relationships are chainlike and not always hierarchical. Fourth, the objectives proclaimed by leaders as national objectives may not always or necessarily reflect the basic values, desires, and aspirations held by the rank and file. Fifth, while the prevailing "ideology" and the resulting choice of sociopolitical goals play a significant role in shaping the nature of economic tools and policies, their relationships are neither direct nor mutually exclusive: different ends-means combinations are possible and desirable.

As indicated before, national economic goals may be a reflection of a single national leader, the value system of a small group of ruling elite at the top, or the aspirations and hopes of the majority (if not all) of the people in society. The term *national* need not always connote the "will of the people"; it simply signifies the course of actions upon which a nation has embarked—willingly, reluctantly, or even against its desires. Goals may also be stated or unstated. Paramount among stated objectives are such widely accepted and familiar aims as growth, full employment, price stability, equity in income distribution, economic security, and individual freedoms. There are also secondary objectives, such as social harmony, national supremacy, and international cooperation. Some of these goals are in conflict with one another; others are in harmony.[1]

Economic Growth and Higher Living Standards

A prime goal of national economic policy is economic growth combined with higher standards and levels of living. The almost universal concern with growth in the world today is rooted in the belief that the fulfillment of many economic goals (full employment, higher material welfare, and fairer income distribution) is not possible without growth. Economic growth is considered desirable because it is expected to increase society's material abundance, reduce the daily toil and burdens of work, enhance individual freedom of choice, and contribute to greater social welfare as well as cultural, scientific, and intellectual progress.

Growth is ordinarily defined as a self-sustained increase in real per capita GNP, or annual increases in the value of total output of all goods and services, adjusted for changes in population and price levels.[2]

For a number of reasons, however, a *per capita* increase in GNP measured in *real terms* may fail to indicate an improvement in the standard of living. First, a real per capita growth consisting mostly of an increase in military hardware may not help improve domestic consumption or living conditions. Second, even if the adjusted increase in GNP should wholly consist of civilian goods, a distinction still ought to be made between current consumer goods, which benefit the present generation, and capital formation, which bears fruit mostly for future generations. Third, a rise in per capita real income tells nothing about the social costs of production, because it may be accomplished at a disregard of environmental factors.

1. Contemporary nations also embrace certain unstated goals such as strategic self-sufficiency, regional or global economic supremacy, leadership in economic blocs, beggar-my-neighbor policy. Here we are concerned merely with explicit or stated goals.
2. When changes in output are adjusted for changes in hours of work, the result would show changes in the productivity of labor.

Most economists also agree that rapid economic growth is only partially a function of the quantity of capital and labor inputs. In the majority view, is economic progress is more significantly a result of the quality of productive factors, enhanced by higher skills, educational levels, and improved technology. The progress of technology is thus a major source of economic growth. Technological progress simply means an increase in the capability of the community for making more and better goods, cheaper and faster. An advanced technology in this context may mean the discovery of resources, invention or innovation of new methods for making a more productive use of available resources, and general reduction of production costs. There is, however, a negative side to technological progress. A technologically advanced society may provide a greater range of individual choice, create new opportunities, and result in greater hopes and confidence; but it may also result in diminished privacy, a sense of helplessness in the face of the machine, pressure for conformity, environmental decay, social conflicts, and public malaise. Many of the fruits of scientific and technological advances (such as deadlier weapon systems, synthetic raw materials, or certain wonder drugs) have not been unquestionable blessings for the majority of the world population.

Full Employment

Another widely accepted objective of modern national economies is full utilization of productive factors, particularly labor. For the classicists, this goal was equated with "maximum production"—what is today called "static efficiency"—because under conditions of perfect competition, unemployment was only a temporary aberration and could not last long without being automatically reversed. Under the influence of J. M. Keynes' *General Theory of Employment, Interest, and Money*, "full employment" itself has become a major goal of economic activity. Today, full employment refers chiefly to the gainful occupation of human labor. Theoretically, however, the idleness, waste, or inadequate use of *any* productive factor is contrary to the goal of full employment.

Needless to say, "full" employment never implies a three-shift operation or a constant engagement of every living soul. The exclusions and qualifications are many. Under-age youngsters and old-age pensioners are generally not counted in the labor force. Neither are housewives, hospital patients, or prison inmates. In Western countries, where work is not an individual obligation, exclusion from the labor force extends to those who do not seek jobs, those voluntarily unemployed: beachcombers, loafers, drifters and others. Even among the involuntarily jobless, full employment does not mean 100 percent occupation. There are always new entrants into the labor force who have not yet found employment, people who are temporarily out of work because they have quit their former positions to seek better ones, persons on temporary layoff with instructions to return to work in a few days, persons waiting to start new jobs within a short period, and so on. This group—a small percentage of the total labor force—is considered frictionally unemployed.

True unemployment exists when workers who actively seek gainful work at the going wage rates cannot find jobs. Unemployment may arise as a result of seasonal variations in demand for labor (for example, winter slacks in farming), or it may develop from an economic slowdown (insufficiency of effective demand by consumers, businessmen, and/or government). This unemployment is called cyclical, because it follows swings of economic activity and is not permanent. Yet a third type of unemployment, structural, may last for a long time. It results from changes in long-term demand and supply, national priorities, or technology— changes that make workers' jobs redundant or their skills obsolete.

The desirability of full or high employment as a prime national purpose is easy to understand. Economic depression and unemployment, associated with low levels of prices, wages, and profits, are likely to cause wastes of resources, create unused capacity of machines and people, and increase individual frustration and despair. Worker idleness usually breeds other national ills, such as business bankruptcies, social unrest, violence, crime, and suicides. Mass unemployment may also involve political hazards: many regimes and political parties in the past have been ignominiously ousted on this very issue.

Price-Level Stability

Another national economic objective is a relatively stable price level. The significance of this objective has been recognized since the dawn of monetary history. The Egyptians under the pharaohs, the Greeks under Alexander, the Romans under Nero, the Spaniards in the seventeenth century, and the Germans after World War I fully realized what havoc inflation could play with their fortunes. With the development of modern economic indexes, the impact of inflation on the national economy has been more intensively underscored.

Price-level stability does not, of course, mean the absence of changes in the prices of individual commodities. Indeed, individual price adjustments to changes in income, tastes, cost of production, and other economic phenomena are considered highly desirable from the standpoint of consumer sovereignty and economic efficiency. Price-level stability means a lack of sharp and sudden fluctuations in the average level of prices, as measured by marked changes in wholesale prices, cost of living, and other indexes. Inflation is an insistent and prolonged period of rising prices (and wages), generally accompanied by upward movements in employment, output, and incomes. A recent and disturbing phenomenon in Western industrial nations, however, is a combination of unemployment and inflation called "stagflation."

Inflation is disruptive of orderly economic progress, but because of its subtly deceptive appearance it is often less understood, feared, or resented than a depression. A gradual increase in the price level over a period of time—sometimes called "creeping inflation"—is often considered a stimulus to business expansion and new ventures. Prolonged and insistent inflationary pressures—branded "galloping inflation"—is more palpably felt, but sometimes still preferred to unemployment. Price increases of significant magnitude and lengthy duration hurt only individuals and groups who live on fixed incomes. Inflation also hits hard at people who hold the bulk of their accumulated wealth in conservative stocks, bonds, mortgages, insurance policies, savings accounts, and cash. Such de facto devaluation of incomes and assets constitutes a baseless redistribution of income.

A significant way that inflation hurts everyone by disrupting orderly economic progress is through its encouragement of unhealthy speculations. With prices going up and the value of money coming down, rational individuals try to protect their liquid assets by placing them in anything that promises to rise in value. Small savers become stock-market players; regular investment pros go after the big game; businessmen's profit delusions begin to mount; and the accuracy of cost calculations and market analyses is impaired. Entrepreneurs become lax, tend to condone inefficiency, fail to pay due attention to technological improvements, and misjudge market conditions. Businessmen tend continually to overexpand beyond what potential markets can absorb. And the ground is paved for a downward spiral.

A further evil of inflation is the pressures it exerts on the balance of international trade by encouraging imports and undermining exports. Domestic inflation reduces a country's ability to maintain (much less raise) the volume of exports it needs for high levels of employment and output at home; it also reduces the means of financing raw materials and consumer imports.

A partial corollary of price stability is the maintenance of equilibrium in the balance of international payments.[3] For most of the major trading nations, balance-of-payments equilibrium has become a very crucial national objective, occasionally overriding many others. No country can incur deficits in its external balances forever; creditors will see to that. Nor can payments surpluses be accumulated year after year before the surplus country realizes its unenviable position of exchanging real goods and services for foreign paper IOUs.

For the world major trading partners, a continuing balance-of-payments deficit would also entail additional harms. By undermining world confidence in the future value of currencies, continued external deficits would encourage unhealthy foreign exchange speculation, disrupt the smooth flow of world trade, foster trade wars, and undermine the fabric of the international trading and monetary system.

---

3. Owing to substantial increases in short-term and long-term capital movements in recent years, the balance of trade (difference between import and export of goods and services) does not always match the balance of payments (difference between total foreign exchange payments and receipts). Countries with trade surpluses may experience payments deficits as a result of lending or investing abroad. The reverse may be true of trade-deficit nations.

Equitable Distribution of Income and Wealth

Equity, social justice, and equality of opportunity in the distribution of income and wealth constitute yet another important national economic goal. An economic system, ideologically speaking, is largely a system of distribution of wealth, income, and economic power among individuals and groups. Equity, justice, and equality, however, are not always treated as synonymous concepts. In fact, distributive equity based on need is sometimes pitched against blind justice based on merit or economic contribution. Absolute equality in distribution is widely considered both unjust and inequitable. In a word, there is no ideal distribution rule except perhaps a vague criterion such as "reduced inequality."

Reduced inequality in the distribution of wealth and income may be considered a desirable social objective for four main reasons. First, because contemporary standards of decency in a civilized society require that a minimum of life amenities be given to all members who, for reasons beyond their control, are incapable of earning it. The second reason is the desirability of the diffusion in economic and political power. Everyone agrees that while power does not emanate solely from economic sources, wealth and income do give individuals and private groups substantial clout. Thus, some measure of equity or equality in the distribution of income and wealth would be indispensable to the realization of a true democracy. Third, reduced inequality increases economic opportunity for all members of a society and enables them to develop fully their personal aptitudes and abilities. Finally, by creating too much savings by the rich and too little consumption by the poor, gross inequalities of wealth and income in economically mature and affluent societies tend to undermine the economy's power to utilize its full productive capacity.

Economic Security

Closely related to the goal of distributional equity is that of economic security. Economic security is in essence an extension of equity over time. As an economic objective, this goal relates to the protection of individuals against the uncontrollable socioeconomic hazards of a complex, interdependent society. Unpredictable adversities that call for community action and protection include natural disasters, accidents, sickness, disability, loss of jobs, property damage, old-age loss of income, and sudden death. Some of these risks are partially insurable; the responsibility for protection against them can, in various measures, be placed upon individuals. Others (like unemployment) are largely or totally beyond personal control and protection; they call for deliberate social intervention.

No matter what one may think of the virtues of diligence, self-reliance, initiative, hard work, and similar puritanical traits, one cannot help but admit that in a modern industrial society, the rugged individualist has been replaced by the organization man. People are no longer the sole master of their economic livelihood. As most of their dependence on society is socially caused, it is "fair" to expect that it also be socially remedied.

Economic Freedoms

Last, but by no means least important among major national goals (although not often explicitly stated) is freedom of choice: the right to determine one's own economic destiny, to live according to one's own choosing, to rely on one's own initiative. Economic freedoms are considered desirable for their own sake and as a means of obtaining employment, a higher standard of living, and self-development. If economic activity is to maximize society's economic well-being, it is argued, individuals must be allowed, within a certain broad framework of law and order, to follow their own self-interest. If this freedom is not restricted by artificial means, individuals are likely to end up serving the interests of society. Some very intelligent people also argue that economic freedom of choice is essential to the preservation of political democracy; people cannot be really free unless they are allowed free forays in the marketplace.

There are reservations and limitations on individual economic freedoms, to be sure. Thus, it is readily conceded even by the staunchest champions of free enterprise that individual freedom of choice, if it is to serve the "good of all," should not be allowed to mean the freedom to make profit at the expense of the community's welfare, to exploit other individuals, to waste natural resources, or to monopolize economic activities. Other restrictions on individual freedom of choice—wartime rationing, emergency wage-and-price controls, compulsory overtime work, and involuntary savings, for example—are commonly accepted and allowed as necessary and legitimate during national or community crises. Furthermore, freedom is not opposed to order and organization. In fact, a truly meaningful exercise of individual freedoms in a complex modern society requires a vast amount of social organization and regulation.[4]

On the whole, human freedom as a desirable social goal is neither easy to define nor easy to maximize. In its most formal definition—the absence of control, coercion, or exploitation by others—freedom may have meaning and significance only for those who enjoy relative affluence. It may be meaningless for the poor, the diseased, the undereducated. For the latter, effective freedom means a positive access to economic opportunities; and freedom from fear, from hunger, from want, from ignorance. If freedom is not to be an empty slogan, it is argued, it must mean

4. A major problem here is that of measuring and evaluating economic freedom. Greater freedom is often identical with a greater number or range of choices, but in reality, the number of choices available is not always crucial; an intelligent exercise of choice making *is*. The availability of numerous choices is often necessary and desirable, but it is not always sufficient. Giving a blind man the choice of ten different color shirts is no better than giving him the choice of one.

the possibility for self-development and self-expression, regardless of aptitude or status in life.

Conflicts and Harmony among Objectives

A cursory look at the basic character and social implications of the objectives discussed in this chapter shows that while they may occasionally support one another, more often than not they are in basic conflict. The goal of full employment, for example, is frequently at odds with the objectives of price stability. It may at times also be inconsistent with the goals of growth, freedom, and efficiency.

Studies made of the relationship between full employment and price stability in advanced economies show the existence of a critical trade-off. That is, beyond a certain point, any attempt to reduce unemployment would result in more inflation. The trade-off point, like the concept of involuntary unemployment itself, is the subject of controversy among economists; it is admittedly different for different countries at a given time, and different for the same country at different times. But the relationship seems to hold for many countries most of the time.

The objectives of economic growth and technological progress may also at times be contradictory to the goals of high employment, economic stability, and individual choice. The accelerated rate of automation (jobs done by machines) and cybernation (automatic controls) have both created and destroyed thousands of jobs. To the extent that this argument has validity, rapidly changing technology and long-run full employment may not be mutually compatible. And unless the structurally unemployed are retrained, rehabilitated, and technically prepared for new and more complicated tasks, an artificial increase in the number of available jobs might sap the economy's total energies and hurt its rate of growth. Technological progress may also prove incompatible with the goal of economic stability. The results of growth-producing scientific research, invention, innovation, and entrepreneurship in an unplanned market economy may not be smooth and gradual; more often than not, they may involve short-run fluctuations in output, income, and employment.

A deliberate achievement of optimum growth in developing countries may also violate the requirements of individual choice. Since suboptimum growth rates may be due to deficiencies of capital investment, lack of technical knowledge and skills, or unfavorable worker attitudes, the remedy may be state intervention to provide the needed stimulus, remove the bottlenecks, or enhance investment opportunities. All of this, however, more often than not involves significant reduction in consumer sovereignty and even consumer freedom of choice.

Even more interesting is that the goal of growth may work against both full employment and equity under different circumstances. In the major industrial countries, growth and employment are almost always considered to go hand in hand, and in a majority of cases, they do. But in the less developed countries that favor heavy industrialization via capital-intensive large-scale industrial projects growth is often realized without increased employment. In fact, capital-based growth works against more effective utilization of human resources.

The conflict between growth and equity is perhaps a bit more farfetched, but it is real. To the extent that faster growth requires more active substitution among resources (greater efficiency) and more active competition among resource owners (greater productivity), better placed resources and more energetic or enterprising resource owners would be likely to move ahead faster than others. The results would thus be greater inequalities of wealth and income.

A similar conflict may exist between the goals of distributive equity and economic security on the one hand, and those of growth, freedom, and efficiency on the other. The distribution of income and the provision of economic security on any basis other than individual productivity in the marketplace, (such as need, merit, equality, or capacity for enjoyment), is bound to have some adverse effects on incentives. A majority of economists believe that these effects, beyond a certain point, become generally unfavorable, if not absolutely damaging. To the extent that a redistribution of income in favor of the consumption-oriented poor adversely affects the supply of domestic savings and the rate of capital formation, greater income equality may also impede economic growth.[5]

Objectives of full employment, growth, freedom, and price stability can be individually fulfilled at a given time, but all four cannot be fully secured simultaneously. Instead of aiming at full employment and maximum growth, plus unrestricted freedoms and zero inflation, every nation has to settle for less: a high level employment, a respectable rate of growth, a good measure of individual freedom, and a tolerable rate of inflation.

The foregoing discussion on the *conflicts* of objectives should not convey the impression that national economic goals are always or irrevocably opposed to one another. In point of fact, within certain ranges and for certain levels of achievement, national priorities may be harmonious or even complementary. The maintenance of an optimum rate of growth, for example, by keeping unemployment of resources to a reasonable minimum, may make unemployment compensation and other transfer payments largely unnecessary. Here the goals of growth, full employment, and economic security go hand in hand.

A successful preservation of basic economic freedoms may help achieve efficiency, growth, high employment, and technological progress. High employment, price stability, and economic security in turn may promote greater individual

---

5. The issue at stake, again, is how to strike a balance between moral, as distinct from functional, distribution of income: how to provide optimum welfare for all, without seriously undermining productive efficiency and needlessly tampering with individual freedoms.

freedoms. A steady job, a healthy body, a stable mind, better education, greater skill, and wider horizons of hope make people more efficient. Greater efficiency guarantees higher incomes and open vistas of fresh alternatives from which to choose. And, this, in a sense, must mean more freedoms. That is why to some liberal thinkers economic freedom is impossible without economic security.

Finally, a fundamental harmony must exist between the objectives of equity and justice on the one hand, and economic security on the other—for obvious reasons. Technological progress and economic efficiency also usually go hand in hand. A rapid rate of economic growth makes a comprehensive and compulsory mobilization of domestic resources less necessary, thus contributing to the enhancement of individual freedoms. Increased investment in public and welfare-oriented projects (skills and education, improved health, adequate nutrition, sanitary dwellings, community development) makes the attainment of growth, self-reliance, and social balance much easier. In sum, many major goals may be, under some circumstances, in harmony.

The Need for Social Balance

Because of the major conflicts among national goals, the need is for the attainment of basic social balance among the freedoms of individuals and the imperatives of society, the needs of the present generation and those to come in the future, and the advantages of economic progress against its major costs.

The most important aspect of socioeconomic equilibrium refers to the necessity of comparing the benefits of economic progress with its major costs. Economic progress in the last 150 years, unprecedented as it has been in terms of rising annual per capita income, a shorter workweek, greater material comfort, and higher output per man-hour, has not been without costs. Progress has been accompanied by the life-threatening environmental decay and alarming exhaustion of essential natural resources, excessive urban congestion and blight, a diversion of human time and energy from intellectual pursuits, excessive conformity, a hectic tempo of life, an atmosphere unfavorable to self-enlightenment, encroachments on personal freedoms, impersonality in human relations, and violent crimes. In the words of a contemporary sage, "We are a generation prepared for Paradise Lost, who do not know what to do with Paradise Found."

Social tensions, individual frustrations, personal neuroses, family breakdowns, group hostilities, and other individual and social ills are also associated with material progress. Whether the prices paid for our present affluence are justified is a matter of value judgment, but losing sight of the costs of progress defies both common sense and conventional wisdom.

Suggestions for Additional Readings

ANDERSON, J. E. *Politics and the Economy.* Boston: Little, Brown, 1966.

ANDERSON, M. *Welfare.* Stanford: The Hoover Institution Press, 1978

BROWN, L. R. *Resource Trends and Population Policy.* New York: Worldwatch Institute, 1979.

DENTON, G. *Planning for Growth.* London: PEP, 1965.

HOOVER, C. B. *The Economy, Liberty and the State.* Garden City: Doubleday, 1961.

MEADOWS, D. H. *Alternatives to Growth.* Cambridge: Ballinger, 1977.

MEADOWS, D. H., ET AL. *The Limits to Growth.* New York: New American Library, 1972.

MISHAN, E. J. *The Economic Growth Debate.* London: Allen & Unwin, 1977.

OKUN, A. *Equality and Efficiency.* Washington: The Brookings Institution, 1975.

OKUN, A. AND G. L. PERRY. *Curing Chronic Inflation.* Washington: The Brookings Institution, 1978.

RAWLS, J. *A Theory of Justice.* Cambridge: Harvard University Press, 1971.

THUROW, L. C. *Generating Inequality.* New York: Basic Books, 1976.

TOBIN, J. "Inflation and Unemployment." *American Economic Review,* March 1972.

WILSON, J. *Equality.* New York: Harcourt Brace, 1966.

4

Economic Agenda in the Modern World

THIS CHAPTER EXAMINES the nature, composition, and relative weight of major national economic goals among various groups of contemporary nation-states: the market-oriented advanced industrial countries (MICs); the centrally directed economies (CDEs); and the less developed countries (LDCs). These groups are also referred to as the first world, the second world, and the third world. The MICs, often called "Western democracies," comprise essentially the United States, the major members of the European Economic Community (West Germany, France, Great Britain, and Italy), Japan, Canada, the Scandinavian countries, and some other advanced members of the Organization for Economic Cooperation and Development (OECD). The CDEs include the Soviet Union, People's Republic of China, Cuba, and the East European economies. The LDCs cover the majority of the United Nations membership in Asia, Africa, and Latin America. Ideologically and organizationally, the LDCs fall in between the other two categories.

Market-Oriented Advanced Industrial Countries

The United States, the members of the European Economic Community,[1] Canada, and Japan—the so-called Western democracies—are market-oriented and market-directed economies in the sense that they either have no national economic plan or their planning is not of the binding prescriptive variety. The basic national objectives of these countries must be searched for in their annual budgets, major economic policy statements, international agreements, or occasional summit communiques.[2]

1. The European Economic Community (EEC) is part of European Communities, which include other agencies (chapter 9).
2. Some observers argue that the very idea of searching for a single-minded national

41

Among the major industrial countries, the United States has as yet no formal national economic plan, although several attempts have been made in the Congress to introduce this concept, such as the Humphrey-Javits bill. From the very beginning of their independence, Americans have favored two fundamental objectives: maximum opportunity for private competitive enterprise, and the widest possible exercise of free personal choice in the area of occupation, expenditure, and investment. In the Employment Act of 1946, the U.S. Congress for the first time called on the federal government to use all practicable means for the purpose of creating and maintaining conditions "to promote maximum employment, production, and purchasing power." In the 1950s and 1960s, the goals of equality of opportunity for the minorities, a minimum of economic security for all, and a better balance in U.S. international accounts were added. In the 1970s, the objective of price stability gradually climbed to the top of the list of national priorities.

Postwar British national economic goals, under both the Labour party and the Conservatives, followed a long-established pragmatic and progressive philosophy rooted in British political and economic thought. Historically, England has been the originator, the architect, the developer, and the promoter of laissez faire capitalism. Yet almost from the start, (and long before Marx), British social philosophers made repeated references to the shortcomings and weaknesses inherent in the capitalist system. The British trade-union movement, precursor of the present Labour party, was born amidst the exploitations, hardships, and inequalities of the British factory system. The 1945 Labour platform of jobs for all, general economic expansion, efficiency, fair distribution of income, and social welfare provided the equivalents of Britain's postwar national economic goals. The Labour party's planks later became a part of British public consensus and acceptable to the Conservatives during their years in power.[3] The essence of these commitments, plus a dash of environmentalism, was later pragmatically and faithfully embraced by the successive Conservative and Labour administrations voted in by the British electorates. A distinct cleavage between Labour and the Conservatives seems to have surfaced under Mrs. Thatcher's leadership since 1979. Thatcherism has clearly sided with the free play of market forces (free collective bargaining, no incomes policy, less government intervention) while Labour has veered distinctly to the left. In a

---

direction in a free-enterprise economy is absurd, if not inconceivable. In an unplanned market economy, they believe economic priorities follow consumers' wishes and manifest themselves in impersonal market forces. Only during a national crisis, may a "free-enterprise economy" embrace some national purpose.

3. In some observers' view, the goals of efficiency and growth have taken second place to those of full employment, distributional equity, enlargement of social security, support for the vested interests, and the maintenance of status quo. This system of priorities is in turn alleged to have had a "disastrous" effect on government-business relations and given rise to "confrontation" between management and labor. See G. C. Allen, *British Industry and Economic Policy* (London: Macmillan, 1979).

statement adopted in May 1980, the Labour party endorsed, among other proposals, the nationalization of North Sea oil and parts of the construction, drug and electronics industries, and called for the protection of certain industries by import controls.

Japan's economic and social development plans in the postwar period have been officially committed to growth, high efficiency, and improved national living conditions. The distinctive thrust of the plans, however, has been centered on one overriding purpose: rapid industrial growth, almost at all costs. Improvements in living standards (particularly in health and education) and productivity have been mostly secondary to the main objective, and incidental to its achievement. With passage of time and the emergence of economic ills and environmental strains, the clamor for a more balanced approach has been increasingly heard. The latest Seven-Year Plan (1979-1986), for example, aims at a slower annual growth rate of 5.7 percent (about half as much as realized rates in the past) and the creation of a new welfare society. The plan's guidelines emphasize full-employment, price stability, economic security, fiscal balance, and "life environment facilities" (public works, housing, education, welfare). The unstated objectives of the Japanese plans have been the establishment of a first-rate industrial base, a rise to the top of the world trading nations, influence over world exchange markets through accumulation of reserves, the perpetuation of small-scale agriculture, the preservation of paternalism between industry and labor, and the maintenance of the symbiotic relationship between business and the state.

The Centrally Directed Economies

Countries that engage in prescriptive (binding) national economic planning, and make extensive use of centralized economic directions, commonly state their national economic goals in the official documents and plans.[4] The pioneer, promoter, and most sophisticated among this groups of countries is the Union of Soviet Socialist Republics. The Soviet Union's basic national economic objectives are largely determined by the political realities of being a world super power as well as a Communist model. Like those of other major world powers, Soviet objectives follow a basically nationalistic philosophy, but this philosophy, depending as it does

---

4. This group includes the Soviet Union, mainland China, Yugoslavia, Hungary, Poland, Czechoslovakia, East Germany, Romania, and Cuba, among others. These countries, to be sure, are not homogeneous in their economic structure or composition of economic policies, but they all fall into the category of the so-called Marxist-Leninist countries, which use a tightly structured party as the apex of decision-making power in the economy.

on the standings and the understandings of successive Soviet leaders, undergoes changes in interpretation and rationalization from time to time.

In a broad historical perspective, the roots of present Soviet objectives can be traced to several underlying factors: first, the global ambitions of the legendary Russian czars, who tried to unify, modernize, industrialize, and, in a narrow sense, even pluralize Mother Russia; second, the lingering legacies of a feudal, authoritarian, oppressive, and basically fatalistic social order; third, the imposing weight of a largely agricultural economy that until the turn of this century, had four-fifths of the population dependent on land; fourth, the dialectical teachings of Karl Marx as well as the untiring efforts of Marxist intellectuals as manifested in a number of socialist movements in Czarist Russia; and finally, technical and managerial difficulties that have plagued the Communist party leaders, and their choice of national priorities.

Against this background, the stated economic objectives of the USSR are detailed specifically in its constitution and periodic development plans. In addition to the universal goals of rapid growth, improvement in national standards of living and fair distribution of income, they call for across-the-board economic security (guaranteed employment), enhancement of efficiency, increased labor productivity, scientific and technical progress, higher levels of artistic and cultural activities, and an overall social balance. The conspicuous absence of such goals as price-level stability and balance-of-payments equilibrium can be explained by the fact that official prices are centrally determined, and external trade is a state monopoly. Individual freedom, as another goal of modern national economies, is constrained by the "obligation" to work on the part of every ablebodied citizen. There is also the prohibition against making private profit at someone else's expense. The freedoms of occupation, expenditure, saving, and inheritance, however, are constitutionally guaranteed—although subject to Soviet authorities' own interpretations. The stated socioeconomic purposes of the Soviet Union are, in a word, designed to create a communist society.[5]

Translated into specific aims of state economic policy, these ultimate objectives are subdivided into a number of programs and targets specified in the Soviet five-year and seven-year plans. They are considered as "transitional" steps at the present stage of development of socialist society toward the eventual (and presumably inexorable) establishment of the Communist ideal.

The People's Republic of China's present national economic goals also bear the imprints of Chinese history and tradition, as well as current international position. The Chinese Communist revolution, rooted largely in Mao's Yenan philosophy, emphasizes the creation of a superpower status through individual puritanism and national self-reliance. Within the framework of this egalitarian

5. The unstated objectives of the Soviet Union (the spread of communism across Soviet frontiers, competition with the United States in world economic power play, maintenance of economic disciplines within Soviet borders, etc.) are perhaps more significant and more "operational" than some of the explicit goals.

philosophy, China's national economic goals in Mao's time emphasized comprehensive industrialization, national provision of basic domestic needs, and the creation of a homogeneous, classless society. Priorities in resource allocation toward these fundamental objectives, in turn, called for rapid expansion of military-industrial capacity and output, collectivization and consolidation of agriculture to ensure national self-sufficiency, and a gradual improvement in the level of living consistent with expected labor productivity. The post-Mao leadership, however, has emphasized modernization of production through adoption of foreign technology, stepped-up programs of increased efficiency through scientific and technical education, increased foreign trade and investment, and the protection of environment.

For the other CDEs, specific politicoeconomic goals have included rapid industrialization, increased economic efficiency through more advanced technology, emphasis on self-sufficiency, greater reliance on intragroup trade, a steady rise in living standards and balanced regional development. The objectives of full employment, internal price and exchange stability, and social security are again not explicitly mentioned in official documents, because these social desiderata are presumed to be imbedded in the fundamental (socialist) ideology. In these countries, as in the Soviet Union, the constitution guarantees every citizen the right to work, as well as the rights to certain life amenities and social security, such as housing, education, medical care, and pensions, along with certain obligation toward the state.

The Less Developed Countries

In their economic characteristics and prospects, this group of countries differs not only from the major industrial and the centrally directed economies; they are a vastly heterogeneous group even among themselves. Their enormous diversity is reflected in their land area, access to sea, size and skills of population, resource endowment, stage of technological advancement, sociopolitical institutions, development experience, managerial talent, and the general standard of living. They are also markedly different in the kind and quality of means at their command to cope with the twin problems of poverty and underdevelopment.

Some countries in this category, like Gabon, Nigeria, Zaire, and Zambia, are poor but have large untapped mineral reserves. Some, like Bolivia, Egypt and Thailand, have somewhat higher per capita incomes than the poorest, but are predominantly rural. Others, like Brazil, India and South Korea, while differing considerably in their per capita income levels, are sophisticated manufacturers and exporters of machinery. Still others are hardly viable economically; some are real basket cases.

In spite of the divergence in economic structures and development capabilities, LDCs share certain common objectives explicitly stated in their national plans or implicitly followed. Development plans of such disparate countries as India, Brazil, and Nigeria all speak of rapid industrialization, employment for the entire labor force, reduction in income disparities, curbing inflation, and improved economic security. As in the case of other groups, however, many stated objectives in LDCs are only expressions of popular sentiments and aspirations without concrete national plans or programs for their realization. Chapter 13 shows that the goals of full employment, economic security, and income equity in particular have, for the most part, remained pious hopes for these countries. Other unstated objectives, such as military strength, regional dominance, and nuclear capability, have occupied leaders' attention and absorbed national resources without being overtly emphasized.

Differences in Economic Goals among Nations

A quick look at the declared platforms, stated priorities, and planned agenda in the three groups of contemporary nation-states shows that the majority differ but little in their explicit and publicized overall economic objectives.[6] Behind the facades of ideological tags or party labels, most countries in these groups *officially* subscribe more or less to the same broad objectives of full employment, adequate growth, reasonable price stability, desirable technological progress, equitable distribution of income, balanced social welfare, and higher levels of living.

Yet it defies common sense to regard such diverse countries as Communist China, Brazil, the Soviet Union, the United States, India, and Japan as having the same national objectives or outlook. There must be a catch somewhere—and indeed there is: while written constitutions and officially proclaimed policies may not differ much, other systemic aspects of social order that relate to the determination, interpretation, and implementation of these objectives, do indeed vary.

As the composition and determination of national objectives are essentially political and ethical problems (and, thus, mainly the subject matter of comparative politics rather than comparative economics), their treatment here must be brief and confined to their inseparable relations to the processes of solving economic problems.

In this context, there are essentially three factors that separate countries with similar economic objectives: first, the special definition or *interpretation* placed by each nation on a given goal, such as freedom or equity or security; second, the particular *priority* attached to identical goals in the country's total scale of

---

6. Noneconomic objectives, and the unstated but observed goals of nations differ widely and are subject to frequent changes. Here we are mainly concerned with economic pursuits, although admittedly the distinction between economic and noneconomic goals is not always clear or uncontested.

preference; and third, the methods of goal *determination*, the processes by which objectives are considered, weighed, decided upon, and changed.

Differences in Conception and Interpretation

Concepts such as individual economic freedoms, equality, security, and justice obviously do not mean the same things to all those who preach or practice them. Countries that officially and in their written constitutions subscribe to these objectives sometimes operate under markedly different rules, either because these concepts mean different things to them, or because the leadership does not intend to observe those objectives to the last letter.

For example, the 1977 Soviet Constitution (the fourth since the October Revolution) guarantees "freedom of speech, of the press, and of assembly." But, it adds that such activities may be carried out only in order "to strengthen and develop the Socialist system." According to the Communist party newspaper *Pravda*, while criticism of Soviet shortcomings, if it serves to strengthen the Russian society, should be encouraged, criticisms from "positions of hostility" that undermine the foundations of the Soviet system should be rebuffed. Freedom of speech thus means one thing to the Russians and another to the Americans. The same applies to the freedom of action. In Western industrial countries, people are free to work for themselves or for others; the state not only recognizes this freedom, but protects it within broad limits. Under Soviet Constitution and in Communist ideology, however, citizens have neither the right nor the liberty to employ other workers for their private benefit. Job freedom, therefore, has different meanings in the West and the East.

In many left-of-the-center countries, political freedom is considered somewhat empty without some measure of economic security. People are considered not really free unless they are given the wherewithal to enjoy a minimum of decent and comfortable life. To many conservatives, on the other hand, a free society is not only consistent with considerable inequalities of wealth and income; it actually requires a good measure of differential rewards to keep it healthy and vigorous. British Fabian socialists, Scandinavian welfare protagonists, and other Western liberals regard individual freedoms under free enterprise as an abstraction in constitutional theory. People, they hold, may possess inalienable freedoms to choose between jobs, goods, and the pursuit of happiness, but they may not necessarily have effective rights to enjoy any of them. Under the democratic states of Western and Northern Europe, the whole society has an obligation to provide assistance to underprivileged individuals on the basis of talent, interest, and potential ability, regardless of socioeconomic background or status in life. The responsibility for self-development is not solely an individual, parental, or parochial responsibility but an obligation of the entire community.

The content and scope of business arrangements too is subject to wide disagreement among nations. West European countries are, on the whole, more lenient toward business concentration, cartel arrangements, and monopolistic practices than is the United States. Individual economic activities, on the other hand, are subject to more cumbersome regulations in Europe than in the United States. Freedom of the press is nowhere as broadly interpreted as in America to justify certain exercises of questionable service to the readership or to the nation.

A difference in interpretation applies equally well to the concepts of *welfare* and *equity*, or "substantive democracy." To the majority of Western conservatives, individual economic security should be acquired by private means: through private foresight, private insurance, and private savings. The responsibility for earning a livelihood, providing for one's old age, rearing and educating wanted (or unwanted) children, and taking care of sickness, disabilities, and disasters rests on the individual's own shoulders. Unfortunate emergencies should be taken care of by relatives, the parish, or mother nature. To socialists and humanists, however, individuals have a right to adequate social protection against natural or human-made disasters. In this view, the community as a whole has an obligation toward its members because they happen to be born without their consent, and because they may have to earn their livelihood in an environment that may be out of their individual control.

Similar differences in definition and interpretation involve the concept of economic *growth* and progress. High growth rates in the Soviet Union and other CDEs are often derided and minimized by Western analysts because they are presumably achieved in a costly and callous way at the expense of such other values as individual freedom, human dignity, and a truly creative society. Communists and socialists, on the other hand, criticize Western measurement of growth as exaggerated because it includes "unproductive" services of bureaucrats, service personnel, "social parasites," and others. They also tend to belittle economic growth in the West, because it is allegedly achieved through monopolies, exploitation, class privileges, and similar bourgeois evils.

Definitions and interpretations placed by different nations and regimes upon the goals of efficiency, full employment, and social balance show equally substantial diversities. In many of the CDEs, efficiency is equated with the fulfillment of planned quotas at predetermined factor prices regardless of true production costs or quality of output. The cleavages between national economies officially committed to the same or similar national goals sometimes also appear in the degree of honesty and sincerity (or cynicism and demagoguery) with which publicly proclaimed policies are viewed in private and pursued in actual practice. Not everything said is always believed or meant to be followed.

Preferences and Priorities

The second distinction among countries with more or less the same national economic goals is the difference in *priorities*. Each nation, depending on the short-run problems it faces and the long-range aspirations it holds, tends to arrange its basic objectives in its own special order. Thus, the United States and other MICs tend to cherish the goal of individual freedoms on a par with, if not in preference to, other objectives. A majority of LDCs and almost all CDEs, on the other hand, tend to give priority to economic growth and the sacrifice of some personal liberties for the sake of other goals.

Among the major industrial countries, Great Britain and the Scandinavians emphasize income equity, economic security, and social balance more than the United States or Canada. In the socialist camp, Yugoslavia and Hungary seem to show a greater concern for consumers' preferences than do mainland China, Cuba, or Albania. Within the LDCs, densely populated and exchange-short India, Pakistan, and Egypt are more seriously preoccupied with ensuring full employment and adequate foreign earnings than are Saudi Arabia or Kuwait, which contain small populations and overly ample external incomes from oil. During most of the postwar years, stopping galloping inflation has been the major concern in Argentina, Indonesia, Brazil, and Chile.

India and Pakistan, dependent during most of the postwar period on foreign aid and external credit, and increasingly disappointed with the pace of outside assistance, have often emphasized self-reliance as one of their highly ranked objectives. Mexico and South Korea, on the other hand, have followed a more open-door policy with regard to foreign trade. Germany and Japan, which have enjoyed high employment for most of the postwar years, have been mainly concerned with price stability. The United States, on the other hand, which has been plagued with high unemployment for many years, has been alternating its priorities between high employment and price stability. Britain's much debated "stop-go" policy, alternating betwen increased growth and restrained inflation, has followed a fluctuating path. France, in its turn, has oscillated between balance-of-payments equilibrium and price stability on the one hand, and economic growth and full employment on the other. In short, each country tends to rank its goals in a somewhat different order according to its short-run needs and its long-range expectations.

Methods of Goal Determination

Nations with outwardly identical objectives may differ in yet a third respect: the way they determine their national aims and establish priorities among them. The differences in the way national goals are determined (and conflicts among them resolved) would show the extent of rank-and-file support.

The determination of national objectives and the relative importance given each goal in a modern society reflects the distribution of power, authority, and control of resources. Where power is monopolized by one individual (a leader or dictator) or narrowly shared among a small ruling elite, the ranking of objectives can

THE TASK OF DIRECTION

be a relatively simple matter. The establishment of priorities is at the discretion of a hierarchy whose only constraint is the difficulty of reaching all goals at the same time.

Where political and economic powers are diffused (as in democracies with an educated electorate and a fairly equitable distribution of wealth and income), the scheduling of social values becomes a matter of majority will. In situations where power is spread but, not fundamentally equal, the process of conflict resolution becomes more complex. Depending upon the number of power centers and the gravitational pull of each, the ranking of national objectives becomes a matter of hard-fought political compromise among major pressure groups.

The five alternative processes of decision-making identified in Chapter 2, help explain the way national economic objectives may be determined under different forms of sovereignty. Under *individual sovereignty* where choices rest with individuals and private groups free from centralized control or coercion, individuals and groups choose "national" objectives by their economic actions in the marketplace. Each person directly participates in the economic goal-setting process through the offer of his services and/or disposition of his income. In this process an individual largely seeks his own interest. To paraphrase Adam Smith's celebrated passage, he neither intends to decide on social priorities nor possibly cares about social welfare; but given the competitive structure in the market, he will end up promoting objectives that are not part of his own design. Prosperity and depression, inflation and deflation, fair and unfair distribution of income, growth or stagnation, and similar national issues are influenced by individual decisions in the market place.

Where individual sovereignty is less than infinite, some of the basic national economic goals may be determined by the legislatures on behalf of the rank-and-file. This method of goals determination called *delegated sovereignty*, exemplifies the indirect expression of preference by the population as a whole. In the more pluralistic societies among the MICs (but by no means only in them) national economic agenda may be arranged by compromise among major pressure groups or lobbies. This mode, termed *multilateral sovereignty*, typifies a situation where national economic priorities are ascertained through the multiplay of vested interests. Finally, in monolithic situations called *unilateral sovereignty*, socioeconomic policies are decided upon by a centralized hierarchy.[7] This authority may reside in an all powerful leader (a monarch, a military strongman, a tribal chief, a community patriarch) or in a single dominant political party.

A final variety of sovereignty relates to a decision-making process that transcends domestic jurisdictions and is in a sense *supranational*. This type of sovereignty, exercised through international cooperation and covenants, determines

---

7. The role played by pressure groups is, to be sure, not limited to "democratic" societies. Every community, even a totalitarian one, embodies certain diverse seats of power. Modern one-party chiefs and enlightened rulers are generally mindful of the attitudes and reactions of their clergy, military commanders, rival politicians, labor leaders, security agents, intellectuals, technocrats, and so on.

many foreign economic policies and postures of modern nations. Policies concerning international transport and communication, postal service, travel, trade, investment, and exchange are largely shaped by agreements among nations. These agreements usually supersede the laws of the land. Bilateral, regional, or global, they limit national economic independence in varying degrees and for different lengths of time.[8]

In the real world, no economy is organized on any one of these mechanisms exclusively; all modern nations use a combination of them. Thus, contemporary national priorities are nowhere the exclusive prerogatives either of "all the people" or "only the leaders." There are significant mutations.

Among the countries examined in this book, the leaders' preferences and priorities predominate in China, the Soviet Union, Yugoslavia, and, to a large extent, in Brazil and Nigeria. By contrast, the population as a whole has more to say about national objectives in the United States, Great Britain, Japan, and India. Disaggregating these two broad categories, one can also see the relatively greater influence of democratic representation in the United States and Britain than in other countries, with India presenting a distant third. The power of vested interests in deciding national objectives is probably largest in the United States, Britain, and Japan, and least pronounced in China, Nigeria, or Brazil. Finally, the MICs and the LDCs on our list, by virtue of their participation in a wide variety of international organizations, allow for a much larger influence of international commitments on their domestic policies than the CDEs, particularly China and the Soviet Union.

Suggestions for Additional Readings

ARROW, K. J. *Social Choice and Individual Values.* New Haven: Yale University Press, 1970.

BUCHANAN, J. M., ED. *Theory of Public Choice.* Ann Arbor: University of Michigan Press, 1972.

KEY, V. O. *Politics, Parties and Pressure Groups.* New York: Harper, 1964.

LIPSET, S. M. *Political Man.* Garden City: Doubleday, 1963.

MARCUSE, H. *One Dimensional Man.* Kansas City: Beacon, 1964.

PRESTON, N. S. *Politics, Economics and Power.* New York: Macmillan, 1967.

8. A somewhat visionary method of goal determination, which we may conveniently term *communal* sovereignty, relates to a voluntary association among community members who are equal, cooperative, and harmonious. In such a society the interests of one coincide with the interests of all, and what is good for the community is also good for its individual members. In this "dream world" of harmony and cooperation, community goals are presumably arrived at in a kind of spontaneous and automatic consensus on the part of all, thus eliminating the need for lengthy deliberations, bargaining, voting, and other forms of policy making.

Part Three

THE TASK OF
MANAGEMENT

IN PART TWO, some of the major national socioeconomic goals of modern economies and the processes through which they are normally determined and altered were reviewed. The professed goals of different countries were found to be partly a matter of interpretation, partly a question of social priority, and partly also a reflection of national resolve in pursuing those goals. Several alternative methods of determining these objectives and resolving conflicts among them were identified in terms of the type of decision-making power or sovereignty.

Part Three deals with the task of management—the mechanism of economic problem solving within the framework of national goals. This part will focus on the five basic mechanisms or processes of calculation, motivation, and coordination outlined in chapter 2. As that chapter indicated, decision making through the market (individual sovereignty) refers to a process under which an "infinite" number of units make independent individual decisions on their own behalf. Decision making by proxy (delegated sovereignty) characterizes a situation where a number of democratic representatives try to reach a decision (either by consensus or by a majority vote) on behalf of their constituencies. Bargaining (or multilateral sovereignty) represents the case of a few bargainers attempting to reach a compromise on behalf of their interest groups; command (or unilateral sovereignty) points to a decision-making process where power is concentrated in a centralized, hierarchical line. Supranational sovereignty relates to a mechanism that goes beyond national frontiers in seeking cooperative solutions to some national problems.

Chapters 5 through 9 examine the basic characteristics, methods of operation, and advantages and limitations of these mechanisms.

5

Decision Making
through the Market

THE MARKET MECHANISM (or individual sovereignty) is one method of organizing economic activity, that is, rationing and allocating scarce resources and output. In this process, production, distribution, consumption, and capital formation take place through the free decisions and actions of individuals or private groups. Under individual sovereignty, identified with the *market mechanism*, or the *price system*, consumer is king and business entrepreneurs are all the king's men. Business enterprises fulfill consumers' wishes by producing the type of things for which there is effective demand in the market. The guide is profit; guideposts are market prices paid by buyers and incomes received by resource owners. The market is free from state intervention except for providing a legal framework for action.

Essential Characteristics

Individual sovereignty is characterized by six essential elements. First, economic activity is organized around the free decisions and actions of independent businessmen, resource owners, suppliers, and consumers. Second, the allocation of scarce resources is facilitated by the division of labor and exchange, for products are made for sale and not for one's own use. Third, the basic motivation for action in the economic arena is essentially personal and private gain: there are no government dictation, community pressure, or overriding national considerations. Fourth, the state provides only the "rules of the game" under which private individuals and households can enter into voluntary contracts. The government serves only as a referee; it monitors the game, interprets the rules, and enforces them. The state's role under this laissez faire philosophy, is limited mostly to preservation of law and order, and the provision of defense, public health, and safety. Finally, planning, controls, and adjustments are largely private: there are no national plans. The separate, self-centered plans by the rational businessman, the intelligent consumer, and the shrewd resource owner are controlled and coordinated by the market. Market planning is private and diffused; market control is spontaneous and impersonal; market adjustments are equilibrating.

The Market Mechanism As a Model

In its pure and idealized form, the market mechanism is a conceptual model, a norm. It is based on certain specific assumptions of human behavior; it relies on certain particular economic tools identified with a free-enterprise exchange economy; and it employs certain decision-making techniques traditionally associated with laissez faire capitalism.

The Concept of the "Economic Man"

In Adam Smith's view, individual self-interest is at the center of all economic activity. Smith regarded man as a creature of passions, but capable of self-regulation by susceptibility to reason. Self-interest was defined as "the uniform, constant and uninterrupted effort of every man to better his condition." The subsequent elaboration of this rational and individualistic philosophy was provided by the British philosopher Jeremy Bentham. Bentham's "utilitarian" philosophy holds that people are motivated in their actions by a desire for obtaining pleasure and avoiding pain. In attempting to achieve these goals, an individual—supposedly the best judge of his own interests—carefully reviews the utilities and disutilities of prospective choices, calculates a balance between them, and reaches a rational conclusion as to the best possible line of action. In this view, work is essentially distasteful and painstaking; consumption and leisure are delightful and desirable.

The market mechanism, upon which capitalism has built its ideological superstructure, thus assumes a hedonistic, acquisitive, and competitive behavior on the part of economic actors—consumers, workers, investors, and others. Implied in this assumption is the argument that the "economic man" is self-serving, rational, and a maximizer of returns to his endeavors.[1] All economic actions—production plans, sale of resources, purchasing decisions, and others—are made to maximize satisfaction or utility. For individuals and households, maximum satisfaction can be achieved by obtaining the highest level of living from a given amount of time, effort, or money expenditure. For private business firms, maximum satisfaction is equated with maximum profit. For resource owners, (workers, landlords, and savers), satisfaction is maximized when the rewards for their services are highest.

Principal Tools

The market system relies on private ownership, profit motive, and uncontrolled prices as its major institutions. The significance of private property is based on an

---

1. A new and controversial theory called bioeconomics or sociobiology also argues that people are "genetically" programmed to be selfish and competitive—even in their seemingly most altruistic actions. Self-interest is ingrained in each individual's genes.

early argument advanced by Aristotle, that the individual's attention to the maintenance and care of property is directly related to the extent of his personal interest and ownership in it. In ancient Roman laws, private property embodied rigid and absolute rights—rights to enjoy, destroy, or bequest. St. Thomas Aquinas held that property ownership was "natural" to human beings. In his early "natural right" theory, individual ownership of property was the foundation of better maintenance, order, and enjoyment—but only so long as it was not misused or abused. To John Locke, property ownership was also an indisputable natural right, along with individual life and liberty. Under contemporary theories of capitalism, private ownership is exercised through claims on incomes and through control of productive factors. The presumption is that only under private ownership of means of production can rational resource allocation be made in accord with consumer preferences.

Profit, as a reward for business ventures, is also considered central to the operation of free enterprise. It is the guide to business activity; a measure of success both for the firm and for its management; a source of saving and capital formation; and an incentive for risk taking and initiative. It is also argued that the imperatives of survival in a world of rapidly changing technology call for a protective shield of business "self-insurance," which can be covered only by profits. Under pure competition, where investments are light, entry and exit easy, and obsolescence can be written off swiftly, normal profits are presumably adequate for survival. Under conditions of imperfect competition (see below), profit assumes a new role as the "protector of the realm" in addition to its traditional function of motivation and rational resource allocation. Competitive or "normal" profits would not be sufficient. Excess or "abnormal" profits would have to be made to cover the imputed costs of contingent risks, future losses, and uncertain technological research and development. High profit levels thus become a cushion against future setbacks.

Market prices serve as the guideposts to profitable enterprise and as incentives to productive economic activity. Prices (including wages, interest and rent) that reflect consumer demand and factor scarcity help allocate resources to their most efficient use. They help distribute society's real wealth and income according to the relative demand for, and supply of, commodities and factors of production. Higher prices (and profits) tend to attract diligent entrepreneurs; higher wages paid for certain skills tend to reward smart and hard workers; higher interest rates encourage savings and facilitate investments; higher rents would put land to better use.

Major Policy Instruments

In its basic techniques, the market mechanism exemplifies private initiative and free enterprise. Initiative is considered private when there is no central planning or direction. Enterprise is considered free when its financing, organization. and management are in the hands of individuals or private groups. Under private enterprise, the objectives of economic activity (often identified with profit making) are determined free from government regulations. The enterprise's motivating force, its business decisions, and its final rewards or losses are all privately assumed.

The preference for private initiative and enterprise is based on two implicit presumptions: a belief in the supremacy of individual liberty and the natural efficiency of competition; and a strong distrust of the state's motives and its competence. In Adam Smith's view, legislatures are often directed by "partial interests," and governments are usually in the hands of "self-serving" groups. Smith and his followers argued that in the conduct of private enterprise (particularly when ownership and control are in the same hands), greater care is taken by owner-operators to estimate realistically costs and returns. Inefficiency and inertia are minimized, because private entrepreneurs are in a better position than public managers to determine the prices of their products and the cost of their supplies.

Free enterprise and private initiative are presumed to serve the public interest best, because they neither recognize nor require central planning, control, guidance, or direction. The government may provide for collective needs when and where private enterprise is unwilling or unable to meet them, but such functions are minimal and incidental to the main tasks of preserving law and order and providing the "rules of the game." The choice of occupation, production, exchange, and consumption is not to be hindered by state intervention or regulation.

Method of Operation Under Ideal Conditions

In its ideal form, the market mechanism is assumed to be operating under conditions for perfect competition where property is totally private, profit is the sole incentive for enterprise, and competition is characterized by perfect knowledge, perfect mobility of workers and resource owners, ease of entry and exit in the market, and homogeneity of goods and services.

A perfectly competitive economy is expected to function under four idealized conditions:

1. Economic decision makers are assumed to be so numerous, so small, and so anonymous that none, by his individual decision, can exert any appreciable influence over prices in his own favor.

2. Information regarding economic alternatives—services, occupations, enterprise opportunities, technological processes, and resource outlets—is available, free, and transferrable.

3. Goods and services, occupations, and investment outlets are homogeneous and standardized; there are no brand names, no real or artificial differentiations among the same products, no job discrimination against identical workers, no special favor given to similar customers, and no personal ties between buyers and sellers.

4. There is maximum freedom of entry and exit to, and from, markets and maximum factor mobility among business enterprises, occupations, and economic activities.[2]

Under these optimal conditions, a perfectly competitive market mechanism automatically tends to achieve the goals of full employment, individual freedom, and efficiency under an "equilibrium" (called the "Pareto optimum," after the Italian mathematical economist of the early twentieth century). The equilibrium is achieved when aggregate demand and aggregate supply are in balance. When there is such a balance, the tendency for further changes is absent. The equilibrium is thus characterized by an (ideal) situation where:

1. no consumer would be better off by trading one good for another;
2. no producer would gain more by shifting from one product to the next;
3. no factor owner would find it advantageous to change employer;
4. no firm would benefit from substituting one factor for another factor;
5. no supplier of any productive factor would be pirated away from his employment by another producer;
6. no resource owner would find it more rewarding to change place;
7. no consumer would receiver greater pleasure from increasing his consumption at any given time as compared to the additional satisfaction he expects to receive in some future time.

The Market Mechanism in the Real World

The abstract character of the Pareto optimum and its presumed social-welfare implications hardly requires emphasis. The basic features of the ideal market mechanism under perfect competition are obviously different from the patterns of production and exchange in the real world (chapter 10).

Human Behavior and Motives

To begin with, the universal validity of the motivational assumptions of people's acquisitiveness, self-interest preoccupation, and hedonism may be called into question. The German theorists of the "historical" school have long challenged the universality of man's individualism and self-interest. Instead, they attribute human motives in each society to its particular historical, cultural, and social traditions.

2. For a concise analytical treatment of this concept, see G. J. Stigler, "Perfect Competition, Historically Contemplated," *Journal of Political Economy*, February 1957.

The twentieth-century American "institutionalist" school, following Thorstein Veblen, also takes issue with the single-motive assumption of the classicists; it claims that human motives are varied and influenced not by rational calculation, but by instinct and environment.

Freud and his successors, Jung and Adler, in their turn attribute individual's basic motives not to calculated rationality but to sensuality, power drives, and ancestral traditions. More recently psychiatrists such as Viktor Frankel have cast aside both instinct and tradition in favor of a new motive: the search for the meaning of life itself. Behavioral psychologists, under J. B. Watson and B. F. Skinner, reject the subjective concepts of motivation altogether and consider human external behavior as largely predictable and subject to "scientific" controls.[3] Newer theories in the West emphasize security, stimulation, and identity as man's major motives in life. Other observers draw a distinction between personal and collective motivation, arguing that individuals are motivated by ambition, masses usually out of fear.

Modern studies of economic behavior—of consumers, businessmen, and workers—equally belie the laissez faire interpretation of the human being as a one-dimensional "economic man." While the assumption of human rationality and independence is still considered of value in economic exploration and business forecasting, it is not taken for granted as a realistic basis for policy determination or public control. People are not found always to be rational, calculating, pleasure-hungry, or leisure-conscious; they are both compulsive and impulsive. Human beings are also often driven by nonpecuniary goals, such as love, compassion, or dedication, on the one hand, and power, prestige, self-esteem, and status, on the other. The "canons of taste," in Veblen's enduring words, are often "pecuniary"; the more expensive an item, the more it is coveted. Consumption is often desired for its "conspicuous" aspects, not for its own sake or for the pleasure it supposedly bestows.

Ownership and Profit

In the real world, entrepreneurs and business managers, too, behave in a pragmatic way; as a rule, they do not insist on profit maximization, but are often satisfied with certain "socially tolerable" rates of profit. Corporations are often run by nonowner executives: business managers, public servants, or similar "organization men." Executives are mostly interested in their own survival, and that of their fiefdoms. Their instinct for survival favors a live-and-let-live course of action over an aggressive and combative policy. Embarrassingly large profit rates are thus not overtly sought

---

3. Learned anthropologists such as Malinowski, Thurnwald, and Mead also tell us that in primitive, economically rural, and culturally fatalistic societies, motivations beyond survival are largely determined by prevailing social institutions: kinships, tribal taboos, religious rituals, and sociopolitical status in life. Acquisitive drives are neither individually developed nor socially condoned. Instead, the emphasis is on gift giving, discharging family obligations, and friendship reciprocity.

after, and if such rates are inadvertently realized, they are subtly camouflaged or cleverly explained and justified.

These clear deviations from the ideal assumptions regarding consumers and businessmen's motivation and behavior directly and substantially modify the conditions of Pareto's general equilibrium. To wit, a laissez faire economy would ensure efficiency only if certain stringent conditions were carefully maintained at all times. In the area of production, for example, the so-called free play of impersonal market forces would bring about desirable resource allocation only if—and these are all very big ifs—businessmen were truly subordinate to the will of consumers; producers were perfectly free to use least-cost methods; competitors were forced to reduce cost and improve quality; production costs were accurately measurable; and there were no decreasing costs to scale of operation—in short, if there were no "externalities." In resource utilization, the preconditions are equally strict. Resource owners must be independent, rational, active, and competitive. Opportunities must be widely known, information must be available and free, and original income distribution should present no substantial gaps between the rich and the poor. In consumption, long-run equilibrium could be optimum only if consumers were the best judge of their needs and interests, fully informed of alternatives, acting rationally, and independent in their choice.

Characteristics of Imperfect Competition

As one can easily observe, the conditions of production and exchange in the real world are very different from the model's. First, information regarding the nature, content, quality, and cost of many products are not readily available. Second, producers in many economic pursuits are few and interdependent; workers are organized, and the advantages of large-scale production or distribution may make atomistic competition inefficient. Third, products and services may be artificially differentiated, making an intelligent evaluation of qualities and comparison of products almost impossible for an average shopper. Fourth, obstacles to entry and exit may include heavy capital outlays required for establishing certain businesses, institutional barriers like union membership or exclusive dealership arrangements, commercial impediments such as prohibitive costs of national advertising or maintaining a vast dealership network, and so forth.

In short, unlike the idealized model, where private cost to the entrepreneur equals total cost to society, these costs often differ considerably in the real world. To a private businessman, motivated by profit, costs consist of direct and indirect outlays that affect the firm's net revenue. Toil, sacrifices, injuries, or damages involved in the production process which are not paid for and which impose no claim on the firm's revenues are not considered a part of costs. They do not enter into private cost-price-profit calculations. Yet almost every productive enterprise involves extra costs to society that are not privately accounted for. These costs reflect hidden or concealed damages inflicted on society as a whole in addition to those reflected in private cost calculations and profit and loss statements of private firms. Glaring examples of social costs are the unpaid damages by power companies and oil refiners who pollute the air or water surrounding their plants, chemical wastes disposal in rivers and water basins with no compensation to injured farmers and consumers, and strip mining without land restoration.

Economists refer to the gaps between private and social costs as "externalities," both positive and negative. "External economies" or savings refer to a favorable effect on a firm's cost as a result of the actions of a different firm or the government. An "external diseconomy" is defined as a burden or harm done to others. The so-called social overhead capital (public roads, state labor, training facilities, employment exchanges) are obvious costs borne by society and benefiting private firms. They are private firms' "external economies." The damages inflicted upon other persons or the environment (pollution, congestion, and noise by motorists) are examples of "diseconomies," or social costs not reflected in the prices of private automobiles. The presence of external economies and diseconomies, in one observer's view, is "one of the major exceptions to the proposition that the invisible hand guides us to a Pareto optimum."[4] Thus, wherever there are externalities—and lapses from the Pareto optimum—a laissez faire, or hands-off, policy by the government would not ensure social welfare. Some kind of group action, or *collective involvement*, may become necessary.

This brings us to the discussion of the type of market mechanism and competition that exist in the real world. As the foregoing discussion showed, the modern market mechanism is "imperfect." The question is: How imperfect can competition become before losing its computing and coordinating grip in obtaining social welfare or the "common good"? Two conceptual standards have been suggested. The first one, called workable competition, emphasizes the structure of the market and seeks to identify the closest approximation to the perfectly competitive ideal. Workable competition requires a considerable number of buyers and sellers dealing in closely related products, the absence of collusion among economic units, effective freedom of entry, the absence of artificial impediments and barriers between buyers and sellers, independent rivalry on prices among a large number of sellers, and the existence of sufficient incentives for innovation.

The second conceptual standard is called effective competition; it emphasizes business behavior and performance. In this concept, any market structure or organization that can approximate the results of perfect competition should be judged as socially acceptable. The key tests of desirable behavior and performance include business responsiveness to changes in market conditions, downward movement of prices and costs in the face of falling demand, the use of the most efficient plant size, efficient adjustment of capacity to output, concentration of

4. See D. K. Whitcomb, *Externalities and Welfare* (New York: Columbia University Press, 1972), p. 1.

competition on product improvement and cost reduction instead of socially wasteful promotional rivalry, a rate of profit not out of line with rates in activities of similar nature, progressive innovation, and a willingness to share the fruits of new processes and techniques with competitors in exchange for reasonable rewards.

Strengths and Weaknesses of the Market

As was indicated in chapter 2, any mechanism of economic problem solving has the basic tasks of calculation, motivation, and coordination. Different mechanisms may therefore be compared by their costs of collecting and communicating relevant information for economic decision making, by the effectiveness of their cues and incentives in encouraging productive economic activities, and by their ability to coordinate economic actions to optimize goal attainment.

Advantages

The first and foremost attribute of the market mechanism lies in the maximizing of individual economic freedoms. This superiority of the market over other mechanisms hardly needs elaboration. Under no other system do people enjoy such discretion in demanding and obtaining what their hearts desire, and nowhere is the opportunity for initiative and self-expression more abundant. The market rations the national product among consumers and motivates resource owners into productive activity with a minimum of government control, coercion, threat, or other forms of intervention.

    The second major advantage is efficiency; that is, the system is likely to obtain the highest GNP commensurate with given resources and technology at least effort (cost). The market reflects individual free choices in a most effective manner through costs and prices; it leaves economic decisions to the free will of the largest possible number of people who are willing to take the irksome or pleasurable consequences of their decisions. Consumers, resource owners, and entrepreneurs seeking to maximize their individual private gains need no other instruction than to keep a watchful eye on price signals.[5] The decentralized mechanism, depending on the nature and extent of competitiveness in the market, tends to solve basic economic problems smoothly, effectively, impersonally, and at less cost than any other apparatus.[6] Efficiency is enhanced by a more direct and accurate manifesta-

---

    5. The analogy with traffic control in a large metropolitan city is of interest here. Instead of every motorist being asked to call a central switchboard at every intersection to find out if he has the right of way, a simple rule (*go*, if the signal is green; *stop*, if it is red; *slow down*, if it is amber) is all that is normally necessary to direct traffic without one single call being made, or one single additional instruction being issued by a central control board.
    6. For a more rigorous analysis of the market's efficiency, see the references to the basic theoretical works at the end of the chapter.

tion of consumer preferences and by the speed with which economic decisions can respond to these preferences. Decision makers can be expected to be more informed, more rational, and more responsible regarding their own interests and actions. Incompetence, miscalculation, and inefficiency are quickly penalized by losses; ability, innovation, and foresight are rewarded by profit. As the individual's own capital, time, and effort are at stake, the incentives to use scarce resources efficiently are stronger than those in the other mechanisms.

The third principal advantage of the market is its inherent tendency toward technological progress. The attraction of anticipated profit and the fear of possible loss tends to exert powerful pressure on entrepreneurs to search continually for cost reduction, product improvement, diversification, and technological innovation. Businessmen are constantly challenged by new materials, new commodities, new technology, and new processes that present competitive cost or quality advantages. Competition is a benevolent intruder that helps shake an established market and destroy its vested interests in order to create a new path to progress.

A fourth, highly admired merit of the free market system is its alleged ability to bring personal gain and public welfare into harmony. While the individual, in Adam Smith's everlasting words, "neither intends to promote the public interest nor knows how much he is promoting it," the invisible hand of competition would see to it that he indeed promote the public welfare—a social objective that is no part of his intention.

The market mechanism, under less than ideal conditions, may not be as free or efficient or progressive as in perfectly competitive situations, but the economy's adaptation to continuous change in consumer tastes, technology, resource availability, and population movements is still considerably more rapid and smooth than in a centrally directed economy. Large-scale private production and distribution may involve internal and external cost-cutting benefits. Similar benefits may also accrue to big-business operation through mergers and conglomeration, benefits derived not necessarily from mass production and large-size operation, but from such possibilities as unified buying, selling, and financing; more efficient utilization of personnel; and increased effectiveness of integrated administration, transportation, marketing, sales, and promotional activities. Here large company size signifies large-scale ownership and management rather than large technological plant size.

Business concentration in the hands of large corporations may equally tend to increase the industry's ability to adapt itself to market shifts and to serve as a basis for more important inventions and innovations through a pooling of money, skills, and management. In many industries, pioneering technical developments may come from larger firms simply because new inventions are not simple or cheap.

Similarly, bigness in business may be a source of vigorous and dynamic competition just as much as rivalry among small units. Large concerns are apt to be more progressive in creating new technologies than small units because they have greater incentives for making larger profits from a larger share of the market. Competition among large concerns is also held to be not only keener but more meaningful and effective as reflected in a wider range of choice for consumers.

A final, but equally significant defense of big private business is the ability and willingness of large corporations to give to a wide range of charitable causes: philanthropic, educational, cultural, and civic. Corporate giving is an effective means—occasionally the only means—of keeping certain socially desirable activities or organizations alive and healthy. Whether based on corporate social responsibility or as a matter of prudent realism, big business grants serve many worthy causes in society.

Disadvantages

The market is a mechanism of reciprocal controls by buyers and sellers that under perfect competition, would tend to insure the common welfare. It is impersonal, responsive, efficient, and exact. Without competition, sellers of factors or products may be tempted to charge exorbitant prices to producers or consumers, and buyers may be encouraged to take advantage of resource owners or suppliers. In neither case would the Pareto optimum and its efficiency implications any longer hold. However, as we shall see presently, even under its most stringent assumptions, a laissez faire system would not be able to obtain all national economic objectives.

Even if people were well informed and economically rational, even if firms were many and small, even if products were simple and undifferentiated, even if entry and exit were easy and frequent—even if all this were true, a perfectly competitive market economy would still not be able to guarantee full employment and economic stability at all times. Market forces, to be sure, would be self-adjusting in the long run, but in the short run there would be no guarantee of price stability, full employment, or steady growth. A highly competitive economy, in short, may be a fairly unstable economy.

Another weakness of the market lies in its inability to ensure an equitable distribution of income. As the ownership of wealth and means of production give certain people greater say (or "dollar vote") in determining the *what* and *how much* composition of the gross national product, two consequences would be inevitable: people who start rich are likely to maintain their privileged positions, and possibly even get richer; and final goods and services may not be those that give greatest satisfaction to the poor majority, may not go to those who may need them most or to those who may derive the greatest pleasure from them. Private wants (lucrative gadgets and profitable trivia) may take priority over social needs (slum clearance, recreational facilities, cultural services). A market economy is thus a basically unequal economy, disinterested in the ideal of distributive justice and income equity.

A third flaw in the market mechanism is its inability to produce public or merit goods (chapter 6). National defense, crime prevention, health delivery, public education or foreign aid are indivisible services which cannot always be produced piecemeal or sold on the basis of ability to pay. These goods cannot be provided by the market, because it would be extremely costly, if not impossible, to exclude reluctant beneficiaries or nonpaying customers.

The same is true of goods and services for which private incentives and the lure of profit are not strong enough or the risks are too formidable to attract private investment (basic research, space exploration, environmental clean-up). Closely associated with the prohibitive risks of certain business ventures as a liability of the market mechanism is the latter's inability to compensate for hazardous tasks not purchasable in the marketplace. War is the textbook example; there are others.

Closely related to the problem of high risk and insufficient incentive in certain types of activity is the inability of the market to ensure rapid rates of growth and capital-intensive technological innovation. Both of these objectives require heavy investment in plant and equipment, which would normally be unavailable without high rates of profit and a high propensity to save on the part of consumers. They may require public subsidies and support.

A fourth inherent incapacity of the market lies in the area of social cost accounting. Competitive markets fail to take into account the total costs of production when externalities are present. Cost figures shown in private producers' ledgers underestimate the total (social) costs when the result adversely affects the welfare of others; they may also occasionally overestimate total costs when there are social benefits involved. Oil refineries, private residential incinerators, and motor vehicles pollute the air without having to pay for its purification. Riverside factories and lakeside plants that discharge their waste into fresh water often escape from bearing the full cost of such pollution. Airplane passengers are not charged for the nuisance cost of their jet noise over airport neighborhoods, nor are automobile companies billed for junked cars and traffic congestion, or billboard advertisers for ruining highway landscapes. In short, these and other third-party damages are seldom accounted for in the private cost-benefit analyses of profit-motivated competitors, and even less frequently compensated for by them.

In the absence of the right signals from the private markets, the system will tend to allocate more resources into the production of goods and services that involve external diseconomies, imposing external costs on innocent third parties. The market may also underallocate resources to areas with external benefits to noncontracting parties.

When the market mechanism is less then ideal, deficiencies associated with it take on even greater proportion. A fundamental indictment of the imperfect market is that it encourages and facilitates business concentration and growth of monopoly power.[7] A market dominated by large private business concerns—usually called shared monopolies or oligopolies—may involve antisocial behavior and antisocial performance. Shared monopolies presumably possess the power to charge higher-then-competitive prices and to sacrifice product safety and realiability on the

---

7. The emergence of big business and giant corporations, while always a result of "imperfect competition," may be due to technical or financial advantages of large-scale operation (economies in the scale of production or benefits of lower-cost finance).

altar of profit. Consequently, they are likely to contribute to income inequality, economic instability, and slow economic progress. In the absence of external sanctions, oligopolists may charge "all the traffic will bear." There may also be attempts at price fixing, market sharing, and industrial collusion. The proliferation of styles, models, and packages, bolstered by a barrage of advertising, may tend to undermine rational allocation and cause needless duplication of production and sales facilities.

Private monopolistic and oligopolistic firms, by virtue of their high profits and accumulated reserves, can effectively ignore national credit policies designed to stabilize the economy, and their investment and employment policies also may prove economically destabilizing. A large business concern may also be reluctant to make use of its research and development discoveries in the service of better quality or lower prices if such innovations should threaten to cut its profit margins.

Even big business efficiency is not a certainty. Many industry studies show that big business and greater economic efficiency do not always go hand in hand. Many small and medium-size businesses are often just as efficient as large firms, and when the business size approaches giant proportions, it may indeed lose some of its dynamism, flexibility, adaptation to change, and overall efficiency. A large business firm may end up as an entrenched bureaucratic organization, with all the latter's shortcomings.

Still another unfavorable aspect of the unregulated, imperfect market is its alleged tendency to weaken economic freedoms. Economic power, even if not used, remains a potential danger to a free society. In the absence of the harsh discipline of perfect competition, there is no built-in antitrust mechanism; and without the forceful and impersonal safeguards of unfettered competition, large business firms are more than likely to throw their weight around at the expense of their smaller competitors, employees, suppliers, customers, potential challengers, and the general public.

A corollary of this type of criticism is the undesirable emergence of pressure groups. Concentration of economic power in the hands of a few large concerns may not only prove harmful to the social interest in itself; it may lead to the rise of countervailing powers on the part of the government, labor, and other interest groups. The victims of monopolistic power—workers, suppliers, consumers—would sooner or later come to the realization that they must either take direct actions to protect themselves or to secure the government's assistance in making up for their disadvantaged position. In either case, the emerging power designed to counter-balance established privileges is most likely to reduce consumer freedom, hurt unorganized workers, and penalize small firms. Many economists believe that big business has given, and continues to give, substantial impetus to the unhealthy growth of big government, big labor, and other powerful vested interests.

Finally, there are criticisms of big business's behavior outside the market: unlawful contributions to political parties, domestic and foreign bribery of government officials, threats by transnational corporations to the political integrity and independence of small nations, and other "white-collar" wrongdoings that infringe on social and moral values.

The Need for Additional Safeguards

As the discussion in this chapter has indicated, the philosophical system of individual liberty (and its economic counterpart, individual sovereignty) is a normative system based on certain rigid assumptions.[8] The criticisms of the market, under conditions of both perfect and imperfect competition, show that for a variety of reasons this mechanism alone cannot be relied upon to ensure all contemporary national goals.[9]

At the same time, it is widely recognized that when the allocative and distributive controls of the market prove ineffective, inadequate, or socially objectionable, the public interest would have to be safeguarded through supplemental mechanisms and corrective measures. The need for such remedial measures relates to the structural as well as the operational shortcomings of the market. Once, for example, it is realized that individuals are neither the best judges of their interests nor absolutely *most* rational in their choices, individual freedom can hardly be defended either as a provider of maximum personal satisfaction or as a contributor to optimum public welfare. Similarly, once it is admitted that consumers are not adequately informed about the qualities of products and services, consumer sovereignty can no longer be considered the best calculating and coordinating force in the allocation of resources.

The same is true of market structure and business behavior. Where small-scale production is costly and inefficient, the promulgation of small production units cannot be economically justified. Or where technological imperatives leave the total industry's production in the hands of only a few large firms, genuine price competition cannot be expected to prevail; nor can some type of price leadership be totally avoided. With the concentration of economic power in a few large corporations, the direction of production and the freedom of investment decisions cannot be left totally to the private sector without jeopardizing the goals of growth, full employment, stability, and equity. Other supplemental mechanisms will be needed.[10]

8. The "Pareto optimum" assumes: people are self-interested, rational, informed, and active; products and factors are standardized; producers, consumers, and resource owners have no control over the market to their own advantage; and resource mobility in any and all markets is unobstructed.

9. We are also told by radical antimarketeers that an unbridled private-enterprise system is bound to turn itself into monopoly capitalism and mindless technology which, acting through an interlocking bureaucratic-industrial complex, may lead the human race into increasingly destructive paths.

10. See "The Future of Consumer Sovereignty," *American Economic Review*, May 1972.

THE TASK OF MANAGEMENT

Suggestions for Additional Readings

ACKLEY, G. *Macroeconomic Theory and Policy.* New York: Macmillan, 1978.

BAIN, J. S. *Barriers to New Competition.* Cambridge: Harvard University Press, 1956.

BERLE, A. A., AND G. C. MEANS. *The Modern Corporation and Private Property.* New York: Macmillan, 1932.

BLAIR, J. M. *Economic Concentration: Structure, Behaviour and Public Policy.* New York: Harcourt Brace, 1972.

BORNSTEIN, M., ED. *Plan and Market.* New Haven: Yale University Press, 1973.

COMANOR, W. S. "Advertising, Market Structure, and Performance." *Review of Economics and Statistics,* November 1967.

LEFTWICH, R. H. *The Price System and Resource Allocation.* Hinsdale: Dryden, 1979.

LINDBLOM, C. E. *Politics and Markets.* New York: Basic Books, 1977.

MAGNUSON, W. *The Dark Side of the Marketplace.* Englewood Cliffs: Prentice-Hall, 1968.

MURPHY, R. E. *Adaptive Processes in Economic Systems.* New York: Academic Press, 1965.

ROUSSEAU, S. *Capitalism and Catastrophe.* New York: Cambridge University Press, 1979.

SCHERER, F. M. *Industrial Market Structure and Economic Performance.* Chicago: Rand McNally, 1971.

SILK, L. "Where the Power of Business Lies." *New York Times,* 4 July 1978.

SIMON, J. L. *Issues in the Economics of Advertising.* Champaign: University of Illinois Press, 1970.

STIGLER, G. J. "A Theory of Oligopoly." *Journal of Political Economy,* February 1964.

SWANN, D. *Concentration and Competition.* London: PEP, 1967.

TELSER, L. G. "Advertising and Competition." *Journal of Political Economy,* December 1964.

TOWNSEND, R. C. "The Root of All Evil—Concentrated Economic Power." *New York Times Book Review,* 30 May 1971.

6

Decision Making by Proxy

As indicated in chapter five, the market can at best achieve economic efficiency; it can ensure neither stability nor equity. Some of the other pressing objectives of modern nations also cannot be left to the automatic free play of market forces. In short, the deficiencies of the market call for supplemental mechanisms and measures to ensure the attainment of other goals.

One method of making up for some of the market deficiencies is decision making by delegation or proxy. *Delegated sovereignty* allows modern society to satisfy part of its members' wants through delegation rather than directly through the market.[1] Decision making by proxy is sometimes referred to as democratic decision making. In the West, it is called democratic capitalism; elsewhere it is known as democratic socialism. We saw in chapter 1 how difficult it was to define capitalism, socialism, or communism as concrete socioeconomic orders. The same ambiguity applies, in no small measure, to the term *democracy*. Democracy means many things to many people. Literally, it means "rule by the masses." The Greek statesman Pericles confined it to an administration "in the hands of the many and not of the few." Aristotle had to qualify the "many" as those who were "also poor." John Stuart Mill defined democracy as a form of government in which the sovereignty, or supreme controlling power, is vested in the entire community.

But the entire community is obviously incapable of running the economy. In a large modern industrial state, a government run by all the people, even if all should mean only the adult population, is an impracticality, if not a myth. A similar difficulty applies to the concept of popular rule. If such a rule means mass participation in the decision-making process, then only a small agrarian society with a simple structure and routinized problems can be really ruled by all the people. As Gladstone once said: "No people of a magnitude to be called a nation has

---

1. Delegated sovereignty, in its broadest sense, is not limited to parliamentary representation on the national or local political arenas. Proxy power given by stockholders to corporate directors and acceptance by rank-and-file workers of wage contracts negotiated by union leadership also involve delegation.

69

ever, in strict sense, governed itself; the best they can do perhaps is to choose their governors."

Essential Features

The first outstanding feature of delegated sovereignty is the *indirect* method of resource allocation and income distribution.[2] Under this process, the allocation of national resources and the distribution of income are determined not by direct private expenditures in the marketplace, but *indirectly* by way of tax collection, budgetary appropriation, and a host of other macroeconomic policies. Individual citizens vote for their favored *representatives*, who will then make certain decisions for them. Elected representatives vote to spend part of their constituents' income for the production of the so-called public goods and merit goods. (See below.) Unlike the situation in the market, however, there is no direct, or one-to-one, link between payment and consumption. That is, one's tax bill bears no direct relationship to the amount of "collective goods" one consumes; one must pay for all tax-supported government projects, like it or not.

Second, in the exercise of this delegation, adult citizens have a right as well as a privilege to cast their ballots in favor of or against opposing candidates, issues, or actions on the basis of one man, one vote.[3] Again, unlike the market's case, the number of votes and the power over the production of goods are not directly related. In the market system, "money votes" determine the size and composition of GNP. People with more money have more to say. In the public arena, however, while each person has one and only one vote, political power is not perfectly equally divided. Some individuals, by virtue of their talent, skill, prestige, or political acumen may indeed exert greater effective influence than others.

Third, in fulfilling the voters' mandates, the representatives use their proxy power to influence the size and distribution of GNP by a majority decision. Even though the public sector proper in a country may be relatively small, the influence of the legislature on the economy as a whole may be extensive. In some cases, almost all aspects of economic life, in one way or another, are affected by democratic assemblies. Once again, in contrast to the market situation, the payment for and the receipt of goods by an individual is not independent of the decision of others. In the private sector, an individual may refuse to buy a ticket to a firemen's ball even if the entire neighborhood should decide to attend. In the public sector, however, the will of the majority almost always prevails, and the minority is virtually compelled to pay for "the ticket," ball or no ball.

Fourth, the policies reached and the decisions made by the delegates are put into effect through a bureaucracy, the government's executive branch. Bureaucrats

2. The delegation of decision making, to be sure, is not limited to the economic sphere. Representative bodies and assemblies exist and thrive in the political, social, cultural, and other domains of human life.

3. If the right to vote is guaranteed to all adults regardless of sex, color, creed, wealth, or other discriminatory reasons, the suffrage is universal. Otherwise, it is limited.

are nonelected officials, subordinate to elected leaders both in the establishment of priorities and the allocation of resources. All bureaucrats receive their mandate for action and means of implementation from elected officials.[4]

Fifth, the delegates are expected to represent the whole nation and not only individual constituencies. That is to say, representatives are free from the constituents' day-to-day instruction, and they are only indirectly accountable to the electorate. They can be defeated in future elections; they can be impeached or recalled upon extremely flagrant abuses; and, in some cases, a general referendum may be allowed to alter or undo democratic legislation. These last two actions, however, are rare.

The question that immediately arises is why people should willingly choose to delegate their sovereignty to a relatively smaller group of individuals. There are several reasons. First, as mentioned before, a piecemeal production and acquisition of certain desirable goods or services is physically impossible through the market, because any beneficiary could refuse to pay his share, knowing full well he could get away with it. For this reason, some analysts believe that no large organization, like a nation, can produce basic public or merit goods and services by the purely voluntary purchase (contribution) of its members.[5] The reasoning is simple: As long as public and merit goods are made available, why not get a free ride? Everyone knows full well that in an epidemic, it would be self-defeating for the authorities to refuse innoculation to those who do not pay their share.

The second reason for the collective production of certain goods or services is that the alternatives available to an individual consumer are so complex as to require either special expertise for selection or considerable cost for acquisition. The choice of a weapons system, weather information, and environmental research are among this variety. In all these situations, individuals may be willing to save themselves time, energy, worry, or high costs by delegating allocation decisions to their representatives.

The third rationale of voluntary delegation is the desirability of maintaining a healthy, viable, and harmonious society. Implicit in this desire is the provision of

---

4. Interestingly enough, while the command mechanism, which also relies on bureaucracy, can function without a parliament, a parliamentary democracy cannot operate without a bureaucracy.

5. *Public* goods are defined as: any product or service (like police protection) that, if available to anyone in society, must be equally available to everyone; or a good in "joint supply," like a lighthouse, which, when made available to one individual can be easily or freely supplied to others as well; or a widely usable good (like a radio broadcast) the consumption of which by one individual does not diminish the amount available to others. *Merit* goods and services are the ones supplied by the state free of charge (or almost free) to its citizens on the basis of individual *need*. Education, health care, community services, and others fall in this category. The dividing line (not always hard and fast) between public and merit goods is that the latter could be purchased by consumers in the market, but that there are socially beneficial reasons for their collective production and, in fact, "free" distribution. A healthy, educated, and contented citizenry, for example, may be considered useful or necessary to attain other social goods. For a fuller discussion of these characteristics, see Mancur Olson, Jr., *The Logic of Collective Action* (Cambridge: Harvard University Press, 1971).

certain safeguards for a full and efficient use of resources, sufficient incentives for the production of socially desirable goods and services, and adequate protection for the victims of uncontrollable hazards—none of which can be produced or purchased piecemeal. Many citizens, for example, may like to make use of public facilities—museums, libraries, concerts, parks, swimming pools, day-care centers, recreation areas—but they may not be able to contribute anything for their provision. Yet, from a social standpoint, they may "need" and "deserve" having these services at their disposal free or at a nominal cost.[6]

Basic Structure

Like other mechanisms delegated sovereignty is structured on certain assumptions regarding human motivation and behavior, some specific tools for action, and a given method of operation.

Behavioral Assumptions

Underlying the rationale for delegated decision making is the (loaded) assumption that people in an organized society are interested in reasoning together and reaching a consensus on major issues, refuse to accept their fate as fixed or predetermined, are bound by a social contract to govern themselves intelligently and in the best interests of all, and are committed to achieving the greatest good of the greatest number. Buttressing this assumption is the (not unquestionable) belief in man's innate intelligence, his fair-mindedness, his reliance on reason, and his ability to make ultimately wise decisions through deliberation and discussion.

Superimposed on this essentially libertarian assumption of man's good-will and rationality is the counterargument regarding human inability for self-fulfillment in a large and impersonal society. In Robert Owen's view, society institutionally incapacitates or emasculates man's benign "propensities, instincts, and faculties." The individual's growing dependence on his fellow men in the modern world makes the emergence of the state as the guardian of individual liberty and the guarantor of individual welfare almost inevitable.

According to Thomas Green, a British liberal philosopher, freedom "in the positive sense" is the unleashing of the capabilities of all men in society in such a

6. Delegated sovereignty may sometimes turn out to be temporarily "involuntary" when people initially agree to delegate part of their economic sovereignty to their elected representatives in a limited way, but the representatives go beyond their mandates (tax and spend more than the voters approve at any given time). To the extent, therefore, that the electorate have to accept the consequences of their initial delegation until the next election, one may consider such proxy decisions "involuntary."

way that one's own good can be found in the "common good".[7] In Green's view, it is the business of the state "to provide the circumstances under which such fullest and freest exercise of human faculties in the service of common good may become possible. The mere "enlightened self-interest" of individuals under a laissez faire system of unlimited freedom of contract, in his view, would not be sufficient to ensure free development of human potentialities. Without a certain minimum standard of "moral and material well-being," the majority of people cannot be expected to recognize, promote, or safeguard their own interests, unaided by proper legislation.

Opposed also to the older individualistic assumption of man's rights and wrongs is the new liberalism of Leonard Hobhouse, another British social philosopher, to whom individual liberty is only one side of social life; the other side is mutual aid and collective action. In his view, individual rights cannot be in conflict with the common good, nor could any right exist apart from the common good. Social harmony is not the absence of conflict but the presence of positive support. Deprecating what he calls the "too optimistic" assumption of a "natural harmony" to be obtained through laissez faire, Hobhouse argues that the "social ideal" lies in an "ethical harmony" that can be attained partly through rational discipline, but partly also by the improvement in the conditions of life. All social distinctions in wealth, power, or position in such an "organic" society must be arranged with a view to maximize community welfare.

In this view, delegated actions to ensure full employment, equality of opportunity, economic security, and social welfare may enhance not threaten individual liberty. Unlike theoretical laissez faire capitalism, where the state's responsibility beyond the preservation of law and order is severely limited and what is not specifically assigned to the government is left to the individual, delegated sovereignty considers public intervention both necessary and legitimate. The legitimacy of public action, both for ensuring greater welfare and higher efficiency, is thus one of the hallmarks of "democracy." Not only has society a right to interfere when market mechanism breaks down, it also has a duty to take rational action whenever individual greed, ignorance, helplessness, or irrationality jeopardize society's welfare.

Institutional Differences from Laissez Faire

Property ownership, economic enterprise, and pricing under delegated sovereignty differ from similar institutions under the market system. Under the market mechanism, property is essentially private and widely diffused. Under delegation,

---

7. Needless to say, the popular concepts of the *common good, social interest,* and *general welfare* are difficult terms to define because of the difficulties involved in interpersonal comparisons of utility, pleasure, and interest. A number of "welfare" economists have tried to establish certain comparative guidelines, but the controversy has not been settled yet.

THE TASK OF MANAGEMENT

there are two important qualifications to this laissez faire rule: control over the disposition of a portion of national wealth and income belonging to individuals and private groups is entrusted to the elected representatives; and while the delegates are not given personal title to those assets, they have total collective control over them. National and local assemblies enact laws and regulations that affect individual wealth, income, and disposition of property. Public revenues and expenditures at various governmental levels also involve obvious infringements on individual property rights. Thus, while property itself is still privately owned and widely spread, the management and control of that property is shared with a number of "trustees."

Economic enterprise is similarly affected by some conceptual modifications under delegated sovereignty. For example, certain entrepreneurial functions related to the provision of capital and assumption of risks are largely separated. That is, a good part of the taxpayers' income and assets is spent not by them but by their delegates on their behalf (and ostensibly for their benefits). Actual decision makers thus possess no property of their own and bear no risks for making wrong decisions.[8]

The pricing process is also somewhat different from the free market's. Under individual sovereignty, the interplay of impersonal supply-and-demand forces determines market prices (as well as wages, interest rates, and rents) in accordance with factor costs and consumer demand. Market prices, in turn, determine the choice of technology, the distribution of the social product among its rightful claimants, and the provision for future needs. Under delegated sovereignty, some prices in certain important segments of the economy may be controlled or affected by legislative decisions. During periods of emergency or hyperinflation, prices and wages may be frozen or allowed to change only within certain guidelines. Certain prices may also be permanently regulated, supported, or otherwise controlled by delegated decisions for specific sociopolitical objectives. Consequently, prevailing prices may reflect neither private demand nor relative factor scarcities very accurately at all times.[9]

Wage-price controls are often part of an overall "incomes policy." Incomes policy is a method of combating inflation without having to undergo unemployment; it is a shortcut around the inflation-unemployment trade-off. As it has evolved in postwar Europe and elsewhere, incomes policy refers to a formal, statutory freeze or limitation on rises in prices and wages; or some voluntary and informal guidelines for limiting wage-price hikes. Statutory incomes policy requires an elaborate administrative machinery to monitor wage-price increases; its effectiveness is also often temporary and mostly psychological. Voluntary guidelines are easier and less costly to establish, but they often favor the unions and businesses that choose not to cooperate with the government's wage and price rules. Like all

8. A parallel with Western large private corporations, foundations, and trade unions is both clear and close.

9. A major difference in price policy between this mechanism and the command process is that here prices are simply *controlled* in the public interest, while there they are centrally *determined* in accordance with the leadership's priorities.

controls, they both shift the criteria for the allocation of resources from consumers' priorities to the delegates' preferences.

Limitations on market-determined prices usually extend to various sectors of the economy quite apart from the "incomes policy." For example, almost all modern countries have usury laws prohibiting the charging of interest on borrowed money over certain percentages. In almost all countries, too, commercial bank rates on saving deposits are subject to various ceilings. Public utility rates (of buses, airlines, water, power, telephones) need the approval of regulatory agencies. Still other prices are supported by the state over and above certain minimum levels: some farm products and other staples are often subject to price supports. Many others are strongly influenced by tariffs, import quotas, public subsidies, exchange controls, discount rates, and similar measures. When not specifically controlled, wages and fringe benefits are subject to minimum wage laws, social security provisions, and the like.

Principal Tools

In between laissez faire and central planning is a host of other techniques and levers a community may use. A mixed economy, which is partly directed and managed by delegation, uses certain techniques that differ from both "doing nothing" and "doing everything."

Broadly speaking, delegated sovereignty uses four principal, closely related techniques. The first category relates to the *stabilization* of economic activity. It includes the prevention of undesirable economic fluctuations (severe inflation or recession); full utilization of national resources, particularly labor; and rectification of certain structural distortions and imbalances in the economy (unemployment caused by automation). The purview of stabilization measures extends from demand management through monetary and fiscal policies to incomes policy covering wages and prices.

The second category embraces the *regulation* of economic activity. It consists of measures designed to improve competition and to prevent possible abuses of market power. Included in this category are measures against monopoly and restraint of trade; safeguards for the interests of consumers, workers, and resource owners; and surveillance over rates charged and services supplied by public utilities. The range and variety of regulatory devices used by the government are extensive. Regulatory agencies use legislative, judicial, and executive controls to mitigate the inequalities and abuses of the imperfectly competitive business firms. Regulation is preferred to both state ownership and operation of a business and to an unregulated business enterprise that can be sued only in a court for violation of the public trust. A regulated private activity is considered preferable to a nationalized firm, because the latter has a tendency to become routinized, rigidified, and self-perpetuating despite clear inefficiency. Regulation is considered preferable to litigation because of great speed of adjudication and less costs. A regulatory body is also considered better suitable to deal with abuses of "national monopolies" for several reasons: a trilateral administrative body that combines the legislative, judicial, and executive functions can develop the kind of expertise unavailable to the legislatures and the courts; it possesses greater operational flexibility than the others; and it replaces political partisanship by independent judgment.[10]

The third basic technique of delegated sovereignty involves the *provision of security*. It is aimed at rectifying certain social inequalities and injustices through public assistance and guidance. This type of action covers, among others, unemployment insurance and old-age pension, retraining and rehabilitation of unemployed or unemployable workers, and welfare payments and disaster relief.

The fourth indirect intervention technique is *promotion* of socially desirable economic activity. It aims at the improvement of socioeconomic infrastructures and needed assistance to the private sector, such as recognition of the creative rights of inventors and innovators, cost sharing with private enterprise in the case of high-risk ventures, protection of home industries against foreign competitors, and public-sponsored research.

The foregoing techniques of stabilization, regulation, protection, and promotion may be obtained through a number of public policies. These policies are too familiar to require much elaboration. Fiscal instruments include government's taxes and expenditures; transfer payments, such as pensions, subsidies, and social insurance; public borrowing and lending; and transactions on public assets. Taxes are often raised and expenditures reduced to realize a surplus during periods of economic booms and undesirable inflationary pressures. Transfer payments may be increased or decreased to make up for the insufficiency or excess of purchasing power of special groups. Borrowing and debt repayments may be used to offset state deficits and surpluses. Public assets may be bought or sold for many of the same purposes.

Monetary tools are more numerous and generally more flexible than fiscal measures. Major monetary instruments in relatively advanced economies include central banks' legal reserve requirements, discount rate changes, open-market transactions in government securities, and selective credit controls. An increase in the reserve requirements or discount rate or sale of public securities tends to contract the supply of money and credit, thus putting a damper on a buoyant economy. Selective credit controls are usually designed to influence consumer decisions in the area of installment purchases, time deposits, housing and home ownership, stock market speculations, and others.

Persuasion, another intervention weapon, uses reasoning instead of dictation. It includes official appeal to large corporate executives for compliance with some

10. The critics of the regulatory technique argue ardently that regulatory agencies are unduly influenced by the industries they regulate, that they are highly sensitive to political pressures, that they are undemocratic, and that their reputed expertise may be highly exaggerated.

nationally significant economic guideposts, or it may involve a variety of actions, such as mediation and conciliation, informal contracts, the establishment of fact-finding boards or other forums for airing group differences to reduce frictions.

Methods of Operation

Delegated decision making, like the market mechanism, is a method of solving economic problems and, by doing so, modifying the solution of others. Public sanction or encouragement of certain activities determines or affects the decisions as to what to produce; in what shape, form and quality; and by what techniques.[11] Economic stabilization measures influence growth as well as saving and investment levels. Regulation of industry influences the type of services offered to the public as well as the technology used in their provision. Statutes dealing with consumer protection and workers' welfare have profound impact on business decisions. The government's promotional activities obviously rearrange economic priorities. All of these interventions naturally alter and modify price ratios, consumers' ability to satisfy their needs, and resource owners' ability to earn a living. In short, delegated sovereignty influences the levels of consumption, investment, and government expenditures, thus determining the magnitude of the gross national product.

The fundamental method of delegated sovereignty is the use of public purse strings. The legislature, having the "tax power," imposes and collects part of the earnings of individuals and private groups, services, and facilities. Legislative bodies at the local, state, or national levels decide on the percentages of private gross incomes which should be turned in as taxes, levies, charges, or fees. They also have the power to determine how tax receipts ought to be spent. The financing of budgetary deficits or the disposal of surpluses are also voted upon by parliaments.

Since the delegates have the responsibility to look after the best interests of their electors, their principal aim would be to please their constituents. To judge the constituents' expectations reasonably well, without making irreversible errors that may prove fatal to both success and survival, the delegates acquire and maintain a certain degree of knowledge about voters likes and dislikes.

Charged with the responsibility of fulfilling many complex roles over a wide spectrum, the delegates try to device policies and programs that in their expert opinion are in the interest of their "public." As politicians, however, the very same representatives have the additional task of convincing the public that the policies and programs so expertly devised are in fact in its interest. In a small agrarian

11. Automobiles, for example, will naturally be cheaper, and clean air far more expensive, than would otherwise be the case as long as there are no effective laws against polluting the air. So will be the price of chemicals and clean water. The prices of most nationally sold goods and services are similarly affected by public laws and regulation voted by representative assemblies.

society, this may not be difficult to accomplish. The constituents are mostly familiar with basic issues and are likely to understand the propriety of policies and programs that promise to serve them. In the technologically dominated democracies with highly complex issues at stake, the public cannot be expected to fully understand the issues or to be readily educated about their pros and cons. The more complicated the decisions, the greater would be the likelihood of their being misunderstood by the public. Complicated issues would thus have to be presented under seemingly simple, easy to understand, attractive covers. Success in winning votes would demand a good deal of sugar coating and magical packaging of hard choices.

The successful vote getters in a complex democracy would, as a rule, have to: subscribe to an eye-catching platform, attractive enough to the majority, if not to everyone; maintain a reputation for efficiency; close credibility gaps between words and deeds by proper public-relations means; operate under a facade of omniscience; and be able to manipulate the constituents' priorities from time to time in order to bring them into line with economic realities. The main task is to lead voters to believe that what they get is truly in their best interest. The crucial test is how good the voters feel about the results of their representatives and how long they are going to remain loyal to them.

Here certain similarities between political elections and market selections may be of interest. In both cases, the "seller" tries to convince his customers that his "cause" or "product" is different from and superior to those of his rivals. He will endeavor to build and maintain his customers' loyalty in the face of his rival's counteroffers. He gives as favorable an impression as possible about his own stuff in order to minimize the possibility of rational comparisons with the rivals. He appeals as much as possible to his customers' impulses, fears, prejudices, and fantasies. And he takes advantage of every effective medium in order to convey his message.

The extent to which delegates might succeed in their efforts would thus depend upon the relative perfection of the "political market," including the intelligence of customers (voters) and the behavior of rivals (other politicians). The degree to which delegated decisions could be considered in the public interest would also depend upon the delegates' own conscience and wisdom. The voters' access to various channels of information and the effectiveness of the election machinery are also of paramount importance.

Conditions of Effectiveness

The effectiveness of delegated sovereignty as a mechanism of economic decision making depends upon the presence of certain operational preconditions. The first and most essential characteristic of these conditions is periodic free elections; that is, an ability on the part of the constituents to elect their representatives freely, to charge them with appropriate authority and responsibility, and to be able to change them at regular intervals and peacefully.

The second imperative of delegated sovereignty is the multiplicity of real choice between alternative candidates, issues, and actions; that is, the existence of more than one slate of delegates, more than one party platform, more than one course of action. It also means the ability of the people to go to the polls, cast their secret votes, and make sure that their choice is properly recorded and reported. An essential reflection of this free choice is not only the existence of familiar political freedoms (of speech, expression, assembly and organization) but also a large measure of social mobility, (a society where new classes and new individuals are regularly coming to power). A democratic society has constantly to find room for people below to move up the social ladder.

The third basic requirement of delegated sovereignty is the "reasonableness" of the majority rule. For this ideal to be maintained, the majority should be willing to exercise a high degree of self-discipline and self-restraint; to be open to a variety of voices and ideas; to tolerate differences of opinion; to face criticisms from the opposition; and, above all, to be ready to accommodate reasonable demands of the minority whenever changes in the social or organizational structure are warranted.

The fourth precondition of democracy is an irrevocable commitment by both the majority and the minority to observe certain basic rules. These rules require that: political office should be open to all regardless of sex, race, color, creed, or status in life; political office should be obtainable only by winning elections; incumbent officeholders should surrender their authority and responsibility to the winners peacefully, without delay, and in an orderly fashion; the electorate should not expect to control the decisions of the elected official directly but only through the ever-present threat of not voting for them again in future elections; and elected officials should be allowed to deviate from their campaign pledges and prior policy commitments only if the interests of all, or the majority, should favor such actions at a later date.

The final prerequisite of delegated sovereignty is a widespread indoctrination on the part of the people in the desirability of democracy itself as a method of resolving conflicts. One of the major manifestations of this faith in democracy is a graceful acceptance of defeat at the polls regardless of the inherent superiority or weakness of the positions lost or won. Another aspect of this conviction in the workability of democracy is the willingness on the part of the majority to hold continuous dialogues with the minority, freely and openmindedly, in order to reach mutual accommodation on major issues.[12]

12. For a full account of these preconditions, see R. A. Dahl and C. R. Lindblom, *Politics, Economics and Welfare* (New York: Harper, 1953).

An Appraisal of Decision Making by Proxy

As a mechanism of economic problem solving, delegated sovereignty presents a number of strong features, but it also contains some thorny problems. Most of these attributes and shortcomings are also applicable to the delegated decision making outside the political sphere. Business corporations, trade unions, and other socioeconomic organizations where decision making is mainly by proxy are subject to similar strengths and limitations.

Advantages

A first great merit of delegated choice is its superior ability in providing socially desirable but indivisible public or merit goods. In all such cases, choice making by proxy is theoretically superior to individual sovereignty on account of both lower overall costs and higher overall benefits as indicated earlier in the chapter.

The second virtue of choice making by proxy (compared with the price mechanism) is its greater suitability for making an appropriate decision when the market falls short of achieving its desirable social goals: full employment, economic stability, and security—the goals that the free market does not automatically achieve. Furthermore, sharable goods like public transportation, day-care centers, museums, and other public facilities provided under delegated sovereignty can partially make up for the income inequalities based on market imperfections. Still further, third-party damages caused but not compensated by a laissez faire system can be covered almost exclusively by delegated or collective action.

The third merit of delegated choice is the possibility of optimizing social welfare for the whole community. Assuming that there is common good and that it can be optimized, the decisions taken by the majority are more likely to lead to an optimum result. As the majority is more likely to look after its own interests, any decision taken in its own favor is, ipso facto, in the interest of more people rather than fewer. The majority rule, however, could be expected to ensure public welfare only when it can be assumed that the majority knows its own best interests, and that individual happiness and welfare are identifiable, measurable, and capable of interpersonal comparison.

The fourth superior value of delegated choice (compared to command) is the possibility of terminating or revising popular mandates at regular intervals. The very assurance that policies and policy makers can be replaced from time to time provides a degree of long-term safety and security not available under other mechanisms, except the market. By virtue of such periodic adjustments, the wishes of the electorate may be more readily conveyed to the elected representatives; the interests of the leaders and the led can also be made to coincide more comfortably and peacefully.

Finally, to the extent that self-determination can be considered an end in itself or a rational means to higher objectives, delegated choice making is a more appropriate solution to certain broad socioeconomic problems than other mechanisms, except perhaps the market. For one thing, it encourages an optimal participation in the decision-making process by a majority of the adult population. For another, it involves extensive deliberations and airings of different viewpoints, thus minimizing the likelihood of hasty and unwise actions that generally result from impulsive or compulsive decisions. Delegated sovereignty is more open to "self-correction" and adjustment to new circumstances than the societies where pluralism and multiple voices do not exist.

Disadvantages

A major disadvantage of economic decision making by representation (compared to the market) lies in the deficiencies of direct representation itself. The electorate, even in the most advanced democracies with high literacy rates, is often uninformed or misinformed about costs and benefits of major collective programs and projects. Nor is there much gain for an average citizen in spending time and effort to acquire information on candidates and issues, for his single vote is not likely to determine the outcome of an election; it may, in fact, be rational to remain ignorant and uninformed.[13] Furthermore, vote-seekers are usually limited to a relatively few professional politicians—and voters are often faced with choices that are unsatisfactory in their totality. This deficiency is further complicated by the deliberate "differentiation" of candidates in the hands of public-relations men, professional image makers, and make-up artists. Campaign promises and debates often consist of vague, nonquantifiable, noncomparable generalities. Still further, despite the popular belief that in a true democracy every poor boy can become president of the republic, political success is neither easy, nor cheap. It usually takes a great deal of political acumen, electioneering savvy, indefatigable energy, strategic connections, financial support, and a particular thickness of skin to withstand the rough and tumble of election campaigns. Political miracles do sometimes happen and maverick candidates do occasionally get elected, but these are exceptions that prove the rule. By and large, the process of delegation is often imperfect, and sometimes unworkable or ineffective, because the delegates are not always the peoples' considered choices.

    The second principal shortcoming of collective choice in a modern large-scale democracy is the difficulty of correcting one's mistake or miscalculation. Choosing a delegate is almost always a "package" deal. Delegates are generally selected, and have to be lived with, for a certain period of time. They also have to be taken as a whole, and not just for that little bit of them that may particularly appeal

---

    13. For further elaboration of this rationality of ignorance see A. Downs, *An Economic Theory of Democracy* (New York: Harper, 1957).

to the voter. By contrast, choice making under consumer sovereignty is both separable and reversible. Goods and services in the free markets can be bought separately; often one can return them to the seller and get one's money back. For most of these goods and services, the costs are individually determinable and the losses due to errors or miscalculation are not usually disastrous. In the case of goods and services purchased collectively, such a separation is almost always impossible. The costs are also unknown. Voters cannot choose between the projects that their elected representatives favor or disfavor. They cannot choose to pay their due taxes to support projects they like and withhold them for those they do not. Nor can they withdraw their proxy power (change the delegates) at will if they realize they have made a mistake. Once they make their choice of a delegate, they pretty much are stuck with it. Often the only hope for remedy comes no sooner than the next election.

The third fault with collective choice is its tendency to fail the test of rationality. Even in situations where the majority of delegates meet the ideal prerequisites of office, individually rational men and women often tend to act in a nonrational manner when making collective decisions. There may be safety in numbers, as the saying goes, but there is no assurance of wisdom. One reason for this paradox is that the electorate, by and large, is incapable of assessing future costs and benefits of public programs and projects. It also naturally dislikes harsh truths. The candidates assess voters' emotions and impulses and act accordingly to enhance their own popularity. Proposals that offer immediate or short-term benefits at the expense of disproportionate future costs usually receive greater popular support, and certain economic falsehoods often become the majority's most effective slogan or argument. Plato considered this tendency toward demagoguery the disease of democracy. Another reason for collective inefficiency is what Tocqueville termed "the errors of temporary excitement," overreacting to popular likes and dislikes.

The fourth weakness of delegated sovereignty resides in the slow and frustrating pace of the decision-making machinery. Apart from lack of necessary expertise, nonfamiliarity with complex issues, and inability to sense crucial social undercurrents, the delegates are often unable to move promptly and at the opportune time. Delegated decision making usually involves three important lags, in problem-recognition, action, and impact. The first delay is caused by the difficulty of recognizing the problems faced by the nation if the majority of decision-making delegates are unaffected by them. That is probably why many important and badly needed laws (particularly in the areas of public safety and welfare) are enacted only after some shocking national disasters. The second lag—the delay in taking speedy action on badly needed legislation—follows from the grinding, slow motion of the modern democratic machinery itself. Part of this difficulty, in turn, is because a good deal of energy and effort are spent by elected representatives to keep themselves reelected through fence mending, entertaining the constituents, and making needless speeches. The third lag is the time involved between the enactment of a particular piece of legislation and its anticipated effect. This lag is particularly bothersome, because each and every piece of democratic legislation has to be implemented either through the market or through bureaucracy. In either case, the implementation process may become subject to the weaknesses of both of those mechanisms.

The fifth, but by no means the least important, defect of delegated choice is the incapacity of most democratic assemblies to produce what Professor Hayek has termed "agreement on everything." In Hayek's view (and, apparently, in Jefferson's), if every assembly member in large industrial societies faced with complex socioeconomic problems be allowed to accept some particular parts of a bill and reject the rest, the resulting legislation may be worse than the status quo. If, on the other hand, assembly members could be persuaded into accepting the bill in toto, then the assembly's vote would become that of a few among its leadership. This difficulty of reaching agreement on everything, in turn, tends to weaken and often incapacitate the decision-making process, making it particularly vulnerable to the pressures and influences of the technocrats.

The influence of technocracy on the national decision-making process usually leads to a weakening of delegated sovereignty in favor either of pressure-group bargaining or a strong executive. When the legislature is large and the typical delegate (like the average voter) knows that his vote in a majority of cases is not going to make much difference to the outcome of the bills under consideration, he may find little inducement to study the issues as carefully as he might have had his decision made any real difference. With many rank-and-file legislators unable to exert any real influence, there would be a tendency in large assemblies for the major decisions to be decided in the committees, party caucuses, and by smaller leadership groups—a tendency toward bargaining among the leaders. If, on the other hand, the legislature is not represented by special interests, or if pressure groups are weak and underdeveloped, the de facto inability of an average legislator to change the outcome of leadership decisions may increase the power of the executive branch and thus put the decision-making process in a unilateral line of command. In that case (as witnessed in the majority of one-party democracies) the representative assembly becomes largely a pawn of central authority dutifully rubber-stamping policies advocated by the executive.

A modern legislative assembly in a large industrial economy, therefore, can function properly only if the scope of delegated decisions is not too extensive, complex, or controversial; the electorate is generally enlightened and mindful of its major interests; and the legislative branch is backed by a highly efficient bureaucracy and manned by competent, responsible, and incorruptible officials. The difficulty of obtaining these ideal conditions in most parliamentary societies has led both Schumpeter and Hayek, economists of the same intellectual background but of vastly different socioeconomic viewpoints—to conclude that the parliamentary process possesses an inherent bias toward antidemocratic tendencies, for popular exasperations with endless debates will sooner or later favor the withdrawal of decision-making power "out of politics" and its placement in the experts' hands.

This is particularly true of societies whose functional requirements call for bigger forms of organization, greater degree of specialization, and the solution of more and more complex issues. In such societies, there are usually very strong trends pushing business, labor, and government together. Delegated sovereignty is a precarious process constantly moving toward the unitary command of a strong leader or the pluralistic compromises of vested interests.

Suggestions for Additional Readings

BERKLEY, G. E. *The Administrative Revolution.* Englewood Cliffs: Prentice-Hall, 1971.

BUCHANAN, J. M. *The Bases for Collective Action.* New York: General Learning Press, 1971.

BUCHANAN, J. M. *The Limits of Liberty.* Chicago: University of Chicago Press, 1977.

BLUMBERG, P. *Industrial Democracy: The Sociology of Participation.* New York: Schocken, 1974.

BUSIA, K. A. *Africa in Search of Democracy.* New York: Praeger, 1967.

CROZIER, M., ET AL. *The Crisis of Democracy.* New York: New York University Press, 1975.

CONNOR, W. D. *Socialism, Politics and Equality.* New York: Columbia University Press, 1979.

FRANKEL, C. *The Democratic Prospect.* New York: Harper, 1962.

FRIEDMAN, W. *The State and the Role of Law in a Mixed Economy.* London: Stevens, 1971.

HAEFELE, E. T. "A Utility Theory of Representative Government." *American Economic Review,* June, 1971.

KOHLMEIER, L. M. *The Regulators: Watchdog Agencies and the Public Issues.* New York: Harper, 1969.

MEADE, J. E. *Efficiency, Equality and the Ownership of Property.* London: Allen & Unwin, 1969.

MUSOLF, L. D. *Government and the Economy.* Chicago: Scott, Foresman, 1965.

RUSSEL, C. S., ED. *Collective Decision Making.* Baltimore: Johns Hopkins University Press, 1979.

SMEAD, E. E. *Governmental Regulation and Promotion of Business.* New York: Appleton-Century, 1969.

TULLOCK, G. "Entry Barriers in Politics." *American Economic Review,* May 1965.

TULLOCK, G. *Private Wants, Public Means.* New York: Basic Books, 1970.

WILCOX, C. *Public Policies Toward Business.* Homewood,: Irwin, 1979.

7

Decision Making through Bargaining

A THIRD MECHANISM of economic decision making is bargaining among pressure groups. Bargaining (or multilateral sovereignty) is based on a desire for mutual accommodation by peaceful means and through compromise. Under this mechanism, as under delegated sovereignty, individuals exercise their economic rights indirectly, but the character and number of the proxies, the terms of representation and the methods of reaching decisions are different. Bargaining takes place formally or informally among vested interests that have different ends in view and varying degrees of market power. The outcome of such bargains does, in the last analysis, influence the allocation of resources, distribution of national income, volume of employment, direction of technological process, and sometimes the whole operation of the economic system.

Under this mechanism, sovereignty is delegated by individuals to their oganization leaders for essentially similar reasons that they do under delegated sovereignty. As indicated in chapter 6, in an industrial, urban economy people are functionally and economically interdependent, and many of their problems can be solved only through group actions. This is particularly true in countries with highly advanced technology, where the growing diversity and complexity of consumer choice (and especially the emergence of varying imperfections in the choice-making process) often makes group assistance and guidance necessary.

One method of dealing with these complexities is making decisions via representative assemblies, but the delegation of decision making through the political process may not always do the trick. Assemblymen, elected from geographic districts rather than economic blocs, usually represent geographic and not economic interests; they are expected to be lawmakers, not advocates. Caught between the conflicting economic interests of their constituents, they may vote in accordance with the national interest or other considerations. Even when mindful of local problems, they may be individually powerless to influence a national assembly. In some circumstances, it may also be considered socially more desirable, as well as economically more efficient, to resolve group conflicts through negotiations among those directly involved, instead of leaving them to the discretion of a large and amorphous legislative body.

The characteristic distinctions between this mechanism and delegated sovereignty are thus basically three in number. First, the nature of representation here is functional and revolves around specific objectives of special groups. Second, the representatives are fewer in number and clearly represent vested interests. Third, the proxies are more professionally skilled in their roles, more aggressive in their specific demands, more securely entrenched in their constitutional bases, and more directly responsible to their constituents.

Essential Features

Multilateral sovereignty can be characterized by five primary features. First, there is a plurality of identifiable vested interests, each with a special ax to grind and sufficient clout to throw its weight around.[1] These groups in a modern economy basically consist of labor unions, business groups, trade associations, special lobbies, and, to some extent, organized consumer groups and the bureaucracy itself.

Second, membership in pressure groups is essentially voluntary, and sometimes only ad hoc. Pressure groups may represent broad economic classes, such as management, labor, and the consuming public; or they may be divided along more functional lines, such as manufacturers, farmers, processors, distributors, and retailers. On occasion, they may also represent geographical or regional causes, as in the case of coastal regions against the hinterland or urban centers against rural communities. But in all cases, the essential characteristic of the group is its basically voluntary pooling of politicoeconomic strengths through a united stand in the service of certain vested interests.[2]

Third, economic decisions are reached through group negotiations. Bargaining takes place because the interests of negotiating parties differ, but each party recognizes that it cannot have it its own way altogether and that some trade-off is necessary to reach a mutually acceptable solution.

Fourth, the scope and extent of bargaining, to a large measure, depends on the number of bargaining groups and the magnitude of initial conflicts among them. The greater the number of bargainers, the less the possibility and magnitude of bargaining. Under price mechanism, economic decision makers are "infinite," and no one has any appreciable effect on the outcome of his bargain; there is thus

1. Special interests are not necessarily always self-centered or antisocial; conservationist groups and humane societies are in fact the opposite. But vested interests are largely subjective, with limited, self-serving goals.
2. Voluntarism itself, however, is subject to different interpretations. The "Right to Work" groups, for example, argue that union membership under the "closed shop" or even the "union shop" clauses (where workers must be union members or promise to join a union as a condition of their employment) is essentially "involuntary."

no point in bargaining.[3] In a centrally directed system too, where all decisions emanate from the center, there are no bargainers outside the central hierarchy. Bilateral monopoly with only two crucial bargainers, offers the widest scope for give-and-take.

Fifth, the magnitude of basic conflicts among major economic groups affects the extent of bargaining the same way as does the number of bargainers. With no conflicts of interests, there would be no need for bargaining at all: total harmony would prevail. Conversely, if group interests are fundamentally irreconcilable, there again is little room for bargaining; if the terms and conditions of each side are non-negotiable, there is no bargain. The actual magnitude of bargaining will thus depend on the possibility of a compromise.

Basic Structure

Decision making through negotiation, like the other mechanisms, affects the solutions of basic economic problems involving, *inter alia*, business investment decisions, consumers' disposable incomes, and the government's expenditures and taxes. The partial equilibrium that this process tends to bring about is based as usual on the behavior of bargainers and the effectiveness of the institutions and techniques that they use.

Behavioral Assumptions

The implicit assumption of economic behavior under bargaining is somewhat different from that under the profit-motivated, self-regulated, and free-wheeling market system. It also represents certain modifications in comparison with delegated sovereignty's. Under bargaining, the economically active population is, to a large extent, regarded as members of various economic blocs or interests. These economic blocs or power centers are, in turn, assumed to be concerned with a national bargain over the production and distribution of the *social dividend*—the GNP. The whole economic arena is thus regarded as a giant "occupational parliament" where major economic problems are negotiated and settled.

Individual members of economic groups are not regarded as purely or solely self-seeking, self-driven, and self-reliant. They are considered interested also in

---

3. The so-called bargaining that takes place in the oriental bazaars is different. That is a sort of bilateral transaction in an imperfectly competitive market. There the seller tries to maximize his advantages by preying on his customer's ignorance of the market, and the customer tries to maximize his "surplus" by pushing the seller as far into the corner as he possibly can. Neither one, however, has any appreciable economic power outside that bargain, and they are both acting on their own instead of bargaining on other people's behalf. The outcome, too, seldom has any influence of impact beyond individual transactions.

organizational identification, inclined toward trading off some economic freedom for more economic security, less prone to gamble, and more inclined to follow bloc leaders. Altogether, while individuals are still assumed to be interested in material self-improvement, they are not considered as always keenly calculating economic people anxious to risk long-term security, status, prestige, and comfort for purely greater short-term material gains.

Top corporate executives running giant and diversified conglomerates are believed to act not like simple profit-maximizing entrepreneurs, but as consummate politicians, bent on playing many different roles: a manager, insuring the firm's stable and sustained growth; a planner, enhancing the firm's relative long term position; a competitor in innovation and salesmanship but mindful of his rival's and public reactions; a fair dealer toward his customers and his employees; a decision maker interested in the welfare of his community, his industry, and perhaps even the whole nation; and above all, an ambitious individual with a craving for personal achievement. An ideal business leader often is likened to Machiavelli's prince: shrewd, ruthless, ambitious, an organizer, a go-getter, and creative.

Top labor leaders in their turn, are expected to act not like old-line militants or uncouth troublemakers opposed to the established order. Nor are they necessarily radical in their demands on management or indifferent to the survival and growth of their companies. Instead, they are regarded as professional stalwarts of powerful organizations, aware of the economic power they possess, interested in their own, as well as their union's survival and prosperity, willing to settle issues with management on a businesslike give-and-take basis, and ready to enter coalitions with other pressure groups to further mutual interests. They usually try to present a self-constrained, statesmanlike facade of good behavior and a bona fide bargaining spirit so as to elicit popular (and political) sympathies for their causes.

Other bargaining leaders in the public or private sectors are similarly regarded as pragmatist officeholders and higher officeseekers, cognizant of society's divided power structure, mindful of the importance of business and labor support in their own survival and success, and ready and willing to go along to their level best with important pressure groups in settling basic socioeconomic problems as long as it is legally permitted, politically prudent, and acceptable to their own personal conscience.

Bargaining Tools

Bargaining, as an extension of the delegated mechanism in a large pluralistic industrial and urban society, relies mostly upon certain economic tools that are themselves logical extensions of those belonging to delegated sovereignty. Thus, private ownership, the nature of enterprise, price ratios, and profit motive are similar to those discussed in chapter 6 except for certain modifications.

Ownership and Enterprise. Individual private ownership here is even more significantly divorced from the management and allocation of resources than in delegated sovereignty. In a large (and often strategic) segment of a modern industrial society, entrepreneurial decisions are made by large corporations. In most of the industrialized countries, the national market in many basic industries is shared by a few corporate entities, which also own a significant share of total industrial assets.

By law a corporation is controlled by its stockholders, who elect its board of directors, who in turn run corporate affairs. In a large, modern industrial corporation, however, the dispersion of stock ownership and the lack of knowledge and expertise on the part of rank-and-file corporate owners leave little effective room for the exercise of ownership rights. Managers in giant corporations are theoretically elected by stockholders as in delegated sovereignty, but they frequently act like professional bureaucrats; they are recruited from within the corporate establishment and usually expected to be self-perpetuating. Top corporate executives may not be necessarily major stockholders in their firms, although various stock options may make them occasional, minority owners. Corporate decisions, including the crucial decision about dividends distribution, may bear little or no correspondence to the wishes of the widely dispersed majority of stockholders. Corporate management responsibility is usually divided up and exercised through corporate bureaucracy. An overwhelming share of corporate financing comes from undistributed profits, over which individual stockholders have little or no influence.

Under this mechanism, private property and individual initiative are thus further radically affected by separation of ownership from management, concentration of much of corporate wealth in a few large corporations, and control of corporate management by a relatively small number of powerful business executives. The significant degree of market power enjoyed by managers of dominant corporations in a large industrial economy puts them in a privileged position to be able to lock horns with top labor leaders and top public officials in determining the direction and management of the economy. Business executives are often responsible only to themselves within the corporate hierarchy; and outside of that hierarchy they are bound only by the terms of the bargains between them and other major bargainers.[4]

Price Administration and Wage Bargains. As indicated fully in chapter 5, under the oligopoly conditions characteristic of highly industrial societies, products are

---

4. Major critics of giant private corporations consider them "private governments" that have the power to tax (through price fixing); the power to coerce (through extraordinary influence over citizens); and even power to take life (by producing unsafe products). These private economic governments, in the critics' view, are largely unaccountable to their constituents: shareholders, workers, suppliers, consumers, local communities, and future generations. See Ralph Nader, "Corporate Democracy," *New York Times*, 28 December 1979.

not standardized, consumers often show loyalty to a specific brand, the lion's share of the market is frequently shared by a few large corporations, and entry is usually difficult. Product prices can, thus, not be expected to follow impersonal market forces: they are set and maintained by the few sellers who, by virtue of control over an appreciable share of the market, can adjust their supplies to the consumer demand in such a way as to optimize their organizational benefits. As every oligopolist's price policy is carefully watched and reacted upon by his rivals, each oligopolist possesses some bargaining power within the industry.[5] Prices consciously set and maintained are called "administered" prices to distinguish them from the market's.

Administered (selling) prices have a number of nonmarket characteristics in common. They are usually set by a price leader in the industry and followed by other firms through gentlemen's agreements, a tacit understanding of expected behavior in the oligopolistic market, or collusion. They are based on a careful calculus of the target rate of return on invested capital, the plant scale and rate of capacity utilization, and the average cost per unit of production. They remain inflexible for a considerable period of time despite changes in demand and supply conditions. And they move generally in an upward direction.[6]

Administered prices may be effectively used or abused. When kept close to marginal costs, they may provide stability and orderliness in the market, prevent costly and socially wasteful price wars, and eliminate certain unnecessary business risks. On the other hand, they may create exorbitant profits, subterfuge wasteful promotional outlays, protect the inefficient, and perpetuate privileges enjoyed by price leaders.[7] The corporate discretion in administering prices and output within an oligopolistic framework is used primarily to maintain and enhance corporate bargaining position in the industry and in the economy. But this discretionary power is often used to raise prices and maintain a targeted level of profit even in the face of changed conditions, such as falling demand.

Wage rates, particularly in unionized industries, also defy impersonal market conditions: they are collectively negotiated by unions and management and may not closely correspond to individual workers' marginal productivity—at least in the short run. A distinctive aspect of collectively bargained wages is a strong correspondence to the particular interests of economically active and influential labor unions. The relationships to consumer wishes, opportunity costs of production, length of training required for a given skill, or the difficulty or disutility of a given task may be faint.

5. Price uniformity among oligopolists, while occasionally a result of collusion, may often be obtained through rational adaptation to price leadership or through experience with market conditions.

6. For a fuller description of oligopoly behavior, see the references at the end of this chapter.

7. Whether or not administered prices are misused depends on the pricing power of the seller in a particular market situation, his "social conscience," and the degree of awareness and intervention on the part of other "publics," such as suppliers, creditors, consumers, and the government.

The wage structure (the relationships among wage rates of occupational groups) under labor-management bargaining is also different for market wages in five particular areas. Collectively negotiated wages are (1) indeterminate particularly in the short-run; they fall within a wide band between the minimum acceptable by the union and the maximum tolerable by management;[8] (2) they are often sacrificed for, and accompanied by, nonwage benefits; (3) they usually remain in force for the life of the contract and take longer to adjust to market conditions, particularly in downward adjustments; (4) they contain a built-in upward trend; and (5) part of their increase usually is passed on to the consuming public in the form of higher prices.[9]

While occupational and industrial wages are still influenced by labor productivity, they are not solely determined by any strict efficiency criteria. For example, the professional cadres of big corporations, and sometimes even the bulk of their highly skilled labor force, are often treated as fixed overhead costs instead of variable charges. Collectively negotiated wages (as well as the statutory minimum wage) frequently reflect various objectives of the union leadership, business's top command, and the state. These objectives, in turn, may reflect such noncompetitive considerations as industrial peace, a sense of fair play in sharing the fruits of economic progress, production continuity, and the like.

Profit and Other Income Shares. Business profits (and to a lesser extent also interest, and dividend) are also partly influenced by noncompetitive forces, and subject to group bargaining and pluralistic considerations. Corporate profit is neither the sole end of corporate activity nor a test of corporate efficiency. Under corporate diversification and the conglomerates, profit is not maximized for each product or in each market. While some products may be designed to be, or may simply turn out as, substantial moneymakers, others may be prestige boosters, image builders, or loss leaders. Such risk sharing obviously blunts the effect of changes in prices, costs, and profits as competitive guides to economic activity. Profit is also partly a status symbol for corporate executives, a measure of executive one-upmanship, a test of personal survival. A good portion of corporate profit is also used for the purpose of self-maintenance or aggrandizement through mergers or conglomeration.

Interest rates and dividends are also influenced (and often actually determined) by collectively organized forces and by nonmarket considerations. The interest structure—the relationship between short-term and long-term rates as well as differentials based on risks—are determined partly by internal government monetary and fiscal policies and partly by the discretion of giant commercial banks. Dividends, while institutionally a management prerogative, are also partly subject to certain trade-offs between stockholders' tolerance, internal requirements for financing, takeover threats, or the corporate lenders' personal ambitions and empire-building tendencies.

8. The outcome depends on the elasticity of demand for the product, possibilities of automation, and the willingness of the union to undergo further unemployment.

9. Some of the characteristics of collectively negotiated wages, such as (2) and (5), also apply to free-market wages under conditions of less than perfect competition.

Even rent, which by its local nature and specific features is perhaps least amenable to organized bargaining, does not usually escape multilateral trade-offs. Apart from statutory rent control in many Western democracies (which falls within the purview of the command mechanism), tenant and landlord groups in non-controlled areas are in almost perennial confrontation over the lease terms. The demands and counterdemands of these opposing interest groups are usually accommodated through negotiations between the parties involved, but not infrequently political pressure and outside intervention are also brought to bear on the outcome of settlements.

Major Policy Instruments

Bargaining is a process of trade-off or give-and-take among two or more parties. Such reciprocity may occur in the political arena among politicians, in the economic arena among trade blocs, and in other segments of society among leaders of organized groups. The bargaining process itself may take different shapes: politicoeconomic "horse-trading" in party caucuses, management-labor negotiations, worker participation in management, government-business cooperation, and multipartite determination (including government mediation and public arbitration). Informal pressures by organized lobbies and other types of influence peddling or wheeling-and-dealing are virtually limitless.

In general, bargaining techniques may be distinguished by their scope, content, and procedures. In terms of scope, the bargaining process may be nationwide, industrywide, or local. In nationwide bargaining, union and industry leaders for the entire nation may engage in negotiations on behalf of their constituents, such as a federation of businessmen or of labor. When consumers are organized, they can be represented as a third group at the bargaining table. In a more pluralistic type of national bargaining, all major social organizations may participate, and the government itself may be a party to the negotiations representing the public interest.

The scope of bargaining may, however, encompass a much smaller arena than the whole nation. Negotiations may take place, for instance, between two groups, say, management and unions only. In a more decentralized manner, bargaining may even be practiced at the level of the firm or the shop, instead of being industrywide or nationwide. Geographically, too, bargaining may cover a city, region, or the whole country. It may be collective on one side when organized labor bargains with a single employer, or it may be collective on both sides when unions bargain with multiemployer teams.

As to the content of bargaining, several alternatives may be highlighted. In a comprehensive national bargain, a whole group of issues—the extent of resource use, control of job opportunities, wages and other compensations, production methods, the rate of technological progress, settlement of disputes, and group security—may be covered. In more limited situations, the substance of bargaining may be concerned with a few basic issues such as organizational rights, bargaining format, jurisdictional representation, and adjustment of local grievances. Prices, wages, and other economic parameters may be left to be determined by other mechanisms.

Some variations in bargaining techniques involving the content of bargains are worth noting. A widely known form is the so-called industrial democracy, or worker participation in managerial decisions, under which production planning, size of labor force, raw materials allocation, product pricing, wage contracts, and expansion of facilities are collectively negotiated. Such participations are generally expected to be accomplished by worker representation in private corporations' boards of directors or in the management boards of nationalized industries. A modern variant of this industrial self-government is *codetermination* or *comanagement*, under which some percentage of the members of the boards of directors may be composed of trade-union representatives.[10]

In addition to differences in scope and content, bargaining may also differ in procedures. As indicated before, the bargaining process may be formal or informal. In formalized bargaining, procedural details (such as frequency of negotiations, rights of representation, requirements of good faith, fair and unfair practices at the bargaining table, and enforcement regulations) may be mutually agreed upon through reciprocal arrangements among bargaining parties themselves, or they may be prescribed by law, binding on all parties concerned, and enforceable in courts. In the most inflexible cases, bargaining rules may even be detailed in the national constitution instead of a legislative act so as to make them subject to fewer modifications by subsequent administrations.

At the other extreme, bargaining may take place with no particularly formalized pattern. Negotiations may be carried out by principal parties informally and behind closed doors, at bridge games, in the sauna section of a city athletic club, or by secret telephone calls to highly placed officials. Groups may make use of every effective channel of communication to get their way. They may cajole, persuade, or otherwise pressure legislators, judges, government officials, and other public leaders in support of their causes.

In its procedures, bargaining may also be direct or indirect. Direct bargaining takes place among parties principally concerned; indirect bargaining is through intermediaries and intervening processes like compulsory arbitration or

10. So far, West Germany, Sweden, Denmark, and Holland have, in various measures, adopted the principle of employee participation in management decisions. This principle has also been considered one of the European Economic Community's "valuable and realistic" long-term objectives. In Britain, France, and Italy, however, there has been little sympathy as yet for codetermination; the idea has been disliked by labor unions (which fear losing their ability to press demands) and the political left, which has always favored nationalization. In Germany and Sweden, the management has been unenthusiastic about the idea for fear of losing its prerogatives.

government mediation. In direct bargaining, compromises are reached as a result of the games bargainers play. These games often contain many of the elements of a poker game—watchful calculation, bluffs, counterbluffs, and luck. They also include the basic elements of bona fide negotiations: the identification of other party's position, persuasive presentation of relevant arguments, narrowing down of the areas of conflict, and cooperation in reaching a compromise.

Indirect bargaining comes about when principal parties, for one reason or another, do not wish direct confrontation (or even direct negotiation). It also occurs when bargaining is hopelessly deadlocked. Compulsory arbitration is suggested when such continued deadlocks and their accompanying (or threatened) strikes are injurious to national safety or security. Mediation is preferred where economic losses for one or both parties are substantial, but there is no probability of a national disaster.

Methods of Operation

Multilateral sovereignty lacks a firmly established theoretical base compared to the market mechanism. In a perfectly competitive situation, each economic actor behaves independently. Thus, no one tries to predict the behaviors of others, and no one anticipates them. But under bargaining, each party has to take into account the reactions of others; he must outguess his opponents but not be outguessed by them—an inconsistent requirement if followed by everyone.

In general, a plausible theory of bargaining must answer several basic questions: What kind of agreement (if any) is likely to result from a bargain? What are the determining or influential factors in producing such agreements? Under what conditions may negotiations break down into a deadlock instead of resulting in a compromise? And how long can a bargained agreement last once it is reached? No single theory succeeds in answering all of these questions.[11]

The closest analytical approximations to an interpretation and explanation of the bargaining process have been the theories of oligopoly and bilateral monopoly, the theory of games, and the decision-expectation-adjustment theory. The bilateral monopoly theory assumes that the total benefit to be shared by two bargainers is fixed and constant; it then proceeds to show how two bargainers with exclusive powers and strictly opposing interests (but without knowledge of each other's exact response) engage in a series of demands and counterdemands leading to an agreement (or a deadlock). The theory identifies a whole range of possible

11. In certain new analyses, a revived concept of the prewar Italian "corporatism" has emerged to describe state-society relations in Latin America. Corporatism is defined as a system of interest representation in which the state grants a representational monopoly to a limited number of interest groups in exchange for their cooperation in some areas of politicoeconomic policy. See F. Pike and T. Stritch, eds., *The New Corporatism* (Notre Dame: University of Notre Dame Press, 1974).

combinations of benefit sharing between the two parties. But beyond the establishment of this range, it is indeterminate as to the final outcome. The same indeterminacy within a range of possible values is attributed to prices and output in the oligopoly case.

The game theory explores the rational behavior of bargainers in situations involving conflicts, outguessing, and negotiations. In this theory, two or more bargainers pursue their own interests under certain rules. Each bargainer has a set of strategies or specific contingency plans designed to be used in the bargaining process. For each set of strategies there is a corresponding outcome or payoff. Every outcome embodies different values or gains for each player, and each player is supposed to know not only the value of various outcomes to himself but the other players' as well. The outcome, again, is indeterminate ex ante.

The expectation-adjustment theory attempts to replace the static framework of bargaining, in which each bargainer expects a single response to his demand, by a dynamic process where each bargainer has certain initial expectations regarding the other's responses to his possible courses of action, and each acts in accordance with his expectations of how the other will respond to his acts. Thus, at any time each party believes that the other will respond to his demands (or decisions) in a particular way until he is proved mistaken by the other's response and is forced to revise his expectations. Each bargainer obviously also has a set of preferences with regard to the possible outcomes and a plan that leads to the best attainable outcome.

In real life, the bargaining process is, of course, far more complicated. The game is not limited to two players only; there are usually many players. The gain by one bargainer may not necessarily be a loss to the other or others. Oligopolists, being few and interdependent, generally find it advantageous to cooperate (through common understandings or other devices) in order to enhance their positions. In the real-life bargaining, each party's strategy is thus to reach, through a compromise, a most satisfactory settlement for itself. The sacrifices made by each bargainer in reaching this settlement—the inducements offered to other parties in order to obtain certain concessions from them—depend upon his relative power position and his knowledge of real costs-benefits involved in his position and those of others.

While the precise outcome of the bargaining process may not be theoretically predictable, and the exact outcome of this mechanism in national resource allocation not determinable, the impact is pretty obvious. Agreements among bargainers relating to output, prices, technological innovations, and so forth all tend to affect national income, consumption, and investment. Collective bargaining with labor unions influences the share of income going to organized workers, prices charged to consumers, and the overall level of consumption. Contracts negotiated between large industrial corporations and public agencies often determine the cost to the government and taxes to be paid by the average citizens, again affecting the type and level of consumption and investment. Research and development activities undertaken through business-government collaboration influence technological development and future growth. Lobbying pressures by vested interests affect the level and direction of government spending and thus the size and composition of the gross national product. Altogether, multilateral sovereignty modifies, sways, and in various degrees determines the solution to basic economic problems.

Prerequisites of Effectiveness

Under bargaining, economic activities are controlled and harmonized by institutionalized checks and balances. Business, labor, and other pressure groups strive for public approval and common consent instead of being forced by impersonal market forces to behave in the public interest. Self-interest on everyone's part is held in check partly through self-discipline (a factor generally absent under laissez faire) and partly by the pressures of countervailing power (including public opinion). Each pressure group survives and succeeds by restraining or negating the abusive power of other groups and enhancing its own market power. That is, each group's desire to influence the market in its own favor would be moderated or cancelled out by an equally strong desire on the part of other equally powerful groups. Thus, a strong seller's desire to curtail outputs and raise prices may be resisted by labor unions, large chain buyers, consumer cooperatives, and state procurement offices. These countervailing groups would try independently or in unison to protect themselves against the impositions by the strong seller and to drive a better bargain for themselves.

For the bargaining process to succeed, however, certain preconditions must prevail. First, no major bargainer should take an "all-or-nothing" position with regard to the settlement most favorable to its own interests. Every bargainer should be willing to engage in give-and-take negotiations involving concessions made and favors received toward a mutually satisfactory compromise.

Second, each bargainer should have a realistic assessment of his relative strength, the total benefits involved in an uncompromising position, the costs of concessions to be made in order to reach a compromise, and the losses (or gains) involved in prolonging the bargaining process. Ignorance of these facts, more than individual or organizational weakness, may indeed lead a party into taking an intransigent stand, thus worsening his own position and hurting others as well. The better the issues are understood by major contenders, the less will be the chances of futile and wasteful struggles.

Third, the mutuality of the most advantageous settlement also depends on improved communications, the ability of the critical contenders to understand each other's constraints and possibilities. An optimal compromise could be reached, and a good deal of unnecessary and costly conflicts eliminated, if all parties to a bargain knew how to communicate with one another.

Fourth, within its own terms of reference, bargaining could serve outsider third parties if any one of the major contenders could insist upon certain concessions that are in the long-term interest of all, but perhaps not in the immediate interests of some. Thus, for example, a consumer's representative at the bargaining table may successfully insist that no compromised wage settlement shall be a prelude to higher retail prices in the industry. Or a public official at a tripartite bargaining session may hold out for a promise from the labor union that increased wages and fringe benefits shall not exceed labor productivity.

Finally, bargaining may serve the public interest if bargainers are sufficiently numerous to represent various socioeconomic classes; if bargaining in good faith is accepted by the community as a means of settling otherwise insoluble issues; and if the cost of the bargaining process is not greater than the expected benefits.

The Bargaining Process: An Evaluation

As a process of accommodation between conflicting group interests, bargaining raises a number of important questions concerning the suitability of this mechanism for obtaining basic socioeconomic goals, the effects of negotiated settlements on economic efficiency and stability, and the net result of bargaining from the standpoint of social harmony and public welfare.

Advantages

The first major advantage of bargaining is the likelihood of its greater acceptability by many different interests. Since major national economic policies almost always require explicit endorsement or tacit approval of major interest groups, bargaining might be more likely to promote the priorities and preferences of a larger number of influential groups. As indicated before, economic vested interests constitute an "occupational parliament" that may be more representative of popular wishes than a national assembly based upon geography, or territorial precincts. In addition to the special zeal and expertise of bargaining leaders, "functional" participation in decision making places responsibility directly and squarely on the participants' own shoulders, thus making ultimate compromises more genuinely acceptable to the membership.

Inasmuch as bargaining is done by the professionally knowledgeable and the politically active among important social groups, it will be relatively free from mistakes, apathy, irrationality and other weaknesses that usually accompany occasional and haphazard individual decisions. The representatives of each group, even in countries where this mechanism is not well developed, may be expected to be relatively more skilled in the art of bargaining; they certainly are in a relatively better position to know their constituents' true interests and bargaining power. Each group's insistence on its demand, in turn, might result in a convergence toward socially desirable compromises.

The second principal merit of bargaining is its built-in safety valve through which the interests of minority groups may be reasonably safeguarded. A strategically situated minority can resist the unreasonable demands of the majority by refusing to go along with it. Minorities can also protect their own legitimate rights by offering, or withdrawing, their support for alternative coalitions. The majority would, therefore, have to reckon with minority wishes and be more attentive to them in order to gather support for its own proposals. The filibuster in Western parliamentary democracies is one such device through which a minority may insist on being heard.

The third basic strong point of bargaining is its possible contribution to the clarification of national issues and social problems. In general, the more advanced and pluralistic an economy, the greater the expertise of its main bargaining leaders, and the more sophisticated its major lobbies. The more skilled the leadership and the more professional the lobbies, the greater may be the light thrown on various sides of major policy decisions. Modern associations of business, labor, consumers, and professional elites are typically run by experts who make use of modern public relations in promoting their interests. They collect and analyze data on various aspects of their demands, employ specialists in various socioeconomic fields to build up convincing arguments for their causes, gather intelligence information on their rivals in order to forestall disastrous surprises, and employ operational research methods to bolster their demands. They are thus in a position to air divergent views and to educate the public. Although each group still tries to follow its own self-interest, the competition among opposing groups for public approval may provide some interesting and otherwise obscured arguments for or against pending resolutions. Strange as it may sound, even totally self-serving lobbies may inadvertently produce a pressure on the opposing party to come forth with a better solution. Union pressure for higher wages, for example, has undoubtedly been responsible for a good deal of productive automation and cost-cutting in industrial countries.

A final merit of bargaining lies in its flexibility in reconciling group conflicts through orderly negotiations instead of costly confrontation. Bargaining provides certain agreed-upon procedures and standards within which the stresses and strains of opposing economic forces can often be reduced, if not eliminated, peacefully and in a more orderly fashion.

Disadvantages

The first great drawback of bargaining is its tendency toward irrationality. This should not be hard to understand. A compromised policy is obviously not an ideal policy. What is not quite obvious is that compromised decisions may not be any better than many of their uncompromising alternatives. It goes without saying that if bargainers are not rational in their demands, the outcome of bargaining would, in all probability, be also irrational. But assuming that each bargaining group is totally rational in its demand from its own point of view, the result may still be less than rational collectively. This is particularly true of policies and practices that favor some private interests, but generally hurt public welfare. Each form of trade restriction can be expected to be in the interest of some private group, geographic region, or special industry. From the standpoint of the interests of that particular group, region, or industry, too, the restriction may be perfectly rational. But since the adoption of each restrictive proposal as a national policy would require the concurrence of representatives from other groups, regions, or industries, certain concessions must be exchanged in order to gain their support. Each new concession, in turn, is rational for some group, irrational for others. Yet, once the whole process of horse trading, back scratching, and log rolling comes to an end, the community may not acquire a policy that might meet everyone's interest partially or halfway. The outcome may prove to be against the overall interest of the whole community.

Another shortcoming of group bargaining is the undue and disproportionate power that it sometimes bestows upon some relatively small, but strategically centered minorities—a power that enables them to block some desirable policy proposals of the majority. This discretionary power, to be sure, is as much a source of good as it is of evil. If the minority is right, and is being victimized by a majority or a coalition of other minorities, the power to resist and nullify the wrong deeds is a highly desirable safety valve. But if the minority is self-centered, unreasonable, and parochial, then its power may be abused. In such cases the authority enjoyed by the minority exceeds its social responsibility, and the question of legitimacy of a nonresponsible power arises. In some Western democracies, a small professional lobby, a secret coalition of a few leaders, or even one single individual sometimes may be in a position to flout the wishes of the majority without being legally responsible to anyone.

A third major flaw in bargaining is that it is a time-consuming and costly process. Bargainers generally have to mobilize their forces long before actual encounter or confrontation. This is an arduous, lengthy, and hazardous task. Real positions have to be kept secret until the last minute; accusations and counteraccusations have to be methodically voiced; the rituals of first presenting "totally unacceptable" demands must be observed; new offers and counteroffers, new demands and counterdemands, must be made. Each party also has to appear triumphant at the end. This process, by itself, and even if it finally ends up with a reasonable and effective agreement, is costly. If agreement is not reached in time and work stoppages ensue, the costs would be often enormous and sometimes staggering. The negotiated settlements themselves may also be costly to the community if they include as in some labor contracts, feather bedding, makework, and other regressive provisions that stifle technological progress or hamper productivity growth.

A fourth disadvantage of group bargaining lies in the possibility of the "in" groups exploiting the rest of the community. When bargaining is not universal (as it usually is), the groups left out of the bargains will eventually turn out to be the losers. Special-interest groups, advocating a particular economic cause or issue, can reap substantial economic gain for their constituents while imposing a relatively small individual cost on a large number of others. The injured parties—unknowingly or otherwise—may not put up much resistance, particularly if the issue is fairly complex and the information cost too large. Special groups, on the other hand, would be most willing and financially able to support those who favor their position (politicians, opinion leaders, negotiators). If the stakes are high and the countervailing forces too weak, it would also pay bargainers to get together instead of fighting among themselves. The outcome may be at the expense of the unsuspecting or powerless public, but the process is economically beneficial to special interests and expedient for the individuals engaged in bargaining.[12]

A fifth major drawback of bargained decisions is their inflationary bias. As one sure way to reach a quick compromise is to accede to each party's demand as much as possible, bargainers are usually more than willing to be generous to one another if their costs can be passed on to outsiders. The classical example of this mutual generosity is typically found in some collectively negotiated wage settlements. These settlements often exceed labor productivity, and their costs are bound to be passed on to the consumers at higher prices. Another manifestation of this inflationary tendency can be seen in the activities of special interest groups. The very purpose of most lobbies is to press the government to establish new programs. There is seldom a lobby for budget cutting or program elimination.

A final weakness of multilateral sovereignty is its inherent tendency toward centralization and perhaps eventual degeneration into unilateral mechanism. Bigness in business is inevitably challenged by labor unions; and both groups stimulate the rise of big government. As bargaining groups become more powerful, the stage is set for the mutation of collective bargaining into a more centralized machinery under which the number of bargainers may gradually become smaller and smaller. The ultimate necessity of safeguarding the public interest against the unpredictable and harmful actions of special-interest groups might eventually force the government to take upon itself the responsibility of coordinating and bringing into line all major bargainers. In societies where the national constitution or tradition protects and supports collective bargaining and special-interest groups, the danger of a totalitarian government taking over the decision-making function is perhaps slim, but in emerging societies where interest groups and political coalitions are formed as fast as they are broken, the danger would indeed be great, because the major bargaining parties would tend to weaken one another through political ineptitude, immature emotionalism, or uncompromising attitudes. The possibility of an eventual rise of the central government as the ultimate arbiter of partisan disputes would thus become both real and compelling.[13]

12. See J. M. Buchanan and G. Tullock, *The Calculus of Consent* (Ann Arbor: University of Michigan Press, 1962).

13. For a more detailed theoretical discussion of bargaining as a decision-making mechanism see R. A. Dahl and C. R. Lindblom *Politics, Economics and Welfare.* (New York: Harper, 1953).

Suggestions for Additional Readings

BANNOCK, G. *The Juggernauts: The Age of the Big Corporation.* London: Weidenfeld, 1970.

DEAKIN, J. *The Lobbyists.* Washington: Public Affairs Press, 1966.

GALBRAITH, J. K. *The New Industrial State.* Boston: Houghton Mifflin, 1979.

GOLDFARB, R. "A Fifth Estate—Washington Lawyers." *New York Times Magazine,* 5 May 1968.

GOULDEN, J. C. *The Money Givers.* New York: Random House, 1971.

KORNHAUSER, A. ET AL, EDS. *Industrial Conflict.* New York: Arno, 1977.

LARNER, R. J. *Management Control and the Large Corporation.* New York: Dunellen, 1970.

MASON, E. S., ED. *The Corporation in Modern Society.* New York: Atheneum, 1966.

MILBRATH, L. W. *The Washington Lobbyists.* Westport: Greenwood, 1976.

MONSEN, R. J., JR., AND M. W. CANNON. *The Makers of Public Policy: American Power Groups and Their Ideologies.* New York: McGraw-Hill, 1965.

SAUERHAFT, S. *The Merger Game.* New York: Crowell, 1971.

SCHIFF, E. *Incomes Policies Abroad, Parts 1 and 2.* Washington: American Enterprise Institute, 1971 and 1972.

SHEAHAN, J. *The Wage-Price Guideposts.* Washington: The Brookings Institution, 1967.

VANEK, J. *The Participatory Economy.* Ithaca: Cornell University Press, 1971.

8

Decision Making through a Chain of Command

WE BEGAN OUR DISCUSSION of problem-solving mechanisms with the market system. Under that mechanism, a large number of private, independent individuals are assumed to be making all economic decisions in society without anyone having any appreciable influence over the market through his actions. In chapter 6 we examined decision making by proxy, under which some major decisions are made collectively and indirectly through delegation. Chapter 7 further narrowed the scope of decision making to a process of bargaining among yet fewer representative leaders. This chapter deals with economic decision making through a single line of command.

Our discussions in chapter 5 showed that individual sovereignty and market mechanism would not solve all the economic problems of a modern industrial economy even under the stringent conditions of a competitive market. And in the absence of workable or effective controls provided by competition, there would be stronger reasons for additional direction, incentives, and controls in order to reach national objectives. The command mechanism is one that provides such needed additional controls through an organized bureaucracy. The use of the command process is rooted in the belief that market imperfections in the real world can and should be dealt with, at least partly, through central planning and management. The preference for this mechanism is also based on the presumption that society is superior to the sum of its individual parts; that social and national interests cannot and should not always be sacrificed for the sake of individual choices; and that these interests should be safeguarded through proper national economic planning, socially oriented enterprises, and social accountability.

Unilateral sovereignty is exercised by a central authority through a hierarchical chain of command. The central authority may be vested in a single national or organizational leader, a group of top leaders, or the bureaucratic leadership of a single party. In all modern economies, even in those where decision-making processes on the national scale are decentralized, and political power diffused, a portion of the economy is centrally directed and bureaucratically managed.[1]

Essential Features

Although centralized direction and bureaucratic management may apply to a variety of decision-making organizations, the essential features of the command mechanism can be generalized in certain basic features. First, in every hierarchy certain national or organizational objectives are prescribed from the top and are binding on all subordinates. Everything else in the organization is subservient to the hierarchy's prime objectives. Leadership in a bureaucracy depends not upon the ability to meet consumers' wishes, as in individual sovereignty; not upon voters' approval, as in a democracy; and not upon the service to special interests, as in group bargaining; but mostly upon the ability to promote national or organizational goals.

Second, the single chain of command allows the leadership to determine priorities among basic objectives, to design proper courses of action in order to optimize net goal satisfaction, and to minimize frictions and bickerings. The attainment of objectives is entrusted to managerial experts, who are expected to see to it that prescribed goals are obtained with a minimum of delay and waste.

Third, individual authority and responsibility in the organizational pyramid are related to individual skill and specialization. That is to say, all regular functionaries (rank-and-file employees, supervisory personnel, and various echelons of intermediate and senior officials) have only limited and rigidly prescribed power. And all decision makers are ultimately responsible to the very top level of leadership or central authority.[2] Regardless of the particular shape of the organizational structure, all subordinates in a hierarchy are also expected to be loyal to their immediate superiors and to the organization's objectives.

Fourth, depending on the extent of centralization or decentralization, the chain of command (and performance criteria) may be detailed and strict or broad and general. Thus, in the highly centralized and authoritarian extremes, subordi-

1. The concept of bureaucracy is used here in its neutral sense of "rule by bureaus" and not in the widely held and derogatory sense of inefficiency and red tape. Bureaucracy and hierarchy are also used interchangeably.

2. The apex of the pyramid may be occupied by an all-powerful leader, but immediately below him there may be a large number of subleaders who report to him directly and not hierarchically. These bureaucracies are called administrations of "the rising sun," because all powers emanate from a supreme source—like sun rays. Central authority may reside in one supreme leader (as in Stalin's Russia or Castro's Cuba) or in a *politburo* (as in many present CDEs).

nates may be given detailed directives by the superiors and may be expected to comply with these directives attentively and assiduously. In the less stringent bureaucracies, subordinates may enjoy considerable leeway in interpreting, modifying, and otherwise bypassing directives if the results of their activities should warrant and justify deviations from the rules.

Fifth, the relationships between subordinates and superiors that are not formally defined in the organizational hierarchy tend to follow the informal requirements for survival, security, or success within that hierarchy. Thus, there may be strong tendencies on the part of the subordinates to try to be in good standing with the "in" groups among the superiors, to enter into formal alliances with the up-coming individuals in order to ensure future survival, and to seek status, prestige, and power not through regular channels but by way of group affiliation, social contacts, family ties, and other means.

Sixth, bureaucracies have a life, and death, separate from, and independent of, their constituents. Each bureaucracy is the collective owner of the organization's physical and institutional assets; it also has its own rationale (or rationalization), its own rites, status symbols, rewards, and punishments. Almost all bureaucracies, too, have a prime interest in their own survival and expansion—an interest that cannot be easily challenged or attacked by outsiders. And while different factions within a bureaucracy may be at odds with one another from time to time, they all usually unite against actual or potential external threats to the organization's existence, jurisdiction, or expansionist ambitions.

Seventh, in order to ensure accurate communication between superiors and subordinates and to guarantee the fulfillment of basic goals, bureaucracies try to identify individual interests with those of the collective. Thus, all viable bureaucracies usually require special ideological qualifications for their potential recruits or employ subtle techniques to bring their employees in line with the leadership's objectives.

Eighth, in a bureaucracy, recruitment is theoretically based on individual competence; promotion within the organizational hierarchy, on the excellence of performance; and tenure, on the continued promise of service to the organization. Within a well-defined division of jurisdictional authority and responsibility, every bureaucratic expert is required to devote his full working capacity to his prescribed duties and to perform these duties according to specific rules and regulations. In the performance of these duties, superiors and subordinates are officially bound by what is good and right for the organization—not by what if fair, just, or proper by external criteria.

Basic Structure

Like other decision-making mechanisms, the command process embodies certain behavioral assumptions, economic tools, and operational techniques. As already indicated, bureaucracy is used not only by nations with authoritarian ideologies, but as an indispensable method of organizing economic activity under delegation and bargaining as well. The difference between totalitarian governments and others in the use of command mechanism is a matter of degree. Yet when differences in degree reach high proportions, they may become differences in kind.

Assumptions Related to Human Behavior

The reader will recall that laissez faire capitalism emphasizes the liberal principles of individual self-reliance, personal liberty, and pursuit of happiness. Under the market mechanism, the purpose of the state and the nation is to serve the individual. Individuals precede society, as society precedes the state. Citizenship is a right, not a privilege. Public laws are for the protection of personal life and property as well as the enhancement of freedom and happiness—all of which are considered the individual's inalienable rights; none is a state gift.

By contrast, communism regards individuals and the state in a totally different light.[3] The communist interpretations of human nature and their assumption of human behavior, while different from those of fascism, are also at variance with Western concepts of individualism and liberalism. Under "full communism," when the means of production will finally belong to the whole society—when labor, in Karl Marx's words, becomes "not only a means of living, but itself the first necessity of life"—there will be no need for the state to exist. Since there will no longer be ruling classes to try to protect their interests against the needs and claims of others in society, the state, as the handyman of the ruling class, will "wither away." There, at the center of the new classless society, will stand a "new man" free of all base drives of selfishness and aggression. The "new man" will be conditioned to be altruistic rather than acquisitive; cooperative instead of competitive; self-sacrificing rather than self-indulgent; a giver instead of a taker. People will work voluntarily and according to their ability; they will endeavor in a cooperative spirit toward greater abundance for all. In Leon Trotsky's words, "Man will master his emotions, elevate his instincts to the pinnacles of consciousness, and create a higher sociobiological type."

In its ultimate nirvana, a classless communist society is to operate without pecuniary motives. A brotherly spirit of cooperation, an altruistic sense of performance without expecting greater rewards than one's basic needs, and a belief in the importance of teamwork would presumably be sufficient to make people toil to the best of their ability. Exhortations are presumed to provide partial substitutes for monetary rewards. The capitalist specter of joblessness and destitution as a

3. Under the 1977 Soviet Constitution (Article 59) "Citizens' exercise of their rights and freedoms is inseparable from the performance of their duties and obligations." The citizens are also expected "to safeguard the interests of the Soviet state and to enhance its power and prestige." Rights are thus not inalienable; they are granted by the state; they can be defined, limited, or suspended by the state.

deterrent to inactivity and inefficiency will be replaced by the obligation to work, fear of losing self-respect, humiliation among one's peers, and other social stigma attached to nonfulfillment of one's duties.[4]

To be sure, not every nation that makes use of the command mechanism subscribes to this view of human nature and motivation. Even China, the Soviet Union, and Cuba, who rely mainly on this process, admit that the "new man" is still in the making, and not yet out. The overriding assumptions in the economies that presently employ the command process—with or without mandates from representative assemblies—are that a modern government cannot be a totally passive agent of its citizens; that the government's role in society is not always or exclusively to follow; that the state leadership can indeed be exercised in the service of national objectives without the people becoming subservient to it. These assumptions, however, like those of the classicists, are clearly controversial. The old-line libertarians and the neoconservatives still deny such a patronizing, big-brother role to the state.

Major Command Tools

A traditional difference between direct rule and the unregulated free enterprise has been the nature of property ownership. Under the command mechanism the ownership and/or control of means of production are to be in state or collective hands. The preference for public ownership is based on both ideological and rational grounds. Ideologically, private property is held in scorn because ownership of natural or god-given means of production belongs to no one but the whole nation. Land ownership in particular has come under brutal assaults by socialists and populists. Since land is created by nature and its supply cannot be increased, only society (the state) has the right to its ownership. This concept has been gradually expanded to cover all "gifts" of nature, such as minerals, timber, and water power. By a clever twist, the necessity for public ownership has been extended to "the commanding heights" of the economy (socioeconomic infrastructures, means of communications, and strategic industries).

On rational grounds, private property is disfavored because it is considered divisive and inequitable. Private ownership is attacked as the cause of social conflicts, economic injustices, and political strife. Individual wealth is criticized for feeding on itself, favoring the rich and the affluent against the poor and the propertyless. Social ownership, on the other hand, is seen as a key to greater social welfare on the assumption that it can eliminate private competitive waste, wipe out class conflicts between propertied and propertyless classes, increase fairness in

---

4. While no modern society has ever been solely organized on nonmaterial rewards, there is evidence that in all modern organized societies, man's altruistic propensities, desire for social recognition, vanity, pride in self-assertion, and even genuine self-interest make him favorably disposed to many nonmonetary incentives.

income distribution, and enhance economic opportunities for many by reducing inheritance and other social privileges.[5]

Wage-Price Determination.   Under consumer sovereignty, it may be recalled, price ratios serve as a common denominator of relative scarcity as determined by the balance between aggregate supply and demand in the free market. Under the command mechanism, prices (including wages, interest rates, rents, and profits) are basically determined by a central authority. Relative price ratios are deliberately arranged so as to obtain basic national priorities and goals. Industrial and raw material prices, for example, serve as accounting units devised to measure industrial productivity. Agricultural and other prices are set with a view to determine workers' real incomes. Sometimes prices are altered in order to correct the national plan's unintended turns. Oftentimes, prices are tampered with in such a way as to maximize state revenues. In some cases, international politicoeconomic motives may dictate different prices to be charged for the same commodities at home and abroad or for sale to different countries. Occasionally, also, some prices may be raised or lowered in order to channel productive factors into (or out of) certain occupations, activities, or geographic regions. Low farm prices, for example, are often used as a means of inducing farmers to seek industrial, urban work.[6] In short, prices under the command mechanism are used mainly as a lubricant and not as a fuel; as a steering wheel, not a compass; as a unit of accounts, not a guide to production. They have limited allocative functions.

Wages and other distributive shares are determined in a similar discretionary manner by central authorities in accordance with national requirements. Wages and salaries have a relatively greater allocative influence, compared to commodity prices, in regulating the supply of special skills and encouraging personal savings. Rentals on land and property are sometimes fixed on a full-cost accounting (by taking into consideration both land values and structural facilities), or they are set on the basis of capital maintenance (interest and depreciation charges of capital invested only). Interest rates are also charged on similar arbitrary criteria. The characteristic distinction in all such valuations is their authoritarian nature as distinct from impersonal market determination.

Mandatory prices and wages are obviously easier to establish by simple executive proclamation, but they suffer from two basic flaws. First, they can hardly ever be set with any great degree of accuracy, regardless of the objectives they are supposed to serve. Second, even if such a feat should be feasible, they frequently get

---

5. The absence of private property, however, is not an indispensable feature of all political regimes based on unilateral sovereignty. Fascism, for example, favored private ownership and individual wealth-holdings as long as they were used in the service of the state.
    6. The difference in price policy between the delegated sovereignty and the command process is the distinction between central price *determination* and price *controls*. In the one case, the decision is a permanent feature of national economic management; in the other, prices are determined by the market but modified or tampered with, temporarily, by the authorities.

out of line as a result of changing conditions of supply and demand. The advantage of stability may thus be eroded by the disadvantage of rigidity. Although centrally determined wages and prices ordinarily follow certain objective rules (relative skills for wages, and the full unit cost plus tax for prices), they may still fail the necessary consistency tests of supply-demand equilibrium.

To get around these basic shortcomings, certain supplementary rules have been suggested to make command pricing substantially achieve the competitive equilibrium in a more subtle way. Given data on consumer preferences and supply of resources, actual prices (or exchange ratios) are to be determined by the central authorities through the technical possibilities of substituting one factor for another. These prices are, in turn, to be adjusted through a trial-and-error method. Factor prices can be chosen arbitrarily at first, and the unit cost of production for each product be determined on the basis of the "least-costs" possible under given technology. If commodity prices thus calculated should produce a shortage in the market, they may be adjusted upward directly or through higher sales taxes. If a surplus should develop, prices can be revised downward until a "competitivelike" equilibrium is reached.[7] The main difference between this equilibrium and the perfectly competitive variety is the absence of "abnormal" profit as an economic incentive, and of monopoly gain as a reward for entrepreneurship.

Despite the theoretical possibility of such a "mathematical solution," the exacting practical task of establishing optimal price ratios at all times can hardly be exaggerated. Constant shifts in consumer tastes and demand, the changing character of technology, and the dynamic effects of changes in prices and incomes on the availability of factors supply would defy mortal planners' knowledge and wisdom. The necessity of changing commodity and factor prices by trial and error would also require repeated shifts of resources among planned programs and projects. Prior planning, under such continuous shifts, would be highly impractical.

For these and other practical reasons, actual price setting under the command mechanism in the present-day world does not follow such a theoretically workable, objective, and flexible process. Many countries that rely mainly on the command mechanism are not willing to go as far as allowing consumer preferences a free rein in the pricing process. Prices are, as a rule, set with broader social goals in mind and with much greater arbitrariness.[8]

7. This process of central price determination is sometimes called "market socialism," under which the central planning board is to fix prices in such a way as to clear the market, and industrial managers are to combine productive factors in such a manner as to minimize average cost. With these two rules, a condition close to the competitive equilibrium could be reached without private ownership of means of production, but with a large degree of consumers' choice.

8. For a discussion of these rules and their criticisms, see E. Neuberger and W. Duffy, *Comparative Economic Systems* (Boston: Allyn and Bacon, 1976), chapters 7 and 8.

Nonmonetary Incentives. The command mechanism puts great stock in non-monetary incentives as a spur to economic activity and efficiency. On both theoretical and empirical grounds, it is argued that neither personal gratification nor national welfare could always be maximized through the sole lure of money or material rewards. Examples are myriad of selfless services provided by men and women who voluntarily forego more lucrative alternatives in order to work in more intellectually or emotionally rewarding endeavors. Modern management experts argue that money and fringe benefits may be only "negative motivators." That is, their absence may render people unhappy or unwilling to take up certain risky or demanding tasks, but their presence may make them neither happier or more productive. In fact, nonmoney incentives, beyond a minimum customary standard of living for a particular class already attained, often seem to work more effectively.

Some analysts have found that offering a successful executive a greater challenge and recognition and a feeling of more responsibility and greater accomplishments may be more attractive than an increase in salary. Loyalty to the organization is often a strong impetus. Patriotic, religious, or ethnic motivations may also play a strong role in urging people toward more productive work. Nonmoney incentives may induce scientists, artists, pioneer technologists, and workers in strategic industries to work harder and better. As a matter of practical considerations, too, such distinctions as greater power in the hierarchy or prestigious titles, may be as important as pecuniary remuneration.

In highly bureaucratized corporations, executives are often interested as much in relative social distinctions as they are in absolute material possessions. If the latter is actively sought after, it is partly because individual success is often measured in, and identified with, salaries. Higher money incomes are an indicator of business performance. Even in capitalistic societies, private wealth is not (at least not beyond certain comfortable levels) desired for its own sake; it is sought as an index of social distinction.[9]

Basic Policy Instruments

The command mechanism is commonly associated—and sometimes loosely identified—with national planning and public enterprise.

Although national planning is theoretically independent of both public ownership and public enterprise, it is often used in conjunction with varying degrees of control over basic means of production. Several combinations of planning and

9. For some Western corporate executives in the top "six-figure" income brackets, and faced with a very steep progressive tax, the annual salary figures are partly a "prestige" symbol.

nationalization may exist. A comprehensive planning of the national economy may be combined with a large measure of private ownership and supervised private activity.[10] Partial planning may be fused with large public holdings and extensive government operations (as in many developing countries). Planning may be thorough while social ownership and state enterprise are also nearly total (as in Soviet Union and China). And there are nations with substantial public ownership and extensive government enterprise, but with little or no mandatory planning (as in Japan and France).

National Planning

National planning refers to a purposeful husbanding of domestic resources toward specific goals over a given period of time. The raison d'être of planning is to minimize (if not eliminate) uncertainties and obstacles to a rational achievement of national objectives. A national economic plan can thus be defined as a rational course of action designed to control and coordinate economic activities in accordance with the planners' preferences. The essential characteristic of national planning is a deliberate, purposeful activity aimed at some predetermined objectives. All planning operates through a special bureau or agency staffed with a technical cadre in charge of the forecasting of future requirements, estimation of available resources, and formulation of projects. All planning relates to allocations among major economic sectors, programs, and projects.[11]

National planning, in its ideal form, could perform the major economic functions of allocation and distribution fairly well. Its main difference with the competitive market system would be the replacement of consumers' sovereignty with planners' sovereignty. In other words, once the planners' preferences are known, the national plan could broadly divide available resources between aggregate consumption and investment outlays, determine the share of private consumption in the total, decide on the choice of technology and innovation to be followed by producing units, distribute national income in such a way as to meet national objectives, and choose different time paths for investment projects.

As in all models, however, the reality is different from the ideal. Apart from the enormously intricate problem of defining and determining national goals (and

10. The 1951 Socialist International, composed of delegates from thirty socialist parties the world over, adopted a resolution specifying that socialism and planning are in fact compatible with private ownership in small farming, handicrafts, retailing, and even small and medium-size industrial undertakings.

11. The reader interested in a discussion of more detailed aspects of planning may consult Jan Tinbergen, *Central Planning* (New Haven: Yale University Press, 1964); G. Sirkin, *The Visible Hand: The Fundamentals of Economic Planning* (New York: McGraw-Hill, 1968); "The Theory of Planning," *American Economic Review, Papers and Proceedings*, May 1971; and Raymond Vernon, "Comprehensive Model-Building in the Planning Process: The Less-Developed Economies," *Economic Journal*, March 1966.

planners' preferences where there are more than one planner), several other complexities exist. First, there is the planners' problem of collecting and sorting accurate and up-to-date information regarding resources availability, consumers' tastes, production functions, and other key economic variables. Second, there is the task of processing collected data, reaching optimal decisions, building an economic model, and relaying commands from the center to the operating units.[12] Third, there is the thorny problem of motivating economic agents to respond fully and faithfully to the planners' wishes—the matter of incentives and penalties. Finally, there is the complexity of a well-developed information feedback system to show how, and to what extent, the planners' commands are carried out.

On account of these complexities, no national plan is an ideal one. Each economy, within its political, technological, and administrative characteristics and capabilities, decides for itself the nature and scope of its plans. National plans thus differ in their duration (short-term versus long-term); their scope (comprehensive versus partial); their binding nature (indicative versus prescriptive); and their methodology (optimization versus mere consistency).[13] All planned economies as a rule have a long-term perspective, a five-to-seven-year plan, and a short-term annual budget. In the CDEs, plans are usually comprehensive, covering the entire economy; in the LDCs, most national plans cover only the public sector. In the Soviet Union, China, and some East European countries, national plans are the mandatory course of action for agencies to follow. In the so-called "planned market economies" (Japan and France), the planning system is indicative, a mere guideline on present and future markets for the public and private sectors to keep in mind in their own production and investment decisions.

Planning methodology differs in preparation and purpose. Comprehensive plans of the Soviet variety comprise highly sophisticated econometric models (with all the paraphernalia of input-output matrices, linear programming techniques, and functional equations). Economic plans of the LDCs (when they are more than mere expressions of national aspirations) enjoy different degrees of practical applicability. In terms of purpose, most plans—even those of the Soviet Union—reach for consistency rather than optimality. The two most important aspects of consistency, in turn, relate to intertemporal consistency, the meshing of long-term perspectives with medium-term plans and annual budgets in order to reconcile short-run and long-run objectives; and material balances, the matching of projected supply with the projected demand for every good or service. (See the conditions of ideal performance, below).

The implementation of national plans commonly takes place in a number of different ways. First, there is the administrative inspection of physical output to

12. By the Russians' own estimation, a complete computer programming of one year's operation of the Soviet economy would require one million high-speed computers operating nonstop for several years. See L. Smolinski, "What Next in Soviet Planning," *Foreign Affairs*, July 1964.

13. See H. S. Levine, "On Comparing Planned Economies," in A. Eckstein, *Comparison of Economic Systems* (Berkeley: University of California Press, 1971).

make sure that quantitative targets are reached. Second, there are controls by state banks over the use of the authorized working capital and allocated investment funds to see to it that all transactions (between firms, their suppliers, and customers) are carried out according to the planned prices or other common denominators of value. Third, there is supervision and inspection by political party officials who serve as a liaison between the firm and the party. And finally, news media and other community organizations act as watchdog over the plan's fulfillment, production failures, and other difficulties.

Nationalization and Public Enterprise

Another principal technique of the command mechanism is nationalization, or public enterprise. Public enterprise may be defined as a type of economic activity in which the initiative, financing, management, and the final decision-making responsibility are borne by the state or the collective. Public enterprise may take a variety of legal or organizational forms. Three major forms of a socialized organization may be distinguished according to the degree of autonomy in managerial decisions, sources of finance, and responsibility to the governmental hierarchy.

First, there is the regular government agency, like the visa office or the ministry of housing or the national park administration, which receives its appropriations directly from the legislature and turns in its revenues to the treasury. It is managed like a typical bureaucratic political organization with its staff and line divisions and chains of command.

Second, there is the autonomous or semi-independent public corporation, operating as a legal entity capable of conducting business like a private corporation. The public corporation's stocks are totally owned by the government, and its board of directors is appointed by the state or by one of its department heads. Management is accountable to the corporate or administrative boards and usually follows a more businesslike and less bureaucratic method of operation and accounting. The corporation can borrow on its own account; its cost and price policies are determined by the boards, which in turn take their cues from the hierarchy.

Third, there is the mixed corporation with regard to both ownership and operation. Corporations that are mixed on both of these scores are governed by a multipartite board representing different interest groups or different institutional owners of the corporate stocks. Management responsibility and financial accountability in mixed enterprises vary according to the legal arrangements in the corporate charter. There are scores of other combinations among these three basic forms of public enterprise.

Public enterprises cover a vast array of economic activities for a variety of reasons. Munition factories, warfare research and development, fissionable sources of energy, basic means of communications, and central banking are usually in the state hands for reasons of national security or independence. In some countries, basic fuels, certain heavy industries, national means of transportation, and regional development activities are state-owned for similar reasons. Basic considerations for public welfare (income redistribution) necessitate the public provision of primary education, health care, recreation facilities, and low-cost housing where risk or time preferences are such as not to attract private funds. Urban transit systems, many public utilities (water, electricity, gas), and other vital public services are often provided by government at or below costs as a means of ensuring adequate supply at modest prices. Efficiency considerations, too, are invoked to justify state ownership and operation in declining-cost industries (like railways), troubled or old industries (like shipbuilding), or infant industries (like steel in many LDCs). The arguments on this account are particularly strong in the case of multipurpose projects such as hydroelectric dams, highway construction, natural resource management, and so on. In many developing countries, direct state intiative and operation, particularly in building infrastructures and industrial development, are considered crucial to economic growth and progress through the proper management of exports, imports, and basic investments. Finally, as a good source of public revenues, state monopolies exist in the manufacturing and sale of tobacco, liquor, and salt; such monopolies also often exist in the operation of national lotteries, banking, insurance, airlines, and foreign trade.[14]

Methods of Operation

Under the command process, the basic economic problems of *what, how much, how,* and *for whom* or which generation are solved by a central authority. Central planners decide on the basic direction and guidance of the economy, work incentives, organization of production and transfer, and effective rewards and punishments. Such basic choices as aggregate consumption versus investment; public versus private use of resources; civilian versus military expenditures; and the volume and composition of private consumer goods are made according to the planners' discretions. The objectives that the delegated sovereignty tries to achieve through a mixture of taxation, subsidies, regulation, and persuasion are here pursued directly.

Private consumption, for example, is reduced or expanded by centrally determined price changes, delays or speed in filling orders, and other bureaucratic measures. The rate and composition of capital formation is determined through direct expansion of productive capacity in certain industries, as well as the direction

14. The reasons why certain industries are or are not in state hands in different countries are many. Ideological considerations usually loom large, but sheer historical coincidence, incurable private-sector inadequacies, and the appropriation of excess profits in highly lucrative industries may provide some of the other incentives.

of research and development activities. The actual assignment of productive factors to various economic activities—how many workers in each plant, how many houses in each locality, how much steel in road building—is made in physical volumes or in monetary terms. Frequently it is a combination of both.

Where the means of production are totally owned by the state, little or no provision needs to be made for assigning accurate monetary values to these factors. Capital and land may be allocated directly according to government plan, based on some arbitrary cost-benefit calculations. In a more decentralized situation, different value coefficients may be assigned to productive factors. These values may not necessarily reflect factor scarcity or marginal productivity but, rather, basic allocative preferences of the planners. Specific monetary incentives, too, may be devised for specific purposes independent of market forces or individual preferences.

Income distribution follows the same pattern as production and exchange. The centralized determination of salaries, wages, and bonuses naturally affects personal income distribution. While a compensation system based on total equality may, theoretically, be devised, the command mechanism allows for notable gradations in pay according to individual skill and experience, job hardships, hierarchical responsibility, and workers' attitude. In addition to wage determination, such factors as consumer prices (including profits of states agencies plus turnover taxes) directly influence the national standard of living. Such additional factors as fringe benefits, pensions, and other bureaucratic allowances also produce effective redistribution results. By manipulating these devices, the central authority can always reduce or increase inequalities of wealth and income.

The command mechanism thus makes effective use of such fundamental instruments as money, prices, wages, and a controlled market process in addition to its own devices such as planning, nationalization, and nonpecuniary incentives. The workability and effectiveness of this process depends on the wisdom and practicality of chosen instruments and their efficiency. The main difference between the methods of operation under delegated sovereignty and the command mechanism lies in the purpose and precedence of public controls. Under delegated sovereignty, social controls usually complement, rather than replace, free-market decisions: they try to rectify imperfections and inequities of the market. They also partly attempt to forestall damages to public safety and welfare, as in the case of consumer protection and environmental quality legislation. The command mechanism replaces the market by directly deciding the pace of economic activity. Social services and infrastructure are provided directly by the state and distributed according to criteria of need. Equity in income distribution is achieved by centralized determination or control of wages and prices. Economic stability is maintained through planning, licensing, and investment controls. Growth is promoted through direct allocation of resources to capital formation. Social costs are supposedly taken into consideration in centralized cost pricing. In short, delegated mechanism tries to make up for market deficiencies; the command mechanism attempts to cope with these imperfections directly.

Conditions of Ideal Performance

There are five prerequisites for an ideal performance of an economy under the command mechanism. First, national or organization objectives, both stated and unstated, must be clear and unambiguous for all concerned. In practical terms, this means that resources and activities should not be permitted to work at cross purposes, bureaucrats should not be allowed to play one unclear goal against another in an effort to camouflage their incompetence, laziness, or personal ambitions; and proper priorities among conflicting objectives should be adequately established.

Second, while no bureaucracy is perfectly harmonious with regard to its members' personal aspirations and ambitions, there must be certain basic agreements among top leaders as to the overriding objectives of the organization itself.

Third, in all bureaucracies, whether pyramidal or otherwise, the relationships between departments, bureaus, offices, sections, and other subdivisions must be well defined and effectively communicated. The same should be true of the lines of responsibility and decision making between specialists, advisors, executives, and policy makers.

Fourth, rational performance in a bureaucracy is much enhanced if there is the expected sympathy among the rank-and-file with the objectives of the top leadership. The ideal situation requires total loyalty to these objectives, but an effective performance needs only a high measure of sympathy and identification. Without such a community of interests, the status gap between members may drive a wedge between purpose and process, and mere compliance may replace genuine achievement.

Fifth, and most crucial, is the command mechanism's planning quality and enterprise efficiency. A good plan is externally balanced and internally consistent. External balances may be characterized by a functional harmony among the plan's objectives, a reasonably accurate calculation of the plan's costs and benefits within a minimum margin of error, the political and administrative feasibility of the plan's execution based on adequate public appreciation or a minimum of conflicts, a realistic assessment of the community's overall capabilities and weakness, and sufficient flexibility in the plan's structure so as to allow necessary adjustments to changing circumstances. Internal consistency requires the maintenance of certain technical checks and balances among the plan's key variables. Total output targets should match the availability of productive factors. Under the so-called crosswise or horizontal balance, there should be physical, spatial, and temporal matching of inputs and outputs in such a way as to prevent unemployment and excess capacity, on the one hand, and product shortages on the other. Under the vertical balance, finished products should match their component parts so that the right people should fill the right jobs; the right jobs and the right resources should be put to work to produce the right goods and services; and the right goods and services should be placed at the disposal of the right uses and users so that the circle be properly closed.[15] A closely related balance that must be achieved in an open economy (an economy with trade windows to the outside world) is the one between the demand and supply of foreign exchange. A plan that relies on foreign finance for domestic development must see to it that foreign exchange required for the importation of capital goods, technical know-how, and other sundry goods and services is matched by the proceeds of exports, foreign borrowing, and/or foreign aid.

Enterprise efficiency is the fifth condition of ideal performance. Efficiency, in a broad sense, requires that a nationalized industry be more responsive to the planners' preferences or to general public welfare than to its own interests. The human frailties that affect private corporate executives (personal ambitions, empire-building tendencies, game plays) should be minimal. Inward-oriented institutional behavior of the type practiced by large private corporations, such as inattention to external costs, should be avoided. Unfortunately, finding competent management for nationalized industries—managers who can combine business acumen with dedication to public service and a knack for efficiency—is harder than many aspiring bureaucrats are willing to admit. Relatively low salaries and fringe benefits, greater degree of subjugation to political superiors, and the inadequacy of perform-ance criteria often deprive nationalized industries of the best talent available in the market.

Command Mechanism: An Appraisal

The command mechanism has very few staunch advocates in Western industrial economies; it is a mechanism to be practiced grudgingly and sparingly, but nothing to be proud of or to preach. But in the socialist East, it is the standard operating process, and it is widely used in the nonsocialist world, particularly among developing nations.

Advantages

The first advantage relates to the merits inherent in national planning and the latter's inherent bias in favor of rationality. This rationality revolves around four basic characteristics: efficient adaptation of means to ends, suitability for major resource transfers, reduction of uncertainties, and better coordination and consistency. Under the command mechanism, as decisions are based on predetermined priorities of the top leadership, a good deal of waste, delay, and frustration that

15. There are also supplemental balances which a good plan must maintain. One such balance is that between money and real factors. Any divergence between the financial and physical resources (prices charged for goods and incomes paid to people) would cause inflationary imbalance or a deflationary rise of inventories.

usually accompanies interparty bickerings (or results from conflicts of private interests) can be eliminated or reduced. National or organizational objectives can be selected, and conflicts among them resolved, at minimum costs and maximum speed. Socially relevant decisions are less likely to be hampered by the weak incentives of the market or by compromised (and naturally watered-down) actions of special-interest groups. And where top leadership is personally outstanding, professionally qualified, and organizationally motivated, the quality of centralized policy and direction may become distinctly superior to the cues and incentives of the free market.

National planning can provide sufficient incentives and disincentives to facilitate the attainment of social objectives. A deliberate shaping of economic resources in the service of high-priority national goals can prevent unnecessary business fluctuations and senseless waste. This advantage, inherent in the command mechanism, is, in turn, partly based on the fact that ownership and control of resources is vested in the organization itself, and that means of production can be rationally employed to further organizational objectives without the necessity of offering excessive private incentives to elicit private responses. Government-owned lands, for example, can be set aside for public parks or designated for low-cost housing readily and without speculative costs. The power to induce top-notch talent into accepting low-paid public-service positions (like the draft into the armed forces) enables the government to satisfy its skilled manpower needs cheaply and promptly—albeit at some financial costs to the draftees.

National planning may also be credited with the ability to reduce economic risks and uncertainties. To be sure, total information is seldom attainable under planning, because planners cannot always know all available courses of action, because costs and benefits of different alternatives are not always precisely measurable, and because each course of action will usually entail certain unexpected consequences that cannot be foreseen and foreclosed. But while all economic uncertainties resulting from changes in consumer tastes, new technology, or population changes cannot be eliminated in the real and dynamic world, better and cheaper information in the hands of central decision makers can reduce most calculable risks.

Better coordination and greater consistency are another hallmark of command. The advantages of specialization and division of labor inherent in bureaucracy tend to make a hierarchical process more stable and consistent, less liable to individual anxieties and frustrations, and subject to better rational coordination. A relatively small group of specialists can supervise and control the decisions and actions of the whole community. A corollary of this advantage is the possibility of eliminating much of the duplication of productive facilities inherent in an imperfectly competitive market. Theoretically, at least, such elements as the plant size, industry location, product differentiation, and distribution channels can be designed in response to public needs.

Production for use and in response to public needs may also tend to result in genuine technological development and progress. The priority of national or organizational interests over private gains would be more effectively amenable to the adoption and utilization of novel ideas and techniques. New inventions and innovations would be less likely to be held back, or permanently shelved, when their adoption might entail the scrapping of huge but obsolete private investments. The government can write off the sunken costs of outmoded facilities as part of the general budget expenditures and give the people added benefits of new and improved products. Often such cost write-offs, which might be ruinous to a particular firm or individual, can be easily underwritten by the community as a whole.

A related manifestation of this consistency and coordination is the possibility of better social cost-accounting. Third-party damages, for example, could be more easily compensated. Public enterprise managers, too, may be directed to include external costs in their unit-cost calculations. Again, while the inclusion of such externalities in production costs may be prohibitive for a private producer or threaten his competitive position, a uniform and centrally determined system of indemnification can be established and efficiently administered by the whole community.

The second set of advantages associated with the command mechanism derives from the merits attributed to public ownership and enterprise. For national security considerations, it is expedient to keep certain strategic raw materials or industries under state ownership and operation. Social-welfare arguments point to a variety of circumstances where incentives for private operation are too weak to bring forth some desirable social services, where risks are too forbidding to attract private investments, where direct public outlays are needed to save some vital services used by those who cannot afford to pay their full costs, and where state monopoly may bring in public revenues better and faster than taxes.

Public enterprise, not motivated by selfish interests in the sale of its products and not engaged in competitive bidding in the employment of resources, can save on many cost elements. It can realize substantial savings by eliminating wasteful competition, excess capacity, and duplication of functions. The unification of control, for example, may reduce unnecessary retail outlets or may locate them in a more socially satisfying manner. The coordination of competing services (rail, bus, trucks, water, and air transportation) may eliminate duplicate terminals, routes, services, and facilities. It may follow a better cost-price policy. There may be no need for costly supervision and regulation of business behavior in regulated private monopolies. A government enterprise may be able to borrow its investment and working capital at lower rates of interest, eliminate quasi-rents paid to factors in short supply, and save substantially by the elimination or reduction of advertising, promotion, and lobbying costs.

Still another argument in praise of public enterprise—ease of administration—is based on the alleged superiority of public ownership and enterprise over public regulation when it comes to natural monopolies. The preference for the nationalization of industries "affected with a public interest" (as compared to private enterprise plus public regulation) is based on the argument that regulation is often inadequate or ineffective in inducing private interests to improve product quality, to reduce operational and promotion costs, to renovate or innovate, to coordinate operations with other social policies—in short, to operate with a view to public needs and aspirations instead of private profit.

The third category of attributes associated with unilateral sovereignty has to do with the alleged superiority of nonpecuniary incentives over material rewards in certain types of human endeavor. The argument is that such problems as employee absenteeism, high turnover, and low productivity can often be dealt with best by exhortation, by praise, and by recognition. The government may be more successful in eliciting better performance from its employees, who are induced to work harder, more devotedly, and more imaginatively for the sake of public service rather than higher pay. The command mechanism's capacity to enlist the energy and talent of superachievers in the service of the community or the nation may be greater than that of the market.

Disadvantages

The disadvantages of command are many, and mostly familiar. Some of these shortcomings, such as high costs of obtaining information and the difficulties of communications, are inherent in the structure of any large organization. Others, like excessive centralization and inexcusable inefficiency, may be extraneous to the system and based on the type and stage of development of a particular bureaucracy.

First and foremost among the command's weaknesses is the charge of inefficiency. In fact, the very word *bureaucracy* is sometimes the semantic equivalent of waste. What gives credence to this pejorative appraisal is the fact that bureaucracy has an inherent tendency to degenerate into its own opposite. Too much attention to rationality, in other words, may become irrational.[16]

One aspect of this unintended irrationality or inefficiency is generally referred to as red tape, or unnecessary delays and frustrations involved in getting things done by bureaucratic methods. Yet the apparent irrationality of red tape is ironically ingrained in the hierarchy's inner necessity for rational performance. Dividing responsibility for technical decisions among competent specialists is necessary for maximum efficiency. But this essential requirement often degenerates into an unnecessary morass of petty rules and regulations. Since in a large bureaucracy no one is supposed to act beyond his own specialty and jurisdiction, a

16. Bureaucracy's alleged inefficiencies have been satirized lately by two astute and witty authors. C. Northcote Parkinson has subjected modern bureaucracy to a few basic "laws," the most celebrated of which are that work expands to fill available time, and that expenditures increase to absorb available revenues. Laurence J. Peter has given us his "Peter Principle," the gist of which is that in a hierarchy, every employee tends to rise to his level of incompetence.

minor but nonroutinized problem becomes the subject of numerous reviews, checks, and approvals. The use of elaborate and extensive rules designed to keep officials from surpassing their authority, while absolutely essential to orderly bureaucratic conduct, has a tendency to expand to the point where the regulations themselves become holier than the purposes for which they were established.

Another aspect of bureaucracy's inadvertent deviation from rationality is the widely known reluctance of most bureaucrats to assume responsibility for risky or unpopular decisions. This shortcoming—popularly dubbed "passing the buck"—is also rooted in the need to limit the specialists' discretionary power within their own expertise in order to safeguard technical efficiency. Yet, in practice, the safety and security of the status quo often leads cautious or timid specialists to evade almost all responsibility for making any important decision and to throw such decisions into someone else's lap. In any organized activity, new and untried decisions involve risks of failure, but these risks are not always commensurate with expected rewards, for in a hierarchy failures have to be accepted by subordinate risk takers, but success has to be shared with superiors. Naturally, therefore, any rational bureaucrat interested in safeguarding his job, rank, and reputation resists untried and risky ventures that might threaten these prerogatives. As a result, bureaucracy often tends to favor simpler and more orthodox policies over radical or innovative measures.

Closely related to the allegation of inefficiency is the second major disadvantage of command: inflexibility. Bureaucracy has an intrinsic tendency to become unduly rigid partially due to the limitations of bureaucratic experts and expertise. In the words of Harold Laski, government by experts would, after a time, become government in the interest of experts and not for the welfare of the common man. By reason of their "immersion in a routine" and their rigid view of their specialized knowledge, the experts possess neither flexibility of mind nor the art of persuasion. They often sacrifice common sense to the depth of their specialty. Bureaucratic inflexibility is also partly a result of its impersonality. Bureaucracy's inherent bias in favor of efficiency tends to downgrade informal personal relationships, such as compassion, tolerance, generosity, intimacy, which are both desirable per se and necessary for achieving other desired ends. This impersonality, in turn, discourages devotion to one's work, individual sincerity, and creativity. Bureaucratic perfection may become an absolutely colorless and insipid bore.

The third principal shortcoming of hierarchy is inertia, a self-serving resistance to change. There are many reasons for this. The presumed expertise of the incumbent technocrats in the hierarchical pyramid often makes them truly indispensable or convincingly difficult to replace. Reform-minded leaders generally hesitate to advocate or undertake wholesale replacement of the staff for fear of upsetting the whole administrative apple cart. Assured of their well-entrenched positions, bureaucrats often tend to cling to their jobs long after outliving their professional usefulness. Furthermore, the risks involved in sticking one's neck out often induce the middle- and lower-echelon leaders to play it safe. This deep-rooted timidity tends to make new ideas and untried methods unduly suspect. In the words of the British economist, Walter Bagehot, bureaucracy will "care more for routine than for results."

Organizational inhibition also tends to shut the door on proposals not originated from within and to regard them as not worth bothering about. Bureaucrats often reject suggestions by outsiders because, to quote Bagehot again, "the trained official hates the rude untrained public. He thinks that they are stupid, ignorant, reckless." Even those who do not resent or resist the public's suggestions usually prefer to listen to the same sources all the time rather than welcome new ideas from diverse sources. And even if bureaucratic regulars should heed outsiders' proposals, changes would not be easy to come by. The necessity, in a very large and complex organization, to go through channels to get new suggestions approved often causes such ideas to be lost or badly smothered along the way.

The fourth drawback of bureaucracy is the bewildering difficulties of communication between superiors and subordinates. Orders issued from the top hardly ever reach the rank-and-file operators without cumulative distortions: they get interpreted and reinterpreted along the way at the subordinates' pleasure and convenience. As a result, much that happens at the operational levels may substantially deviate from the real national or organizational goals. At the same time, badly distorted information reaching higher-ups may give the latter an unduly rosy and optimistic picture of what goes on at the bottom.

The difficulty of establishing proper communication between order givers and order takers also tends to discourage innovations and adventures; instead, it tends to reward unimaginative and routine performance. Since a person's advancement in a hierarchy depends on pleasing a superior, there will always be a bias in favor of telling the boss what the subordinates think the boss wants to know. The very nature of hierarchy thus tends to prevent accurate information from reaching the higher layers. Instead of being able to act, promptly and progressively, bureaucracy becomes an instrument of procrastination, a vehicle for conformity, an easy way for failing safely, a mechanism for preserving the status quo.

Fifth, the command mechanism, like all forms of entrenched power, tends to feed on itself: it moves in the direction of greater and more abusive power. The necessity of placing responsibility for coordinating diverse decisions and actions in the hands of a small number of people (so as to prevent duplication and waste) may place undue power in the wrong hands. Thus, a coordinating committee may soon assume dictatorial might; inspectors may become commanders; watchdogs may turn rabid. The inequality of social prestige, political status, and economic rewards also gives top leaders manipulating power to perpetuate their own positions within the organization and to ward off outside threats to their hegemony. Political leaders often use their office, their staff, their patronage power, their exposure to the public, and even public funds to strengthen their hold on the job.

Finally, the more centralized and the more complex a bureaucratic organization, the more difficult will be the task of its administration. As the gap between the interests, motivations, and identities of policy makers and policy takers widens under an immense and impersonal bureaucracy, the virtues of hard work, self-improvement, diligence, and plain integrity begin to erode. Work shortcuts, nepotism, favoritism, misuse and abuse of personal position, and similar improprieties tend to rise. Overstaffing, underproduction, lax supervision, camouflaged incompetence, and outright corruption slowly emerge.

Another direct result of excessive centralization, tight controls, and bureaucratic red tape is a system of wheeling and dealing through which transactions are handled illicitly or extralegally by a group of go-betweens who know how to find their way around public bureaus. The younger and faster-growing a bureaucracy, the greater its chances of getting energetic and dedicated officials devoted more to achieving organizational goals than their own self-aggrandizement. Bureaucratic efficiency, like that of centralization, is curvilinear. As bureaucracies grow up from infancy, they learn to become more efficient; but as they grow older, their interest in self-preservation, security, and power begins to override other considerations.

The scope and intensity of these limitations are thus not always directly related to the size of a bureaucracy. A weak and decentralized governmental structure is more vulnerable to the most costly types of corruption than a strong central administration. Supervision laxity, on the other hand, seems to go hand in hand with the height of the pyramidal organization. Overstaffing and underemployment may exist at all levels, from a small factory to a very large government bureau. The prevalence of incompetent staff generally reflects the incompetence of the top leadership, which is both incapable of recognizing ability among subordinates and afraid of it. Favoritism, however, is usually more prevalent in societies with distinct class barriers than in equalitarian societies. The relative costs and benefits of each bureaucracy, thus, have to be investigated and analyzed separately in each case in order to reach an objective judgment.[17]

Suggestions for Additional Readings

BERGSON, A. "Market Socialism Re-Visited." *Journal of Political Economy*, October 1967.

COHEN, S. S. *Modern Capitalist Planning: The French Model.* Berkeley: University of California Press, 1977.

COOMBES, D. *State Enterprise: Business or Politics?* London: Allen & Unwin, 1971.

17. Dahl and Lindblom consider red tape, passing the buck, inflexibility, impersonality, and excessive centralization as bureaucracy's *minor* disadvantages; failures in economizing, inequality of status, and independence of leaders from nonleaders, as *major* shortcomings. For a discussion of these "costs," see their *Politics, Economics, and Welare,* chapters 8 and 14. The first part of this section draws on some of their main arguments.

DOWNS, A. *Inside Bureaucracy.* Boston: Little, Brown, 1967.

FRIEDMAN, M. "The Market v. the Bureaucrat." *National Review,* 19 May 1970.

HAVEMAN, R. H. *The Economics of the Public Sector.* New York: Wiley, 1976.

HORVAT, B. *Toward a Theory of Planned Economy.* Belgrade: Yugoslav Institute of Economic Research, 1964.

JEWKES, J. *The New Ordeal by Planning.* London: Macmillan, 1968.

JEWKES, J. *A Return to Free Market Economics?* London: Macmillan, 1978.

KAUFMAN, H. *Red Tape: Its Origins, Uses and Abuses.* Washington: The Brookings Institution, 1977.

KOHLER, H. *Welfare and Planning.* New York: Wiley, 1966.

LANGE, O. *Essays on Economic Planning.* London: Asia Publishing House, 1960.

LEEMAN, W., ED. *Capitalism, Market Socialism and Central Planning.* Boston: Houghton Mifflin, 1963.

LIPPINCOTT, B. E. *On the Economic Theory of Socialism.* New York: McGraw-Hill, 1964.

LUTZ, V. C. *Central Planning for the Market Economy.* London: Institute of Economic Affairs, 1969.

NISKANEN, W. A. "Non-Market Decision Making: The Peculiar Economics of Bureaucracy." *American Economic Review,* May, 1968.

NISKANEN, W. A. *Bureaucracy and Representative Government.* Chicago: Aldine, 1971.

OLLMAN, B. *Alienation: Marxist Conception of Man in Capitalist Society.* Cambridge: Cambridge University Press, 1977.

PETER, L. J. *The Peter Principle.* New York: Bantam, 1969.

PRYKE, R. *Public Enterprise in Practice.* New York: St. Martin's, 1972.

REID, T. E. H., ED. *Economic Planning in a Democratic Society.* Toronto: University of Toronto Press, 1963.

SPULBER, N. *Socialist Management and Planning.* Bloomington: Indiana University Press, 1971.

TANDON, B. C. *Economic Planning.* Allahabad: Chaitanya Publishing House, 1970.

TURVEY, R. *Economic Analysis and Public Enterprises.* London: Allen & Unwin, 1971.

ZIELINSKI, J. G. "Centralization and Decentralization in Decision-Making." *Economics of Planning,* December 1963.

9

Decision Making through International Cooperation

MODERN NATIONS do not live in isolation. In addition to the traditional bonds of history, geography, religion, and culture, they are also signatories to many political treaties and agreements, and participate in a large number of global, regional, and bilateral economic agencies and schemes.

International economic interdependence, to be sure, is not a new phenomenon. Treaties of "friendship, navigation and commerce" concluded between sovereign nations in more distant times underscored the desirability of making some sacrifices of national sovereignty in order to promote world trade, investment, and mutual assistance. The novelty of contemporary international economic cooperation is their inescapable necessity: nations and national economies are being drawn together with or without their will.

For this reason, the way in which certain basic national economic problems are resolved is not always a matter of independent national choice. Important national economic decisions with significant bearings on the destiny of other nations—tariffs, quotas, currency valuations, export drives, investment ventures—are often made with due concern for possible international repercussions. Sometimes policies of worldwide importance are agreed upon through official governmental conferences, conventions, and organizations. In other cases, private multinational corporations are supplementing or supplanting international arrangements. Worldwide cartels, exclusive patent pools, market sharing, and price agreements, are common features of private global interdependence.

Prices, production cost, and profits of many goods and services, particularly those that cross international frontiers, are thus determined by a process of collective action and involvement that transcends national frontiers. We may term this process "supranational sovereignty," or decision making through international cooperation.[1]

1. The terminology is not strictly correct, because supranational sovereignty is commonly associated with a world government capable of exercising both tax and police powers. In none of the cases discussed in this chapter does such an authority exist. But to the extent that rules and regulations made beyond national jurisdictions are binding on national governments, supranational sovereignty may be a useful first approximation.

Supranational Sovereignty As a Decision Making Process

The supranational process is, in fact, a combination of delegated and multilateral sovereignties on a global scale. It thus may present a not too distant parallel to the other mechanisms discussed earlier, but it has its own distinctive features. First, economic decisions under this process are made by a multinational institution charged with the task of unifying or coordinating members' actions or empowered to act on behalf of members in matters of mutual interest.

Second, each participant in an international scheme is willing to give up certain rights, privileges, and prerogatives considered part of national sovereignty as a price for membership. In other words, there is a membership fee paid, partly, at least, through concessions or sacrifices in domestic sovereignty.

Third, the powers and responsibilities of a multinational organization vis-à-vis its individually sovereign members are clearly defined or agreed upon in advance so that the vital interests of no member can subsequently be infringed. Leading members, too, usually enjoy a statutory or practical veto power over the organization's major decisions.

Fourth, the association's objectives and interests, while aimed at maximizing the welfare of all, are theoretically independent of the nationalistic interests and motivation of each. Thus, membership involves not only some concessions on national sovereignty, but also certain sacrifices of national interest.

Fifth, the power, status, and benefit of each participant depend on the institutional structure of the association itself. In some international economic organizations (like many UN affiliated agencies), each member has one vote; in others (like the International Monetary Fund, the World Bank and regional development banks), voting rights are based on the size of capital subscription.

Finally, the association serves as a forum where members can informally discuss (and sometimes solve) matters of common concern that cannot be handled within the formal organizational machinery.

The Rationale of Cooperation

The underlying premise of decision making through international cooperation is the belief (not altogether uncontested) that world peace and prosperity are indivisible; that no country can live as an island of tranquility and affluence in a sea of turmoil and poverty; that economic instability in any major area of the world is a threat to both world peace and affluence; that poverty and frustration are inimical to politicoeconomic order; and that the dynamics of present-day technology, population explosion, and nationalism require certain supranational arrangements through which domestic and foreign economic policies can be coordinated and stabilized.

The growing significance of this premise is largely a product of three recent and mostly nonviolent "revolutions": the quickening pace of new technology binding nations together as never before in both war and peace; a deepening of conflicts between nationalistic economic policies and world economic stability; and the widening of horizons of expectations by the newly independent, emerging countries.

The effects of new industrial technology on the nature and pattern of world trade have indeed been revolutionary. As is generally recognized, the present pattern of world commerce bears only a faint resemblance to the conditions assumed by the classical theory of international trade (and its concomitant, international laissez faire). David Ricardo's theory of comparative advantage was based on the assumption of perfect competition on the global scale: free movements of commodities and capital, unrestricted shipment of gold across frontiers, and a close adherence by national monetary authorities to the gold standard's "rules of the game." In the same way that *national* welfare was to be maximized through competition among firms and individuals, so were attitudes and actions of self-centered nations expected to result in maximum *global* welfare through international exchange of goods and services.

The shortcomings of the comparative advantage theory in the contemporary setting need not be belabored here. The spectacular postwar growth of "space-age" industries has dramatically changed methods of production, transport, and communication in the leading industrial countries. The gaps in technology, organization, and management between the innovating countries (the United States, West Europeans, and Japan) and their trading partners have placed the latter at a competitive disadvantage. The result has been a new series of economic relations between the nations.

The need for international cooperation is also accentuated by the growing conflicts between goals of domestic policy and those of international welfare—themselves a product of greater interdependence. National goals of full employment, rapid growth, and economic security now clash more than ever before with the objective of expanding world trade and investment. Domestic full employment can often be achieved by import restrictions, export subsidies, and barriers against investment abroad. But, as is often said, no one wins a trade war, and unemployment cannot be remedied by exporting it. A restrictive trade policy may help a nation temporarily, but as soon as other countries begin to retaliate by introducing similar measures, the flow will be reversed. And at the end everybody is poorer. Accelerated economic development and increased national security can likewise be attempted—as they were during the 1930s—through the so-called beggar-my-neighbor policies, with similar dire consequences.

International economic cooperation has become the focus of attention for yet a third reason: the need for improving the plight of the relatively poor, underdeveloped countries. The concern of affluent industrial countries about the widening gap between their prosperity and the poverty of others has been intensified by the increasing number of independent but poor countries. These nations are now in a majority—in terms of territories, population, raw material resources, and number of votes in many United Nations agencies. Accordingly, the goal of wealth sharing and greater income equality has officially become part of the rich nations' foreign economic policy.

Institutions, Techniques, and Methods of Operation

The institutions and techniques of supranational sovereignty are not altogether well defined or sharply drawn. In general, contemporary multinational economic arrangements may be classified into governmental and private. Governmental schemes are established among sovereign nation-states. Private agreements are concluded among business corporations and trade associations. Governmental agencies and organizations may, in turn, be divided into geographical and functional. Public arrangements of a geographical or regional nature comprise customs unions, currency blocs, free-trade areas, and common markets. These schemes have two common characteristics. They are usually established among a limited number of countries, and they ordinarily include more than one aspect of intercountry economic relations.

In contrast to the regional economic schemes, functional arrangements ordinarily envisage certain limited objectives but enjoy much broader geographic coverage. Within this category, for example, are worldwide monetary or financial organizations designed for the specific purpose of promoting world monetary and financial orders. There are trade-oriented arrangements for the purpose of expanding international commerce through the reduction of trade barriers. There are also development agencies created for the transfer of real resources from richer to poorer countries.

Side by side with public agencies and schemes, one also finds interindustry or intercorporate arrangements among private groups and companies. Some of these arrangements are of the traditionally oligopolistic type (cartels, gentleman's agreement, patent pools) with narrow group interests. Their immediate objectives include concerted or coordinated actions to restrict supply, fix minimum prices, ward off potential competitors, or protect their investments and assets against the onslaught of new technology.

Other types of private, intercountry setups have broader and more universal goals, such as taking advantage of greater economies of scale available in a larger territorial market, using cheaper foreign labor and raw materials in conjunction with domestic technical and management know-how, or trying to escape discriminatory tariffs by establishing subsidiary plants with a foreign economic bloc.

When supranational sovereignty is exercised through interregional or international organizations, the method of operation would be similar to that of delegated sovereignty, except that representation would be multinational. Some distinctions, however, are to be made here between different voting procedures. The geographical or functional organizations in which each member officially has one and only one vote, as with many United Nations agencies, would be like national parliaments, where decisions are finalized by a simple majority vote. The only major difference is that almost no intercountry assembly possesses a tax or police power of its own. Thus, the enforcement of majority decisions would require voluntary compliance by all, particularly the minority of rich nations that often will have to supply the means of implementing those decisions.

In the specialized and functional organizations, like the International Monetary Fund, where membership votes are weighted on the basis of quota subscriptions, organizational policy is mainly determined by the largest share-holders, as in an a national or international business corporation. But even in organizations like the IMF, different coalitions of small and large members on different issues may significantly affect the outcome of the issues.

International Organizations and National Policies

The world economy in the last quarter of the twentieth century is becoming increasingly international in structure, transnational in orientation, and open in receiving and transmitting capital, technology, management, and even labor. A not insignificant part of domestic economic policies in most countries is subjected to international commitments under various arrangements. The emphasis here is on those commitments that exemplify supranational influence on national economic policies.

International Trade and Commodity Agreements

Agreements among nations for the purpose of facilitating commercial contacts and improving trade relations are numerous and varied. Some are of a broad nature, dealing with general problems of external trade and balance of payments. Others deal with special commodities or services. Some are formal and binding on members; others are informal and voluntary. Two important contemporary schemes that contain extranational obligations and affect domestic economic policies deserve special attention: intergovernmental commodity agreements, and the General Agreement on Tariffs and Trade (GATT).

International Commodity Agreements. ICAs are formal arrangements between nations for the purpose of regulating trade and stabilizing prices of certain raw materials and agricultural products in international markets. These agreements are, as a rule, concluded between the governments of producing and consuming countries in order to safeguard the interests of both and to ensure maximum compliance with the provisions of the agreement. Commodity agreements are mainly concluded with the essential purpose of regulating production, eliminating excess capacity, fixing prices, and getting rid of actual or potential surpluses.

The rationale of subjecting the national production and trade of certain primary products to international agreements is based upon five major considerations. First, supply and demand for some raw materials and farm products are not sufficiently price elastic, resulting in erratic shortages and gluts. Second, because of such relative inelasticities, the markets for these products are subject to wide fluctuations in prices and incomes for the producers. Third, as a result of the development of synthetic materials, foreign demand for some of these products is growing less rapidly than productive capacity. Fourth, the terms of trade between raw materials and manufactured products are in some cases worsening from year to year. Finally, as almost one half of raw materials producing countries depend on only one commodity for more than 50 percent of their total exports and exchange earnings, their ability to obtain needed foreign exchange almost totally depends on the level of economic activity in the industrial countries.[2] To reduce excessive price fluctuations in primary products, stabilize foreign-exchange earnings, and improve the level of income, a number of intergovernmental agreements have been concluded under the auspices of the United Nations Conference on Trade and Development (UNCTAD). These agreements, to be sure, are not universally admired or supported. The "free-marketeers" consider commodity agreements barriers to free trade. The agreements are also charged with tending to distort both the economic level and geographically rational location of supply. They are blamed for perpetuating production in areas that no longer offer competitive advantage and for freezing opportunities for competitive newcomers. The supporters, however, point out such merits as the assurance of adequate production and supply at relatively stable prices, removal of wasteful speculations, guarantee of quality standards, aid to poor producers of primary product, and greater overall certainty in development planning. The consensus among both opponents and supporters however, is that commodity agreements do influence the pattern of domestic production and the direction and composition of world trade. In satisfying responsibilities and obligations under these agreements, domestic policies—and national sovereignty—are thus partly affected.

Commodity agreements cover a whole range of metals and raw materials. Their origin goes back to the collapse of commodity prices after World War I. The idea was extensively discussed in the League of Nations in the interwar period. Since 1964, UNCTAD has been spearheading the drive for stabilizing prices of seventeen raw materials and sustaining revenues of their exporting countries. Here we shall

2. For example, Bolivia on tin; Ceylon on tea; Cuba on sugar; Chile on copper; Colombia and Haiti on coffee; Egypt and Sudan on cotton; Ghana on cocoa; and Malaysia on rubber.

deal with four commodity agreements to which many countries in our future discussion belong: wheat, sugar, coffee, and tin.

The International Wheat Agreement was first concluded in 1949 and renewed several times, last in 1971. The previous agreements established minimum and maximum prices at which exporting and importing countries could expect to receive or pay for the sale and purchase of wheat. About 80 percent of the world commercial trade in wheat during much of the 1960s was covered by such cooperation among more than fifty countries, but the main provisions of the 1967–71 grain agreement proved unworkable, and market instability continued during 1968–70. The 1971 agreement consisted of a trade convention and an aid convention. The trade part provided only for cooperation and consultation on supply and prices and contained no minimum and maximum prices or other provisions. The aid convention called for contributions by rich grain-producing countries to needy countries, with the United States assigned the largest share of such contributions. Originally due to expire in 1974, the agreement has been extended by successive protocols. Under UNCTAD's lead, a conference was convened in 1978 to replace the existing agreement, but the conference adjourned in 1979 because it could not agree on the price levels at which the reserve stocks were to be accumulated or released, the amount of reserve stocks and their distribution among members, and the share of aid contributions. Consequently the old agreement was extended to 1981. Brazil, India, Japan, the Soviet Union, the United Kingdom, and the United States are some of the participants in the wheat agreement.

The International Sugar Agreement is a relatively modest arrangement in comparison with others. As about 75 percent of world trade in sugar is covered under preferential and bilateral trade agreements, the ISA attempts to regulate only the residual "free" sector. First concluded in 1954 and renewed in 1958, the agreement worked well for several years thanks to the adherence of major trading countries. Adjustable export quotas were set for the producers under the supervision of the International Sugar Council, and exporters agreed to maintain certain stocks in order to prevent prices from rising beyond the prescribed maximum. Importers, in turn, agreed to limit their purchases from nonmembers. Following the breakdown of U.S.–Cuban relations, the agreement became unenforceable, and prices gyrated dramatically up and down. New understandings were reached in 1968 and 1973 in setting export quotas, minimum and maximum prices, and the producers' commitment to holding national stock. Under UNCTAD's auspices, in 1977 a new agreement was successfully negotiated between forty exporting and sixteen importing countries. The 1977 agreement is designed to stabilize sugar prices within a range, through a system of export quotas and national stocks. Brazil, India, Japan, the Soviet Union, the United States, and Yugoslavia, among others, are party to this agreement.

The International Coffee Agreement was signed in 1959, covering some 90 percent of all internationally traded coffee in the world and comprising forty-one exporting and twenty-one importing countries in North and South America, Europe, Africa, and Asia. The main purpose of the original agreement was to put a floor below coffee prices and to bring about a long-term equilibrium between supply and demand. The ICA was renewed in 1962 and 1968 for five years, setting annual, adjustable market shares or quotas for each of the forty-one producing countries on the basis of world import demand. Each producing member undertook to limit its domestic production to its domestic needs plus an alloted export quota in addition to a national stock. Export quotas were to be increased or suspended if market prices remained above a "trigger level" for several days. A special fund from the proceeds of supplementary quotas was set up to help diversification in the producing countries.

Despite occasional noncompliance by members and intrusion by nonmembers, the agreement succeeded in stabilizing the chaotic world coffee market (and keeping coffee prices above what consumer countries consider "fair") for some time. But under pressures of soaring coffee prices in 1972 and the refusal of consuming countries to agree to a higher trigger level, quotas were temporarily abolished, and the stage was set for a new round of negotiations in 1973. After two extensions of the 1968 agreement, a new six-year agreement between forty-three exporting and twenty-four importing countries entered into force in 1976. The 1976 agreement provides for the regulation of exports and imports under certain price conditions. Brazil, India, Japan, Nigeria, the United Kingdom, the United States, and Yugoslavia are among the signatories of this agreement.

The International Tin Agreement was first concluded in 1956 and renewed several times thereafter between the six principal producing countries (including the leading producers—Malaysia, Indonesia, and Bolivia) and many importing nations (with the notable exception of the United States). As in other agreements, a minimum and maximum price range, to be determined periodically by the International Tin Council, was set and specific export quotas for each supplier, adjustable to world market conditions, were duly established. A unique feature of this agreement has been the existence of an international buffer stock through which purchases and sales of tin are made in order to keep prices within the prescribed range. The buffer stock is supplied by the producers. The votes in the council, which effectively regulate outputs and exports, are divided equally between producers and consumers and, for each member, based on volume of production or consumption. The 1976–81 agreement among seven producing and twenty-three consuming countries is designed to prevent excessive price fluctuations through buffer stock operations. India, Japan, the Soviet Union, the United Kingdom, the United States, and Yugoslavia are among the importing signatories; Nigeria is among the exporters.

Some of the countries in our study belong to other commodity organizations. Brazil is in the Cocoa Organization. India is in the Coconut Community and National Rubber Association. Japan is in the Cotton Advisory Committee. Nigeria is in both Cocoa and Cotton, as are the Soviet Union and the United Kingdom. Yugoslavia is in the Copper Council and the Bauxite Association, among others. As indicated before, while some of these agreements are often inoperative because of market buoyancy, and others are unenforceable during depressions, the obligations and responsibilities accepted by the signatories are part of a voluntary sacrifice in national sovereignty.

The General Agreement on Tariffs and Trade. GATT came into existence in the wake of the U.S. Congress's refusal right after World War II to ratify the Charter for the International Trade Organization. It was meant to be a makeshift arrangement, pending the fate of a more permanent institution to deal with the rules of conduct for world trade and commercial policy.[3]

GATT is a voluntary, informal association of some ninety-nine countries accounting for 80 percent of world trade. Its main purpose is to reach certain mutually satisfactory accommodations out of diverse and often contradictory national policies in the area of commercial relations. The agreement is based on four basic principles: "most favored nation" treatment of all contracting parties; gradual elimination of quotas and other quantitative restrictions, with tariffs remaining the sole means of protecting home industries; settlement of trade disputes through direct consultation and discussion; and progressive reduction of all tariffs through successive rounds of negotiaton. These general principles are elaborately expressed in a large number of specific articles in the agreement, with a long list of exceptions, waivers, and escape clauses.

Any country that wishes to join GATT and to benefit from the tariff concessions already made by its contracting parties must agree to four principal rules: to offer tariff reductions in exchange for reciprocal privileges; to extend concessions obtained by some members to all other members; to commit itself not to withdraw its concessions except as permitted by the agreement; and to work toward further reduction of tariffs and trade barriers.

Although GATT has no formal authority, it provides the institutional machinery for regular consultation, mediation, and amicable settlement of commercial policy disputes among its contracting parties. It also organizes periodic rounds of multilateral conferences for tariff reduction. The last one of the seven such post-1947 gatherings—the "Tokyo Round" (1974–79)—succeeded in an across-the-board reduction of thousands of tariff items.[4]

The "sacrifices" of national sovereignty in matters of foreign-trade policies under GATT are many. First, the principles of nondiscrimination and most favored nation treatment make it difficult for a country to use special tariffs or other restrictive measures against another country in order to exact a bargain. Second,

3. For an analytical examination of the functions of GATT, see G. Curzon, *Multilateral Commercial Diplomacy* (London: Michael Joseph, 1965).
4. The Tokyo Round, which finished in 1979, produced a customs valuation code for imports, a government procurement code, a code on subsidies and countervailing duties, a standards code to prevent unnecessary obstacles to imports, and an agreement on import licensing procedures—among others.

once a country's negotiated tariff schedule is approved and made part of the agreement, further tariff increases (and other duties, domestic taxes, or unequal treatment of imports) would be difficult, unless, of course, the country should plan to abandon GATT. Third, antidumping and other retaliatory measures against other countries would be normally limited to the extent of injuries received. Fourth, new trade restrictions (other than tariffs) and exchange control would be permitted only under stringent conditions and on a nondiscriminatory basis. Fifth, export subsidies established by a member must not unduly burden other members. Finally, while the less developed countries are permitted to take protective measures in favor of their infant industries, their power in this respect is measurably circumscribed.

International Monetary Order

Economic cooperation through multinational economic agencies has a long history. The International Telegraph Union was founded as far back as 1865 to regulate telegram transmission across national frontiers. The Universal Postal Union, which constitutes a single postal territory for the entire world, unifies postal charges, and allows freedom of transit by mail, was established by the Treaty of Berne in 1874. In this century, the International Labor Organization was established in 1919 to set up international labor standards and to promote technical cooperation in manpower training and management development. These and dozens of other international economic organizations play important roles in shaping domestic economic policies and influencing world resource allocation.[5] Our discussion here will be limited to a brief examination of one international organization with considerable influence on domestic price and foreign exchange policies in the postwar period—the International Monetary Fund (IMF).

The IMF is the offspring of an international conference of the Allies held at Bretton Woods, New Hampshire, in 1944 to lay the foundations for a new international monetary order after the war. The Fund was created as a new "adjustable-peg" system of exchange rates to put an end to recurrent changes in domestic levels of output and prices under the old gold standard, and to remove foreign exchange uncertainties and fluctuations under the gold exchange standard. In the Bretton Woods Conference, a majority of nations agreed to peg their foreign exchange rates to the U.S. dollar and use the IMF machinery for adjusting those rates from time to time.[6] The par value of each country's currency was established in terms of the U.S. dollar at the time of joining the Fund. Each member agreed to keep the price of its currency in terms of other currencies within 2 percent of its par value through sales or purchases of foreign exchange. Once the par value of a

5. For a comprehensive listing of these organizations, see *The Europa Year Book, 1980* (London: Europa Publications, 1980).

6. The Soviet Union participated in the Bretton Woods Conference, but later refused to join the Fund.

currency was determined, its upward or downward revisions for the correction of a fundamental disequilibrium could be made by the country itself by as much as 10 percent without Fund approval.[7] Further changes in the exchange rate made necessary under persistent disequilibrium required prior consultation and approval by the Fund. Fund approval was also normally required for changes in exchange restrictions on current international transactions. Failure to comply with these provisions by a member could result in its ineligibility for the use of the Fund's resources and facilities. The rewards for compliance, for instituting effective stabilization programs at home to deal with internal inflation and external deficits, would be available in the form of foreign exchange credit by the Fund.

Under the Bretton Woods Agreement and its two subsequent amendments, the Fund is to undertake certain functions of a world central bank for its member countries. Each member is given a share or a quota in the Fund's total capital subscription, based on its importance as an international trader (as measured by such factors as GNP, exports and imports, and foreign exchange revenues). Quotas determine each member's voting powers in the election of the executive directors and the formulation of Fund policies; and the extent to which each member can borrow from the Fund. Quotas are revised every few years according to changes in economic conditions in member countries.

In addition to the regular drawing rights, since January 1970, each member has also become entitled to the Special Drawing Rights (SDRs). The SDRs—popularly dubbed "paper gold"—are simply additional credits given member countries (based on their quotas) to be used as reserves for contingency. Since 1963, the Fund has also stood ready to help primary producing countries with temporary balance-of-payments difficulties arising from shortfalls in export earnings. During the 1970s, several other "facilities" have been made available to members with temporary problems in their external balance.

The original Bretton Woods scheme worked reasonably well up to 1970, as long as the U.S. dollar was convertible into gold at the fixed prices of $35 an ounce. But consecutive monetary crises during 1971–73 drastically reduced the Fund's effectiveness as a stabilizing institution. Fundamental imbalances in international trade, such as chronic U.S. deficits vis-à-vis continuing surpluses for Japan and West Germany, and disequilibrating flows of short-term capital led, in early May 1971, to the floating of the German mark and, in August 1971, to the abandonment by the United States of the dollar's convertibility into gold. After a few months of general uncertainty, the Smithsonian Agreement of December 1971 provided for a realignment of exchange rate relationships and a new procedure for currency adjustments. The U.S. dollar was devalued by 7.89 percent in terms of gold and of Special Drawing Rights in exchange for the appreciation of the Japanese yen and the German mark, among others. A temporary regime of wider margins (4.5 percent) was established, within which a member's currency could move in relation to other

7. For a full account of the Fund's evolution and operations, see J. K. Horsefield et al., *The International Monetary Fund, 1945–1965*, vols. 1–3 (Washington: IMF, 1970).

currencies. Heavy flows of speculative capital, resumed in mid-June 1972, led to the flotation of the pound sterling and similar actions by most of the Commonwealth countries. Later in the year, the mark again came under heavy pressure, and the exchange market had to be closed temporarily. Early in 1973, the U.S. dollar was devalued by another 10 percent against gold, and the Japanese yen was set afloat in a move to establish closer parities. The system of floating exchange rates was thus put unofficially in place.

Under the second amendment to the IMF's Articles of Agreement, in 1976 the concept of the par value system and fixed exchange rates was formally abandoned. Members became legally free to choose their exchange arrangements, including floating. Monetary stability was to be achieved not necessarily through stable rates, but by orderly economic and financial conditions that would promote a stable system of exchange rates. In order to achieve this objective, members are now subject to certain obligations in relation to their internal and external policies. The Fund, in turn, is required to maintain "surveillance" over members' compliance of their obligations. Another significant feature of the second amendment is the abolition of an official price for gold and the elimination of the role of gold as a denominator in exchange arrangements. A concomitant aim is to make the SDR the principal reserve asset of the international monetary system.

The Bretton Woods system, by requiring members to maintain relatively stable official rates of exchange, established an international legal obligation that preceded domestic policies. Fixed exchange rates were in a sense the impersonal rule of law that guided sovereign nations in the pursuit of national monetary policy. Again, while national sovereignty in matters of national interest was not ever abandoned, obligations toward the IMF provided a discipline in controlling the money supply—and, thus, the domestic rates of growth, employment, and inflation.[8] At present, the Fund's "supranational" power has become more limited and, at best, somewhat unclear. Jurisdiction to control certain activities and behavior of members in relation to exchange rates is relegated only to the "surveillance" of international liquidity, yet members are still under numerous obligations in their external payments and transactions.

International Economic Integration

Economic integration or union refers to various degrees of collaboration, harmonization, and unification among independent states with respect to certain international economic policies. The Organization of African Unity, the League of Arab States, the Regional Cooperation for Development, the European Free Trade

8. In a different vein, some of the LDC leaders have occasionally accused the IMF of demanding that client nations surrender their decision-making power and change their national policies in the areas of price controls, exchange valuation, interest rates, and public spending.

Association, the Organization for Economic Cooperation and Development, the Caribbean Community, and the Latin American Free Trade Association are among the more than fifty such regional economic organizations on four continents. Here we discuss only two of these organizations: the European Economic Community, widely known as the Common Market, and the Council for Mutual Economic Assistance.

The European Economic Community (EEC). The EEC is part of the larger European Communities (comprising European Coal and Steel Community and the European Atomic Energy Community). Born of the Treaty of Rome in 1957 between France, Germany, Italy, and the former Benelux Customs Union (Belgium, Holland, and Luxembourg), the Community was the culmination of persistent efforts by a number of leading European statesmen toward an eventual United States of Europe.[9] Great Britain, Ireland, and Denmark joined the EEC in January 1973. Greece, Portugal, and Spain are to join in the early 1980s.

The EEC came into force in January 1958, designed to promote coordinated economic development of member states under conditions of stable, full employment, growth in the service of higher standards of living, and greater common politicoeconomic strength. These objectives were, in turn, expected to be obtained by: the gradual elimination of customs duties and other trade restrictions between members; establishment of a common tariff against outsiders; harmonization of commercial, agricultural, transport, and welfare policies; free movement of resources, including capital and labor; promotion of fair competition and prevention of monopolistic practices; and the creation of a Social Fund and a European Investment Bank. The latter was to aid poorer areas of member countries and poorer countries associated with the members by former colonial ties. The Social Fund was to help geographical and occupational mobility of workers within the Community.

The Common Market was to be gradually established, within twelve to fifteen years and in three stages, based on the principles of: nondiscrimination against member countries' goods, services, and people; nonreversibility of concessions made to other members; and the possibility of membership or association with the Community for other countries and communities.

Under the intra-Community policy toward agriculture (worked out in 1963), the market for basic foodstuffs had to be stabilized through a system of: minimum price supports at some internal target level; restrictions against outside imports of farm products at prices below internal targets; subsidies to high-cost exporters in surplus countries (principally, France); and preferential treatment given to associated overseas territories (chiefly, France's former African colonies).

The EEC has an elaborate "supranational" organization. The Community possesses a 410-member, quasi-legislative body—the European Parliament—com-

9. For a detailed analysis of the EEC's evolution, see the references at the end of this chapter.

posed of directly elected representatives from member countries who discuss broad questions of policies and practices related to matters of Community interest and make recommendations to other Market agencies. All basic policy decisions are taken by the executive branch, the Council of Ministers. The Council, composed principally of foreign ministers, but also attended by other cabinet officials in various economic fields, is the highest and most powerful organ of the Community; it acts on proposals submitted by the Parliament and the Economic Commission; its majority decisions are effective in all member countries.

The workhorse of the Community is the Economic Commission, a tight, thirteen-member body elected unanimously by the member governments each four years and sworn to serve the Community impartially and free from nationalistic tendencies. The Commission can investigate breaches of Community rules, impose fines on offenders, and take members to the Community's Court of Justice for noncompliance. It also makes proposals to the Council of Ministers to advance Community policies. The Commission's large staff prepares background materials for policy decisions, and every decision and action by the Community, or related to its operation, has to be approved by the Commission before being submitted to the Council of Ministers. There are numerous specialized committees under the Commission. The Court of Justice supervises the enforcement of the Treaty of Rome and interprets Community laws and rules. Its rulings have precedence over domestic law, but in practice it lacks sanctions and has to leave enforcement to the Commission or national courts.

The initial successes of the six economies in achieving the Community's goals have been remarkable and swift. The Customs Union, among the original six members, became effective in 1968, a year and a half ahead of the original timetable. The common external tariff also was instituted in 1968, a year sooner than scheduled. Tariffs among all nine members were abolished in 1977. The Community has also succeeded in removing essential restrictions against labor emigration and immigration; in facilitating transfers of capital for investment purposes; in moving towards a unified commercial policy; and in extending sizable loans for the development of depressed areas in and out of the EEC. Trade within the area and with nonmembers expanded considerably faster than in other countries and economic communities.

Despite its outstanding successes in the industrial and trade fields, agriculture has remained the Market's biggest economic headache. Labor-intensive, small-scale, old-fashioned, and heavily protected from the start, the EEC's high-cost farming (with the possible exception of France) has had to be supported ever since the Community's establishment. Under the common agricultural policy referred to above, every farmer in any member country is entitled to receive a guaranteed minimum price (usually much above world price) for his crop. If the market price within the Community falls below the internal target, the crop is turned over to the Agricultural Guidance and Guarantee Fund. Surpluses are then stored or dumped in world markets. Some 85 percent of total EEC produce is supported at an annual cost of several billion dollars, mostly contributed by manufacturing member countries and received by those with extensive farming. In this manner, the EEC acts like a federal government, taxing some states and helping others. For the same reasons as in the United States (farmers' political clout), surpluses of unwanted commodities (butter, soft wheat, and sugar) are piling up, but prices of supported products remain high, and some commodities, such as maize, are heavily imported.

In the summit conference of EEC leaders in September 1970, it was agreed to move toward the final phase of economic integration: complete economic and monetary union. In April 1972, agreement was reached on the first stage of the eventual currency union. In September 1972, another modest but significant decision was made toward establishing a European Monetary Fund to help member countries out of temporary balance-of-payments difficulties. Formally established in 1973, the fund was regarded as a European "central bank" and as a key first step toward a single EEC currency and a monetary union.

In December 1978, the heads of state of the Community—the European Council—adopted a resolution on the establishment of the European Monetary System. The EMS was ostensibly designed for the creation of closer monetary cooperation and the promotion of exchange stability in Europe. At the center of the scheme stands a new European currency unit, called ECU (consisting of a basket of European currencies), in terms of which the value of each member's currency is to be fixed. Deviations from this central rate are allowed within small margins (2.25 to 6 percent), but beyond the so-called thresholds of divergence, each member has the obligation to intervene in the market to bring the rate back into line. Members are allowed to draw on the resources of the EMS for the purpose of intervention. EMS resources consist of 20 percent of each central bank's gold holdings and 20 percent of its gross dollar reserves.[10]

In other areas, the EEC Commission has also moved aggressively against intrabloc cartels, multinational mergers, price fixing, and other anticompetitive practices. The Commission can fine offenders and take them to court.

As can be seen from the foregoing discussions, while the goal of a United States of Europe envisaged by the Community's founding fathers is still far from a reality, the Common Market is asserting itself as an independent and quasi-sovereign power. And while no member nation has given up its sovereignty, part of the internal affairs of every member is now run by the Community. And despite the lack of effective legal or administrative sanctions, members have been able to forge a series of significant common policies in trade, monetary issues, agriculture, and taxation.

The Council for Mutual Economic Assistance (COMECON). COMECON was founded in 1949 as a kind of counterpart to the OECD, established in 1948 under

10. For details of the EMS, see *Texts Concerning the European Monetary System* (Brussels: European Monetary Cooperation Fund, 1979).

the impetus of the U.S. Marshall Plan to coordinate postwar European reconstruction. The Council, in addition to the Soviet Union and Mongolia, includes all East European countries, except Albania—with China, Cuba, North Korea, North Vietnam, and Yugoslavia as observers. The publicized purposes of the COMECON are to promote "the most rational" development of member economies, to raise their standard of living, and to strengthen the "unity and solidarity." In accordance with these basic objectives, the Council is to coordinate member countries' national economic plans; to organize economic and technical cooperation among members with a view to increasing country specialization and to maximizing the benefits of large-scale production and "socialist division of labor"; to develop joint enterprises in industry, agriculture and transportation; to expand trade and investment between members; to exchange information on scientific and technical data; and to make recommendations to members on matters of mutual interest.

COMECON has an elaborate Moscow-led organizational structure. Its supreme organ is the Council itself, composed of government chiefs, which meets at least once a year to consider proposals from members, the Executive Committee, and other organs to design basic policies and to lay down programs of action. A committee, made up of deputy prime ministers or foreign trade ministers, is convened several times during the year to examine proposals from members, to coordinate the operations of the permanent commissions, and to assess the bloc's progress and take appropriate actions between Council sessions. Decisions and recommendations have to be approved by unanimous vote. The Moscow-based Secretariat employs hundreds of technical and administrative civil servants drawn from each member country. Within the organization, some twenty permanent commissions, made up of cabinet ministers, deal with agriculture, industry, transportation, money, taxes, and scientific research. There is also an International Bank for Economic Cooperation (IBEC). Half of the bank's capital is subscribed by the Soviet Union and East Germany.

The central COMECON tenet originally was a move toward community-centered economic planning to forge a self-contained (if not totally self-sufficient) communist bloc to be mutually interdependent, but outwardly independent of the rest of the world. In practice, however, East European developments have not followed the dictates of such an economic alliance. The economic reforms instituted in Poland, Hungary, East Germany and Czechoslovakia in favor of more decentralization, and independent tendencies emerging in Yugoslavia, Romania, and Hungary, have markedly eroded the COMECON's solidarity. This is chiefly because COMECON, unlike the EEC, is not a closely knit regional association with a central executive power binding on member states. Instead, it is a loose arrangement between largely self-contained economies bound together mainly through bilateral trade.

Although initially envisaged by the Soviet Union as a supranational socialist economic community, COMECON has remained essentially a trading bloc. Since 1964, it has officially accepted Romania's argument that the planned management of the national economy is an "inalienable" responsibility of the socialist state. It has thus substituted voluntary cooperation for regional integration. Romania's active resistance has blocked successfully Polish and Russian attempts to increase cooperation in planning, product specialization, regional investment, and trade relations within the organization.[11]

In 1971, the member governments agreed that the ultimate aim of COMECON should be to integrate member economies stage by stage over a period of fifteen to twenty years, but there were no indications that the proposed integration would have such elemental features as a common COMECON currency, specialization by each member in a particular branch of industry, or radically greater intrabloc trade. The practical objective of the new accord seemed to increase ad hoc cooperation in multinational projects.

The success of COMECON has been uneven from the standpoint both of its organizational objectives and also the interests of member states. The Soviet Union's hope for economic integration of Eastern Europe—with coordination of national plans, joint policies on investment, and a controlled interregional division of labor—has not yet materialized. While intrabloc trade has markedly increased in the last two decades, trade imbalances within the bloc and with the outside world have continued to plague many partners. Mutual convertibility among member currencies, an essential aspect of any real integration, has not yet been achieved. But despite some members' dismay, COMECON has indeed influenced their internal economic development. The most notable success of COMECON has been in increasing trade among members and in keeping intrabloc trade at a constantly high rate.

Since 1970, improved relations between West Germany, the Soviet Union, and other bloc members have produced new opportunities for increased trade between the two sides of the Iron Curtain. The same has been true of trade between the United States and the Soviet Union, and recently with China.

Suggestions for Additional Readings

BALASSA, B. A. *European Economics Integration.* New York: Elsevier, 1975.

COFFEY, P., ED. *Economic Policies of the Common Market.* New York: St. Martin's, 1979.

COHEN, S. D. *The European Community and GATT.* Washington: EC Information Service, 1975.

DAM, K. W. *The GATT.* Chicago: University of Chicago Press, 1970.

11. For a brief analysis of COMECON developments, see H. W. Heiss, "The Council for Mutual Economic Assistance—Development Since the Mid-1960s," in *Economic Development in Countries of Eastern Europe,* Joint Economic Committee, 91st Cong., 2nd Sess. (Washington: GPO, 1970).

FRANK, I. *The European Common Market.* New York: Praeger, 1961.

GEORGE, K. D. AND C. JOLL, EDS. *Competitive Policy in the United Kingdom and EEC.* Cambridge: Cambridge University Press, 1979.

INTERNATIONAL MONETARY FUND. *The International Monetary Fund: Purposes, Structure and Activities.* Washington: IMF, 1980.

KOSTECKI, M. M. *East-West Trade and the GATT System.* New York: St. Martin's, 1979.

KRAUSE, L. B. *European Economic Integration and the United States.* Washington: The Brookings Institution, 1968.

LEWIS, W. A. *The Evolution of the International Economic Order.* Princeton: Princeton University Press, 1973.

SWANN, D. *The Economics of the Common Market.* New York: Penguin Books, 1978.

Part Four

THE TASK OF PORTRAYAL

PART FOUR PRESENTS an examination of the relative significance of the five decision-making processes among a selected number of contemporary nation-states. Selection is made from among the major industrial nations, the centrally directed economies, and the less developed countries.

As chapters 10 through 12 show, a modified market mechanism, superimposed by delegated and multilateral sovereignty, provides the main decision-making framework in the major industrial nations while unilateral sovereignty is somewhat reluctantly used. Among the centrally directed states, the processes of delegation and bargaining are usually overshadowed by the dominant role of the command mechanism while some measures of the free market are tolerated for various internal considerations. In the less developed nations, because of the need for rapid economic growth and industrialization, the market mechanism is often supplemented by unilateral sovereignty and a large dose of government regulation; delegated sovereignty is often exercised through a one-party system or through revolutionary councils that combine the legislative and executive functions; and the bargaining process often verges on the rudimentary.

More specifically, the market mechanism plays a significant role in influencing economic policy, both internal and international, among the major industrial nations. In the less developed countries of Africa, Asia, and Latin America—despite their impatience with the slow process of market-dependent growth—the role and influence of private enterprise are also pervasive for both historical and practical reasons. Even in the centrally directed economies that are ideologically opposed to private ownership and private gain, individual sovereignty has some limited use.

Delegated decision making has increased in scope and intensity in the postwar period because of the inadequacy of market mechanism to cope with modern socioeconomic problems and expectations. The most conspicuous programs of postwar national legislatures in Western democracies and in many newly emerging nations have been socioeconomic, attempting to supplement market forces with indirect state controls in order to improve national and individual economic conditions.

Multilateral sovereignty has for long been the characteristic process of decision making in Europe and North America. Bargaining among organized groups has, to a large extent, also influenced the process of translating national objectives into specific policies, programs, and projects. In the major industrial countries, this is candidly acknowledged. The significance of group bargaining in each country depends on the number, political power, economic strength, and the skill of organized groups.

Unilateral sovereignty and direct state control of the economy have now become permanent features of the contemporary economic order throughout the world. In the developed Western democracies, government ownership and operation are limited to certain basic sectors of the economy. The centrally directed economies, on the other hand, rely mainly on direct controls in almost all economic sectors. The less developed countries fall somewhere in between.

Chapter 10 discusses the relative significance of the four processes of decision making in some of the major industrial nations. Chapter 11 examines the application of these processes in some of the centrally directed economies, while chapter 12 outlines the functioning of these mechanisms among selected LDCs.

10

The Market-Oriented Advanced Industrial Countries

THE MICS INCLUDE some eighteen countries in Western Europe, North America, Asia, and Oceania—all members of the Organization for Economic Cooperation and Development (OECD). They represent some 670 million people, living in over 30 million square kilometers. While they are often collectively referred to as "Western democracies," they are not all in the West, nor do they all have exactly the same democratic regimes. The United States and Canada are in the Western Hemisphere, but Japan, Australia, and New Zealand are in the East and the South. The Scandinavian and Benelux countries are constitutional monarchies; others are republics with varying democratic traditions (the oldest being the United Kingdom; the newest, Japan and West Germany). In terms of annual GNP per capita, too, they range from $4,000 for Ireland to $11,000 for the United States.[1] In land area, they comprise Belgium, with only 31,000 square kilometers and Canada, with 9,976,000. The size of population varies from about 3 million for New Zealand to 225 million for the United States. Nevertheless, they all have certain structural features more or less in common.

First, these countries are the originators, developers, and users of high technology (nuclear fission, space exploration, cybernetics, semiconductors, lasers, advanced computers, and similar knowledge-intensive industries). Second, a relatively small percentage of their labor force is engaged in agriculture,[2] and a relatively large portion of their GDP is derived from industrial production (mining, manufacturing, power, and construction). Third, no more than half of GDP passes through state hands for current expenditures on goods, services, and transfer payments. Fourth, a relatively high standard of living is enjoyed by the majority as measured by high private per capita consumption and such other indicators as

1. For the origin and methodology of calculation of comparable GNP figures, see *World Development Report, 1980* (Washington: World Bank, 1980).
2. Ireland is the only exception, with 20 percent of the work force in farming.

energy consumption per capita; the number of passenger cars, telephones, and TV sets; university enrollments; and number of physicians per capita. Fifth, more than half of the merchandise exports consists of machinery, transport equipment, and other manufactures.[3]

Owing to significant differences in geography, land area, population, natural wealth, and even relative advances in technology, the MICs' individual approaches to decision making naturally exhibit certain national nuances and specifics. While all nations in this category are by definition market oriented, the structure of the market itself and the extent of reliance on consumer sovereignty vary widely. There are also variances in the degree of state intervention, governmental attitude toward business concentration, the influence of economic pressure groups, and the functional relationship between the executive and legislative branches of the government.

Consumers' Sovereignty

The MICs, as a rule, rely mainly upon private enterprise and the free market for the production of goods and services. The United States, the West European countries, Scandinavia, Canada, Australia, New Zealand, and Japan are often called the "capitalist" world because their major mechanism of economic decision making is consumer sovereignty. The bulk of domestic resources and means of production is privately owned, and economic activity is conducted by private firms. The lion's share of consumption, saving, and investment is concentrated in the private sector. The choice of occupation, expenditure, trade, enterprise, and innovation is open to individuals and private groups. Not an insignificant part of national economic policy, both internal and international, is in varying degrees influenced, if not dictated, by private businessmen.

The unregulated and unplanned sector of the MICs usually comprises the wholesale and retail trade, the self-employed professionals, nonsubsidized agriculture, small-scale manufacturing industries, and most services. Most of these businesses are organized on a single proprietorship or small partnership basis. By contrast, manufacturing, utilities, banking, and finance are fairly concentrated. In most of these activities, public ownership and operation are exceptions, not the rule. Part of the government intervention in the economy is designed only to safeguard, promote, and bolster the free market.[4]

3. Australia and New Zealand are the only two exceptions, showing figures of 21 percent and 17 percent, respectively. Japan, on the other hand, shows a figure of 97 percent.
4. Interestingly enough, almost all "socialist" parties in the MICs throughout the postwar period have supported and endorsed the free-market mechanism. Germany's ruling Social Democratic party, which has been partly responsible for the German "economic miracle," has as its motto: "As much competition as possible; as much planning as necessary."

The private sector, however, is private predominantly in terms of ownership. In operation and decision making, it is, at least partly, regulated by the state. This sector displays the modern characteristics of so-called mature capitalism. That is, the markets are less than perfectly free. The manufacturing sector shows considerable concentration of control by a few large firms, bank holding companies, diversified conglomerates, and other forms of supercontrol by private interests. Deviation from competitive standards exists in varying degrees in the vital matters of nonmarket pricing, difficulty of entry and exit, brand promotion, and advertising.

The concentrated control in Europe and Japan, however, seems substantially greater than in the United States. So is the degree of official and public tolerance of monopolies, mergers, and cartels. Ideologically, the West European democracies seem far less wedded to the free-enterprise dogma. Business mergers and industrial concentration are far more widely tolerated (not to say officially encouraged) than in the United States. Industrial concentration in Germany draws significant support from the lukewarm enforcement of German antimonopoly laws, particularly with regard to intercompany ownership of stock and the mutuality of directorship in closely related companies. On the other hand, both industrial plants and firms in Western Europe are smaller than in the United States. The number of firms in each industry is also much larger in Europe than in the U.S.[5] Business concentration in France, for example, is established and maintained largely by family ownership, but also extensively by means of intercorporate stock ownership, interlocking directorates, minimum price maintenance, joint sales efforts, and other types of close cooperation.

Although postwar antimonopoly legislation has ruled against flagrantly restrictive practices, enforcement is undermined by exempting those combinations approved by the government for the national interest. Unlike in the United States, therefore, a distinction is made between good and bad cartels. Good cartels are not only permitted but also actively supported by the government as a means of rebutting foreign—particularly U.S.—competition. In Scandinavia, too, cartel and other noncompetitive arrangements are widely prevalent. There are hundreds of cartels registered with the government. Postwar legislation only forbids "antisocial" cartels, but is not opposed to the growth of private power per se.

Decisions through Proxy

The second half of the twentieth century has witnessed a conspicuous trend toward representative or participatory democracy. In the advanced industrial states, national assemblies have become more representative and increasingly more involved in

5. For a detailed comparison of size and efficiency between EEC countries and the United States, see D. Swann, *Concentration or Competition* (London: PEP, 1967), pp. 7–12.

legislating socioeconomic measures. The most conspicuous programs of postwar national legislatures have been welfare oriented. There has been a marked tendency in almost all democratic assemblies to supplement market forces with group action in order to improve national and individual economic conditions.

The growth of indirect state intervention among advanced industrial nations has been a result of further industrialization and mechanization, technological progress, urbanization, and the revolution of popular expectations. The advance of modern technology has resulted in the concentration of management, capital, and manpower in fewer and fewer industrial units. Business concentration has, in turn, required fresh evaluations of existing antitrust policies and the devising of effective new instruments to cope with the new forms of monopoly and oligopoly. The enormity of risks and financial outlays involved in developing modern, science-based, and internationally competitive industries has called for state promotion of technological research and development. The adverse effect of new technology on social and environmental conditions has invited the government to take protective measures.

As indicated in chapter 6, governments have also been drawn increasingly into the provision of supplementary income assistance, unemployment compensation, health insurance, old-age pension, and industrial mediation, because of intensified industrialization and the gradual breakdown of automatic market controls. With individuals becoming increasingly dependent on the state, the pressure of rising popular demand on the state has ushered in state-supported measures toward higher growth, equality, equity, and welfare.

Wage-price policies have also been a frequent feature of major industrial economies. In addition to the United States, Great Britain, and Japan (whose incomes policies are discussed in more detail later in this chapter), West Germany, France, Canada, and the Nordic countries frequently resort to such policy in order to combat wage-price spirals. While the postwar successes of incomes policies are at least spotty—and mostly of a very short duration—these policies are considered the only positive alternative to traditional monetary and fiscal measures, which often prove sluggish, ineffective, or risky.

A combination of unemployment and inflation prevailing in the MICs through most of the 1970s has led these countries to restructure and upgrade their welfare schemes. Consequently, both social security taxes and budgetary deficits have been on the rise. A guaranteed minimum income has been instituted in some countries. In others, pensions have been adjusted for the rise in the cost of living. Unemployment benefits and unemployment assistance have been increased and extended. Among various welfare measures adopted by the MICs, old-age pensions now take the lion's share of total social security spending (from a third to well over one half in different countries). Sickness and disability benefits rank second (between a quarter and a third). Family benefits and unemployment insurance follow.

State indirect interventions to correct free-market deficiencies are pervasive not only in the MICs with long welfarist tradition (the United Kingdom) or those with close government-business collaboration (Japan and France), but also in others. For example, despite its postwar reputation as a market-oriented, private-enterprise economy, Germany is now a full-blown "welfare state." The German economy under the Christian Democrats was one of the largest and costliest such states in the world, and the Socialist-Free Democrats coalition has, if anything, moved faster in that direction. Subsidies to specific segments of the economy (apart from social welfare payments and general tax concessions) have been a common feature of postwar German economic policy.

The same is true of France. The French social security system is the world's most comprehensive. Despite a long tradition of laissez faire going back to the Physiocrats, indirect state control of the economy is second to none among the MICs. In the French view, government intervention is aimed at avoiding both total government direction and complete laissez faire. Under this hybrid policy, industries in distress and areas in decline become "wards" of the state and receive various measures of aid. In short, the desirability and necessity of offsetting the free market's shortcomings and amplifying its beneficial effects are universal in the MICs. The differences are only in the priorities and in emphasis.

Decisions through Bargaining

The characteristic process of determining national socioeconomic goals in Western Europe and North America is one of bargaining among organized groups in search of a consensus. The same is true to a large extent of the process of translating national objectives into specific policies, programs, and projects. The postwar economic developments in MICs, based on the rising number and influence of economic pressure groups, has made multilateral bargaining increasingly widespread. Not only in traditionally pluralistic societies of the United States and Great Britain, but also in other MICs, an important part of basic economic decisions is now influenced by formal and informal bargaining among major interest groups.

"Live-and-let-live" policy, for example, is now at the core of French business conduct. Cooperation and compromise among business firms and the government, are an accepted and legitimate mode of economic behavior. The government, instead of taking a clear-cut attitude toward either unfettered competition or authoritarian paternalism, tries to bring special-interest groups together under its own auspices and direction. France's indicative plans are the result of extensive consultation (bargaining) among representatives from manufacturers, suppliers, trade unions, customers, and public agencies. In this bargaining process, officialdom usually offers some important favors—import restrictions, easy credit, fiscal subsidies—in order to obtain big businesses' cooperation in pursuit of the plan targets. The large firms, the trade associations of many small businessmen, and the bureaucrats in specialized ministries often bargain on behalf of sectoral interests, albeit in the name of national welfare. It is often argued that if French planning has anything to do with good economic performance, it is because the "3,000 or so" people who are involved in it constitute a sort of club for likeminded technocrats in government, business and labor, who are often educated at the same *grandes écoles*.

Another MIC with growing interest-group pressures is West Germany. The West German economy is called "organized private enterprise." As the centralized power of the state in the management of the economy has been deliberately downgraded in the postwar period, the influence of special-interest groups has correspondingly been enhanced. The bargaining process is most formally reflected in West Germany's "labor-management" scheme, generally known as codetermination or comanagement. Under the law, all corporations with more than five hundred workers have to give one-third of their seats on their supervisory boards to workers' representatives. Labor supervisors thus have a direct opportunity to participate in corporate decisions. Decision making through group representation exists also in other segments of the German economy. The governing board of the German TV networks, for example, consists of over sixty members from all walks of German life: political parties, religious organizations, labor unions, industry groups, farm blocs, retailers, professional associations, and public officials.

Sweden presents another political economy of consensus at its practical best. It has highly organized interest groups that constantly strive to better their group position within the national economy. While these groups do not enjoy legal recognition or privileges (as lobbies do in the United States), they provide a workable and effective mechanism for influencing basic national economic decisions. Almost all major governmental policies are reached as a result of extensive consultation between special-interest groups.

The United States, Great Britain, and Japan show further clear examples of the way the bargaining mechanism works among the MICs, as will be seen.

Command Features

Direct state control of the economy through planning, public enterprise, and wage-price controls is now a semipermanent feature of contemporary economic order in most industrial countries. The United States, Western European countries, Japan, and other MICs have mixed economies that make effective use of many command techniques. Planning, for example, as an exercise in long-term goal achievement, is no longer limited to the CDEs. Among the MICs, Austria, Belgium, France, Italy, the Netherlands, Norway, and Sweden have already joined the planning club. Among the giants, the United States is the only country without a formal national plan. Even Japan and West Germany make use of some long-term or medium-term forecasting.[6]

French planning is called "indicative," as distinguished from the so-called prescriptive planning of the Soviet variety, although French planners themselves prefer to call it "active" planning to distinguish it from a purely advisory scheme. French plans are actually an official guide for economic decision makers to follow—voluntarily, under some stimulation and controls. Germany's so-called medium-term Fiscal Plan, while not an imperative plan for the whole economy, contains an action program for public authorities to follow in preparing annual welfare and investment budgets with a view to combatting cyclical fluctuations. Swedish planning, like that of the French, is the forecasting of development tendencies for an essentially free-market economy. The basic purpose of preparing such a perspective is to draw attention to the need for larger investments in certain neglected infrastructural areas as housing, roads, and hospitals. Part of the planning strategy is also to identify the kind and number of skills and talent needed and to provide necessary incentives, training, and mobility for their supply. Although these plans are very broad, flexible, and not binding even on the government, their influence on private decisions and public policy is not insignificant.

In addition to planning, public enterprise is another command technique used by the MICs. The growing shortcomings of price mechanism since World War II, and the difficulties and frustrations involved in preserving vigorous competition among private firms through indirect controls, have moved many governments to take up new types of public enterprise. Such industries as atomic energy, space exploration, commercial aviation, and even some mining, manufacturing, and trade have become candidates for public ownership and operation. Traditionally, and particularly since World War II, France has had a partly nationalized economy. At present, the French government owns public utilities (gas, water, electricity, and coal); news media (newspaper, radio, and television); four of the largest commercial banks; almost all major insurance companies; the largest automotive firm; all the equity in Air France; the French Shipping Line; and part of petroleum refining. In some of these activities (gas, coal, mines), the government has a monopoly. In others (newsprint, automobiles, oil, aircraft), it shares the market with private enterprise. In Germany, despite its reputation for championing the free market, the government owns and operates railroads; most transportation and communications facilities; public utilities; and vast commercial and industrial assets in coal, steel, aluminum, and shipbuilding. The provincial (*Laender*) governments also own several hundred enterprises of their own. In Sweden, state ownership and enterprise exist in some specific undertakings: railways, air and bus transportation, communications, savings and investment banking, and a few joint-stock corporations (mining, steel, tobacco, and liquor).

6. Paradoxical as it may seem, a strong impetus for the evolution of planning among the MICs came from the United States. Under the Marshall Plan, the European recipients were required to prepare *plans* showing the areas in which American aid was to be applied.

Direct wage and price determination are also used in a selective manner and during national "emergencies" in MICs. The changing nature of industry and the incapability of indirect controls (such as antitrust laws) to cope with corporate power have made some direct controls inevitable.[7] Temporary wage-price freezes put into force in a number of European countries, however, have often been replaced by some forms of "incomes policy."[8] The French government exercises price control in establishing both the maximum and minimum levels for certain basic commodities. Since the end of World War II, the French Ministry of Finance has possessed legal standby powers to set prices on all products and services. In the fairly large nationalized sector of the economy, the government obviously has control over prices of key products. Among these, railroad and urban transit fares and utility rates for coal, gas, and electricity are the outstanding cases. Germany, too, has exercised direct control over some products affected with social welfare, such as foodstuffs like milk and sugar, drugs, and some rentals. The government has "transitional" standby power to fix prices under emergencies and as long as such a decision is not permanent.

In short, while the MICs have little or no ideological fondness for command techniques, they embrace these techniques from time to time. The discussions of the United States, Great Britain, and Japan show in more detail the prevalence of command in these so-called free-market economies.

7. For an elaboration of this view, championed by Professor John K. Galbraith, see his *The New Industrial State* (Boston: Houghton Mifflin, 1979), particularly chapters 25, 26 and 35.

8. For an assessment of price controls in the MICs, see Eric Schiff, *Incomes Policies Abroad* (Washington: American Enterprise Institute, 1972); and "Price Controls Assessed," *European Community*, February 1972.

THE UNITED STATES

The United States of America, with 9,363,000 square kilometers of land and more than 220 million people, is the world's sixth largest nation in size (after the Soviet Union, Canada, China, Brazil, and Australia) and fourth in population (after China, India, and the Soviet Union). In terms of national resources, highly skilled people, advanced technology, productive power, and military might however, America is second to none. With only 7 percent of the world's territory and about 5.5 percent of its population, the United States has more than a third as much productive capacity as the rest of the world combined. While naturally unable to sustain its enviable lead in living standards without substantial imports, the United States has a far greater potential for high-level self-sufficiency than most other major industrial countries. The U.S. economy is a mixed economy where the responsibility for economic calculation and coordination is shared by the market and nonmarket mechanisms. Even in the market sector, competition can best be described as imperfect or monopolistic (chapter 5). On the whole, only a relatively small percentage of national economic activity may be classified as largely competitive.

Data published by a study of the U.S. economy show that some 70 percent of U.S. GNP is market determined; some 15 percent is somehow regulated by the government (as proxy);[9] and 12 percent is under command.[10] In the market sector, some 6 to 7 percent of activities approximate pure monopoly; nearly 50 percent or so is highly concentrated; and only 13 or 14 percent is basically competitive (although again with varying degrees of imperfection).[11] An examination of the role of each decision-making mechanism in the U.S. economy makes these points clear.

The Market Sector:
Scope of Individual Sovereignty

The American private sector overshadows the public and the regulated sectors. The bulk of economic activity in the United States is determined by private decisions and

9. As we shall see later, there is hardly any economic activity in the United States that is unaffected by government supervision or controls of any kind. The percentage cited here refers to the public utilities and others that are most closely regulated by the federal government.

10. The actual scope of decisions made through bargaining is hard to assess because, as we saw in chapter 7, pressure groups often affect economic decisions in ways that cannot be easily scrutinized or quantified.

11. See F. M. Scherer, *Industrial Market Structure and Economic Performance* (Chicago: Rand McNally, 1970), pp. 57–60.

THE UNITED STATES: BASIC DATA

LAND AREA (sq. km.)	9,363,000
POPULATION (1980 estimate)	225 million
Net annual increase (1970-78 yearly average)	0.8 percent
Urban (percent of total, 1980)	73 percent
Working Age (15–64) (percent of total, 1978)	65 percent
LABOR FORCE (total civilian, 1979)	103 million
Agriculture, forestry, fishing (percent of total)	2 percent
Mining, manufacturing, construction (percent of total)	33 percent
Services, etc. (percent of total)	65 percent
GROSS DOMESTIC PRODUCT (market prices, 1979)	$2,370 billion
Per capita (1979)	$10,700
Average annual increase (1970–78)	3 percent
Public consumption (percent of GDP)	18 percent
Private consumption (percent of GDP)	64 percent
Fixed capital formation (ratio to GDP)	19 percent
Savings (ratio to GDP)	18 percent
GROSS DOMESTIC PRODUCT (market prices, 1979)	$2,370 billion
Agriculture, forestry, fishing (share in GDP)	3 percent
Mining, manufacturing, construction (share in GDP)	34 percent
Services (share in GDP)	63 percent
FOREIGN TRADE	
Exports (percent of GDP)	7 percent
Imports (percent of GDP)	8 percent

reflected in private enterprise. More than two-thirds of U.S. GNP is probably generated in the predominantly private sector. There are an estimated 14 million U.S. private business firms, mostly small and medium-size enterprises in industry, agriculture, trade, services, and construction. Although the number of U.S. farms has been steadily declining over the past decades, rural America in 1980 still had 2.7 million farm units—70 percent small family owned and operated. The primacy of private activity can be seen everywhere. Some 450,000 private trade marks are registered with the U.S. Patent Office. Thousands of new products are introduced in the market each year in consumer package-goods alone. There also seems to be no end to private ingenuity, private brand names, privately produced goods, and private services.[12]

As was indicated before, however, the U.S. private sector should not be totally identified as a "market" sector. The arena of consumer sovereignty and effective competition is much smaller than these data suggest.

Market Imperfections

The U.S. economy, like that of other private-enterprise MICs, is neither totally *private* nor perfectly *free*; nor does the private sector correspond to the theoretical norms of *competition* in structure, behavior, or performance. The basically competitive segment of the U.S. private sector includes non-government-supported agriculture, most services, most real estate, part of retail trade, and local contract construction. Outside these areas, which account for probably no more than 25 percent of GNP, the market is circumscribed by a host of imperfections. That is to say, in many essential lines of private economic activity, firms are not numerous; products are not, for the most part, standardized; and exit and entry are neither always free, nor always easy. Information about alternative goods, techniques, or opportunities is neither widespread nor reasonably accessible; and individual economic agents are not always acting as "economic man."

Number of Firms and Size of Enterprise. While small firms and farms in the American economy still numerically outnumber large and medium-size enterprises, the United States is often categorized by "corporate giantism" and large transnational corporations. For example, America's four largest producers of aluminum, light bulbs, glass, cereals, cigarettes, sewing machines, tires, toys, and motor vehicles control between 75 and 100 percent share of the market. In such industries as beet sugar, liquor, photographic equipment, vacuum cleaners,

12. The U.S. is sometimes called a "service economy," for the balance of employment once largely concentrated in agriculture and later in manufacturing is now shifted to services. In 1980, three out of every five working Americans were employed in service jobs. See Victor R. Fuchs, *The Service Economy* (New York: Columbia University Press, 1968).

scientific instruments, and electrical applicances, between 50 and 75 percent of the market belongs to the four largest manufacturers. The two hundred largest U.S. corporations control 64 percent of all manufacturing assets.[13] Altogether some 85 percent of all U.S. manufacturing and mining assets are held by approximately 2,400 corporations.

In many other sectors of the economy, the trend is toward conglomeration and merger of smaller firms into larger concerns. In the 1973–78 period, there were nearly 15,000 mergers and acquisitions, totalling $125 billion in assets.[14] In 1978 alone, there were more than 2,100 corporate mergers, with an aggregate acquisition of $34 billion in assets. Professional firms providing individual services are also getting bigger as time goes by. Doctors, lawyers, and engineers find it increasingly more profitable to operate under one roof and take advantage of internal and external cost savings. Even retail outlets, long considered the symbol of small-scale efficiency, are not immune from the merger fever. In the opinion of a majority of the National Commission on Food Marketing, retail chains, in general, have grown larger than necessary for their efficiency, increasing their market power vis-à-vis their suppliers and weakening price competition at the consumer level. There is also growing concern among economists and government officials that "giant investors" —mutual funds, pension funds, insurance companies, and commercial banks' trust departments—may eventually take the stock market away from the "little man."

U.S. House and Senate staff studies indicate that virtually all of America's biggest and most powerful corporations are linked together directly or indirectly by the men and women who sit on their boards.[15] Almost all commercial banks are involved in hundreds of interlocking directorates with the top five hundred U.S. corporations. While being on the boards of competing companies is prohibited by the Clayton Act of 1914, there is virtually no limitation against the number of "noncompeting" firms in which one may be a director.

Experts do not all, or always, agree on what "bigness" in business really is or what harm can come from such linkages among big corporations. The magnitude of corporate assets, the percentage share of the market, the annual sales revenue, the number of people employed, and other criteria are all relevant, but none has proved satisfactory for the purpose of divestiture. Nor is a general trend toward business

13. For further information on the degree of business concentration, see J. M. Blair, *Economic Concentration: Structure, Behaviour and Public Policy* (New York: Harcourt Brace, 1972); and G. Bannock, *The Juggernauts: The Age of the Big Corporation* (London: Weidenfeld, 1971). See also Stan Sauerhaft, *The Merger Game* (New York: Crowell, 1971); and Isadore Barmash, *Welcome to Our Conglomerate—You're Fired!* (New York: Delacorte Press, 1971).

14. Conglomerates refer to mergers that link companies and concerns operating in diverse and unrelated fields in such a way as to defy identification with any particular industry. Since these mergers do not usually reduce competition in any one industry, they cannot be stopped by the existing antitrust laws.

15. The Morgan Guaranty Trust Company of New York, for example, by virtue of its trust and pension funds, sits on the boards of at least twenty-seven of the major U.S. corporations. Morgan is also among the top five investors in fifty-six major U.S. firms.

concentration easy to identify. In the postwar period, for example, there has been greater concentration in automobile manufacturing (from ten to four firms), but a decline in the relative position of steel and aluminum giants. Furthermore, giant U.S. firms typically defend their structure and performance by nonclassical criteria. They point out that: each large company in an oligopoly has two or three large and vigorous rivals to contend with; the competition among big and sophisticated rivals is generally stiffer than rivalry among "atomistic" competitors; that the dominance of large firms in the market results not from sheer size but from "superior management, sales, and technical skills"; and that size alone is neither bad nor antisocial; what matters is how it is attained and used. It is further argued that no monopoly unaided by the government is ever truly immune from an outsider's challenge. When General Motors was organized, the Ford Motor Company was the dominant firm in the auto industry. Univac lost its early lead in commercial computers to IBM. Sylvania successfully challenged General Electric's hegemony. Despite all of this, however, those who are opposed to bigness per se argue that even though giantism may harbor no economic ill, bigness is intrinsically bad because of its social and political implications. Big business, it is argued, influences social attitudes through its command over advertising, philanthropy, and politics.[16]

Brand Names and Lack of Standardization. Almost everything bought and sold in an average U.S. retail market is nonstandardized. Food items, articles of clothing, cosmetics, over-the-counter drugs, minor and major household appliances, and leisure goods and services are sold largely under national or local name brands. Some brand-named articles advertised and sold as competitors may also be made by the same company.[17] Many consumer products, ranging from toothpaste and baby food to liquor, cigarettes, tires, television sets, and household appliances, are sometimes made by a few large manufacturers (General Electric, Goodyear, Magnavox, Hoover, Singer) and sold under private brands in large department stores. Every year, Americans reportedly spend some $2 billion on nearly five thousand brands of over-the-counter remedies. Paramount among these are painrelievers (Bayer Aspirin, Bufferin, Excedrin, and Anacin). The essence of all of these pain-killers is aspirin. Basic aspirin is produced by the Monsanto Chemical Company and supplied to different laboratories. Each laboratory adds something to it and sells it under a national brand name. Price differentials between plain aspirin privately labeled and the most heavily advertised compound have been as high as 1000 percent. Cold remedies, sleeping pills, cough medicines, and throat lozenges that also differ only in name often sell at different prices. Choosing the right name for a new product is as important as its inner qualities, sometimes even more important.

16. *New York Times*, 31 August 1979.
17. Proctor and Gamble, for example, makes Crest and Gleem toothpastes; Joy, Ivory, and Thrill dishwashing liquids; Zest, Lava, Ivory, Camay, Safeguard hand soaps; Spic and Span, Mr. Clean, and Top Job cleaners; and Tide, Cheer, Oxydol, and Bold detergents.

The arguments in favor of brand-name marketing are familiar. Consumers are able to distinguish and choose the products of reputable manufacturers and reject those with poor reputation. Consumer loyalty to a brand name is a kind of reward for efficiency and a punishment for shoddiness or poor service. Continued consumer confidence in a manufacturer's integrity and its trademark help establish and enforce high-quality standards and good designs among all competitors. And so forth. The debate over the actual benefit of such differentiation, however, is as profound as it is heated. The ability to make a meaningful selection among competing products is based upon the assumption of the consumer's necessary and accurate knowledge of alternatives. In the absence of adequate information, there would be no *real* choices in most markets.

Freedom of Entry and Exit.   The barriers to entry and exit in the American private sector are numerous and of varied origins. Some are technological in nature, such as large initial capital requirements or ownership of raw materials. Others are institutional and legal, such as patent protection given to inventors, franchises granted to public utilities, and statutes restricting competition in public utilities. Many hurdles are artificially created by incumbents to ward off potential competitive challenges. Examples are large outlays in advertising, exclusive dealership arrangements, and threats of patent litigations. Other obstacles may be financial.[18]

Effective control of a strategic product, process, or raw material is always a powerful instrument for restricting entry into a lucrative market, such as IBM in punch-card tabulating machines. So is the misuse or abuse of a patent right for anticompetitive practices, such as fixing prices of patented products, warding off competition by refusing to grant licenses to rivals, dividing the market among licensees, determining the volume and conditions of sales, and otherwise forcing the licensee to act in a manner approved by the patent holder.

State and local governments are sometimes the worst offenders against competitive market operations. State "blue laws" prohibit some activities between midnight Saturday and midnight Sunday. "Fair trade" laws permit manufacturers to determine and enforce minimum retail prices of their products, and licensing regulations are used to block outsiders' entry into a protected market. State health and sanitation regulations often serve as economic barriers to the inflow of food products from outside localities and states. For fifteen years up to 1970, the U.S. Congress and the Federal Communications Commission effectively blocked entry by prospective entrepreneurs into a legitimate private enterprise: pay television.

Artificially created private barriers to entry (apart from occasional physical violence, price cutting, threat of litigations, and other unsavory practices) include the restrictions imposed on the number of persons who can enter a given occupation

18. According to one estimate, in 1970 it would cost a company nearly $800 million to enter the auto industry, some $725 million of which is required for annual style change capability and only $55 million for productive capacity. See J. S. Cohen and M. Mintz, *America, Inc.* (New York: Dial Press, 1971).

or trade. Labor (craft) unions, for example, frequently restrict entrance into their ranks by a variety of regulative devices. Plumbers and carpenters are the most widely cited examples of restrictive unions, but they are not alone.

Nor are restrictive practices characteristic only of the labor unions. In a highly critical book on the state of American health, the American Medical Association is accused of direct or indirect responsibility for the shortage of doctors in the United States, for higher infant mortality, and shorter longevity in America, for the high cost of medical care, and for the low quality of health services offered to minorities.[19]

The AMA is clearly not alone in this respect. In recent years the Justice Department has charged the American College of Pathologists with conspiracy to charge artificially high prices for laboratory tests. American Orthodontists have been accused of cornering the teeth-straightening market. The American Society of Civil Engineers, the American Institute of Architects, and the American Institute of Certified Public Accountants have been sued by the Justice Department for having fixed the fee schedules for members and eliminating competition among them. All three have agreed to discontinue the practice.

In some experts' opinion, the high cost of style changes, the expensive packaging, and particularly advertising on TV is one of the important factors in driving small companies out of business and preventing potential competitors from entering consumer-goods industries. While the effect of national advertising on the long-run sales, or market share, of basically standard products is hard to assess, the relative competitive strength of large advertisers over their weaker rivals can hardly be denied. In recent years, one cigarette manufacturer's annual advertising budget for one single brand amounted to about $5 million per word of its advertising message. A manufacturer of toothpaste spent even more per copy word. Such heavy costs of national advertising clearly leave many lucrative markets out of reach of many small firms with low advertising budgets.[20]

Information: Scanty and Expensive.   If effective competition is the heart of free enterprise, market information is the key to effective competition. Yet in the modern industrialized economy of the United States, information available to individuals about prices, product quality, employment opportunities, and other relevant data is often inadequate, costly, or both. An average consumer more often than not has little information about the technical quality of the merchandise he buys or the services he receives. Workers often lack information on job opportunities. Small investors often lack access to pertinent market data and technical know-how. In the words of *Consumer Reports*, a monthly magazine devoted to improving consumer information, "It takes a lawyer to figure out what a guarantee really covers. A research chemist to determine whether additives make any

19. Roul Tunley, *The American Health Scandal* (New York: Harper, 1966).
20. See J. L. Simon, *Issues in the Economics of Advertising* (Champagne: University of Illinois Press, 1970).

difference. An automotive engineer to help you decide between a Mustang and a Camaro. A mathematician to figure out exactly how much food you are getting for your money."

Millions of corporate stockholders do not know the type of business they partially "own," or the kinds of product *their* corporation makes; they buy and sell shares of stocks on the advice of their brokers or their friends or on tips they pick up over a bar corner or at a cocktail party. Numerous surveys around the nation have shown that the poor unknowingly pay more and get less for their money through inferior quality products, two to three times higher costs for an identical article, and exorbitant interest rates.[21] All experts agree that the most important reasons for the continuation and increase of such practices are lack of information.

Information on the technical processes used in manufacturing, costs of production, and the prices actually charged to different customers by different companies are also usually matters of utmost secrecy. Covert price cutting and under-the-table deals by large sellers frequently escape individual customer's knowledge and cunning. Sometimes even rivals do not know exactly what goes on in a firm with regard to costs, prices, and discount policies. U.S. corporations are repeatedly charged by private investigators and government agencies with attempts to delay the development and/or use of technological devices that threaten existing investments or cut down their future profits.

Due to the deficiency of buyer information, the price for the same product—even the same brand name—in the same area at the same time often varies considerably. A report by the American Medical Association found that the price of the same prescription drug could vary from drug store to drug store by as much as 1,200 percent. Interestingly enough, even when different prices are publicly *advertised*, public misinformation (or apathy) lets the disparities persist.

Lapses from Consumer Sovereignty. U.S. consumers, like most buyers in a modern economy, are not always rational buyers in the Sombartian sense.[22] Faced with a bewildering array of goods and services, and equally bewildering claims and counterclaims, they cannot and do not always pick and choose in a calculated manner. They, like the average buyers anywhere in the modern world, are also creatures of habit, style, fads, and plain impulses. They cannot always know what is in their best interest. Small savers, investors, and businessmen are usually no better. They, too, are not the classical "economic man."

In the case of relatively standardized purchases, the U.S. consumer is probably a fair judge of quality. Their tastes and distastes are routinely conveyed— sometimes unequivocally and emphatically—to producers. Most housewives plan

21. See F. D. Sturdivant, ed., *The Ghetto Marketplace* (New York: Free Press, 1969).

22. Werner Sombart, the German "cultural economist" of the early twentieth century, considered rationality one of the three basic concepts of the capitalistic "spirit"; he characterized it as a reasoned choice of carefully calculated alternatives arrived at in defiance of tradition, custom, and authority toward an acquisitive goal.

their budgets fairly carefully, and in a limited range of information at their disposal, they probably act as wisely as possible. But when confronted with branded and differentiated items, there is not assurance of informed and rational purchases.[23] Daily releases by the Federal Trade Commission show how millions of people every day voluntarily fall prey to a barage of quack health remedies for anything from arthritis and cancer to baldness and rundown feeling; to retirement land sales; to dancing instruction; and to phony correspondence schools. As indicated by the President's Consumer Advisory Council, faced with a perplexing myriad of choices as to the characteristics, contents, components, weights, and prices of similar goods and services, the average consumer is often at a loss to make a rational decision without a great deal of time and effort for research and comparison.

A vivid example of the gradual loss of consumer sovereignty in much of the American retail scene may be sought in the influence of commercial television. As the critics point out, what the American public sees on commercial TV (and indirectly pays for through purchase of advertised goods and services) is based neither on individual choice nor on its sovereign preference, The big national networks that originate most of the packaged programs for affiliated stations take their cue mostly from large sponsors (cosmetics, beer, automobiles, over-the-counter drugs, and other large suppliers of consumer goods). Sponsors, in turn, generally listen to a half-dozen major rating services that keep score on the size of the audience attracted to a particular program. Apart from allegations of tampering with the ratings results and the statistical shortcomings of audience measurement, the "voice of the people" in TV programing is not reflected in a direct market choice, as in a theater ticket or concert fee. Television programs are in effect a kind of "centrally determined" viewing paid for by TV viewers (and nonviewers) through a sort of private "tax" imposed and collected by private economic entities. As is often contended, U.S. commercial TV programs in the prime evening hours of affiliated stations are, in the last analysis, determined (if not dictated) by the leaders of the three or four national networks. The sovereignty does not always rest with consumers.

Shortfalls from Ideal Conditions

The roots of market imperfections are embedded in the very nature of almost every modern industrial economy. Modern technology often precludes efficiency in small-scale operations save in personalized services. Highly efficient firms are

23. Supporting business opposition to the so-called truth-in-packaging bill in the mid-1960s, one of the staunchest advocates of free enterprise dismissed the rationality assumption altogether. "It is not part of the nature of a housewife," he said, "to be rational. The housewife is not buying a detergent; she is buying a dream. It is purposeless to demand that the makers of breakfast cereals label their packages by the ounces, for she is not buying ounces; she is buying the stuff that goes snap, crackle and pop. [The bill's sponsors are] seeking to be rational. A free society cannot work that way." See J. J. Kilpatrick, "Illusions and Truth in Packaging." *Washington Evening Star*, 7 April 1966.

often—although not necessarily—large firms having appreciable influence over the price and quality of the goods they sell. Furthermore, consumers' ever increasing taste for variety, novelty, and exclusivity rules out uniformity of both substance and appearance among similar products. Differentiation is what people generally want. Still further, the complicated and diffused nature of goods, services, and economic opportunities is such that knowledge can be neither universal nor free. Finally, entry and exit is neither easy nor costless. Even without the artificial and institutional barriers raised by statutes or public regulations, some natural obstacles (high initial capital outlay, ownership rights, locational problems) would tend to prevent open entry and exit.

The American market economy is a prime example of a large, affluent, and highly industrial economy that displays these modern-day deviations from the norms of classical pure competition. The "market" features in the United States are markedly different from the classical norms.

Nonprice Rivalry. In the "market" sector of the American economy where competition still prevails, rivalry among producers is only infrequently based on prices. For most large industrial sellers, price competition signifies price war. Instead, changes in product style or quality, credit and after-sales service, promotional devices, and advertising are employed to attract consumers and maintain their loyalty.[24] Prices quoted are often "administered prices" established and maintained by sellers. Price discrimination in professional services is the rule rather than an exception.[25] Rivalry in the sale of many consumer products among major producers is frequently on the basis of real or superficial differences in quality. Trading stamps, prizes, gifts and giveaways are endlessly used to lure both the gullible and the sophisticated consumers. A good example of this oligopolistic behavior—reacting to the competitor's strategy—is to be found in national radio and TV advertising. As soon as a serious challenger defies a leading brand, through advertising or promotional baits, a whole barrage of retaliatory actions gets underway almost overnight. As company officials often admit, it is necessary to go along with the rivals' advertising fads or lose business. Investigations by the Federal Trade Commission and others have shown that dealers, most customers, and many companies are not usually happy about gimmicks and contests, but no one dares back out. Games and gimmicks, in the opinion of many observers, in one way or another add to the price of articles. Only the game makers and inventors of frills, often the only ones who get rich from nonprice competition, deny this. According

24. The competition in product introduction is sometimes so fierce that according to authoritative sources, about five hundred new products come on the market each month—and 90 percent fail for lack of consumer interest. See *U.S. News and World Report*, 1 May 1978.

25. Doctors, dentists, lawyers, and architects do not as a rule compete overtly and publicly. There is seldom a single market price for a given service. Substantial price differentials and much price discrimination exist in the same market, and clients are often charged according to their ability to pay and what the traffic will bear.

to some estimates, food prices could be cut from 6 to 9 percent if housewives were willing to forego such frills as trading stamps, giveaway games, carry-out service, piped-in music, check-cashing privileges, late closing hours, and thousands of items from which to choose. Some of these extras (helping with grocery bags and remaining open in the evening and on Sundays) may be genuine conveniences for which most shoppers would gladly pay. A few, like piped-in music, for example, are of questionable value.

Central to the nonprice rivalry in the market sector of the United States is the $40 billion a year advertising industry. As a means of informing the consumer about the nature, weight, quality, availability, price, and conditions of sale, proper advertising performs a rational and useful service. Consumers are regularly informed about available alternatives, from Thursday bargain ads in the local newspaper to special private-sales notices, mail-order catalogues, and myriad items about new and improved products. A good many excellent news stories, educational materials, plays, concerts, entertaining programs, and public discussions are also made freely available to an average American family by commercial advertising. Most marketing managers also believe that no major inroads can be made in a vast and complicated U.S. national market without extensive national advertising; products, like performers (and politicians), need promotion in order to get somewhere.

But much advertising on the American economic scene is not of this informative variety. In fact, one of the basic characteristics of American advertising (which is probably more or less true of commercial ads elsewhere in the Western world) is that it is often not true to itself. It is not really informative; it is often directed toward persuasive and motivational considerations or "conditioned-response purchasing behavior." Its claims often play upon man's incurable frailties, fears, and hopes: the fear of ill health, obesity, old age, social failures, loss of job, respect, or love; and the hope for eternal youth, vitality, beauty, popularity, fame, or success. Examples run into the thousands. Insurance ads, for example, subtly scare families about the possible loss or incapacity of their breadwinners. Mouth washes and deodorants scare young men and women about losing prospective customers and/or suitors. Auto tires are often portrayed as life savers.[26]

U.S. advertising is also criticized for its alleged creation of demand for socially useless products in much the same way as command economies are blamed for producing not the goods and services their people *want*, but those the government thinks they *need*. Some critics believe that in America's "affluent society," consumer demand is also managed by advertising and salesmanship; that many consumer wants are in fact contrived and promoted. The "general rule,"

---

26. The Parliament cigarette ads once claimed, "Tobacco tastes best when the filter's recessed"; Winston rebutted by claiming, "It's what's up front that counts." The Atlas Company emphasized its "round tire," and Firestone came back with its "wide oval tire," both touted as safety features. Sometimes the absurd exceeds the irrelevant. American Petrofina Inc. once promised motorists "pink air" for their tires as the "ultimate additive."

according to an astute observer, is: "If they make it, we will buy it." The rejects and the flops (the proverbial Edsel and Corfam shoes) are the exceptions.[27]

Wasteful Competition.   Another feature of the U.S. modified market sector is a proliferation of slightly differentiated goods and services by a few large sellers. In the area of brand competition, for example, this proliferation is monumental. Among an estimated eight thousand items in an average U.S. supermarket or drug store, there are hundreds of foods, drinks, and household items that are differentiated from one another by only slight features. There are more than 60 major brands of cigarettes; 190 cold pills; 70 different potato chips; more than 50 toothpastes; 20 detergents; upward of 30 paper towels; and 3,600 basic drugs sold in 18,000 different combinations. In the "big ticket" category, such as automobiles, outward differentiation is extensive, but qualitative differences are minor. The four big U.S. auto makers offer each year more than 150 different model automobiles with a variety of optional accessories. The possible combinations of cars and accessories theoretically reach into the million. One obvious result of such diversity is higher manufacturing and servicing costs, which consumers ultimately have to pay. It is not always clear whether in most such instances the increased choice is illusory or real.

Duplication of effort and extensive rivalry also exist in U.S. retailing. There are reportedly some 220,000 gas stations around the country—three or four of them often at one intersection, selling practically the same commodity, and frequently operating at sizable excess capacity. Partly because of this extensive competition, it is estimated that a very large percentage of those who enter the retail business each year fail. While no demonstrably objective criteria exist to gauge the magnitude of excessive facilities in retailing, the low average daily sales volume in the majority of sales outlets—one-third making less than $100 in sales a day—may be an indication.

Other services, too, suffer from similar duplication of facilities. In health care, for example, which in recent years has had a higher inflation rate than the national average, the major cause of increasing costs has been the proliferation of costly equipment, excess capacity in numbers of unused beds, unneeded surgery, and other wasteful efforts. The United States spends more of its GNP on health than any other nation, yet the quality of national medical care ranks below many European nations. The reasons are an excessive congregation of physicians in affluent centers; the piece-rate system of medical payment based on the number of visits to the doctor rather than flat fees for an ailment; and the overuse of medical services by privately insured, affluent families.

Social Costs.   A third feature of the U.S. "market" sector is its tendency to distort or ignore many of the social costs of private business activities. U.S. private industry

27. See, J. K. Galbraith, *The New Industrial State* (Boston: Houghton Mifflin, 1967), pp. 204–07 and 272–73; and Andrew Hacker, "Country Called Corporate America," *New York Times Magazine*, 3 July 1966, quoted ibid., p. 205.

has been blamed as one of the main causes of resource waste. The charges are particularly strong against too rapid exploitation of natural resources like oil, coal and timber; wasteful extraction methods; scattered and inefficient prospecting; and environmental damage through indiscriminate use of chemicals.

The damage to the environment results from industrial air and water pollution, soil erosion, toxic wastes, excessive use of pesticides, strip mining, and a host of other predatory practices.[28] These losses are caused largely by private industries, public utilities, and incinerating firms, but minicipal sewage plants and state and federal establishments also bear a share of the blame. Costs of these pollutants—in terms of lost incomes, medical bills, deterioration of buildings and equipment, crop and vegetable damages, and fish and wildlife losses—are differently estimated. The Harvard Center for Pollution Studies estimates the cost of controlling such pollutants as air, water, and solid waste to be $13.5 billion a year. In some especially "dirty" cities like New York and St. Louis, the annual per capita cost may approach $200.[29] Other estimates reach even higher.[30]

The accumulated cost of environmental clean-ups shows that the free market does not automatically allocate resources to their socially most desirable alternatives, but rather to their privately most profitable outlets. The pollution problem is thus often called a "competitive" problem. As an industry spokesman puts it, "It is frightening to see how the competitive structure of our economy has played the devil with pollution." Companies are often slow to install even minimum antipollution controls because the cost would allegedly "impair or destroy their ability to compete." And many communities "wink" at pollution violations in order to attract new business.[31]

The "Quality of Life." Consumer sovereignty in the United States portrays yet another deficiency described in Chapter 5: inability to enhance the social quality of life through market incentives. That is to say, public services and "merit" goods do not always get the priorities they deserve. The critics' argument is that although private enterprise has brought the United States unprecedented prosperity in terms of material welfare, no such progress has been made in the social quality of living.

28. For a disturbing account of the effects of pesticides on soil, see R. Carson, *Silent Spring*, (Boston: Houghton Mifflin, 1963); and F. Graham, Jr., *Since Silent Spring*, (Boston: Houghton Mifflin, 1970). For an illuminating account of the misuse of environment, see John Hay, *In Defense of Nature* (Boston: Atlantic-Little, Brown, 1969); and P. Shepard and D. McKinley, eds., *The Subversive Science* (Boston: Houghton Mifflin, 1968).

29. Public enthusiasm for air-pollution control does not seem to be matched by their eagerness to share its costs even moderately. For example, when St. Louis residents were polled in early 1970s on how much they would be willing to pay in higher taxes for air-pollution control, the answer was between $0.50 and $1.00 a year!

30. The Council on Environmental Quality puts the cost of pollution-free water (zero discharge) by the year 1985 at the staggering figure of $316.5 billion. See *U.S. News and World Reports*, 21 February 1972. The cost of cleaning the Great Lakes alone is estimated to be about $20 billion up to 1990.

31. "Industry and Pollution," *Wall Street Journal*, 26 November 1965.

They argue that the American mixed, capitalist economy is likely to neglect many social needs because it unduly glorifies private enterprise, because it is politically influenced by essentially rural folks who are insensitive to urban problems and because, under pressures of expensive advertising, it tends to misallocate resources in favor of meaningless private gadgetry, at the expense of sorely needed public goods and services.[32] A manifestation of this imbalance is seen in the public arena, where one finds the blight of municipal services (schools, health centers, sewerage facilities, refuse collection, parking space, parks and playgrounds), undermanned police forces, dirty and inefficient public transportation, polluted water and air, traffic congestion, noise, slum housing, and so on. At the same time, the private sector keeps producing color-toned and power-packed automobiles, assorted electronic toys, and ready-mix foods. Deodorants, mouthwashes, vitamin pills, laxatives, dog foods, and similar symbols of satisfied affluence lengthen the list. The U.S. case shows that the market by itself is incapable of insuring social harmony, or establishing a public-private balance.[33] The need is for government intervention.

Government's Indirect Controls:
Decisions by Proxy

The interventionist role of the legislature, or the "government," in the U.S. economy has been on the rise almost from the establishment of the republic.[34] The growing pressures of modern technology, accelerated urbanization, and growing individual dependence on the community have further forced public authorities to widen the network of controls, regulations, and surveillance. Today, in virtually every major economic activity in the United States, the Congress, as well as state and local legislatures, are involved in controlling and/or regulating basic relations between business and its employees, suppliers, customers, creditors, stockholders, competitors, and the general public. Federal, state, and local regulatory agencies, in one way or another, now affect business conduct, consumer safety, purity and effectiveness of food and drugs, rates and services of public utilities, purchase and sale of real estate or securities, standards of air and water quality, and a host of other areas.[35]

32. For a more detailed discussion of these factors and their relative role in creating social imbalance, see C. R. McConnell, "Social Imbalance: Where Do We Stand?" *Quarterly Review of Business and Economics*, May 1961.

33. For a critique of individual sovereignty in practice, see R. C. Edwards et al., *The Capitalist System: A Radical Analysis of American Society* (Englewood Cliffs: Prentice-Hall, 1978).

34. The term *government* is a generic reference to a complex network of departments, agencies, bureaus, and services at the federal, state, and local levels that are engaged in direct or indirect control of economic activity.

35. In some states and localities, the authorities regulate days and hours of work and play, business opening and closing, noise decibels in motor vehicles, and the size and color of outdoor billboards. Federal law even tells people when it is daylight saving or standard time.

Government intervention in the U.S. economy has risen because of a combination of several social objectives: a politicoethical responsibility on the part of the "collective" for correcting market "failures" in the areas of economic stability and individual security; a sort of nostalgic desire to preserve the competitive character of the early American economy by protecting small businesses and small farms; the promotion of economic activities that, for a variety of reasons, require government protection, assistance, or subsidy; and the pressures of interest groups to use the machinery of the state for their own objectives. State interventions, in turn, have encompassed both microeconomic policy, i.e., the level of economic activity in the economy and microeconomic considerations, i.e., individual industries, groups or circumstances.

Economic Stabilization

The notion that deliberate government policy ought to supplant the market's cyclical malfunctions gained substantial ground in the United States during the Great Depression. The Employment Act of 1946 and the more recent Full Employment and Balanced Growth Act of 1978 have given the federal government a clear mandate to combat economic fluctuations with all macroeconomic means at its disposal.[36] In accordance with this mandate, postwar economic stabilization has relied on a combination of fiscal, monetary, incomes, and exchange and trade policies to keep the economy on a path of sustained noninflationary growth. The variety of these countercyclical devices (and their mixed results) show the bewildering complexities of a modern-day economy.

Fiscal Policy. The U.S. Constitution gives Congress the power to levy taxes "to provide for the common defense and general welfare" of the people of the Union. Under these broad objectives, taxes are frequently raised or cut by Congress for a variety of reasons: to raise public revenues and to manage demand; to discourage certain expenditures (outlays on cigarettes, liquor, gambling, imports); or to encourage certain activities (homebuilding, plant investment, charitable contributions). They are also increasingly used by the federal, state, and local governments in transfer payments from the rich to the poor to support and subsidize low-income groups.

Up until World War I, the bulk of government revenues at all levels was derived from excise, customs, and property taxes. Income taxation was introduced first in 1913. Since then, the federal tax system has been subject to many revisions, the most recent and the most comprehensive being those of 1969 and 1978. Many states (and some cities) have enacted their own income taxes in addition to sales taxes, property taxes, and others. As shown below, the federal government relies

36. For details of the earlier activist and expansionist role of the government in the U.S. economy, see Walter E. Heller, *New Dimensions of Political Economy* (New York: Norton, 1967); and A. M. Okun, *The Political Economy of Prosperity* (Washington: The Brookings Institution, 1970).

more heavily than most MICs on income taxes (both on individuals and corporations). Individual income tax rates range from a minimum of 14 percent to a maximum of 70 percent (on income over $100,000 a year).[37] There are, however, a large number of exemptions, deductions, exclusions, and credits that blunt this extreme progressivity.[38] Corporate incomes are taxed at rates between 17 and 46 percent for incomes below $25,000 and over $100,000. Investment tax credits, special treatment of corporate capital gains, and other allowances make the effective rates lower.

Total federal government income in fiscal 1981 was about $613 billion. Of the total income, over 45 percent was derived from taxes on individual incomes and 12 percent on corporate profits, bringing direct taxes to 57 percent of total. Social insurance taxes contributed nearly 30 percent; excise taxes, about 6 percent; and other taxes, about 2 percent. Nontax income amounted to 5 percent of the total.

On the expenditure side, total federal outlays in fiscal 1981 were to match revenues. The biggest single item in total expenditure was national defense, with about 24 percent, but the largest single program was direct benefit payments for individuals: social security, over 22 percent; health care, 10 percent; public welfare, over 6 percent; education and social services, 5 percent; aid to veterans, over 3 percent; civil service retirement, about 3 percent; and unemployment compensation, over 3 percent—totaling over half of the entire outgo. Subsidies to agriculture and industry took another 5 percent. Direct aid to states and local governments amounted to about 3 percent. Interest on public debt absorbed over 12 percent. The rest went for the development of energy and other resources, pollution control, research and development, and foreign aid.[39]

In the opinion of some tax experts, the United States has one of the best tax systems in the world by most tax criteria: productivity, ease of compliance, and cost of administration.[40] As the lion's share of the tax bill falls on individual and corporate incomes and is mostly progressive, it conforms to the "fair" principle of ability to pay. Compliance with tax laws is readily assured because wage compensation accounts for 75 percent of national income. And the administrative costs of tax collection are no more than 1 percent of the amount collected.

However, in terms of other traditional criteria of simplicity, certainty, equity, neutrality, and countercylical potency, the federal tax system is judged differently. The tax code is an incredibly complex document made up of more than one thousand sections full of a huge patchwork of special provisions. Because of different interpretations by the Internal Revenue Service and the courts, no tax calculation is

37. Marginal rates on personal incomes reached 95 percent during World War II; the corporate rate was over 50 percent during the Korean War.

38. The effective rates range from 5.5 percent in the $5,000–$10,000 brackets to a maximum 30 percent on incomes of over $200,000.

39. For details, see *The Budget of the U.S. Government, Fiscal Year 1981* (Washington: Office of the Management and Budget, 1980).

40. See Joseph A. Pechman, *Federal Tax Policy* (New York: Norton, 1971).

absolutely certain to meet the rules.[41] In many respects, also, the U.S. tax structure is considered "inequitable, capricious, and economically damaging."[42] Despite its overtly progressive appearance, income taxation has only a scant income-leveling effect on final distribution of income, because of the many legal loopholes, shelters, and preferences. Sales and other major excise taxes are distinctly regressive. Regardless of how one decides to measure economic inequality, an increasing number of middle-class Americans believe that their tax system is inequitable, because the main burden of taxation falls on the middle-class professionals, salary earners, and people with no tax loopholes.[43]

The neutrality and countercyclical effectiveness of the U.S. tax system are also subject to question. Since the same income from different sources is taxed differently in the United States (homeowners versus those who rent), not only is horizontal equity denied, but neutrality is also sacrificed and efficiency undermined. By allowing special depreciation, depletion, and exemptions, the government is in fact directing investment into certain unrelated and dubiously productive activities (oil drilling, cattle raising, pistachio growing, real estate speculation, and a host of others.)[44]

A change in the composition of federal expenditures has, in turn, reduced efficiency of the budget. While the total outgo as a percentage of GNP has remained fairly stable over the last thirty years, a persistent shift has occurred in the makeup of federal outlays. In the 1960s, some 56 percent of total spending on average went to buy goods and services (including military hardware). Transfer payments (social security, welfare, and so on) accounted for less than 26 percent. In 1980, the purchase category was down to less than 35 percent, while transfers exceeded 41 percent. In just ten years to 1980, social security benefits nearly quadrupled.

Increased transfer payments certainly serve important social goals, but their rapid rise presents notable budgetary and economic consequences. From a fiscal standpoint, the marked increase in transfer payments has persistently raised the proportion of total spending that is "least controllable" by the authorities in any one year. These payments are largely "open-ended," that is, based on previous substantive legislation and responding to the composition of population, the state of the economy, and other trends. These items, plus those that are "relatively uncontrollable" (interest on debt, price support, routine government expenditures,

41. A legion of tax lawyers and accountants actually constitute a $2 billion-a-year "tax industry."

42. See "Why Tax Reform is So Urgent and So Unlikely," *Time*, 4 April 1969; see also L.C. Thurow, *Distribution and the Possibilities of Economic Change.* (New York: Basic Books, 1979).

43. In 1969, some 300 Americans with annual incomes of more than $200,000 (including 56 persons with an income of $1 million or more) paid no federal income tax at all, taking advantage of special preferences and allowable deductions.

44. For a discussion of some of these issues, see "Carter's Tax Plan," *Business Week*, 29 August 1977.

and prior-year contracts), make up more than 75 percent of outlays. The authorities' power to combat cyclical fluctuations through fiscal policy, by raising or reducing public expenditures, is thus limited at best to only 25 percent of the budget.

In addition to the relative weakness of fiscal policy caused by the "uncontrollable" outlays, the shift of public expenditures from goods and services to transfer payments has two further serious effects on individual saving. First, to the extent that these payments involve the redistribution of income from the "rich" (with higher saving propensity) to the "poor" (with relatively lower willingness to save), expanded transfer programs would lead to reduced personal saving. More generally, the greater measure of economic security provided by these programs would reduce the need for individuals to save for rainy days and thus the magnitude of national savings.[45] Second, to the extent that social security and other transfer programs are not self-financing on an actuarial basis, the expansion of transfers would tend to have adverse effects on the size of the annual budget deficit.[46]

Monetary and Exchange Policies. In the immediate postwar period, and particularly during the 1950s, the recurrent recessions of 1949–50, 1953–54, and 1957–58 were fought mainly through monetary, debt management, and credit measures. In the latter two recessions under President Eisenhower's balanced-budget policy, the Federal Reserve discount rate was brought down to as low as 1.5 percent. The Korean War inflation was, in turn, lowered partly by a reduction in money supply through orthodox measures (higher rediscount rates, larger legal reserve requirements, and appropriate open-market operations). During the Kennedy-Johnson administrations, the focus of governmental anticyclical policy was shifted from the control of money supply to the Keynesian-type fiscal policy (tax reduction and budgetary stimulus).

In the decade after August 1971, when the dollar convertibility into gold under the 1944 Bretton Woods Agreement was unilaterally suspended by President Richard Nixon, U.S. monetary policy followed three main objectives: reduction of inflationary pressures; stabilization of world exchange markets; and support of economic growth.

Since the passage of the Federal Reserve Reform Act of 1977, the monetary control of inflation has rested with the determination by the Federal Open Market Committee (FOMC) of quarterly and annual growth targets for the money supply (M1, M2, and M3)[47] and control over interest rates. These controls have been implemented mainly through the provision (or reduction) of bank reserves. The

45. The United States has one of the lowest savings/GNP ratio among MICs.

46. In the two decades between 1960 and 1980, the federal government budget was in small surplus only in two years (totalling $3.5 billion) as against nineteen years of deficit totalling $401 billion.

47. M1 is commonly defined as currency plus demand deposit; M2 is M1 plus savings deposits in commercial banks; M3 is total currency, demand, and savings deposits in the whole banking system.

linkage between reserves and the growth of monetary aggregates was, until late in 1979, achieved by setting an interest target range each month for federal funds (the money commercial banks lend each other over night to cover their legal reserve obligations); and a two-month range for M1 and M2. In actual practice, the Federal Reserve Bank of New York, as the agent for the Federal Reserve System, was ordered by FOMC to raise or lower the federal funds rate whenever the growth of M1 and M2 appeared to be moving away from the two-months' tolerance range.

In line with this basic policy objective, federal fund rates and rediscount rates have been frequently raised to stem the tide of money growth.[48] In 1978, a series of innovative financial measures were also taken to increase personal savings and ease bank liquidity. Among these pressures have been permission to commercial banks to pay interest on demand deposits (by a circuitous way of "automatic transfer" from checking to savings accounts); allowing savings and loan associations to issue money market certificates at attractive interest rates; authorized expansion of highly liquid money market mutual funds; and exemption from interest ceilings of large certificates of deposit.

The critics maintain, however, that up until late in the 1970s, the Fed did not abandon interest rate targets, because it was not sanguine about reaching the announced money targets. Thus, up until late in 1979, the Fed's main weapon to slow inflation and strengthen the dollar was a change in short-term interest rates, through the basic federal funds rate. The growth of money was often far above or below the announced targets. After October 1979, the focus turned to controlling the growth of money supply by controlling bank reserves. It was apparently decided that no matter how high the interest rate was fixed, the expectation of further inflation (caused partly by the "free" growth of money supply) would not dampen individual or business appetites for further borrowing. The solution was to control the money supply and let interest rates fluctuate in the market. Accordingly, the Fed raised some legal reserve requirements in early October 1979, pushed the discount rate to 13 percent—the highest ever—and announced its intention strictly to control bank reserves. Subsequently, the commercial banks' prime rate reached 20 percent in early 1980—also the highest in U.S. history, before it began to plummet as the 1980 recession intensified.

Part of the blame for the relative ineffectiveness of U.S. monetary policy rests with the incompatibility of the three objectives of monetary policy mentioned before. Every time that the Fed tried to bolster the value of the U.S. dollar in world exchange markets by raising domestic short-term interest rates (when dollars began to pour out of the United States seeking safer currencies or higher foreign interest rates), foreign currencies would flow in, and their conversion into dollars would increase bank reserves and money supply. Part of the problem has also been the

48. Between 1972 and 1979, the basic money (M1) increased by nearly 40 percent, and M3 by 65 percent, while real GNP went up by about 16 percent. During this period, federal funds rate went up as high as 13 percent in 1974, dropped to less than 5 percent late in 1976, and rose back toward double-digit figures in 1979-80.

political difficulty of pushing short-term interest rates high enough to discourage borrowing without at the same time triggering or intensifying recessions. The Fed, conceding the difficulty of sticking to monetary supply targets over any short-term period, has for the most part tried to control interest rates. But the right level of interest rates capable of slowing down money growth, avoiding the risk of recessions, and moderating dollar flows has not been easy to find. As a result of unavoidable miscalculations, the Fed has been intermittently blamed for helping to prolong inflation or for pushing the economy into a recession. For this reason, some monetarists argue that the Fed should announce its monetary growth targets for several years in advance and avoid shifting between tight and easy credit.

Exchange Policy. The U.S. exchange rate system is one of "floating," under which the spot and forward rates of the dollar are determined in the market. However, the authorities "intervene" from time to time in the spot market to offset disorderly fluctuations in the dollar value. The official policy has persistently favored a stable dollar in terms of foreign currencies, but the actual performance has been far from that ideal.

The United States enjoyed a comfortable surplus in its annual balance of payments during and immediately after World War II, when it served as the world's readiest supplier of war materiels, consumer goods, reconstruction equipment, and development machinery. After 1951, however, the federal government's increasing worldwide commitments finally caught up with the economy's productive capacity. While the U.S. balance of trade (the difference between exports and imports) continued to show a surplus until 1970, the government's foreign aid and foreign military expenditures, tourist outlays, and particularly private business investments abroad more than offset the trade surplus, and the balance of payments showed persistent deficits.

The Kennedy-Johnson administrations, backed by Congress, took a series of remedial measures. An "interest equalization tax" was voted by Congress in 1963 to discourage foreign borrowing in the United States. A program of voluntary guidelines was announced early in 1966, under which private industry was urged to reduce its foreign direct investment, to repatriate part of its foreign incomes, and to expand its export promotion efforts. Increased foreign expenditures caused by the Vietnam War and continued outflow of U.S. funds for private investment and tourism forced the Johnson administration to announce early in 1968 a temporary mandatory program of reduced foreign investment and foreign loans and, among other measures, to ask Congress to enact new taxes on travel abroad.

Faced with an unprecedented balance of payments deficit of $10 billion by the middle of 1971, a reduced gold reserve of just about $10.5 billion, and the possibility of a first U.S. trade deficit in this century, the Nixon administration, on August 15, 1971, announced some drastic new measures to safeguard the value of the dollar. As part of these measures, the United States suspended "temporarily" the convertibility of dollars into gold, imposed a 10 percent surcharge on U.S. imports, and proposed a reduction in American foreign aid by 10 percent.

After floating for a while in world exchange markets, and losing part of its pre-1971 value, the dollar was finally devalued officially by 7.89 percent in March 1972, raising the price of gold from $35 to $38 an ounce. After other necessary exchange rate adjustments were made in the major surplus countries, the U.S. import surcharge was removed early in 1972, and the dollar's value again headed toward stabilization.

Under continued speculative pressures on the dollar, the United States again announced a reduction in the par value of its currency in terms of the Special Drawing Rights by another 10 percent in February 1973. The Smithsonian Agreement of 1971 regarding central rate arrangements therefore ceased to be effective. Owing to further frequent changes in relationships among major world currencies, and the decision in March 1973 by nine European countries to maintain a narrow margin of 2.25 percent among their currencies and jointly to float against the dollar, the U.S. currency began to seek its value freely in the market.

Subsequently, U.S. exchange policy was focused on keeping the market value of the dollar from wide fluctuations. By special "swap" arrangements with some of its trading partners, U.S. authorities intervened from time to time to maintain relative stability in the market. After a temporary balance-of-payments improvement in 1975, however, the U.S. current account again faced a dramatic deterioration. To counteract the sharp decline in the dollar value in foreign exchange markets, a package of measures was announced in November 1978; they included (in addition to fiscal, monetary, wage-price, and energy measures) special provisions for export promotion, a monthly sale of Treasury gold, and larger foreign-exchange resources borrowed from other countries to support market intervention. Subsequently, the Treasury started offering for sale part of its gold holdings to "mop up" part of the excess dollars and issued foreign currency-denominated securities on the German and Swiss capital markets in 1978 and 1979.

Trade Policy. The U.S. trade policy, while more liberal than those of many of its major trading partners in many respects, is not totally free. There are tariffs, quotas, import and export licensing, and other barriers. The importance of U.S. trade restrictions in world trade has also increased owing to the growing significance of foreign trade in the U.S. economy. In 1960, U.S. imports and exports together accounted for only 10 percent of GNP. By 1980, the figure was around 15 percent. Furthermore, U.S. private foreign investments were worth more than $150 billion (as compared to some $35 billion of foreign firms' investment in the United States).

The United States is a party to the General Agreement on Tariffs and Trade (GATT) and follows its tariffs arrangements. Import quotas apply to a number of items ranging from peanuts, dairy products, fish, sugar, and meat to cotton textiles and steel products. In addition, imports of some petroleum products require an import license. With respect to exports, licenses are required for munitions, strategic materials and equipment, and crime-control devices to certain countries. Total prohibition of trade exists with regard to certain countries. Capital movements are not subject to control, except transactions with a limited number of countries.[49]

Incomes Policy. Unlike the situation in some major European countries, wage-price controls were never considered as part of U.S. peacetime economic weapons. The War Labor Board and the Office of Price Administration during World War II kept wages and prices within the limits deemed in the national interest. The same type of controls was used briefly during the Korean War, but these measures were regarded as the tools of last resort. For much of the early postwar period, the conventional anticyclical levers seemed to suffice. The 1949–50 recession (with its 7.6 percent peak unemployment) was fought mainly through monetary and credit measures. So was the recession of 1954. The subsequent 1955–56 inflation was attacked by a balanced budget approach.[50]

The emergence of inflation as a major economic worry after recovery from the 1958 recession, however, renewed the demands for a national wage-price policy similar to those of the Western Europeans. A voluntary scheme of wage-price guideposts appeared in the 1962 *Economic Report of the President*. These voluntary guideposts had some salutary effect in limiting wage-price increases up to 1966, when unemployment was still relatively high and industry was not working at capacity. But as inflation continued unabated with the escalation of the Vietnam War, the need for taking additional anti-inflationary measures was more urgently felt.[51]

Bowing to increased public pressure, in June 1970, the Nixon administration proposed three new policy measures, the new "game plan." The Council of Economic Advisers was asked to issue an "inflation alert" to call public attention to major wage or price increases. A twenty-three-man board composed of business, labor, and public officials was established to suggest ways and means of improving labor productivity. And an anti-inflation "review board" was set up to look over federal purchasing programs and regulations to see how they could be changed to fight price rises.

With no effective results from these measures, and with continued high inflation and unemployment, the Congress passed the Economic Stabilization Act in early 1970, authorizing the president to establish temporary controls over prices, wages, and rents, if and when economic situations in the country warranted such actions. All during the year there were signs that the "game plan" was failing.

49. For details, see *Annual Report, Exchange Arrangements and Exchange Restrictions, 1980* (Washington: International Monetary Fund, 1980).

50. See John Sheahan, *The Wage-Price Guideposts* (Washington: Brookings Institution, 1967).

51. See *The Wage-Price Issue: The Need for Guideposts*, Joint Economic Committee, 90th Cong., 2nd Sess. (Washington: GPO, 1968).

Inflation had not been brought down from its 6 percent a year level and unemployment stood stubbornly at 6 percent of the labor force. For the first time since the 1890s, too, the United States faced a deficit in its balance of trade as imports exceeded exports. And the long weakened dollar came under heavy new attacks in international money markets.

Thus, on August 15, 1971, President Nixon announced his New Economic Policy, dealing with the suspension of dollar convertibility; imposition of an import surcharge; reduction of government spending and foreign aid; lowering of automobile excise tax; restoring investment tax credit; and increasing personal income tax exemption. At the same time, the president invoked the extended Economic Stabilization Act of 1970 to announce a total freeze (with minor exemptions) on all prices, wages, and rents at the existing levels for a period of ninety days. Profits, interest rates, and dividends were not included in the freeze, but the president asked corporations not to increase dividends. The new measures introduced mandatory government wage-price controls for the first time in U.S. peacetime economic history.

In October 1971, Phase II of the incomes policy was announced to deal with inflation after the ninety-day freeze. A new Price Commission was set up to develop price and rent guidelines and supervise their enforcement. A tripartite Pay Board, consisting of government, business, and labor leaders, was established and charged with the responsibility of setting wage policy, issuing wage guidelines, approving wage contracts, and providing sanctions against violators. An Interest and Dividend Committee was instituted to monitor interest rates and watch over dividends. A Committee on Health Services Industry was to deal with the costs of health care. The Construction Industry Stabilization Commission (established earlier) was to continue its task of stabilizing wages in the construction industry. And the ten-member Productivity Commission (also previously established) was expanded to thirteen to continue its study of finding new ways to improve output per man-hour and to cut labor costs. The Cost of Living Council was to act as the supreme organization in this elaborate hierarchy. Legislation for institutionalizing the new control devices was approved by both the House and the Senate in December 1971.

In January 1973, President Nixon unfurled Phase III of his anti-inflation program, designed to give more freedom to business and labor while retaining some jawboning power with teeth for the government.[52] Under Phase III, government controls over prices were abolished, except on food, health care, and construction. Federal rent controls were terminated. The Pay Board and the Price Commission were disbanded. The Cost of Living Council was put in charge of the new phase, with power to go along with noninflationary wage and price changes, pare down

52. Persuasive diplomacy by the chief executive to bring industry and labor leaders into line had previously been used by President J. F. Kennedy in rolling back steel prices in 1962, and by President L. B. Johnson in rescinding the aluminum price hike in 1965. The 1965 railroad and steel wage disputes were also settled under the aegis of the White House. So was the strike by the copper mines in 1968.

proposed changes beyond its guidelines, or roll back excessive wage and price boosts. The authority for controls under Phase III was approved by Congress under an extension of the Economic Stabilization Act to April 1974.

Phase III expired in June 1973 and was followed by a short, selective price freeze until August, at which time Phase IV was introduced. Under a most complicated new set of controls, selective and limited increases were allowed for different categories of goods and services (food, oil and gas, industrial products, health care, insurance premiums, wage rates). Most of these controls were abandoned in April 1974.

Persistent inflationary pressures in the wake of a sharp crude-oil price adjustment by the Organization of Petroleum Exporting Countries in 1974 renewed the clamor for a new inflation fight. President Gerald Ford's anti-inflation campaign did not go much beyond exhortation—"Whip Inflation Now." President Carter began his anti-inflation program by a limp voluntarism (Stage I) in April 1978, a jawboning effort that had little bite. This was followed in October by Stage II, wage-price guidelines. Under this program, workers were asked to settle for wage and benefit increases averaging 7 percent over the 1978–80 period. Price boosts were expected to be limited to a half point below the average of the 1976–78 years, or no more than 9.5 percent. Profit margins were to remain at the average of the best two years of the 1975–77 period. There were additional promises of a freeze on new federal hiring, a reduction in the budget deficits, and a careful cost-benefit analysis of various regulations. The Council on Wage and Price Stability was given the mandate to monitor compliance with voluntary guidelines. Some exceptions were envisaged for hardship cases, both in business and among workers.

In September 1979, President Carter announced a "national accord" with the AFL-CIO and other major unions on a common commitment to deal with inflation. The administration's anti-inflation program included a "disciplined" fiscal policy, job training and improved housing, continued voluntary programs of pay and price restraint, and reduced dependence on imported oil. Two advisory committees were set up under the Council on Wage and Price Stability to deal with wages and prices. The Pay Advisory Committee was to advise the Council on general pay guidelines and specific dispensations to assure fairness and equity in individual cases. The Price Committee was to recommend general price standards.[53]

None of these programs achieved what was expected of them—a permanent solution to a virulent inflation. In fact, the consumer price index in 1979 rose by 13.3 percent, the highest since World War II. As a result, public attention focused on a new variant called tax-based incomes policy (TIP). Rooted in a growing conviction that the underlying causes of both high U.S. unemployment and high inflation are wage increases that far outstrip productivity gains (over 8 percent a year

53. Numerical targets for prices, wages and profits were also announced by the Council effective to September 1980. For details, see United States (Paris: OECD, November 1979).

wage hike since 1973 versus 1.2 percent growth of productivity), suggestions were made to combat inflation by discouraging business-labor coalition from raising wages and prices. The policy would penalize companies with a surcharge on their corporate income tax if they grant their employees wage increases in excess of government guidelines. Similarly, a tax credit would be granted to companies that keep wages below government-set standards. As expected, both labor and management showed opposition to this scheme.

The inability of voluntary wage-price guidelines to stem the tide of inflation forced President Carter to propose a series of new measures affecting just about everyone. The signals of an economy in trouble were becoming increasingly clear in the early months of 1980 as the prime interest rate jumped to 20 percent and the consumer price index presaged an annual increase of more than 18 percent. Under the weight of the new inflationary pressures the bond market was in disarray, and the exchange value of the dollar was kept high by inflows of funds in pursuit of record high interest rates. To cool off the accelerating annual price rise, the new anti-inflation plan was unfolded in March, 1980. The centerpiece of the plan was a balanced federal budget for 1981, the first in more than a decade. Other key elements were a boost in gasoline prices, a reduction in aid for cities and states, a number of specific controls on individuals' use of credit, some changes in the welfare system, and the "tougher" monitoring of the voluntary wage and price guidelines.

Regulation of Micro-Economic Activity

Public regulation of economic activity in the United States at the federal, state, and local levels is considered a midway point between the impersonal controls exerted by the free market and the self-imposed controls theoretically assumed under the command system. Government regulation covers a wide range of activities.

Maintenance of Competition. The American philosophical and cultural commitment to individual freedom and the free-enterprise system calls for the preservation of competition in the economy. Since the end of the nineteenth century, U.S. antitrust and monopoly have fought—not always satisfactorily—against restraint of trade and abuses of economic power. The oldest and best known federal antitrust law is the Sherman Act of 1890, which forbids monopoly, restraint of trade, and attempts to monopolize any segment of interstate commerce. Elaborating on the Sherman Act, and putting additional teeth into it, is the Clayton Act of 1914, which specifically prohibits price discrimination, tying contracts, exclusive dealership arrangements, intercorporate stock ownership, and interlocking directorates whenever the results "substantially lessen competition or tend to create a monopoly." The 1914 Federal Trade Commission Act outlaws "unfair methods of competition" such as mislabeling; misbranding; false, deceitful, or misleading representation; trade espionage; boycotts; and altogether more than thirty different "sharp" practices. These basic laws have been amended and supplemented by scores of others in the last fifty years. There are parallel laws on a state level.

The effectiveness of U.S. antitrust laws in promoting vigorous and healthy competition has been a matter of unending controversy. The successful judicial enforcement of these laws in this century has produced a number of "landmark" decisions. Thus, such predatory practices as price cutting to drive competitors out of business, spying on competitors' activities, cornering supplies of strategic raw materials, obtaining secret rebates from customers, forcing customers not to compete with the seller, and binding dealers not to deal with other sellers have all been ruled unlawful. The same has been true of agreements among independent sellers to fix prices or to limit sales. Price discriminations and discounts unwarranted by cost differentials have all also met similar verdicts.

Yet critics have been unmerciful. Professor Galbraith, for example, has called antitrust laws "a charade" designed to placate and fool the incredulous public about the underlying nature of modern capitalist enterprise.[54] It is argued that these laws have provided neither a deterrent to continued and persistent abuses nor a block to the rise of mergers and conglomeration. Enforcement has also been time-consuming and costly. In recent years, as in the past, charges of restraint of trade, conspiracy to monopolize, and actual monopoly have been leveled against the bluest of the blue-ribbon U.S. corporations, trade associations, and professional groups. Yet, in many of these antitrust litigations, the government's success after costly and time-consuming battles with the smart and well-defended violators has resulted in punishments that can hardly be said to fit the crime.[55]

In the eighty-year enforcement of U.S. antitrust laws, jail sentences for law violations have been unusually rare and extremely mild. A good majority of cases have involved "civil suits." Corporations and corporate executives charged with flagrant antitrust violations have merely entered a plea of *nolo contendere*, or not contesting the prosecution's allegation and simply promising not to continue their wrong deeds.[56]

Regulation of Business. There are reportedly eighty-seven federal agencies and offices with 100,000 employees exercising control over private economic activities in the United States. Among these organizations, fifty-five major regulatory agencies have specific jurisdiction over private economic activities. These agencies can be

54. See J. K. Galbraith, *The New Industrial State* (Boston: Houghton Mifflin, 1979).

55. In 1967, for example, three men who had conspired with a physician to promote a worthless weight-reducing scheme and succeeded in selling 2,000,000 copies of the book, *Calories Don't Count*, along with $500,000 worth of oil and vitamin capsules, were given a fine of $1,000 each.

56. According to a task force report, American consumers pay between $48 billion and $60 billion a year in artificially inflated prices due to market concentration and lax enforcement of antitrust laws. See Ralph Nader, *The Closed Enterprise System* (New York: Crossman, 1972).

divided into five distinct categories: industry specific; financial reporting; energy and environment; job safety and working conditions; and consumer safety and health. [57]

Of these fifty-five agencies, five regulatory commissions are "industry specific," that is, concerned with the daily operation, rates, services, and other aspects of public utilities engaged in interstate commerce and related business of great social concern. The fifty states have their own regulatory agencies. The regulatory commissions policing "natural" monopolies are considered the "fourth branch" of the U.S. government. They are independent, semiexecutive, semijudiciary, and semilegislative bodies created by Congress as watchdogs over private business "affected with the public interest."[58]

The oldest regulatory commission is the Interstate Commerce Commission, created in 1887 to check the abuses of railroad monopolies. By virtue of the Interstate Commerce Commission Act of 1887, the Hepburn Act of 1906, and the Transportation Act of 1920, the U.S. railroads are now regulated in their rates structure, finances, safety, adequacy of service, contraction of existing lines, and expansion into new territories by the ICC. The Motor Carrier Act of 1935 gives the ICC the authority to issue or deny the "certificate of convenience and necessity" (license) to bus, truck, or cab companies engaged in interstate traffic. Since the passage of the Transportation Act of 1940, federal regulation of domestic water transportation is also vested in the ICC.

Airlines were regulated up until 1938 by the Department of Commerce and between 1938 and 1958 by the Civil Aeronautics Administration in both safety rules and conditions of service. They are now regulated by the Civil Aeronautics Board and the Federal Aviation Agency. The CAB has the responsibility for issuing certificates of convenience and necessity to new carriers, approving rates, authorizing route changes and, lately, encouraging healthy competition among major carriers. The FAA, established in 1958, has the authority to establish safety rules, coordinate military and civilian flight, examine air accidents, and revoke or suspend pilots' operating permits. The Maritime Administration and the Federal Maritime Commission have jurisdiction over shipping and shipbuilding.

The Federal Water Power Act of 1920, which created the Federal Power Commission, is the mainstay of federal regulation of the sale of electricity and piped natural gas in interstate commerce. The commission's responsibility includes rate determination, issuance of licenses for hydroelectric plants on federal government lands or on navigable waters, surveillance of mergers, inspection of records, and establishment of a "fair" return on a fair value of facilities.

Since 1934, the Federal Communications Commission has regulated all means of communications under one integrated control. The FCC act gives the

---

57. For the problems and prospects of the regulatory commission in the United States, including their costs and benefits, see P. W. MacAvoy, ed., *The Crisis of the Regulatory Commissions* (New York: Norton, 1970); and M. L. Weidenbaum, *Business, Government and the Public* (Englewood Cliffs: Prentice-Hall, 1977).

58. Other regulatory commissions dealing with the protection of consumers, workers, and investors will be discussed below in appropriate sections.

commission power over facilities, service, connections, expansion, and other activities in interstate and overseas commerce. In the case of radio and television, the commission has authority over the assignment of frequencies and channels. This power also involves a good deal of influence over the use of air time for advertising, public affairs, news broadcasts, and other programs.

The actual performance of U.S. regulatory agencies in the past has called into question the effectiveness and benefits of the regulatory process. Almost from their beginning, the regulatory commissions have come under severe criticism for inactivity, submissiveness to political pressure, bureaucratic bungling, mediocrity, undue influence by the very industries they are supposed to regulate, and lately for contributing to inflation through costly edicts, and for impeding industrial growth.

Protection of Consumers and Resource Owners.   Another major aspect of government regulation involves protection of uninformed or mistreated consumers against possible abuses by greedy or unscrupulous sellers. Despite occasional furies, boycotts, and picketing by the public at large, individual consumers and resource owners often find themselves powerless to deal with antisocial business practices. The American consumer may indeed think of himself as a "sovereign," but as a Presidential Commission on Food Marketing has noted, he is not an "all-knowing, all-powerful and fully-served sovereign." The same is true of an individual worker and investor.

Consumer Protection.   Elementary measures of business regulation by the state and local governments in the United States, such as standardization of weights and measures, date from early colonial days, but consumer protection by the federal government is of more recent origin. After the publication of Upton Sinclair's *The Jungle* in 1906, which caused a public uproar over unsanitary conditions in Chicago's meat-packing industry, the first Pure Food and Drug Act and a Meat Inspection Law were passed. In 1914, the Federal Trade Commission Act gave the FTC the task of definind and preventing "unfair trade practices." The Wheeler-Lea Amendment, passed in 1938, gave the Commission direct authority to stop false, misleading, and deceptive advertising.

After the publication of another best-seller, *100 Million Guinea Pigs*, by Kallet and Schlink in 1938, the Food, Drug and Cosmetics Act was passed in the same year, replacing the 1906 statute. This was followed by the Wool Products Labeling Act of 1951. The Kefauver-Harris Amendment to the 1938 drug act was passed in 1962, requiring drug manufacturers to prove the safety, purity, and efficacy of their products before they can be marketed.

Another widely circulated book, *Unsafe at Any Speed*, by Ralph Nader in 1965 gave rise to the National Traffic and Motor Vehicle Safety Act of 1966, establishing requirements for auto safety (seat belts, headrests, blow-resistant tires). In 1966, the U.S. Congress also passed the Fair Packaging and Labeling Act—the so-called truth-in-packaging law—in order to protect U.S. shoppers against product misrepresentation. The Consumer Credit Protection Act—the so-called truth-in-lending act—was passed in 1968 to give borrowers comprehensive and easily understood information on their loans from banks, finance companies, and other lenders. The Congress also passed the Wholesome Meat Act of 1967, Radiation Control for Health and Safety Act of 1968, Wholesome Poultry Products Act in the same year, and a Toy Safety Act in 1969. In 1970 cigarette commercials were outlawed on radio and TV, and stricter health warnings was required on cigarette packages and printed advertisements. The Consumer Product Safety Act was passed in 1972, establishing a new five-member commission to devise mandatory safety standards for consumer products and to supervise their adoption and sales by manufacturers.

Altogether, the U.S. Congress has already passed more than twenty major pieces of legislation dealing with consumer protection. At present, a half-dozen federal agencies are involved in this endeavor. The President's Office of Consumer Affairs deals with legislation and recommendations to the president on all aspects of consumerism. The Consumer Product Safety Commission is in charge of unreasonable risks of injuries associated with consumer products, fabrics, and hazardous materials. The Federal Trade Commission, the Food and Drug Administration, and the Civil Aeronautics Board also partly handle other aspects of consumer protection in their respective jurisdictions. In addition, there are state public service commissions, state banking and insurance departments, local health departments, local consumer affairs departments, and so forth.

Protection of Resource Owners. Government regulation is also used to protect the interests of workers, savers, investors, and other resource owners. Protective labor legislation with respect to industrial injuries, employment of women and children, hours of work, and minimum wage goes back to the middle of the nineteenth century, when Massachusetts pioneered an anti-child-labor law in 1842. The first comprehensive U.S. federal statute in this regard is the Fair Labor Standards Act of 1938. The act established a minimum hourly wage for workers in industries engaged in interstate commerce, excluding farm workers and a few other occupations. The standard workweek for nonseasonal industries was reduced from forty-eight to forty hours, with overtime pay beyond that limit. The law has been amended several times, and the "minimum" wage has been raised periodically.[59]

Since 1938 all industrial states in the Union have also passed minimum wage laws of their own. Almost all states also have laws regarding sanitary working conditions, workingmen's liens on employers' property in case of bankruptcy, regulation of apprenticeship, and workers' compensation for injuries, disability, or death. Since the passage of the Social Security Act of 1935, an increasing number of workers and self-employed people have been covered under state unemployment

59. In 1981, the minimum wage was $3.35 an hour for about 5 million people at the lowest rungs of the work force.

compensation systems, aided by the federal government, to be paid for the loss of income due to joblessness.

The Occupational Safety and Health Administration was set up in 1973 to develop and enforce safety and health regulations for some 50 million workers in 4 million places of work. The agency's code book is reportedly seven-feet thick. The Equal Employment Opportunity Commission, established in 1964, has the responsibility of investigating and ruling on charges of racial and other discriminations by employers and labor unions.

In the area of investors' protection, the government's involvement is also extensive. The stock market crash of 1929, and widespread reports of flagrant abuses of the securities market by certain large investors, corporate insiders, and bankers, prompted congressional actions for the protection of small investors. Based on some twenty years of experience by many state governments with stock exchange regulation under the so-called "blue-sky" laws, the Securities and Exchange Act was passed in 1934, establishing the Securities and Exchange Commission for its enforcement. The Securities Act requires prior registration of new stock offerings with the commission before their sale to the public and giving sufficient information regarding new issues to potential buyers in a prospectus. It forbids stock manipulations by insiders and regulates margin requirements for the purchase of stocks on credit. In 1970, Congress passed the Securities Investor Protection Act, whereby a semipublic insurance corporation was to be established under the SEC's supervision to insure investors against the loss of cash and securities left in the hands of stockbrokers.[60]

Provision of Equity and Economic Security. The U.S. national objectives of ensuring equity in the distribution of income and providing economic security are based on dissatisfaction with other deficiencies of the market. These deficiencies are, in turn, rooted in the inequality of opportunity that a free-market economy usually imposes on its less fortunate members, and in the differences in income, wealth, and power which result from initial differences in economic opportunity. To make up the deficiencies in income, and hence economic power, the federal, state, and local governments have, in varying degrees, assumed responsibility for a number of remedial actions, particularly since the Great Depression.

The post-Depression proposals for eradicating poverty, increasing economic opportunity, and instituting a fairer distribution of income have been based on convincing indications that poverty is not always self-imposed. The American puritanical tradition has often tended to link poverty with laziness, apathy, lack of motivation, self-pity, and other defects of character. In latter-day thinking, however, the plight of the poor in a good many cases is considered a direct outcome of

60. In recent years, the SEC has censured, suspended, or penalized some of the largest and most reputable brokerage houses in the United States for the alleged violation of federal securities laws, such as giving inside information to favored investment company clients.

deficient aspirational, educational, housing, and employment opportunities imposed upon them by the more affluent majority for an inordinately long period of time [61]

For this reason, the scope of federal involvement in income redistribution has increased considerably in recent years, as witnessed by the magnitude and variety of government services and aids to individual citizens. The 1,000-plus-page *Encyclopedia of U.S. Government Benefits* singles out some two thousand different ways that Americans might avail themselves of the government's generosity from cradle to grave. Starting at the outset, (and to name just a few) there are hospital care for premature babies; hot lunches for millions of schoolchildren; monthly checks for orphaned and disabled youngsters; even allowance for returning runaway teenagers to their homes. There are various kinds of national scholarships, fellowships, and research grants to individuals; retraining and rehabilitation programs for the disadvantaged; placement service for job seekers; and so on. In the prime of life, there are government loans for establishing small businesses; subsidies for staying in favored-crops farming and low-interest loans to family farms; loans for mining explorations; government-supported housing and homeownership programs; assistance for building recreational facilities and personal hobbies; unemployment compensation, disability payments, and veterans' benefits. At old age, there are social security, medicare, medicaid, and sundry other programs. At the state and local levels, there are more of the same. [62]

These various redistributive measures are for the most part embodied in three basic programs: unemployment compensation; social security (old-age, survivors, and disability benefits); and welfare—under the general banner of "income security." The rationale of unemployment compensation has been the compulsory provision for occasional slack periods during which workers laid off involuntarily can manage to offset loss of earnings; it is a built-in stabilizer of recessionary periods out of the proceeds of full-employment incomes.

The goal of social security has been a forced savings program out of which a certain amount of income is set aside for retirement needs so as to obtain the objective of individual equity. Welfare has been based on the goal of "social adequacy," insuring a minimum income to poor retirees and their dependents. The unemployment compensation program, enacted in 1935, is financed by a federal tax on employers and is administered by the states. Social security—also enacted in 1935 and amended several times since—covers old-age, survivors, and disability benefits; workmen's compensation; and public employees and railroad retirement. The program is financed by a tax on both employers and employees which goes into

61. See Michael Harrington, *The Other America* (New York: Macmillan, 1970); H. P. Miller, *Rich Man, Poor Man* (New York: Crowell, 1971); and A. M. Okun, *Equality and Efficiency*, (Washington: The Brookings Institution, 1975).

62. President Johnson's antiproverty program included such projects as the Job Corps, Neighborhood Health Centers, Volunteers in Service to America, Legal Services for the Poor, and many others.

a trust fund from which some millions of retired and disabled workers are paid.[63] Tax rates and the tax base are determined by Congress from time to time in order to keep the trust fund solvent.[64] Benefits depend on the duration and amount of contributions made by employees. The program is administered by the federal government, and benefits are uniform for all the states. Over a million retired civil servants and nearly 5 million veterans or their survivors have their own separate pension programs.

The third category—the most widely criticized for inefficiency and inequity, and the most controversial in its basic premises—is welfare. The welfare program includes a welter of schemes with different origins, durations, purposes, benefits, and beneficiaries. They are financed by federal and state appropriations and administered by the states and local governments. There are three basic categories of welfare: the federal Medicare and the state Medicaid (health and hospital care) for over 35 million old and poor people; aid to families with dependent children; and general relief assistance to a variety of individuals. The last catch-all category includes such items as free food given to the needy, food stamps sold to the poor at low or no cost, and hot school lunches for millions of children at subsidized rates.[65]

The 1972 Social Security Act passed by the Congress after three years of debate raised social security taxes, linked payments to the cost-of-living index, and federalized welfare payments for the aged, the blind, and the disabled (providing for a uniform minimum payment to the sick and the elderly in all fifty states). The 1977 act substantially raised employee and employer contributions and placed new curbs on benefits in order to save the program from impending insolvency.

Social Accounting and Third-Party Compensation. The federal, state, and local governments have, in recent years, gradually moved toward rechanneling some social costs back to their sources. Concern about deteriorating quality of the environment in the United States has been aroused by the alarming increase in air, water, and noise pollution, soil toxity, harmful substances in the atmosphere, and other ecological problems.

Federal and state rules regarding such undesirable phenomena have usually followed industry's alleged disregard of its "social responsibility."[66] Thus, as part of President Johnson's Great Society program, Congress passed the Water Quality Act

63. In 1980 an estimated 36 million Americans—one out of every six—received retirement checks or other pension-related benefits.

64. In 1980, the tax rate for each employee and employer was 6.13 percent, and the maximum tax per worker about $1,588.

65. For an analysis of U.S. public welfare programs, see G. Y. Steiner, *The State of Welfare* (Washington: The Brookings Institutions, 1971); M. J. Ulmer, *The Welfare State: U.S.A.* (Boston: Houghton Mifflin, 1969); and A. H. Munnell, *The Future of Social Security* (Washington: The Brookings Institution, 1977).

66. In the area of air pollution, for example, some auto industry leaders admit that antiexhaust devices would not have been added to new cars had California not passed a law requiring them.

of 1965 and Clean Water Restoration Act of 1966 for water purification and sewage treatment plants; the Clean Air Act of 1965 and Air Quality Act of 1967, seeking air purification; the Solid Waste Disposal Act of 1965; and the Highway Beautification Act of 1965. Under a subsequent strong bipartisan effort, a new National Air Quality Standards Act was passed in 1970 amending and strengthening previous laws. The Council on Environmental Quality was established in the Executive Office of the President to provide broad policy recommendations on ecological problems. The National Environmental Policy Act of 1970 established a new Environmental Protection Agency to deal with polluters.

In other cases of third-party injuries, some states have enacted laws to compensate crime victims. It has long been considered ironic that public authorities should take care of convicted criminals—providing them with food, shelter, medical care, and even rehabilitation during their prison terms—while ignoring the innocent victims of the crime, who often lost their breadwinners, their savings, or their livelihood. Following the examples of Britain and New Zealand, California took the first step in 1965 toward compensating such victims. Massachusetts, Maryland, New York, Hawaii, Nevada, and New Jersey followed suit.

Legal aid to the accused poor has also received growing support. In the words of a *New York Times* editorial, in "both civil and criminal courts there is a law for the rich and a law for the poor. Equal justice under law simply does not work unless people who cannot afford legal representation are considered as clients instead of charity cases."[67] Some states have thus begun to improve the operation of their legal aid societies.

Promotion and Support of Private Business

In spite of its avowed commitment to a free-enterprise economy, the U.S. government has always been a protectionist government. In the very midst of rejecting British mercantilist hold on America, the original thirteen colonies were engaged in mercantilism in almost all its promotional and protectionist manifestations: tax exemption to favored industries; patents and monopoly grants to investors and innovators; free land and cheap loans for high-priority goals; export promotion; and protection of local industries.[68]

Grants and Subsidies. Under Alexander Hamilton's centralist thesis, the U.S. Congress adopted many promotional measures as national policies. Through enormous grants of lands to the states and private concerns, the federal government was instrumental in building a solid national infrastructure, including a vast

---

67. "Legal Inequities," *New York Times*, 13 February 1969.
68. For further discussion, see E. E. Smead, *Governmental Promotion and Regulation of Business* (New York: Appleton-Century, 1969).

network of transportation. A consistently rising tariff wall provided sufficient protection for new industries to grow and prosper.

The scope and variety of promotional activities of government in the United States today defy a cursory look. For the federal government alone, some 170-odd programs are identified by a congressional committee. These programs include direct cash subsidies, credit subsidies, benefits in kind, and concessions running into nearly $100 billion. [69] Among these variegated programs, both old and new, one of the most extensive and expensive has been transportion—railways, highways, waterways, and airways. The U.S. Merchant Marine has been kept alive for years under the Merchant Marine Act of 1936 by government subsidies and government cargoes under the banner of national security and national interest.

The agricultural subsidy program, costing the government about $3–4 billion in annual direct outlays (and about $4.5 billion in higher farm prices paid by consumers each year), covers a variety of activities designed to cut production, raise farmers' incomes, and improve their well-being. It includes a price-support program that guarantees a minimum price for certain farm commodities; a surplus disposal scheme under which farm surpluses are bought by the government at higher-than-market prices; an export subsidy program that helps move some high-priced American products in world markets; and a cash payment program for taking land out of production. The total government aid to agriculture, however, extends much beyond these subsidies; it includes the offer of free land and free extension services, flood control, irrigation, credit, insurance, and electrification. Agricultural price support has helped mainly the big corporate farms, which constitute only 20 percent of all farms but received 60 percent of the subsidies.

Other government subsidy programs include: tax benefits to specific industries (more than 100 different depletion allowances, accelerated amortization of defense facilities, investment credit allowance, aid to small business); disposal of surplus property at low prices and stockpiling of "strategic" materials at high prices; free or below-cost services such as statistical and other information; and investment and trade promotion. [70] The United States is reportedly spending about $24 billion a year on scientific research and development, $15 billion of which comes directly out of federal funds. The federal government, under the 1965 National Foundation of Arts and Humanities, subsidizes poets, novelists, actors, painters, dancers, and other performing artists.

Protection of Private Business Activities. Government support of private business in the U.S. has a long tradition. The history of U.S. foreign commercial policy up

69. See *Subsidy and Subsidy-Effect Programs of the U.S. Government*, Joint Economic Committee, 89th Cong., 1st Sess. (Washington: GPO, 1965).

70. In the summer of 1971, the U.S. Congress voted for a large new federal fund to guarantee commercial loans to big corporations in financial trouble. The first beneficiary was the Lockheed Aircraft Corp., which was on the brink of bankruptcy; a similar loan was made to the Penn Central Railroad in an identical situation; a special federally guaranteed loan was also made available to the Chrysler Corp. in 1979.

until the end of World War II was essentially a history of protecting domestic industries. While in the early years of the republic (and briefly during the Civil War), tariffs were used principally to raise federal revenues, the Tariff Act of 1816 was ostensibly designed to protect Eastern manufacturing interests. Subsequent tariff laws, with minor exceptions, raised custom levies to higher and higher levels and made home-industry protection an almost permanent feature of U.S. foreign economic policy. The Smoot-Hawley Act of 1930, under nationalist and isolationist pressures on the part of both political parties, brought the protectionist drive to its most notorious culmination. Under this act, duties were levied not only on goods similar to those produced in the United States, but also on a multitude of other items not domestically produced and not commercially competitive with American products.

The Trade Agreement Act of 1934 and its subsequent extensions and amendments gave the president authority to lower duties by as much as 50 percent through bilateral negotiations. Despite a number of concessions made by the United States under these acts, and even through the machinery of the General Agreement on Tariffs and Trade (including the all-important Kennedy and Tokyo Rounds of tariff liberalization since 1963), the United States remains wedded to the policy of protecting its home industries—infant and not-so-infant. In addition to tariffs, the federal government has been using a number of other devices—import quotas, "buy American" regulations, border taxes, discriminatory methods of tariff valuation, voluntary restraints by foreign exporters—to stem the tide of imports. Of these measures, import quotas are the most significant, and among quota-regulated imports, oil and sugar are the most controversial.

Another aspect of U.S. assistance to private industry is the recognition of patents, copyrights, and trademarks for inventors and innovators. Under the U.S. patent law passed in 1790, seventeen-year patents are issued to individuals who claim to be "the sole and true inventor" of a machine, a design, or a product. Under a revised law in 1977, copyrights are registered in the name of writers, composers, publishers, and radio and TV talent; they run for the lifetime of the author, plus fifty years. Trademarks are registered in favor of the applicants in the form of words, symbols, or service marks; they are good for twenty years and may be renewed for similar periods afterwards.

In all these cases, state-sanctioned rights effectively prevent competitors from using the patented item, copyrighted material, or registered trademarks without somehow compensating the rightful owner. In some cases, however, patents are used, or rather misused, as a means of perpetuating private monopoly, gobbling up unpatented goods, usurping other inventors' rights, controlling output, dividing markets, and engaging in a variety of similar practices. In others, inventions and innovations made with government funds or in government-financed research facilities are patented by private contractors, particularly in the Defense, Treasury, and Post Office departments.

Decision Making through Bargaining

The U.S. political economy may be described as an economy governed largely by compromise. In fact, if the United States were to be characterized by only one major process, it would probably be pluralistic bargaining, a process under which various social groups and independent economic powers are in a perpetual tug-of-war to determine the direction and management of the economy. "Everybody in America has a lobby," declares a frustrated House Speaker. The ability to find a workable compromise out of the conflicting interests of diverse pressure groups has often been considered the "genius of American politics." A major means of reaching such compromise is bargaining among major interest groups.[71] Important economic decisions by the legislative and executive branches of the government are often influenced, if not altogether determined, by skilled efforts of special interests jockeying for special treatment.

The essence of American pluralism is to be found in the constitutional separation of power among the congressional, executive, and judiciary branches, and also between the responsibilities of the federal versus local governments. The origin of American pressure-group lobbying also goes back to the First Amendment to the Constitution, which guarantees the public right "to petition the government for a redress of grievances." At present, more than two-thirds of the states and the federal government have explicitly recognized this important safeguard and have sanctioned lobbying.[72] At the root of the prolobbying sentiment is also the business argument—not totally without merit—that in the U.S. mixed economy the government's presence is felt everywhere by top corporate management. And this "presence," according to industry leaders, ought to be "preconditioned" in favor of business by appropriate lobbying.

In the following sections, we shall first briefly discuss some of the major bargainers in the American scene and then examine some of the most widely used techniques.

Major Bargainers in the U.S.

America's "participatory democracy" consists of an endless series of actions, reactions, and interactions by power blocs and pressure groups. These groups tend to coalesce with, or diverge from, one another as their organizational interests coincide or differ on each major issue. The principal "bargainers" can be divided

71. For a more recent treatment of this long-established thesis, see A. M. Rose, *The Power Structure: Political Process in American Society* (New York: Oxford University Press, 1967).

72. For a brief period following the Depression of 1929–32, the National Industrial Recovery Act of 1933 provided for "codes of fair competition" in each industry through collective bargaining between all parties concerned. The "codes" were to set forth maximum hours of work, minimum wage and fair prices, a set of labor standards, and permissible trade practices.

into several categories: giant business corporations, labor unions, public agencies and officials, special private lobbies, and the "outsiders" (foundations, universities, think tanks, pollsters, and individuals of great national stature).

Private Corporations. Giant corporate managers constitute one of the principal bargaining forces in the U.S. economy. In addition to their formalized and legally sanctioned bargains with trade unions, they take part formally or informally in almost all collective decisions that involve the direction and management of the economy, such as the composition of goods and services, location of plants, organizations of work, and the choice of technology. The crucial role of business leaders in deciding major issues is rooted in the strategic powers of the modern giant corporation itself. These powers, in turn, stem from corporate size, the separation of management and ownership, the possibility of administered price determination, and the personal make-up of business leadership. Corporate power is also said to derive from the "goodies" that business is able to give: jobs, incomes, status, security, and a sense of order. In some observers' opinion, these privileges give corporations a degree of influence over the decision-making process that no other interest group can aspire to match.[73]

Big corporations in America are big by almost all standards: assets, sales, employment, and power. As few as 120 large corporations account for more than 40 percent of the market value of all outstanding common stocks in the United States. The Standard Oil Company of New Jersey employs more people in its various subsidiaries than the majority of the world's nation-states. General Motors has an annual sales volume larger than the gross national product of all but the seventeen biggest non-communist industrialized countries. The fifty largest U.S. corporations have more people working for them than the fifty largest federal agencies. Three companies—General Motors, Standard Oil of New Jersey, and Ford—receive more income each year than all U.S. farms. The economic life or death of many products, processes, plants, and even towns throughout the United States often depend on decisions taken at corporate boardrooms in New York, Wilmington, or Jersey City. Publicity-shy corporate managers are often more powerful than national politicians.

Large corporations influence social policy through their lobbying before the Congress and statehouses. More than five hundred corporations have representatives in Washington to plead their individual cases. Collectively, too, they support the U.S. Chamber of Commerce and the Business Roundtable in an effort to stake out positions on pending legislation and adopt strategies to influence the outcome.

At the helm of U.S. corporate bureaucracy stand the professional corporate managers trained in law, engineering, business administration, and finance. Many own little stock in their company. In the opinion of a keen observer, these individuals are often self-made, with ambition, drive, and willingness to make

73. See, for example, C. E. Lindblom, *Politics and Markets* (New York: Basic Books, 1977); and Leonard Silk, "Where Power of Business Lies," *New York Times*, 4 July 1978.

company business the center of their lives. They are men and women of middle-class tastes and values, attracted by the monarchic principles of tradition, continuity, and past glories. They are subject to less criticism than most public figures because they do not have to face elections and because capitalist ideology insulates them from public scrutiny.[74] Unlike the original "rugged individuals" who started their corporations, they are not great risk-takers—certainly not with their own funds.

So much has been made of the separation of ownership and control in corporate America that the dictum increasingly sounds like a worn-out cliché, yet the supreme significance of this phenomenon is as fresh today as it was in the 1920s. In their classic study,[75] Berle and Means showed that in 1929 about 44 percent of the two hundred largest nonfinancial corporations in the United States were governed by "self-perpetuating" managers. Robert Larner has found that in the 1960s, some 85 percent of the two hundred top-ranking companies were dominated by their management; that is, no group of stockholders owned more than 10 percent of the corporations' voting stock.[76]

In 1978, a Senate Subcommittee on Finances found that in 122 of America's largest corporations, accounting for 41 percent of the total outstanding common stocks in the United States, the big institutional investors (commercial banks, insurance companies, and mutual funds) throw their votes behind management, keeping in power executives who may not be working in the best interest of all stockholders. One of the subcommittee's conclusions was that control of as little as 1 or 2 percent of a company's voting stock can exert a disproportionate leverage on its policy.

Small stockholders' scrutiny into U.S. corporate practices have so far been limited to some noisy barrages of criticism by a number of "professional gadflies" who attend annual meetings of corporations in which they own a few shares and confront the company's management with their inquiries. The power of individual shareholders to change the company's management or policies is almost nil. All they can do is to sell their shares.[77] In some states, the law allows a majority of the stockholders to dispense with annual meetings altogether.

Corporate bureaucracy—which Professor Galbraith prefers to call *technostructure*—manages, in his opinion, to preserve its "autonomy"—from its shareholders, creditors, and even the state—by becoming administratively self-centered, financially self-sufficient, and technologically more complex.[78] In the stinging words of a former corporate executive: "In the Consciousness Zero land of

74. See Andrew Hacker, "The Making of a (Corporate) President," *New York Times Magazine,* 2 April 1967.

75. A. A. Berle and G. C. Means, *The Modern Corporation and Private Property* (New York: Macmillan, 1932).

76. R. J. Larner, *Management Control and the Large Corporation* (New York: Dunellen, 1970).

77. General Motors has nearly 300 million shares, owned by over a million stockholders. But no shareholders' proposal opposed by management has ever been approved by the annual meeting in GM history.

78. See J. K. Galbraith, *The New Industrial State,* chapters 6 and 7.

the corporate giants, competition where it counts is a joke, the market place where it matters is a myth, and what is left of free America is being eaten alive by a few hundred monster corporations while government branches, departments, bureaus and agencies serve as chefs, waiters and busboys."[79]

In the opinion of other critics, the U.S. managerial elite are more likely to run publicly owned corporations in their own private interests than in the interests of corporate owners. Others believe that U.S. big business has now an effective veto power over the solutions to collective problems such as energy and the environment. But Berle and Means, who first attracted America's attention to the managerial power, later agreed that the exclusion of giant corporations from shareholders' pressures is bound to make them more socially responsible and even more efficient. And as management is not under much pressure to reach for maximum profits, administered prices may not be raised as high as corporate power would allow or as much as the market would bear. A more sympathetic book argues that U.S. corporate bureaucracy is being gradually modified in favor of "participatory management," which tends to reward education and expertise more than seniority and conformity, and to embrace more imaginative approaches to corporate planning with a view toward social welfare.[80]

The rosier side of the corporate picture is not hard to see. Affluent America owes much of its wealth, vitality, and enviable power to the ingenuity, effort, and productivity of some giant corporations. Corporate bureaucracy has been largely responsible for the continuity of operation, accumulation of technical knowledge and experience, training, and improvement of specialists. Many corporate managers have become first-class public servants. Big business has also been a main source of large private philanthropy. A large part of anticorporate criticism, it seems, is due to the fact that many people refuse to accept modern corporations as a bureaucratic entity engaged in high-level bargaining with other entrenched bureaucracies: labor, government, foundations. Modern large corporate giants present some of the same weaknesses (and strengths) as a full-blown government or labor bureaucracy. Administrative inefficiency, intramural rivalry, and empire building are often found in many large firms. The same type of politicking for appropriations, scheming for greater publicity, secrecy, backbiting, friction, personnel raiding, proliferation of research, and duplication of services that one ordinarily expects to find among governmental agencies also hold sway among corporate divisions.[81]

---

79. R. C. Townsend, "The Root of All Evil—Concentrated Economic Power," *New York Times Book Review*, 30 May 1971.

80. See G. E. Berkley, *The Administrative Revolution* (Englewood Cliffs: Prentice-Hall. 1971).

81. In an immense wealth of materials on modern corporations, the reader may wish to consult some of the "classics": E. S. Mason, ed. *The Corporation in Modern Society* (New York: Atheneum, 1966); Andrew Hacker, ed., *The Corporation Takeover* (Garden City: Doubleday, 1965); T. M. Garrett, *Business Ethics* (New York: Appleton, 1966); Paul A. Baran and P. M. Sweezy, *Monopoly Capital* (New York: Monthly Review, 1966); and R. J. Barber, *The American Corporation* (New York: Dutton, 1970).

Labor Unions. Another principal bargaining group in the United States is organized labor. Trade unions take part not only in collective bargaining with management over wages and working conditions; they also serve as a key agent in most social bargains. The big powerful unions—AFL-CIO, Auto Workers, and Teamsters—exert a crucial influence in ordering national priorities, shaping resource allocation, and determining the pace of technological innovation.

Union influence is exerted through different channels. Labor leaders are influential in helping politicians get elected to public office; they have a lot to say in the passage of socioeconomic legislation; their support is often sought for patronage dispensation; and they play a key role in the success of government incomes policies. Trade union's bargaining power emanates from their membership size, their leadership's skills, their legally recognized bargaining rights (including the right to go on strike), their lobbying tactics, and their restrictive practices.

Membership in U.S. unions, totalling 22.5 million by latest count, represents about 30 percent of nonfarm labor and about 22 percent of the total work force—smaller than in most industrial countries and down from a 34 percent peak in 1955. There are 114 trade unions affiliated with the giant American Federation of Labor and the Congress of Industrial Organizations, having a total membership of about 14 million. Another sixty or so independent or unaffiliated unions claim an additional 6 million members. Of the latter, the Brotherhood of Teamsters and the United Automobile Workers, both formerly affiliated with the AFL-CIO, are the largest, with a reported membership of 1.9 million and 1.4 million, respectively. The National Education Association, with 1.9 million membership, is technically not a union, but serves as such for its members.

Of the 15 million federal, state, county, and city workers, some 3 million are reportedly union members. Public employee unions—the American Federation of Government Employees, the American Federation of State, County and Municipal Employees, the American Federation of Teachers, and, to a much larger respect, the postal unions—are actually better organized than unions in the private sector. They exert increasing pressure on all levels of government for higher salaries, for changes in civil service regulations, for a greater voice in management policies, and, in general, for sharing power with government administrators.[82]

Based on the original notion of industrial democracy, American labor leaders often call their unions "brotherhoods" of one thing or another. In reality, however, most U.S. labor unions, particularly at the national level, operate through a hierarchy similar to that of government and business corporations. Union "democracy," except for being younger and less sophisticated than political democracy, shares with business and government many problems of representation and control. As corporate managers are often independent of corporate shareholders in managerial decisions, and congressmen are disowned by their constituents in

82. Public unions also play an important role in airing employee grievances before the public, combating race, age, and sex discrimination within the federal bureaucracy, and educating the government to be a "good" employer.

some of their votes, so are labor leaders divorced from their rank and file on many important issues. Frequent polls taken among workers from a dozen big unions repeatedly reveal union members' disavowal of their leaders' stand on some social issues.

The American trade union's right to negotiate collectively with management was legally sanctioned in the National Labor Relations Act of 1935 as amended by the Taft-Hartley Act of 1947 and the Landrum-Griffith Act of 1959. The bargaining process is characterized by four distinctive features. First, most bargaining, even by large unions, is decentralized and fairly democratic. Industrywide bargaining is limited to a few unions, notably coal and steel. Second, because of the basically centralized nature of bargaining, as well as the union's ability to withstand fairly prolonged strikes and its insistence on direct bargaining without government intervention, the extent of industrial conflict is relatively high. Third, government intervention in union affairs is largely limited to the regulation and mediation of the bargaining process rather than the substance of the bargains. Finally, the basic philosophy of American unionism has been businesslike, conservative, and apolitical, within the private enterprise system and away from radical ideological movements of their European counterparts.

Presently, in some important industries (auto, steel, railroads, and trucking) the entire work force is covered by collectively bargained wages. Union contracts usually cover, in addition to the hourly wage rates, such issues as union shop, the work load and work speed, production methods, union security, seniority rights, grievance procedures, and fringe benefits.

U.S. labor unions are unquestionably a dominant bargaining force in the major mass-production industries, transportation and communications, public utilities, housing and construction, mining, and increasingly in the city, state, and federal services. In some important industries, almost all workers are union members.[83] Although the net effects of trade unionism on labor's share in GNP is a matter of dispute, organized labor credits itself with gains resulting from its direct bargainings. Indirectly, too, labor is active in political propaganda, in helping or hindering the election of political candidates, in exacting better deals from the Congress and state legislatures, and in offering advice and support in various national advisory councils. Of greater importance to political elections, perhaps, is the nonmonetary contribution by trade unions, volunteer workers doing all types of vote-getting chores. On top of this comes the money spent by unions on "political education," subtle propaganda in favor of or against individual candidates and issues. Unions are showing increasing interest in such areas as import restrictions, tax reform, national health insurance, aid to education, social security benefits, civil rights, and foreign aid.

Labor unions like to call themselves "the people's lobby." Their variegated lobbying techniques match other interest groups' efforts in both magnitude and

83. An estimated 20 million nonunion workers also have their pay tied directly to union wage levels.

scope. Among them are deluging Congressmen with letters, persuasion-and-pressure contacts with members of Congress and statehouses by special representatives, flooding influential decision makers and molders of public opinion with briefs showing the labor side of social issues, and indirect political contributions to favorite members' campaigns. There are an estimated one hundred or more union lobbyists in Washington, one-third of them full-time professionals, dealing with the White House and Capitol Hill. The labor lobby is also reportedly one of Washington's most influential and effective as well as generous.

Bargainers within the Government.   Under U.S. pluralism, the government is an unmatched bargainer. Within the federal executive branch, there is constant bargaining among bureaus for funds and favor from the chief executive. There is bargaining between the president on the one hand, and Congress and special-interest groups, on the other. And peculiar as it may seem, public departments and bureaus, too, often serve as a kind of informal, if not disguised, lobby in Congress for their "constituents."

At the very top of the executive "bargaining team" is the president of the United States. By virtue of his specific constitutional power independent of the legislatures, his direct responsibility to the electorate, and his titular leadership of the party in power, the chief executive gives final effect to the will of the majority. He is the supreme administrator of the "spoils system" (where party workers are given public office as a reward for their services to the party); the final arbiter of rivalry among government bureaus that report directly to him; the main formulator of the administration's legislative programs; and the "bargainer-in-chief" among competing pressure groups.[84] He is the head back-scratcher, the master log roller, and the paramount dispenser of patronage positions. Other members of the executive team consist of the White House staff, cabinet officers, independent agency heads, top military leaders, state governors, heads of presidential advisory commissions, presidential appointees, and other top-ranking bureaucrats.

Influential members of Congress (party leaders, commitee chairmen, and popular mavericks) form another powerful bargaining group. By virtue of their safe seats in Congress, their seniority, or personal talent, they are usually in a position to exact a fairly high price for their concurrence in bargainable issues. While individual congressmen and senators, as a rule, serve as effective lobbyists for their districts and states when it comes to federal appropriations, it is usually the chairmen of standing committees and appointees to the House-Senate Conference committees that wield greatest power. Certain congressional committee chairmen are matched in their bargaining position perhaps only by the president himself.

The much publicized "military-industrial complex" is one of the outstanding public lobbies.[85] This power bloc is composed of the Pentagon, the defense

---

84. For a discussion of the different styles of presidency, see Richard Neustadt, *Presidential Power* (New York: Wiley, 1960).

85. This expression was first used by President Dwight Eisenhower in his oft-quoted "farewell address," in which he warned against "the disastrous rise of misplaced power" by the military and industrial establishments over the traditionally democratic life of the American people.

industry, a host of military research facilities, and the military's friends in and out of Congress. The significance of this "complex" lies in its huge size (accounting for more than 8 percent of the GNP) and particularly in its crucial influence in determining national priorities. The defense establishment, according to one estimate, constitutes the nation's largest single activity, employing nearly one-tenth of the labor force, dealing with some 120,000 defense suppliers, and having impact on more than 80 percent of all congressional districts.[86] The military-industrial complex probably has as many articulate defenders as it has detractors, but one noticeable effect of its bargaining power seems to have been an almost continuous expansion of military spending in the postwar years through an effective lobbying operation in Congress and with the executive.[87]

The Post Office lobby is another strong and expert public pressure group. The three postal unions have always had recourse to Congress directly and, until the establishment of the new Postal Service in 1971, used their bargaining leverage in obtaining wage increases from the lawmakers. But while the military and postal workers are usually singled out as the most powerful of bureaucratic pressure groups, public-sector lobbying is by no means limited to them.[88] Any large appropriation in the U.S. federal budget (and in the budgets of populous industrial states and large metropolitan cities) has its own strong pressure group that constantly presses for that item's undiminished continuation, if not substantial increase. This is as much true with defense as it is with the highway program, the agricultural price support, research grants to universities, free milk in public schools, or government reorganization.[89]

Special Private Lobbies. U.S. private pressure groups present perhaps the most picturesque mosaic of the American pluralist system. The Americans for Democratic Action support social-welfare measures; the John Birch Society and the American Conservative Union oppose welfarism. The Women's Christian Temperance Union fights for prohibition; distillers push for lower excise taxes on liquor and stiffer fair-trade laws. Dairymen and dairy-state congressmen push for government school milk programs. The American Legion and the Veterans of Foreign Wars seek expanded benefits for American servicemen. The National Association of

---

86. For a more detailed and critical discussion, see H. I. Schiller and J. D. Phillips, eds., *Super-State: Readings in the Military Industrial Complex* (Urbana: University of Illinois Press, 1971).

87. Well over 2,000 high-ranking former military officers are reportedly in the service of 100 big defense corporations.

88. In some years, the United Federation of Postal Clerks (the biggest of the three) has been at the top of the list in Washington big spending lobbyists.

89. Examples abound. Labor unions, manufacturers, and farmers effectively blocked President Johnson's proposal for the establishment of a single department of "economic affairs" for fear that the voice of their particular spokesmen in the existing departments of Labor, Commerce, and Agriculture would be lost in the combined agency. The maritime lobby forced Congress to exclude the Maritime Administration from the Department of Transportation, which had been advocated as the only means of establishing coordinated policy in the four major means of transportation.

Manufacturers and the U.S. Chamber of Commerce fight for tariffs and oppose taxes. Environmentalists try to mobilize the public into a vocal constituency for conservation. The National Association of Professional Bureaucrats is the spokesman for the "unsung heroes" of the U.S. bureaucracy. The League of Women Voters champions various causes, not necessarily involving either women or voting. The National Welfare Rights Organization is described by its leaders as a "card-carrying, dues-paying organization" of poor people.

There are an estimated six thousand trade and professional associations in the United States. The *Congressional Quarterly*, which publishes expenditures reported to Congress by registered lobbyists under the 1946 Federal Lobbying Act, lists over three hundred organizations engaged in lobbying and spending millions of dollars on various causes. Each industry, and in fact each major economic activity, has its own association. There is the Iron and Steel Institute, the Tobacco Institute, the Association of American Railroads, the American Petroleum Institute, and so on.[90] The number of active lobbies in the U.S., however, substantially exceeds the reported figures, for many pressure groups, such as the U.S. Chamber of Commerce, do not consider themselves a lobby on the ground that their principal objective is not lobbying. Many government units, municipalities, and public agencies make frequent use of lobbyists in Washington without ever registering. According to one estimate, there are some two thousand registered lobbyists in the capital, but the actual number is probably close to fifteen thousand—or about thirty lobbyists for every member of Congress. Due to innumerable loopholes in the 1946 law, the bulk of lobby spendings usually go unreported. The law is not strictly enforced, and perhaps not enforceable.[91] Private lobbies usually work through their "men in Washington" or at the state capitals. Most of these men are meticulously familiar with the U.S. politicoeconomic system. Former Congressmen, aides and friends of former presidents, ex-cabinet officers, ex-federal regulatory commission members, former agency heads, Pentagon officers, and other assorted retired bureaucrats form a colorful coterie of lobbyists by the Potomac. They have their fraternal ties with their former colleagues; they have privileged entrée to high offices; they know the pitfalls and dark corners in the legislative and bureaucratic labyrinths. Each statehouse, also, has its own lobbyists.[92]

Not all U.S. lobbying activities are necessarily harmful to society, nor always a distortion in resource allocation. Knowledgeable and seasoned lobbyists often

90. Foreign governments, too, make ample use of counsel and contacts of special lobbyists. Under the Foreign Agents Registration Act, there are reportedly five hundred active registrations on file with the Justice Department.

91. For a detailed account of lobbying activities in the United States, see James Deakin, *The Lobbyists* (Washington: Public Affairs Press, 1966); L. W. Milbrath, *The Washington Lobbyists* (Chicago: Rand McNally, 1963); V. O. Key, *Politics, Parties and Pressure Groups* (New York: Harper, 1964); L. H. Ziegler and G. W. Peak, *Interest Groups in American Society* (Englewood Cliffs: Prentice-Hall, 1972); and "Rise of the Power Brokers," *U.S. News and World Report*, 10 March 1980.

92. See Ronald Goldfarb, "A Fifth Estate—Washington Lawyers," *New York Times Magazine*, 5 May 1968.

exercise a moderating, public-oriented influence on their clients, while, at the same time, they educate public officials and their aides against the pitfalls of too hasty or emotion-packed decisions. Almost all lobbying activities, however, affect the production and/or distribution of income.

Among private pressure groups, the "farm bloc" usually stands out as a powerful lobby, with the million-member American Farm Bureau Federation probably the strongest political force in it. The Farm Bureau is on record against government regulation of farming, against agricultural subsidies, and for free markets; it opposes the unionization of farm workers and the extension of the Fair Labor Practices Act to agriculture. But it provides a strong countervailing force to supporters of protectionist measures. The National Farmers Union, by contrast, is for continued and expanded farm subsidies.[93] Under "farm bloc" proddings, Congress has passed among a host of statutes affecting agriculture, the Agricultural Fair Practices Act of 1968 which protects the rights of farmers to join voluntary bargaining associations to deal with big canning and processing companies.

The oil lobby represents an industry vital to the security of the United States and a heavy contributor to electoral campaigns of both U.S. major political parties. Under the oil lobby's pressure, oil imports into the United States have been restricted by a system of quotas; and U.S. oil companies have been allowed to deduct a sizable percentage of their gross income as depletion allowance for federal corporate income tax purposes. This efficient and influential lobby is also credited with successful efforts to shelve an Interior Department plan for low-sulphur, less-pollutant oil production; to block a consumer-backed proposal for a foreign trade zone and oil refinery in Maine; to secure lucrative offshore oil leases; for oil price decontrol; and for a continued round of price increases and extraordinary profits.[94]

The medical lobby is another powerful pressure group in America. The median net income of U.S. physicians is probably close to four times the national average, and much larger than the average for other professions requiring similar training and skill. Doctors' fees and hospital costs have also been rising much faster than the national average of either prices or wages in recent years. At the core of this sustained prosperity is the 122-year-old American Medical Association. The AMA has for years kept a tight rein over U.S. health care, the number of medical schools, and hospital privileges for practicing physicians.[95] The policy has been defended

93. Despite demonstrable proof that agricultural subsidies do not help the small farmer, the practice continues. Large and prosperous producers (including some influential members of Congress) are major beneficiaries of the farm subsidy. See C. L. Schultze, *The Distribution of Farm Subsidies* (Washington: Brookings Institution, 1971).

94. A *New York Times* editorial said, "The American oil industry is a kind of private government, an entity which has had sufficient political power to shape the petroleum policies of the Government in Washington, not only through its influence in key Congressional committees but by direct pressure on the White House." See "Oil and Inflation," 10 March 1969.

95. See Ed Cray, *In Failing Health: The Medical Crisis and the A.M.A.* (Indianapolis: Bobbs-Merrill, 1971); and B. and J. Ehrenreich *The American Health Empire: Power, Profits and Politics* (New York: Random House, 1971).

ostensibly in the name of maintaining high standards of medical care in the U.S. Throughout its history, however, the AMA has consistently supported conservative political causes. In recent years its main political effort has been focused on defeating national health insurance schemes.[96]

The "education lobby" is the outcome of the spectacular rise in U.S. school enrollment in the immediate postwar period and the increasing responsibility placed on the federal government for aid to education. This lobby is a loose coalition of more than eighty groups consisting of teachers, school officials, trustees and board members, publishers, equipment makers, and consulting groups benefiting from the education market. The coalition works through a dozen or more seasoned professional lobbyists in Washington. Their methods of operation follow standard procedures. They draft education authorization and appropriation bills, organize local pressures on individual members of Congress, contact key congressional leaders at the Capitol, pack the galleries with educators flown in from the districts of politically troubled Congressmen, and physically haul lawmakers to the House floor to cast a crucial vote.

The "Outsiders." Among the organizations not directly involved with the government, but trying to influence social and economic policies, are the "outsiders," the news media, private foundations, research groups, and advisory councils. There are nearly 2,500 daily and Sunday newspapers and 7,500 broadcasting stations in the United States. The majority, however, are not independent voices of the people. About 60 percent of the dailies are owned by a few giant publishing houses that also own radio and TV stations, although not all in the same locality. Furthermore, "canned" editorials, "canned" cartoons, and syndicated columns carried by a large number of independent newspapers in different cities reflect rather narrow and sectarian viewpoints. For these reasons, a few East-Coast newspapers and the four or five national TV networks wield extraordinary influence on the Congress, the bureaucracy, and the White House in the formulation of socioeconomic policies.

Private, largely tax-exempt philanthropic foundations and charitable organizations form another pressure group in the United States. There are reportedly more than 26,000 foundations with total assets of more than $20 billion, disbursing about $1.5 billion in gifts each year.[97] The Ford Foundation alone has reportedly more than $3.5 billion in assets, disbursing more than $100 million annually. These foundations use their bargaining power, both material and nonmaterial, in taking on the problems of income distribution, race relations, urbanism, and political representations. Some top foundations have been called a "political lobby." Private foundations play a vital social role in the American economy by providing financial

96. One of the association's past presidents called health care a "privilege" and *not* a "right" for individuals and urged his fellow doctors to resist government health planning as inimical to the "American way of life—capitalism."

97. Most of these foundations, however, are very small and for very limited purposes. Foundations with assets of more than $1 million are fewer than 3,000. Those with more than $10 million, fewer than 250.

assistance to activities constitutionally forbidden to the government, such as aid to religion; they promote operations that are politically impractical or difficult for the state, such as controversial research; and they support institutions that are economically unprofitable to private industry, such as education, art, and health care.[98]

There is also what may be called a "research lobby," a congeries of researchers in government laboratories or on various types of federal grants in universities and private foundations, which press both the White House and the Congress for more money. Congressional and administrative appropriations for scientific research and development generally respond to the pressures exerted by members of various research groups, most of whom have direct or indirect professional connections with defense contractors, business laboratories, university departments, and government agencies.

There are also some two hundred independent "think tanks," such as the Brookings Institution and the American Free Enterprise Institute, along with broad public-interest groups like Common Cause and the Ralph Nader organization, and hundreds of "single-issue" lobbies (fifty-three for minorities, thirty-four for social welfare agencies, thirty-one for the environment, fifteen for the aging, and six for population control). There are lobbies in behalf of foreign countries (over sixty for Japan). Finally, connections with the chief executive and Congressional leaders by hundreds of "advisory councils" give them a crucial voice in policy formulation, both in the public and private sectors. Both political parties make frequent use of such councils and committees in order to gain support of the business community for their particular policies and also to learn a good deal in the area where business expertise is urgently required.

Formal Bargaining Techniques

As can be seen from the foregoing discussion, in a very large, although not precisely measurable sector of the U.S. economy, resource allocations and income distribution are essentially determined by direct and indirect bargaining among pressure groups. The techniques of bargaining in the U.S. differ among different groups and on the different issues. Most formal bargains are made collectively between labor and management, largely outside the political arena. Some important compromises, however, involve direct or indirect use of politics. Congressional budgetary appropriations, for example, present largely above-board bargains between democratic representatives and special-interest groups, including "professional" bureaucrats. Nonbudgetary legislation favoring special interests (tariffs, quotas, tax exemptions) are obtained through various forms of indirect political maneuvering.

98. For further discussion, see *Tax Exempt Foundations and Charitable Trusts: Their Impact on Our Economy*, Select Committee on Small Business, U.S. House of Representatives, 89th Congress (Washington: GPO, 1966) pp. 3–14. See also J. C. Goulden, *The Money Givers* (New York: Random House, 1971).

There are also almost always some behind-the-scenes machinations, in and out of the government, in determining national priorities.

Labor-Management Bargains. Union-industry collective bargaining is the most open and above-board of all social bargains. The overriding function and preoccupation of labor unions, as an organized lobby for the aspirations of working men and women, is collective bargaining with employers. U.S. labor unions are commonly referred to as the "bread-and-butter" unions, because they emphasize greater material gains for their members and treat social issues and political activities as only auxiliary actions.[99]

U.S. labor economists generally credit American union leaders with five broad common objectives in the process of collective bargaining: the union's survival and strength as a viable institution for collective action; the desire for raising wages and improving working conditions; the perennial demand for acquiring certain managerial prerogatives with respect to control over jobs, automation, profit sharing, and job security; a kind of flirtation with the old, humanistic drives for making industry responsive to human needs; and personal ambitions for greater prestige, power, income, and social recognition.

On the management side, the main objectives in collective bargaining have to do with developing a strategy for accommodating union demands without abandoning management prerogatives, hurting stockholders, or losing customers. Within this context, management is believed to follow five specific goals: an obvious interest in preserving the identity, strength, and efficiency of the business enterprise; a concern with safeguarding managerial power; a desire for increased labor productivity; an "ideological" concern with promoting free enterprise; and a drive toward empire building and greater prestige, status, and power.[100]

Collective bargaining provides a civilized, businesslike, and orderly vehicle for harmonizing the objectives of the two parties. While frustrating stalemates, costly strikes, occasional violence, and eventual government intervention can not always be prevented through amicable union-management relations, successful collective bargaining is often responsible for finalizing an overwhelming majority of wage contracts without difficulties.

The extent to which U.S. labor unions are able to affect the structure and level of wage rates (and hence the allocation of the "social dividend") is still a matter of controversy. Union leaders naturally tend to claim credit for substantial

99. In France and Italy, by contrast, trade unions are fundamentally political movements engaged in direct political action. And in Great Britain and Scandinavian countries, unions show interest in both political action and economic benefits.

100. See F. H. Harbison, "Collective Bargaining and American Capitalism," in A. Kornhauser, ed., *Industrial Conflict* (New York: McGraw Hill, 1954). The election of Douglas Fraser, President of the United Automobile Workers, to the Board of Directors of the Chrysler Corporation in May 1980, is considered a landmark decision. For the first time in the history of U.S. labor relations, management responsibility has been given to a union leader.

improvements in labor incomes in the past few decades. Some economists, on the other hand, argue that much of what labor has gained in the postwar period has been due to the progressive and dynamic nature of the American economy, which would have come about with or without unions. The consensus is that labor unions certainly serve their own members, at least, in the majority of industrial disputes. Unions have secured for organized workers not only higher wages but also important fringe benefits: pensions, insurance, paid vacation, layoff pay, and health care.

Abstracting from the merits or demerits of arguments about the net effects of unionism on the welfare of the working classes, certain observations are probably incontestable. First, collectively bargained contracts for a length of time introduce a certain rigidity in wage rates adjustment, particularly downward. Second, workers usually expect to receive increases in wages and fringe benefits every time their contract is up for renewal. Third, unions tend to exert a steady upward pressure on wage rates. Fourth, when labor's bargaining power exceeds management's, wages may rise faster than productivity. Fifth, higher negotiated wages may produce unemployment, at least in the short run. Sixth, when unemployment exceeds the politically irreducible minimum, the government is generally expected to create new demand, directly or indirectly, with assured inflationary consequences.

Government Mediation. Government participation in multilateral bargaining with unions and employers in the United States has, for the most part, been limited to mediation and conciliation efforts. Part of these efforts have been prescribed by law and put forth through such agencies as the National Mediation Board (for railroads and airlines) and the Federal Mediation and Conciliation Service (for other industries). State and local governments often offer their own services for settling local disputes. Mediation and conciliation efforts by the government are to a large extent voluntary.

Government intervention in settling industrial disputes through mediation or political persuasion has come about gradually, reluctantly, and under the pressure of imminent dangers to national safety and security. In the aftermath of postwar strikes, wage-price spirals, and labor's increasing political power, some angry demands were made by the public for labor-law reforms. The 1947 Labor-Management Relations Act (the Taft-Hartley Law) defined new standards for union conduct and business practices and gave the government new power to intervene in certain labor disputes.

Since then, whenever labor disputes have threatened national security or public welfare, the government has intervened in a number of different ways, from frequent declarations of eighty-day cooling-off periods to an occasional temporary "takeover" of the industry.[101] Compulsory arbitration, by the state, widely used in

101. Under the Kennedy-Johnson administration, occasional "arm twisting" by the White House and routine intervention by the secretary of labor influenced the outcome of many labor settlements. The Nixon administration, on the other hand, believed that labor and management should work out their own disputes.

Europe and elsewhere, has been employed only occasionally in the United States—and mostly by the federal government during wartime emergencies.[102] While the government and a few industry leaders in railroads, airlines, and steel have supported compulsory arbitration, a majority of union members and corporate executives oppose the idea. Some unions have rejected even a voluntary agreement to submit unresolved issues to binding arbitration. In most cases, management and labor believe that their disputes should be solved through their own bargaining power, without outside interference. The essence of this argument is that compulsory arbitration would virtually put an end to collective bargaining.[103]

Informal Bargains by Pressure Groups

The objectives of lobbying in the United States, as elsewhere, are to secure, for a given interest group, the optimum possible benefits from the government or to minimize its losses through legal and extralegal means. The main instrument of such return optimization is influence peddling in the right places and with the right people.

"Influence peddling," states a *Time* essay, "is, in a sense, what democracy is all about." Adds another *Time* article, "Without lobbying, Goverment could not function." The American democracy recognizes lobbying as a legitimate activity in promoting group interests as long as lobbyists register as such. This recognition is evidently rooted in a traditional American belief in the desirability of *dispersion* of power if *diffusion* should prove impossible.[104] Lobbying, according to the *Wall Street Journal*, has been transformed from "a haphazard, often crude practice" into "a calculated, sophisticated science." The modern lobbyist, contrary to the old image of "an affluent, swaggering individual, manipulating votes, throwing lavish parties," and operating in secrecy, is more likely to be "a polished, businesslike technician who deals largely with facts and, as a rule, works out in the open."

Other means of securing special favors through lobbying are endless. As a *Time* cover story indicates, a single clause inserted in, or removed from, the 32,000-page *Federal Register* of regulations can put a small-town manufacturer out of

102. In the postwar period, the U.S. Congress on several occasions has ordered compulsory arbitration to settle railroad and airline disputes in order to avert nationwide strikes.

103. In the area of tripartite government-business-labor settlement of issues, two U.S. experiments are worth noting here. In the spring of 1971, a twelve-member Construction Industry Stabilization Committee composed equally of the representatives of government, labor, and management was set up to review and approve all wage settlements in each craft, and to establish guidelines for further settlements. In 1971–72, a fifteen-member tripartitie Pay Board had the power to set noninflationary wage guidelines and to approve collectively bargained wages and fringe benefits within the framework of those guidelines.

104. Many people believe that if it were not for Ralph Nader's persistent prodding, Congress would not have bothered about auto safety, tire quality, unhealthy meats, poultry and fish, leaky gas pipelines, and excess radiation from X-rays.

business or rejuvenate a near-bankrupt industry. The strategy against a particular measure to minimize possible losses runs on similar lines. The lobbyists first try to defeat or postpone its passage through the legislature, regulatory commissions, or administrative agencies. Failing to do so, they may try to water down the objectionable parts of the measure by diluting amendments, provisos, and preconditions. If the measure is passed despite their opposition, they may attempt to challenge it in the courts on constitutional grounds. If this should prove costly or impractical, they may try to persuade legislators not to appropriate sufficient money to carry out the law's provisions. Should they fail on this score, too, they may attempt to prevail on the executive branch not to spend the money appropriated by the legislature. Failing this, strong lobbies usually see to it that public officials unfriendly to business interests are not appointed or reappointed to the enforcement agencies.

Bargaining as a Major Decision Making Process

American capitalism has been called a system of power play among countervailing forces. Bigness in business, in labor, in government, in the press and mass media, and even in universities has been a self-reinforcing trend in modern American history. The emergence of power groups in the American society has, in turn, followed the progress of the U.S. economy.

Professor Galbraith shows how U.S. farmers, since the colonial days of the mid-eighteenth century, have tried to offset their relatively weaker bargaining power in the market, first by expanding demand for farm products; then, by supporting antitrust legislation against industrial and processing trusts; and, finally, by organizing cooperatives and obtaining government price guarantees for basic farm products in exchange for accepting limited marketing quotas.[105] Professor Perlman traces the origin of the American labor movement to the time and circumstances under which "the sovereignty of American government was confronted with the apparently stronger sovereignty of American business."[106] Unionism has developed to match the monopolistic power of employers. Professor Lindblom, and others, contend that American labor unions' success in their persistent pressures for higher wages and more extensive fringe benefits has undermined price stability and/or full employment. Unchecked inflation and/or mass employment, in their view, has in turn weakened the foundation of the private enterprise system and invited a gigantic government bureaucracy.[107]

There is much talk about "union conglomerates" (a single negotiating team

105. See J. K. Galbraith, *American Capitalism: The Concept of Countervailing Power*, (Boston: Houghton Mifflin, 1956).

106. Selig Perlman, "The Basic Philosophy of the American Labor Movement," *Annals of the American Academy of Political and Social Science*, March 1951.

107. C. E. Lindblom, *Unions and Capitalism* (New Haven: Yale University Press, 1949).

made up of all the unions involved) to deal with multimarket and multi-industry corporations. Such concerted and conglomerate bargaining among big business and big labor, if and when practical, would involve inflationary pressures, work stoppages, and threats to national safety and security; it would also inevitably set the stage for the government's direct entry into industrial disputes. In such national issues as inflation, foreign competition, cheap labor immigration, consumer protection, and technological change, the government cannot simply remain silent or uninterested. The ever increasing influence of government over the American economy—itself ever increasing in complexity—naturally leads to the expansion and significance of lobbying activities.

Thus, apart from that portion of GNP directly allocated and used by the formal process of collective bargaining between labor and management, a very large part is also informally determined by the actions of pressure groups. Without the risk of much exaggeration, one may argue that the entire federal, state, and local budgets are for the most part extensively influenced, if not altogether determined, by group interests. Every dollar collected, as well as every dollar spent, by the government at all levels is based on a piece of legislation that is, in the final analysis, a compromise between the conflicting objectives and interests of major pressure groups (and recently of single-issue organizations).

Organized interest groups work on all levels and among all agencies of government. The games they play include influencing public opinion by overt propaganda or subtle subliminal persuasion; logrolling and back-scratching with other lobbies; manipulating political elections by campaign contributions and other means; serving in governmental advisory committees; organizing grass-roots support (pickets, marches, letter-writing campaigns); the use of "key resource people" (those who have special influence on a legislator—a campaign contributor, an old army buddy, or a law partner); and a host of other highly sophisticated measures.

Some of the most familiar techniques used on U.S. legislators and government officials include drafting bills, amendments, and speeches for friendly high officials; buttonholding undecided legislators at opportune moments; issuing pertinent newsletters; giving testimony before congressional committees; explaining intricacies of a complex legislation to undecided representatives; dispensing gifts (anything from campaign contributions to tickets to cultural and sport events, to company airplanes for private travels); and extending subtle personal favors. Among the positive ways that pressure groups obtain optimum benefits from the government is the enactment of special tax treatments for various economic activities: a deduction, an allowance, an exemption, a credit, a loophole, or a preferential rate. Although not all such breaks presently included in the U.S. Internal Revenue Code has been acquired through pressure-group techniques, many of them (oil depletion allowance, investment credit, tax preferences) were so acquired.[108]

108. For a further discussion of the role of pressure groups and some handy references, see J. E. Anderson, *Politics and the Economy* (Boston: Little, Brown, 1966); *The Washington Lobby* (Washington Congressional Quarterly, 1971); "The Swarming Lobbyist," *Time*, 7 August 1978; "Single-Issue Politics," *Newsweek*, 6 November 1978; and "Who Owns Congress," *Washington Post Magazine*, 8 June 1980.

The Scope of Command

While the command mechanism occupies the least important role in the U.S. economy, its manifold use and growing significance should not be underestimated. The federal government's *direct* involvement in the economy goes back to the beginning of the republic itself, but its recent spectacular growth dates from the middle 1930s, when the National Resource Planning Board was established, among other things, to provide jobs for the Depression-ridden industrial workers of urban America. The Works Projects Administration, under President Roosevelt's New Deal, brought the government to the very center of public ownership and operation. Today, Washington is not only a policeman, a regulator, and a bargainer, but also a large employer, an industrialist, a guardian of financial order, and a direct dispenser of enormous sums of money.

The federal bureaucracy is America's biggest business: it buys more goods and services, builds more structures, employs more people, handles more money, and spends more for scientific research than any other U.S. organization—or any agency in the whole non-centrally directed world.[109] The governments in the United States—federal, state and local—are the country's biggest growth industry. At the turn of the century, only 4 percent of the work force was on the public payroll; in 1980, the percentage was nearly 17. In 1929, all governments accounted for only 10 percent of GNP; in 1980, the percentage reached 33. The federal budget submitted under President Harding, by the first Budget Bureau, amounted to only $3.2 billion. President Carter's expenditure budget for fiscal 1981 amounted to $613 billion. Total spending by state and local governments in fiscal 1981 was estimated to be an additional $350 billion. By some conservative estimates, some 65 to 70 million persons—nearly a third of all Americans—depend on the government for their income.[110] The federal government alone had nearly 5 million employees in 1980.

The raison d'être of government ownership and enterprise in the United States follows by and large the traditional rationale of public enterprise the world over. National defense and public security have been two of the most crucial considerations in the establishment of U.S. weapons system development, space exploration, postal service, and atomic energy research. Some public services, like public lending, education, and housing, have been undertaken on social-welfare grounds. The Alaskan Railroad and the Panama Canal were built by the government because profit prospects were too low and the risks too high. The TVA and rural electrification have been established on the basis of alleged public efficiency in offering ample, low-cost electricity. The ease of administration has been a main reason for "nationalizing" various public utilities at the local level.

109. For a quick education about the U.S. economy, see "The ABCs of How Our Economy Works," *U.S. News and World Report*, 1 May 1978 (Special Section).
110. About half of these are social security recipients; 15 to 20 million are on welfare.

Public Ownership

On account of these considerations, and partly also by historical circumstances, a significant amount of property has fallen into the U.S. government's hands. At present, the federal government is the world's biggest landlord and its richest property owner. More than one-third of the nation's land—most of Alaska, nearly half of eleven Western states, and 4 percent of total acreage in the thirty-eight remaining states—is estimated to be in federal ownership. The bulk of the 16,000 square miles of oil-shale land around the Rocky Mountains, with an estimated deposit worth billions of dollars, belongs to the federal government. While most of the federal land consists of national parks, forests, land preserves, and wilderness, the size of the public commercial domain is still noteworthy. State, county, and municipal landholdings amount to over 120 million acres. An estimate by the Bureau of the Budget puts the federal government's belongings at several hundred billion dollars. While nearly half of these holdings consist of military property, supplies, and equipment, the federal government still owns sizable amounts of buildings, nondefense installations, owership claims, cash, and other financial assets.

Public Enterprise

The federal, state, and, local governments in the United States are all, in varying degrees, engaged in a variety of business activities.[111] Federally owned or operated enterprises[112] comprise over eighty separate entities, from the giant, multibillion-dollars-a-year national postal corporation to a small laundry shop on a military base. Some of the enterprises, like the Commodity Credit Corporation, incur a deficit year after year; others, like TVA, are profitable. Some of these entities, like the CCC, are in the form of a public corporation; others, like park services, are unincorporated establishments. Federal, state, and local governments in the United States directly provide education, health, banking, insurance, real estate, power, transportation, and a host of other services.

Despite their variegated nature and vast scope, public enterprises still account for a very small part of the giant U.S. economy. Altogether, only about 1 percent of GNP is contributed by what the Department of Commerce classifies as "public enterprise."

111. For a more detailed discussion of various government enterprises, see Clair Wilcox, *Public Policies Toward Business* (Homewood.: Richard D. Irwin, 1979), part 4; and L. D. Musolf, *Government and the Economy* (Chicago: Scott, Foresman, 1965), chapters 5 and 6.

112. The term *public enterprise* is used here to include government activities dealing with the provision of goods and services, either for itself or for the public, that can be provided also by private enterprise. Thus, defense and justice, for example, are excluded, but postal service and insurance, among others, are included.

Postal Service. The mail service is probably the oldest federal enterprise in the United States. Created in 1789 by the Constitution as a special agency, and until 1971 a cabinet-level department, it symbolized by far the largest business-type public enterprise in America.

In 1971, the Post Office was converted into a new U.S. Postal Service as a nonprofit public enterprise. The service is run by an eleven-member governing board, a postmaster-general, and a rate commission. It has the power to borrow money, bargain collectively with its employees, and set postal rules and rates outside of direct congressional control.[113] The federal government continues its subsidy to the service for twelve years, after which it is expected to become self-supporting. Labor disputes are subject to compulsory arbitration. Strikes by local postal employees are outlawed.

Power. The production and distribution of electricity at the federal level goes back to the sale of power generated from dams built by the Bureau of Reclamation as early as 1906. A more outstanding example of federal power projects presently is the Tennessee Valley Authority. Created by an act of Congress in 1933, the TVA is a gigantic public enterprise directed by an independent board appointed by the president. The Authority is given the multipurpose task of flood control, navigation, and generation of electricity related to the first two objectives. The Authority produces electric power from its hydroelectric and steam plants; sets its own rates under broad congressional guidelines but subject to no other regulations; follows its own personnel policy; covers its operating costs out of its own business revenues; and finances its investments, partly by borrowing in the market. It pays no taxes, but its administrative budget and expansion plans have to be approved by Congress; its borrowing terms, by the Treasury. The federal government also owns and operates power projects built by the Bureau of Reclamation and the Corps of Engineers in the Colorado, Columbia, Missouri, and St. Lawrence basins.

Another outstanding example of federal enterprise in the power field is the Nuclear Regulatory Commission. As an outgrowth of U.S. atomic weapon development during World War II, the Atomic Energy Commission was established in 1946 as a public monopoly and given exclusive rights to the ownership, production, trade, patents, and private licensing related to fissionable materials. The NRC is now charged with the promotion of mining and exploration of atomic materials; it is to build and operate atomic power plants or license private contractors to provide such facilities; stimulate research; and supervise the dissemination of technical knowledge in the field.

At the state and local levels, power projects are also numerous. Several states are generating and selling hydroelectric power from multipurpose dams. Several hundred U.S. cities, too, have municipally owned and operated electric systems,

---

113. The service's authority for deciding rates is thus more limited than that possessed by the TVA and some municipal transit systems, which can unilaterally determine their own rates.

generating and/or distributing power from their steam plants or transmission facilities. In many cases, gas and water are also nationalized at the local government level. Like federal power projects, municipal enterprises enjoy the tax and borrowing advantages of a public enterprise and usually charge lower rates, but they are not always as efficient as private companies, largely because of the small scale of their operation.

Transport and Communications.   In addition to a mammoth, worldwide network of transport and communications services owned and operated by the various branches of the armed forces, the U.S. government currently operates the Panama Canal under a special treaty, runs the Alaskan railroads, owns and operates the National Railroad Passenger Corporation (Amtrak), and has a remnant of a commercial shipping operation under the Maritime Administration. The governments in some states operate barge canals, intercity transit systems, harbor facilities, grain elevators, air terminals, and industrial depots.

The construction and maintenance of major U.S. highways are in the hands of the states, which administer them partly out of federal revenues and partly through tolls collected and spent by special turnpike authorities. The urban transit systems in scores of American cities are publicly owned and operated by local municipalities.

The Communications Satellite Act of 1962 established a unique federally chartered quasi-public corporation—the Comsat—to build and operate a network of satellite and ground terminals for domestic and international transmission of telephone and TV messages. In 1968, the pioneering Corporation for Public Broadcasting was officially established by the federal government to originate and expand noncommercial TV programs as a supplement to the advertising-supported commercial networks.

Lending and Insurance.   In the broad fields of banking and finance, the federal government's lending organizations make loans to financial institutions as well as to individual borrowers. The twelve Federal Reserve Banks, the Federal Home Loan Bank, the Rural Electrification Administration, the Rural Telephone Bank, the Farmers' Home Administration, the Maritime Administration, and the Small Business Administration make loans to member banks, savings and loan associations, farmers, and small family-type business concerns. The Export-Import Bank of the United States finances American foreign trade. The Commodity Credit Corporation makes nonrecourse loans for the purpose of supporting the prices of certain agricultural commodities.

In the field of insurance, the Federal Deposit Insurance Corporation and the Federal Savings and Loan Insurance Corporation offer insurance on checking and savings deposits; the Federal Housing Administration and the Veterans' Administration, on home mortgages. The Government National Mortgage Association guarantees real estate loans. The Federal Crop Insurance Corporation protects farmers against crop failures. The Social Security Administration and the VA carry the largest life and annuity insurance policies in the world. The Overseas Private Investment Corporation provides insurance and investment guarantees for American private investment abroad.

Trading, Manufacturing, and Development. The federal government, through its various agencies—notably, the General Services Administration, the Commodity Credit Corporation, and the Defense Materials Service—buys and sells billions of dollars of commodities each year. The GSA procures general supplies and equipment. The federal and state governments buy a multitude of goods and services (from battleships to peanuts) on behalf of their constituents. Public purchases from private concerns serve a dual purpose of providing certain indivisible goods and services (defense, justice, health care) and propping up certain laggard industries or regions (agriculture or urban slums). Some state governments operate liquor stores; others sell lottery tickets. The government is also engaged in manufacturing. At the federal level, the armed forces produce weapons, ammunition, and other military wares. The Virgin Islands Corporation produces sugar cane. The Federal Prison Industries uses federal inmates in producing a variety of goods. The Government Printing Office has a thriving business producing and selling government documents. Some states are engaged in low-cost housing construction.

In the management and development of natural resources, the Federal Forest Service deals with logging, grazing, and other timber operations. The National Park Service administers parks, campsites, and other recreational facilities. The Fish and Wildlife Service manages and maintains hatcheries and preserves. The Bureau of Land Management has the responsibility for looking after the vast federal public domain. The National Science Foundation is charged with the advancement of American scientific endeavors through research. The federal and local governments maintain and operate libraries, museums, zoos, and other facilities. The Synthetic Fuel Corporation is in charge of developing new sources of energy.

Economic Planning

The United States is the only major industrial country in the Western world with no formal national plan of any kind. While federal and state governments have played an active, dirigist role in promoting economic growth for more than a century, there has never been a single, central framework for national policy making.[114]

114. Economically, there has been relatively less compelling reasons for a big, rich, and relatively self-sufficient country like the United States to be overly preoccupied with a strict husbanding of its resources. And as long as increased productivity kept ahead of population growth, the need for a long-term natural planning was not strongly felt.

American democracy has been regarded by the business community as the "political counterpart" of private enterprise and opposed to central planning. Constitutionally, the American system of government is based on the separation of power between federal, state, and local units. Even in the executive branch, the statutory "independence" of certain public agencies (the Federal Reserve Board and the regulatory commissions) make it difficult, if not impossible, to develop anything like a long-range economic plan. This, however, has not precluded short-term national budgeting or long-term *partial* planning for specific problems, like interstate transportation, urban renewal, and energy conservation.[115]

The annual federal budget serves as a short-term plan for the public sector and as a powerful device for managing the whole economy. In the words of a congressional committee chairman, U.S. budgets "set goals, chart courses of action, outline expectations, and embody anticipations." And this is the stuff that goes into an economic plan. The director of the Office of Management and Budget, serving directly under the president, is in a sense a master national planner. States and cities also normally engage in a good deal of planning in some of their activities without much public opposition. Virtually every American city has a planning commission and a "master plan" to guide its development.

As a result of a combination of stubborn inflation and persistent unemployment in the mid-1970s, however, voices from the organized labor, the academia, and even certain business circles were raised in increasing support of the argument that a large, complex, technological society without national planning is bound to invite massive economic dislocations. A change in thinking in this direction was perhaps responsible for the Humphrey-Javits Bill, introduced in 1975 to create the Economic Planning Board as a new federal agency. Because of insufficient public understanding and enthusiasm, and strong business opposition, no serious action was taken on that bill.

The closest that the United States has come, so far, to national planning has been the provisions of a recent full-employment legislation by Congress. The Humphrey-Hawkins Act on Full Employment and Balanced Growth, a 1978 updating of the 1946 Employment Act, sets out the main goals of countercyclical policy up to 1983, along with structural policies, institutional procedures for monitoring, and other employment principles. The medium-term (five-year) priorities of the American economy as outlined in the act were: restoring U.S. international competitive position; encouraging the growth of productive investment; reducing the ratio of public outlays to GNP; and establishing budgetary balance. The goals to be achieved by 1983 were: a reduction of unemployment to 4 percent; a cut in consumer price index to 3 percent (and zero in 1988); an annual GNP growth of 4 percent; and productivity gain of 2 percent a year.[116]

---

115. Gerhard Colm and L. H. Gulick, *Program Planning for National Goals* (Washington: National Planning Association, 1968).
116. For details, see U.S. Congress, 95th Session, Act No. 95-523, 27 October 1978.

Wage-Price Determination

Direct and extensive determination of prices and wages is only a wartime phenomenon in the United States. In times of peace, most prices are left to be determined mainly by the market, albeit often under varying degrees of indirect regulations and controls. The Emergency Price Control and the Stabilization Acts of 1942 gave the federal government the power to control prices, wages, and rents. During World War II, these controls were extensively used and proved relatively effective. During the Korean War, the Defense Production Act of 1950 empowered the government anew to control prices and wages in a selective or comprehensive way. Some use of this power was attempted during 1951–52, but with little overall success.[117]

Despite the absence of across-the-level wage and price determination, however, the United States has not been totally free from "fixed" prices even in peacetime. Under the Agricultural Adjustment Act of 1933, an elaborate scheme of loans, purchases, and storage operations by the federal government is designed to ensure the price of certain agricultural commodities at the 1909–14 parity and often higher than world market prices. Federal and state "fair trade" laws often place a *price floor* below a countless number of manufactured items. The rates of almost all public utilities in interstate commerce are fixed by federal agencies. In intrastate commerce, too, although outright price determination is an exception to the rule, exceptions are frequent. Local fresh milk prices, for example, have been controlled at various marketing levels by state and local governments. Local boards set fares for buses and taxis. There are numerous other goods and services whose prices are fixed by local authorities.

The minimum hourly wages paid to millions of American workers is also in a sense centrally determined. The Fair Labor Standard Act of 1938 covers the minimum daily earning of men and women engaged in interstate commerce, except for certain exempt categories, such as professional and administrative personnel, farmers, and domestics. Three-fourths of the states have some type of minimum wage laws of their own. The extent of coverage under the federal and state laws varies, depending on industry and occupation. There are probably more than 45 million workers in the United States whose minimum wage rates are determined by the state under the Fair Labor Standard Act. The federal minimum wage rose from $0.25 in 1938 to $3.35 in 1981.

To a significant degree, interest rates also have been influenced, if not determined, by government decisions. The official rediscount rate and the federal fund rate are determined by the Federal Reserve Board. By controlling the supply of money in the economy through various means at its disposal, the board also plays a pivotal role in determining the whole structure of interest rates in the nation. In addition, the board controls the rates that commercial member banks may pay on

117. Under the abortive National Industrial Recovery Act of 1933, some wages and prices were also fixed and written into the so-called industrial "codes".

their savings deposits. The maximum interest paid by savings and loans associations and other financial institutions is fixed by various agencies of the federal government. Many states have their own ceilings interest rates, usually through state usury laws.

Nonmonetary Incentives

The U.S. government bureaucracy is able, by and large, to attract men of great talent and intellect into its service by offering them rewards other than monetary compensation. There are such honors as a presidential appointment, national meritorious medals, active or honorary titles, as well as prestige, status, and power that go with certain jobs. Top men and women in government often can make more money in the private sector, yet they choose to devote part, or all, of their energies to public service.[118] There are tens of thousands of talented but unsung bureaucrats—lawyers, doctors, engineers, administrators—who work for the government at relatively lower salaries than their counterparts in the private sector. The reasons lie in the imponderables of patriotism, pride, respect, and self-satisfaction that drive them to seek challenge, adventure, and danger. These nonmonetary incentives, at least at certain levels of income, seem to provide greater attraction for America's "supermen" than cold cash.

The United States: An Overview

A widely held view of the American economy—both at home and abroad—is that it is essentially a free-market economy where output, prices, wages, savings, and investments are nearly all determined by private, profit-seeking entrepreneurs in a largely competitive market. In U.S. business circles, it is still fervently claimed that consumers are the real "bosses" of the American economy and that both business and government take their cues from consumers. As our discussion showed, however, this view is at best a very simplistic assessment of the U.S. economy. Neither business nor government is in fact the consumers' lackey.

Our examination of the U.S. market sector demonstrated that the complexity of modern American society and the inadequacy of pertinent information on goods and services does not allow U.S. consumers clearly to recognize and identify their true preferences; that the pervasive influence of clever advertisements and other promotional activities on personal selections negate the dominance of free choices;

---

118. In every president's cabinet since FDR, there have been individuals who gave up annual private incomes of up to ten to fifteen times their public salaries in order to serve their country (and their own egos).

and that the existence and increasing diversity of public and merit goods on the American scene show that not all U.S. goods and sources are produced in response to individual choice. The crucial role of U.S. federal, state, and local governments in directing, managing, and regulating economic activities also shows the extent of lapses from the free-market norms.

Government regulations, ranging from the design of atomic power plants to the size of toilets on construction sites and the minimum quantity of cream in ice creams, directly and indirectly affect consumers' decision on where to live and how to work, how much to spend and on what. Government rules also influence business decisions on investments, production, and the choice of technology.[119] Business, in turn, is neither an idle bystander nor a passive agent. The five hundred largest companies (a mere 0.1 percent of all U.S. manufacturing enterprises, but accounting for more than half of all sales and three-fourths of all corporate profits) are the most active and aggressive shapers of things in America. By virtue of their control over capital, raw materials, and huge advertising outlays, they create consumer's demand for goods and services, mould consumer tastes, administer prices, and maintain their profits at all times. In the opinion of a business observer, the giant corporations have become so important to the U.S. economy in terms of jobs and incomes that no government dares let one go under. National policy is thus often shaped in terms of protecting the big corporations instead of letting the market rightly penalize inefficiency, bad judgments, or poor management. A good deal of state intervention and control, in turn, is the result of *ad hoc* and unplanned responses to the shortcomings of the market forces, and the corresponding public clamour for rectification. Part of the government's intervention may also be attributable to a desire to placate some influential or vocal pressure groups, and not necessarily calculated to serve the best interest of the nation.

In short, neither by the classical libertarian standards, nor by the early 19th century American example, can the current U.S. economic "system" be characterized as a private enterprise market economy. The stretched hand of the bureaucracy over nearly all aspects of economic life in the United States makes the classification of America as a capitalist country not only simplistic but highly misleading. The United States economy, like those of the other market-oriented Western countries, presents a complex system where the state's direction, supervision, and influence permeate almost all economic decisions made by individuals and private groups. What distinguishes the U.S. economy from the centrally directed ones (despite its extensive government intervention) is not so much the exclusive presence of capitalist institutions or techniques, but instead, the absence of national commitment to a non-capitalist ideology.

119. According to a recent three-volume academic study of the case, a staple, quick hamburger purchased at the corner stand is the subject of 41,000 federal and state regulations based on 200 laws and 111,000 court cases. Another study by the Small Business Administration estimates that nearly $13 billion are annually spent by America's small businesses to complete some 850 million pages of government forms.

THE TASK OF PORTRAYAL

Despite all this, the U.S. economy is probably better prepared to respond to consumer needs and wishes than other economies, and more prone to function in a competitive fashion. The twin problems of inflation and unemployment which have stubbornly plagued the United States in recent years may be an indication that the American economy has lost some of its traditional resilience, flexibility, and adjustment capacity, but this has been mostly unavoidable. As an economic pundit puts it, just as American political democracy no longer corresponds to the New England town meetings, neither does the U.S. marketplace quite correspond to the norms of consumers' sovereignty. Interestingly enough, most Americans still seem to prefer their economic system over others. And this is what probably counts most.

THE UNITED KINGDOM

The United Kingdom of Great Britain and Northern Ireland has a total population of about 56 million in a land area of nearly 244,000 square kilometers. It is the birthplace of modern constitutional monarchy, classical economics, traditional free-enterprise capitalism, and the Industrial Revolution. With limited farmland and few natural resources except coal and North Sea oil, Britain, like Japan, is a very large importer of food and raw materials and an exporter of manufactured products, such as iron and steel, machinery, chemicals, textiles, and miscellaneous consumer products. Unlike Japan and other MICs, however, it is self-sufficient in energy sources.

Although one of the world's most highly industrialized countries, with a tradition of political stability, economic ingenuity, and psychological steadiness, the British economy has been trapped in a vicious circle of low investment, lagging produtivity, slow growth, and stubborn inflation. Responsible for this plight have been repeated shifts in power between the Tories and the Labour party at the hands of a frustrated and impatient electorate; the emphasis by both parties on greater social justice through income redistribution, nationalization and controls; and a succession of labor-management strifes.

Starting the post-1946 period with the third highest standard of living among MICs, Great Britain has acquired the unenviable distinction of experiencing a continued decline in economic growth and prosperity. In per capita GNP, the United Kingdom is now behind all major European countries except Italy. Britain's long-lost prosperity and its present fossilized economy show the direct effects of its choice of economic direction and management. The British political economy thus presents an interesting contrast to the dynamic case of Japan, and the still mildly vigorous case of the United States.

Like the United States, Great Britain has a "mixed" economy, but a mixture that tries to accommodate both a typically "capitalist" infatuation with free markets, and a typically "socialist" distrust of the private market forces. The structure of Britain's mixed economy thus shows the interplay of different processes of decision making. The market mechanism operates almost freely in the case of commodities and currencies, and with some oligopolistic elements in manufacturing and certain services, such as banking and insurance. Public and merit goods and services are supplied mostly outside the market through delegation or public enterprises. And in much of the nonmarket sectors, pressure-group tactics exert a very strong influence on the allocation of resources.

The British government manages, directly or indirectly, the larger share of national income. The state's share of GDP has also rapidly increased in recent years. Total public expenditure has ranged from 38 percent in 1971–72 to a peak of 46 percent in 1975–76. The public sector proper, however, is much smaller. General government expenditure on goods and services has ranged from 22.5 percent to 27 percent. Public sector broadly defined absorbs some 25 percent of total work force. Despite different official attitudes by the two main political parties, Labour and

THE UNITED KINGDOM: BASIC DATA

LAND AREA (sq. km.)	244,000
POPULATION (1980 estimate)	58 million
Net annual increase (1970-78 yearly average)	0.1 percent
Urban (percent of total, 1980)	91 percent
Working Age (15–64) (percent of total, 1978)	64 percent
LABOR FORCE (total civilian, 1979)	25 million
Agriculture, forestry, fishing (percent of total)	2 percent
Mining, manufacturing, construction (percent of total)	43 percent
Services, etc. (percent of total)	55 percent
GROSS DOMESTIC PRODUCT (market prices, 1979)	$300 billion
Per capita (1979)	$5,500
Average annual increase (1970-78)	2.1 percent
Public consumption (percent of GDP)	20 percent
Private consumption (percent of GDP)	59 percent
Fixed capital formation (ratio to GDP)	19 percent
Savings (ratio to GDP)	20 percent
GROSS DOMESTIC PRODUCT (market prices, 1979)	$300 billion
Agriculture, forestry, fishing (share in GDP)	2 percent
Mining, manufacturing, construction (share in GDP)	36 percent
Services (share in GDP)	62 percent
FOREIGN TRADE	
Exports (percent of GDP)	23 percent
Imports (percent of GDP)	25 percent

Conservative, toward state intervention in the economy in the pursuit of social welfare, they both have used such a mixed bag of tools as planning controls, depreciation allowances, and subsidies to entice private investment in the economy and to encourage industry into depressed regions. The Labour party, officially committed to the "common ownership of means of production, distribution and exchange," has acted rather cautiously in its program of nationalization. The Conservative party, supporting the cause of private enterprise and the free markets, has leaned toward a more or less "mixed" position.

The Regulated Sector: The State As a Proxy

Since the end of World War II, Great Britain has faced nearly a dozen economic crises, which have been dealt with through indirect governmental intervention. The range of indirect measures taken to influence the economy has been wide. Under both Labour and Conservative administrations, the state has used its arsenal of traditional (monetary and fiscal) and modern (incomes) policies to guide the economy toward national objectives. The government policy has influenced the economy largely through indirect controls over the levels of demand and supply. Aggregate demand has been manipulated through money supply and credit policy, taxation, and welfare assistance. Aggregate supply has been stimulated through changing interest rates, regulating trade and exchange policies, tax exemptions, subsidies, and more active competition.

Fiscal Policy

Given the main postwar British preoccupation with full and stable rate of employment, higher rates of economic growth, and the maintenance of Britain's position as a reserve currency country, the principal objectives of postwar fiscal policy have been a containment of consumption (through income and sales taxes); encouragement of production for domestic needs and exports; reduction of cyclical fluctuations; and, under Labour, a fairer distribution of income. Social welfare services, taxes, and subsidies have been cut under the Tories, and increased under Labour.

The British budget is the traditional "centerpiece" of British fiscal management. The budget document, unlike the one in the United States and most other countries, is not only a plan for government expenditures, but also a proposal for the economy's overall direction, a program of income redistribution, and a source of stimulus or restraint for the economy.

The British tax system is a combination of levies on income, expenditure, and capital gain, but the Treasury relies largely on income taxation as a source of public revenue. (The first income tax law was passed in 1799). The tax base and tax rates change frequently, with almost every annual budget, and far more often than in any major industrial country. Shares of various levies out of the total tax receipts (or total public revenues) are thus subject to periodic changes. On the whole, however, about half of the annual central government taxes is derived from personal and corporate income taxes and a surtax on dividends and interests (the "unearned" income). Personal incomes, accounting for about 40 percent of total taxes, are basically taxed at a rate of 25 percent on incomes of over £1,075 (33 percent before 1979) subject to a number of allowances, deductions, and exemptions. Under the 1979 Tories budget, the top marginal tax on "earned" income (wages and salaries) was reduced to 60 percent from 83 percent and for "unearned" income to 83 percent from 98 percent (on £25,000 annual income).[120] Corporations are taxed at a flat rate plus an additional excess profit tax. Various allowances for depreciation and modernization alleviate the corporate tax burden. Corporate taxes usually amount to about 10 percent of total taxes. There are other minor direct taxes on capital gains, inheritance, petroleum, and stamps.

In addition to direct income taxes, there are customs and excise taxes (value added tax, taxes on oil, tobacco, alcohol, gambling), accounting for about 45 percent of total general government taxation.[121] Total government receipts include incomes from national insurance contribution, rent, interest, and dividends from public corporations.

On the expenditure side, the outlays are for current public services, capital investment by nationalized industries, and grants, loans, and subsidies. Of the total annual expenditure by the central government, a little more than three-fourths involve current outlays on regular activities. Well over 50 percent of regular public outlay is earmarked for housing (8), health (12), education (14), and social security (22). Defense absorbs some 11 percent. The total public-sector transactions include receipts and expenditures by local authorities and those of public corporations.

Since the war's end, both Conservative and Labour governments have used fiscal measures to keep full employment at all times—and, until recently, at all costs. They have both followed a "stop-go" policy of increasing taxes and reducing investment allowances when aggregate demand began to look excessive and reversing gears whenever the economy seemed to falter. They have both used a kitful

120. Despite such steeply progressive rates of taxation, the average tax rate on all incomes in early 1970s was reportedly only 13 percent, and on taxable incomes no more than 32 percent. And due to a large number of legal loopholes, only 40 percent of total personal income was taxed. See J. A. Kay, *The British Tax System* (London: Oxford University Press, 1978). See also "Britain's Tax Expenditure," *The Economist*, 27 January 1979.

121. The 1973 VAT replaced the existing purchase tax (called sales tax elsewhere) and the selective employment tax (a flat-rate levy on the services and the construction industry for every worker in their employ in order to penalize them for labor-intensive operation). The 10 percent original VAT was subsequently broken up into 8 percent, and 12.5 percent taxes on different commodities. These taxes were again unified—at 15 percent— under the 1979 Tory budget.

of fiscal measures (flexible tax rates, selective levies, changes in public expenditures and investment, subsidies, rebates, and loans) to manage aggregate demand and stimulate supply.

The new Conservative government that took office in 1979 blamed the deteriorating performance of the British economy on heavy taxes, high government borrowing, and excessive public expenditures. In its first one hundred days, it cut income taxes substantially, increased expenditure taxes sharply, and ordered deep cuts in public spending. The new fiscal philosophy emphasized three central objectives: to bring down the rate of inflation, to restore incentives, and to relate public spending to the prospects for growth.[122]

Monetary Policy

With the Bank of England remaining in private hands until 1945, the British government had no official monetary policy. As a private control agency, however, the bank had a self-imposed responsibility for money and credit regulation. The Labour government made little use of money and credit policy in its first tenure of office (1945–51). The Bank of England, nationalized in 1946, kept its rediscount rate at the very low 2 percent. Excessive corporate expansion was held in check by controlling issue of securities. The increase in money supply was less than 2.5 percent a year. The flow of credit into high-priority activities (public utilities, export industries, and agriculture) was encouraged via qualitative controls over commercial banks.[123] For much of the postwar period, too, monetary policy was used in the traditional, nondiscriminatory manner to fight inflation and balance-of-payments deficits. A mildly active money and credit policy, designed to maintain full employment and growth, was developed during the 1950s. During the early 1960s credit rationing was adopted by private banks in favor of productive investments and exports, and against imports. Some credits were also made available to particular industries or regions in distress through the (now defunct) Industrial Reorganization Corporation.

Thus, the government, long indifferent to a heavy reliance on monetary policy, turned to these instruments in varying degrees by the mid 1960s. Until early 1971, quantitative ceilings were placed on lending of major commercial banks, and a priority list of borrowers was established in all private banks. Installment-buying regulations were frequently used to dampen excessive consumer demand. As of the middle of 1971, quantitative credit ceilings were abandoned in favor of changes in reserve requirements. In September 1972, the government announced the abolition

122. See *The Government's Expenditure Plans 1970–81* (London: HMSO, 1979); and *Financial Statement and Budget Report 1979–80* (London: HMSO, 1979).

123. For a detailed account of British monetary policy in the immediate postwar period, see J. C. R. Dow, *The Management of the British Economy* (Cambridge: Cambridge University Press, 1970).

of the fixed discount rate (which for 270 years had been the standard bearer of monetary policy and the peg for commercial rates). In its place, the Bank of England adopted a flexible minimum lending rate tied to the average discount rate for ninety-one day Treasury bills, with no connection with the Treasury's desire to expand or restrict money supply. This was generally considered a subtle move to increase the effective discount rate charged to commercial banks without the adverse psychological and political implications of raising the official rate. This policy, however, was again changed in 1978 in favor of an administratively determined rate, which reached 17 percent in 1979, the highest ever in any major MICs since World War II.

Since 1974, monetary policy has been used essentially as part of the government's overall counterinflationary strategy. The emphasis has been increasingly on the control of the growth of the monetary aggregates (total money supply). Since mid-1976 quantitative targets have been set and publicly announced. The announcement and observance of monetary guidelines have been considered as a framework for protecting internal and external financial stability and as a signal to the private financial community of the government's resolve to control inflation. Under this policy, interest rates have been allowed to move more flexibly in the market instead of being fixed as a pivot for monetary management.[124] In addition to the control of the money supply through the Bank of England, the government has also resorted to use of a supplementary deposits scheme—called "corset"—to limit the growth in private bank liabilities. Under this scheme, a guideline is set for the maximum growth of the bank's interest-bearing liabilities, with a progressive schedule of penalties for exceeding the guideline.

Exchange Rate Policy

One of the difficulties of managing monetary conditions in the United Kingdom is the large external capital flows. Thus, the main objectives of external policies in recent years have been the avoidance of too sharp fluctuations in the sterling value, the promotion of British industrial competitiveness in world markets, and the support of anti-inflationary policy through domestic monetary restraint. The road to success, however, has been very bumpy.

After refusing for three years to accept expert advice to devalue the pound sterling (despite continued balance-of-payments difficulties), the Labour government finally had to give in to increased pressures on its dwindling foreign exchange reserves and to devalue the pound by 14.3 percent (from $2.80 to $2.40) in 1967. As part of the currency realignment effectuated under the Smithsonian Agreement of 1971, the pound was upvalued by 8.57 percent to $2.61. The resulting competitive

124. The 1978–79 target for the growth of the total money supply was to be between 8 and 12 percent; for 1979–80, 7 to 11 percent. Neither of these targets, however, was achieved, and inflation passed the 20 percent mark.

exchange-rate disadvantage vis-à-vis the United States put sterling under severe new pressures. Unable to support the pound at the official (and evidently overvalued) rate, the Heath government in June 1972 decided to float the pound in exchange markets. Following the summer "float," the sterling value in terms of dollar and other currencies gradually overshot its pre-Smithsonian level and reached as low as $2.32. Since then, the pound sterling has been floating in the exchange markets, fluctuating between a low of $1.60 in late 1976 to a high of $2.32 in July 1979. Toward the end of 1979, the Tory government abolished all exchange controls on sterling flows, which had existed since the beginning of World War II.

Incomes Policy

Between 1945 and 1980, the United Kingdom made six successive attempts to cope with cyclical crises through controlling prices and wages to throttle inflation. The first peacetime shot at incomes policy was a voluntary wage standstill proposed by the Labour government in 1948, which the Trades Union Congress supported. While the intended wage freeze was not realized, the annual rise was within the improvements in productivity. The exercise later proved ineffective in the face of rising inflation after the Korean War, and the government was forced subsequently to devalue sterling to reestablish British competitive position on the world market. In the mid-1950s, attempts to restrain wage-price inflation consisted of pleas for voluntary restraints, but the TUC refused to cooperate. In 1957 a Council on Prices, Productivity and Incomes was established by the Tories as an independent body to examine the relationships of wage-price increases to national productivity. The commission's reports dealt mainly with generalities concerning imperfections of the British markets and the need for better labor training and less restrictive business practices.

In 1961 the Conservative government, facing a new balance-of-payments crisis, ordered a complete pay pause in the civil service for several months, hoping this would be emulated by trade unions. The TUC rejected the appeal. In 1962 a new National Incomes Commission was established with the same task of reviewing major agreements on wages and fringe benefits negotiated by labor and management, and reporting on their compatibility with the national interest. Because of a refusal by the Trades Union Congress to participate in the membership of this commission, little was accomplished by the nonlabor members except for conducting some public hearings.

After the victory of the Labour part in 1964, a National Board for Prices and Incomes was organized to look over all incomes: profits, rents, and dividends, in addition to wages. The new board was to be a semijudicial body independent of the government administration and outside of party politics. It was composed of the representatives of business, labor, and government and was empowered to investigate and publicize all pay and price increases; to study any boosts in wages and prices not warranted by a rise in productivity; and to focus public attention (and perhaps public pressure) on the companies and unions that violated productivity guidelines. The program did not work. Growth was sacrificed to avoid devaluation and to secure the balance of payments—with accelerated inflation. The term *stagflation* was coined.

Faced with another sterling crisis in the summer of 1966, the government introduced the first wage controls backed by law and ordered a complete standstill in wages, salaries, prices, and dividends for six months, to be followed by six more months of severe restraints. Later, the freeze was extended to a full year with some modification. The freeze succeeded, and inflation was reduced to 3 percent a year in 1967.

Under a stronger National Incomes Policy Act passed in 1968, the PIB had to be notified in advance of all planned increases in prices, wages, and dividends. Pay raises had to be limited to the case of workers in short supply, workers with increased productivity, and workers who refrained from restrictive practices. Dividends had to remain within productivity limits. Rent increases also had to be limited. While the absolute income freeze of 1966 achieved its objective of keeping the index of hourly earnings stable, the productivity guidelines suggested for the post-freeze period were systematically ignored by unions and management.[125]

The five-year-old policy was finally abandoned by the newly elected Conservative government in 1970 in accordance with campaign promises of freeing the economy from state controls. In January 1971, a new Office of Manpower Economics took over part of the disbanded PIB's functions in regard to the government's own pay scale. Later in the year, the Confederation of British Industry was persuaded to hold price rises to 5 percent for a year voluntarily. Unable to stem the tide of inflation or to improve lagging productivity, the Heath government, disregarding its past opposition to an incomes policy, proposed a program of voluntary wage and price restraint in September 1972. Failing to obtain TUC's cooperation (and faced with inflation at an all-time high and sterling's value at an all-time low), the Conservative government, in a more dramatic about-face, introduced its first statutory wage controls and ordered a ninety day freeze on wages, prices, rents, and dividends.

This "first-stage" of the anti-inflationary policy was extended for another sixty days and was successful. In January 1973, the Heath government unveiled its Stage 2 program, designed for strict controls on prices, pay, dividends, and rent for nine months, to be replaced by a longer-duration Stage 3. The existing freeze was extended for another sixty days. Prices were allowed to increase only by cost of production. Wage boosts were limited to a flat rate of £1 a week plus 4 percent of the workers' wage bill subject to a top average ceiling of about 7 percent. Profits were to remain within the average of the best two of the previous five years. Similar limitations were placed on dividends and rent. A Price Commission and a Pay Board were established in 1973 to enforce the Prices and Pay Code. The new code embodied the postwar's toughest and the most comprehensive program of controls.

125. Average hourly earnings rose 8 percent in 1968 and 1969, and 14 percent in 1970, when suggested wage hikes were between 2.5 and 4 percent.

The new Labour government elected in 1974 put an end to the statutory wage controls, but kept the lid on prices and profit margin. The consequent rise in wages and the statutory ban on passing wage hikes onto prices squeezed profits and increased unemployment. Later in the year, price controls were also eased. Instead, a voluntary wage policy called the "social contract" was introduced with a set of guidelines dealing mostly with maintaining workers' real incomes, limiting wage hikes to every twelve months, and allowing specific wage increases commensurate with productivity. Under the new voluntary program, some TUC leaders tacitly acknowledged that free collective bargaining was no longer consistent with either controlling inflation or obtaining social justice; some form of wage-price policy was needed. For this reason, a flat £6 a week limit on wage hikes was announced in 1975, the 5 percent limit on low wages in 1976, and the 10 percent limit on earning in 1977 were not opposed by the trade unions. But the 5 percent limit proposed for 1978 ran into strong labor opposition, and the Labour party itself rejected any new pay restraint. The new victory by Mrs. Thatcher's Conservative party in 1979 coincided with the end of the final stage of Labour's formal incomes policy. The Tories terminated prices and dividends controls as well.[126]

The British experience with incomes policy during 1955–1980 is credited with some short-term success (in 1961, and the 1966–67 wage-price freezes), a milder medium-term impact on wages and prices in certain years (1975–77), and a questionable long-term effect. In general, the evidence seems to show that: a short-lived freeze works in as much as wages remain lower than would have been expected; the ground gained in the freeze period is, however, often subsequently lost; a voluntary policy with the unions' assent can result in a significant drop in inflation; and no incomes policy can take the place of monetary and fiscal disciplines.

Regulation of Industry

Competition has never been a norm or a popular practice in England after the Industrial Revolution, but it was only toward the end of World War II that the government, anxious to ensure postwar full employment, decided to revive a workable competitive climate in the economy. Both the Labour and Conservative governments have supported legislation regarding monopolies, mergers, and restrictive practices. The widespread nature and extensive abuses of economic power through well-entrenched restrictive practices (resale price maintenance, market-sharing quotas, collusion on contract tenders, exclusion of outsiders from access to raw materials and markets, price discrimination, and agreements to limit imports) gave rise to the Monopolies and Restrictive Practices Act of 1948. The act declared restrictive practices contrary to the public interest and set up the Monopolies Commission to receive complaints and to report to the Board of Trade, which then

126. The government's new strategy seemed to abandon all serious efforts toward holding wages down in the hope of combating price rises. Instead, the emphasis shifted toward reducing money supply, reduced public spending, and reduced income taxes.

could propose legislation to outlaw them. Several reports on specific industries were made, and as a result, collective resale price maintenance was outlawed in 1964.[127] Restrictive practices among professions, however, remained strong.

Under a new Restrictive Practices Act of 1956, monopolies and formal cartels were prohibited. Unfair competitive methods, and specifically collusive agreements, were outlawed. All mergers and business takeovers had to obtain prior approval of the government's Monopolies Commission. Resale price maintenance practice was outlawed in 1965. But plagued by low productivity, old-fashioned management, scant financial resources for renovation, and a relatively small size for competition in world markets, many British companies kept following the merger road. The Labour government itself, under the banner of "rationalization," actively promoted industrial consolidations. Labour's Industrial Reorganization Corporation, set up in 1966, had in fact the task of acting as "marriage broker for corporate weddings." A major change in government policy surfaced toward the end of the 1960s, when some proposed mergers were delayed by the commission's review, and the commission itself was destined to become a part of the Prices and Incomes Board.

The Labour government that came to power in 1974 set a definite course of action against anticompetitive behavior. A spate of new laws was subsequently passed by Parliament to deal with the issue. The 1973 Fair Trading Act had already set up the Office of Fair Trading to protect consumers against harmful trading practices, monopolies and mergers, and even some restrictive labor practices. The Restrictive Trade Practices Act of 1976 consolidated earlier legislation covering the registration and judicial investigation of restrictive agreements. The Resale Prices Act of 1976 also updated earlier legislation prohibiting collective and individual resale price maintenance.

The Conservative government of Mrs. Thatcher in 1979 got through Parliament a new Competition Act designed to abolish the Price Commission and to give the Office of Fair Trading (created under the 1973 law) and the Monopolies and Mergers Commission (established under the 1948 law) a new "competition reference" power. Under this new procedure, any anticompetitive practice would be referred to the MMC by the OFT. If the MMC finds that the investigated firm is engaged in the alleged practices, is anticompetitive, and is acting against the public interest, then the commission will report the case to the Department of Trade for remedial actions. Nationalized industries are also covered by the law. The focus of the act is to control not prices or even market structure, but competitive behavior.

In other areas of business regulation, Britain also has a long tradition. Since the last quarter of the nineteenth century, Britain has been in the forefront of the market economies in introducing regulatory legislation in almost all aspects of the economy. In making up for the deficiencies of market mechanism and curbing

127. For a history of these practices and measures to prevent them, see G. C. Allen, *Monopoly and Restrictive Practices* (London: Allen & Unwin, 1968).

modern urban plagues,[128] the United Kingdom has usually been ahead of the United States in this century. A Clean Air Act, for example, was passed in 1956 to reduce air pollution by industry and households. The government's policy vis-à-vis the industries affecting general public welfare is also stricter. Supervision over TV performance and the independence of TV programs from advertisers' control, for example, are two of the main features of TV broadcasting in England.[129]

Consumer Protection

Protection of buyers against shady or unscrupulous behavior of sellers has also always been one of the long cherished principles of democratic government in Britain. British legislation safeguarding the consumer goes back to the 1878 Weights and Measures Act, and the 1893 Sale of Goods Act, which required "merchantable quality" and reasonable fitness for use of all goods sold in the market. The 1955 Food and Drugs Act and the 1961 Consumer Protection Act deal with food purity and product safety. The new 1963 Weights and Measures Act deals with accuracy of statement on quantity and packaging. The Misrepresentation Act of 1967 and the 1968 Trade Descriptions Act call for accurate description of goods and services offered for sale and cover such violations as misleading advertising, misrepresentation, and deceitful promotional activities. The old common law doctrine of *caveat emptor* (let the buyer beware) has become a sort of *caveat vendor* (let the seller think twice).

The responsibility for consumer protection, however, has been spread among many government agencies. A Consumer Council was established in 1963 by the Conservatives to carry out comparative testing of the products and advise shoppers. Under an economy move by the Heath government, and based on the government's arguement that increased competition is the consumers' "best safeguard," the council was abolished in late 1970. Instead, the old Department of Trade and Industry was replaced by a new Ministry of Trade and Consumer Affairs late in 1972 to be in charge of antimonopoly activities as well as consumer protection against unfair trade practices. The Fair Trading Act of 1973 provides the department with a watchdog unit on all matters of interest to consumers.

Since 1967, a British ombudsman, called the Parliamentary Commissioner for Administration, has been in charge of reviewing specific cases of administrative wrongs referred to him by a Parliament member. The commissioner can only declare an "injustice" if it is caused by maladministration rather than on sociomoral

128. The Criminal Injuries Compensation Board, established in 1964, has the task of rewarding the innocent victims of violent crimes.

129. The Greater London Council has been able to clean the Thames—polluted since the Industrial Revolution—so that fish can live in it. Air pollution has been cut by 80 percent.

consideration.[130] In related areas of environmental protection, the British Ministry of Environment has statutory powers for conservation and pollution control, and Great Britain leads many Western democracies in its fight to save the environment.

Promotion of Private Business

In addition to its high tariffs and various import restrictions against non-EEC countries, Britain has a comprehensive system of subsidies and tax concessions to the private sector. Subsidies are given in the form of grants and loans to such economic sectors as agriculture and related activities, industry and trade, and local housing. Under the 1947 Agricultural Act and through the Annual Review between the government and the National Farmers' Union, British farmers were subsidized by the Treasury, largely for wheat, barley, beef and milk. Consumers paid additional covert subsidies in the form of higher fixed prices for farm products. Government subsidies, called "deficiency payments," were supposed to make up the difference between average domestic costs and imported prices. After joining the European Economic Community (EEC), and in a move to bring British agriculture more in line with the Community's, the Heath government in July 1971 revised its national farm support price policy from one of government subsidies to that of import levies. New tariffs were imposed on non-EEC cereals, meat, and dairy products in order to increase farm production and raise farmers' incomes. Since 1973, British farm policy has followed EEC's.

Promotion of private industry has been concerned with incentives to businessmen to invest larger sums in plant and equipment, and with regional dispersion of new industrial enterprises in order to solve localized unemployment. Under the first objective, both Labour and Tories, blaming Britain's stagflation on a lack of investment and shortage of investment finance, have tried to pump funds into industry through various financial institutions, including Labour's Industrial Reorganization Corporation (IRC) and the National Enterprise Board (NEB). As to the second objective, the 1945 Distribution of Industry Act and the 1966 Industrial Development Act allowed up to 40 percent grants toward the cost of new plant and equipment in manufacturing industry. The Labour's industrial modernization policy favored operational grants, research grants, labor-reducing rebates, and reorganization and merger contributions. Shipyards, aircraft, computers, machine tools, atomic energy, and other industries for which Britain has no "natural" domestic market have been the major beneficiaries.

The Tories have generally favored tax incentives instead of investment grants or industrial subsidies under the banner of "disengagement from industry" and on the grounds of greater efficiency. The Heath government in 1970 thus abolished IRC, and introduced investment allowances and free depreciation. But under

130. The complaints about aircraft noise around Heathrow (caused partly by the government-owned airline), for example, do not fall within the injustice category.

pressures from rising unemployment and unexpected bankruptcies (Rolls-Royce and Upper Clyde Shipbuilders), the 1972 Industry Act was passed by the Conservatives to save private corporations from collapse and regions from unemployment. The newly established Industrial Development Board was empowered to make investment grants, take equity holdings, and provide loans to companies in distress. Labour's 1975 Industry Act set up the National Enterprise Board as a holding company for the so-called "lame ducks." In a related field, the 1973 Employment and Training Act attempts at improving labor skills, mobility and placement.

Social Welfare System

The origin of the British "welfare state" can be traced back to the "poor laws" of the Elizabethan era.[131] The present scheme was established in 1946, under the Labour government, largely upon Sir William Beveridge's Report of 1942. The system is a comprehensive national insurance plan financed by everyone and for everyone's benefit, regardless of need. Under this scheme, every resident has a "right" to government services, regardless of ability to pay. The entire welfare system was until the late 1960s universal and indiscriminate, requiring no "means test." Rent subsidies, family allowance, and free milk were given to both rich and poor.

Benefits have ranged from prenatal medical care given to expectant mothers, all the way to funeral expenses paid to the deceased's survivors. In between, there has been insurance against every hazard that may unfavorably affect one's income: unemployment, disability, sickness, old age, and even unusually heavy expenditures. Family allowances as cash payments to families with two or more children are paid out of general revenues. There is no means test or income limit, but allowances are taxable. The family allowance represents only a small part (about 6 percent) of the average recipient's income—(as compared to more than 30 percent in France). There are also supplemental benefits to certain groups (the aged, widows, mothers with children, the disabled) on the basis of need. Supplemental benefits include free school meals, free welfare milk, rent rebates, free prescription drugs, and assistance for unavoidable expenses given to the poor on a selective basis and with means tests.[132]

Prominent among the British social welfare services is the pioneering national health program. The National Health Service provides nearly free medical care of all types—doctor's visit, hospitalization, maternity care, convalescence

131. For a succinct examination of the early British welfare programs and their comparison with other European countries, see *Guaranteed Minimum Income Programs Used by Governments of Selected Countries*, Economic Policies and Practices #11, Joint Economic Committee, 90th Cong., 2nd Sess., (Washington: GPO, 1968), pp. 34–47.

132. After 1968, social security benefits and free services are partly distributed on a "selective" basis, only to the needy minority. The principle of "selectivity"—still much resented in the United Kingdom—is generally interpreted to mean different services for different classes of people, thus violating the idea of equality.

facilities—to all British residents, including foreign citizens. Prescriptions, dental care, dentures, eyeglasses, hearing aids, and other medical supplies are provided at reduced costs. The service is financed 80 percent out of the general budget, 16 percent by employees, and 4 percent by employers. Nearly all general practitioners and many specialists belong to the service and are paid fees by the government. Some specialists have their own private practice. Patients can choose their own doctors.

Of equal significance is the National Insurance Program, which provides regular social security benefits: maternity benefits, unemployment insurance, sickness benefits, old-age pensions, disability compensation, and funeral expenses. Participation is compulsory for all the working population, regardless of age and income. The program is financed by management and labor contributions and by the general Treasury. Benefits vary with individual contributions. For a flat-rate contribution, a flat-rate compensation is paid in the case of unemployment, sickness, and retirement. Additional benefits can be secured by paying graduated premiums.

Social security spending now accounts for 30 percent of total public spending. Yet, in spite of the huge public outlays on social welfare, the amount of benefits received by needy families and individuals is rather meager. The free and subsidized services are estimated to have ranged between 14 percent and 20 percent of the GNP in recent years. Yet due to its basic universality of distributing aid regardless of need, Britain has lagged behind most Western democracies in the magnitude of its pensions and other benefits. Another peculiar implication of the British indiscriminate welfare system is that while the British income tax is steeply progressive, total annual British consumption expenditure takes more of the GNP than is the case in some other advanced countries. Part of the reason is that Britain generously subsidizes private consumption and then has to tax it back from richer tax payers in order to finance the scheme.[133]

Britain's complex welfare system, put together in the last thirty years, has been designed to accomplish both individual equity and social adequacy through a welter of forty different programs dealing with unemployment and poverty. As in the United States, however, the British welfare system has been criticized for gross abuses and for increased unemployment due to reduced incentives for work.[134]

British Pressure Groups

Great Britain has often been called the most "pressure-group organized" country in the world—in many ways, even more so than the United States. One observer goes

---

133. For a concise history of social security in Britain, see John Walley, *Social Security: Another British Failure?* (London: Methuen, 1972).

134. Mrs. Thatcher's Conservative government, which came to power in 1979, promised to reduce the portion of Britain's resources being spent on social services.

so far as to claim that: "For better or worse, self-government as we now enjoy today is one that operates by and through the lobby."[135] The traditional British view of politics has favored separation in all its forms. This philosophy is considered essential not only in government-business relations, but also within the various branches of government itself. As in other Anglo-Saxon countries, the relationship between the public and the private sectors is one of arms-length bargaining. The difficulty of mixing public-private power in a combined machinery for economic decision making (as is the case in Japan and France) thus makes Britain's pressure-group politics all the more significant.

In addition to the two major political parties that by and large represent business and labor interests, there are innumerable organizations representing business, professional, charitable, religious, ethnic, cultural, and scientific communities within British society, with varying purposes, memberships, and powers. Most of these groups—even the Lord's Day Observance Society—exert some direct or indirect influence on the processes of resource allocation. In the economic arena, the bulk of politicoeconomic decisions is directly affected by the maneuvers of business interests, professional societies, trade unions, and, to a smaller scale, consumers.

Business Interests

Among the business groups, the Confederation of British Industry is most outstanding, both for its considerable financial contributions to Conservative members of Parliament, and its claim to a large number of MPs within its own affiliated businesses. It includes more than 10,000 firms, 200 trade and employer organizations, and even some nationalized industries covering about half of the work force. CBI advises its members on labor issues, consults with government agencies, and presents business views on socioeconomic problems. The Institute of Directors, the British Bankers' Association, the Chambers of Commerce, the National Farmers' Union, the Federation of Property Owners, and a large number of other trade associations constitute the bulk of business interests' organizations. It is estimated that more than 90 percent of Conservative MPs have some industrial ties. Such organizations as the Aims of Industry and the Economic League can also be classified as business associations, for they seek to promote the cause of private, free enterprise. Besides providing technical services to their members, many employers' associations in different industries often engage in industrywide collective bargaining.

The *professional* pressure groups include such diverse organizations as the influential British Medical Association, the Society of Civil Servants, the National

135. For a lucid examination of the British pressure groups, see R. M. Punnett, *British Government and Politics* (New York: Norton, 1971), chapter 5. See also J. D. Stewart, *British Pressure Groups* (Westport: Greenwood, 1979); and A. M. Potter, *Organized Groups in British National Politics* (London: Faber and Faber, 1961).

Teachers' Union, and the University Teachers' Association. These groups do not have particular party affiliations, but fill the membership of numerous outside advisory committees that provide the civil service and other agencies of the British government with expert information and advice. The powerful National Farmers' Union, for example, has its members in some fifty consultation committees set up by the Ministry of Agriculture. There are also local government lobbies, such as County Councils' Association and the Municipal Corporations' Association, that bargain with the central government over local administration. And there are organized groups, such as the Law Society and the Accidents Prevention Society, that administer certain laws on behalf of the government or as a government agent.

Labor Unions

Organized labor presents another powerful lobby in the British economic arena. Labor organizations consist of more than six hundred individual unions, with a total membership of nearly 12.4 million, or about 50 percent of the labor force. Of these, some 111 unions are affiliated with the British Trades Union Congress (TUC).

The dominant Trades Union Congress—the world's oldest labor federation, extablished in 1868 with barely 120,000 members—has now a membership of more than 11 million workers. The affiliation is extremely loose: national officials do not have the power to control individual union's day-to-day activities. The unions themselves are also often helpless to prevent unauthorized behavior of shop stewards or rank-and-file members.[136] Among TUC unions, the "Big Six," with nearly 6 million members, constitute about half of all British trade unionists. Of the six, the Transport and General Workers' Union, with over 1.9 million members, and the Amalgamated Union of Engineering Workers, with nearly 1.4 million, form the two largest unions. The other four are General and Municipal Workers' Union, National and Local Government Officers' Association, National Union of Public Employees, and the Union of Shop, Distributive and Allied Workers, with a total of 2.7 million members.

The Labor movement, with its closely associated Cooperative Union, is formally affiliated with the British Labour party. Over 40 percent of the party's National Executive Council are union members. Some 40 percent of Labour MPs are usually sponsored (their campaign financed) by the unions. Many others have various labor ties. The trade unions' pressure is exercised through direct parliamentary maneuvers and indirect political clout created by strike threats. When the government is in Labour's hands (as in 1945–51, 1964–70, and 1974–79), the

---

136. Over 90 percent of British strikes in the 1960s were believed to be unofficial, of the brief, local, wildcat variety ordered by the local shop steward. The strikes also are frequently over extremely trivial issues: sympathy with a dismissed apprentice who had refused to cut his long hair; or a dispute over the right of shipwrights versus boilermakers as to who should draw a pencil guideline on metal for tools to follow; or disagreements between two rival unions on who should press the switch for operations to begin.

unions' influence is brought to bear directly on individual ministers and agency heads—but not always to the unions' satisfaction.

In fact, substantial cleavage exists not only between the Labour government and organized labor, but also between the Labour government and the Labour party, and between unions and their rank and file.[137] The party harbors several factions from the center to the extreme left, while the government usually represents the centrists and moderates. The interunion rivalry is also extensive and sometimes bitter. Usually nonmanual (minority) unions are opposed by the manual-union majority.

Industrial Relations. Up until 1971, labor-management relations in Britain were voluntary and totally informal; there was virtually no labor law as such. Contracts were gentlemen's agreements not always enforceable in courts. There was no legislation nor legal procedure defining bargaining units and representatives.[138] Up until then, also, there were no industrywide unions such as the auto or steel workers in the United States. Many industries had to bargain with as many as a dozen or more unions at a time. In 1970, three-quarters of the union members in Britain worked alongside members of other unions—sometimes twenty in all—in the same plant.

The first labor law, widely described as a milder copy of the U.S. Wagner and Taft-Hartley acts plus European labor laws, was introduced by the Heath government in 1970 and approved by Parliament in March 1971. The comprehensive legislation made labor contracts legally binding on both parties; it banned closed shops and declared secondary boycotts, refusal to bargain in good faith, and unauthorized strikes "unfair" industrial actions. A new National Industrial Relations Court was given the power to issue cease-and-desist orders and to make labor or management pay penalties for contract violations.

To obtain benefits from the new law, labor unions had to register with the chief registrar of trade unions. Failure to register limited a union's recruitment drive and bargaining rights; it meant a loss of tax exemption status on investment income and a loss of immunity from suits brought by third parties injured by labor strikes. Despite these penalties, the Trades Union Congress, which considered the law antiunion, asked its affiliates not to register.[139]

The Trade Union and Labour Relations Act of 1974 and its subsequent amendment under the Labour government repealed the 1971 legislation and

137. The TUC, for example, always keeps its distance from the Labour party by not allowing its leaders to sit on both the TUC General Council and the party's National Executive Council.

138. Minimum standards for safety, health, and welfare at the workplace, however, were governed by an old law enacted as early as 1871.

139. In its first test of the law in early 1972, the National Industrial Relations Court successfully caused striking railway workers to return to work while bargaining was continued, but it proved ineffectual (despite sending some union leaders to jail) in preventing a costly dock strike later in the same year.

restored some of the old legal protection for trade-union activities. The Employment Protection Act of 1975 established certain individual and collective rights to employees and trade unions regarding leave, layoffs, trade-union duties, and bargaining procedures. The Employment Act of 1980 aimed at certain other reforms concerning lawful picketing, closed shop, and union elections.

Under these laws, collective bargaining takes place in a variety of forms. In some industries, industrywide collective agreements are reached on minimum rates of pay, hours of work, paid holidays, and overtime work. Effective rates of pay and working conditions (including grievance procedures) are then determined by negotiations at the company or plant level between the shop steward and business representatives. Industrial disputes not settled by the parties are referred to the Advisory, Conciliation and Arbitration Service (ACAS), composed of labor, management, and independent members. Disputes not resolved by the ACAS are handled by Industrial Tribunals.[140]

Farmers

Of the pressure groups that exert notable influence on the British economy, particular mention must be made of the National Farmers' Union. Although farmers account for about 3 percent of the British labor force—far below the West European ratios—their union is well run and efficient. The influence of the National Farmers' Union on legislators is disproportionate to its small size and economic power. Public subsidies to agriculture—the so-called deficiency payments, or the difference between prices of unrestricted farm imports and the government's guaranteed minimums—are determined by bargaining.

At the annual price review conferences, where the estimates of costs and productivity are presented by government officials and farm representatives, the union invariably presses for higher farm prices (and, hence, larger subsidies). Supporting devices—marches on Parliament, tractor parades along major highways, boycotts of farm markets—are also used to influence the bargaining outcome.

Consumers

As in all other economies, consumers are the least organized and least influential. The National Consumer Council is active and articulate, but without much clout. Claiming that consumers are the only group with a "single-minded interest" in price stability, the council has tried, mostly in vain, to be consulted by the government on pay and price policy on an equal footing with business and labor. The council's

140. For details, see *Profile of Labor Conditions: United Kingdom* (Washington: U.S. Department of Labor, 1978). See also "Who are the Masters Now?" *The Economist* 23 February 1980

position, as expected is for lower rates of inflation (as a cause not only of unemployment, but also of crime, violence, and terrorism); consumer representation in economic decision making; and pay raises commensurate with economic need or social justice, not economic power. It is against uncontrolled business mergers, import controls, and state support of industries that are no longer internationally competitive.

Pressure-Group Activities

As in the United States and other MICs, the pressure groups in Britain operate at various levels of the government and use both formal and informal means. The bulk of lobbying, however, is directed toward the executive branch, where influence peddling is usually most direct and often cheapest. Pressures are also applied to members of Parliament by financing election campaigns or contributions to party coffers. The third domain of pressure-group activity involves appeals to public opinion as a means of indirectly influencing certain legislative actions or forcing the executive to adopt certain public policies. In all three levels of activity, the approach may be open and above board or subtle and less publicized. As in other pluralistic countries, too, each lobby has to contend with a rival and countervailing group.

One of the interesting cases of group bargaining in postwar Britain has been the short-lived attempt at national planning. The National Economic Development Council consisted of representatives of the government, the trade unions, and industry, plus some independent members. According to a competent observer, the NEDC structure shifted "the locus of decision in national economic policy from Parliament to another body in which the representatives of the country's major economic organizations deliberate in secret and bargain with one another."[141]

The more structured, and by far the most publicized, process of give and take is, of course, direct collective bargaining between employers and unions. But the proliferation of local unions makes the outcome of annual bargains confused, unpredictable, and often independent of government policy. Another multilateral method, increasingly favored by the TUC and Labour party leaders, is the European-style worker participation in management decisions. Since 1967, workers have been appointed to the divisional boards of the British Steel Corporation. The government has the discretion of appointing worker-directors to the boards of other nationalized industries. But both the trade union movement and business interests have so far been cool to the idea—labor not willing to give up bargaining for participation; management for fear of losing power.

The British "incomes policy" has also been a basis for bargaining among government, business, and labor leaders. In recent years, trade-union opposition has often modified government programs for wage and price stability, modernizing

141. See Andrew Shonfield, *Modern Capitalism* (New York: Oxford University Press, 1969), p. 161.

nationalized industries, increasing industrial efficiency, and improving technological methods. At the bargaining table, the government has consistently appealed to trade unions for restraint in their wage demands. Many threatened strikes have also been averted as a result of direct government mediation.[142]

Some outstanding pressure-group triumphs in recent years attest to the importance of multipartite bargaining. The passage of the Independent Television Authority Act of 1954 is generally considered such a bargain. Up until the middle of the 1950s, radio and TV broadcasting in England was a monopoly of the BBC, which did not allow commercial advertising in its broadcasts. The 1945–51 Labour government was adamantly against changing the status quo. The victory of the Tories in 1951 saw the emergence within the Conservative government of some influential personalities favoring commercial TV. The 1954 Bill was a compromise between the "popular TV" lobby of private industry, advertisers, and bankers, on the one hand, and the National TV Council, a counterlobby opposed to commercialism. In another widely publicized case, a coalition of TUC leaders, left-wing intellectuals, and Labour party backbenchers successfully blocked the Wilson government's effort to enact a relatively tepid labor reform bill in 1969.

The quantitative role of economic pressure groups in the British economy (the percentage of GNP determined through bargaining) is hard to assess, for even in industries whose prices are directly influenced by collective pay bargains, other forces and considerations are not totally absent. In other areas of group influences, the assessment is much harder.

On the whole, the record of group bargaining in improving British economic growth, living standards, and welfare is at best controversial. On the positive side, the trade unions have fought successfully for reducing inequalities of rank and status in the class-ridden British society. And as a redoubtable social force in the economy and in Labour party politics, they have been instrumental in influencing British socioeconomic priorities and in giving Britain a more economically egalitarian society. How well they have done in raising British productivity and growth is a different story. So is the story of how well they have done for their membership, materially and financially.

British organized labor has a reputation for inefficiency, costliness to the industry, restrictive practices in the economy, and lackadaisical attitude toward national economic crises. It is often claimed that in much of the British manufacturing and construction industries, three or more workers do the job that only one American or German worker does under comparative circumstances. According to one estimate, 4 million of Britain's nearly 25 million workers are redundant at their jobs. Featherbedding exists in its most flagrant forms in railroads, trucking, shipbuilding, and other industries.

Some critics also point to the frequency and illogic of British wildcat strikes

142. In 1975, for example, the trade unions and the government agreed to voluntary wage restraints as a counterinflationary measure which also included promised price controls.

as a drag on British economy.[143] Britain has probably lost more of its national income through work stoppages than other industrial countries because both Tory and Labour governments have been compelled to sacrifice economic growth in order to combat wage-push inflation, and the British industry has found it impossible to plan for a steady industrial progress without fear of sudden walkouts by union workers.

Doubts have also been raised about organized labor's ability to lift the workers' share of national income over the long run through collective bargaining much more than they would have achieved in a faster-growing and more efficient British economy. The same may be said about big business's push toward a greater concentration of economic power in the face of the declining profit rates and rising social tensions.

The indisputable fact, however, is that the trade unions have markedly increased their political power in the postwar period. Owing to the increasing impact of pay hikes in accelerating inflation and the crucial role of the unions in moderating wage demands and preserving industrial peace, labor has acquired greater new leverage. The defeat of the 1971 Industrial Relations Act at the hands of the TUC—albeit through noncooperation—showed that labor is in fact a formidable force. This legislation, which had considerable popular support and was voted by a clear parliamentary majority, was still unable to control the unions. The "social contract" concluded between organized labor and the Labour government was clearly a political bargain under which the unions promised their anti-inflationary cooperation as a price for a number of pro-union policies. The promised legislations by the 1974 Labour government were the repeal of IRA, a new Employment Protection Act, more nationalization and state intervention to save jobs, and greater redistribution of income through higher taxes on the rich.[144]

Bargaining may, theoretically, provide a better safeguard for minority interests and a more balanced allocation of resources, but in the British case there is no evidence that all sectoral interests are equally represented in the bargaining process, that the leadership in each group has succeeded in promoting group interest, or that the coalition of some interest groups has been in the best interest of the rest of the community.

The Command Sector

The British democracy is characterized by a fairly disciplined parliament under a strong, party-based executive. Some critics claim that the parliamentary system has

143. In the decade to 1978, an average of more than 2,630 work stoppages occurred each year, resulting in more than 9,450 million work days lost annually.
144. For a detailed analysis of the British labor movement, see Robert Taylor, *The Fifth Estate: Britain's Unions in the Seventies* (London: Routledge, 1978); and "Do Unions Rule Britain?" *The Economist,* 29 November 1975.

actually "collapsed" under the excessive power of the prime minister.[145] Most objective observers, however, agree that the British cabinet, if not the prime minister himself, rules the country as long as its party has a comfortable majority in Parliament. Backbench MPs as a rule have neither the power nor the inclination to challenge party leadership. The prime minister has the power to dissolve Parliament (thus terminating MPs tenure of office) at will. The separation of powers between the British executive and legislative branches is nowhere near as great as in the United States.

Yet, while the central government at Whitehall plays an important role in the British economy, the instruments and techniques most readily identified with the command mechanism—planning, public enterprise, and direct wage-price controls—are not at all as extensive or effective in Britain as they are in other Western European MICs.

Planning

Despite the Labour party's long identification with "socialism," there was no economic planning in prewar Britain. The cornerstone of British national planning was laid in the program of the Labour party in 1945. At the time, planning was regarded as a means of establishing national priorities in such a way as to secure full employment, a balanced growth of the economy, and public welfare. After the Labour victory in 1945, planning was more specifically advocated as a means of influencing resource allocation in the desired directions without interfering with democratic freedoms.

The most serious attempt toward sustained long-term indicative planning, however, came with the establishment of the National Economic Development Council in 1961, under a Tory government dissatisfied with the slow pace of UK economic growth and state direct intervention in the economy.[146] The conversion to planning was inspired by the French experience, and the NEDC was in fact modeled after the Commissariat du Plan and charged with drawing up a program for realizing potential growth.[147]

The NEDC's plan for 1962–66 called for an annual growth rate of 4 percent. It was a modest plan dealing with only seventeen industry groups. As some critics have said, the document was not a directive or a government commitment, but a guide and a stimulus. The plan failed to achieve its growth target in the first two years. The victory of the Labour party at the polls in 1964 shelved it.

Labour's full-blown National Plan presented to Parliament in September 1965 called for the elimination of the balance-of-payments deficits, an annual

145. See Humphry Berkeley, *The Power of the Prime Minister* (London: Allen & Unwin, 1968).

146. A Tory minister said at the time that it was not "planning" to which the Conservatives were opposed but "socialist planning."

147. See Geoffrey Denton, *Planning for Growth* (London: PEP, 1965), pp. 79–80.

growth rate of 3.8 percent, and a number of subtargets for various sectors. Major priorities were placed on an increase in productivity to the tune of 3.4 percent a year, as well as maintenance of wage and price stability. The Labour plan was described as both "a commitment to action by the government" and "a guide to action" by the private sector.[148] There was no mention, however, of how the government was going to induce, let alone direct, private business into action.

The plan was far from successful. It failed to achieve its intended targets and was unceremoniously abandoned in July 1966.[149] The demise of the Labour plan—officially blamed on the sterling crisis and the "gnomes of Zurich"—is generally attributed to its lack of strategy; it had no coordinated policies for achieving the plan's stated goals.[150] Determined to keep the unemployment rate below 2 percent, and unable (and perhaps unwilling) to check the pressure of demand, the Labour government was continually faced with one balance-of-payments crisis after another. The government's insistence, until November 1967 (when sterling was devalued) on keeping the exchange rate at its overvalued 1949 level made the plan's overall goal virtually impossible. Planning was used mainly to get the economy out of a depressed state without giving up any other socioeconomic goal as a trade-off. The expectation proved impossible to achieve. Thereafter, national planning remained dormant, although the NEDC continued to produce sectoral plans for various industries, without much influence.

State Enterprises and Nationalization

British nationalization of the industries "affected with the public interest" goes back to a post-World War I movement called "gas and water socialism." Prior to the Labour party's victory in 1945, the British Broadcasting Corporation, much of the national electric power grid, the overseas airlines, and London urban transit system had been "nationalized" and operated by public authorities under state-chartered corporations. The largest extension of the public sector took place within five years after World War II.

The Labour government's nationalization program during 1945–51 was presented to the electorate and the Parliament as a move toward: better coordination of public policies in the areas of transportation, energy, money, and credit; consolidation and concentration of many small and inefficient concerns; improving the welfare of working men; and reduction of private monopoly power. The targets were the so-called "commanding heights" of the economy, i.e., fuel, power, and transportation. As part of this program, the Bank of England was nationalized in 1946. Coal mining, electricity and gas, railways, civil aviation, cables and wireless,

148. See *The National Plan* (London: HMSO, 1965:), pp. 1–3.
149. For a critical evaluation of British planning, see John Jewkes, *The New Ordeal by Planning* (London: Macmillan, 1968), Part One.
150. For a balanced evaluation of British planning, see Samuel Brittan, *Inquest on Planning in Britain* (London: PEP, 1967).

waterways, and, finally, steel came under government ownership and control before the Labour Party was voted out of office in 1951. The Conservatives reversed some of these measures, and the new Labour government reinstated them after 1964.[151]

In the wake of the Conservatives' victory in 1979, the British nationalized sector included nine industries whose assets were totally owned by the state and whose boards of directors were appointed by the government. They were British Airways, British Gas, British Rail, British Steel Corp., Central Electricity Council, the National Coal Board, the Post Office (including telephones), National Bus Co., National Freight Corp., British Aerospace, and British National Oil Corp. Other public enterprises not primarily engaged in industrial activities included British Airports Authority, British Waterways Board, a number of regional water and port authorities, and a host of others, such as the Bank of England and the National Enterprise Board. The state also had various stakes in hundreds of other firms, ranging from the giant British Petroleum to a soccer club. In 1975 the National Enterprise Board was established by the Labour government as a kind of state holding company to manage sundry public entities and to buy and keep a stake in any manufacturing company.

Altogether, the nationalized industries account for about 11 percent of GDP, 8 percent of the work force, nearly 20 percent of all fixed investments, and 24 percent of industrial investments.[152] The rationale for nationalization in the United Kingdom is not so much the old "socialist" dogma regarding job provision and consumer protection. It is, instead, mainly concerned with preventing the abuse of private monopoly power in a strategic industry, achieving economies of scale, shoring up a declining industry, increasing research and development for higher efficiency, and supplying essential goods and services that are not competitively produced and cannot be very well regulated by public utility commissions.[153]

The British nationalized industries have shown different rates of profitability at different times. British Rail—dubbed the "worst organization"—has been losing money year after year as a result of administrative inefficiency, featherbedding, and other problems. The Postal Service (including telecommunications) is another nationalized activity often in the red. The coal industry, despite heavy government protection (monopoly pricing, ban on imports, taxes on competing fuel) has had

---

151. The British steel industry, for example, which was denationalized in 1953 under the Tories, was renationalized in 1967. But unlike the 1951 steel nationalization, which placed the entire industry under public control, the 1967 move left about 250 small firms (producing about 10 percent of total output) in private hands.

152. The public sector, however, including all government services not sold in the market (police, courts, defense, welfare, etc.), is much larger, with 6.5 million workers in public employ.

153. Steel renationalization by the Labour government in 1967 was defended on the grounds of a need for modernization and reorganization of the stagnant steel industry to make it competitive in world markets. The takeover of British Leyland, ICL, and Rolls Royce during the 1970s was justified on grounds of keeping Britain in high-technology and defense-related fields.

half of its pits in perpetual deficit because of overstaffing and low productivity. The Electricity Council, British Gas, and Waterways have also been money losers from time to time. The government annual subsidies to the money-losing nationalized industries have run as high as one billion pounds sterling. Deficit industries have also been helped with social grants, capital write-offs, and tax exemptions. The British National Oil Corp., on the other hand, has been a very lucrative public enterprise.

The blame for the losses in nationalized industries, however, may perhaps have to be placed partly on the conflicts of objectives in those industries. Public enterprises in Britain have been saddled with a compulsory range of activities they cannot easily modify, an inherited work force they cannot readily reduce, a wage scale that has escalated under political pressure more than the private sector's, and prices that have not always been allowed to rise as fast as costs.[154] Undue centralized control, sheer size, inflexible manpower budgets, small supervisory staff, and a ban against diversification have also been responsible for the poor performance.

On the whole, the considered view of some careful analysts is that the postwar British nationalization efforts have satisfied nobody: not the Labour politicians, who saw public ownership as a means of increased efficiency and fairer share for all; not the trade unionists, who aspired to run the nationalized industries once the capitalist managers were ousted; not the consumers, who hoped that nationalization would mean a better deal for them; not the social reformers, who wished to abolish the conflict between workers and management.[155] Nor has it made any difference which political party has been in power. In the opinion of the British historian C. Northcote Parkinson, who believes that nationalized industries have a built-in tendency to go bankrupt, the difference between the British Conservatives and Labourites with respect to nationalized industries is that Tories expect state corporations to make money or break even through restriction of domestic and foreign competition, and Labour is willing to subsidize them directly.[156]

In retrospect, one reason for the British stagflation has been the relatively large size and the relative autonomy of the British public sector, making it possible for nationalized industries and local authorities to disregard the government's monetary and fiscal policies. Public enterprises also enjoy special borrowing privileges and fund-raising opportunities on the one hand, and monopoly power in setting utility rates and prices on the other. And those industries that cannot raise their prices at will, usually fall back on government subsidies.

154. For an analysis of pricing and productivity in public industry, see Ralph Turvey, *Economic Analysis and Public Enterprises* (London: Allen & Unwin, 1973). For a brief account of public enterprises see "Doing the Sums for Britain's Nationalized Industries," *The Economist*, 15 March 1980.

155. See "Living with the Leviathans," *The Economist*, 26 July 1975.

156. For further evaluation of British nationalization, see Richard Pryke, *Public Enterprise in Practice* (London: MacGibbon, 1971); David Coombes, *State Enterprise: Business or Politics?* (London: Allen & Unwin, 1971); and D. N. Chester, *The Nationalization of British Industry, 1945–51* (London: HMSO, 1975).

Nonmonetary Incentives

Great Britain makes an effective use of nonmonetary incentives to elicit greater achievements from its citizens. The Queen's Annual Honors List, giving such prizes as a life peerage and knighthood in various "orders," recognizes exemplary accomplishments such as improving the British balance of payments (the Beatles), fighting a good boxing match (Henry Cooper), or exhibiting mastery at *haute politique* (former foreign secretaries). While some recipients may not be enormously excited about their honors (and a few occasionally return them), the vast majority of the British people envy such recognition. And the British economy, particularly in its public sector, is considerably influenced by such incentives.

Wage-Price Determination

Direct wage and price determination was extensively used in England during the Second World War and continued until the early 1950s. Since then such actions have, as a rule, been exerted mainly in the nationalized industries (railroads, coal, gas, electricity, and steel) and in supporting agricultural prices.

Prices in nationalized industries (or state monopolies) are all set by the government on a variety of considerations ranging from consumers' welfare to enterprise's profits. For years, prices in many of those state activities were kept down for political expediency (to restrain general inflation). Since 1975, utility rates, postage stamps, and transport fares have been raised periodically.[157] Outside the nationalized industries, the minimum lending rate of interest by the Bank of England is government determined. The agricultural support prices are also centrally determined according to a complicated formula in line with Britain's rights and responsibilities vis-à-vis the European Community.

The Market Sector: Consumers' Influence

Great Britain was the originator and, for long, the most ardent practitioner of laissez faire capitalism. The British economy was until World War II a largely free-market economy with characteristic concentration of economic power and a philosophical aversion to governmental interference. Since the war, however, it has drifted back and forth between an activist Labour government and a Conservative administration. Even today, however, Britain's economy is predominantly governed by individuals and private groups who direct and manage some 60 percent of the GNP.

157. In April 1978, nationalized industries were given responsibility for their own pricing policy (and more flexibility in financing) in exchange for a 5 percent required rate of return on new investment.

The "nonmarket" sector (where output is not sold privately to individuals but paid for out of taxes or financed by other state revenues) accounts for about 40 percent of the economy (compared to 30 percent in the 1960s).

The market sector is also far from perfectly competitive. The "near-perfect" sector includes the *commodity* market (gold, metals, raw materials) and the *currency* market (spot and forward exchange trading).[158] The "imperfect," or "monopolistic," sector includes agriculture (subsidized and protected) and services (diffuse in small retailing and concentrated in banking and insurance).

Agriculture, a small but important British economic activity, is in the hands of well over 200,000 private farms (mostly family units) employing directly about 3 percent of the labor force and producing about 3 percent of the GDP. All arable, grazing, and pasture lands are privately owned. Even two-thirds of the woodlands belong to private interests.

A large part of manufacturing, employing nearly one-third of the labor force and accounting for about 30 percent of Britain's output of goods and services, is in private hands. There are an estimated 50,000 private manufacturing concerns, mostly small and medium sized. Except for iron ore and coal (the only major mineral resource in the United Kingdom), all mining and quarrying activities are done by private enterprise. The construction industry, employing some 5.5 percent of the labor force and contributing about 7 percent of the GNP, is mostly private, although some of its projects are undertaken for the public sector. Transportation is partly private. Commercial banking, shipping, insurance (except social security), wholesale and retail trades, and almost all professional services (with the notable exception of health care) are almost totally private.[159] Perhaps more important than most of these sectors, foreign trade is a crucial element in the British standard of living and is almost totally dependent on private enterprise.

Counting farmers, professionals, small retail shops, and others in the service trade, Britain has close to 3 million privately owned and unquoted enterprises. Eliminating agriculture, the professions, financial services, and "tiny" shops, there are more than 800,000 small firms divided almost equally between manufacturing and retailing. They employ one-third of the work force and account for one-fifth of GDP. The average small retail establishment employees three or four people, and has an annual sales of about $100,000.

158. In both markets, particularly that of foreign exchange, there are large numbers of buyers and sellers (hundred of dealers in London and throughout the world); the products traded (pound, yen, or gold) are homogenous; and there is also near-perfect knowledge of prevailing prices at any given time during trading days. But the ideal conditions of perfect competition are still wanting, because entry is often limited to authorized dealers, and large buyers and sellers actually do influence prices. For details of a currency market operation, see "Pound Dealing," *The Economist*, 16 October 1976.

159. Even in the area of medical and old-age pension insurance, an estimated 2 million Britons reportedly subscribe to private health insurance plans, and some 4 million use private doctors at one time or another. Some 12 million are also covered by private pension plans.

The British private sector governed by consumer sovereignty, however, is subject to all the important modifications of a purely competitive system. Furthermore, the decline in the number of small firms over the last twenty-five years has been more pronounced in Britain than in the United States and Japan. The top one hundred British firms share more than one-third of total manufacturing employment, 40 percent of output, and 45 percent of sales. In such British manufacturing industries as mining (except coal), food and drink, chemicals, metals, electronics, and vehicles, more than half of total output is produced by only five large firms in each industry. Thus, while the average size of big businesses in England may be smaller than the corresponding figure in the United States or Japan, bigness is by no means absent in the British economy. Some 40 percnet of annual private investment is made by no more than seventy-five concerns. Giant firms, however, account for only a small percentage of total British business concerns. Firms employing more than two thousand workers are less than 1 percent of the total.[160]

In general, while the conditions for pure competition rarely apply over a wide range of products in private manufacturing, genuine competitiveness in retailing remains relatively strong.[161]

The British Economy: A Shrinking Giant

Postwar Britain presents a curious and somewhat uncommon case of a major industrial economy suffering a relative decline in economic power and prosperity.[162] Those concerned with the British "national malaise" often note that the United Kingdom, before World War II, had a per capita income twice that of France's or Germany's. By 1980, the ratio was nearly reversed. Even in the mid-1950s, the United Kingdom was among the world's top ten richest nations, with a per capita income about one-fourth larger than West Germany's and five times as large as Japan's. In 1980, Japan's income per head was more than 50 percent higher, and West Germany's nearly twice as high.

Some commentators, both in England and the United States, attribute this poor economic performance to a persistent move by both Tory and Labour administrations to a "corporatist" and "collectivist" economy, increasingly bent on providing added social services and larger public ownership and operation. The Tory leadership during the 1979 election referred to the British postwar experience as a "failure" and argued that only through greater reliance on the private enterprise and market incentives could Britain once again become a dynamic and prosperous economy. Previous governments were indirectly criticized for failure to strengthen

160. For a detailed account of business mergers in Britain, see L. Hannah and J. A. Kay, *Concentration in Modern Industry* (London: Macmillan, 1977).
161. For more details, see "Britain's Small Businesses," *The Economist*, 29 September 1979.
162. See W. Beckerman, ed., *Slow Growth in Britain* (London: Oxford University Press, 1979).

individual incentives by denying people the right to keep more of their income; failure to enlarge freedom of consumer choice by reducing state intrusion in the economy; failure to reduce public borrowing from the market in order to leave more room for private commerce and industry to finance their projects; and failure to make those who engage in collective bargaining responsible for the consequences of their actions.

The intensity and duration of the British disease, however, cast doubts on the validity of such simplified, unilinear explanations. The behavior of the British economy since Mrs. Thatcher's accession to power clearly shows the stubborn nature of British stagnation, inflation, unemployment and labor strife. In the first year of the new Tory rule, inflation rose from 8 percent to nearly 20 percent; the discount rate rose from 12 percent to 20 percent; unemployment rose from 1.3 million to over 1.6 million and headed toward the previously unthinkable level of 2 million; private capital spending was down by 3 percent; the 1978 trade surplus of $1.5 billion turned into $7.3 billion trade deficit in 1979; and the 1980 economic slump promised to be worse than the 1973–74 decline.

A more plausible diagnosis must therefore be sought in the fundamental economic and social conditions of postwar British society and, in particular, in a juxtaposition of several growth-inhibiting factors in the economy.

Past governments, both Labour and Tory, may in fact have been too activist and too expansionist in the public sector for a weak economy to withstand or endure. Taxes may have been too punitive in their extreme progressivity, (98 percent on marginal "unearned" annual incomes over a mere $20,000). Money supply may have been too excessive in the face of sluggish (a mere 2.5 percent a year) productivity. Foreign exchange controls may have been too rigid for a reserve currency country. But none of these factors—or even their combination—is uniquely British or capable of causing such a prolonged stagflation.

A recent analysis offers some penetrating, nonideological explanations. Of the major factors responsible for the poor British economic performance, attention is drawn to political setbacks from the position of imperial power, the demise of sterling as a world currency, a natural "catching up" by new industrializing LDCs, the inability to weed out aging and lame-duck industries, and failure to wind inflation down to the level of international competitors. The resulting industrial ossification and endemic inflation are, in turn, attributed to labor immobility, low investment and scant innovation, poor management-labor relations, internal social division, and regional rivalries. Juxtaposed to these growth-impeding causes are excessive expectations by the rank and file of what government can deliver, persistent demands by voters for income distribution by the state rather than stimulation of production, the acceptance by the government of an unsustainable dominance in the economy, and, last, but not least, the behavior of trade unions in featherbedding, interminable internal rivalries, and attempts to usurp the role of the state and of management.[163]

163. For a most concise examination of these issues, see "The British Disease," *The Economist*, 10 November 1979.

JAPAN

With a population of more than 115 million, crammed into some 372,000 square kilometers of land scattered over an archipelago of more than a thousand islands with precious little natural resources, Japan is a study in wonders. Militarily defeated, psychologically demoralized, and economically devastated at the end of World War II, Japan today is the third largest country in the world in GNP (after the United States and the Soviet Union), with a per capita income several times higher than the Russians and fast approaching the Americans'.

Third in industrial production and international trade, behind the United States and Germany, Japan is now an economic superpower. She presently leads the world in shipbuilding; second in steelmaking and in automobile production. Japanese industries, long-identified as "the world's leading copycats," are now taking the lead in many scientific and technological areas and selling their patents and processes abroad, particularly in electronics and optics but also in chemicals, steel, aircraft, nuclear power, antipollution devices, and oceanography.

Japan's postwar "economic miracle" is attributed to a host of diverse factors, among which the choice of the decision-making mechanisms has been of crucial significance. While most foreign specialists on Japan tend to credit her success to the traditional Japanese virtues of diligence, hard work, frugality, organizational loyalty, modesty, self-discipline, and eagerness to learn, others seem to place more stock on the vital influence of a national purpose, the consistency of economic policy, and conscious planning.[164] Others point to such factors as a markedly light burden of expenditures for defense and social security, an unusual talent for borrowing and adapting the best in foreign technology, a typically Japanese esprit de corps or teamwork, a highly successful domestic protection policy, and a largely undervalued currency for a good number of years after the war.[165]

Consumers' Sovereignty

The Japanese economy is commonly considered a market economy, because nearly all major economic activities are ostensibly under prvate ownership and management. Outside the traditional sphere of government enterprise and operation, this is certainly true, but the emphasis on the market is primarily instrumental, not ideological. That is, the Japanese system is neither structurally liberal nor economically free. In fact, Japan's economy is highly regulated internally and, until recently, strongly protected against foreign competition. Although the government plays a crucial (if not determining) role in shaping private business decisions, the private economy regards the state not as a regulator, controller, or rival but rather as a protector, a guide, and a partner.

164. See E. Neuberger and W. Duffy, *Comparative Economic Systems* (Boston: Allyn and Bacon, 1976). ch. 18; and Ezra F. Vogel, *Japan as Number One* (Cambridge, Mass: Harvard University Press, 1979).

165. For an earlier discussion of Japan's phoenixlike rise to prominence, see Robert Guillain, *The Japanese Challenge* (Philadelphia: Lippincott, 1970).

JAPAN: BASIC DATA

LAND AREA (sq. km.)	372,000
POPULATION (1980 estimate)	117 million
Net annual increase (1970-78 yearly average)	1.2 percent
Urban (percent of total, 1980)	78 percent
Working Age (15–64) (percent of total, 1978)	68 percent
LABOR FORCE (total civilian, 1977)	54 million
Agriculture, forestry, fishing (percent of total)	13 percent
Mining, manufacturing, construction (percent of total)	39 percent
Services, etc. (percent of total)	48 percent
GROSS DOMESTIC PRODUCT (market prices, 1979)	$1,100 billion
Per capita (1979)	$9,560
Average annual increase (1970–78)	7.7 percent
Public consumption (percent of GDP)	10 percent
Private consumption (percent of GDP)	58 percent
Fixed capital formation (ratio to GDP)	31 percent
Savings (ratio to GDP)	32 percent
GROSS DOMESTIC PRODUCT (market prices, 1979)	$1,100 billion
Agriculture, forestry, fishing (share in GDP)	5 percent
Mining, manufacturing, construction (share in GDP)	40 percent
Services (share in GDP)	55 percent
FOREIGN TRADE	
Exports (percent of GDP)	10 percent
Imports (percent of GDP)	8 percent

An estimated 14 percent of the Japanese labor force is engaged in agriculture, which is both private and small scale (1.14 hectare per farm household). Farming is concentrated on little over 16 percent of the total land area and accounts for about 5 percent of GDP, but Japanese agriculture is relatively modernized and highly efficient. For some crops, such as rice, the yield per acre is the highest in the world. Mining, manufacturing, and construction account for about 37 percent of GDP and about 37 percent of the labor force. Tertiary activities (trade, public utilities, services, and the government) account for nearly 60 percent of GDP and 49 percent of employment.

Domestic trade and services (excluding transport and communications) are small scale and in the hands of nearly 2 million private concerns.[166] Department stores, however, are among the world's largest. Banking and financial institutions (including credit associations and farm cooperatives) are largely private. Except for publicly held long-distance railway hauling and freight, land, sea, and air transport is also private.

The Japanese private market economy is dualistic in character, consisting of a large number of small firms beside a small number of giant concerns. Of an estimated 4.8 million Japanese enterprises, more than 75 percent are unincorporated. In terms of unemployment, more than 95 percent of all establishments employ less than four persons, and only 1.5 percent have more than 1,000 people on their payrolls. Of the medium-size companies employing more than thirty workers, nearly 88 percent have less than two hundred employees. Despite the numerical superiority of small and medium-size private firms, the giant corporations are highly visible. More than 25 percent of the entire labor force depends for its livelihood on the 1.5 percent companies employing more than 1,000 people. Furthermore, small companies are mostly suppliers and subcontractors for larger firms.

Japanese industrialization, beginning in the late nineteenth century and benefiting from developed Western technology, was initially concentrated in light industries. In the postwar period, steel, heavy engineering, shipbuilding, electrical and chemical industries, automotives, and other science-based manufacturing sprang up very rapidly, bringing Japan up to the level of the most developed industrial countries. In spite of Herculean efforts by Allied powers after World War II to break up the traditional economic power of the Zaibatsu, the large-family holding company structure,[167] the three largest firms in aluminum, lead, automobiles, glass, tin cans, zinc, and beer and ale still control the bulk of output in each industry. In some fourteen industries, the three largest firms have a more than 50 percent share of the market. Industry concentration is actually far more significant than these figures indicate, for many "independent" firms are linked together through a maze of reciprocal deals, financial affiliations, and close business

166. Japan's domestic trade employs 22 percent of the work force and accounts for 18 percent of the national income.
167. Under the order of Occupation authorities, the existing Zaibatsus were dissolved and their senior executives purged under a Law for the Elimination of Excessive Concentration of Economic Power (1947).

ties. Nevertheless, the large postwar conglomerations—the Keiretsus—provide for more intramural and interfirm competition than before, at least in terms of diversified stock ownership. Postwar business concentration is largely reflected in specialized associations of firms with mutual economic self-interests.

Indirect Controls: The State As a Proxy

Competent observers are unanimous in their belief that Japan's postwar "miraculous" growth has gained its major stimulus from government regulation, guidance, and direction. Abandoning its prewar role of a direct major economic decision maker, the state has assumed a new responsibility for bringing together various groups in the service of national goals, a process aptly called "sponsored capitalism." Among the many factors underlying Japanese postwar recovery (including American aid and the absence of heavy armament), three public policies stand out: a monetary policy that provided growth industries with needed expansionary finance and cut credit quickly when pressures rose against price stability; a fiscal policy that was all for expanding private industrial investment and encouraged private initiatives through tax holidays, export subsidies, and sensible taxes; and an effective foreign-trade policy (including quotas, tariffs, and commodity taxes) that kept the balance of payments in a fairly healthy state.[168] As we shall see, the Japanese public sector as such is fairly small in comparison with other advanced industrial countries. Most of the strategic controls by the government are uniquely indirect and embedded in a sort of close cooperation between economic authorities and big corporations.

The ostensible aims of economic policy under Allied dictation was the creation of a competitive market structure and the establishment of a "just" income distribution. In the immediate postwar period, a strong antimonopoly law was passed and the tax system was overhauled in a progressive direction, but under subsequent cold war politics and heavy pressures from the old-line military-industrial coalition (which saw quick Japanese recovery as essential to peace in Asia), a greater degree of leniency toward business concentration and a tougher line against equality was followed.[169]

Fiscal Policy

Taxation and credit policies are extensively relied upon not only for income redistribution, social-welfare provisions, and monetary control, but also to spur modernization, export promotion, and economic growth. The Japanese tax system (relying on personal and corporation income taxes for more than half of the

168. See G. D. Allen, *Japan's Economic Expansion* (London: Oxford University Press, 1965), pp. 249–250.
169. See Kozo Yamamura, *Economic Policy in Postwar Japan* (Berkeley: University of California Press, 1967).

government revenue) is geared through a number of special provisions to the basic national objectives of encouraging personal savings, stimulating industrial modernization, promoting research and development of new products, and expanding exports.

Fiscal policies and incentives are also employed by the central government, as in France, to ensure compliance with the basic directions of the socioeconomic development plans. Through appropriate changes in regular government expenditures and its public investment programs (as well as changes in public loans, subsidies, and tax credits), the Japanese government is able to channel aggregate demand and supply toward nationally desired targets. Because of the buoyancy of the Japanese full-employment economy for most of the postwar period, up to 1973 fiscal policy was rarely needed to stimulate demand, and there was relatively little deficit financing. The recession of 1974–75 and the deflationary effects of the oil price rise on the oil-starved Japanese economy gave rise to a gradually increasing deficit spending, so much so that by fiscal 1979, some 40 percent of state expenditures was made up by bond issues—the highest of any MICs.

In frequent revisions of the original, Allied-imposed tax law of 1946, the Liberal-Democratic government's policy until recently was to encourage savings through a reduction in income tax progressivity for both individuals and corporations; to increase investment through generous depreciation allowance, preferential tax treatment and numerous exemptions given to business firms in the name of rationalization; to allow some income redistribution by reducing tax burdens on lower-income groups in times of high corporate profits and lower corporate taxes during recessionary periods; and to alter interest and dividend tax rates to combat economic fluctuations.

The share of the Japanese tax burden (including social insurance contributions) in the national income is around 28 percent. Expenditures by all levels of governments is less than 22 percent of the GDP—the lowest among all industrialized countries. More than 60 percent of government revenue is derived from direct and indirect taxes, an additional 2 percent from state enterprises and monopolies, and the rest from miscellaneous sources, including public bonds. About 24 percent of total revenue is raised from individual incomes; another 22 percent, from corporations; 18 percent, from customs and excises (mostly customs, liquor, and stamp duties); and the rest is from miscellaneous levies. On the expenditure side, about 24 percent of the total public expenditure is spent on pensions and social security;[170] 16 percent on social infrastructures (housing, roads and ports, land conservation, and development); about 11 percent, on education; some 5.5 percent, on national defense—the lowest of any major country in the

---

170. Japan's social security covers old-age pensions, welfare assistance, unemployment insurance, health insurance, workers' compensation, family allowances, and others. Almost the entire population is covered by these schemes. The benefits, however, are generally lower than in Western Europe. Financing is divided between the national government, local governments, and the beneficiaries.

world; and the rest is spent on regular government services and transfer to local governments.[171]

Monetary Policy

Despite extensive government involvement in the economy, economic growth in Japan has been accompanied by frequent business fluctuations and pressures on the balance of payments. The government, through the Central Bank of Japan, has used various indirect monetary controls to cope with the emerging situations.

Monetary policy has been by far the strongest arm of government indirect intervention. This is largely because the bulk of domestic savings in Japan is based on individual thrift; a sizable portion of domestic private investments is financed through corporate bank borrowings; individual investment opportunities in the securities market are limited; and savings accounts still provide the most readily available outlet for private individual savings. The banking system thus plays a crucial role in Japanese economic development, for mobilizing small private savings, for lending to industrial corporations, and for combating business fluctuations.

Monetary and credit policies are formulated and carried out by the Central Bank and a host of government financial institutions. The principal policy instruments are the familiar ones: changes in the official discount rate, requirements for legal reserves, open-market operations, and "window guidance" (ceilings on commercial bank loans). The most effective and most frequently used device has been the discount rate, on funds provided to the usually liquidity-short and overlent commercial banks. Reserve requirements on demand deposits during the 1970s ranged between 4.25 percent in 1974 to 2.5 percent in 1978. The discount rate has been as low as 4.25 percent in 1972–73 and as high as 9 percent in 1974–75, and 1980. Monetary policies of the Bank of Japan are determined by a Policy Board composed of government officials, commercial banks' representatives, and industry leaders, which has somewhat similar functions as the U.S. Federal Reserve Open Market Committee.

Trade and Exchange Policy

Japan follows a freely floating exchange rate policy under which the value of Japanese yen is determined, in principle, on the basis of underlying demand and supply conditions in the market. However, Japanese authorities intervene from time to time to combat disorderly fluctuations. Thus, when the yen becomes inor-

171. For details, see the annual *Statistical Handbook of Japan* (Tokyo: Bureau of Statistics); and annual *Statistical Survey of Japan's Economy* (Tokyo: Ministry of Foreign Affairs).

dinately undervalued and Japanese raw materials become too costly for domestic anti-inflationary policy, the authorities dip into their substantial foreign-exchange reserves to offset the trend.

Japanese external trade has also received a good deal of official attention and intervention in recent years. Imports have been subject either to individual licensing by the government or, if liberalized, to declaration. Certain items have been controlled by the import quota system. The importation of items on "the negative list" has been restricted because of direct state trading in them, for the protection of home industries, or for other reasons. Items under state trading include cereals, salt, and tobacco. Items not under the quota system have been free of quantitative restrictions and licensing; they required only notification to an authorized bank.

Exports have also been subject to government controls. Under the Export and Import Transaction Law, restrictions on export volume, export prices, or other conditions may be imposed in the case of some sixty items on global exports to particular destinations. Some items have required special licenses under the Foreign Exchange and Foreign Trade Control Law. Restrictions on these goods have included certain destinations, temporary halt due to domestic shortages, and precautionary measures to forestall the imposition of import restrictions by other countries.

Foreign investments in Japan in the form of purchases of stocks and bonds or loans by foreign investors are generally subject to government approval. Foreign direct investment is also subject to approval by the Foreign Investment Council.[172]

Antimonopoly Policy

On paper, Japan possesses a rather strong antimonopoly law. The Act Relating to Prohibition of Private Monopoly and Methods of Preserving Fair Trade, passed in 1947, aimed at preventing the revival of the Zaibatsu private empires; but the law, amended several times, permits mergers and cartelization when justified by external economies or in order to deal with industrial depression. Intercorporate stock ownership and interlocking directorates, even among competitors, is allowed when competition is not substantially lessened. Resale price maintenance is legal in many lines. Cartelization of small enterprises and export-import cartels are in fact encouraged and sanctioned by the government itself.

Japan's anticartel law is administered by a Fair Trade Commission, but the commission, working against the public opinion which considers corporate giant-ism vital to Japanese "national survival," rarely moves seriously to block proposed mergers. According to Western obervers (and fiercely denied by the Japanese themselves) cartels, monopolies, price fixing, and market splitting, are accepted facts of life. This attitude has been responsible for the reemergence of the prewar

172. For details, see *Annual Report on Exchange Arrangements and Exchange Restrictions 1980* (Washington: International Monetary Fund, 1980).

Zaibatsu system (vertical integration and control of financial, operating, and trading activities under one holding company).[173] Nevertheless, the FTC has remained an important feature of the government's anti-inflation fights as it is often supported by the public in its curbs on price fixing. At the same time several features of the Japanese economy (rivalry among big corporations, the supervision of private banks, and cost-cutting drives) play into the commission's hand.

Business Promotion

The type of help that Japanese business receives from its government is the envy of businessmen the world over. Big Japanese corporations can get together and act in concert not only free from government intervention, but with considerable official blessings.[174] This is particularly true with respect to foreign trade, the mainstay of Japanese postwar prosperity. In addition to having one of the lowest corporate taxes among industrial countries, Japanese business has been sheltered from world competition by high tariffs, import restrictions, and exchange control. As indicated before, there are quotas against scores of imported commodities and various restrictions against foreign direct investment in Japanese enterprises. Even under the investment liberalization adopted in 1973, some twenty-two categories of Japanese industries were excluded from 100 percent foreign ownership. Until 1964, Japan refused to make its currency fully convertible, thus giving its exporters a competitive edge over their rivals by keeping the yen distinctly undervalued. Government ministries and agencies regularly prepare or underwrite studies of overseas markets with a view to Japanese export sales. A persistent surplus in the balance of trade has helped increase Japanese foreign-exchange reserves to one of the highest in the world—although the trend seems to be changing.

In the area of public subsidies, various government financial institutions have been established to help small business and agriculture. The Small Business Finance Corporation and the Japan Development Bank provide credit for plant and equipment modernization; the People's Finance Corporation covers smaller business credits; and the Small Business Credit Insurance Corporation provides guarantee and insurance against private loans to small business. The Agricultural Finance Corporation makes low-interest, long-term loans to small farmers with low credit standing. The heavy burden of Japanese corporate financial structure (80 percent debt versus 20 percent equity) is reduced through low-interest public loans.

173. The Mitsubishi complex, for example, is engaged in manufacturing, mining, transportation, real estate, banking, insurance, electric and gas utilities, and retailing. Its manufacturing segment alone covers oil refining, copper and zinc extractions, machine tools, electrical equipment, major household electrical appliances, shipbuilding, automobiles, chemicals, glass, rayon, cement, textiles, and ceramics.

174. In return, decision on industrial capacity expansion and new plants location must meet the prior approval of the government. In agriculture, too, the government annually announces the minimum purchase price for a number of agricultural commodities.

Intergroup Bargaining

Almost all sectors of the Japanese economy—agricultural, industrial, commercial, and professional—are organized in special-interest groups. So are workers and consumers. Farmers band together to raise governmental price support for agricultural products and to establish barriers against foreign competition. Professional associations coordinate their efforts to regulate fees and services. Consumer groups engage in activities that may produce better terms for them. Industrialists have their horizontal, vertical, and criss-cross federations.

Pressure groups formally operate outside the government, but in reality, there are very close ties between business associations and the ruling Liberal-Democratic party. One observer, in fact, considers Japanese interest groups "an organic part of the government mechanism" because of the homogeneity of industrial and government leadership, the tradition of government intervention in the economy, and the largely oligopolistic nature of Japanese business competition.[175] In addition to their close personal and professional ties with Diet deputies, Japanese lobbyists influence state decisions through participation in a number of "advisory committees" established by the government, in addition to their regular lobbying activities.[176]

The Japanese economy thus displays its own brand of multilateral choice making. Cooperation between government, business, and labor is very close and fairly extensive. In fact, one of the main responsibilities of the state is described as "the search for a consensus on national economic goals." The bulk of major economic decisions at the national level are made by consensus. Companies readily accept administrative guidance from the government and accommodate retired government officials as their executives and directors. Large corporations also work closely together in matters of common interests—sometimes in areas that would be patently illegal under the U.S. antitrusts laws—although they compete actively in gaining market shares. The consensus among companies, in turn, helps to coordinate business (particularly investment) decisions and to foreclose a good deal of uncertainties, surprises, and duplications. In a sense, Japan's "free-market" economy is run at the top by a complex alliance of financial, industrial, and commercial interests aided by the government.

Prior to World War II, all major politicoeconomic decisions in Japan were taken by four powerful Zaibatsus. Legally broken up during U.S. occupation, they later came back under loosely knit confederations of former members. Behind the new confederations are the major Japanese banks, which hold more than 20 percent of total stocks in Japanese industries, provide needed capital for expansion, participate in management decisions, and arrange mergers. At the core of the

175. W. M. Tsuneishi, *Japanese Political Style* (New York: Harper, 1966), p. 165.
176. An estimated 95 percent of all the leaders in government, business, industry, and banking come from no more than six big universities and have known each other for a long time.

Zaibatsu is a trading company, like Mitsubishi and Mitsui, which buys, sells, and gathers intelligence for the group. The three new big Zaibatsus together own some 40 percent of Japanese industry. They themselves are knit together through interlocking shareholdings, mergers, and joint ventures. This big business community, in its turn, is on intimate terms with the government. Government-business relations in Japan have few parallels among industrial countries. Students of the Japanese economy are all in agreement that while the state's statutory control over business is more limited than in most MICs, its informal powers are much more effective. Government and business leaders seldom make major decisions without consulting one another.[177]

Management-labor relations in Japan are moderately cooperative. Present-day Japanese unions are the creation of the Allied powers' desire to democratize Japan's postwar economy and to build up a new countervailing force against the Japanese military-industrial complex. The total trade-union membership is about 12.5 million (33 percent of the industrial labor force) divided among 70,000 unions. The core of Japanese unionism is the "enterprise union," organized from among all workers in a single plant or company regardless of occupation. Nearly 90 percent of union membership is organized along this line. There are few industrywide unions, the seamen's being the notable exception. Unions in the same industry form industrywide federations, which in turn make up the membership of one of four national labor centers or confederations. Of the latter, the General Council of Trade Unions is the oldest (established in 1950) and largest (with fifty affiliated federations and over 4.5 million members); it is also the most militantly socialist. It includes mostly public-sector employees, such as the Teachers' Union and the Local Government Workers' Union. The General Confederation of Labor, with thirty federations and nearly 2.2 million members, has 90 percent of its membership in private employment and is a bread-and-butter socialist; it generally supports the Democratic-Socialist party. The other two, the National Federation of Independent Unions, with 1.3 million members, and the National Federation of Industrial Organizations, with only 61,000 members, comprise a very large number of small union shops in the private sector. Owing to serious differences in the organizational philosophy among the four confederations, there is no united labor front. None of these centers directly engage in collective bargaining, although there is some degree of cooperation among them toward a uniform annual wage hike.

On the management side, there are also several major confederations. The Federation of Economic Organizations (Keidanren), for example, consists of more than a hundred large commercial, financial, and industrial associations comprising several hundred leading corporations. It is the voice of big business on all policy

177. Such actions as the "voluntary" quotas on some exports or a temporary cutback in steel output are decided upon and enforced by close consultation between industry and the state. See K. Yoshitake, *An Introduction to Public Enterprise in Japan* (Beverly Hills: Sage Publications, 1973); and W. W. Lockwood *(The State and Economic Enterprise in Japan)* Princeton: Princeton University Press, 1965.

matter except industrial relations and decides financial campaign contributions to political parties. The Federation of Employers (Nikkeiren), comprising nearly one hundred business associations, is the main spokesman for employers in all labor matters before government bodies. The Chamber of Commerce and Industry is made up of all companies but largely serves small-business interests, trying to represent smaller firms before government agencies. The Committee on Economic Development deals with a broad range of policy issues.[178]

Labor-management relations fall within the jurisdiction of four key acts: the Labor Standards Law, the Trade Union Law, the Labor Relations Adjustment Law, and the Unemployment Insurance Law—all enacted in 1947. Collective bargaining takes place at the enterprise level between the company and its union. There are, however, a handful of agreements on a multiemployer basis, as in shipping and private railways. Usually a key bargain is struck first in a leading industry and then becomes the model for other settlements.

Traditionally, Japanese organized labor has been largely a loyal, cooperative, partnership type. Workers and union leaders have often found their interests linked to those of their companies. Big business, in turn, has shunned labor-management strife. In large companies, workers have seldom been fired en masse, even during lean times; they, in their turn, infrequently resort to strikes and stay with one company until retirement. But this is all changing now.

The Japanese industrial relations system is thus said to be based on four pillars: lifetime employment, seniority wages, enterprise unionism, and company paternalism. Under lifetime employment, labor is frequently considered a "fixed cost," and workers are really big business's charge in a "cradle-to-grave" manner. Japan has no national minimum wages, but minimum wages are set by the government by industry, occupation, or region. Wage differentials in each industry or firm are related mostly to years of continuous service with the company rather than the job performed. Enterprise unionism allows many unions in various companies not to conclude collective bargaining agreements even though legally eligible to do so. Under company paternalism, the enterprise assumes a social nature, where there is a much stronger identification by workers with their employers.[179]

A large part of the annual income of Japanese workers frequently consists of fringe benefits like family health insurance, allowances for children, company pensions, housing, vacations, and other nonwage benefits. Familylike obligations of employees to their place of employment and a paternalistic attitude of Japanese entrepreneurs toward their workers continue to be an important social force in

178. There are also: organizations of firms from a single industrial sector (electrical or chemical) that specialize in looking after the common interests of that special sector, and groups composed of one firm from each sector that represent broad mutual interests (the Zaibatsus).

179. For details, see *The Development of Industrial Relations Systems: Some Implications of Japanese Experience* (Paris: OECD, 1977); and *Japan: Country Labor Profile* (Washington: U.S. Department of Labor, 1979).

Japan. Like other Japanese traditions, however, the "family enterprise" seems to be showing signs of change.[180] The same is increasingly true of such traditional fundamentals as job security, worker-management solidarity, and cooperation for technological innovation. As in other affluent societies, younger workers shun overtime in favor of holidays and days off in order to enjoy themselves; there is a new mobility among skilled workers from one company to another.

Government's Direct Controls

Japan's phenomenal postwar economic success is often attributed to its basically "free-enterprise" system. This is true in the sense that public ownership and operation of industry and imperative planning do not loom large in the Japanese economy. But from the standpoint of independent private economic decision making, Japanese business is far from free. As mentioned before, government agencies, including the Central Bank and the Ministry of International Trade and Industry, closely supervise business decisions, actively participate in corporate planning, serve as umpires in business disputes, and provide nonmonetary incentives to spur labor productivity. In fact, nowhere in the non-communist world do business and government work so closely together.[181]

Economic Planning

The Japanese economy is not unplanned, but economic planning is of the *indicative* variety, aiming to guide government agencies and private business in their investment decisions. The attempt at planning is attributed to the prevailing fashion in much of the postwar world. In the case of Japan, it is also based on a strong belief in the necessity and efficacy of government-business cooperation.

In addition to the early postwar reconstruction schemes (starting with the Five Year Plan for Economic Self-Support, 1953–58), two major indicative plans should be mentioned. The Plan for Doubling the National Income, 1961–70, envisaged an average annual growth rate of 7.2 percent through a much increased share of total investment in the infrastructure (transportation, and urban development) and public guidance, encouragement, and assistance to the private sector (for making long-term plans within the projections and targets of the main plan). As in the event of the two previous plans, the actual performance of the economy surpassed planned targets by substantial margins. The annual growth rate averaged

180. The government's welfare rolls are also increasingly replacing company obligations. The Japanese poor can now qualify for several types of welfare benefits: livelihood, housing, education, medical care, and vocational training.

181. See *Japan, The Government-Business Relationship: A Guide for the American Businessman* (Washington: GPO, 1972).

over 10 percent in 1961–65. Private investment in manufacturing industries also exceeded planned outlays in infrastructure. A new Social and Economic Plan for 1967–72 was similarly overtaken by events. As a result, planning was downplayed after the 1973–74 oil price shock and the considerable decline in economic growth. Later in the decade, in 1979, however, a Seven-Year Plan was announced, projecting a 5.7 percent annual expansion, and a much greater emphasis on the prerequisites of a new welfare society.

The significance of Japanese planning for private investment decisions (or even for the conduct of public agencies) is highly debatable. So is the planning's impact on the economy's actual performance. The real influence of the plans probably lies in their suggestive power over the private sector, and in their Japanese-style challenge to business firms to outperform each other. The plan's decisive powers are largely minimal. The enthusiastic response of Japanese industrialists to their national plans, however, is in sharp contrast to the scepticism of British firms with respect to Britain's 1962 and 1965 plans.

As in the case of French planning, Japanese plans are developed by an Economic Council composed of government and business leaders. The plans are worked out and coordinated by the Economic Planning Agency as an adjunct to the Prime Minister's Office. The main functions of economic planning, in addition to formulating public investment projects, are to use tax privileges, subsidies, and easy credits to stimulate private business firms to move along national economic lines. As in the French case also, the formal structure of the EPA is supplemented by an informal process of consultation between public officials and interested groups (large business firms, research organizations, academicians, trade unions, and others).

Public Enterprise

The public sector proper in Japan is not large, but varied. There are reportedly over one hundred public corporations engaged in basic services, social infrastructure, banking, administrative services and regional development. They differ not only in their functions, but also in their organizational control and sources of finance. Some, like Japan National Railways and Nippon Telephone and Telegraph, are run along close lines to a regular government department. Public financial corporations (such as Housing Loan Corporation) are administered and financed by the central and local governments. There are mixed enterprises, like Japan Airlines, which are capitalized and managed jointly by the state and private interests. Another group consists of semi-independent and joint public-private agencies responsible for such administrative functions as agricultural price support, social security, or environmental protection.[182]

182. For the list and more detailed description of these enterprises see G. C. Allen, "Government Intervention in the Economy of Japan," in Peter Maunder (ed.) *Government Intervention in the Developed Economy* (London: Croom Helm, 1979).

The central and local governments own over 40 percent of Japan's forests, and forests constitute nearly 70 percent of Japan's total land area. The central government has a monopoly on the production of salt, tobacco products, alcohol, and camphor. Railways, as a major means of transportation and an instrument of Japanese rapid modernization, are mostly in government hands. Post, telegraph, and telephones are under a public corporation. In finance, the government owns or operates Japan's Export-Import Bank, Japan Development Bank, Small Business Finance Corporation, Postal Savings, and the life insurance handled by the Post Office. Seven percent of the population live in public housing. Others are helped by the government through its Housing Loan Corporation.

Public ownership of industry, however, is insignificant. The income generated in the public sector proper is only 4 percent of the GNP. Government employment is an insignificant 4.5 percent of the labor force. General government consumption—about 8.5 percent of the GNP—is much less than in Western Europe and the United States. However, the public sector has been responsible for about 25 percent of annual gross domestic capital formation in the postwar period. Almost one-third of total investment has also been, in one way or another, influenced by government loan and investment programs. Extensive infrastructural inadequacies (transportation, environmental sanitation, housing and urban facilities) have increased governmental investment in major projects in housing sewage facilities, and road building.

Japan, Inc.

The whole Japanese economy is sometimes called "Japan, Inc." The designation refers to a constellation of closely linked efforts by Japanes politicians, business leaders, the bureaucracy, bankers, academia, and trade unions, as though everyone worked for a giant corporate enterprise.

This unique feature of Japanese society has produced Japan's postwar "economic miracle." With the highest population density among major industrial countries, heavy dependence on food imports, and virtually no oil, coal, iron ore, and other strategic minerals, Japan has managed to create an industrial base larger than the Soviet Union's. It has become the third largest trading nation (after the United States and Germany). It has overtaken Western countries in some of their traditional industries (British motorcycles, Swiss watches, German optics, American audiovisuals). And it has acquired a commanding position in many industries with highly sophisticated technology.

By taking advantage of a low-cost, disciplined, and hard-working labor force, economies of large-scale production (mostly due to unrestricted access to the rich U.S. market), and a highly efficient organization, Japan has managed to turn around its prewar reputation for poor quality goods to become an efficient innovative industrial and trade leader.

A large part of Japan's economic success is due to the Japanese special system of direction and management of the economy. Paramount among the distinct features of this system are a strong sense of national unity among the Japanese (partly reinforced by the result of World War II defeat); the concentration of economic power in large corporations and the tradition of paternalism in the private sector; a curious blend of cooperation and competition within the business community; and an open popular acceptance of the dominant role of the government, and the bureaucracy, in reaching major national decisions. Despite its avowed commitment to the free market, Japan is in many ways an "administered economy," where the adversary relationship between government and business, common in other free-enterprise countries, does not exist. Under so-called administrative guidance, the business sector solicits government advice, assistance, and protection all the way along. The state, in turn, expects private companies to heed its counsel when in the national interest. There is, indeed, an implicit and unwritten "partnership" between business and government that governs state-business relationships and behavior.

This partnership has undoubtedly worked well so far to bring about Japan's spectacular success story. This success, however, has not been without heavy costs: air and water pollution, traffic congestion, crowded quarters, inadequate health care, shortage of public services, and poor socioeconomic infrastructures have been the costs of building up industry. There are, however, increasing popular demonstrations protesting social disamenities and demanding more leisure time, better housing, greater social security, and more attention to other social problems.

There are also signs that the super growth, full employment, and the surplus position of the Japanese economy is encountering new strains. Unemployment, hidden and counted, is rising in the labor-intensive industries such as textiles, shipbuilding and steel that feel the competitive pinch from newly emerging industrial countries like South Korea and Taiwan. Jobless rates are also expected to increase in relatively less efficient service sector of the economy that is being rapidly modernized.

Yet, what distinguishes Japan from the other MICs is its fundamental attitude toward finding practical and expedient solutions instead of bothering with ideological or abstract debates; relentless dynamism in the pursuit of daily productivity; the characteristically enterprising spirit of its people; the meticulous care of its workers for making defect-free products; and its reliance on a mutually accommodating consensus instead of searching for flawlessly right decisions. These are the qualities that are most likely to endure.

Suggestions for Additional Readings

ABEGGLEN, J. C., ET AL. *Japan in 1980*. London: The Financial Times, 1974.

ABEGGLEN, J. C. *Management and Worker.* Tokyo: Kodansha, 1973.

ALLEN, G. C. *British Industry and Economic Policy.* London: Macmillan, 1979.

AUSTIN, L., ED. *Japan: The Paradox of Progress.* New Haven: Yale University Press, 1976.

AVERITT, R. T. *The Dual Economy: The Dynamics of American Industry Structure.* New York: Norton, 1968.

BIEDA, K. *The Structure and Operation of the Japanese Economy.* New York: Wiley, 1970.

BROADBRIDGE, S. *Industrial Dualism in Japan.* Chicago: Aldine, 1966.

CAMPBELL, J. C. *Contemporary Japanese Budget Politics.* Berkeley: University of California Press, 1977.

CAVES, R. E. *American Industry: Structure, Conduct, Performance.* Englewood Cliffs: Prentice-Hall, 1977.

CHRISTOPHER, J. B. "Consensus and Cleavage in British Political Ideology," *American Political Science Review,* September 1965.

COATES, D. *Labour in Power?* London: Longman, 1980.

DENISON, E. F., AND W. K. CHUNG. *How Japan's Economy Grew So Fast.* Washington: The Brookings Institution, 1976.

DIMOCK, M. E. *The Japanese Technocracy: Management and Government in Japan.* New York: Walker, 1968.

FRIEDMAN, M. AND R., *Free to Choose,* New York: Harcourt Brace, 1979.

GIBNEY, F. *Japan: The Fragile Superpower.* New York: Norton, 1975.

HACKER, A. *The End of the American Era.* New York: Atheneum, 1971.

HANNAH, L. *Concentration in Modern Industry.* London: Macmillan, 1977.

HEILBRONER, R. L. *The Limits of American Capitalism.* New York: Harper, 1966.

HIRSCHMEIER, J. *The Development of Japanese Business, 1600–1973.* Cambridge: Harvard University Press, 1975.

JOHNSON, C. *Japan's Public Policy Companies.* Stanford: Hoover Institution Press, 1978.

KAHN, H. *The Japanese Challenge.* New York: Crowell, 1979.

KALDOR, N. *Causes of the Slow Rate of Economic Growth of the United Kingdom.* London: Cambridge University Press, 1966.

KAPLAN, E. *Japan: The Government-Business Relationship.* Washington: U.S. Department of Commerce, 1972.

MATSUMOTO, Y. S. *Contemporary Japan: The Individual and the Group.* Philadelphia: American Philosophical Society, 1960.

MAUNDER, P., ED. *Government Intervention in the Developed Economy.* London: Croom Helm, 1979.

OKOCHI, K., ET AL. *Workers and Employers in Japan.* Princeton: Princeton University Press, 1974.

PATRICK, H., AND H. ROSOVSKY, EDS. *Asia's New Giant*. Washington: The Brookings Institution, 1976.

PATRICK, H., ED. *Japanese Industrialization and Its Social Consequences*. Berkeley: University of California Press, 1976.

PEMPEL, T. J., ED. *Policy Making in Contemporary Japan*. Ithaca: Cornell University Press, 1977.

REISCHAUER, E. O. *The Japanese*. Cambridge: Harvard University Press, 1977.

SCOTT, A. M. *Competition in American Politics—An Economic Model*. New York: Holt, Rinehart, 1970.

SCOTT-STOKES, H. *The Japanese Competitor*. London: The Financial Times, 1976.

SEGAL, R. *The Americans: A Conflict of Creed and Reality*. New York: Viking, 1969.

VERNON, R., ED. *Big Business and the State*. Cambridge: Harvard University Press, 1974.

VOGEL, E. F. ED. *Modern Japanese Organization and Decision Making*. Berkeley: University of California Press, 1975.

WALLERSTEIN, I. M. *The Capitalist World-Economy*. Cambridge: Cambridge University Press, 1979.

YOSHINO, M. Y. *Japan's Managerial System: Tradition and Innovation*. Cambridge: MIT Press, 1969.

YOSHINO, M. Y. *The Japanese Marketing System*. Cambridge: MIT Press, 1971.

11

The
Centrally Directed
Economies

THE CENTRALLY DIRECTED ECONOMIES (CDEs) principally comprise the Union of Soviet Socialist Republics, the People's Republic of China, the Eastern European members of the COMECON, and a few smaller countries such as Albania, North Korea, and Cuba. The CDEs, comprising nearly 35 million square kilometers and 1.3 billion people, possess about 27 percent of the earth's land mass and nearly 30 percent of global population. In terms of average GNP per capita, the CDEs assume a position between the third world and the MICs.

Centrally directed economies are not monolithic. Today, there are fourteen full-fledged communist governments in the world. There are more than one hundred active communist parties, most of them with no hope of gaining power. Of the ruling communist parties, China, Albania, and possibly North Korea constitute one group that more or less follows the Mao road to communism. Cuba and the six East European nations—Bulgaria, Czechoslovakia, East Germany, Hungary, Poland, and Romania—are usually classified as Soviet-type economies, following more or less the Russian lead on politicoeconomic matters. Yugoslavia is a maverick, with a somewhat less than orthodox communist ideology and vastly more unorthodox economic policy.

There are also significant points of divergence within each category. In the Eastern European bloc, for example, Yugoslavia and Romania have been more defiantly nationalistic than others. As a matter of practical economy, too, communist countries have followed different and somewhat divergent ways. Many have reversed their basic policies of economic reforms and liberalization—sometimes more than once. For these reasons, and also because of their basic ideological orientation, the use made of the four basic decision-making mechanisms vary in extent and intensity among these countries—and between them and the other groups.

Despite these important differences, certain fundamental features are common to all countries in this category, characteristics that more or less distinguish the CDEs from Western industrial countries and the less developed nations. First, as a matter of basic philosophy, the lion's share of national resources, means of production, and financial assets belongs to the state. Second, the largest share of gross domestic product investments and expenditures is planned and carried out by the state or state-controlled agencies and enterprises. Third, a distinctive majority of the economically active population is in the state's employment. Fourth, most major prices, wages, and salaries are determined by the government. Finally, the state has a virtual monopoly over foreign trade and investment.

Command Features

The most widely used mechanism of decision making in CDEs is command. The Soviet economy is a pioneer and a prototype of a modern command system among the CDEs.[1] Production and exchange in these economies are organized mainly through hierarchical lines that recognize the sole sovereignty of the Communist party and, theoretically, communist ideology. Resource allocation, output, consumption, and savings are publicly controlled through central directives or plans. Ownership is mainly public. Prices, wages, and distributive shares are largely and essentially determined by the state. Credit creation is a state monopoly. Private profit making is frowned upon. Nonmonetary incentives are made to play an important role in promoting initiative and innovation. The CDEs, however, use most of the instruments and many of the techniques of Western economies: money and banking, wages and interest payments, profit incentives, tariffs, taxes, and so forth.

Except for relatively minor differences in public ownership, administration of public enterprises, and the content of national plans, most CDEs follow the Soviet model in basic planning techniques and in decision-making mechanisms. The one major exception is Yugoslavia. To some extent, Hungary too has moved into certain novel experiments under its New Economic Mechanism. Of the six East European CDEs, Bulgaria is the least industrially developed; agriculture still absorbs nearly 40 percent of the labor force but produces only 25 percent of the GNP. By contrast, Czechoslovakian agriculture takes less than 20 percent of the work force and accounts for about 11 percent of GNP, while its industrial sector uses more than 40 percent of labor and turns out nearly two-thirds of the GNP. Romania and Hungary are moderately industrialized, with about 40 percent of their labor force and about half of their GNP associated with manufacturing. Poland employs

1. The Soviet economic system, however, is no longer an archetype of the CDEs. In some respects—particularly in attitudes toward totalitarian controls—such countries as Albania, Cuba, North Korea and Vietnam seem to be in favor of broader and more stringent intervention in the economy.

slightly more than one-third of its workers in each of these two sectors, but its industry produces three times as much as its agriculture (50 percent versus 17 percent). In East Germany, agriculture absorbs less than one fifth of the active population and accounts for about the same percentage of the GNP.

The East European economic plans are usually prepared under their own Communist party directives and are largely approved by their parliaments with little or no substantive changes. Until recently, economic planning was centralized in almost all its major aspects, with physical quotas, prices, and wages centrally determined. Since 1965, there has been a trend toward liberalization.

Industry in the CDEs (again with the notable exception of Yugoslavia) is almost totally nationalized and is pretty much directed and managed according to central plans. State industrial enterprises are, with minor differences, modeled after the Russians. Company managers are appointed by the government. Prices for almost all industrial goods are centrally determined or allowed to fluctuate within certain ranges. Credit control and investment in new industries are in state hands. Transportation, communications, banking, insurance, and foreign trade are almost totally nationalized and run by the state. The only real systemic difference between the Eastern European countries is in the treatment accorded agricultural and retail trade. Under Soviet tutelage, agricultural collectivization was undertaken in all Eastern European countries after 1949, but the pace of progress differed in different countries. At the start of the 1980s, Bulgaria, Czechoslovakia, East Germany, Hungary, and Romania were distinguished by their predominantly nationalized agriculture, where more than 85 percent of farmlands were in collectives or state farms and only 15 percent in private plots and/or cooperatives. Poland and Yugoslavia, on the other hand, had predominantly private agricultural sectors, where more than 80 percent of agricultural land was in private ownership and management, and the rest under state farming. Collectives accounted for less than 1 percent.

After Stalin's death in 1953, a trend got under way in Eastern European countries toward a profit-motivated management of the economy and away from the highly centralized postwar planning. This movement reached its zenith in the middle of the 1960s, when the Soviet Union itself began to grant more decision-making power to its plant managers.[2] These reforms—dubbed "creeping capitalism"—have been largely keyed to greater enterprise autonomy, production for sale instead of quota fulfillment, and the increased use of monetary incentives and individual initiatives. The broad aims of the reforms in almost all cases have been: to introduce greater flexibility in annual and medium-term planning, to give enterprise managers greater decision-making powers, to establish salability and profit as "success indicators," instead of physical volume and product quotas, to upgrade quality, and to rationalize costs and prices by allowing interest on capital outlays.

2. The first move actually came in Yugoslavia after its break with Moscow in 1948. It was followed by Poland's far-reaching reforms after the 1956 riots. The trend was then sanctified by the Soviet Union and copied by other satellites.

As a general rule, the extent and intensity of transition to the new reforms in each country have been related to the country's stage of economic advancement, its dependence on foreign trade, and its previous experience with Stalinist-type central planning and control. Thus, the Soviet Union and Czechoslovakia have found their industrially advanced economies more amenable to modern management reforms. Hungary and Yugoslavia have been heavily dependent upon foreign trade, and this almost forced them to establish closer links between their internal cost-price relationships and international ratios.

Decisions by Proxy

In the centrally directed economies, usually only one political party is legally allowed to operate—the Communist party. The opposition is either nonexistent, unorganized, or underground. The one-party political system is commonly justified by communist governments in a straight Marxian dialectic fashion. As all conflicts, in Marx's view, are class conflicts, and as classes are divided on the basis of private property and ownership, differences in political coloration are a characteristic of capitalist societies. Without large-scale private ownership, there would be no class distinctions and no sociopolitical heterogeneity. In a largely homogeneous society, there is no basis for political parties with opposing ideological or even practical platforms. A socialist societ is thus, by nature, a one-party society.

"The dictatorship of the proletariat," said Lenin, "is the highest type of democracy." To China's Mao Zedong, democracy was represented by the "joint dictatorship" of several revolutionary classes in the form of "democratic centralism." What is called democracy in the West, according to Mao, was a "militaristic dictatorship of the bourgeoisie." In Eastern Europe, too, the "forces of counter-revolution" are excluded from participation in the political life of the community, and all non-Communist political parties are excluded from legal participation in national political life, on the grounds that Communist party members are a select group of competent, trained, tested, and disciplined individuals who are ready at all times to subordinate personal interest to the interests of the party and the people.

The delegation of sovereignty in the Western sense obviously cannot be duplicated in CDEs. The absence of political parties, the frequent expression of unanimity in the election of representatives, and the seemingly perfunctory decisions and sanctions of national and local assemblies in these countries do not allow an objective evaluation of the free and voluntary nature of their citizen's delegation of decision making. Yugoslavia presents a somewhat different situation in this regard, but in general, the delegated mechanism plays the least significant role in CDEs. For this reason, the government's direct and indirect interventions are largely indistinguishable and gain their legitimacy essentially from the same source—the leaders' preferences and pleasure.

Group Bargaining

The CDEs with a one-party political regime ostensibly present the examples of nonpluralistic, highly centralized, economic decision making. To a large extent, this observation is correct. The hegemony of Communist party apparatus over the administrative machinery and the influence of party leaders in determining national socioeconomic objectives obviously symbolize monolithism. Closer examination, however, shows that even in these nations, decision-making is not totally unilateral.

As shown below in the study of the Soviet Union, the Communist party itself is not an entirely homogeneous institution. In other Eastern bloc countries, too, the party harbors divergent views among its formal organs and informal elements. Government and party leaders are not always the same individuals with exactly the same personal convictions or ambitions. It is often argued that Eastern Europe's old political pressure groups (the court, the landed gentry, the church, the army, and the business elite) are now replaced by half a dozen other power centers. Apart from the Communist party itself, which bears the responsibility for overall guidance of the economy, the army, the urban proletariat, the farming communities, the press, the intellectuals, and various professional organizations also wield power, and some basic economic decisions doubtless result from implicit bargaining among these groups. Trade unions, too, while representing no particular economic interest, are nevertheless engaged in intramural rivalry with other state entities.

While communist sympathizers try to regard these groups as "a coordinated authority with constituent parts fitted together in a tightly knit working organization," there is much evidence that they act just as the old groups—in their *own* interest. In almost all communist countries, the constant and sometimes fierce rivalry between "professional communists" and "communist professionals" tends to favor multilateral compromises and to temper ideological dogmatism.

There are also some formal manifestations of multilateral sovereignty. Labor unions, for example, have the power to bargain collectively. They theoretically have the right to strike—and sometimes exercise it. Except for basic wages, which are centrally determined, other aspects of labor-management relations are subject to some forms of negotiations—formal and informal, voluntary or induced.

Consumers' Sovereignty

Since the mid-1960s, there has been a move in East Europe toward greater reliance on market prices, profitability, and competition. Of the six countries in this bloc, Hungary has been the pioneer and is now the most market-oriented economy in Eastern Europe, with a reported 60 percent of its prices free of controls. Romania has been next. Yugoslavia boasts of a socialist market economy as the centerpiece of its regime.

In all of these economies, private home ownership is allowed and encouraged. So are personal possessions, savings accounts, and consumer durables. There are hundreds of thousands of private shops or businesses engaged in professional and commercial services, retail trade, home construction, road transportation, handicrafts, and food processing. Moonlighting and part-time private work are widespread. Private farming is in varying degrees tolerated or authorized. Farmers are allowed to cultivate various percentages of the cultivable land and sell their yield in the private market. Private plots are also allocated to farmers for market-priced fruits and vegetables.

Material incentives (both rewards and penalties) have been instituted for workers and enterprise managers in the form of bonuses and pay cuts. Foreign private investment in minority joint ventures is sought by some countries.

THE UNION OF SOVIET
SOCIALIST REPUBLICS

The Soviet Union is the world's largest country in land area, with some 22.4 million square kilometers stretching across two continents. It has the second largest economy in the world, after the United States. With nearly 264 million people, it is the third most populated country on earth, after China and India. Russia has a wealth of natural resources and is a leading producer of many commodities, including steel, pig-iron, cement and crude oil.

Officially committed to implementing Karl Marx's communist philosophy, Soviet leaders have combined Russia's long tradition of government paternalism with largely borrowed Western technology to transform a relatively backward agricultural country with a population two-thirds illiterate in 1919 to an industrial superpower in a span of sixty years. The Soviet Union is now a world leader in many scientific and technical fields: space exploration, aviation, irrigation, medicine, atomic energy, and heavy machinery.

The Soviet public sector is by far the world's biggest "single" economic enterprise. Soviet planning authorities have to manage and coordinate some 350,000 economic activities (over 200,000 industrial enterprises, nearly 13,000 state farms, over 36,000 agricultural collectives, and hundreds of thousands of wholesale and retail outlets, schools, hospitals, resorts) everything from a repair shop to a research organization. Soviet planners also have to cope with some 5,000 product groups in an estimated 45,000 different business enterprises in fifteen federated republics.[3] The enormous complex of this task is a testimony both to the Soviet Union's administrative skills and its well-publicized inefficiencies and shortcomings.

A detailed discussion of the whole Soviet system is obviously beyond the scope of one chapter. Consequently, attention here will be focused only on the relative significance of the various decision-making processes in the Soviet economy.

Government's Direct Role:
The Command Process

Historians of the Russian economy are quick to point out that neither the command mechanism nor the leading role of the state in national economic affairs has been a

---

3. The largest of these republics is the Russian Soviet Federal Socialist Republic, with almost 80 percent of the Soviet territory and 55 percent of the population of the Soviet Union. Seventy percent of USSR's industrial and agricultural output is from this republic.

THE SOVIET UNION: BASIC DATA

LAND AREA (sq. km.)	22,402,000
POPULATION (1980 estimate)	266 million
Net annual increase (1970-78 yearly average)	0.9 percent
Urban (percent of total, 1980)	65 percent
Working Age (15–64) (percent of total, 1978)	65 percent
LABOR FORCE (total civilian, 1979)	140 million
Agriculture, forestry, fishing (percent of total)	17 percent
Mining, manufacturing, construction (percent of total)	47 percent
Services, etc. (percent of total)	36 percent
GROSS DOMESTIC PRODUCT (market prices, 1979)	$1,500 billion
Per capita (1979)	$5,700
Average annual increase (1970–78)	5.3 percent
Public consumption (percent of GDP) ⎫	
Private consumption (percent of GDP) ⎭	73 percent
Fixed capital formation (ratio to GDP)	26 percent
Savings (ratio to GDP)	27 percent
GROSS DOMESTIC PRODUCT (market prices, 1979)	$1,500 billion
Agriculture. forestry, fishing (share in GDP)	17 percent
Mining, manufacturing, construction (share in GDP)	62 percent
Services (share in GDP)	21 percent
FOREIGN TRADE	
Exports (percent of GDP)	5 percent
Imports (percent of GDP)	5 percent

Communist party initiative in the Soviet Union. They point to Russia's long history of totalitarianism and the active participation of the state in domestic economic development, necessitated by Russia's relative economic underdevelopment.[4] The concept of a centrally planned economy, however, was first embraced by the Soviet leadership in 1928 and introduced into the Eastern European countries (and the third world, as well as China) after World War II.

The Soviet leadership's uninterrupted grand strategy of rapid industrialization and high economic growth has been implemented mainly through a very high degree of central control. Under this process, basic national objectives have been determined by Communist party leaders and put to work with the help of an all-pervasive bureaucracy, using central planning, price manipulations, and material rewards—along with other noneconomic incentives, coercions and sanctions. The two most notable features of the Soviet economy are the almost total ownership and operation of the basic means of production by the state and the primacy of development planning. State ownership and control of resources is both an ideological imperative as well as a means of achieving broader sociopolitical goals. The Soviet Union is also a planned economy in the full sense of the term.

According to the 1977 Soviet Constitution, the ownership of all essential means of production and distribution is entrusted to the state on behalf of "the whole people." Thus, all lands, mineral wealth, waters, forests, all major industrial enterprises and construction firms, all means of transportation, the entire communications network, all financial institutions, and the major portion of urban housing belong to society. Collective and cooperative ownership is allowed in the case of farm machinery, rural buildings, small industrial equipment, and handicrafts facilities.

Pervasive also is state operation. The Soviet public sector produces some 98 percent of the gross value of industrial output, with the other 2 percent supplied by cooperative workshops and collective farms. The state sector is directly engaged in about half of the agricultural production, the rest being largely produced by collective farms. More than two-thirds of all retail sales are transacted in state retail shops; consumers' cooperatives have nearly 30 percent; and collective farm markets, the rest. The state transportation network accounts for over 90 percent of the traffic and haulage, with the remainder in collective and cooperative hands. One hundred percent of banking, insurance, and other financial services are provided by the government. Only in livestock production is the state's share less than one-third of the total. Well over 60 percent of urban housing is public. All welfare services (including education and health) are made available by the state. Almost 80 percent of the labor force work for the government.

No private citizen can legally engage in entrepreneurial functions for private

---

4. See, for example, Alexander Gerschenkron, *Economic Backwardness in Historical Perspective* (Cambridge, Mass.: Harvard University Press, 1962).

gain. Individual professional activity and owner-operator shops do exist. Bookkeeping profit (excess of revenue over costs) is also realized in such shopkeeping, but shops are usually part of the cooperatives, and profits are mostly wages of the shopkeepers. No private commercial enterprise, with hired workers, is allowed to operate for "capitalistic" profit. State enterprises, however, make profits, which are mostly paid out to the government.

Soviet Planning

National planning determines and directs the economic life of the Soviet Union. Every industrial enterprise, every collective farm, every state agency, every geographical subdivision, every one of the fifteen republics, the autonomous regions, and the federal union has its plans. There is, in fact, an elaborate hierarchy of plans for a single factory, for a region, for a republic, for a ministry, and for the whole union.

Traditional Soviet economic planning—going back to the establishment of the State Planning Committee, or Gosplan, in 1921—has aimed at a centrally controlled mobilization and use of Russia's resources in the service of national goals. Soviet national planning is the oldest in the modern world.

Nature and Types of Plan.   There are three time plans in the Soviet Union: a long-term twenty-year *general* plan, which sets forth certain long-range national goals for key sectors of the economy; a medium, five-to-seven year plan, or *perspective*, which is the core of Soviet medium-term objectives, particularly with regard to capital investments, and a guide for the preparation of short-term plans; and an annual, or *operational*, plan, similar to national budgets. Each plan specifies key output targets, manpower requirements, capital investments, and consumption objectives in physical and monetary terms. Perspective plans are nonoperational; they merely reflect the desired direction of economic activity. The only truly operational plan is the annual plan that prescribes actual production and distribution schedules for operating units. Annual operational plans are subdivided on the basis of operational periods (quarters and months) and operational levels (regional, district, or local).

The medium-term plans, usually for five to seven years, consist of a series of input-output targets that foresee the course of development of national resources during the plan period, project certain growth rates to be attained in each sector and subsector of the economy at the end of the period, and prescribe, in detail, the institutional and organizational framework under which resources can be mobilized and put to use. Microeconomic targets for individual enterprises, sectors and subsectors (steel, cement, electric energy, or grains) are normally set up in physical volumes: tons, kilowatts, or bushels. Macrotargets such as the GNP, national income, public budget, savings, investment and foreign trade are presented in monetary terms (so many rubles). The overriding consideration in preparing the plans is not optimality and perfection, but practicality and chances of success.

The mid-term national plan is normally concerned with basic "leading links" or priorities on defense versus civilian production; industry versus agriculture; heavy capital industries versus light consumer products; and, in each category, some group of items versus others. Each plan is divided into basic economic sectors: agriculture, industry, transport and communications, construction and housing, and so forth. Each sector has a growth target for the duration of the plan made up of subtargets for each year. Detailed planning of this type relates only to the high-priority undertakings, such as defense, space, and research. In other areas, and particularly in the case of consumer goods, significant leeways are allowed to local governments, regional economic councils, and republics.

The annual plan is the concrete blueprint of detailed economic decision making. Each annual plan takes its cue from the main socioeconomic objectives of the five-year or seven-year plan, as the latter follows the broad perspective of the general long-term plan. The main task of each year's plan is to obtain three balances: a physical balance between inputs and outputs so as to ensure both full resource employment and efficiency, a monetary balance between total purchasing power of households and enterprises, and total value of goods and services so as to avoid shortages or unused inventories, and a foreign trade balance to make up domestic input requirements through imports and to pay for them by means of exports.

Thus, each annual plan contains several equations with respect to raw material supplies, labor force, output and consumption, money and credit, taxes and expenditures. The raw material balances or equations involve the allocation of basic industrial, agricultural, and processed resources among thousands of production units. The labor balance consists of matching the supply of various kinds of available workers with employment positions that demand their services. Output and consumption balances aim at the division of total output between a physically "irreducible" minimum (or a politically safe maximum) of consumer goods and the requirements for defense and capital investment. Money and credit equations are to guarantee sufficient cash for wage payments and consumer transactions, working capital of enterprises, and investment funds for expansion. Taxes and expenditures balances are the two sides of the balanced Soviet government budget dealing with "nonproductive" activities.[5] In each equation, the *sources* and *uses* naturally balance.

Soviet Five-Year Plans. The First Five-Year Plan was put into operation for the 1928–32 period. It tried to retrieve Lenin's liberal and somewhat decentralized New Economic Policy (1921–27) from its major contradictions to Marxist ideology and redirect that policy toward the establishment of a transitional *socialist* society.[6] The Second Plan (1933–37) gave some recognition to the badly needed expansion of consumer products, but its chief attention was still directed toward heavy metal industries. The Third Plan (1938–42) was to move toward the final goal of *Communist* construction, but was interrupted by the German invasion of Russia in June 1941, and was inevitably redirected toward essential defense requirements.

No plan was announced until after the war, when a new Fourth Plan (1946–50) was promulgated, with its major emphasis on postwar restoration and reconstruction. The Fifth Plan (1951–55), coinciding with Stalin's death in 1953, moved toward increased production of consumer goods and improvement in the Soviet standard of living. The Sixth Plan (1956–60) launched an overly ambitious program of capital investment in both industry and agriculture, as part of a broader plan for the economic integration of Eastern Europe under the Council for Mutual Economic Assistance (COMECON). A year after its start, however, intramural difficulties within the Communist bloc made a substantial revision of the new plan necessary. It was replaced by a new Seven-Year Plan (1959–65), which promised to produce, in conjunction with other communist nations, more than half of the world's industrial output by 1965 and to obtain the world's highest standard of living for the Russians by the early 1970s. The Eighth Plan (1966–70), reverting to the regular five-year duration, called for an increase in GNP of nearly 40 percent, a real per capita income growth of about 30 percent, and a narrowing of the gap between living standards of the rural and urban populations. It also promised better-quality goods, greater leisure time, and more material benefits for all. The Ninth Five-Year Plan (1971–75) puts its major emphasis for the first time in the Soviet planning history on consumer welfare, calling for the production of light consumer industries to expand by 44 to 48 percent during the plan period, and for heavy industry (including military hardware) to grow by 41 to 45 percent.

The Basic Orientation of Economic Development of the Soviet Union for 1976–80, as the Tenth Five-Year Plan is called, aims at strengthening the technical and material base of communism through intensified production, utilization of economic potentials, improvement in defense capability, and raising the material and cultural standards of life for Soviet citizens. With these objectives in view, the

5. In the Soviet Union's national income accounting, all services not directly connected with production of material goods are considered "unproductive" and thus excluded from the "gross social product." Thus, outlays for personal, domestic, and public services (including health and education) do not enter into the composition of GNP.

6. In Lenin's pragmatic approach to Russia's postwar problems, only key industries, banking, and foreign trade—the so-called commanding heights—were in state hands. Small industries, agriculture, and domestic trade were given considerable freedom.

plan calls for a stable growth of the economy, a hike in labor productivity through mechanization and automation, a reduction in the urban-rural gap, a strengthening of research and development, and effective measures for environmental protection.[7]

As indicated in Chapter 3, national objectives are not all or always publicly stated. This is true of many countries, but particularly of the CDEs. Among the unstated objectives of the last plan, four pivotal aims are worth mentioning: first, effective control by the Soviet Communist party over the national economy; second, strengthening the military-industrial posture of the Soviet state vis-à-vis an allegedly hostile external world; third, fulfilling traditional national prestige of the Soviet Union in international political, scientific, technological, and cultural competitions; fourth, satisfying personal interests, ambitions, and priorities of the Communist party and Soviet government leaders.

Plan Formulation. Officially and theoretically, national plans are the products of the "initiative and spontaneity of the working masses." In reality and in actual practice, the general tenor and direction of state economic plans are decided upon by the fourteen-member Communist party Presidium (the Politburo) and approved by the 287-member Central Committee of the Communist party, and by the party's Congress in its periodic conventions. In the Soviet economy, the "planner's preference" overtakes consumers' preference and sovereignty. The nexus of economic activity is the decisions made and the top of the hierarchical pyramid.

The formulation of the Soviet annual plan takes place in a hierarchical fashion in two directions: by individual enterprise proposals at the bottom up the bureaucratic ladder to the enterprise associations, regional economic councils, and the appropriate ministry all the way to the top party leaders in Moscow; and by master planners at the apex of Soviet hierarchy down the administrative chain of command to managers, workers, and peasants on production lines. The Gosplan in Moscow and its branches in the republics review ministerial requests for resource allocations and their planned outputs. After a good deal of "coordination and reconciliation" (bargaining) within the economic cabinet, the total available resources are allocated, on a "first-thing-first" basis, by the leadership. The "leading links," or top-priority items, present primary claims on resources, and they are served accordingly and in a fairly detailed fashion. Lower-priority targets receive their shares after the leading ones, and so it goes down the line until the resource supply is totally allotted to the competing claimants. Each ministry or agency proceeds to allocate its share of resources among its assigned tasks in the various

---

7. For a more recent and specific comparison of Soviet plans, see V. B. Singh, *Soviet Economic Development and Rising Living Standards* (New Delhi: Sterling Publishers, 1977). See also A. Katsenelinboigen, *Soviet Economic Planning* (White Plains: M. E. Sharpe, 1978).

republics. Ultimately, each industry, enterprise, collective farm, or distributing unit will receive its production quota and its materials ration. A similar procedure is followed in the allocation of consumer goods among wholesale and retail outlets, in the choice of investment projects, and in foreign trade (based on availability of foreign exchange).

The main directives or general guidelines of the plan are initially approved by the party Congress, with instruction to the government to work out the detailed document for subsequent ratification by the Politburo and the Central Committee. Upon their approval, the entire plan is submitted as a whole to the Supreme Soviet or the legislature. The exact role of Soviet legislators in amending planned provisions is not known to outsiders. The common guess is that deputies do not, as a rule, cause any major changes in the plan. The published version of the plan document contains only a limited number of important targets in a percentage form. Detailed targets, absolute figures, and supporting data are not normally made public.

Planning Machinery and Supervision. Plan directives are communicated to the Council of Ministers or the cabinet by the party hierarchy. The ultimate responsibility for drawing up the plan document and supervising its execution rests with the State Planning Committee. At the operational levels, there are planning sections of government ministries, agencies, factories, and farms and service organizations. On the side, there is a large number of specialized and mainly advisory committees at the federal and republic levels, dealing with agriculture, construction, machine building, defense, and scientific research.

The plan's implementation, or "fulfillment supervision," is controlled and coordinated through several channels. First, the planning committees normally have their reports in every major enterprise and can at all times discover sources of difficulties or negligence. Second, all transactions between state enterprises take place under formal contracts. These contracts specify the purchase of input factors from some factories and the sale of outputs to others. A failure to honor such commitments serves as an indication that the failing enterprise is not fulfilling its plans. Third, as every enterprise's deposits have to be kept in the state bank (Gosbank) and all transactions must be made by check, the failure to draw on these deposit accounts for the purchase of materials or to replenish these accounts through the sale of outputs may give warning signals. Fourth, both the government and the Communist party make official inspections of plant activities and report inefficiencies or wrong-doing. Finally, trade-union leaders in each enterprise are expected to serve as watchdogs of plan fulfillment, both as a duty and as a matter of self-interest in bonuses and premiums.

Soviet Financial Plans. The only other type of Soviet planning that matches the physical product or real output plan in magnitude and significance is the *financial* plan. Despite traditional socialist calls for abolishing money and credit, the Soviet Union is a thoroughly monetized economy, where money, prices, savings, and bank credits are vital to the everyday functioning of the economic system. All incomes and all bonuses in the Soviet Union are paid and received in money. Transactions among individuals, enterprises, buyers, and sellers are conducted in monetary terms. Economic values, taxes, savings, and enterprise profits are expressed in monetary units.

The Soviet annual financial plans are prepared and administered by the Gosplan, the Finance Ministry, and the Gosbank. The principal aim of financial planning is to provide necessary and sufficient funds for the proper fulfillment of the physical plan. Funds are supplied in appropriate amounts by the state bank for consumer transactions, individual savings, and tax payments.

Performance of Soviet Plans. The Soviet government and the Russian press seldom publish detailed (particularly critical) accounts of Russia's economic performance beyond specific production data, but, on the whole, Soviet planning seems to have been successful in mobilizing domestic resources, and channeling them into high-priority investment outlets from the very beginning of the Soviet regime. Planners have also been able to force-feed the relatively backward Soviet economy of the pre-1917 era with modern (and mostly borrowed) technology to the point that the Soviet scientific and technological community has obtained a position of leadership in a number of major areas. Ambitious and knowingly unreachable targets determined from above have kept labor and management on their toes and under constant pressure to produce one of the world's highest rates of economic growth for a long time. Consolidation and "rationalization" of industry, transportation, and even agriculture under the plans have brought about considerable economies of scale.

On the negative side, Soviet planning, particularly in the early stages, has clearly been a process of trial-and-error, with each new plan trying to rectify the errors of the previous one. And the process is continuing. The results have obviously been less than optimal. The monumental task of bringing an intricate and sprawling economy under one centralized direction, coupled with an almost total lack of experience with planning on the part of early revolutionaries, must also have cost the Soviet Union and the Soviet nation an untold amount of waste and needless sacrifices.

State Enterprises

The whole of the Soviet economy, in effect, resembles a single mammoth business enterprise, made up of diversified units, directed by the Politburo of the Communist party and managed by state ministries and agencies on behalf of the silent shareowners, the Soviet people. The directors of this "USSR Ltd." (the communist hierarchy) are bent on ensuring the enterprise's continuity and growth, extending and strengthening effective communist control over it, and apportioning just enough dividends (life amenities) to the stockholders to secure their passive consent, if not active support. In this gigantic operation, political and ideological considerations usually outweigh economic criteria.

As in a modern giant corporation, the underlying philosophy of Soviet planners is that "the whole is greater than the sum of its parts." Constituent units are directed and controlled by top management in such a way as to ensure the fulfillment of the conglomerates' objectives—not those of individual firms, subsidiaries, or factories. The supergiant Russian economy is, in a sense, an "autoplex": a complex of separate units tied to headquarters through planning and financing.

Every nonfarm enterprise—be it an electric power station, a newspaper publishing house, a sanatorium, or a department store—is a legal entity, chartered by the state for specific activities. Under the so-called *Khozraschet* (full-accounting) principle, each enterprise is also operationally independent and fully responsible for its accounts; that is, it can buy, sell, and enter into contracts. The enterprise's initial assets, its working capital, and its operational policy are essentially provided by the state. It ordinarily buys its materials at stated prices, and in the amounts appropriated to it, from other enterprises, paying them by checks on its bank deposits; it gets paid for selling its goods or services to other enterprises or to households. And it has to make a profit—mostly for the state—by adhering to its production schedule and target, carefully and diligently.[8]

The Soviet industrial enterprise is headed by a director, often an engineer, appointed by the appropriate ministry. The director is solely responsible for the enterprise's performance under the Soviet "one-man rule" system.[9] The main responsibility of the director is to fulfill (or preferably, exceed) his plant's quota, to reach the "success indicators."[10]

In 1965, a new economic program was inaugurated with the avowed aim of

8. Some enterprises, like schools, hospitals, and welfare organizations (and, of course, all regular governmental agencies), are included in the state budget.

9. For a comparison of enterprise responsibilities, see B. M. Richman, *Soviet Management with Significant American Comparisons* (Englewood Cliffs: Prentice-Hall, 1965). See also D. Granick, *The Red Executive* (Garden City: Doubleday, 1960).

10. Until the 1965 reforms, the enterprise's workforce, wage bill, input-mix, output, inventories, prices to be paid for materials, and those received for product, the expected profits, and allocation for expansion and improvement were all centrally determined. The temptation was thus great to outsmart the planners by underestimating productive capability, overestimating costs, or using other tricks, thus ensuring planned targets and qualifying for bonuses.

loosening centralized direction and increasing the economic "levers" of profits, pay bonuses, and interest charges on capital as a means of raising productivity. Thus, factory operations were placed under the direction of factory managers within certain broad (mostly sales and profit) targets, instead of rigid physical production quotas by volumes. Success indicators became salability, not mere production. A greater share of profit was left to the discretion of enterprise managers to use for workers' bonuses or further reinvestment. New investments in plan expansion or new enterprises were to be financed mostly through interest-bearing loans, instead of direct budgetary appropriations. Selected enterprises were required to pay a fixed return out of their annual profits to the government on the basis of the total value of their fixed assets.

Light industry goods have since been turned out with due attention to market conditions and with some price flexibility. Styles and prices are allowed to be altered by managers to make them more attractive. Central planning directions are allowed to be bypassed in certain plants for the sake of higher quality and greater salability of consumer products. Under the new system, factories may receive orders directly from retail stores instead of the central planning agency. Nevertheless, managers still have to produce the types of things that the planners want. They must also fulfill some monetary quota—so many rubles' worth each year. They must make a certain minimum profit on their sale and turn a large portion of it over to the government. And they have to sell their products at predetermined, centrally imposed prices.

As an adjunct to the 1965 reforms, there has also been some recent experimentation with the reduction of underemployment in Soviet mechanized plants. By raising production targets but freezing total wages paid by a factory, Soviet planners, have, in effect, induced some plant managers to lay off redundant workers, with amazing results in higher productivity. Under the new and limited experiment, the number of factory employees is left pretty much to the discretion of the plant manager. The factory "wages fund" is left intact, despite a reduction in employment. So is the size of the plant bonus.

As a still further step in the direction of profit-oriented reforms, the Twenty-fourth Communist Party Congress in 1971 approved a plan to reorganize Soviet industrial plants into larger "production associations," linking each plant with its own suppliers, sales outlets, marketing and research divisions, and designers. Under the new system—considered the most comprehensive since 1965—industrial plants in different provinces are to be placed under mid-level corporations, which can get their basic policies from the ministries, and direct individual plants accordingly. In this manner, the larger associations or public corporations are expected to be better able to attract skilled manpower, make a more rational use of resources, and take advantage of computerized technology. The role of industrial ministries is to be largely limited to overall planning, investment policy, and technological innovation.

Agricultural Organizations

The Soviet economy is still partly agricultural. In 1980, about 17 percent of the Soviet labor force was on the farm (as compared to only 2 percent in the United States). Although Russia produces more barley, cotton fiber, wheat, oats, sugar, and rye than any other country, the Soviet Union is not yet self-sufficient in farm products. The direction and management of Soviet agriculture have changed frequently and drastically in the postwar period, particularly in the 1950s and 1960s. Emphasis has shifted back and forth between state and collective farms. Farm prices have been restructured time and time again to spur production. However, the basic responsibility for agricultural production still remains with state and collective farms. There is also a small, but crucial private sector, discussed in a later section.

The state farm (*sovkhoz*) is an idealogically preferred form of agricultural production in the Soviet Union. Other farm organizations are expected to move into this type in the future. A state farm is a publicly owned and operated agricultural enterprise, organized and managed much the same as an industrial enterprise. The government owns the farmland, livestock, machinery, and equipment. The sovkhoz's production plan is determined by the state; its products belong to the state. Like an industrial enterprise, it has three main annual plans for output, labor, and finances. The farms are under the direction of state managers appointed by the appropriate republic's ministry of agriculture. The work force is hired for wages, plus bonuses and premiums for increased production. Farm workers enjoy fringe benefits similar to those of industrial workers with respect to pensions and disabilities. They also have the same privileges as *collective* farmers in regard to home ownership on the farm and the use of a small "private" plot for their own cultivation.

State farms are fairly large enterprises (varying in size in different regions and for different crops), with an average farm area of over 120,000 acres, a sown area of nearly 18,000 acres, and a work force of nearly 650. They are generally specialized in a few crops, mostly grains. Most state farms have routinely operated on "planned losses" and survived on state subsidies, owing to a combination of unrealistically low output prices fixed by the state, bureaucratic inefficiency, and excessively centralized regulations. Although these farms sow more than 45 percent of the farm land, they account for only 25 percent of farm output in most years.

Soviet *collective* farms are a hybrid form of agricultural organization. Although the backbone of Soviet agriculture in terms of output, labor force, and number of units, they are still regarded as a makeshift arrangement by communist ideologists. A collective farm (*kolkhoz*) is, theoretically, a *voluntary* association of farmers. The purpose of such collective endeavor is to reap the benefits of large-scale production and other economies associated with unified purchases and sales. Each collective member contributes his time, energy, and skill in return for a proportional share of the collective's net profits. Each member has a vote in the collective's administration. Incomes are to be received in cash and kind as a share of profits—not as wages. The collective's net income (total revenues minus fixed obligations, expenses, capital depreciation, and taxes) is to be divided among members in accordance with their contributions, the number of workdays devoted to the collective each year. Legally speaking, if there is no net income, there could be no income distribution.

The kolkhoz is a chartered enterprise after a uniform model. It has legal title to the use of land permanently secured from the state. All the communal structures, livestock, machinery, and equipment are its property. Investment in collective farms is financed out of their own incomes. Each collective farm buys its capital equipment from the state and sells all or most of its produce to the government. The kolkhoz is, in theory, managed by its members on a democratic basis. All matters of major policy—membership responsibilities in the production plan, labor rules, investment programs, members' share of income—are voted on in a collective assembly, independent of the government. The collective's managing board, its director, and other officials are elected by the membership. In actual practice, however, collective farm members normally vote for the nominees of the local Communist party cells or local state officials. Usually, a number of collective farms are grouped under a farm "trust" for the purpose of output coordination, exchange of information, and modernization.

Until the recent reforms, collective farms were expected to deliver part of their output to the state at fixed prices. Additional output could be sold to state purchasing agencies or consumers' cooperatives at higher (fixed) prices. Only the output of "private" plots was allowed to fetch their market worth. Because of high costs and low output prices imposed by the state, many collectives had little residual income to divide among members. Collective farmers left the farms for the cities en masse. Those who remained on the farms tried to make ends meet by directing most of their skill and initiative to their own tiny private plots. This, in turn, aggravated the collectives' plight.

Consequently, the system of dual pricing was abolished late in the 1950s and a series of single higher prices was established for all output of the collectives. In the mid-1960s, a guaranteed monthly wage, corresponding to that of state farm workers, was established for collective farm members, to be paid if necessary by borrowing from the State Bank. A modest pension plan was instituted for these farmers and a tax break was granted to the collective's income.

Collective farms are now also encouraged to set up sidelines, or "subsidiary enterprises," for processing food, producing construction materials, and making household articles and industrial by-products. These enterprises are allowed to decide on their own production plans without Moscow's permission, to borrow money from the State Bank for their capital needs, to establish plants, to make contracts for the sale of their wares, and even to sell them through their own retail outlets.

There are more than 36,000 kholkhozy in the Soviet Union. They comprise 15.5 million peasant families, working nearly 54 percent of the total sown area, and producing more than half of all Russian grain; 80 to 90 percent of cotton and sugar beet; and one-third of the total livestock, eggs, and dairy products. The average collective farm has about 400 farm households and almost 7,500 acres of cultivated land and 31,000 acres of land area.

Price Policy

With a notable exception of certain farm produce, almost all wholesale and most retail prices in the Soviet Union are fixed by the government. The State Committee on Prices, ministries at the union and republic levels, and other organs of the state take part in price determination. The committee makes its decisions presumably on the basis of ideology ("socially necessary labor time" embodied in various products, according to Marx's labor theory), strategic national interest, and the leadership's view on the desired direction of aggregate consumption and investment. Production costs usually take second place to these priorities. That is, the quantities of goods and services are first determined according to the leadership's preferences, and prices are set to serve as guides to desired production and as rationing devices for limiting aggregate consumption to the planned level. Thus, certain raw materials are priced deliberately below cost to stimulate industrial production and growth, and certain "luxury" products, such as vodka and automobiles, are priced far above costs to discourage consumption. These prices reflect neither relative scarcities nor social values. Their role (along with that of wages) is to apportion goods and services among consumers and to allocate the work force among enterprises. Prices and wages, in other words, substitute for rationing and direct labor assignment.

There are actually three types of administrative prices in the Soviet Union. First, industrial wholesale prices, at which Soviet enterprises buy, sell, and transfer goods to one another. As a rule, these prices are based on three elements: the average cost of production or processing in major plants throughout the nation, including raw materials, labor overhead costs, depreciation, and interest paid on working capitals—all of which are also priced by the state; planned profit, ideologically corresponding to the surplus created by labor in the process of production, but in practice set at a percentage of cost; and delivery expenses to buyers at different areas, usually borne by the seller. Since 1966, under a new price policy, the cost of investment capital is also taken into account. In the case of certain items, produced under different natural circumstances, such as gas and oil, the basic cost is calculated on the basis of "marginal" production, and enterprises enjoying comparative advantages are required to pay a "rent" to the government.

The second category of Soviet prices are state retail prices for food and other consumer goods. They are based on industrial wholesale prices, plus certain additional marketing costs, markups, and taxes. Marketing costs include services of labor, transport, storage, packaging, advertising, and retailing. A small planned profit or markup is added at different stages of wholesaling and distribution. The principal surcharge, however, is the turnover tax (or final users' sales tax) levied on almost all items sold to consumers in state stores. Retail prices are supposed to be set in such a way as to clear the market, but in actual practice shortages (and black markets) often occur in the case of goods whose fixed prices are still too attractive. There are also frequent inventories of unsalable goods due to high prices or poor quality.

Agricultural procurement prices constitute the third category. These are prices at which state and collective farms deliver their goods to state purchasing organizations, and from them to industrial and retail establishments. These prices differ in different regions; for compulsory and voluntary deliveries; for buying and selling; and between state and collective farms and sometimes in good and bad harvest years.

Soviet prices are determined through an arduous and intricate process of data collection and calculation;[11] they are to be changed every five to seven years. The intervals for wholesale prices have recently been longer, but individual price changes among nearly 10 million controlled items are frequent. There have been numerous price cuts or upward hikes on prices of individual goods and services in response to consumer demand and taste.[12]

The Soviet pricing system is a curious blend of Marxist fetish, standard accounting procedures, and genuine Russian pragmatism. Price setters, although evidently more realistic under the new reform than during Stalin's days, still cling to Marxist dogma by refusing to allow full interest and full rent in their full-cost pricing.[13] Soviet pragmatic ingenuity, however, has tried to circumvent Marx's anachronistic dogma by introducing through the back door some measures of social cost accounting and relative scarcity. For example, the so-called coefficient of relative effectiveness is the difference in annual operating costs of two projects

11. Russian economists admit that their price determination is a "laborious and complicated" process requiring "scores of research and design institutes" to calculate, analyze, and draw up thousands of price lists for the planners' consideration.

12. Between 1977 and 1980, there were reportedly four waves of price increases on items ranging from books to gasoline, plane fares, restaurant meals, and automobiles.

13. A disregard in cost calculations of interest charges on capital value has led to an industrial tying up of scarce capital resources in heavy projects with slow capital turnover and a long gestation period.

divided by the difference in initial capital outlays; it plays the role of interest—with the important exception that Western interest rates bear greater affinity to the market, or "natural," rates, whereas Soviet CRE is largely arbitrary.[14]

Rent, as the differential due to the inherent superiority of certain scarce resources over others, is also given a de facto recognition as indirect labor costs.[15] Thus, the opportunity costs of natural and man-made resources—differences in location, fertility, productivity, approximity—are taken into account by a circuitous process of converting these scarcity values into labor units.

A major shortcoming of Soviet pricing, apart from the nearly insurmountable difficulties of accurate data collection, has been the length of time in which everyday changes in costs and productivity can be detected, analyzed, and acted upon before national production and exchange become badly distorted. As a result, not only do prices fail to perform the calculation and coordination functions in allocating resources, they also fall short of optimally implementing the planners' preferences.

Wages Policy and Incentives

By World Bank estimates, some 65 percent of the Soviet Union's population are between the ages of fifteen and sixty-four (the same percentage as in the United States). Of these, some 53 percent are in the labor force (compared to 46 percent in the United States). Women constitute about half of the total Soviet labor force (up from 24 percent in 1928). In all sectors of the economy except farming and industry, women outnumber men. Eighty-five percent of workers in the health services are women. The female share of employment in teaching and the civil service is more than two-thirds.

Wages are the main legal source of individual income in the Soviet Union. The total share of national income going to wages is predetermined by the planners in accordance with the planned availability of consumer goods. During the Stalin era, labor employment and allocation were both solved by assigning workers to factories and requiring factory managers to hire and keep them there. Permission for changing jobs was not easily obtained. Force and coercion were often used in lieu of monetary incentives to lure workers into unpleasant regions in Siberia. Under post-Stalin liberalization and reforms, workers are promised higher pay, larger allowances, housing priority, service facilities, and other economic rewards to go to regions with labor shortages and unattractive climates.

By law, every Soviet citizen has a "right" to gainful employment and is

14. Regular interest is, however, paid on savings accounts and also charged to enterprises for inventory accumulation.
15. Rent on residential housing is also recognized and collected by the state, but the amount is usually below full costs.

guaranteed a job. The Soviet wage system, rooted in Marx's distribution theory, is based mainly upon productivity and scarcity of labor.[16] Monetary wages and bonuses are used as chief incentives for both greater quantity and better quality work. Wage and salary differentials exist between easy and difficult skills; between safe and hazardous occupations; between diligent pacesetters and run-of-the-mill workers; between high- and low-priority positions; and between Moscow and hardship locations such as northern Siberia.[17]

Wage and salary payments take three basic forms. First, *time* rates (so many rubles per month) are paid to workers in mass production or service industries where final products cannot always be identified with individual workers and quantitative standards cannot be established for the amount of work performed. The second type of wage payments involves *piece* rates (so many rubles per unit of output) paid to the majority of Soviet labor force. The third form of "earned income" is *salaries* paid to enterprise managers plus bonuses received along with workers for outstanding performance. Professional personnel and white-collar workers also receive salaries according to their skill requirements and occupational priorities.

In a Marxian fashion, higher wages for more difficult skills, harder jobs, or inclement regions are calculated as simply multiples of the basic legal minimum wage. Wages and salaries, as well as the total wage bill, are determined by Soviet authorities through the State Committee on Labor and Wages. There is no collective bargaining on basic wages or fringe benefits, yet the scarcity of certain skills and the managers' determination to fulfill their quotas have often given workers an opportunity to earn more through upgrading of the scarce labor within the enterprise or lowering production norms. The statutory minimum wage is raised periodically as productivity increases.

Wages are generally supplemented by a number of fringe benefits, such as free education, free health care, low-cost housing, and vacations.[18] Family incomes are normally much larger than the breadwinner's wage, for many wives also work. Under the 1965 reform, special bonuses are paid to workers whose enterprise is successful in fulfilling its sales and profits targets. Although "profit sharing" has always been an effective monetary incentive to Russian workers, the new bonuses are to be paid out of a new "material incentives fund" established particularly for this purpose under the banner of "socialist competition" to supplement regular bonuses paid out of the wage fund.

16. Marx advocates a sharing of social dividends among all: "from each according to his ability, to each according to his need." During the "socialist" transition to full communism, however, Lenin allows the substitution of "work" for "need."

17. The difference between the lowest legal minimum wage paid to unskilled workers, such as cleaning women, and the highest paid, to a skilled technician, shows a ratio of 1:6.

18. Big Soviet enterprises have their athletic teams, country places, resort establishments, art groups, and handicraft shops.

The Soviet Union relies to a degree also on nonwage and nonmonetary incentives to elicit favorable response from its labor force. To increase efficiency (and presumably to speed up the Soviet journey to full communism) workers and peasants are rewarded by membership in such societies as the Shock Brigades (the Stakhanovites) and the more recent Movement of Communist Labor. In addition to obtaining greater power in the hierarchy, workers vie for prestigious titles, meritorious citation, and even the macabre expectation of a burial site among the nation's heroes. Honors bestowed upon working citizens for outstanding achievements range from a simple badge, a red banner, and local press publicity to the Order of Lenin, Hero of the Soviet Union, and Hero of Socialist Labor. These awards, in addition to being highly coveted by the Soviet citizenry for their honored distinctions, also often open many doors in Soviet society, economy, and administration.

Indirect Controls: Reflections of Democracy

As indicated before, the economies of the Soviet type leave little room for indirect monetary and fiscal controls. The allocative and redistributive functions of taxes, credits, and subsidies are generally performed by direct state allocation of resources into consumption, investment, and budgetary assistance; wage and price determination; and credit rationing. Since full employment and the composition of national income are predetermined in the state plans, there are theoretically no trade cycles—and no need for countercyclical measures. The same is true of other indirect controls to deal with market failures or deficiencies. Such measures as antitrust legislation, public utility regulation, unemployment compensation, consumer protection, and business promotion have very little meaning and purpose in the CDEs.

If the Soviet Union were a nonmonetized and closed economy—with everyone working for the state, all wages and fringe benefits paid in kind, and all investment decisions made by direct allocation of labor and materials—there would indeed be no place for monetary, fiscal, or welfare policies. But Russia is no such microstate. It is one of the largest countries in the globe, thoroughly monetized, and connected with the rest of the world in many respects (trade, travel, communications). Not all the decisions are taken centrally. There is freedom of consumer choice and labor movement, and millions of transactions take place every day in monetary terms. Consequently, in order to influence individual decisions in some key areas, a resort to certain indirect state measures are necessary.

The scope and significance of indirect controls in the Soviet Union are thus related to the degree of reforms and liberalization measures allowed in the economy. The more the government relinquishes its direct controls on microeconomic allocation at the local and enterprise levels, the more intervention must be focused on indirect methods of charting the economy's course of development such as monetary policy, credit allocation, taxation and welfare measures.

Banking and Monetary Policy

The Soviet monetary apparatus is geared to three state institutions: the All-Union State Bank (Gosbank); the Investment Bank (Stroibank); and the Foreign Trade Bank (Vneshtorgbank).[19] The State Bank, directly responsible to the Council of Ministers, serves as both a central and a commercial bank. It issues currency and regulates money supply, and it serves as the fiscal agent of the Soviet treasury. Through its thousands of commercial branches and savings offices, it engages in routine banking operations for all Soviet enterprises and account holders. The Gosbank is responsible for the preparation of the credit and cash plans as adjuncts to the national production plan. Under this responsibility, it serves as the general "inspector of finances," supervising the fulfillment of the national plan through its control by the ruble. Initially, the State Bank was authorized to supply short-term and planned working capital to Soviet enterprises. Under subsequent reforms, the bank can also make medium-term (five- to six-year) loans to both industrial plants and collective farms for expansion and mechanization.[20]

The Investment Bank is responsible for financing long-term capital needs of Soviet industry, cooperative housing, school and hospital construction, and residential homes. It receives its loanable funds through state budget allocations, deposits of social insurance contributions, and depreciation setasides by industrial firms and collective farms. It finances almost all new, and part of recurrent, investments by Soviet enterprises and farms in accordance with the national plan. Financing includes nonreturnable grants as well as low-interest loans. The Bank for Foreign Trade has the responsibility of financing the bulk of Soviet state-controlled foreign trade in conjunction with Soviet-owned banks abroad.

On the whole, monetary policy in the Soviet Union has a limited function: to provide a lubricant for the grinding machinery of national planning; to ensure plan fulfillment; and occasionally to mitigate hidden or suppressed inflation. In the narrow context, credit is provided by various state banks for working capital, expansion of facilities, and new investment ventures. To a much smaller scale, financing is also provided for installment purchases. The banks' more important role is the inspection of intra-firm money flows. In the absence of diverse financial assets, monetary instruments, and private banking, however, monetary policy is only a very minor branch of statecraft.

19. For details, see *Soviet Financial System* (Moscow: Progress Publishers, 1966), and G. Garvy, *Money, Banking and Credit in Eastern Europe* (New York: Federal Reserve Bank of New York, 1966).

20. The credit plan specifies the total amount of credit to be allocated to Soviet enterprises during the plan period broken down in terms of short, medium, and long terms. The cash plan determines the amount of money in circulation; it is similar to the Western national cash-flow accounts.

Fiscal Policy

Among the Soviet financial plans, the comprehensive budget is by far the most important and the most elaborate. The Soviet state budget covers over half of the Soviet national income. State revenues are derived essentially from profits and interest paid by state enterprises and a general turnover (sales) tax on all final transactions—from the sale of raw materials to the final delivery of finished products to consumers. These two items account for about two-thirds of total revenues. Deductions from profits—the most important source of revenue and accounting for over one-third of the total—are that part of the enterprise's net revenues paid to the budget as capital charges (interest), investment returns (dividends), and loan repayments. Total "deductions" vary from industry to industry and enterprise to enterprise. Some lose money during the year and have to be subsidized.

Of total profits made by successful enterprises, some 80 percent is returned to the state. The remaining 20 percent is retained by the enterprise for various purposes. The turnover tax is a complex levy imposed on articles sold by enterprises. The rates vary according to regions, industries, and nature of the product. Luxury items (liquor, jewelry, furs, caviar) have the highest rates of 100 percent or more. The lowest rates of 10 percent or less are levied on children's clothing, kitchen utensils, and the like. Some products, such as export items, are exempt.

There are two types of direct taxes in the Soviet Union: personal income tax and a variety of local taxes and charges. All earnings from labor above the minimum are taxable. Incomes from nonwage sources are liable to tax except for certain exempt categories (interest, prizes, welfare receipts). The standard marginal rate on incomes of more than 100 rubles a month is 13 percent. For income earners with more than four dependents the rate is 9.1 percent; for bachelors, 19 percent. Social insurance taxes are imposed as a percentage of wages and salaries paid out by industrial enterprises and state and collective farms. Other minor taxes account for less than 1 percent of the revenues.

Public expenditures include, first and foremost, the financing of the national economy by providing investment funds, working capital, subsidies, and appropriations for related facilities. Such financing absorbs 44 percent of total budgetary expenditures. Defense expenditures in the budget account for about 13–14 percent of annual outlays, but many Western analysts believe that part of the defense budget is hidden under other categories, such as space and scientific research.[21] Free education for all in all levels and for all ages absorbs about 16 percent of the total; free medical and health care for all, about 6 percent; comprehensive social security and pensions, nearly 16 percent. Altogether, nearly 38 percent of the Soviet state budget is devoted to social and cultural measures. Soviet budgets are normally in balance or show a slight surplus, which goes into the capital of the Gosbank.

21. Western estimates put total defense-oriented expenditures in the Soviet Union at as much as 13 percent of the national income.

On the whole, fiscal policy plays a minor role in Soviet economic management. It has little or no countercyclical responsibility, as there are theoretically no cycles. It has little or no redistributional function, because personal income distribution is handled directly through administrative (manipulative) prices and wages. Owing to its crudity, inflexibility and relatively low rates, direct taxation is neither a source of significant revenue nor a means of levelling incomes. It is only an important device to exact funds from farm cooperatives; to discourage private artisan activity and craftsmanship; and to foster marriage and family life. Occasionally the policy tries to curtail or stimulate consumer purchases of certain specific items or to siphon off consumers' excess purchasing power through the turnover tax.

Welfare Policy

Economic security and the distribution of income in the Soviet Union are part of the considerations for setting wages and salary scales, but earnings from employment are not the only source of income for Soviet citizens. In addition to the public and merit goods and services that Soviet households can obtain free or at subsidized prices (free education, free medical care, and generously subsidized housing), there is a broad range of transfer payments available under the social security and social insurance system. What Soviet authorities call "social consumption expenditures," constitute the welfare aspect of the Soviet state and the second set of instruments for income redistribution.[22] In the 1970s, social consumption per capita amounted to some 28.5 percent of total per capita income.

The Soviet social security system consists mainly of cash transfers to compensate for the permanent loss of earning capacity. Thus, there are old-age pensions, incapacity pensions, survivors' pensions, long-service pensions for certain categories of white-collar workers, and meritorious personal pensions for those offering special service to the state or to the cause of revolution.[23] The social insurance system covers financial assistance in certain cases of temporary earning incapacitation, such as pregnancy. There are sickness benefits, sick leave with pay for women workers before and after childbirth, maternity grants to low-income families, and holiday pay.[24] The system also provides child allowance to mothers with two or more children; family income supplement to poor households, stipends for academic and vocational education, and, finally, burial grants.

22. For details regarding costs, principles of entitlement, and benefit calculations, see A. McAuley, *Economic Welfare in the Soviet Union* (Madison: University of Wisconsin Press, 1979).

23. Old-age pensions and survivors' benefits vary from 50 to 100 percent of earnings, depending on size of earnings, nature of job, duration of employment, and number of survivors.

24. Disability, sickness, and injury payments start from 50 percent of earnings and reach as high as 90 to 100 percent, based on the type and duration of disability and years of service to the enterprise.

Welfare outlays account for about one-sixth of the total Soviet budget. Social insurance contributions are made entirely by public enterprises in the form of payroll taxes. These taxes vary from 4.4 percent to 9 percent of an enterprise's payroll, depending on the type of industry. Workers pay nothing. The gap, if any, between the system's income and outgo is financed by the state. The collection of payroll taxes and disbursement of benefits is handled by the trade unions. Coverage extends to all industrial workers, and, since 1964, also to workers in agricultural collectives.

The Soviet social security system compares favorably with Western schemes in comprehension and generosity.[25] Unlike the European and American varieties, however, the Soviet welfare policy is an integral and coordinated part of income distribution rather than an adjunct or supplement to it. Thus, pensions are higher in unpleasant, strategic, and hazardous occupations. State industrial and farm workers are more favorably treated than collective farmers. Trade-union members receive more sickness and maternity benefits than nonmembers. Labor turnover is penalized by relatively lower pensions, permanent disability benefits, and other compensations. The family allowance program rewards only families with four or more children as compared with one or more in France and two or more in Germany and the United Kingdom.

Group Influence: Diversity in Unity

The Soviet Union, by virtue of its single-party rule and its totalitarian superstructure, should by definition leave little room for economic conflicts, class interests, and group quarrels over the allocation and distribution of resources. The one-party system in politics, the "classless" orientation in society, and the emphasis on labor as the sole source of value and its sole claimant, *prima facie*, preclude formal collective bargaining. In the opinion of Western observers, however, the post-Stalin era, despite its monolithic appearance, is as "complex and stratified" as any other society, divided into heterogeneous social classes and subject to various forms of group pressures.

Most students of the Soviet Union also agree that despite the Communist party's dominance over the Soviet economy (and the Politburo's primacy over party members and the government), Russia is not yet a homogeneous, classless society. In addition to party and government leaders who may represent certain personal or parochial interests, major bargainers in the national scene consist of the leaders of

25. Since unemployment is not officially recognized, there is no provision for unemployment compensation, and until recently, workers laid off would not receive any income before they were placed elsewhere. Recently, however, administrative personnel laid off as part of the new reforms have been paid for nearly a year while being trained for new jobs.

different nationalities in the union, the party *apparatchiki*, the police, the armed forces, the managerial elite, the state bureaucrats, the intelligentsia (writers, jurists, economists), and such mass associations as the trade unions, women's committees, and the unions of writers and journalists.[26] Within each group, too, there are usually certain subgroups, ranging from conservatives to reformers and radicals.

These variegated elite groups of roughly one million individuals form a relatively small part of total Soviet population and a relatively minor proportion of Russia's active labor force. Furthermore, of these individuals, only a small fraction is actively engaged in multilateral decision making. Still further, the pluralistic participation and influence of the major bargainers are not reflected in massive identification or action; rather, Soviet pluralism manifests itself in interactions among "leadership echelons" and political activists.

Much of the bargaining within the Soviet society and across its sprawling institutions is thus informal, behind the scenes, and scantly publicized. But there are also provisions for formal and open negotiations between labor and management in certain areas of industrial relations. To be sure, multilateral bargains are neither notably formalized nor markedly strong. Pressure groups (with the notable exception of the trade unions) are not usually organized, or if organized, they are not "democratically" structured.

Labor Unions and Industrial Relations

The provision for formal collective bargaining is included in Soviet law for trade unions,[27] but ideologically there is no room for elaborate or extensive bickering. Since the Soviet government is the government of workers and farmers, and since the state is almost the sole employer of the work force, the interests and objectives of labor and management are naturally to coincide. Furthermore, there is a paucity of bargaining issues. Wages and labor laws are for the most part centrally determined; job security and employment are guaranteed; and party control over working men is fairly strict.[28]

The Soviet trade unions are, in a sense, the popular and presumably "democratic" arms of the state and the Communist party, although legally and constitutionally separate and independent from both party and the government. The

26. For an elaborate discussion of this topic, see H. G. Skilling and F. Griffiths (eds.), *Interest Groups in Soviet Politics* (Princeton: Princeton University Press, 1973).

27. Leonid Brezhnev's report to the twenty-fourth Party Congress in 1971, for example, promised something to almost every faction within the Soviet power structure: the party hardliners, the liberal intellectuals, the military men, the reform-minded managers, and the consumers. It is generally conceded that the continuity of collective leadership in the post-Krushchev years was largely due to continuous compromises by the top Politburo leaders.

28. Mary McAuley, *Labour Disputes in Soviet Russia* (London: Clarendon Press, 1969), quoted in the *Economist*, 22 March 1969.

smallest unit of organized labor is the enterprise union, to which almost all workers, employees, and middle-echelon personnel belong. These plant or shop unions are vertically grouped in a national organization corresponding to their industrial function and horizontally aligned in interunion councils of the city, province, or republic. The supreme labor organization is the All-Union Congress of Trade, with its permanent All-Union Central Council. The All-Union Congress is composed of some twenty-five labor organizations established along industrial lines (transportation workers, coal miners, farm workers, railway employees). Unions must be recognized by the government. Membership is voluntary; dues are uniform and relatively low; and benefits are attractive. Consequently, more than 95 percent of workers and employees in the Soviet civilian labor force belong to unions.

Theoretically, the unions are "democratic" and the leadership is elected by union members, most of whom are not party members. In fact, the Communist party provides the dominant influence over the selection of union leaders and the management of union affairs. Workers in each local union are represented by a union committee elected by the membership of the enterprise. The committee represents workers' rights before the management, advises the management on the enterprise's production plan, and signs collective agreements. These agreements, patterned after standard models, specify the rights and responsibilities of each party. The management agrees to maintain safe working conditions, provide for further training, use recommended production methods, and spend part of the enterprise's income on health, recreational, and cultural services. The union, in turn, pledges to accept predetermined wages, fulfill production norms, work loyally and diligently, promote competition among workers, and supervise management's adherence to all government regulations concerning wages, working and living conditions, welfare services, and bonus payments.

Labor unions do not engage in real collective bargaining at the industry or plant levels, because the total industrial wage bill and its total real purchasing power are both predetermined in the national plan. Such matters as wage rates, working conditions, output norms, and many of the fringe benefits are also not subject to free collective bargaining. But, there are also indications that the All-Union Central Council is "consulted" by the party hierarchy at the time of drawing national plans.

A primary function of the Soviet labor unions is to increase labor productivity and to assist the management in fulfilling overall production quotas. This task includes the maintenance of labor discipline; labor training and education; encouragement of socialist emulation among individual workers and work brigades; rewarding leading performers and efficient innovators with a variety of monetary and nonmonetary prizes; cooperating with management in assigning workers to various factory jobs; and last, but perhaps most important, determining how bonuses shall be used.

Another major task of the unions is to sponsor cultural and recreational activities. The unions are also given both the ownership and management of welfare facilities and services. The social insurance administration is in the unions' hands, although insurance premiums are totally paid by the government and not the workers.

A third major activity of the unions is the joint arbitration of labor disputes. Each shop has a "labor dispute committee," composed of equal numbers of management and labor representations, in charge of resolving conflicts that may arise from the interpretation of the collective agreements. The grievances not resolved by the committee can be taken to the people's court by the worker or workers who originally lodged the complaint, and by the management under certain circumstances. The committee handles disputes related to work norms, wage differentials, job assignments, and so forth.

Finally, the unions may occasionally engage in a limited consultation process. Since 1957 the State Committee on Labor and Wages has been required to consult with the All-Union Council in adopting major policy decisions. Local union committees, too, enjoy similar rights to participate in personnel decisions, drafting of the factory's plan, establishing production norms, and determining wage differentials for various job categories. They also have veto power over dismissing employees.

Thus, although the Soviet trade unions cannot bargain over wage rates, the wage bill, or other centrally allocated funds for services, they do have consultative, supervisory, and even controlling rights in Soviet enterprises. In some sense, they also participate in minor managerial decision making not yet practiced in the West, such as participation in production goal conferences with the management. In short, unions are not a mere rubber stamp for the party or the management; they are, in a sense, the "loyal opposition" to the regime. They do not yet elect the managers (as in Yugoslavia), nor do they fully participate in managerial decisions (as in West Germany), but they seem to be moving in those directions.

Informal Pressures

Repeated shake-ups of the Soviet leadership and the frequency of changes in the Soviet hierarchy indicate that spontaneous self-government is not yet at hand. That is, some conflicts of interest still exist not only between the governing and the governed, but also among governors themselves. According to a noted Kremlinologist, such intraparty maneuvers often end in compromise. In this view, the Soviet society is now a full-fledged oligarchy ruled by special lobbies that represent organized interests—the party, the military, the secret police, the technocracy, the ethnic minorities, the hard-liners, the coexistentialists, and the dissidents—mostly in the name of communist ideology and Marxian dialectics.[29] Other experts on Soviet affairs confirm the presumption that Soviet leaders now make major decisions on a collective basis. They also agree that there is a kind of special group

29. See Michel Tatu, *Power in the Kremlin* (New York: The Viking Press, 1968).

representation within the Politburo itself. In the opinion of some observers, each member has a specific area of responsibility or interest for which he must continually lobby for budget funds, key personnel, and recognition.[30]

To be sure, the basic decision-making power in the Soviet Union still lies in the hands of top party leaders, and it operates chiefly through a command process. Leaders themselves decide when and with whom, to consult. They may ignore group pressures or even defy them, if necessary, or they may use one pressure group against another for their own political objectives. Yet the evidence presented by Western analysts and others indicates that the final decisions are, sometimes, affected by the competing and conflicting tendencies of the unorganized, somewhat amorphous, but influential pressure groups. The influence on policy is often exerted through coercion or persuasion in informal and often uninstitutionalized methods. The security police, the military, the party *apparatchiki*, and the bureaucracy often lean toward coercion by reward and punishment, although they sometimes engage in propaganda as well. The intelligentsia, on the other hand, must rely only on mobilizing public opinion.

Outside the strict political arena, too, group influences are clearly visible. In the opinion of one expert observer, what actually occurs in Soviet economic planning is an unavoidable process of bargaining among planners and those who have to implement the plans.[31] In the matters of wage and price determination also, the political leadership and planning authorities seem to be mindful of the workers' views and expectations. Periodic increases in wages and fringe benefits are a clear indication of this concern by the leadership. Given the political underpinnings of Soviet economy and industry, it is not difficult to see the necessity of bargaining among the counterveiling forces of ideology, bureaucracy, and technological efficiency.

The "Private Sector": Consumers' Influence

Despite its basic commitment to a socialist command regime, unilateral control in the Soviet Union is far from total: the Soviet state is not the sole owner of everything. While admittedly a relatively minor feature of national decision making, consumer sovereignty prevails in a small sector of the Soviet economy.

Under Soviet law, individuals have the right to own *personal* property, as long as such ownership is for one's own private use. Privately owned means of production can also be used by their owners to earn income, but there is a ban on the hiring of labor for private profit. Individuals and households own their personal

30. Divisions and conflicts of interests are generally worked out and resolved inside the party or government machinery.

31. K. W. Ryavec, *Implementation of Soviet Economic Reform* (New York: Praeger, 1975).

effects: furniture, appliances, automobiles, motor boats, art objects. Productive capital tools and equipment used in one's own profession or craft are also privately owned. One-fourth of the urban population owns private houses and condominium apartments, and space in them is semilegally rented to others. Most rural dwellings—dachas, beach houses, and peasant cottages—are also privately owned.

Private land ownership is not allowed, but space in the city and homesites in the suburbs can be leased from the state at relatively nominal prices. The state also assigns part of its landholdings for cooperative ownership in farming. Private home construction on leased sites is both lawful and economical. Many people, particularly in rural areas, build their own homes. Private savings are increasingly invested in cooperative apartments. Inheritance is also a right fully recognized by Soviet law. All personal property, bank accounts, and savings deposits can be willed to heirs. So may residential homes and country retreats.

Private economic activity, while not officially encouraged, is permitted under two conditions. First, such activity must be personal, and individual, not entrepreneurial. Thus, a barber, for example, cannot hire extra help in his barber shop. Second, private enterprise must be directly involved in the production of goods and services, and not in trade alone. Thus, professional men and women—lawyers, physicians, artists, artisans, craftsmen, and repairmen—may chose to sell their services and works privately instead of offering them to state enterprises.[32] There is also a good deal of "moonlighting" on the part of professionals and artisans who normally work for the state. One may hire domestic help, and private tutoring and professional services are also legal.

The law bars purchase of goods and services by private individuals for resale. All private sales must be made by the owner. Thus, the private growing of fruits, vegetables, and flowers is permitted as a legal private enterprise on small "private" plots or gardens adjacent to peasants' and farm workers' homes. The size of the plots ranges from 1 to 2.5 acres, depending on geography, climate, and market. Collective farmers, state farmhands, and even some urban workers with small backyards near urban centers usually devote part of their free time to cultivating such cash crops. In Moscow's Central Peasant Market, farmers and middlemen from as far as Tibilisi and Tashkent peddle their produce in the midst of winter. There are several thousand such farmers' markets in the Soviet Union, where profit-minded country folk come from thousands of miles to make a legal ruble. Weekend fishermen and hunters are also permitted to offer their fish and game for sale in these markets. In the private farmers' markets, prices are not regulated and fluctuate daily under supply and demand situations. "Private plots" constitute about one percent of Russia's cultivated land, but in some years they have been responsible for a third to a half of the country's supply of milk, meat, and vegetables and some 80 percent of its eggs. Altogether, Soviet private agriculture accounts for between a quarter and a third of total agricultural output; 50 percent of livestock population,

---

32. According to one estimate, between one-third and one-half of all consumer expenditures for repair services pass through private hands.

and a hefty 30 percent of agricultural labor. Incomes from private farms are estimated to be ten times more than earnings on collective farms.

Freedom to dispose of one's income at will is both guaranteed and extensively exercised. Private consumption, except for unauthorized travel abroad, is an individual decision. Private savings and a limited type of "investment" are allowed and often encouraged by the state. Soviet citizens can open a savings account at any one of more than 80,000 branches of the Gosbank, the world's largest state-owned bank. Interest on savings is paid by the bank (although in deference to Marxist dogma, it is called "a charge for use of money"). Soviet citizens can also use their spare incomes to buy a cooperative apartment or art objects as a means of building a nestegg.

In addition to the freedom of consumer choice in the area of consumption, saving, and investment, individuals as workers can usually pretty much choose their own jobs and change them at will. Labor mobility is, in fact, extensive, and labor turnover is a headache for state planners. Since the mid-1950s, workers have been allowed to quit their jobs on short notice.

Beyond lawful private ownership and legitimate private enterprise, there is reportedly a vast amount of unlawful and forbidden private production and trading. Articles in short supply—from knitwear to bootleg jazz records and tapes—are profitably produced, sometimes in small underground "factories" employing scores of moonlighting workers. There are flea markets where brand new goods are sold as second-hand stuff at higher prices. While these activities are severely punished when discovered, they are evidently both extensive and frequent.

Another manifestation of greater Soviet attention to consumer demand may be found in the new emphasis on the kind and quality of goods and services. Since the middle of the 1960s, concerted efforts have been made by the Soviet hierarchy to upgrade the quality and increase the quantity of consumer items—from shoes and men's suits (the traditional subjects of caricature in Soviet humor magazines) to furniture, appliances, and services.

Ideologically, too, service industries, which classical Marxism considered "unproductive" (as against industry and agriculture), are now extolled as "honorable" social undertakings. Workers in Soviet trade are, for the first time since the Revolution, considered as important as those working in production sectors of the economy. In the same context, the Soviet Union has used advertising media in the West to promote its tourist and export trade. Domestic advertising, however, was for a long time limited to "institutional" uses, such as exhortations to put money in savings banks. There was no industry or factory advertising.[33] Under the policy of greater consumer satisfaction, emphasized by Nikita Krushchev in the 1960s, new attention was paid to commercial art, attractive industrial design, and sales promotion, including Western-style advertising. For obvious ideological reasons,

33. The official Soviet attitude toward advertising as late as the 1940s was that such sales promotions were "a means of swindling the people, and of foisting upon them goods frequently useless or of dubious quality."

product advertising was rationalized as an "educational service" to consumers, acquainting them with the nature, quality, and uses of new products.

With hundreds of consumer-goods factories now converted to demand-oriented production, Soviet sales promotion through advertising has begun to push such items as baby foods, radios, refrigerators, sewing machines, clothing, and color TV. All major media—billboards, local newspapers, trade magazines, radio and TV—are used in product advertising. *Pravda* and *Izvestia* still refuse to carry ads, but another Moscow newspaper has started a weekly advertisement supplement with success.

Consumer sovereignty in the choice of household appliances, service facilities, and food items has in turn given rise to the gradual emergence of brand names and trademarks. As a means of identifying the shoddiness and poor quality of nearly identical consumer products made by different factories, Russian authorities have found it convenient to place a "factory mark" on finished products. By this method, consumers' refusal to buy poor reputation "marks" helps authorities to discover inefficient plants, and to penalize shoddy producers. Such "brand" identifications have also allowed planners to bother less with detailed quality standards and the bureaucratic problems of inspections and enforcement.

Other "capitalist" trappings long associated with consumer sovereignty are also making an increasing appearance. Installment credits, for example, are available for many household items. Fashion shows are used to attract customers. There are lotteries, layaway plans, and even bank secrecy. Market research, once almost unknown in Russia (and somewhat unnecessary in the light of consumer goods shortages), has become both respected and useful in determining Soviet consumers' likes and dislikes.

While capitalistic profit making is legally forbidden to private citizens, the Soviet government is keen on using capitalistic devices to earn foreign exchange or to acquire foreign technology. Some stores in Moscow, for example, sell their wares to foreigners only for hard foreign currency. The Soviets have also set up joint distribution ventures in Western Europe with local capitalist partners. In France, Britain, and Belgium, the Russians show classically capitalistic attention to consumer tastes in modifying their export items—from watches to tractors. The Russians' eight foreign banks in Western Europe and Asia, established to help finance East-West trade and sell Russian gold, have proved able capitalists.

The Soviet Experience: Some Lessons from Central Direction

After more than sixty years of trials and tribulations under a largely command mechanism, the Soviet Union can boast of many accomplishments. For the masses, living conditions have, by almost any standard, vastly improved; illiteracy has been virtually eliminated; health care and education are freely available to all; and individual economic security is guaranteed.[34] For Mother Russia, many spectacular scientific and technological feats in engineering, medicine, and space probes have been achieved. In the international arena, the Soviet Union is now matching the United States in global military pre-eminence. The Soviet's sphere of political interest and influence is spread the world over. And stability and security— the two objectives that the Russians value above all else—have been attained.

Yet Russia's "socialism" is not anywhere near Marx's (or Lenin's) dreams of an egalitarian, classless society where a new breed of men and women work cooperatively without hindrance or interference from the state. In reality, not only has the state failed to "wither away"; it has become the nexus of almost all activities. A new Soviet-man has yet to emerge; a classless society is neither established nor on the horizon. Wide differentials in incomes and wealth among individuals are not only tolerated but respectably practiced.

The Soviet economy also shows extreme paradoxes.[35] A system that is second to none in the world in the most advanced production of space stations, long-range rocketry, and supersonic planes has one of the industrialized world's worst distribution systems, and is perennially short of basic food, proper housing, high-quality clothing, and other consumer amenities. Missing also are the level and quality of services that usually go hand in hand in countries with indigenous high technology. Soviet advances in pure science and theoretical economics are not matched by advanced enterprise management and plant efficiency. A country with vast arable lands, abundant minerals, plenty of water, and the advantages of a fairly early start in industrialization, which could have easily caught up with Western standards of living, has not even approached them. Instead, the Soviet leadership has focused its ideological preferences and priorities on obtaining a superpower status in military strength, and it has achieved this goal with remarkable success. The lessons from the Russian experience are still fragmentary and inconclusive. In attempting to produce both guns and butter, the Soviet leadership is still groping for the answers. Post-Stalin Russia, in particular, has been a peculiar mixture of regulation and freedom, centralization and decentralization, functional and regional organization. In the ten years between 1955 and 1965, the state's economic organization chart was rearranged six times in the hope of achieving a better utilization of the country's industrial potential.

34. President Brezhnev told the twenty-fifth Party Congress: "One of the greatest achievements of socialism is that every Soviet man is assured of his future . . . His work, his abilities, and his energy will always find a fitting use and aspiration . . . His children will be given a free education . . . Society will never abandon him in a misfortune . . . He will be given free medical treatment, a pension in the event of permanent disability, and security in old age."

35. On a per capita income basis, the Soviet-American ratio at about 40 percent is almost the same as the relationship was in 1860! Even among the CDEs, Soviet per capita GNP is still only about two-thirds of East Germany's; it is behind Czechoslovakia's and slightly ahead of Poland's.

Soviet centralized planning, under which almost all major decisions are made by planners thousands of miles away, still remains an experiment in the making. It certainly has coordinated the sprawling Russian economy, both in war and peace, without a breakdown, but its efficiency still remains in doubt—even by the Soviet's own reckoning. Under a system of largely centralized direction, factory managers seem to have become indifferent bureaucrats; their initiative, ingenuity, and imagination have often been focused not on innovation, but on outsmarting Moscow planners. Thus, when the output target is set in terms of volume or weight, a smart manager has tried to fulfill his obligations by producing unneeded heavy or bulky articles rather than badly needed lighter or more delicate merchandise. On the other hand, if the quota is set in monetary terms—so many rubles' worth of hats or shoes a year—a seasoned operator has been inclined to use more expensive materials, regardless of costs or market demand, to reach or surpass his quota the easy way. If overfulfillment of quota is not rewarded, then the managers try to keep their annual production capability deliberately down so as to avoid getting a larger quota next year. If, on the other hand, larger-than-quota output should command appropriate rewards, then they would tend to inflate and exaggerate their needs for raw materials, equipment, and workers.[36]

Rational resource mobilization has also been largely hampered by inadequate material incentives for a rational use of land and work force. Individuals and households have little or no incentive to save, for they normally receive very low interests on their savings deposits. Soviet enterprises and collective farms, too, prefer to spend their surpluses on bonuses or uneconomic reinvestments, because Soviet factories and industrial units receive little or no interest on their bank deposits.

Rational resource use has also been admittedly undermined by an economically nonrational capital investment policy. For a long time in the past, Soviet planners ideologically favored charging no, or only nominal, interest on budgetary appropriations for investment purposes. The result was that managers were often inclined to come up with larger and more numerous projects regardless of return, since they cost them nothing in government appropriation; to hoard raw materials, equipment, and production facilities for a long time without use; and to postpone loan repayments for as long as they could.

Prior to the 1960s reforms, Soviet state farms operated on an industrial basis, with workers and management receiving fixed wages and salaries regardless of crop yield or sale. Agricultural machinery and equipment were in turn allocated to them free of cost. Most managers thus ordered, and often received, a far greater amount of equipment than they really needed. As a result, many state farms showed a loss year after year. Part of the blame for the disastrous agricultural performance (apart from the very serious vagaries of the weather with which the Russians have to contend) has rested with rigid planning and the absence of local initiatives. Despite very large

36. Countless examples of mismanagement, waste, and inefficiency in Russia's so-called "hyperbureaucracy" regularly fill the pages of the Soviet press, particularly *Pravda*, the organ of the Communist party.

investment outlays ($500 billion in the last fifteen years) on Soviet farming, agriculture remains Russia's Achilles' heel. Employing eight times as many farm workers as the United States, and with five times the capital investment, Soviet farm output is still only 80 percent of the United States'.

In industry, the difficulties lie partly with the shortcomings of Soviet pricing and allocation practices and partly with overstaffing. Industrial managers have been prone to thwart excessive centralization by masquerading economic folly as rationality. In an almost ritualistic exercise, Soviet enterprises desperately try to spend their appropriated funds before the end of the year (in a practice called "storming") because a ruble saved is a ruble lost in the next year's budget. Since Moscow planners often have no way of assessing agency needs precisely, nor of evaluating an agency's accomplishments accurately, they usually look at what is completed. An agency that can show all its budget allocation spent can legitimately claim its task "completed" and can proudly expect to receive more.[37]

The misallocation and misuse of resources and significant unused capacity in the Soviet Union have caused growing concern among Soviet leaders in recent years,[38] particularly because of growing manpower imbalances by the low birth rate, the energy crisis resulting from resource exhaustion outside of inclement Siberia, and falling labor productivity. The declining growth in Soviet labor productivity (only 1 percent in 1979 as against the 4 percent planned target) has also been partly blamed on the relative abstraction and practical barrenness of some Soviet research and development efforts. Many of these efforts have not been directly tied to manufacturing plants or readily available to those who can put the results to work. There is also a bureaucratically rational reluctance on the part of Soviet managers toward radical innovations, and in favor of status quo.

Curiously enough, despite the command mechanism's bias towards full social cost accounting and the disregard of profit in the service of conservation and environmental quality, the Soviet record in this regard is admittedly a poor one. In the push for rapid industrialization, Soviet industries (particularly oil and electric energy) seem to have followed their capitalist counterparts in ravaging nature. Air and water pollution, inadequate waste treatment, and damages to soil and wildlife are reportedly as bad as elsewhere in the capitalist world. Strong antipollution laws on the books since 1963 have been ineffective and ignored. Managers have often found it profitable to pay the fine and continue polluting.[39] Soviet officials concede

37. Other "smart" responses by enterprise managers to circumvent planning rigidities include a system of mutual back-scratching with suppliers and customers, use of go-betweens to expedite deliveries, and exercise of personal influence.

38. All the so-called capitalistic crimes are also apparently rampant in the Soviet Union. Stealing, embezzlement, price rigging, black marketing, fraud, bribery, false bookkeeping, and faking statistical reports are some of the examples of wrongdoing levelled against state officials. See George Feifer, "Russia Shoots Its Business Crooks," *New York Times Magazine,* 2 May 1965.

39. See Marshall I. Goldman, *The Spoils of Progress* (Cambridge: MIT Press, 1972); and *New York Times,* 20 September 1972. For more recent accounts of the Russian economy

that air pollution in large Soviet cities and industrial centers exceeds permissible limits. Only recently have the Russians seriously engaged in quickening their pollution control programs.

All in all, the Soviet's dream of turning Russia (and the rest of the world) into a peaceful, proletarian, progressive, and classless society remains as distant as ever. The leaders' revolutionary exhortations still have modest effects on the essentially conservative and pragmatic Russian citizens. Surprisingly, some of the most basic institutions are avowedly little changed from czarist days. The most intractable problem is still the organization of the economy toward transition to full communism. Even by the Russians' own reckoning, the Soviet economy is facing serious difficulties in the 1980s: rising materials costs, energy shortages, slower growth of the labor force, and sluggish labor productivity. At the same time, the growing diversity and complexity of the Russian economy is making central planning and control less effective. And the heavy reliance on the command mechanism and the overgrown bureaucracy militate against real reforms, as the 1965 experiment with "liberalization" and decentralization seems to indicate.

see D. A. Dyker, *The Soviet Economy.* (London: Granada Publishing, 1976); A. Nove, *The Soviet Economic System* (London: Allen & Unwin, 1977); and C. A. Krylov, *The Soviet Economy* (Lexington; D. C. Heath, 1979).

THE PEOPLE'S REPUBLIC OF CHINA

China is heir to the world's oldest uninterrupted civilization. It is a potentially powerful but presently underdeveloped nation. With almost 9.6 million square kilometers of land and near a billion population,[40] the People's Republic is one of the major powers by virtue of sheer size. In global power equations, however, China lacks both the military ability to project its power beyond its frontiers and the economic means to challenge the other two superpowers. In high technology, the country is at least thirty to forty years behind the West and the Soviet Union. In per capita income, it is the poorest of all CDEs, and ranks with Pakistan and Tanzania among LDCs. Its standard of living, measured by per capita GNP, is only about 2.2 percent of the United States and only 4 percent of the USSR. Seventy-five percent of the people still live in the countryside, but compared to its own pre-communist status, China's accomplishments are indeed noteworthy. It has a large industrial base, built up almost from scratch; it has a nuclear capability; it is self-sufficient in most of its essential needs; it possesses a small but complete cadre of scientists and engineers; and it has little external debt.

In politics, the People's Republic is somewhat to the left of the Soviet Union in Marxist-Leninist orthodoxy. Up until recently, Soviet leaders were denounced by the Chinese communist hierarchy as "revisionists" who sacrificed the Marxist concept of the dictatorship of the proletariat under the policy of peaceful coexistence and competition with the West. Kremlin leaders, in turn, accused the late Mao Tse-tung and his associates of being dogmatists who could not adapt Marxist-Leninist teachings to the exigencies of a changing world.

Government's Role in the Economy

Historically, China has always been considered a "monolithic, oppressive, totalitarian state" while harboring some of the world's most educated, creative, resilient, and hard-working people. It still remains so, with a one-party system and a discipline that requires subordinates to follow superiors and the minority to obey the majority. Although in the last thirty years or so since the communist takeover the country has gone through three different constitutions and several major organizational upheavals and ideological convulsions, this basic discipline has remained firm.[41]

---

40. China has not published a census since 1953. Estimates of present population and demographic growth vary considerably, even among China watchers and Western experts. Estimated total population figures range from 850 million to over 1 billion; estimated growth rates stretch from 0.8 percent to 2 percent a year.

CHINA: BASIC DATA

LAND AREA (sq. km.)	9,597,000
POPULATION (1980 estimate)	977 million
Net annual increase (1970-78 yearly average)	1.6 percent
Urban (percent of total, 1980)	25 percent
Working Age (15–64) (percent of total, 1978)	61 percent
LABOR FORCE (total civilian, 1979)	415 million
Agriculture, forestry, fishing (percent of total)	62 percent
Mining, manufacturing, construction (percent of total)	25 percent
Services, etc. (percent of total)	13 percent
GROSS DOMESTIC PRODUCT (market prices, 1979)	$245 billion
Per capita (1979)	$250
Average annual increase (1970–78)	6 percent
Public consumption (percent of GDP)	14 percent
Private consumption (percent of GDP)	51 percent
Fixed capital formation (ratio to GDP)	35 percent
Savings (ratio to GDP)	35 percent
GROSS DOMESTIC PRODUCT (market prices, 1979)	$245 billion
Agriculture, forestry, fishing (share in GDP)	36 percent
Mining, manufacturing, construction (share in GDP)	50 percent
Services (share in GDP)	14 percent
FOREIGN TRADE	
Exports (percent of GDP)	6 percent
Imports (percent of GDP)	6 percent

Eight distinct episodes characterize the changes in the government's direction and management of the economy between 1950 and 1980. The first episode, 1948–52, involved a period of communist reconstruction and rehabilitation. In this period, the Chinese leadership was struggling against an inflation-ridden, financially bankrupt, and strife-torn economy. The new communist rulers were most anxious to obtain the widest possible popular support. Thus, private ownership and free enterprise was tolerated in most economic sectors. A unified currency was introduced through the People's Bank of China, and wages and prices were stabilized. During the latter year of this limited "free-enterprise" episode, however, private firms were gradually and systematically regulated. Under a land-reform program, some 300 million peasants became the private owners of 117 million acres of land confiscated from big landlords and rich peasants for whom they had worked as sharecroppers.

In the second episode, coinciding with the First Five-Year Plan (1953–57), based on a Stalinist development pattern, the pressure on private businessmen was stepped up. The government established a joint state-private partnership with the avowed purpose of eventual nationalization of all private business. As small and poor peasants became unable to eke out a livelihood from their meager landholdings and began to sell their lands to richer farmers, they were voluntarily encouraged to join "mutual-aid teams" for the purpose of joint use of animals and farm implements. Gradually, these voluntary teams became mandatory, and farmers were forced to join agricultural cooperatives. At the end of 1956, private enterprise both in industry and agriculture ceased to exist except for a very small segment of retail trade and some peasant households. The free agricultural market was abolished, and peasants were forbidden to take their produce to the cities or to deal through channels other than state channels.

The third period (1956–58) witnessed a policy of relative economic liberalization on a limited scale. Under the influence of the "moderates," free markets were reopened for some commodities in certain areas. Some new decision-making authority was given to local governments and enterprise managers. Individual initiatives and profit making in state enterprises were again stressed. Centralized distribution of important commodities was somewhat relaxed. The size of agricultural cooperatives (for which farmers had shown scant enthusiasm) was reduced and the size of "private plots" expanded.

The fourth phase (1958–60) began with a fairly sudden change of policy toward tighter controls. When the liberalization movement began to spread beyond its expected limits, a political drive, led by Mao Zedong and his radical associates,

---

41. These frequent seesaws in basic approaches to economic problem solving in China have been commonly attributed to a constant struggle within the Chinese Communist party between the "moderate liberals," who advocate central planning, maximum growth and material incentives, and the "radicals," who favor decentralization, noneconomic objectives, and "permanent revolution."

got underway under the banner of the Great Leap Forward toward four main campaigns: water conservation and flood control; technological innovation; small-scale, labor-intensive industry; and the total communization of agriculture. Hundreds of millions of peasants, soldiers, workers, and intellectuals were mobilized through agricultural and urban communes to increase industrial and agricultural output. Iron smelting was done in homemade furnaces; irrigation works were started with crude tools; coal, cement, and other basic raw materials were produced in small-scale factories. "Private plots" and the free market were banned again. Soon after, however, the Great Leap had to be stopped because of three bad years of crop failures (1959–61); the glaring inefficiencies of "backyard" factories; poor quality and unusable products of new industrial units; the formidable resistance of farmers and urban workers to communization; the dislocations in transportation and construction; and the withdrawal of Soviet aid after the 1960 Sino-Soviet dispute.[42]

A fifth episode thus began in the light of the bitter lessons learned from hasty industrialization, excessive regimentation, and the irrationalities of the communes. The new period (1961–65) was generally considered a readjustment and consolidation period marked by "prudence and restraint." The development strategy again emphasized restructuring of incentives to relieve shortages, paid renewed attention to agriculture, and reintroduced central planning and greater reliance on Western scientific and technical know-how.

The sixth period (1966–69) witnessed a resurgence of ideological impatience with the pragmatic policies of the post-Leap years. For reasons never made clear, the Chinese leadership encouraged millions of youngsters, as Red Guard members, to start the Great Proletarian Cultural Revolution against established authority, bureaucracy, and intellectuals. Schools were closed and students were sent all over the country to propagate the thoughts of Mao, to purge bourgeois intellectuals and managerial elites. Central planning was downgraded, and decision making at the enterprise level was entrusted to workers, revolutionary committees, and the People's Liberation Army. Sweeping changes occurred in the structure of the party and the government. The results were work stoppages, transport congestions, reduced output, and dwindling foreign trade.

The seventh phase (1970–76) was accompanied by a new political soul-searching. There was a serious attempt by Chou En-lai and his associates toward a return to the orthodox communist centralism. Part of this new strategy was the resumption of central planning, a revival of the universities, emphasis on retraining and rewarding manpower, and expansion of foreign trade. The new economic policy still rejected profitability as a measure of enterprise efficiency, but emphasized proper cost accounting, better management, and higher productivity. As a sign of

42. The dispute was triggered by Russia's frustration and dissatisfaction with the objectives and methodology of the Great Leap.

the new mood, a series of concessions to free enterprise (the right to farm private plots and to own a house) was inserted in a new draft constitution. Material incentives also were reintroduced under the name of "rational rewards." Maoist work style was replaced by resumption of systematic planning. Chou's plans were, however, not unanimously supported. A powerful faction—later denounced as the Gang of Four—took strong exceptions to the proposed central planning and the use of foreign trade for modernization. As a result of strong opposition and criticisms in the party and in the press, there were a series of strikes, disruptions, and chaos in the economy.

The eighth episode—a New Long March—followed Mao's death in 1976. Under the Hua-Deng leadership, the priority was given to reversing the disruptive effects of the Cultural Revolution's ten years of politically inspired experimentation. The new motto was "four modernizations" in agriculture, industry, the military, and technology—aiming to transform China into a real military and economic superpower by the year 2000. The most outstanding feature of this phase has been a sharp break with Mao's principles of national self-reliance and independence from foreign sources. The new philosophy is based on learning from foreign science, technology, culture, and management. The emphasis is on efficiency in production, competence (instead of political loyalty) in management, and merit (instead of adventurism) in education.

These political and ideological zigzags are reflected in the still unsettled state of Chinese planning and economic management.

Development Planning

Between 1949 and 1980, China had five official five-year plans, mostly tentative and experimental. During the thirty-year period, the leadership has toyed with three or four different development patterns. Planning objectives, however, have remained essentially the same: to build a modern, powerful, socialist economy, mainly through indigenous efforts and an egalitarian sharing of both inputs and outputs.

The goal of self-reliance, the main pillar of Chinese development throughout Mao's life, involved the pursuit of economic independence, reliance on domestic initiatives, and emphasis on internal efforts. As an operational policy base, it meant exhortation to maximum toil, appeals toward eventual national self-sufficiency, keeping foreign ideas and influence from spoiling the purity of China's socialist system, regional and local reliance on local industries to meet local needs, and a move toward decentralization of industry location.

The egalitarian objective manifested itself not only in very narrow income differentials among individuals in various walks of life, but also, and more important, in a constant struggle against the rise of elitism, job status, and "bourgeois" rights. Periodic campaigns to bring together intellectual and manual labor, as well as urban and rural folks, by assigning urban cadres (bureaucrats, professors, researchers, and managers) to periodic farm work on the agricultural communes were another instrument of harmonization.

Much of this has changed in the post-Mao modernization drive, but the planning strategy basically has followed the Soviet lead in its emphasis on high investment ratio to GDP, heavy industrialization at high costs, and democratic centralism. In its quest for modernization, rapid growth, and technological progress, China's strategy also resembles that of the LDCs. However, certain specific characteristics of the Chinese model are worth noting at the outset. First, unlike the Soviet case, the methodology of economic planning has never been published in detail. Second, there seems to have been a gradual shift from the strictly Russian-type planning to the ones suited to China's own underlying economic condition. Third, the very word *planning* in Chinese politicoeconomic terminology has meant "proportional" development, a systematic integration of various sectors of the economy.[43] Fourth, the concrete application of balanced planning has been carried out through the formulation of three tables: material balance, labor balance, and money balance—each constructed in such a way as to accommodate the other two. Fifth, from the Second Plan onward, a broad range of day-to-day economic responsibilities have been transferred to the provincial authorities, so the national plan now also reflects the decentralized participation of economic decision makers at the regional and local level. Finally, while administration and management of the national plan is fairly decentralized, the economic planning and resource allocation functions are retained by the central government and the Communist party.[44]

On the fundamental and philosophical levels, such factors as scant priority given to a rapid rise in the standard of living, strong commitment to self-reliance, stress on egalitarianism, attacks on status and class barriers, glorification of manual work, and considerable autonomy, flexibility, and initiatives given to lower echelons of decision makers have been some of the other most distinctive features of Chinese development planning for much of the postwar period.[45]

The responsibility for national planning in China is shared by the State Planning Commission (SPC) for medium and long-term planning, the State

43. Planning is considered a "balanced method" of obtaining maximum economy and effective utilization of resources in contrast to the "massive waste and destruction of social labor" resulting from "competitive and chaotic production." See N. R. Lardy (ed.), *Chinese Economic Planning* (White Plains: M. E. Sharp, 1978), p. 4.

44. Strictly speaking, Chinese planning also consists of *long-term* plans (twelve years or more) embracing the whole economy or a special sector; *medium-term* plans (five years); and *annual* plans (the budget).

45. For a detailed discussion of this strategy based on "scarcity, ideology and organization," see Alexander Eckstein, "The Chinese Development Model," in *Chinese Economy Post-Mao* (Washington: GPO, 1978); and N. R. Lardy, "Economic Planning in the People's Republic of China," in *China: A Reassessment of the Economy* (Washington: GPO, 1975).

Economic Commission for annual economic plans, and many ministries and agencies for specific operations. The national plan consists of a series of domestic sectoral plans, a labor plan, a plan for materials, a foreign trade plan, the financial plan, (including the state budget), and the capital construction plan.

The national plan is constructed through a two-way hierarchical process of direction and communication at the central and provincial levels, and at the levels of the government and the Communist party. "Control figures" are first issued by the SPC to the central and provincial ministries and agencies for transmission to their subordinate agricultural communes and industrial enterprises. These figures contain production targets, input coefficients, cost data, and other relevant information. After direct consultation and bargaining between communes and enterprises—mostly at the provincial levels—unit plans, including input requirements and output capabilities, are constructed. These plans are then sent to higher levels of the government and the party for subsequent integration and coordination until they reach the SPC again. Revised (and presumably balanced) control figures are then prepared by the commission and, after ratification by the government and the party leadership, become official and mandatory directives for all individual enterprises. Chinese plans allow a greater degree of flexibility than in other CDEs, for the targets are fixed below the levels normally attained.

The first Chinese Five-Year Plan (1953–57), dubbed "Stalinist" in conception and implementation, was a plan for the "transition to socialism." Prepared with the help of Soviet experts and following the Soviet pattern, it emphasized rapid growth via heavy industrialization and nationalization of private holdings. The planned rate of annual growth was 14 percent. The plan was largely financed out of domestic resources, but the Soviet Union, under its 1950 treaty of friendship and assistance, offered nearly $450 million in low-interest loans and extensive technical assistance in the form of advisors, technicians, engineers, demonstration machines, and blueprints.

The Second Five-Year Plan (1958–62) was for the "construction of socialism." Like the previous plan, it stressed again top priority for heavy industry—60 percent of total allocated investment funds—with agriculture receiving only 10 percent. It was superseded by the Great Leap Forward, the "General Line of Going All Out and Aiming High to Achieve Greater, Quicker, Better and More Economical Results in Building Socialism." The Leap was generally regarded as a desire on the part of Mao and his associates to shorten the time interval necessary for China to become a self-sufficient industrial and military world power. The strategy was to use the massive hordes of seemingly underemployed Chinese peasants in the service of some highly labor-intensive projects (road building, irrigation work, dike repair, handicraft production) through political and ideological exhortation. Western observers are not unanimous in their appraisals of the Great Leap Forward. The common view is that the movement did not result in markedly increased production beyond the level reached in 1957, but that the country was nearer to the goal of economic independence.

The 1963–65 period became one of recovery from the far-reaching dislocations of the Great Leap and economic readjustment to labor and materials bottlenecks that developed during that aborted movement. At the end of the period, the Chinese entry into the world "atomic club" was a tremendous boost to the national spirit. During this period, economic planning was carried out on a year-to-year basis.

Between 1963 and 1975, two new five-year plans—the Third for 1966–70 and the Fourth for 1971–75—were hinted at without much detail. Figures obtained from different sources suggested an annual growth rate of 4.4 percent for agriculture and 12 percent for industry during the latter part of the 1960s. The launching of the Fourth Plan was also reported in the Chinese press without the statistics of plan targets or other figures. Agriculture was declared the basis of the economy. Fragmentary information indicated priorities in favor of small and medium-sized industrial plants, more agricultural decentralization, greater attention to water management, increased foreign trade and improved transportation. From all indications, during these ten years planning was carried out on a year-to-year basis through the annual economic plans.

An ambitious ten-year development plan (1976–85), the Fifth, was ratified by the Fifth National People's Congress in 1978. The new plan promised higher standards of living (explicitly for the first time), the modernization of the military, a renewed but more serious emphasis on agricultural development, increased foreign trade, and advances in scientific and technological standards. The targets reported by Chairman Hua suggest an overall annual growth rate of 8.4 percent, with agriculture expected to grow by 4.5 percent; industry, 10–11 percent; and services, 6.2 percent a year. This plan was to be further revised in 1981.

China's almost total silence on its economic planning and performance makes any comparison of plan targets and plan results extremely difficult. An official announcement by the Chinese early in 1971 claimed that all Third Plan targets were "successfully" reached, but no details were given. During earlier plans, however, substantial difference could be detected between the abstract plans and concrete results. There are uncontested indications also that in the 1974–76 period there were sharp reversals in achieving planned targets. Outstanding among factors that have caused Chinese national planning to diverge from reality have been inadequate preparation and the neglect of certain strategic industries (coal, electric power, and transportation); the increasing burden of newly born population (15 million persons per year); the preponderance of political considerations over rational use of resources; exogenous, uncontrollable climatic and natural factors; a long-term decline in labor productivity; the basic self-reliant nature of Chinese development; and, above all, a compulsive, impetuous haste in trying to correct whatever went wrong in the plan's performance. As of 1979, the all-inclusive planning has been modified in favor of certain "market adjustments" at the discretion of industrial enterprises.

Public Ownership and Operation

Following the takeover of the government in 1949, the Chinese Communist party became heir to the ownership of a number of public industrial enterprises built by the Japanese in Manchuria and handed over to China after Japan's surrender. The so-called commanding heights of the economy (railroads, communication facilities, oil, and steel) were already partly or wholly nationalized. Later on, the state followed a deliberate and calculated policy of extending its close ownership and control. By 1952, more than a third of retail trade, about half of all modern industrial enterprises, some two-thirds of wholesale trade, and nearly all of foreign trade were in public hands. By the end of 1956, over 95 percent of Chinese agriculture was collectivized, and industry was publicly owned and operated. Since then, all basic means of production—land, mines, and raw materials; buildings, machinery, and equipment; and financial assets—have been reverted to the "whole people," that is, placed under state control and Communist party direction. At present, some 97 percent of fixed assets, 63 percent of employment, and 86 percent of gross output in industry belong to the state. In agriculture, approximately 90 percent of arable land and 80 percent of farm equipment are collectively owned. In commerce, over 92 percent of sales is in state hands, and over 7 percent is carried out by the collectives. Private employment and trade are minuscule.

Social ownership of means of production takes different forms both in agriculture and industry. In rural areas, there are four types of property rights, corresponding to the four organizational divisions in the rural commune. At the lowest level of agricultural hierarchy, there are small plots over which individual households have the rights of free cultivation and sale. At the higher level, there are the production "teams" (corresponding to a whole village) that, as a collective, own the land, the manual and semimechanized farm tools, draft animals, and irrigation works. At a still higher level, there are production "brigades" that collectively have ownership rights over those assets that exceed financial resources and technical competence of the teams (such as orchards, hatcheries, heavy farm machinery and equipment, and some small rural industries). At the top, there are the people's "communes," whose collective assets ownership includes large rural industries beyond the capabilities of production teams or brigades; some farmland for research and extension work; fixed assets related to social services; retail stores and cooperatives; communications facilities; and power and water stations.

In the urban sector, assets are owned by the cooperatives or by the state enterprises. Most of the more traditional labor-intensive and semimechanized industries, small workshops, service enterprises, and handicrafts are owned by the cooperatives on behalf of their members. The modern, capital-intensive industries are owned by the state. Urban cooperatives are capitalized by three sources: original capital contributed by members, retained earnings from profits, and the state. They are, on the whole, self-financing, but State enterprises receive their original capital and expansion budget from state grants.[46]

---

46. For a more thorough examination of sectoral organizations and finances on which our discussion is based, see J. S. Prybyla, *The Chinese Economy*, (Columbia: University of South Carolina Press, 1978), chapters 1, 3, 4, and 6.

Industrial Enterprises

Under the industrial policy in effect since 1962, the Chinese industrial enterprises are owned and operated at various levels by the central government, provincial and municipal administrations, and rural communes or urban cooperatives. The enterprises producing nationally important goods, defense items, and export products are mostly under the direction of central ministries. Those that produce local goods and small-scale industries are directed by lower-level authorities (provinces and municipalities). A small enterprise may have as few as ten workers, and a large enterprise as many as thousands.

In the state sector (all levels of administration) there are centrally run enterprises, enterprises run by provinces and municipalities (considered "decentralized"), and jointly run enterprises over which both the central and local governments exercise power. Juxtaposed to the state sector is the so-called cooperative sector, composed of enterprises owned and operated by regions and counties, commune-run rural enterprises, enterprises in the hands of urban neighborhoods, and block and street authorities, and jointly run enterprises in various urban-rural and regional-provincial combinations.

Enterprises run by a central ministry receive their detailed directions from Peking on such matters as their production plan, input mix (raw materials, labor, fixed and circulating capital), expansion, innovation, and manpower training. Enterprise products are to be delivered in specific quantity and quality to other enterprises, cooperatives, or trade establishments, as planned. Except for a small portion of the enterprise's net revenue of about 2–3 percent set aside for bonuses and other welfare funds, the rest of the profit (which often reaches 30 percent of the enterprise's turnover) must be handed in to the state. In the case of jointly run enterprises, some portion of the profit is retained by lower-level authorities involved.[47] Losses are also covered by the state.

Industrial enterprises run by communes are mostly engaged in the production of light consumer goods or spare parts—using local raw materials, unemployed or underemployed farm labor, and supplying a limited geographic area. Urban industrial cooperatives consist of urban-type establishments offering daily used industrial goods and services; they are owned and managed by their own workers and management.[48] These outfits have been upgraded in recent years because of their relatively greater decentralized efficiency, flexible entrepreneurial innovations, and their crucial role in alleviating supply shortages and enhancing the welfare of participants.

---

47. As in all centrally planned economies of the communist variety, "profit" has little or no allocative, nor even much of a distributive, role to play. It is only an accounting device and an indication of enterprise productivity and managerial efficiency.
48. While consumer goods reportedly account for only 10 percent of China's total annual industrial output, nearly 80 percent of them are turned out not only by the state but by some 57,000 collectively owned firms.

Legally, each enterprise is an independent business and accounting unit. The enterprise's independence is manifested in arranging loans and credits with the state banks, signing contracts for purchases and deliveries, using its surplus capacity, if any, to fulfill additional local orders subject to approval of higher authorities, exchanging excess raw materials saved through efficient management for capital goods from other enterprises in order to improve or expand its own production, making marginal changes in some prices, and distributing its authorized excess profit among its workers as bonus. This management system is supposed to combine "centralism and democracy, discipline and freedom, unity and will."

Every state industrial enterprise is managed by a director appointed by a technical ministry in Peking or by the provincial or local authorities. The director operates under the collective leadership of a factory party committee and a revolutionary committee, of which he is a member. The party's guidance is crucial; the most important man in an enterprise is the party secretary. Routine operations are carried out under regular conferences between management and workers' representatives. The conference hears, discusses, and approves internal production plans; supervises their implementations; allocates the enterprise's various welfare, medical, and other funds; and distributes bonuses within the broad directives from central authorities. In other technical respects, the operation of Chinese enterprises resembles that of Western factories.

While state industrial enterprises are allowed a certain degree of autonomy in running their business, their power over investment decisions is rather limited. Fixed and working capital of industrial enterprises are normally provided by national and provincial budgets and also by the Capital Construction Bank, under the control of the Finance Ministry. Enterprise revenues are divided among normal costs of producing goods (including wages and salaries), turnover taxes, and profit levies. Enterprises are not required to repay the fixed capital or any interest on it. Tax and profit rates vary in different industries, but they are fixed in such a way that even the least efficient enterprise in an industry can pay. Extra profits made in excess of those stipulated in the official plan are divided between the enterprise and the central and local authorities.

Farm Enterprises

Agriculture has persistently been declared the mainstay of the Chinese economy. While only 11.5 percent of China's land area is cultivated, some 75–80 percent of the population is still dependent on land. This sector accounts for about 36 percent of GDP, nearly two-thirds of national employment, and the bulk of Chinese exports. Before the communist takeover in 1949, China's agriculture—private, semifeudal, backward, and inefficient—accounted for 60 percent of GDP.

The communists' agricultural development policy has attempted to expand farming capacity and output through consolidation and collectivization of the traditional system. The policy is aimed not toward the liquidation of the middle-class farmers, but toward their integration. Beginning with the First Plan, farm households were "urged" first to join temporary or permanent "mutual-aid teams" under which they could pool their resources to their mutual benefit. Later on, they were "encouraged" to set up lower-level or semisocialist cooperatives of thirty to forty households under which participating members received incomes according to their contribution of land, labor, and tools. The next stage was compulsory participation in higher-level, or fully socialist, collectives (like the Soviet kolkhoz) under which land was collectively owned and used, and members received their incomes on the basis of their labor time and skill, supplemented by some shares for animals and implements. By 1957, collectivization of the land was virtually completed, but small plots and minor tools remained private, and output of "private plots" could still be sold in private markets.

The Great Leap Forward introduced a totally new institutional concept of farm management in the form of the "people's commune." The commune was actually more than a giant agricultural enterprise; it was to be a "laboratory" of communal living, a basic unit for all aspects of social life—economic, cultural, administrative, and military. The commune had responsibilities for farming, small-scale industries, and handicrafts, banking, retail sales, tax collection, welfare dispensation, health and education, communications, public safety, and the local militia.

The major objectives of communization (over which the Sino-Soviet dispute arose when the Russians refused to support the new Chinese policy) were mostly sociopolitical and reflected Mao's personality. The aim was to mobilize under-employed resources of rural China (especially women) in the service of labor-intensive projects and small-scale industries. One obvious goal was to abolish the last vestige of private ownership and operation and to make the people's commune the basic institution of rural life. Another goal was industrialization without urbanization.

By 1959, nearly all Chinese peasants had become members of communes, and except for several hundred state farms (mostly research and experimental), the whole of Chinese agriculture was communized. But the excessive regimentation of the new communes was apparently too much even for the hard-working, docile, and frugal Chinese peasantry. The peasants resented (and reportedly revolted in some areas against) the breakdown of family life, barracks existence, harsh discipline, and lack of initiatives. Calamities of nature in 1959–61, coming on top of man-made errors and miscalculations, brought the Great Leap Forward experiment to a rather unceremonious end. Errors were admitted, exaggerated statistics were corrected, and a poorer but perhaps wiser China began the task of recovery and readjustment.

The 1961–72 strategy turned in favor of upgrading agriculture. Since then, the farming sector has received substantial and increasing amounts of necessary equipment, machinery, fertilizers, pesticides, water, and power. The communes, although still an agricultural and administrative unit, have been modified, "rationalized," and reduced in size. There are now reportedly about 50,000 communes. An average commune has fifteen production brigades, 100 production teams (roughly 100 villages), some 3,500 households, and nearly 15,000 members. There are small communes with 5,000 members and large ones with 40,000.[49]

At the core of the commune system is the production team (roughly, the village).[50] Production teams collectively own the land they cultivate, control the labor power supplied by their members, and have property rights over all production equipment, draft animals, and waterworks. Beyond mandatory deliveries under the state plans, they have extensive rights over the disposal of their surplus outputs. Each team is under the control of its members' congress, which elects the team (management) committee, composed of a team leader and other administrative officials. Teams are both a production and a distribution entity. Their production responsibilities consist of carrying out the state mandatory procurement plan for essential goods (grain, oilseeds, cotton) and delivering other goods to various users under contractual arrangements. The team's revenues are divided between the state, the collective itself, and members. The state's share is determined by planned deliveries and taxes. The team's share is devoted to depreciation allowances, repair works, authorized expansions, and welfare funds. Team members are remunerated by some basic "work points" depending on the time spent and the nature of the task involved. Peasants are not wage-earners; their incomes depend on the volume of farm output and are subject to the harvest's fortune. State farms cultivate mainly large plots and are highly mechanized, but they account for only five percent of total arable land, and are not very efficient.

Domestic and Foreign Trade

A tight control of domestic and foreign commerce is an integral part of Chinese national planning. Domestic purchases and sales of certain key products (grain, edible oils and fat, and cotton) are state monopolies. Most of the small retail stores have been turned into cooperatives, and most of the former shopkeepers and traders have become retail distributors or commercial agents for the state trading agencies.

There are now essentially three distribution channels in China. State trading agencies handle the bulk of domestic commodities and all of China's foreign trade. Cooperatives handle mostly agricultural and handicraft products. Rural and local markets (wherever allowed) deal with farm products of small "private plots" and other sideline occupations by individual farmers.

The direction and composition of foreign trade are predetermined in the five-year and annual plans. The main emphasis in imports has been directed toward the latest technology and modern capital goods from Japan and Western Europe. Trade with non-communist countries is, for the most part, multilateral. Accounts are settled in convertible currencies. Large deficits with developed countries are

49. There are also state farms, generally larger and more mechanized than communes, that are engaged in experimental and extension works, and production of special crops and livestock.

50. Communes are made up of households (five persons on the average), teams of fifteen to fifty households, and brigades of eight to twelve teams.

financed by trade surpluses with developing countries and Hong Kong. Trade with communist nations is bilateral, and settlements are in kind.

An inseparable part of China's foreign trade is its foreign aid. In recent years, 0.33 percent of GNP has been given away in the form of technical services, machinery, materials, and weapons. Overseas remittances by Chinese nationals, in turn, have by far surpassed the aid-flow, and China has become a net exporter of services in recent years.

Price Determination

Except for periodic relaxation of the farmers' fruit and vegetable markets, where prices are determined by supply and demand, all prices in China are fixed by the central or provincial governments and kept overtly stable. Under recent reforms, an increasing number of farm sideline and handicraft prices are allowed to be determined through negotiations between buyer and sellers.

Industrial wholesale prices and prices of farm products subject to mandatory delivery to the state are determined by the central government or by provincial and local authorities. These prices are fixed "empirically." They normally cover the average cost of production for the relevant branch in the industry, a planned profit margin (ranging up to 100 percent of the cost price), and turnover taxes. Considerable local variations are allowed in setting prices in different regions. The same is true of differences between ex-factory, wholesale, and retail prices.

Retail and consumer prices are set by the central or regional authorities in such a way as to clear the market; that is, to match the planned supply with the disposable incomes available to consumers. Individual items are priced partly on the basis of costs but also partly according to social and political considerations. "Essential" goods (food grains, textiles, cooking oil) are rationed and given low and occasionally below-cost prices. Equilibrium is obtained, if necessary, by rationing and other physical distribution methods.[51] The items considered "everyday necessities," such as coal, are based on cost plus a profit margin, or a "surplus for society." The nonessential goods are priced well above cost and contain a turnover tax and a "monopoly" profit for the state; prices depend on planned availability and the planners' objectives of encouraging or discouraging consumption. Unforeseen disequilibria between planned production and demand in "essential" commodities are corrected through rationing instead of raising prices. Farmers' incomes are also boosted occasionally by offering manufactured goods at lower prices instead of increasing farm output prices. In the case of "nonessentials," however, price adjustments are made from time to time.[52]

51. The total number of rationed items is large, but varies from time to time. In some cities as many as three hundred articles are rationed.
52. In November 1979, for example, more than 10,000 consumer items—foods grown by farmers or articles produced by cottage industries—accounting for about 20 percent of the total value of merchandise sold in China, were freed from all price controls. At the same time, other food prices were raised 33 percent and urban workers' wages 40 percent.

Price policy is thus used directly not only for physical distribution of GDP among consumers, but also as a means of internal income redistribution as well as inflation control. Prices, however, serve chiefly as "coefficients of choice" and not as guides for the movement or transfer of resources. While little is known about actual criteria used in price determination, indications are that four basic considerations are heeded by the planners: the "social" value of the commodity in terms of the quantity of labor required for its production in the pure Marxism sense; the necessity of a long-term balance between politically sanctioned consumer demand and aggregate supply; the need for a politically expedient parity between incomes of various socioeconomic strata (farmers versus urban workers, for example); and the state revenue needs to be siphoned off from enterprise profits.

Interests and rents are also determined by the state, but they play a very insignificant role in income distribution and resource allocation. Interest is paid by the People's Bank on time deposits and for some properties previously confiscated. Different interest rates also are charged on borrowed capital by industrial and commercial enterprises, communes, and others. The rates vary according to the priority of the proposed undertakings in the national plan. Rent is paid by tenants in public housing, but the amounts paid and received bear little direct relation to the opportunity costs of the assets.

Wage Policies

As in other centrally planned economies, wages (and bonuses) are the dominant form of income (and material incentive) in urban China. Wage-earners are divided between factory workers and employees (management, technical, professional, and administrative personnel). Production workers in industrial plants are graded from one to eight (as in most CDEs), corresponding to the degree of skill—grade one being the least skilled, and eight, the highest. Wage coefficients, or the multiples of grade one, vary with the job's inherent difficulty, working conditions, hazards involved, physical discomforts, plant location, priority in the planners' scale of preferences, and differences in the cost of living. Basic wages are also supplemented by labor insurance, welfare payments, and fringe benefits. Labor insurance covers disability compensation, accidents, medical expenses, and pensions. Welfare benefits include maternity, child care, and subsidized education. Fringes consist of communal consumption, recreational facilities, and subsidized rent. The coverage of "social wage," however, extends to workers in modern industrial establishments, perhaps no more than 30 percent of all industrial workers. The cost also is estimated at no more than 20 percent of the total wage bill.

Employees wages are determined by a different set of schedules containing as many as twenty-five grades for the civil service, with each grade having as many as eleven regional variants reflecting different geographical characteristics and living costs. Technical personnel in industry has its own grades, with variants for enterprises of different sizes. Top-grade scientists, political functionaries, and others also have their own pay scale. In general, however, industrial wages (and farmers' incomes) are kept deliberately low to divert a substantial portion of GDP to investment. The difference between the minimum unskilled wage rate and the highest graded skill remuneration is the smallest of all the CDEs. Rural incomes are based, as indicated before, on a work point system.

Nonmonetary Incentives

Throughout his long life, Mao Tse-tung strove to change human "nature," so to speak, and to condition the Chinese soul into accepting a new motive for work. Material incentives were frequently denounced as a bourgeois relic and a capitalist "rat poison." People were encouraged to show selfless revolutionary zeal. This has been in sharp contrast to Khrushchev's "goulash communism," based on consumerism and increased material standards of living. The Cultural Revolution was evidently launched to stimulate productive capacity more strongly than monetary rewards. Income equality, glorification of manual labor, and the simple pleasures of rural life were to replace anxiety, greed, and the urban race for luxuries. In Mao's thoughts, basic and widespread Chinese poverty was intolerable and could be remedied only through egalitarianism and the removal of class distinctions. Maoist ideology thus pointed toward the eventual suppression of material incentives toward reliance on workers' "socialist conscience," their devotion to the national interest and their spirit of sacrifice, to transform China into a powerful, modern nation.

With a far deeper egalitarian philosophy than the Russians, the Chinese leadership has thus consistently placed much greater emphasis on nonmonetary incentives. Drawing heavily on the Chinese tradition of self-reliance, hard work, group spirit, self-sacrifice, self-criticism, and an authoritarian social organization, Chairman Mao and his associates tried to create a new Chinese man.[53] Chinese loyalty to family and clan was to be diverted toward the state. Workers were exhorted to toil out of devotion to the homeland and communism—not for personal gain or promotion. Patriotic and antibourgeois motives were always stressed. The motto was "Serve the People." Nobody was to work harder for money, but only to be a better worker, one who welcomed tasks of greater difficulty. Negative attitude and performances were to be penalized by public criticism, demotion and other sanctions.

Moral incentives have been used to motivate groups as well as individuals. Factories, departments, teams, or groups within an establishment have been urged to vie with one another in the overfulfillment of their tasks. On the individual level, diligent, cooperative, and spiritual workers have been given such nonpecuniary honors as press write-ups, medals, merit certificates, and honorific titles. As in the Soviet Union, these symbols of recognition also carry other awards and are prerequisites for elevation through political and party ranks.

Under the Hua-Deng leadership, however, monetary rewards have been re-

53. See D. J. Munro, *The Concept of Man in Contemporary China.* (Ann Arbor: University of Michigan Press, 1977).

emphasized. The majority of the nonagricultural workers received a wage increase in 1977 after almost ten years of stagnation; the size of the increase was the largest in twenty-eight years. Piecework and bonuses are again defended as a "necessary material encouragement" and useful in mobilizing the "socialist initiative of the masses." In agriculture, too, "distribution according to labor" has again come into vogue. Although the importance of moral and normative incentives is still stressed by the leadership, much greater emphasis is being given to the necessity of raising the pay of low-income earners.

Indirect Controls

As in the Soviet Union, delegated decision making has very little relevance in the Chinese economy. Indeed, the very rationale of economic direction and management by proxy loses much of its fundamental significance where there is no free-market mechanism and all major economic decisions are made by administrative bureaucratic means, according to the preferences of a relatively small leadership group. There are, in other words, no perceived market inequalities, deficiencies, and cyclical swings to rectify through delegated remedial measures.

Constitutionally, the decison-making system in the People's Republic is called "democratic centralism" under which the rank and file are supposed to be involved in all decisions. The National People's Congress meets from time to time to approve the central government's plans and programs.[54] References to "mass democracy," or mass participation and reduction of status differences, frequently appear in the press and wall posters. The final communiqué of the plenary session of the Central Committee of the Chinese Communist Party held in December of 1978 states that "Socialist modernization requires centralized leadership," but "the correct concentration of ideas is possible only when there is full democracy."

Most China hands, however, believe—and the post-Mao leadership agrees—that in the past there had been more centralism and less democracy. Nevertheless, the process of consultation and genuine discussions between team leaders and members, teams and brigades, brigades and communes, communes and provinces, regions and Peking is more widespread than elsewhere in the CDEs, except perhaps Yugoslavia. The use of indirect policy measures, particularly fiscal and monetary policies, as an inseparable part of the planning process itself is very limited, but their effectiveness is probably still significant. State budget in particular is a pivotal element in rational planning.

---

54. Each commune also has its people's congress, composed of members or their delegates. Production brigades and teams have their members' congress, which elect the management committees.

Fiscal Policy

The central planners, through their control over the public budget and the banking system, are able to control financial flows in the economy and the rate and direction of China's economic development. The major role of fiscal policy in the Chinese setting (in addition to taking care of regular administrative needs) is to syphon off all the profits of state enterprises (above those earmarked for internal working capital, workers' bonuses, and small investment projects) in order to finance planned capital investments. The other conventional tasks of budgetary policy (income redistribution, demand management, social security) are mostly preempted by the planners' direct actions.

Budgetary revenues consist of tax receipts and nontax incomes. Tax revenues are derived chiefly from turnover levies and taxes on profits, both imposed by the central government, with local authorities permitted to add a surcharge. Turnover taxes are levied on almost all economic activities—industrial, commercial, trades and services. Rates vary among products and services and range from less than 2 percent to nearly 70 percent. The profits tax is a progressive one, imposed on incomes of enterprises not under direct state control, such as the collectives and communal industries. There is a minor agricultural tax levied on the "normal annual yield" of the communes, and there are minor taxes on salt, imports, and other items. Nontax revenues consist mainly of profit remittances from state enterprises. Half of the total budgetary revenues comes from taxes, and 90 percent of taxes come from turnover and profit levies.

On the expenditure side, major categories include capital construction (35 percent); defense (18 percent); social services, including education, culture, health, social security and welfare (13 percent); general administration, including foreign aid (7 percent); subsidies (6 percent); and miscellaneous, including research and development (21 percent). Losses by state enterprises are also covered by the state budget. The central budget is normally balanced, but provincial budgets show deficits or surpluses which are transferred between provinces via the central government.[55]

Despite the transfer of a broad range of economic powers to the provinces in the post-1958 decentralization reform, the central government has continued to exercise highly centralized budgetary controls over public expenditures on current and capital outlays in all the provinces. Wealthier regions with revenues in excess of their authorized expenditures are required to remit the balance to Peking. The

---

55. The Chinese social security system is an integral part of the Chinese command mechanism. All major costs are borne by the state. There are no employee contributions except for partial costs of medicines. All workers are covered. Benefits include old-age, disability, maternity, sickness, and injury. There are also special lump-sum grants for childbirth, funerals, and survivor's compensation.

capital, in turn, through its relatively centralized control of economic planning, allocates these resources to other needier provinces. Some 80 percent of all state revenues are collected by the provinces, a large part of which is returned to the center for interprovincial redistribution. The Chinese fiscal system is thus a very effective means of implementing the national plan objectives, particularly in the area of geographic allocation of investment resources.

Banking and Monetary Policy

China's monetary system, like its fiscal order, is a means of implementation and control of the national economic plans. The primary function of monetary policy is to permit the fulfillment of the national plan at stable prices. The main instrument of monetary management is the control of currency in circulation. Reliance on interest rates both on loans and deposits is very limited. Monetary policies are carried out by the People's Bank of China, with its more than ten thousand major branches throughout the mainland, under the direction of the State Council. Special organs of the People's Bank, such as the Bank of China, the Capital Construction Bank, and the Bank of Agriculture are considered "functional banks". There are also credit cooperatives.

Like the Soviet Union's Gosbank, the People's Bank is both a central and a commercial bank; it has similar functions and responsibilities. It issues currency, regulates the money supply, fixes interest rates on loans and deposits, serves as a fiscal agent for collectives and state enterprises, holds savings accounts of individuals, prepares the credit and the cash plans, and supervises the operation of these plans by various means including regulation of commercial transactions and technical assistance on financial management.

All state organs, public institutions, collectives, communes, industrial and other enterprises must keep accounts with the People's Bank. All financial transactions among these agencies are made exclusively by bank book transfers. All taxes and enterprise profits must be deposited with the bank. No transactions among public entities are allowed in cash. All enterprise funds beyond a modest amount of petty cash must be turned over to the bank. All deposits and withdrawals, as well as all book transfers, must take place in conformity with the national plan and the agency's own approved plan.

The People's Bank is the only source of credit and loans. Short-term credits (less than a year) are made at varying modest interest rates to agricultural, commercial, and industrial enterprises for "production expenses," such as building up inventories of raw materials, purchasing of agricultural inputs, and stocking up on finished goods. Medium-term loans of up to five years, called "loans for production equipment," are offered also at moderate rates to communes and industrial enterprises for the purchase of farm equipment and the acquisition of livestock and industrial needs. For no other purposes can the public agencies borrow funds. In order to obtain authorized credit or loan, the agency's financial plan must first be approved by the People's Bank.

There are no checking accounts for individuals in China; only personal savings accounts are allowed (and encouraged) at modest annual interest rates. Individuals cannot obtain loans from the People's Bank except in the case of natural disaster or high medical expenses. Withdrawals of savings are on demand, but the use of savings for "trivial" purposes is shunned by one's peers. There are reportedly some 35 million depositors, with the bulk of the funds contributed by the urban population and in the form of time deposits.

The People's Bank is thus a nationwide clearinghouse for all economic transactions among public agencies, a depository of private savings, a controller and auditor of the administration, and a supervisor of the national plan's execution. The bank revenues derive from the currency issue, state budgetary allocation for medium-term loans, and interest charged on credit and loans. Its expenditures consist of regular administrative outlays and interest paid on the deposits of agencies and individuals. The net receipts are divided into a tax paid to the state and accumulated reserves.

The Bank of China is responsible for conducting China's external financial transactions (foreign exchange, trade credit, overseas remittances, etc.). The Capital Construction Bank, as an agent of the Finance Ministry, controls and handles funds allocated in the state budget for investment; it also extends loans for capital formation. The Bank of Agriculture supervises the allocation of funds to agricultural pursuits; it supplies funds to credit cooperatives, and offers technical assistance to brigades and teams.

Incomes Policy

China's incomes policy has changed frequently with each phase of its post-1949 development. In general, three features of this policy have been fairly persistently followed. First, where politically feasible, wages have been kept below rises in productivity and prices kept reasonably stable in order to finance development projects. In other words, forced savings has been accomplished through low wages and stable prices, rather than high nominal wages and higher prices. Second, there has been a constant concern to prevent urban and rural wage differences from further widening. Finally, wage rates have been scarcely used as a means of labor mobility between positions or geographic areas.

The chronology of changes in incomes policy is most interesting. Between 1949 and 1957, urban and rural incomes were raised systematically, and wage differences were used as material incentives. However, the rise of the industrial labor force toward the end of the 1950s, their rising incomes vis-à-vis the rural folks, and their increasing demands on food and other supplies forced the leadership into a reversal of that policy. A total freeze on wages and an emphasis on further egalitarianism followed up to 1963. Under an anti-Leap policy and a movement toward wage incentives, some adjustments were made for lower-paid workers. The Cultural Revolution again put an end to the restoration of central planning, and to wage increases, until 1972, when the policy was once again reversed. Certain small adjustments in industrial grades were made. The 1975 Constitution confirmed the desirability of economic incentives. A long period of internal conflicts and struggles followed until 1978, when the first major wage adjustment in almost twenty-eight years was allowed.

Countervailing Powers

The course of economic development in the People's Republic of China during Mao's life and in the post-Mao period has been influenced by some deep-seated conflicts at various levels of decision making.

The interplay of countervailing powers is, of course, not of the Western variety, where group bargaining is well structured and formalized. In the absence of independent trade unions, and with virtually all enterprises in state hands, the possibility of labor-management negotiations (as in MICs) or the tripartitie resolutions of disputes (as in LDCs) is almost nonexistent. Instead, there are special coalitions of claimants, unique to China, for the allocation of material resources and the distribution of political power. The outcome of these coalitions has, in the past, been reflected in a strategy of politicoeconomic compromise among contending forces (the radicals, the pragmatists, the military, the professionals, the rural youth, and others).[56]

Throughout the 1950–80 period, there has been a conflict between communist ideology and economic and technical realities. On the one side, a small group of ideological romanticists (of whom Mao himself was the unquestioned leader) wanted to push China toward a totally egalitarian, permanently revolutionary, and basically self-reliant, isolated nation. Opposed to these visionary and impractical concepts have been such moderate pragmatists as Chou En-lai, Deng Xiao-ping, and Hua Guo-feng, who have persistently emphasized modernity, political power, technological progress, rapid economic growth, and rising standards of living within a socialist framework. The balance of power has thus swung back and forth between the radical left and the moderate pragmatists.[57] The result has

---

56. These forces are sometimes identified as "generational, regional, bureaucratic and ideological interests" whose convergence is necessary for politicoeconomic stability. See W. W. Whitson, "The Political Dynamics of the PRC," in *Chinese Economy Post-Mao*, (Washington: GPO, 1978), pp. 63–79.

57. Thus, the speed of industrialization and modernization has been kept in check by those who have been opposed to the emergence of a bureaucratic-management elite and a widening of income gaps. Conversely, the emphasis on socialist egalitarianism and income equality has been resisted by the pragmatists.

been frequent trade-offs between egalitarianism and self-reliance, on the one hand, and growth and modernization, on the other.

The economy's growth cycle, has, in turn, been determined by the vacillating leadership choices between military expenditures versus consumer welfare; efficiency versus expediency; self-reliance versus foreign trade; specialization versus import substitution; and domestic education versus cultural exchange. In the post-Mao economy, there have been reports of a serious debate between the Chinese leaders who preferred to defer military modernization in favor of investments in other sectors (particularly agriculture) and the other leadership groups who favored strengthening defense and heavy industries over farming and consumer goods.

The influence of countervailing powers, however, has not been limited to political infighting and career rivalries among leadership groups and ambitious individuals for deciding the direction and rate of domestic economic development. At the very core of decision making, there has also been disagreement among leaders and their immediate supporters on the essence of economic direction and management. In the post-Cultural Revolution period, for example, the question of centralization versus decentralization has been a major bone of contention between various factions in the Chinese political hierarchy.

The 40-million-member Communist party itself has not been immune from internal factionalism and external challenge. In spite of the apparent pervasiveness of the party over mainland China's national economy, expert opinion points to some "nonconstitutional checks" on its hegemony. The very fact that the Great Proletarian Cultural Revolution was allowed to attack many Chinese institutions and leaders (including President Liu Shao-Chi) is an indication that these institutions and leaders must, at some point, have threatened Chairman Mao's supreme authority.

The People's Liberation Army, for example, by virtue of its crucial role in the establishment of the People's Republic and its professionalism in modern warfare (compared to the old revolutionary guerrillas), considers itself entitled to a final say in matters of national security. By virtue of their expertise in running a vast, complicated bureaucracy, the professional corps of technocrats, economic managers, and midlevel administrators are, in a large measure, apolitical and thus often consciously skeptical of ideological dogma.[58] These elements have been largely interested in pursuing a pragmatic and reformist course. And workers, mostly uneducated and classically anti-intellectual, have nevertheless been demanding a voice in management.

There are also conflicts within the army and among bureaucrats themselves. Young professional military officers are usually opposed to the policies and programs of the old guerrilla leaders, particularly to the latter's desire for the army's involvement in economic tasks. Within the bureaucratic hierarchy, too, "experts" have often been motivated by self-interest and less blindly influenced by party

58. See Franz Schurmann, *Ideology and Organization in Communist China* (Berkeley: University of California Press, 1968).

loyalty. There has thus been a tendency toward some polarization between the party, as the haven for workers and peasants, and the technocrats, as representative of a sophisticated class immune to ideology. The Red Guard's Cultural Revolution was partly directed against academicians, writers, artists, and the entrenched bureaucratic machine.

While the complexion of the 1970–76 leadership is still somewhat obscured by the paucity of information leaking out of China, the multilevel and multilateral pattern of decision making seems to have been enhanced. China's Revolutionary committees, organized after the 1966 purges, were three-way coalitions of professional party members, the armed forces, and the Red Guards. The composition of these committees reflected bargaining between various leaders in Peking, each jockeying for greater power. The government, in turn, operated through "consultation and compromise."

While very little is known about the structure and function of labor unions in China, recent indications point to the development of new labor-management relations in industry, aptly called the stage of "struggle-criticism-transformation." In this new stage, enterprises have been virtually run by a new triumvirate composed of management officials, party cadres, and representatives of workers (or peasants). Participation by workers through their representatives in management decisions has been claimed to be part of the revolution's achievements to insure political control, ideological discipline, and work methods. Workers' "formal" participation in management takes place in the enterprise conferences. Social security and welfare administration also is in trade-unions hands. The All-China Federation of Trade Unions, which was disbanded early in the Cultural Revolution, shows signs of revival.

A very distinctive and somewhat unique feature of the multilateral model in China has also been the use of "mass campaigns" and "peer-group pressure" in the management of the economy. The mass campaign has been described as an instrument of mass participation, through "wave-by-wave" assaults on the managerial-bureaucratic elite to combat apathy, routinization, immobilism, and the rise of privileged classes. The Great Leap and the Cultural Revolution were examples of these "hurricane-type" movements, and served as a counterweight to creeping elitism. The peer-group pressure is a kind of public reaction to an individual's behavior in order to secure compliance with the mass line. Individual actions have been subjected to scrutiny by the family and in the workplace. Both of these methods have the effect of influencing economic decisions at the macro and micro levels in a way that is unrelated to other processes of decision making.

In short, despite strong and consistent verbal adherence to communist ideology, Chinese leaders have been neither unanimous in their interpretation of Marxism-Leninism nor united in their actual policies and programs. Intraparty rifts and clashes have been numerous, and the party hierarchy has gone through several reorganizations. In turning China into a "powerful, modern, socialist state," there has been conflict between the goal of economic modernity and that of socialist transformation. Policy changes have thus been frequent, drastic, and often contradictory. This ambivalence is reflected in a repeated centralization-decentralization seesaw and in compromises resulting from informal bargains and trade-offs. The post-Mao leadership has shown a clear tendency toward greater centralization, more pragmatic operations, more worker discipline, better management, stricter accounting procedures, and a return to monetary incentives. But there is no assurance that the latest orientation is indeed the last.

The "Private Sector"

Consumer sovereignty is by far the least important decision-making mechanism in China. Private property ownership is mostly residual and marginal; it extends to personal and household stuff for personal or family use, tools owned by individual craftsmen, rural houses, and a de facto right to the small plots allocated to farmers by their team. The "private" plots and the community's fairgrounds as their marketplace are the most vivid (and legal) example of the market system in China. Having ranged in size from 1 to 7 percent of the team's arable land during various phases of the Chinese development, the plots, now reportedly covering between 30 to 300 square meters, are at the household's disposal for supplementary production and income. Households own the produce from private plots, their handicrafts, and poultry, pigs, and fruits raised on these plots. These items may be sold to other households or to commune or cooperative stores. Subsidiary incomes from "private" plots are almost the only financial assistance to families in seasonal or other ordinary financial difficulties. It is estimated that about 20 to 30 percent of total household incomes in rural areas is derived from private plots.[59] The "private" sector in agriculture also probably produces 30 to 50 percent of vegetables, fruits, pigs, and poultry, although it takes up only 5 percent of the total arable land.

The exercise of the limited individual sovereignty—such as there is—thus manifests itself in the basic choice between consumption and saving and in choosing among items that are not rationed or received in kind, but purchasable by cash. On a supply side, a supervised "market mechanism" also exists in the production and sale of fruits, vegetables, and handicrafts out of "private" land. While both of these decisions are bound to affect the planners' calculations and policies, their immediate day-to-day significance on resource allocations is clearly minimal. This is even truer in China than in the Soviet Union, because consumer goods are generally not plentiful in China, and China's poor majority cannot be very choosy.

The market sector also includes a small minority, (some 200,000 out of a total industrial labor force of nearly 100 million) of individual craftsmen, street

59. "Private" plots have at times been vilified as "supplying blood to capitalism," and thus were destined for extinction under the Cultural Revolution. But the post-Mao leadership seems to consider their existence (and production sidelines) as part of the newly emphasized material incentives and "necessary adjuncts of the socialist economy."

vendors, small traders, and others whose services were grudgingly tolerated up until Mao's death.[60] Since then they have been more favorably treated as the residual suppliers of goods and services in high local demand.

The Chinese Economy: An Overview

Of the three countries discussed in this chapter, China is probably the most disciplined and the most dogmatic, despite some recent moves toward pragmatism. In Mao's time, the traditional Confucian ideal of harmony was often denounced in favor of constant struggle. Similarly, the Western values of individual rights and material incentives gave way to the primacy of social groups; Western democracy, to the Chinese "mass line"; Western regard for individual privacy, to the Chinese emphasis on the community.[61]

China, at least until recently, more strongly disfavored and deemphasized private ownership and material rewards than the Soviet Union and Yugoslavia (which allows the widest measure, particularly in land ownership). Unlike the Russians, who have always allowed the sway of individual self-interest and monetary incentives as a means of eliciting cooperative responses from the populace, and the Yugoslavs, whose main incentives are monetary, the Chinese emphasize egalitarian values. In running public enterprises, despite many changes in the postrevolutionary period and marked heterogeneity in different parts of the economy, China still offers its managers considerable authority in internal management. The party influence on Chinese managers' decisions (through the mass education programs) is probably greater than the state bureaucrats, in contrast to the Soviet Union.[62]

In the field of development planning, while the Soviets have followed the so-called technocratic strategy (using highly centralized directions, coercive methods of operation, emphasis on rapid industrial growth, material incentives, and modern technology), the Chinese up until 1979 followed the "mobilization strategy,": encouraging growth from the grass roots, deemphasizing monetary remuneration, making appeals to mass solidarity, eliciting voluntary efforts and initiatives on the part of individual citizens, and glorifying ideological purity. Thus, these two command systems, both working toward the ultimate goal of a classless society, have chosen different paths to growth and development.[63]

60. Estimates of total employment and the national labor force in China are as varied and unvarifiable as its population. By certain guesstimation, some 45 percent of the population is active, but this figure is not broken down by subsectors (agriculture, part-time, or female forces) and fails to take account of the contribution of children below the age of fifteen, an age group that constitutes almost 40 percent of the Chinese population.

61. For an interesting contrast between Chinese and Western culture and values, see Ross Terrill, ed., *The China Difference* (New York: Harper, 1979).

62. An interesting feature of the Chinese policy is the variations around official prices paid to the enterprise based on the *quality* of goods produced. For this reason, the quality of Chinese consumer goods is often higher than in other CDEs.

63. Cf. Neuberger and Duffy, op. cit., chapters 13 and 15.

In the sphere of participatory democracy and group decision making, while the Yugoslavs have steadily moved toward decentralization and the reliance on consensus, the Chinese have veered back and forth between mass participation in management and substantial obedience to central authority. Decentralization and greater freedom of consumer choice have been a slow, steady, and seemingly irreversible trend in the Soviet system.

In the area of consumer sovereignty, the Chinese system grants the least important role to individual preferences and tastes compared with the other two nations (and, for that matter, less than any other major contemporary economy). Prices, profits, and wage incentives have so far played a negligible role in resource allocation. Instead, for a better part of the revolutionary years the leadership has emphasized the principles of "solidarity," national unity, and disciplined uniformity. In private consumption, for example, temporary imbalances between demand and supply are infrequently corrected through price changes. Excess supply and inventory stocks are adjusted by reduced production, and excess demand is rectified by rationing.[64] Also, unlike the other two "socialist" countries, there is no systematic link between enterprise profits and wages in China, nor are there relative wage differentials to encourage movement between jobs. Even in the consumers' freedom of choice, the Chinese have so far lagged behind the Russians and even further behind the Yugoslavs. Rationing and the direct allocation of the work force are still some of the hallmarks of the Chinese economy, while free movement of workers and the choice of consumption are pretty much routinized in both Russia and certainly in Yugoslavia.

All this, however, seems to be undergoing serious "readjustments" under the new Chinese leadership. The aim of "socialist production" has recently been declared to be the satisfaction of the "people's needs." Under the pressures of such unconventional problems (for a communist country) of budgetary deficit, inflation, and unemployment, the official strategy is shifting from forced savings toward larger consumer spending; from heavy industry to agriculture and social services; and from controlled prices cum rationing to more realistic cost-based pricing.

This shift toward "radical moderation" is affecting almost all aspects of the Chinese economy. The new slogan, "Find truths from facts," by appealing to doubt and by challenging both communist certainty and authority, seems to be stressing pragmatism over all else.[65] Mao's spiritual exhortations for superhuman efforts are being partly supplemented by material incentives, attention to consumer demand, and some plainly materialistic values. A small percentage of state-owned and state-dominated industrial enterprises are opened to new "self-management" experiments under which central control and planning directives are to be combined with local

64. Delays in purchasing consumer items in the Soviet Union and the allocation of "rights" to obtain such items through management or trade unions to "good workers" are, of course, often considered by Western analysts as a thinly disguised form of rationing.

65. For a fuller detail of new measures, see "China in the 1980s," *The Economist*, 29 December 1979. For the background of these measures, see "Chairman Hua's China," *The Economist*, 6 January 1978.

initiative and market cues; that is, workers are given bonus incentives to produce more and managers are granted more leeway to organize production, personnel, and marketing, albeit still within broad state mandates. The authorities are becoming less zealous about strict egalitarianism. The experiments are still "untidy," but practice and pragmatism seem to be increasingly regarded as "the only test of truth."

The changes in the government hierarchy, approved by the September 1980 session of the National People's Congress, spotlighted the promised new order of things. Among a number of new economic directives, the scrapping of the 1975–86 plan and its replacement by a new 1981–96 plan, the planned introduction of income taxation, the extension of experimental self-management autonomy to all state enterprises, a gradual liberalization of the rigidly centralized planning, and the expansion of monetary incentives as rewards for individual creativity and initiatives were more significant and most innovative.

The new leadership, bent on building a "socialist democracy" under "democratic management," has an enormous task ahead of it in furthering past achievements, and making up for past failures. The major accomplishments are generally acknowledged to include eradication of absolute proverty and provision of a minimum (if low) level of living for all; improvement of health conditions as reflected in a rise in life expectancy and a reduction in infant mortality; extension of practical education to an increasing number of Chinese children; attainment of rural high employment; and progress toward the national objective of establishing an egalitarian society. Shortcomings relate to the extensive restrictions on individual freedom and privacy and to a low rate of economic and industrial growth relative to China's ethnic neighbors Taiwan, Hong Kong, and Singapore (not to mention Japan and South Korea).

YUGOSLAVIA

The Socialist Federal Republic of Yugoslavia, with 256,000 square kilometers of land and some 22 million people, is composed of six republics and two autonomous provinces. Each republic has an administration modeled after the federal republic, with a constitution, parliament, presidency, executive council (cabinet), and public departments and agencies. Each republic or province is the aggregation of many communes, of which there are 510. These political entities are called sociopolitical communities. The state and Communist party organizations are now built along the republic's lines, with the power of the federal government gradually diminished. Since 1948, Yugoslavia has tried to play an independent, nonaligned role between East and West, between Moscow communism and Western capitalism.[66]

Yugoslavia is relatively underpopulated by European standards. In terms of industrialization and the standard of living, Yugoslavia ranks with Romania and Portugal. In per capita GNP, however, the country probably trails behind other Eastern European economies except Albania and Romania. There are also marked disparities in the level of economic development among various regions.[67]

The two most salient features of the Yugoslav politicoeconomic system are its concepts of workers' self-management and a socialist market economy. Under the self-management philosophy, economic enterprises belong to society, but are administered by the workers themselves. Under the socialist market regime, the responsibility for resource allocation, investment, and income distribution is shared by political entities and economic units through voluntary agreements among producers and consumers taking certain cues from the market.

Yugoslavia's self-management socialism is often publicized as a mechanism sui generis, a variant neither of a pure market model nor of a purely centrally planned economy. In reality, it is an experimental offshoot of both, an imperfect market system superimposed on a multilateral regime. Under the 1974 Constitution, the Yugoslav system is probably the most pluralistic of all centrally directed economies. Within this system, the role of the state (at the federal, republican, or communal levels) is limited to selective interventions. The government's direct controls over economic activity have been concentrated in three basic areas: financing of investment projects in priority sectors, control of economic activity in the private sectors, and the use of foreign exchange. Indirect interventions cover monetary, fiscal, incomes and trade policies.

---

66. The discussion on Yugoslavia draws on the references mentioned at the end of this chapter, and on a recent and thorough study by the World Bank, *Yugoslavia: Self-Management Socialism* (Baltimore: Johns Hopkins University Press, 1979).

67. Over 3 percent of Yugoslavia's "gross social product" (GSP) is set aside annually for the purpose of aiding the less developed regions of the country.

YUGOSLAVIA: BASIC DATA

LAND AREA (sq. km.)   256,000

POPULATION (1980 estimate)	22 million
Net annual increase (1970-78 yearly average)	0.9 percent
Urban (percent of total, 1980)	42 percent
Working Age (15–64) (percent of total, 1978)	66 percent

LABOR FORCE (total civilian, 1978)	11 million
Agriculture, forestry, fishing (percent of total)	33 percent
Mining, manufacturing, construction (percent of total)	32 percent
Services, etc. (percent of total)	35 percent

GROSS DOMESTIC PRODUCT (market prices, 1978)	$52 billion
Per capita (1978)	$2,380
Average annual increase (1960–77)	5.6 percent
Public consumption (percent of GDP)	17 percent
Private consumption (percent of GDP)	55 percent
Fixed capital formation (ratio to GDP)	33 percent
Savings (ratio to GDP)	28 percent

GROSS DOMESTIC PRODUCT (market prices, 1978)	$52 billion
Agriculture, forestry, fishing (share in GDP)	16 percent
Mining, manufacturing, construction (share in GDP)	45 percent
Services (share in GDP)	39 percent

FOREIGN TRADE	
Exports (percent of GDP)	12 percent
Imports (percent of GDP)	21 percent

The "socialized" sector employs over 5 million people and accounts for some 82 percent of the "gross social product."[68] There are also some 800,000 workers temporarily employed abroad. Industry and construction account for about half of GSP. Agriculture, both state and private, provides about 16 percent, and the rest comes from services. Agriculture, however, still employs about 40 percent of the active population.

Government's Direct Role in the Economy

Yugoslavia's self-styled road to communism emphasizes the supremacy of "social self-management" over state ownership and operation.[69] The basis of Yugoslavia's social system is social ownership of means of production and the right of all workers to work with the means in social ownership. Neither the individuals, nor groups, nor even the state own the basic means. Ownership resides in the association of producers' or workers' organizations. Social aggregation of workers and machines is achieved through autonomous enterprises managed by workers themselves. This shift from *administrative* socialism (centralized planning and state management) to *market* socialism, (enterprise autonomy and social bargaining) has made the structure of Yugoslavia's direct role in the economy substantially different from that of other centrally directed economies.

Social Ownership and Enterprise

The contemporary Yugoslav model is the result of some thirty years of Yugoslav experimentation (and four different constitutions) dealing with the management of political, social, and economic affairs. In the immediate postwar period up to 1948, Yugoslavia's administrative socialism had all the principal features of a Soviet-type command economy. Under the 1946 Constitution, virtually all vital industries, all means of transport and communications, banking, finance, domestic distribution, and foreign trade were nationalized and managed directly by the state. After the

---

68. In the Yugoslav system of national income accounting, "nonproductive" services (services rendered to individuals, like domestic help) are excluded from the real GDP. By various estimates, if the Yugoslav GDP could be measured on the same basis as a typical MIC, it would be probably about 15 percent higher than GSP.

69. The semantic replacement of the concept of *state* ownership with that of *social* controls was intended to show that in the transition of bourgeois capitalism to full communism, there is no need for an interim state ownership. Workers can immediately take over social ownership and management without waiting for the state to "wither away."

traumatic break with Moscow in 1948 and expulsion from the Cominform, there was a significant turnaround. Comprehensive state ownership and controls were denounced as "state capitalism" and against the true interests of the working man. The 1950 Law on the Management of Government Enterprises and Economic Association by Workers' Collectives and the 1953 Constitution introduced the two new concepts of social ownership of the means of production, and that of workers' participation in the management of their production unit.

The basic law on the Management of Government Enterprises was based on the simple concept that all means of production belong to the society, to the people as a whole, but are entrusted to workers for management. The law thus placed the operation and management of all factories, mines, farms, and other state economic enterprises having more than a certain number of employees in the hands of workers themselves.[70] The difficulties and failures associated with the implementation of the law, and particularly the ill-defined responsibilities of the government and the collectives, gave rise to a prolonged national debate which culminated in the "liberal" Constitution of 1963.

The "economic reform" that followed during 1964–65 ushered in four new changes: a large part of the federal government's responsibilities was transferred to the republics; the Yugoslav economy was further exposed to world market competition through curtailment of price subsidies, more import liberalization, and the unification of a complex system of multiple exchange rates; the task of resource allocation was largely taken away from the state and given to economic enterprises and financial banks; and enterprise autonomy was expanded to include price formation and the distribution of enterprise income (into wages and reinvestments). The objectives of the 1965 "reform," which was subsequently dubbed "market socialism," were to give greater autonomy to the republics, to enhance enterprise efficiency and quality of output, and to improve national income distribution.

As a result of these reforms, federal responsibilities in the management of the economy were further reduced to economic relations with foreign countries; regulation of special funds for financing developments in less developed regions; coordination of monetary, fiscal, and foreign-exchange policies, price controls over certain selected goods and services; and the adoption of social five-year plans. Almost all of these fell into the realm of indirect intervention.

The post-1965 developments of the Yugoslav economy—a too liberal interpretation of the concept of enterprise autonomy, lack of policy coordination, and inability of the state to regulate aggregate demand and supply—produced

70. Workers' self-management in Yugoslavia should be distinguished from "workers' participation" and the so-called comanagement practiced in some Western European countries after World War II. The difference, simply stated, is that in the European models, workers *share* management responsibilities with managers and stockholders. In the Yugoslav case, they are the *sole* decision makers.

inflation, unemployment, and excess industrial capacity. A series of constitutional amendments in 1967, 1968, and 1971 finally culminated in the new Constitution of 1974, which promised to extend the self-management principle to the macroeconomic areas of foreign-exchange allotments, allocation of savings, and distribution of income, prices, wages, and employment.

Self-Management

Economic "self-management" in Yugoslavia is widely publicized as a "democratic" system under which decision-making power is assigned exclusively to those directly affected by the decisions, and individual decision makers exercise their mandate directly without sharing power with others. In turn, the proper functioning of self-management is based on three basic presumptions: the decision makers are homogeneous in objectives, interests, and outlook; the organization of decision making is small enough to allow members personal contacts and direct dialogues on matters of common interest; and decisions made at numerous small units are coordinated with each other (and with the national interest) through further delegations to ascending layers of assemblies all the way up to the federation. Workers are to exercise their socioeconomic and self-management rights through decision making at meetings, delegates in workers' councils, and delegates in the assemblies of the "communities of interest" and in the sociopolitical communities. [71]

The workers' organization on a self-management basis is the main form of decision making in all spheres of socioeconomic activity. It is the right and duty of the workers to belong to a basic organization, for it is through such an association that workers exercise their self-management rights. Workers engaged in economic activities belong to a basic organization. Employees performing administrative or technical tasks or auxiliary services and those working for the state organs belong to "work communities." Those engaged in social activities (education, culture, public health, and social welfare) belong to self-managed "communities of interest." The self-management principle is thus carried out through a number of special organizations and legal instruments.

At the bottom of the organizational hierarchy is the Basic Organization of Associated Labor (BOAL), a technical unit that produces a marketable good or renders a service. A BOAL may have as few as a dozen or as many as several hundred workers. Under the 1974 Constitution, the BOAL is the major decision-making entity. Every BOAL has the right to join or to leave an existing enterprise or to form

71. The "delegates" differ basically from "representatives" in Western "parliamentary" democracies in that they are obliged, under sanction of recall, to solicit and present the views of their constituents exactly as they are.

a new one. The BOAL's net income is separately calculated and can be distributed between wages, accumulation, and reinvestment at BOAL's discretion, but within the limits of its own obligations under "social compacts" and "self-management agreements" (the legal instruments discussed below).

A group of BOALs form a "working organization," a Yugoslav name for the enterprise. An enterprise is a voluntary and ad hoc association of organized workers who are linked by common working interest or by a unified process. (An integrated cotton textile mill, for instance, may have technical BOAL's such as spinning, weaving, finishing, all the way up to retail outlets.) Enterprises may be established by organizations of associated labor, self-managing communities of interest, local communes, sociopolitical communities, or other legal persons.

The bulk of Yugoslav industrial enterprises is socially owned and operated. Any enterprise that has five employees or more is considered a social enterprise and is run by those who work in it.[72]

The Yugoslav industrial enterprise is, within its variegated commitments, free to pursue its business and expansion policies. It plans and implements productions, trade, or services in line with its financial resources and possibilities. It decides for itself the volume and range of its products and its own price policy. It chooses its method of production, its supplies of material and equipment, and its customers at home and abroad. Thus, while workers and managers do not legally own the enterprise's assets, they have effective control over them.[73]

The income earned (what is left of receipts after covering business costs) is the yardstick of economic justification and success. The distribution of this income is decided by the workers. The net income (what is left after all financial obligations such as taxes and other dues have been met) is allocated by the workers, according to the self-management agreement, to gross wages and salaries, funds for the satisfaction of common needs (cafeterias, houses, sports facilities), and reserves for expansion and improvement of plant facilities. Contributions for common services (education, health protection, and social security) are made out of gross personal incomes in accordance with the "exchange of labor" agreements with the relevant "communities of interest."[74]

The modus operandi of self-management is multilayered. Every BOAL or enterprise has three main organs: the "workers' council," the business executive, and the "executive organ." The workers' council consists of delegates elected by members

72. Deviations from the rules are sometimes overlooked and occasionally tolerated. Some businesses employ more than the maximum five without having their assets turned into "social property" or submitting their policies to the workers' council.

73. This is often likened to the old English system of leaseholding, where land itself belonged to the crown, but tenants had the rights to their leases on the land. The emphasis on self-management is also partly expected to broaden the scope for nonmaterial incentives and greater social consciousness in economic decisions.

of any BOAL or enterprise having more than thirty workers. There are more than 10,000 industrial councils, ranging from 15 to 120 members, representing twenty times as many workers. The council is the highest management organ of the enterprise; all basic policies (the approval of the enterprise's plan and its financial budget, distribution of income, election and dismissal of the business executive of other organs) are formulated by the council. The business executive is appointed from among a list of candidates by a special commission composed of the representatives of the workers' council, the trade unions, and the professional associations selected by the local commune. He carries out the council's decisions and directions.

The business executive has a dual responsibility to the enterprise and to the society at large. On the one hand, he is in charge of the day-to-day business according to the enterprise's plan, policies, and commitments under appropriate self-management agreements and social compacts. On the other hand, if the council or the executive organ tries to take actions contrary to those commitments, he has the duty to inform the respective sociopolitical unit. The executive organ can be set up by the council for specific tasks within its jurisdiction. All business decisions regarding work assignments, product design, output planning, wage rates, pricing, sales promotion, and profit distribution are to be made jointly by the workers' council, the business executive, and the executive organ in accordance with all relevant directives, including the national economic plan. In reality, however, only a very small percentage of decisions are taken in a "self-management" way. Managers, professional staff, and administrators usually take an upper hand over inexperienced manual workers.

Self-management is legally and administratively based on a number of unique instrumentalities, such as agreements and compacts. Social compacts are concluded among sociopolitical communities, economic chambers, trade unions, and associations of economic enterprises. They stipulate the rights and responsibilities of each party in the execution of broad national policies. Issues regulated by the social compacts include basic priorities of the social (national) plan, principles regarding prices, employment and foreign trade, and distribution of income between consumption and investment. Social compacts set out the agreements on principles.

Self-management agreements specify rights and obligations of each economic organization (BOALs, enterprises, and banks) in accordance with broad principles. These agreements include the legal status of BOALs, enterprises, and banks; the distribution of joint incomes earned by the contracting parties; transfer prices among parties; criteria for the distribution of BOAL income into current

74. For details, see *Facts About Yugoslavia* (Belgrade: General Secretariat for Information, 1979).

expenditures and reinvestment; and placement of investible funds generated within BOALs or enterprises.

Communities of Interest

Among other institutions unique to Yugoslavia, the "communities of Interest" (CIs) deserve special attention.[75] CIs are organizations formed by producers and users of certain goods or services. The production and distribution of public goods—goods the market price of which cannot be relied upon to match supply and demand—are by law in the hands of CIs. Thus, education, public health, utilities, transportation and communications, and foreign trade are to be organized by CIs. Outside the social services, such communities can be voluntarily formed by enterprises and consumer groups through self-management agreements. CIs replace both the market's role as a mechanism for computation and coordination, and the government's role as a regulator of economic activities. The CIs, both at the federal and provincial levels, also serve as a vehicle for a two-way flow of consultation—upward from enterprises to the federation, and downward from the center to the operating units—until a consensus is reached between enterprise plans and national objectives.

Agricultural Enterprise

As in industry, the structure of agricultural enterprise has changed several times since the war. First there was confiscation of land from big landlords, churches, and other private owners who did not farm themselves. This was followed by limited landholdings for peasant-cultivators; compulsory peasant cooperatives; and forced delivery of farm products to the state. Thus, there was intensified "voluntary" collectivization of free lands during 1950–53 through state assistance to the collectives, on the one hand, and high taxes and other discriminations against freeholders, on the other. Finally came the replacement of agricultural collectives by voluntary, self-managed agricultural cooperatives, where agriculture is privately run on independent farms with limited acreage. Private farmers may voluntarily join

75. Mention ought to be made also of the composite organization, which is a legal entity comprising several enterprises in vertical or horizontal chains of production distribution; reproduction entity, which consists of a group of enterprises linked together vertically by forward or backward delivery relationships, as from coal mining to electricity consumption; and the industry association, to which all enterprises in an industry must belong at the republican and federal levels. Associations, in turn, form the economic chambers.

in producers' or consumers' farm cooperatives for the purpose of benefits from cheaper mass purchasing of machinery and equipment as well as more productive sales and marketing efforts. The five thousand or so general cooperatives own their own land and are managed by private farmer-participants. They combine both buying and selling functions; they are also assisted by the state materially and technically; they have access to low-cost credit of the State Agricultural Bank, subsidized farm supplies, and research facilities. The general cooperatives do a good deal of farming in addition to their trading activities.

Some 16 percent of the farmland and about 7 percent of the active population are now part of "socialized agriculture," mostly in the hands of state experimental farms and collective farms established on confiscated land. State farms are large-scale, self-managed, agroindustrial enterprises. Collective farms lease their land from the state and operate much like the Russian variety. Yugoslavia still hopes to reduce the peasant's resistance to collectivized farming through such aggregative institutions as the Cooperatives Union and the Agricultural Chamber.

State Planning

Yugoslavia's postwar social (national) planning has changed four times with each of the four new constitutions (1946, 1953, 1963, and 1974). By 1980, there had been six medium-term plans, representing four basic planning philosophies.

After a short-lived and unsuccessful experiment with the Soviet model between 1947 and 1952, Yugoslavia abandoned central planning. As state management was replaced by self-management, so was centralized planning replaced by planning in terms of global balances; or basic proportions between aggregate consumption and investment, between shares of investment in different sectors, and between exports and imports. During 1956–61, the content of the social plan was reduced to coordination and guidance in such broad macroeconomic variables as the rate of aggregate investment, the distribution of investable funds, and aggregate consumption. On the basis of these rates, the Federal Planning Institute made forecasts of sectoral growth rates. Enterprises, in turn, prepared their own operative plans based on those projections.

Encouraged by the success of the Second Plan and the conceived compatibility of planning and the market mechanism, further liberalization in the planning process was widely advocated. Thus, between 1961 and 1975, Yugoslav planning became largely indicative in nature. The main tasks of the plan—a medium-term prospective—were to provide a forecast and a basis for decisions by enterprises and a set of objectives for the government to follow. The prospectives dealt mostly with politicoeconomic policies (regional, national, and international) and socioeconomic instruments (taxes and interest rate) necessary to implement them. Annual social plans were more detailed, dealing with the rate of private and public consumption, gross investment, foreign trade, industrial and agricultural outputs, and employment and productivity. With minor exceptions, investment decisions were influenced by market criteria and backed by self-managed all-purpose banks.

Each annual plan was accompanied by a financial plan (a comprehensive social budget) which dealt with wage and price guidelines, credit distribution, and capital use among industrial enterprises. The Federal Secretariat for Finance insepected enterprise accounts and ensured the fulfillment of contract obligations among enterprises. Corporative economic chambers had the task of coordinating output of different enterprises in each branch of industry. Local communes and local Leagues of Yugoslav Communists exerted political and persuasive pressures on workers' councils and enterprise managers to follow the plan's directions.

The experiment with this type of planning, however, was not very successful, for the economy went through a series of internal and external imbalances and gyrations. There was also much disenchantment with too much dependence on impersonal market forces. It was generally conceded that investment decisions by enterprises were not properly coordinated and that investable funds were not always put to optimum use. The market was also blamed for growing income inequality among republics and among individuals in each republic; concentration of economic power in the hands of banks, managerial elite, and various strategic enterprises, such as foreign trade; and the government's inability to prevent duplications, inefficiencies, and misuse of precious investment resources.

Under the 1974 Constitution, the self-management principle was extended to planning. In a radical shift from the past, the planning exercise was divided among all decision makers, instead of being assigned to the Planning Institute, and the plan's directives became legally binding instead of mere indications. According to the new Law on Planning (1976), the planning process is to be carried out simultaneously by all organizations affected and at all levels. The process is a continual one, with the progress and failures of each annual plan serving as the basis for revision of the five-year plan, and each medium five-year plan is part of a longer-term plan.

In the 1976–80 plan, enterprises were expected to prepare their individual plans based on a common methodology, common assumptions, and a common plan period; to coordinate their programs horizontally at the level of the republics; and to reconcile these programs vertically with other interdependent firms at regional levels.[76] The operational part of the plan consists of major investment projects, physical output and financing agreed upon in the legally binding self-management agreements and social compacts. Republican and federal planning

---

76. The final draft of the plan had to be harmonized with some 55,000 individual plans for enterprises, banks, local communes, and republics.

institutes are to aggregate and reconcile individual plans and come up with an overall plan to be submitted to the Federal Assembly for final approval and adoption. Enterprises are committed to planned output and wage and price targets under the self-management agreements. The implementation of the plan is supervised by local overview committees composed of enterprise and consumer representatives.[77] The Federal Planning Institute handles deadlocks in the process of planning and implementation. To implement specific projects outlined in the five-year plan, each republic or provincial authority concludes social compacts with various enterprises.

One of the main tasks of Yugoslav planning—which is not now strictly binding on all enterprises—is to reduce undue dependence on imports of raw materials and equipment and to eliminate major impediments to growth in energy, agriculture, and transportation. The 1976–80 plan is thus aimed at the development of energy, especially through hydroelectric potential and coal; agrobusiness, especially food processing; mining; and machine tools and metalworks. The annual average target growth rate is 7 percent. The 1981–85 plan which is still at the preliminary stages of preparation is expected to provide for a slightly lower target for growth, has as its main priorities raw materials extraction, energy, food, and transportation.

Indirect Interventions

Yugoslavia's "people's democracy," while markedly different from the Soviet and Chinese varieties, is still based on "democratic centralism" and one-party rule. The League of Yugoslav Communists (LYC) and its adjunct organization, the Socialist Alliance, are, in the official view, the only organizations that give citizens an opportunity to participate in political life, in the discussion of sociopolitical issues, and in the presentation of proposals.[78]

Within the framework of this one-party democracy, Yugoslavia is the only country among the CDEs with the broadest use of Western-type interventionist policies to direct and manage the economy. The extent and scope of these public levers, in turn, have increased throughout the years since 1950, with the spread of decentralization measures.

77. In order to guarantee the desired pattern of investment, the plan envisages a number of policy measures such as the use of public loans and bond issues to obtain funds for high priority projects, preferential treatment of capital goods imports, special credit terms, tax breaks, and possible obligations imposed on enterprises to invest in certain specific projects.

78. Democratic centralism refers to a process by which people engage in free deliberations and discussions of issues, but once decisions are made, they have to abide by them.

Fiscal Policy

Public finance in Yugoslavia is divided between the federal government, the governments of the republics, and other social entities. The federal government is responsible for defense, subsidies to lesser developed regions, and general administration. Republics and local communes take care of all other expenditures. Revenues are also correspondingly divided. The tax system, contributing 90 percent of budgetary revenues, essentially consists of three categories: income taxes (including taxes on incomes of enterprises, personal incomes of social-sector workers, incomes from private-sector activities, and incomes from property ownership; turnover or excise taxes on goods and services; and customs duties. Public revenues are shared by social entities. The basic source of federal revenues, since 1978, is contribution from republics and provinces originating from excise or turnover tax receipts (50 percent).[79] All other taxes are imposed and collected at the republic-provincial and communal levels.

Since 1974, there has been a distinct trend toward decentralization of fiscal power and the creation of a number of special-purpose public-sector institutions, such as the social security fund, fund for public services by regional and local communities of interest, and special projects funds. Almost all essential social services—public utilities, road maintenance, housing, health, education, disability insurance, and child care—are now provided by the "communities of interest" at the local and regional levels. The intent of the law is to put the burden of financing these services directly on their beneficiaries. The extent of these services is thus determined by the BOALs that form the membership of the CIs. About three quarters of all public expenditures are out of the reach of the federal and republic governments and in the hands of the CIs social security funds and special funds.

The main objectives of fiscal policy in recent years have been to maintain the rate of growth of public revenues below that of nominal GSP in order to check the rise in social services expenditures, to minimize resources taken from the "productive sector" and spent on nonproductive activities; and to reduce the federal budget deficit. The structure of the tax system, however, has left little room for maneuver by fiscal authorities in dealing with cyclical fluctuations.

The new Law on the Financing of the Federation (1977) seeks to regulate revenue sharing between the federal government and the republics in such a way as to give the former greater autonomy and certainty in revenue collection. At the same time, the responsibility for promoting foreign trade, such as tax rebates to exporters, and domestic subsidies (mostly for guaranteed food prices) was taken away from the federal government in 1978 and given to two special bodies. The size of the federal budget and the amount of the deficit financing in the future should therefore be substantially reduced.

79. Prior to 1978, customs duties were exclusively a federal tax. Since then, they have been collected by the Self-Managed Community of Interest for Economic Relations with the Rest of the World—to be used for drawbacks on exports.

On the whole, fiscal policy, as exercised by the federal government, has not been an effective instrument in demand management because the federal budget's share of total public revenues and expenditures has been on the decline, and lately somewhat less than one-fourth of total; federal revenues based on the republics' contribution could not be geared to the levels of domestic economic activities; budgetary expenditures have proved to be fairly inflexible; and the multiplicity of public institutions—running virtually into the thousands—has not been conducive to a centrally directed anticyclical policy.

Monetary Policy

Because of the particular weaknesses of fiscal policy for demand management in the Yugoslav setting (and the difficulty of ensuring an effective incomes policy), the responsibility for anticyclical interventions rests basically with monetary policy. The policy stance is ordinarily defined in the annual economic policy resolutions adopted by the Federal Assembly. The general scope for monetary policy usually takes into account the main objectives of the plan. The annual resolution defines the targets for the rate of growth of money supply (M_1); reserve money creation; selective credit policy; and the debt of the federal government.[80] Open-market operations are still not very significant.

The implementation of Yugoslavia's monetary policy is the responsibility of the Yugoslav National Bank and the national banks of the republics and autonomous provinces. The governors of these banks constitute the Board of Governors of the country's National Bank. The latter's main task is to regulate the money supply, which is geared, as a rule, to the planned rise in GSP. The National Bank finances the federal budget deficits and may guarantee foreign loans.

The country's banking system under the 1976 banking law is made up of internal banks, which are subsidiaries of public enterprises and whose services are not available to the general public; basic banks, which are full-fledged commercial banks owned by internal banks or other economic interests; and associated banks, which are formed by basic banks and carry out special banking activities, such as foreign-exchange operations, assigned to them by basic banks.[81] A-l banks are required to prepare annual and five-year plans and to integrate them with those of their trade members and ultimately with the overall social plan.

The annual scope for monetary policy, in recent years, has included the sustenance of the desired increase in the general level of economic activities; the control of inflation; a balance between aggregate supply and demand; and balance-of-payments support. The money supply target is commonly regulated by the manipulation of the monetary base. The Law on National Bank Operation

80. For details of these measures, see *Yugoslavia* (Paris: OECD, 1980).
81. The fact that the commercial banks are owned and controlled by their enterprise customers is one reason for the tendency toward keeping interest rates low.

enumerates the instruments of monetary policy and the regulation of the reserve money base as: compulsory reserves of commercial banks and other financial organizations held with the National Bank of Yugoslavia (YNB)—the maximum rate (25 percent) being fixed by law and the actual rates by the Federal Executive Council and YNB; extension of short-term documented credits to commercial banks; purchase of short-term securities such as treasury bills; issue and cancellation of national banknotes; rediscount rate; and restrictions on the volume of bank credit.

In general, the authorities' aim in determining and maintaining the money supply (M_1) at a projected level has gone hand in hand with a desire to keep interest rates at a fairly low level in order to promote investment. Without an internal capital market and with rigid controls on foreign borrowings by individual enterprises, the Yugoslav banks are the main source of credit finance. At the same time, the strict limitations on interest rates charged by the banks in the face of persistent high inflation have resulted in credits being normally rationed. Low interest rates, in turn, have tended to reduce the supply of individual savings and to encourage excessive investment.

Price and Incomes Policies

Yugoslavia's price policy has passed through various phases of regimentation and liberalization but has never been totally controlled or completely free. There has always been some state intervention. As a result of many policy changes in the last three decades, the process of price formulation has become exceedingly complex.

Prices are generally determined at the producers' level (wholesale); trade margins are allowed for retailing. Most prices are under federal jurisdiction and handled by the Federal Bureau for Prices. Within this jurisdiction, there are basically four principles or processes for price formulation. First, the prices of certain products are not under direct control, and there is a wide margin of discretion, based on market forces, for fixing these prices. Second, some products (mainly oil derivatives and consumer items) are, by contrast, under direct control of the state and can be changed only by administrative decisions. Third, the price of other products is based upon self-management agreements among producers of different production levels; they include raw materials and ferrous and nonferrous metals, whose prices are known in world markets. Finally, there are still other products (mainly intermediate materials, chemicals, and equipment) whose prices are under agreements between producers and/or consumers, but must also be approved by the Federal Bureau for Prices.

Price formulation takes place principally through two kinds of agreements. First, agreements among sociopolitical communities define broad lines of policy to be followed in a given year, including price rises that will be tolerated.[82] Second,

---

82. The Annual Economic Policy Resolution for 1978, for example, allowed an inflation rate of 12–13 percent.

within the framework of these "political" accords, there are agreements among producers and/or consumers on prices and price changes for particular groups of goods. All prices—even liberalized ones—must fall within the general price policy guidelines. Price categories can be changed by the state if conditions so warrant, or if self-management agreements do not comply with administratively established criteria. There can be a general freeze on all prices (as in 1971 and 1980) or a selective freeze for some prices.

Incomes policy relates to the principles of the distribution of enterprise income between gross personal incomes (wages and salaries) and the accumulation of investment reserves. Workers in the basic organizations receive their incomes from sales of goods and services by their unit, shares from joint activities with other organizations, and free "exchange of labor" (fringe benefits in the form of education, health care, etc.). Personal incomes are based on the twin principles of individual contribution to the creation of the organization's revenues; and "solidarity," a cross between equity and efficiency. Every worker, however, is guaranteed a minimum personal income enabling him to enjoy a degree of national and social status. Since 1965, the workers' control over the enterprise's income distribution has been on the rise. For this reason, there has been a continuous tendency to increase nominal wages at the expense of savings. Enterprise expansion has, thus, had to be financed through public budget or bank borrowing.

Foreign Trade and Exchange Policies

Yugoslavia's foreign trade and exchange policies are dictated by two statutes enacted in 1977, which consolidated several previous edicts and brought them into line with the 1974 Constitution.

The Federal Executive Council, through its mandate from the Federal Assembly, establishes the day-to-day trade and exchange policies. The Federal Secretariat for Foreign Trade prescribes rules and regulations governing foreign trade and issues import and export licenses when required. It also has the responsibility of securing balanced trade under bilateral arrangements with other countries. Foreign trade is subject to a plethora of regulations necessitated by the five-year development plans and Yugoslavia's persistent and substantial trade deficits.

Imports are classified according to the manner in which foreign exchange is made available: liberalized imports, goods subject to foreign-exchange quotas, commodities subject to physical limitations, and items subject to ad hoc licensing. Liberalized imports, for which foreign exchange is readily available, include mainly raw materials and spare parts; they constitute more than half of all imports. Limited items, accounting for roughly one-fifth of imports, include essentially agricultural and mineral products, machine tools, and equipment; allocation among importers is made by the Chamber of Economy. Goods requiring ad hoc licenses include motor vehicles, aircraft, oil, pharmaceuticals, and firearms; they cover less than 10 percent of imports.

Commercial imports may be brought in only by registered economic organizations. Individuals who hold foreign-exchange accounts with Yugoslav banks may use these funds to import goods for their own use. Self-employed Yugoslav nationals also are allowed to import small capital goods for their own operation up to a certain amount. There is no exchange allowance for tourist travel abroad. Payments for services and invisibles, such as royalties, are allowed. Tariff rates are stipulated in the Customs Tariff Law of 1977 on an ad valorem basis. In addition to customs levies, imports are subject to a variety of taxes and surcharges earmarked for specific purposes. The Federal Executive Council is authorized to raise basic duty rates up to 50 percent when needed to protect domestic industries.

In principle, exports are unrestricted except for some raw materials in short supply on the domestic market. Exports to bilateral trading partners are subject to conditions specified in the bilateral agreements. Proceeds from exports must be repatriated within a specified period, but they need not be surrendered. In fact, foreign exchange earned through exports theoretically belongs to the exporting entity. It can normally be kept in a foreign-exchange account to be used later, used for imports, or be sold to authorized banks.

Economic organizations may borrow abroad in accordance with the self-management agreements. Foreigners also may invest in Yugoslavia through joint ventures up to 49 percent of capital. Repatriation of profits is allowed in specific ways. Economic organizations participating in foreign enterprises may be allowed to transfer the necessary capital under certain conditions, but outright capital transfer by individual residents is not allowed.[83]

The complicated trade system is geared to serving the cause of Yugoslavia's industrial development, turning back the perennial tides of external deficits; and maintaining sufficient foreign-exchange reserves. Under the new trade law, responsibility for maintaining the country's balance-of-payments equilibrium is transferred to the republics and provinces. In each of these political subdivisions, an organization called Yugoslav Community of Interest for Economic Relations with Foreign Countries is formed to supervise the external account.

Foreign exchange is controlled by the state through the Federal Secretariat for Finance, the National Bank of Yugoslavia, and the national banks of republics and autonomous provinces. All foreign-exchange transactions must be carried out through the authorized banks. Payments to and from bilateral trade partners are made in currencies and under terms set forth in the bilateral arrangements. However, residents and nonresidents can maintain foreign-exchange accounts in convertible currencies and may use them freely for payments in Yugoslavia and abroad. The national banks play an important part in implementing the foreign-exchange policy through managing the foreign-exchange value of the national

83. Yugoslavia maintains bilateral clearing arrangements with some CDEs and a number of LDCs, but the share of trade with these partners has been on the decline.

currency, the dinar; financing Yugoslavia's international payments; and influencing foreign borrowing. Up to July 1973, the exchange rate for the Yugoslav dinar was fixed by the authorities. The currency was devalued by 66 percent in the context of the 1965 reforms and the unification of multiple exchange rates. Two more devaluations occurred in 1971, but these rate changes failed to halt the steady rise in imports or to increase exports. In July 1973, the dinar was floated in the exchange market, and the government only intervened from time to time to smooth out drastic fluctuations. None of these measures, however, was able to stem the tide of foreign-trade deficits (reaching $6 billion in 1979) and foreign debt exceeding $13 billion.

Consequently, after the 1979-1980 oil price rise in the midst of rapid growth in domestic demand and strong inflationary pressures, a new and drastic devaluation of the dinar (from 21 to 27.3 dinars for the U.S. dollar) was again announced in the spring of 1980. Many analysts blamed Yugoslavia's inability to generate enough exports on the substantial overvaluation of the Yugoslav dinar, but the balance of payments is now expected to be helped by the most recent devaluation and a new investment law promulgated in 1979, which encourages investment in export-oriented and import-substitution industries and bans investment in "nonproductive" schemes.

Foreign Investment Policy

Yugoslavia is ahead of the other CDEs in seeking to attract foreign private investments in order to substitute imports, increase exports, and acquire modern management and technology. Minority joint venture is the only acceptable form. The new Joint Venture Law of 1979 defines the activities in which foreign partners can participate (not in commerce, public service, or insurance) and the conditions for repatriation of dividends and principal, taxation, and management prerogatives. Foreign investment has to be approved by the appropriate republic or province, the Federal Institute of Economic Planning, and the Yugoslav Chamber of Economy before being licensed by the Federal Committee of Energy and Industry.

The inclination toward joint ventures with foreign partners has been based mainly on the desire to strengthen domestic competitiveness. There is a minimum and maximum of total investment (10 percent and 49 percent) for foreign participation, as there is an absolute minimum amount of capital (5 million dinars).[84]

84. By OECD estimates, between 1967 and 1978, about 150 joint ventures were undertaken in Yugoslavia.

Intergroup Bargaining

Despite its hierarchical political regime under the supreme guidance of the Communist party, Yugoslavia's great ethnic and religious diversity invites a good deal of intergroup dealings and cooperation. For this reason, although the League of Yugoslav Communists has the principal responsibility for establishing economic objectives and for overseeing their achievements, all important policy decisions are reached through consensus. Thus, the LYC seeks to institute inter-republic agreements and secure the approval of the political subdivisions in the determination of national socioeconomic goals and the resolution of problems of common concern. The LYC also endeavors to conclude, in collaboration with trade unions and the Chamber of Economy, regular social accords in various parts of the industrial sector.

By one interpretation, the very system of self-management in Yugoslavia is an attempt to manage the economy by agreements between the various groups in society, to create national unity be recognizing Yugoslavia's diversity, and to reconcile conflicts through compromise. The multitiered structure of self-management is designed for this purpose.

The pluralistic process of haggling, negotiations, and compromise permeates almost all aspects of Yugoslav economic life. Starting at the top, the self-management and multilevel planning requires horizontal and vertical harmonization and coordination between planning agents: sociopolitical communities, planning institutes, economic chambers, and producers' associations. At the midlevels of aggregation, large industrial complexes, trade unions, and various CIs have to harmonize their "assumptions, expectations and ambitions" as to the prospective level and composition of the social product. At the bottom, BOALs and enterprises have to exchange and adjust their projections, possibilities, and potentials. The whole exercise is thus aimed at fusing the varied interests of party leaders, managers, professional cadres, workers, and others into one consistent master plan for the allocation of resources and the distribution of income.

Among the Eastern bloc nations, Yugoslavia is without doubt the only country with a formalized technique of multipartite decision making. When the system of "workers' self-management" was first introduced in June 1950, many critics in the West dismissed it as socialist "window dressing," while non-Yugoslav socialists called it capitalist revisionism. Yet this somewhat unique mélange of multilateral bargaining, state direction, and workers' self-determination seems to have offered a viable, if not ideal, alternative to centralized command.

As outlined in a previous section, decision making in the Yugoslav economy, especially at the enterprise level, is shared by "society," which legally owns the enterprises and their assets; the rank-and-file workers, who have a stake in the enterprise's productivity and profit; and the party élite, which is ultimately responsible for the enterprise's success or failure and follows the party's directives. All decisions regarding the use of the firm's resources, setting personal incomes (above the minimum set by the state), determining prices (where they are not fixed by the government), and reinvesting part of the enterprise's profits are made by continuous "negotiations" among these elements. Workers' participation in self-management is also facilitated by a general workers' meeting where individual workers can present their view, and by the referendums through which the entire enterprise votes on specially important matters. Each enterprise is also partly controlled by the local economic chamber and producers' associations to which it must belong.

Labor unions and trade associations in the Western sense do not exist in Yugoslavia, but both strikes and unemployment do. Yugoslav trade unions are voluntary and essentially political organizations of workers. These organizations, along with the League of Communists and the Socialist Alliance, form the so-called sociopolitical organizations.[85] Almost all workers in the public (social) sector are trade-union members. The major tasks of the unions are to assist self-management through the preparation of procedures and guidelines, and to initiate self-management agreements on income distribution and other matters of material interest to workers. In the performance of these tasks, labor unions put up the list of candidates to be elected to the workers' councils and cosign the self-management agreements.

Chambers of worker organizations, made up from workers' councils at the local, regional, and national levels, cooperate with government agencies in formulating broad policies on matters of common interest to all working men. Similarly, there are associations of state enterprises on an industry basis for the purpose of cooperation in the exchange of information, scientific research, competitive price policy, and so on.

The multiplicity of these organizations and controls, which gives Yugoslavia a pluralistic makeup, is also the cause of delays, deadlocks, and inefficiencies. Economists and the press are dissatisfied with workers' frequent disregard of long-term productivity and modernization, and their great preoccupation with high personal incomes not commensurate with their productivity. The charge is that workers put too much stress on "self" and too little on "management."

On the whole, Yugoslavia's innovative system of self-management through compromise has not been able satisfactorily to solve the country's continued economic problems: insufficient growth, unemployment, and inflation. While the federal government's scope for influencing the economy has been gradually pared, the increased power of the workers' councils has fueled incipient wage and price inflation. The low average level of skill and education of most council members, the political nature of many managerial appointments, and the self-centered behavior of

---

85. Sociopolitical organizations, in turn, are *territorial* political units that constitute the "state." They consist of the federation, the six republics, the two autonomous provinces, and some 510 local communes.

industrial workers have been responsible for much of the persistent difficulties. Yugoslavia's claim to have found an original means of eliminating class conflicts between workers and management through their fusion into one unified body still remains to be demonstrated.[86]

The Socialist Market Sector

Yugoslavia's socialist market economy provides for only a moderate exercise of consumer sovereignty, but compared to other CDEs, private ownership, operation, and initiatives are by far the most extensive.

The 1974 Constitution authorizes certain activities (small farming, skilled crafts, services) to be carried on by personal labor and with minor means of production owned by individuals. Professional activities may also be pursued on the basis of self-employment. This limited private sector allows ten hectares of arable land in agriculture, and five salaried workers in any other business activity. Permitted also are cooperatives formed by farmers or craftsmen in which they can maintain ownership rights and dispose of them freely. Private individuals and cooperatives may also conclude long-term association agreements with public enterprises, obtaining the right to full participation in the latter's self-management. Finally, the Law on Associated Labor allows individual working people to pool their financial resources in a contractual organization that could operate as a business unit, employ salaried workers without limits, receive extra income in accordance with their share of ownership, and reinvest these incomes in the business for expansion.[87]

The private sector presently consists of small, individually owned peasant farms, professional services, and catering run by self-employed individuals, and industrial small enterprises. The sector accounts for about 18 percent of the social product. Under the Yugoslav constitution, land ownership is essentially private. Some 84 percent of the country's farmland (8.5 million hectares) is farmed by 2.6 million private farms of between two to ten hectares. Private farms employ some 33 percent of the resident labor force and account for about 58 percent of marketable agricultural production. There is no mandatory delivery of farm products to the state at fixed prices. Except for certain staple food products, the prices of which are fixed and also supported by the state, farm products are controlled by supply and demand in the free market. Farm prices have moved almost relentlessly upward since the

86. The only other such experience—that of postindependence Algeria—has already withered away. See Ian Clegg, *Workers' Self-Management in Algeria* (London: Penguin Press, 1971).

87. Under a law passed early in 1979, individuals and groups of citizens can operate private shops and workshops; they can also invest their savings jointly with "socialist" enterprises, earning a part of the profit.

early 1950s as a result of high production costs and heavy demand pressures from expanding population.[88]

There is an estimated coterie of 250,000 small businesses in small manufacturing plants employing five workers or less, in restaurants, inns, beauty parlors, repair shops, and retail stores in private, self-employed hands. More than half the taxis and thousands of commercial trucks are owner-operated. Many homes, apartments, and villas are privately owned. The majority of residential housing is privately constructed. Fixed-interest bonds are issued by enterprises and owned by private individuals. People are also encouraged to buy interest-bearing government bond issues. After the 1965 reforms, some of the major characteristics of a market economy—decentralized decision making at the enterprise level, the limited role of interest in both saving and investment decisions, and freedoms in setting production and price policies—became increasingly common.[89]

As indicated before, Yugoslavia since 1967 has welcomed foreign private investors to take advantage of the country's cheap labor, industrial base, and hydroelectric potential to set up 49–51 percent joint ventures with Yugoslav firms. The foreign investment law allows foreign corporations to share in the profit of local companies with freedom to take back all their investment and most of their earnings. The aim has been to gain access to Western private know-how, patents, processes, and marketing techniques.

The Yugoslav Economy: An Overview

In Yugoslavia's maverick system, neither a centralized hierarchy nor the free market has the ultimate decision-making power; they both have limited functions. A complex array of delegated and multilateral processes, assisted in various forms and degrees by the state and the market, are responsible for the management of the economy.[90]

Under the 1974 Constitution, the state functions are decentralized to the largest possible degree among lower echelons of political organizations. Further-

---

88. Mandatory limits of twenty-five acres on private landholdings (state and collective farms, are exempt) and prohibition against hiring farmhands, however, are considered major obstacles to increased farm productivity and the principal reason why agriculture remains Yugoslavia's most lagging sector.

89. General Export, founded in 1952 to facilitate Yugoslav exports to hard currency markets, is a commercial enterprise in everything but legal structure. Although legally operated as a collective, under worker self-management, it is, in effect, run by an enterprising general manager. Genex operates a commercial airline (the first in the Communist world), a commercial radio station, and has large interests in Yugoslav banks, industrial companies, and tourist facilities.

90. A Yugoslav industrial expert is reported to have said, "Our self-management is a mixture of totalitarianism and anarchy, but it is the best we have."

more, the government is freed to the largest possible extent from the management of the economy. Specifically, the state does not own or operate the means of production; it has no financial or administrative control over the production and distribution of social services; its revenues are limited to what is necessary for financing current classical functions, such as defense and justice. The state role in the economy is thus largely residual and restricted to: resolving conflicts and establishing consensus between competing organs and institutions in society, particularly in matters of social priorities; monitoring the fulfillment of social plans; and implementing a few direct controls affecting the national interest, such as fixing prices of a few key items. The actual state involvement in the economy takes place mostly through social compacts.

The market also enjoys very limited functions on the Yugoslav scene. Market socialism simply means a complex set of social actions and transactions in the marketplace, broadly defined. Indeed, with the exception of a variety of goods and services (mostly consumer items) for which the market is competitive and prices determined by supply and demand, the market mechanism has no part to play in Yugoslav economic management. The market for labor is rejected on ideological grounds in order not to treat workers as a "commodity." Wages and labor remunerations are part of the residual incomes of BOALs enterprises (after all other expenses but before taxes); they are determined within certain criteria and limits defined in social compacts and self-management agreements. Similarly, there is no capital market. The decision regarding reinvestments is made by enterprises themselves within broad guidelines. Much investment is thus self-financed. Banks do exist, and credit is extended to borrowers at interest. There are also interenterprise investments based on income and risk-sharing arrangements. But interest rates are administratively determined, and thus not equilibrium rates. Rents, too, are mostly fixed in interagency agreements and are not necessarily equilibrating.

With regard to goods and services, except for certain items mentioned before, there is no real market in the classical sense. For public goods and social services supplied by communities of interest, the market mechanism is ruled out by definition. All transactions between suppliers and users are in a sense rationed and categorized as "free-exchange of labor," making participants in the CI directly responsible for financial arrangements to cover cost. In the case of goods and services transferred and delivered among BOALs or enterprises, the self-management agreements regulate the terms. Transfer prices are thus a matter of agreement among interested parties; they are often not paid or received, but accounted for in income-sharing formulae. These prices may differ substantially and for some time from the true equilibrium prices. Finally, there are certain basic or strategic goods and services for which prices are controlled by social compacts or administrative decisions.[91]

91. There also have been complete price freezes on a range of goods and services, and limits on prices normally allowed to fetch their own level in the market, as in the 1980 summer, when the inflation rate threatened to reach 20 percent.

In short, neither the state nor the market in Yugoslavia is relied upon to ensure a supply-demand equilibrium or a welfare optimum. They are both expected to give certain signals for the decision makers to follow. State signals are meant to show the way toward a stable equilibrium and an optimal welfare. Market signals are expected to reflect consumers' reactions to the state directions.

The weaknesses of this hybrid system are not few. Despite considerable measures of price controls on which the Yugoslav authorities have relied heavily in recent years, the rate of inflation has often been far larger than planned (23 percent rise in the cost of living in 1979 as against the projected 13 percent) and higher than in most other European countries throughout the 1970s. Despite a very generous official policy in favor of very low interest rates, the total cost of ongoing investment projects have far exceeded the amount laid down in the Social Plan (1976–80). Despite heavy emphasis on self-management and planning, investment in certain sectors (energy, transportation, and shipbuilding) have recorded increases well in excess of those planned, but in other sectors, such as agriculture, tourism, and housing, it has fallen short of official targets. Industrial productivity at only 2.2 percent a year has been nearly half of the planned 4 percent. Despite the elimination of capitalist entrepreneurs, Yugoslav unemployment has recently been one of the highest in Europe (around 7 percent)—not counting some 800,000 workers abroad. And most interesting of all, despite the prevalence of self-management by workers, Yugoslav industries have been facing a rising number of strikes (called "work stoppages") with an increasing number of workers taking part in them.[92]

Except for a very respectable rate of growth, and for personal incomes that have been rising faster than labor productivity, Yugoslavia's record in internal and external economic instability (inflation and balance-of-payments deficits), high foreign indebtedness, unemployment, management efficiency, capacity utilization, and material waste has paralleled the poor performance of countries in both socialist or nonsocialist camps. If history is any guide to objective judgment, it looks like it will be some time before Yugoslavia, too, finds its ideal path to an incontestably successful economic direction and management.

Suggestions for Additional Readings

AMES, E. *Soviet Economic Processes*. Homewood: Irwin, 1965.
ASCHER, I. *China's Social Policy*. London: Anglo-Chinese Education Institute, Modern China Series, No. 3, 1976.

92. One Yugoslav trade-union leader has defined Yugoslav strikes as "a specific form of the working-class struggle taking place after specific mechanisms of the self-management system have failed." See "Jugoslavia," *The Economist*, 11 August 1979.

BARNETT, A. D. *Cadres, Bureaucracy, and Political Power in Communist China.* New York: Columbia University Press, 1967.

BERGSON, A. *The Economics of Soviet Planning.* New Haven: Yale University Press, 1964.

BERGSON, A. *Planning and Productivity Under Soviet Socialism.* New York: Columbia University Press, 1968.

BERGSON, A. *Productivity and the Social System.* Cambridge: Harvard University Press, 1978.

BERNARDO, R. M. *Popular Management and Pay in China.* Quezon City: University of the Philippines Press, 1977.

BROEKEMEYER, M. T., ED. *Yugoslav Workers' Self-Management.* Dordrecht: D. Reidel, 1970.

BURKI, S. J. *A Study of Chinese Communes.* Cambridge: Harvard University Press, 1970.

CAMPBELL, R. W. *The Soviet-Type Economies: Performance and Evolution.* Boston: Houghton Mifflin, 1974.

CAMPBELL, R. W. *Soviet Economic Power: Its Organization, Growth, and Challenge.* Boston: Houghton Mifflin, 1966.

CHANG, P. H. *Power and Policy in China.* University Park: The Pennsylvania State University Press, 1976.

CHEKHANIN, E. *The Soviet Political System Under Developed Socialism.* Moscow: Progress Publishers, 1977.

CHEN, N., AND W. GALENSON. *The Chinese Economy Under Communism.* Chicago: Aldine, 1969.

CHU, L., AND T. CHIEH-YUN. *Inside a People's Commune.* Peking: Foreign Languages Press, 1974.

COHN, S. H. *Economic Development in the Soviet Union.* Lexington: Heath, 1970.

COOPER, J. F. *China's Foreign Aid: An Instrument of Peking's Foreign Policy.* Lexington: Heath, 1976.

DELEYNE, J. *The Chinese Economy.* New York: Harper, 1974.

DONNITHORNE, A. *China's Economic System.* London: Allen & Unwin, 1967.

ECKSTEIN, A. *China's Economic Revolution.* New York: Columbia University Press, 1977.

ECKSTEIN, A. *China's Economic Development.* Ann Arbor: University of Michigan Press, 1975.

ECKSTEIN, A. "The Chinese Development Model," in *Chinese Economy Post Mao.* Washington: GPO, 1978.

Economic Developments in Countries of Eastern Europe. Washington: GPO, 1970.

EVENKO, I. A., *Planning in the U.S.S.R.* Moscow: Foreign Languages Publishing House, 1961.

GROSSMAN, G., ED. *Value and Plan.* Berkeley: University of California Press, 1960.

HANSON, P. "East-West Comparisons and Comparative Economic Systems." *Soviet Studies,* January, 1971.

THE CENTRALLY DIRECTED ECONOMIES

HANSON, P. *The Consumer in the Soviet Economy.* Evanston: Northwestern University Press, 1969.

HARDT, J. P., ED., *Soviet Economy in a New Perspective.* Washington: GPO, 1976.

HOFFMANN, C. *Work Incentives in Communist China.* Berkeley: S.S.R.C., 1964.

HOFFMANN, C. *The Chinese Worker.* Albany: State University of New York Press, 1974.

HOFFMAN, G. W., AND F. W. NEAL. *Yugoslavia and the New Communism.* New York: Twentieth Century Fund, 1962.

HOLZMAN, F. D. "Soviet Inflationary Pressures, 1928–1957." *Quarterly Journal of Economics,* May 1960.

HOLZMAN, F. D., ED. *Readings on the Soviet Economy.* Chicago: Rand McNally, 1962.

HORVAT, B. ET. AL., EDS. *Self-Governing Socialism.* White Plains: M. E. Sharpe, 1975.

HORVAT, B. *The Yugoslav Economic System.* White Plains: M. E. Sharpe, 1976.

HSIAO, G. T. *The Foreign Trade of China: Policy, Law, and Practice.* Berkeley: University of California Press, 1977.

HSIAO, K. H. *Money and Monetary Policy in Communist China.* New York: Columbia University Press, 1970.

HUNTER, H., ED. *The Future of the Soviet Economy, 1978-1985.* Boulder: Westview Press, 1978.

ISHIKAWA, S. *National Income and Capital Formation in Mainland China.* Tokyo: Institute of Asian Affairs, 1965.

KAHAN, A. AND B. RUBLE. *Industrial Labor in the USSR.* New York: Pergamon Press, 1979.

KOLAJA, J. *Workers Council: The Yugoslav Experience.* New York: Praeger, 1966.

LEEMAN, W. *Centralized and Decentralized Systems.* Chicago: Rand McNally, 1977.

LIU, T. C., AND K. YEH. *The Economy of the Chinese Mainland: National Income and Economic Development.* Princeton: Princeton University Press, 1965.

MACESICH, G. *Yugoslavia: The Theory and Practice of Development Planning.* Charlottesville: The University of Virginia Press, 1964.

MAO, TSE-TUNG. *On New Democracy.* Peking: Foreign Languages Press, 1960.

MILENKOVITCH, D. D. *Plan and Market in Yugoslav Economic Thought.* New Haven: Yale University Press, 1971.

NOVE, A. *Economic Rationality and Soviet Politics.* New York: Praeger, 1964.

NOVE, A. *Political Economy and Soviet Socialism.* London: Allen & Unwin, 1979.

PEJOVICH, S. *The Market-Planned Economy of Yugoslavia.* Minneapolis: University of Minnesota Press, 1966.

PRYBYLA, J. S. *The Political Economy of Communist China.* Scranton: Intext, 1970.

RAWSKI, T. G. *Economic Growth and Employment in China.* New York: Oxford University Press, 1979.

REYNOLDS, L. G. "China as a Less Developed Economy." *The American Economic Review,* June 1975.

RICHMAN, B. M. *Industrial Society in Communist China*. New York: Random House, 1969.

SCHWARTZ, H. *An Introduction to the Soviet Economy*. Columbus: Charles E. Merrill, 1968.

SELUCKY, R. *Economic Reforms in Eastern Europe*. New York: Praeger, 1972.

SHAFFER, H. G., ED. *The Communist World*. New York: Appleton, 1967.

SHAFFER, H. G., ED. *The Soviet Economy: A Collection of Western and Soviet Views*. New York: Appleton, 1969.

SHARPE, M. E., ED. *Planning, Profits, and Incentives in the U.S.S.R.* New Brunswick: Rutgers University Press, 1967.

SINGLETON, F. *Twentieth Century Yugoslavia*. New York: Columbia University Press, 1976.

SMOLINSKI, L. "What Next in Soviet Planning?" *Foreign Affairs*, July 1964.

SOLOMON, R. H. *Mao's Revolution and the Chinese Political Culture*. Berkeley: University of California Press, 1971.

SPULBER, N. *Soviet Strategy for Economic Growth*. Bloomington: Indiana University Press, 1964.

SPULBER, N. *Organizational Alternatives in Soviet-Type Economies*. Cambridge: Cambridge University Press, 1979.

TREML, V., ED. *The Development of Soviet Economy: Plan and Performance*. New York: Praeger, 1968.

U.S. CONGRESS, Joint Economic Committee. *Mainland China in the World Economy*. Washington: GPO, 1967.

U.S. CONGRESS, Joint Economic Committee. *Allocation of Resources in the Soviet Union and China—1977*. Washington: GPO, 1977.

U.S. CONGRESS, Joint Economic Committee. *East European Economies Post-Helsinki*. Washington: GPO, 1977.

U.S. CONGRESS, Joint Economic Committee. *Soviet Economy in Time of Change, Vols. 1 and 2*. Washington: GPO, 1979.

VANEK, J. *The Economics of Workers' Management: A Yugoslav Case Study*. London: Allen & Unwin, 1972.

VANEK, J. *The General Theory of Labor-Managed Market Economies*. Ithaca: Cornell University Press, 1970.

VELJKOVIC, L., ED. *Economic Development in Yugoslavia*. Belgrade: Interpress, 1968.

VUHINICH, W., ED. *Contemporary Yugoslavia: Twenty Years of Socialist Experiment*. Berkeley: University of California Press, 1969.

Why China Has No Inflation. Peking: Foreign Language Press, 1976.

WHYTE, M. K. *Small Groups and Political Rituals in China*. Berkeley: University of California Press, 1974.

Yugoslavia: Development with Decentralization. Washington: World Bank, 1975.

12

The
Less Developed
Countries

OF THE 4.3 BILLION PEOPLE in the world, roughly two-thirds live in nations called "less developed." There is no universally accepted definition of the term because of the enormous differences among the 110 disparate nations in this group. In this study, "less developed" refers to countries that portray all or most of the following characteristics.[1] First, the level of indigenous technology—perhaps the most important single criterion for separating LDCs from the major industrial countries and from each other—is extremely low. Second, financial and development institutions for absorbing external capital, management, and technology are inadequate. Third, the standard of living of the majority (as measured by food and energy consumption, housing, access to higher education, and life expectancy) is markedly depressed. Fourth, a very large percentage of the labor force is engaged in agricultural pursuits, and a relatively small portion in the industrial sector. Fifth, average per capita GNP is several times smaller than the corresponding level in the industrial countries.[2]

The less developed nations are commonly divided into two subgroups; some eighty or so relatively poor countries in Asia, Africa, and Latin America, which comprise the so-called third world, and around thirty absolutely impoverished nations in Southern Asia, Black Africa, and the Caribbean representing one-fourth of humankind—the fourth world. The relative poverty level is delineated by an annual average GNP per capita of less than $4,000 (in 1978). Absolute poverty is the plight of those with less than $360 yearly income.

1. Strictly speaking, part of the second world (the centrally planned economies) is also less developed. This chapter, however, refers only to the less developed countries in the third and fourth worlds.
2. As indicated above, these characteristics are not mutually exclusive. Some countries, such as, Kuwait, Libya, and Qatar, claim a GNP per capita of over $5,000, and yet they are underdeveloped by other criteria.

Although poor by comparison with income levels in both MICs and CDEs, LDCs themselves exhibit substantial differences of income and economic welfare. In the third world (excluding some rich oil exporters), Israel has a per capita income of over $4,000, while Egypt's is barely $390. In the fourth world, there are nations like Laos and Bangalesh with only $90 per capita GNP, and those like Senegal and Indonesia with $350. Adult literacy rates among LDCs range from 5 percent in Upper Volta to more than 94 percent in Argentina. Life expectancy stretches from a mere thirty-nine years in Ethiopia to seventy-three years in Spain and Greece.[3]

These differences in incomes and standards of living are a reflection of disparities in population density and growth, resources endowment, stage of economic development, state of technology, geographic location, and a host of other historical and cultural elements. These elements, in turn, have affected, and continue to influence, political orientation in the choice of decision-making mechanisms.

By Western standards, the majority of less developed economies are managed by a strong central government or other basic forms of command. Freedom House, an American private group that monitors levels of political freedoms around the world, lists only twenty-five developing nations as totally "free," meaning countries whose peoples are able to bring about changes in government at national and local levels peacefully and periodically. Some forty-eight others are considered "partly free"; the rest are judged "not free." Altogether, according to this survey, only one nation in three around the world lives in "freedom."

Contrary to the widely held assumptions in the conservative Western camps, the existence of political liberties in LDCs is not always correlated with greater emphasis on the market mechanism or higher priority for private enterprise. In almost all LDCs, it is generally recognized that private market forces and incentives cannot be solely relied upon to fight abject poverty and widespread inequalities of opportunity. Some of the countries on Freedom House's politically "free" list (India, Israel, Jamaica, and Turkey) possess very large and economically substantial public sectors. By contrast, some of the nations among the "not free" (Argentina, Haiti, Jordan, Sudan, and Zaire) have a larger private sector than public.

In much of the developing world, the economic structure of the national economy is divided into three basic, although overlapping, sectors. First is the state-owned and state-operated "public" sector, which is often subject to some kind of central planning and is most responsive to the national plan.[4] Second is the joint-enterprise sector (including the largely regulated sector) in which the state offers assistance and protection, but actual operation and management is left to private entrepreneurs. Third is the private sector (including the cooperatives), which in reality is neither totally free nor totally private, but is more or less independent of national planning and by and large subject to free-market forces.

---

3. For comparison of basic indicators, see *World Development Report, 1980* (Washington: World Bank 1980).
4. Thus, in the five-year economic plans of many countries, the planned figures for the private sector are only recommended, but for the public sector, they must be carried out to their fullest extent.

Consumers' Sovereignty

On the whole, by virtue of a large agricultural and largely self-sufficient base, a small-scale services sector, and traditional business mores rooted in individual ownership and operation, the size of the private sector in the majority of LDCs is relatively large. In most of the developing economies of Asia, Africa, and Latin America the private sector is also thriving. This reliance on the market is rooted in the fact that most LDCs try to avoid the excessive individualism of "capitalism" and excessive rigidities of "communism." India's Jawaharlal Nehru, the patron saint of younger and more radical nationalist leaders in the third world, recognized the significance of private initiative and private enterprise in his *democratic collectivism*. The private sector, he argued, was necessary to keep the public sector "up to the mark"; to provide an urge and a push behind it; to use the surplus energies of those not in the public employ; and to give people room to exercise initiative.[5] Many African leaders, although avowedly "socialist," have consistently pleaded for a type of "African socialism" in which individual freedom and initiative is given an important role. Even left-of-center leaders in Africa and Latin America have been strongly in favor of private activities. While "capitalism" per se is regarded as a "dehumanizer" of society and conducive to the concentration of economic power in a few hands, due respect is paid to the "benign" necessity of individual liberty, personal property, and private initiative and enterprise.[6]

Unlike the situation in the major industrial countries, however, the spread of private ownership and management do not go hand in hand with the relative influence of consumer sovereignty and the sway of market mechanism in each country. On the contrary, private ownership and operation in LDCs often accompany a good dose of planning, tight regulation of business activities, controlled prices, trade licensing, exchange restrictions, and various other forms of public intervention.

In fact, the driving force in most LDCs largely flows from the state in the form of national plans, direct government investments in infrastructures, public education and training, subsidies, tax reliefs, and supervised industrial relations.

Command Features

In the majority of developing countries, planning and public outlays serve somewhat broader and more comprehensive goals than in the West. Faced with specific underdevelopment problems—low levels of skills, underemployment, capital shortage, technological infancy, and inadequate financial institutions—LDCs often turn to planning in the hope of bridging the gulf that separates them

5. *Toward a Socialistic State* (New Delhi: All-India Congress Committee, 1956).
6. For details of these views, see P. E. Sigmund, Jr., *The Ideologies of the Developing Nations* (New York: Praeger, 1973), chapters 15, 16, 24, and 25.

from their richer neighbors. Planning in this larger part of the world is used to achieve rapid and deliberate industrialization. In many less developed countries, some of the more remarkable industrial achievements of the Soviet Union are paraded as living proof of the wisdom of industrial policy. Most of the difficulties resulting from the neglect of agriculture are overlooked or underrated.

This particular bias in favor of industrialization and socially oriented priorities is not hard to understand. First, most of the rich, advanced, and powerful nations are *industrialized*. Agricultural orientation is too often and too readily associated with backwardness or colonial status. Second, industrial growth can be achieved more easily than advances in other sectors, particularly agriculture: automated factories can be expected to produce regularly, but the weather is terribly unruly; urban workers can be brought under industrial discipline, but farmers are a peculiarly independent lot. Third, market-oriented historical development of America, Europe, or even Japan is considered slow, frustrating, socially inequitable, and—odd as it may sound to many Westerners—undemocratic. The favored development path in the underdeveloped world is thus planning for rapid, rational, and self-sustaining growth without the oppressions, hardships, and inhumanities that accompanied industrialization in the nineteenth-century.

Economic planning among the developing countries is frequently elite-directed, inward-oriented, and sometimes even romantically egalitarian. Not all planning by developing countries is necessarily geared to rational economic consideration, however, nor does it always result in economic gains. In some developing countries, the ruling elite, temperamentally or traditionally anti-Western or anticapitalist, often favors planning, because planning evokes both socialist idealism and Soviet economic successes. In others, planning occasionally serves as a kind of modern "opiate" for the masses, mesmerizing them with promising growth models that help to portray bleak futures as make-believe nirvanas. In still others, planning is a show of administrative respectability designed to attract foreign assistance, capital, and know-how. Successful plans in the developing world are those led by pragmatic politicians who manage to mobilize available resources within their cultural and administrative capacities toward obtaining realistic and feasible goals.

Indirect Controls

The public sector in the LDCs is managed on the same principles, and to a large extent by the same bureaucratic rules, as in the MICs. But in the private and regulated sectors where decisions are made or influenced by market forces or through delegation of power, there are additional reasons for state intervention. Two-thirds of the world's nations are *poor* by Western standards. Many of them are poor by almost *any* standards. Poor resources base, lack of productive facilities, the pressure of a growing and unskilled population, skewed internal distribution of income, and an ingrained sociocultural attitude toward work, leisure, saving, and enterprise are some of the major reasons for persistent reliance on state initiatives.

Almost all poor countries have an ambivalent, if not overtly unsympathetic, attitude toward "capitalism" (free market, private enterprise, and unbridled competition), but they all aspire to *development*, to a higher material standard of living. And they largely believe, with some theoretical justifications and for certain mundane reasons—that the key to their economic salvation is collective action.

At the core of this belief lies a strong conviction in the futility of incrementalism in the process of growth. The gist of this conviction is that piecemeal adjustments in the market are too slow or too feeble to produce desired reactions; that any realistic effort to get the underdeveloped countries off dead center involves a massive reallocation of resources; and that such drastic redeployments and radical readjustments require central direction.

Another common feature of the LDCs' delegated sector is a preference for a "democracy" of their own making and their own flavor. In postwar Asia, President Sukarno's "guided democracy" in Indonesia emphasized strong leadership and shunned "free-fight liberalism"; it allowed discussion and disagreement for the sole purpose of helping the leader make educated decisions without any process of voting. Nehru's British-style parliamentary democracy in India was to serve as a vital instrument for fitting individual initiative and freedom into the whole pattern of centralized social control of the economic life of the people. Ayub's "basic democracy" in Pakistan favored participatory politics only up to the level of the citizens' "mental horizon and intellectual caliber" and only for the purpose of producing a strong and stable government. Proponents of this brand of "democracy" argue that people do not have sufficient political maturity to determine who should govern them; that complex issues of a modern society are much beyond the personal knowledge and understanding of the rank and file; that national destinies cannot be made subject to individual exercise of sovereignty on the basis of Western-style representation; and that the most workable democracy in the developing nations is a choice of leaders, not one of issues.

In 1980, twenty years after the apogee of decolonization and political independence, three-fourths of African nations had chosen to live under a one-party system or military rule. Most Westerners attribute the growing popularity of one-party rule to Africa's tribalism, low literacy rates, poverty, disease, and a shortage of seasoned politicians and good administrators, but many African intellectuals believe that Western democracy is not the answer to Africa's problems.[7] To many non-Westerners, peace, national dignity, and long-term prosperity require a delegation of sovereignty by the people to their leaders, and not necessarily to their peers. Many, like Kenneth Kaunda of Zambia, see a true participatory democracy in a popularly approved one-party rule.

7. See, for example, K. A. Busia, *Africa in Search of Democracy* (New York: Praeger, 1967).

Latin America also has a long military tradition deeply ingrained in its entire sociopolitical fabric. In 1980, some three-fourths of South American land and almost half of the population were under the control of one-party systems or military regimes. Elsewhere on the continent, a major part of power, prestige, and money rested with the military. Many politicomilitary leaders defiantly claim that Latin America needs enlightened military authority against communism, atheism, political chaos, and public corruption. In economic policy, most Latin American governments are interventionist—with different emphases.

Pressure Groups

In the less developed countries of Asia, Africa, and Latin America, the scope of pressure group politics varies considerably. Where a relatively greater degree of trade-union traditions, notable advances in industrialization, and concentration of economic power exist, there is a mildly pluralistic situation. Rural one-party nations, on the other hand, function (and disfunction) with little or no countervailing forces. Others are situated somewhere in between.

In LDCs, the largely agricultural base of the economy, the significance of land ownership as a source of income and farm occupation, the prevalence of self-employment in the rural areas and the urban service sector, and the infancy of industrial development have not been conducive to the emergence and rapid growth of economic pressure groups. The function of unions in most LDCs is political rather than economic; virtually all are closely associated with some party or with the government. Unions with no political association are usually company unions or are an artificial creation of the state. LDCs' "political unionism" is often contrasted with "business" unionism in the major industrial countries and "productionist" unionism in the Soviet Union and other CDEs. The operating method of political unions is regarded as "political bargaining," as distinct from MIC's collective bargains.

Among other factors, labor's predisposition towards political objectives and the use of political means is attributed to the unions' connection with nationalist movements in Asia and Africa, the strategic position of industry in underdeveloped economies, and the relative weakness of the domestic political system. Thus, while most labor unions in LDCs are not yet a match for the dominant employers in the market, their political influence is considered quite disproportionate to their memberships, finances, or apparent organizational viability. Lacking industrial and economic parity with employers at the bargaining table, these unions have to rely on government support.[8]

8. In the majority of low-income LDCs, more than 60 percent of the labor force is still self-employed, while in the major industrial countries, the percentage of wage employment reaches as high as 80 percent.

But as the pace of industrialization and urbanization quickens along with bureaucratic growth; as a growing portion of the labor force comes to depend on wage employment; and as the power and activities of private business expands, strong internal forces gets underway toward the establishment and expansion of professional associations and organized groups[9] labor will be better able to organize and operate trade unions. The concentration of business activities will be boosted by the spread of manufacturers associations. Similarly, the state will assume an increasingly bigger role in determining wages and working conditions and in settling industrial disputes.

This chapter discusses the nature and scope of the various decision-making mechanisms as they presently exist in Brazil, India and Nigeria, the largest economies of Latin America, Asia and Africa. The examination of these countries mainly emphasizes the comparative significance of each mechanism. For a more thorough and comprehensive account of each economy, the reader should consult some of the references at the end of the chapter.

9 See Robin Cohen, *Labour and Politics in Nigeria* (London: Heinemann, 1974), chapter 8.

BRAZIL

The Federative Republic of Brazil, with over 8.5 million square kilometers of land and nearly 126 million people, is the largest country in Latin America and has the largest economy. In natural resources, too, Brazil's wealth is second to none. But in terms of per capita GNP, adult literacy, and life expectancy, the country trails Argentina, Uruguay, and Venezuela.

Brazil's political system has been one of a strong presidency with a sequence of military leaders at the helm since 1964. The direction and management of the economy have been entrusted to an accomplished cadre of technocrats and administrators responsible to the president of the republic.[10] Two special offices within the presidency—the Economic Development Council and the Secretariat of Planning—supervise the functions of economic ministries and entities. Government authority is divided among twenty-three states, four federal territories, a federal district, and four thousand municipalities within a federal system.

As in most Latin American countries, close relations exist between the government and the private sector. The regime has also been enormously successful in attracting foreign credit and venture capital. The avowed economic philosophy is free enterprise guided by the state.

Brazil owes its outstanding, even imposing, achievements in the areas of economic diversification, industrial progress, and rising exports (it is the world's second largest food exporter after the United States) mainly to its enormous domestic market. The latter has justified massive import substitution and an unparalled potential for sale of agricultural and mineral resources. The success is also partly due to the government's determination to create a modern, competitive, and dynamic economy. This determination is reflected in the iron grip with which the federal government has retained economic control over the allocation of investment capital in profitable ventures and in the way wages have been kept behind gains in productivity.

As in many other semi industrialized countries, such as Colombia, Egypt, Mexico, the Philippines and Turkey, Brazil shows a very rapid rate of population growth, a fast expansion of gross domestic product, and a relatively high spread of poverty. By a World Bank estimate, while the GDP growth in the 1970s has been nearly 10 percent a year, the average annual growth of population has reached 2.8 percent, and between 15 to 30 percent of the population have remained below the poverty line, that is, not able to purchase basic requirements of food, clothing, and shelter.

---

10. The Brazilian system has been described as "bureaucratic authoritarianism" based on a type of corporatism in which the state is supposed to cooperate with large national and international business interests and the technocratic middle class to the exclusion of other groups, particularly organized labor.

BRAZIL: BASIC DATA

LAND AREA (sq. km.)	8,512,000
POPULATION (1980 estimate)	126 million
Net annual increase (1970-78 yearly average)	2.8 percent
Urban (percent of total, 1980)	65 percent
Working Age (15–64) (percent of total, 1978)	55 percent
LABOR FORCE (total civilian, 1978)	45 million
Agriculture, forestry, fishing (percent of total)	41 percent
Mining, manufacturing, construction (percent of total)	22 percent
Services, etc. (percent of total)	37 percent
GROSS DOMESTIC PRODUCT (market prices, 1978)	$190 billion
Per capita (1978)	$1,570
Average annual increase (1970–78)	9.2 percent
Public consumption (percent of GDP)	10 percent
Private consumption (percent of GDP)	69 percent
Fixed capital formation (ratio to GDP)	23 percent
Savings (ratio to GDP)	21 percent
GROSS DOMESTIC PRODUCT (market prices, 1978)	$190 billion
Agriculture, forestry, fishing (share in GDP)	11 percent
Mining, manufacturing, construction (share in GDP)	37 percent
Services (share in GDP)	52 percent
FOREIGN TRADE	
Exports (percent of GDP)	8 percent
Imports (percent of GDP)	11 percent

Thus, despite the "economic miracle," over 40 percent of the national labor force is still employed in agriculture, producing about 11 percent of GDP with an annual growth of a mere 4 percent. By contrast, only about 22 percent of the work force in industry contributes some 37 percent to GDP with a growth rate of nearly 9 percent. The implication of this production pattern is an accute maldistribution of income to the detriment of rural areas.

Government's Direct Role in the Economy

The real size, scope, and influence of the Brazilian public sector are difficult to measure. This large and complex sector includes the central government (comprising the federal treasury, four large autonomous funds, and several hundred decentralized agencies and foundations). The government sector also encompasses the state and local political administrations, including their respective decentralized units. The central state and municipal governments also own productive enterprises. The state, in short, is the most important agent in contemporary Brazil.

State Planning

State dominance of Brazil's remarkable economic growth in the 1960s and 1970s has been exercised through a series of *indicative* plans in which public infrastructural programs have loomed singularly large. Brazil's first national plan was a three-year plan for 1963–65, which never got off the ground. A program of Economic Action was established for 1964–66. This was not a comprehensive plan but a program of coordinated work, setting forth the list of production and investment goals to be attained by the federal government, by public enterprises, and by the private sector. A really comprehensive attempt at planning took place under a new First National Plan for Economic and Social Development (1972–74), with the main objective of 8–10 percent real annual growth of the economy and 3 percent in employment. The Second National Development Plan (1975–79) aims at maintaining the 10 percent yearly growth achieved in the past. Planned projects totaling $100 billion are in basic industries, science and technology, and economic infrastructure. Industrial emphasis is in such areas as capital goods, steel, fertilizers, nonferrous metals, minerals, petrochemicals, paper and cellulose, pharmaceuticals, and electronic equipment. In agriculture, special attention is paid to livestock development.

The plan outlines the government's fiscal, monetary, incomes, foreign investment, and demographic policies. In qualitative terms, the plan aims at balancing the growth of various sectors instead of singling out the most dynamic one; a better distribution of badly skewed national income in order to expand the domestic market for Brazilian manufactures; a reemphasis on import substitution by assisting national firms; and long-term self-sufficiency in energy. The private sector is expected to provide the bulk of resources and managerial talent.

Public Enterprise

Despite the reputation for a capitalist-oriented economic management, the Brazilian economy is dominated by the state sector.[11] Public ownership and operation cover such activities as mining, railroad and coastal transportation, public utilities, iron and steel, petrochemicals, communications, credit and banking. Petroleum production and refining is a state monopoly. The central government wholly or partly owns almost two hundred productive enterprises. States and municipalities own another four hundred.

By some estimates, 70 percent of existing investments are in state-directed sectors and 35 percent in the state hands. Of the twenty-five largest firms in the economy in terms of assets, one-third are state enterprises, which account for more than 80 percent of total assets in the group. Of the top twenty-five in sales, eight are government firms responsible for over 30 percent of sales. Of the top twenty-five in employment, seven are public enterprises providing for more than half of all jobs. Furthermore, public firms, accounting for two-thirds of the hundred largest firms in the country, have been the pacesetter of Brazil's dynamic growth since 1968.[12]

Brazil's so-called "economic miracle" has thus been extensively underpinned by government planning, strengthened by heavy public investments, and accompanied by an ever-expanding public sector. On the whole, however, the general government's contribution to GDP (excluding public enterprises) is no more than 15 percent. The federal government's direct investment is small, and there seems to be of late a shift toward checking the growth of state involvement in the economy. Furthermore, the expansion of public economic activity has not been based on an explicitly "statist" ideology, but is a logical response to the imperatives of supporting economic growth.[13]

Indirect State Controls

Brazil's dynamic and bursting economy may be under tighter state control than any other economy outside the CDEs. Almost all major economic decisions are affected

11. The enormous escalation of "statism" in Brazil since 1964 continues to remain a controversial issue among practical politicians and members of the academic establishment.
12. By another estimate, in the more than five thousand larger Brazilian firms, over 37 percent of net assets belong to public enterprises, concentrating in certain basic industries.
13. See W. H. Overholt, ed., *The Future of Brazil* (Boulder: Westview Press, 1978), chapter 5

by the government in one way or another—directly or indirectly. The state uses its powers to finance and subsidize various economic activities.

Fiscal Policy

In fiscal policy, the role of the state is largely catalytic. The federal budget usually moves parallel to the growth of GDP, but state budgets and those of decentralized public units play a decisive part. Publicly affected investments—broadly defined to include investment by the general government, by public enterprises, and public-sector financing of private investment—come under a multiyear special budget and account for perhaps as much as two-thirds of total fixed capital formation in the economy. The government has been successful in both mobilizing domestic savings and in attracting foreign capital to finance this investment, particularly in the public sector. The total federal, state, and local tax burden in Brazil is also rather heavy, about 30 percent of GDP. Taxes account for between 90 and 95 percent of federal revenues. The main federal tax is a value-added-tax, called the industrial products tax, which brings in about 40 percent of current federal revenues. Federal income tax on individuals and businesses provides about 30 percent of total state revenue, and municipalities share the income from certain federal taxes; they also have a value-added tax levied on the various stages of production from manufacturing to consumption.

Financial assistance of many kinds is part of the budgetary expenditures. The federal government guarantees minimum prices to farms for certain commodities. A large part of the credit extended by the central bank and the financial system, particularly to the country's underdeveloped regions, involves interest subsidies. Basic food items are also subsidized by the state. Various fiscal incentives are offered to more than seventy favored industries in the private sector. Recent moves, however, have been in the direction of reducing these subsidies.

Monetary Policy

The federal government plays an important role as a financial intermediary through its National Monetary Council. The council is responsible for supervising the Central Bank and the Bank of Brazil, controlling monetary policy, regulating transactions in gold and foreign exchange, authorizing currency issue, regulating credit and lending operations of banks, determining minimum capital for financial institutions and minimum reserves requirement, and regulating securities exchanges.

Under the council's directives, the Central Bank of Brazil performs its monetary control functions (issuance of currency, control of money supply and credit, regulation of capital flows, transactions in government securities, and others) and also serves as a development bank. The publicly owned Bank of Brazil is not only the Treasury's fiscal agent, but the largest commercial bank and a substantial source of development finance. Large amounts of credit are supplied to the private sector by these two banks for a variety of objectives: agricultural investment, farm price supports, export promotion, and others. The two banks together account for about two-thirds of total credit extended by the monetary system. In addition to these main banks, Brazil's fairly sophisticated financial system includes several specialized federal development banks, private investment banks, commercial banks, savings banks, finance and credit institutions, credit cooperatives, stock exchanges, and other financial entities. Of these, the National Development Bank and the National Housing Bank are largest.

To control excessive expansions of monetary assets resulting from domestic commercial credits and inflow of funds, the Central Bank frequently resorts to raising rediscount rates, open-market operations, and legal reserve requirements. But because of the concentration of credit supply in the public banking system (and because some 40 percent of the population is still outside the money economy) effective use cannot always be made of these usual control instruments. Instead, monetary expansion is usually controlled by means of direct credit ceilings and the use of selective credit allocations—neither of which has been very effective. Other curbs are placed from time to time on consumer credit and housing finance.

Incomes Policy

Another instrument of monetary policy is a fairly extensive system of direct and indirect price and wage controls. By World Bank estimates, some 60 to 70 percent of industrial output is subject to some form of price control at the production level by an Interministerial Price Council. The key sectors of the economy—steel, petrochemicals, pharmaceuticals, cement, fertilizers, and automobiles—have their prices set by the council. Prices charged by commercial enterprises, nonpriority industries, and others enjoy "controlled freedom"; they must justify their increases before the council after the fact. Nonpriority or nonexempt products (utilities, gasoline, and subsidized items) must obtain authorization *before* changing prices. The prices of key items in the family basket at the retail level are decreed by the National Supply Commission. Price policy is also used to stimulate output. For example, a system of minimum producer prices for forty-two farm products is designed to ensure agricultural self-sufficiency.

Wages are variously regulated by the state. Since 1940, there has been a minimum monthly wage rate for unskilled workers. This minimum not only sets the pace and regulates all wages in the economy, but serves as a key norm for the establishment of some major indexes. The minimum wages (different for different regions) are adjusted twice a year by regional wage boards. While these adjustments are supposed to correspond to increases in the cost of living, actual revisions usually fall short of the inflation level. In addition to these minimum increases, overall salaries are periodically readjusted for inflation and productivity by the government on a set formula. Since 1978, there has been considerable scope for collective bargaining due to changes in labor legislation.

Monetary Corrections

A somewhat unique feature of the Brazilian incomes policy is *indexation*. Indexation is a system of "monetary corrections" whereby key prices (wages, salaries, utility rates, mortgages, rents, savings accounts, bonds, and the majority of other financial instruments) are periodically (and after a time lag) adjusted to the increases in the overall wholesale price index. This policy ploy is designed to help Brazilian income earners withstand high rates of annual inflation without serious erosion of their earnings. The same correction concept is applied to the exchange rate under the so-called "crawling peg," or minidevaluations (1 or 2 percent in the exchange rate every two weeks or so).

Most wages in the industrial sector and in public enterprises are further adjusted to rises in productivity through collective negotiations. In addition to annual indexation, most interest rates charged in the loan operations by financial institutions are subsidized by the monetary authorities and do not reflect market conditions. They include subsidized rates on most loans to the agricultural sector, loans for development projects in small and medium industries, and housing loans. Truly determined rates in the makret, non-indexed for inflation, run considerably higher.[14] Some of the interest subsidies were removed recently.

Trade Policy

Brazil's trade system is known for its long-standing policies of import substitution[15] and export promotion. The National Council of Foreign Trade formulates foreign-trade policy. The Customs Policy Council is in charge of formulating guidelines for tariff policy. The import policy of the public sector is coordinated by the Secretariat of Planning. In addition to fairly high ad valorem duties, the import substitution policy includes quantitative restrictions (or prohibitions) of imports into Brazil of items considered nonessential or superfluous. Ministries and public agencies are, as a rule, prohibited from importing machinery or capital goods if domestic equivalents are available. Almost all imports require a license. For certain imports, prior

14. In 1978, the rate on the indexed treasury bond fluctuated around 50 percent, and for consumer credit was around 70 percent.
15. This policy calls for the progressive increase of the share of local inputs in Brazilian manufactures, acceleration in the purchase of foreign technology, and an orderly substitution of all raw materials.

government approval is needed. There are other means for discouraging imports. Occasionally, import restrictions are lifted to help moderate prices of essential food items. Payments for current invisibles are regulated. The Foreign Investment Law stipulates repatriation of incomes from foreign investments, royalties, and technical-assistance payments. Travel abroad by Brazilians is free, but subject to a limited sale of foreign exchange.

Exports need a certificate to ensure compliance with exchange and trade regulations. Some exports are free from controls, but many others require prior approval of the government, and some are prohibited. Exports of certain commodities, such as beef, are subject to an annual quota. Exports of coffee are subject to authorization by the Brazilian Coffee Institute. Export policy includes a broad set of subsidies and fiscal incentives (exemptions from income taxes, customs duties, and other charges; tax credit; low-interest loans; export insurance and guarantees), particularly for manufactures. Capital inflows as loans or investment are subject to ceilings and require the Central Bank's approval. Occasionally there are taxes on exports for fiscal purposes.

Exchange Policy

Since 1968 Brazil has adopted a flexible exchange-rate policy whereby the exchange rate for the cruzeiro is adjusted frequently in relatively small amounts and at relatively short intervals vis-à-vis the U.S. dollar. These adjustments, under the so-called "crawling-peg" system (or minidevaluations) take into account the movements in Brazilian prices relative to those in the main trading partners, the level of foreign-exchange reserves, export performance, and the overall balance-of-payments position. The National Monetary Council handles the overall foreign-exchange policy.

To maintain a competitive export position, Brazil's exchange system involves extensive restrictions on current international payments and transfers. The country also engages in multiple currency practices for official payments, while also tolerating a grey exchange market for the cruzeiro at some discount from the official rate.

Social Welfare Policy

Since 1974, there has been a clear shift in the public sector in favor of a very significant expansion of social services in such areas as nutrition, education, health, housing, water supply, and old-age care. Government's other promotional activities include a state marketing agency that buys and sells certain key food items at fixed prices, agricultural credit at subsidized interest rates, a low-cost crop insurance, tax incentives in forestation projects and for fisheries, and financing and guarantees to private exploratory activities in mining.

Social insurance policy has been an integral part of Brazilian national objectives since 1923. Various civilian and military governments since then have expanded and reformed the original law to increase social equity. According to official figures, more than 90 percent of the Brazilian population (insured and dependents) receive some form of social insurance protection. There are several separate systems for different groups; the military, the civil service, urban workers, farmers, and so on. The largest system, with a budget second only to the federal budget, covers about 20 million urban workers and their families, or over 80 percent of the urban population. Benefits include cash assistance, medical care, and relief payments. The system is financed equally by both employers and employees, with a government subsidy to cover administrative costs.

Because of the enormous size of the country and its diversity of social forces, benefits and privileges available under the social insurance policy are not evenly divided among beneficiaries. A recent study of the Brazilian systems concludes that despite substantial reforms since 1964, the policy remains internally stratified and continues to have potentially regressive effects on income distribution.[16] Medical personnel and facilities, for example, are badly distributed, to the detriment of the poor and the rural people. Politically effective urban workers receive several times larger cash benefits than distant farmers. On the whole, the benefits from social insurance received by the poor and the rural population may not have compensated for development costs borne by them, as indicated by the continued regressive distribution of income.

Intergroup Bargaining

As in other developing countries with authoritarian regimes, the plurality of social forces is either relatively underdeveloped or kept strictly in check by the government. In Brazil, multilateral power centers do in fact exist, but their functions are limited to what the government considers "legitimate activities," that is, activities "socially-oriented" and in the national interest as defined by the state.

The major institutional groups in Brazil include the military, the Catholic Church, organized labor, and special-interest groups (employer organizations and the so-called economic oligarchies, such as the coffee interests, industrial interests, public employees, associations of professionals, communications media, and

16. According to the same study, social insurance policy has also been used by the authorities as a means of asserting government control over "unruly" groups, such as organized labor, resulting in the latter's "political emasculation." See J. M. Malloy, *Politics of Social Security in Brazil* (Pittsburgh: University of Pittsburgh Press, 1979).

sometimes university students).[17] Of particular relevance is the status of labor management relations.

Brazil, with its long history of strong state control over the economy and of military rule since 1964, is not a fertile ground for strong trade unionism or free collective bargaining. But within a narrow legal framework, the trade unions and the employers' unions provide the only faint challenge to the military regime. Ostensibly, the federal government strives to strengthen and multiply labor unions, to protect workers' legitimate rights, and to mobilize labor's cooperation in the service of national economic development. In ten years, for example, the number of Brazilian labor unions has risen from less than three thousand to nearly seven thousand. The Ministry of Labor offers credits and grants to trade unions for purposes ranging from the acquisition of headquarters to teaching of union administration. In return, the unions are expected to hew fairly closely to the official line.

Union Organization and Functions

Brazilian trade unions, while not exactly a creation of the state, have largely evolved and prospered under federal controls. Brazil's present labor code, tracing back to 1930s, is largely based on the Consolidated Labor Laws of 1943, the gist of which is preserved in the current constitution. Labor legislation is rooted in the concept of the "corporate state," according to which each economic sector, profession, and occupation has a single labor union matched by a parallel union of employers, and the government has the sole authority and responsibility to recognize these unions and to resolve differences between workers and employers. The labor code, while regulating detailed employment rules and working conditions, the minimum wage standard, a national social security system, and a series of social welfare benefits, severely restricts trade-union jurisdiction. The emphasis is on "collaboration" rather than conflict between employers and employees, and the duty of the state is to protect the rights of both groups.

Under the present federal legislation, the scope of bargaining between labor and management is relatively limited. Union organization in Brazil goes back to the 1890s, but labor militancy, industrial disputes, and strikes did not become matters of national concern until the 1950s and 1960s. The military government that came into power in the aftermath of the labor revolt in 1964 sanctioned the right of workers to organize, but under rigorous state control.

According to the prevailing Labor Code, a union is a voluntary association of employees, self-employed workers, or even employers engaged in the same or related activities. The main objective of unionism, according to the law, is to study,

---

17. For a discussion of the roles of these groups, see P. Raine, *Brazil, Awakening Giant* (Washington: Public Affairs Press, 1974), chapter 5.

protect, and coordinate economic or professional interests. Legally recognized unions can negotiate collective agreements on behalf of all workers in their technical or professional category (whether dues-paying members or not), represent these workers before other agencies, and charge dues. Unions have the obligation to collaborate with public authority to develop "social solidarity," to establish consumer and credit cooperatives, and to refrain from activities incompatible with "the interests of the nation." Furthermore, the Labor Code forbids the establishment of any single nationwide labor organization.[18]

Apart from these specific legal injunctions, Brazilian trade unions have a very narrow scope for collective bargaining maneuvers, because the law stipulates in detail worker benefits, working conditions, and even automatic wage adjustment procedures. As a result, the unions' functions are limited to providing social welfare benefits (medical facilities, vocational training, legal services, summer camps), monitoring employers' compliance with the Labor Code and bringing labor grievances before conciliation and arbitration authorities. The right to strike does exist, but is very narrowly defined within rigid, strictly enforced criteria. Furthermore, the incentives for strikes are weak: wages and salary revisions are automatically set; illegal strikes are severely punished; and most disputes are promptly settled by the state. Consequently, strikes up until recently have not been frequent or extensive. The labor scene, however, seems to be changing rapidly.[19]

Collective Agreements

While the right to free collective bargaining is guaranteed under Brazil's Labor Code, the issues normally subject to negotiations are better working conditions and fringe benefits. Wages are pretty much regulated by the government through periodic and automatic adjustments. Under the law, only officially recognized labor unions and employer associations may negotiate collective agreements. To become effective, these agreements must be subsequently approved by two-thirds of the membership of each party and by the Ministry of Labor.

Industrial disputes are resolved informally through Ministry of Labor intervention, conciliation and arbitration by the judiciary, or by the labor courts. Individual grievances not settled informally go to the Conciliation Board composed of the representatives of labor, management, and the state. If no agreement is reached, the board is authorized to arbitrate. Appeals of board rulings as well as

18. A minimum of five labor unions may form a federation, and three or more labor federations may establish a national confederation. There are presently eight separate labor confederations representing Brazil's major economic or professional sectors—in industry, agriculture, commerce, transportation, banking, communications, education.

19. Owing to the unions' limited power, de jure membership is not large. By current estimates, no more than a third of the work force (and perhaps as few as one-fifth) are formally affiliated with the country's 6,700 unions.

collective disputes are referred to the regional labor courts and finally to the Superior Labor Tribunal.

On the whole, the extensive direct role of the Brazilian state in the economy, specific Brazilian measures for combating inflation, and the widespread scope of the mulitnationals' ownership and operation are the main factors inhibiting the evolution and power of organized groups, particularly of labor. For this reason, the bargaining process is probably weakest in comparison with other decision making processes—and certainly dwarfed by the command mechanism.

Economic group pressures within the Brazilian economy thus derive from the business community, mainly through the National Federation of Industries, and from increasingly vocal trade unions. With prices constantly rising and the government anxious to project an image of being on the side of the workingmen and the poor, labor demands are on the rise. So are the strikes, which were dealt with severely under previous military regimes. With trade unions flexing their muscles in growing intensity, wage rates are likely to be influenced by the relative strengths of the bargaining parties.[20] The state, however, will continue to moderate wage demands through wage boards, industrial tribunals, and labor courts.

Private Sector and Consumers' Sovereignty

Notwithstanding the large and pervasive role of the state in the economy through the twin processes of command and delegation, major roles remain for private enterprise and consumer sovereignty in Brazil.

Private consumption accounts for over two-thirds of GDP, most of it on privately produced goods and services. Some two-thirds of domestic investment is also in private hands. All of agriculture (including livestock, forestry and fishing) employs two out of five persons in the labor force, produces some 10 to 12 percent of GDP, and is in the hands of nearly 3 million small, and over 350,000 large, private landowners.

The bulk of extensive and rich mineral resources (except oil and iron ore) is privately held. A growing and diversified industrial sector, composed mostly of small firms accounting for some 37 percent of GDP, is partly private. Foreign trade is in private hands, as are many services.

Brazil's Economy: An Overview

Brazil has achieved its breathless economic pace under strong government direction, protection, and controls. Thanks to a series of centralized and subsidized

20. In some observers' view, the present government's "opening to democracy" would have its immediate manifestation in the relations with trade unions and with wage policy bargains.

measures in exchange, trade, and related fields (minidevaluations, tariffs, import deposits, export subsidies, fiscal incentives, cheap credit, and a liberal policy toward foreign investment), the Brazilian economy ran farther and faster than almost all other developing economies between 1965 and 1980—becoming the world's tenth largest economy.

At the same time, however, under strong pressures from heavy costs of energy imports and an overly buoyant economy, the rate of inflation climbed to 77 percent in 1979 (not far from the rate in 1964, when the military took over), and to over 100 percent in 1980; the federal government's debt passed a staggering $50 billion, the highest for any LDCs; the balance of trade turned into increasing deficits, reaching $2 billion in 1980; and real wages declined by 20 percent in the same fifteen year period, thus worsening internal income distribution.

In the face of aggravating economic difficulties, far-reaching policies were adopted in December 1979 to combat inflation and external imbalances. The cruzeiro was devalued by 30 percent (on top of 19 previous minidevaluations during 1979 of more than 56 percent). Because of this large "maxidevaluation," export subsidies were eliminated. An export tax was established on primary products to divert some of the windfall export profits to help bail out companies with dollar debts. Government-subsidized credit was reduced. The budgets of large state monopolies were placed under tighter scrutiny. Prior import deposits were abolished. Further incentives were offered to capital inflows.

These measures reflected an apparent shift of policy in the direction of reducing somewhat the weight of the public sector in favor of greater scope for the private sector. But despite the austerity measures and the decision to reduce the government's involvement in day-to-day business transactions, the authorities seem committed to continued economic growth (at double the rates in Europe and the United States) and increased exports as the only way out of Brazil's raging inflation, lopsided income distribution, and foreign investors' growing reluctance to risk their capital.

The Brazilian experience shows that a pragmatic and forceful course of action between liberal laissez faire capitalism and doctrinaire socialism—the so-called state capitalist development strategy—may indeed achieve a high rate of economic growth, but it also demonstrates that the social, economic, and political costs of such growth miracles may be high—and may fall mostly on unskilled labor, the urban poor, and the rural masses.[21]

21. See D. E. Syvrud, *Foundations of Brazilian Economic Growth* (Stanford: Hoover Institution Press, 1974), chapter 11; see also J. M. Malloy, chapter 5.

INDIA

The Republic of India, with some 3.27 million square kilometers of land (the seventh largest country in the world), and some 675 million people (the second most populous) is a less-developed country which combines Western parliamentary democracy with central government controls in an Eastern setting. The Indian economy is one of the few exceptions among LDCs where economic decision-making is widely shared. At the same time, the country has one of the most elaborate planning apparati in the third world, and is also one of the world's poorest.

According to its constitution, India is a federated "socialist secular democratic republic" with twenty-two States and nine Union Territories. The Union (Central) Government has extensive powers in relation to the states. Local governments have relatively limited authority.

Under India's concept of a mixed economy, the responsibility for national direction and management is thus shared by the central and state governments and the private sector. Despite impressive advances in education and technology, India remains a critically poor country. More than one-third of the world's poor live in India, a large percentage of them in absolute poverty, and most of the rest with low incomes. Eighty percent of the Indian people live in rural areas, and seventy percent are illiterate. There are over 38,000 more Indians born every day. Forty percent of the population lives below the poverty line.

From independence in 1947 to March 1977, Indian democracy was dominated by the Congress party. The ideological basis of the Congress party under Jawaharlal Nehru and Indira Gandhi was a vaguely defined "democratic collectivism" with accompanying commitments to "pragmatic and flexible socialism."[22] In line with this basic orientation, development priorities tilted toward heavy industrialization, curbing of private economic power, and a mixture of high technology with traditional craftmanship. In early 1977, after coming into power of the Janata party, domestic economic philosophy veered somewhat from Nehru's time-honored populism to private enterprise. The industrial policy announced in 1977 sought to promote labor-intensive technology, to favor agriculture and small-scale industries, and to reduce regional industrial concentration. Industrial "self-reliance" and the stimulation of the internal market in preference to export led growth was emphasized. Income and employment generation for the lowest 40 percent of the population was the new objective. The return to power by the new Congress party in 1979 augured new changes once again.

---

22. In the All-India Committee of the ruling Congress party two resolutions were adopted late in 1972: (1) the takeover of wholesale trade in foodgrains, and stricter government control over the distribution of essential consumer goods; and (2) total government involvement in the "core-sector" industries.

INDIA: BASIC DATA

LAND AREA (sq. km.)	3,288,000
POPULATION (1980 estimate)	675 million
Net annual increase (1970-78 yearly average)	2 percent
Urban (percent of total, 1980)	22 percent
Working Age (15–64) (percent of total, 1978)	56 percent
LABOR FORCE (total civilian, 1978 estimate)	265 million
Agriculture, forestry, fishing (percent of total)	74 percent
Mining, manufacturing, construction (percent of total)	11 percent
Services, etc. (percent of total)	15 percent
GROSS DOMESTIC PRODUCT (market prices, 1978)	$115 billion
Per capita (1978)	$180
Average annual increase (1970–78)	3.7 percent
Public consumption (percent of GDP)	10 percent
Private consumption (percent of GDP)	70 percent
Fixed capital formation (ratio to GDP)	24 percent
Savings (ratio to GDP)	20 percent
GROSS DOMESTIC PRODUCT (market prices, 1978)	$115 billion
Agriculture, forestry, fishing (share in GDP)	40 percent
Mining, manufacturing, construction (share in GDP)	26 percent
Services (share in GDP)	34 percent
FOREIGN TRADE	
Exports (percent of GDP)	7 percent
Imports (percent of GDP)	9 percent

Government's Direct Role in the Economy

India's mixed economy is divided between a relatively small but influential public sector and a large (and markedly regulated) private sector. In terms of direction, influence, and the ultimate decision-making power, the Indian government relies heavily on delegated and command mechanisms. India, in fact, presents the most outstanding example of a large and developing mixed economy that makes significant use of planning and public directives outside the framework of communist ideology, and under a Western-type democracy. It also has vast public industrial undertakings. Given the character of the mixed economy, planning of the large self-employed sector in agriculture, household industry and services is minimal.

Development Planning

Since independence, India has directed its economy through a series of five-year plans, setting development objectives and allocating resources for their achievement. India's economic planning dates back to the establishment of the National Planning Commission in 1950. By 1980, six five-year national plans had been put in operation—the last one for 1978–83. This early and strong preference for planning, although never precisely defined by Indian leaders, is based on the assumption that the classical static equilibrium theory has little relevance for rapid economic growth in LDCs, and that balanced and democratic economic development in a poor country like India requires deliberate planning by the government.

The First Plan (1951–56) was aimed at creating a "just" social order in which every citizen had a right to an adequate livelihood; wealth and economic power were diffused; and ownership and control of productive factors were distributed in such a way as to ensure the common good. Subsequent plans have echoed the same objectives. The principal objectives of the Sixth Plan (1978–83) are: (a) the removal of unemployment and significant underemployment; (b) improvement of standard of living of the poorest segments of the population; and (c) direct provision by the state of some of the basic needs of those income groups.

Indian planning strategy has followed the Russian model in its comprehensive orientation, and the Western variety in flexibility and lack of direct pressure. Target rates of growth have been set for the whole economy. Each economic sector has its own target with varying rates for agriculture, industry, and so on, set for each plan. There is a target for total investment as a percentage of the GNP. The plans encompass both the public and the private sector. In the public sector, investment outlays are divided among various public projects and carried out by government agencies.[23] In the Sixth Plan, a new development strategy was envisaged. Past

---

23. The Sixth Plan's four-pronged strategy consists of (i) a rapid expansion of investment; (ii) an increase in the labor content of production; (iii) the provision of social services through a Minimum Needs Program; and (iv) area development at the block level. The average annual growth rate is targeted for 4.7 percent a year, with agriculture expected to grow by 3.8 percent, and industry by 6.7 percent.

experience had revealed that formulating the objectives of a particular plan period merely in relation to a specified target of growth for the economy had not proved helpful. It was realized that what matters is not the precise rate of increase of GNP but whether, in a given time frame, the planning process could ensure a measurable increase in the welfare of the millions of the poor.

The fulfillment of the private sector's investment outlays have been effected—with varying degrees of success in each plan—through government control and regulation of foreign exchange, investment licensing, tax concessions, and credits. On the whole, the plans have relied on price mechanism, collective-bargaining and profit incentives for their basic computation and coordination. For example, policies to promote small-scale industries under the Sixth Plan include credit allocation policies and such fiscal incentives as excise tax relief; advice on administrative, financing and marketing problems; and other assistance. The plans have tried to achieve simultaneously the somewhat conflicting goals of increased GNP, greater equality of income, increased competition, and social welfare. The Indian government prides itself on the fact that it gives every one of its citizens, political leaders, industrialists, economists, and labor leaders the opportunity to participate in making development planning a truly social process.

India's national planning has been perhaps the most comprehensive outside the Communist world. But the planning process as such has been subject to many criticisms for being too ambitious in its growth targets, too unrealistic in its projection of available resources, too centralized in its directed allocations, too concerned with urban development at the expense of rural construction, too reliant on foreign assistance, and often too wide of the mark in its results.[24]

Under the Janata government a new "rolling" concept was adopted under which a fifteen year "perspective plan" will be divided into three five-year periods: a detailed plan, an indicative plan, and a broad outline. Each plan would be in turn modified and extended every year with a five-year perspective so that policies could be adjusted to unforeseen developments. The technical advantages claimed for the rolling concept are that it would introduce a significant degree of realism and flexibility in the planning process and reduce the chronic and increasing shortfalls in targets and achievement observed in the past.

State Enterprise

Indian state involvement in the economy through ownership and operation was, for some thirty years under the ruling Congress party, essentially based on three basic

24. For further information on Indian planning see J.N. Bhagwati *India: Planning for Industrialization* (Oxford: Oxford University Press, 1970); A. Mehta *Economic Planning in India* (New Delhi: Young India, 1970); S. Swamy, *Indian Economic Planning: An Alternative Approach* (New Delhi: Vikas, 1971); and B.R. Nayar, *The Modernization Imperative and Indian Planning* (New Delhi: Vikas, 1972).

socioeconomic objectives: (a) a reduction in social and economic inequality inherited from the British colonial rule, a semi-feudal princely aristocracy, and a regressive caste system; (b) a centralized and coordinated development of critically important industries through state initiative, control, and direction; and (c) a benign surveillance over the direction and progress of the private sector (including the promotion of small industry, and import substitution). As a result of nearly three decades of planning, the public sector has acquired a dominant and pace-setting role in the economy. India's public sector now accounts for some 15 percent of GNP, and more than 15 percent in the total wage employment.

The bulk of government direct involvement in the economy has been concentrated in industry and basic services, while private enterprise has covered almost all of agriculture, small industries and craft, and sundry economic activities. The adoption of the socialist pattern of society as the national objective, as also the need for planned and rapid development, required that all industries of basic and strategic importance or in the nature of public utility services should be in the public sector. The Second Plan therefore classified industries into three categories, having regard to the part the state would play in each of them. The first category listed in Schedule A included seventeen strategic industries, ownership and control of which were vested in the government. These, among others, were atomic energy, iron and steel, heavy machinery, coal, oil, air and rail transportation, communications media, and aircraft. The future development of these industries was made the exclusive responsibility of the state. The second category comprised twelve industries: non-basic mining, aluminum, machine tools, ferro alloys and tool steels, chemicals, drugs, fertilizers, synthetic rubber, coal, chemical pulp, and road and sea transport, and in these the government would generally take the initiative in establishing new units with private enterprise supplementing the state effort. All other industries (including lucrative jute, cotton and tea) fell into the third category and their development was left to the initiative and enterprise of private individuals and private groups. However, industrial undertakings in the private sector had necessarily to fit into the framework of the social and economic policy of the state and be subject to control and regulation in terms of the Industries Development and Regulation Act. In general, however, it was recognized that such undertakings should develop with as much freedom as possible.

The Indian government presently controls 100 percent of the output in shipbuilding, aircraft manufacturing, coal mining, newsprint, telephones and cables and non-ferrous metals like copper. The state shares with the private sector between 25 and 90 percent of the output in machine tools, oil refining, steel, pesticides and fertilizers. Since 1971, the country's twenty largest domestic private banks, and all private general insurance companies have been nationalized. Between 1950 and 1980 state-owned or controlled enterprises rose from five to nearly 100 with their capital going to 47 billion rupees from a mere Rs 29 million.

Under the Janata party's new development strategy, the direction of the pattern of investment shifted to reflect the prevailing socioeconomic situation. In the new plan, since the highest priority was attached to tackling problems of unemployment and poverty and providing minimum needs, the investment strategy was directed to channeling resources to sectors such as agriculture and allied activities, irrigation, and cottage and village industries. The public sector was also made responsible for implementation of the Revised Minimum Needs Program, which included the provision of drinking water, adult literacy, elementary education, health care, rural roads, and housing in rural areas, as well as environmental improvements of slums in urban areas.

Indirect State Measures

As indicated, the Indian government, in addition to its direct involvement in the economy, uses a variety of economic and administrative measures to secure cooperation of the private sector in the fulfillment of the national plans.

Since 1947, India has tried to use the Western democratic decision-making mechanism in an Eastern, formerly colonial, setting. A resolution adopted by Parliament in December 1954 declared that the objective of economic policy would be to build "a socialist pattern of society." This pattern under Congress party rule called for appreciable increases in national income and employment, but also stressed greater equality of incomes and wealth. The resulting development strategy was thus based on the concept of social gain instead of private profit, and was meant to secure economic growth along democratic and egalitarian lines so as to reduce existing social and economic inequality. It was recognized that major decisions regarding production, investment, distribution and consumption had to be made by agencies enthused by social purpose if the benefits of development were to percolate to the lower stratas of society.

Thus, in addition to the vast number of *direct* controls on the economy, the Indian government has relied on a large array of *indirect* devices to ensure social justice. Various tools of economic policy—monetary, fiscal and others—have been employed in the service of these objectives. But, as in many developing countries with widespread poverty, a largely self-sufficient and poorly-monetized rural sector and underdeveloped money and capital markets, the use of monetary and fiscal policies have had a limited impact.

Monetary Policy

Control of the currency (rupee), money supply, and prices has been assigned under the constitution to the Union government. The state exercises this right through the Reserve Bank of India (the Central Bank). The Reserve Bank has the responsibility for note issue, control of foreign exchange, coordination of banking and credit with the five-year plans, and supervision of the domestic monetary system.

Modern instruments of monetary policy, however, have been effective only in industrial and urban sectors of the economy, largely in the four metropolitan regions of Bombay, Calcutta, Delhi, and Madras. The vast, non-monetized, rural areas have pretty much escaped such controls. Social control over a fair distribution of money and credit has been attempted since 1969 mainly through the nationalized commercial banks.[25]

Recent developments include commercial banks' branch expansion policy directed towards a reduction in rural imbalances, implementation of various measures to speed up the flow of credit to weaker and priority sectors like agriculture, small-scale industries, and small borrowers.

The creation of the innovative credit planning cell in the Reserve Bank was designed to draw up a plan for regulation and distribution of credit. More recently, the new rural credit planning cell has been created to ensure proper implementation of multi-agency approach to credit in rural areas.

Throughout the period of early planned development, the aim of the Reserve Bank's credit policy had been to restrain overall credit expansion and also to relate the expansion to the increase in production, and economic activity. More recently, it has been aimed at employment creation. Some of the measures employed to control credit have been the raising of liquidity ratios, imposition of penalty for default in maintaining SLR and cash reserve ratios, and requiring banks to restrict effective drawing power under cash credit limits in respect of large borrowers and raising of lending rates. The Credit Authorisation Scheme, introduced in November 1965, was a measure to align bank credit with plan priorities. Under the scheme, banks were required to obtain the Reserve Bank's prior authorization before releasing fresh credit facilities in excess of certain specified levels. The scheme has been a fairly effective instrument of credit regulation. Likewise, there is the framework of selective credit controls which seek to regulate advances against sensitive commodities such as cotton, sugar, oilseeds and foodgrains. The selective credit directives are modified from time to time to take account of the supply and demand and price position of the commodity, and to prevent speculative buildup of stocks.

The Differential Rates of Interest Scheme, operative since 1972, has been designed for the benefit of the weaker section of the population. Under the scheme, individuals below a certain level of income (not exceeding Rs. 2,000 in rural areas and Rs. 3,000 in urban areas) are eligible to obtain limited finance at 4 percent from banks. Credit policy has also continued to accord preferential treatment to exports

25. The nationalization of banks and insurance companies has been defended on the grounds that their private ownership and operation (a) neglected weaker sectors of the community; (b) did not effectively participate in the financial needs of the development plans; and (c) reinforced the economic power of vested interests in industry, agriculture, and trade.

in the form of refinance facilities to commercial banks and through concessional preshipment and postshipment credit. The Export Credit (interest subsidy) Scheme has been in operation for the last ten years and the scheme provides for compensating the banks for extending export credit at reduced rates to make up for their losses in interest earnings.

A few incomes policy measures have also been adopted to fight against inflationary pressures. For example, the Compulsory Deposit Scheme Act of 1974 required that taxpayers earning beyond a certain income level to deposit a variable portion of their income with the Central Bank at 10 percent interest. The Bonus Act of 1975 set the maximum bonus that could be offered to employees by private firms. However, in the context of the need to maintain price stability and to mobilize resources for investment in the public sector, a national policy of incomes covering wages, profits, rents and the income from self-employed with a redistributive bias is not yet in place.

Fiscal Policy

Taxation and expenditures are in the hands of the Union government and the states. Fiscal policy is used not only for the purpose of demand management, but also as a stimulus to production and exports. Conventional tools such as changes in the rate and base of taxation, tax holidays for industry, agricultural price support, export rebates, and incentives to savers are employed. Revenues are shared between the Union government and the states as determined by a Presidential Finance Committee. Central and state budgets are normally separated for current expenditures and for capital formation. Four-fifths of government revenues are derived from taxation.

The tax structure relies heavily on excise duties on consumer goods (40 percent of total). Personal and corporate income taxes produce 25 percent. Foreign trade taxes are responsible for nearly 20 percent. The rest emanates from state commercial activities and others. Since the early years of independence, a part of the growing capital expenditures has been financed by domestic and foreign borrowings. All levels of government also float their securities in the private market. Foreign, bilateral and multilateral assistance has covered a part of the deficit. The major public enterprises (e.g., electricity boards, irrigation projects and the coal industry) have been incurring losses in recent years and have had to be subsidized. Other smaller state undertakings have shown modest net profits. The central and state budgets provide famine relief to needy families, cost-of-living allowances to state employees, and also bear an element of food subsidies.

Due to the limited effectiveness of monetary and fiscal policies in the Indian setting, the central government has resorted to other devices for influencing the level and composition of economic activity. In addition to foreign trade regulations (which in many instances are akin to direct controls) the government's intervention has involved direct equity participation, quantitative credit allocation, foreign borrowing, and external assistance. The central government, through a wide range of measures (licensing, price controls, and investment) plays a significant role in the direction and expansion of private sector, the choice of industrial development and the fate of agriculture. Despite a huge inflow of foreign funds into India in the form of grants, the public debt (domestic plus foreign debt) now exceeds the total GNP.

Trade and Exchange Policy

Foreign trade policy is governed by the Imports and Exports (Control) Act of 1947. Under the act, the government is authorized to prohibit, restrict or otherwise regulate imports. India's import/export licensing system has the twin objectives of providing: (a) maximum support and protection for domestic industries to increase production and exports; and (b) conserving scarce foreign exchange resources. Import and export licenses are issued by the Controller of Imports and Exports. There is an elaborate and complex scheme for import licenses according to categories of imports. The importation of certain commodities (e.g., foodgrains, certain drugs, most fertilizers, some metals, and some raw materials) is reserved for the government or state trading companies such as the State Trading Corporation, the Jute Corporation, Steel Authority, or the Minerals and Metals Trading Corporation. Tariffs on imports are relatively heavy. Exemptions include foodgrains, raw cotton, and books. In recent years, the strict import policy has been liberalized, and India's industry exposed to more international competition.[26]

The objectives of liberalization were to transform a part of foreign exchange into resources for development; to buy cheaper imports to stimulate competitive exports and reduce industrial costs in the domestic economy, and to provide an element of competition in certain sectors of industry whose efficiency had suffered on account of excessive overprotection. On the export front, while the thrust of the policy towards promotion of exports has been maintained, the emphasis shifted from the earlier strategy of export-led growth to one where the selection of commodities for export promotion was to be made, mainly on the basis of dynamic comparative advantage, taking into account the domestic resource cost of the exportable commodity.

Export licenses are required for only a few items, and a few others are subject to annual quotas. Some exports (for example, tea, coffee, iron ore, and chromium ore) are subject to export duties. Others (such as mica, tobacco and handwoven carpets) are subject to minimum prices. A substantial number of manufactures receive cash compensatory support for export, and special facilities for import of raw

26. For elaborate details of trade and exchange regulations, see *Annual Report on Exchange Arrangements and Exchange Restrictions*, Washington: International Monetary Fund, 1980.

materials. The government also offers such incentives as cash subsidies, duty drawbacks, liberal credit facilities and the sale of industrial inputs to exporters at world prices. Part of India's trade is subject to bilateral agreements and payments.

India's exchange rate policy is administered by the Reserve Bank in accordance with the general policy laid down by the government in consultation with the Bank. The rupee, formerly linked to the pound sterling, is now valued on the basis of its relationship to a weighted basket of currencies of India's major trading partners. This has proved effective in combining flexibility with a degree of stability. The Bank, and its authorized agents, are ready to buy and sell foreign exchange at fixed prices. There are no taxes or subsidies on exchange dealings. The inflows of capital for direct investments in India are screened by the Foreign Investment Board. Payments for services require approval. Travel abroad is regulated under the Foreign Travel Scheme. Export proceeds for goods and services must be surrendered to the Reserve Bank within a specified period. Inflow of private capital requires Reserve Bank permission for initiating, expanding or continuing any business activity by non-residents. There are also certain restrictions on non-resident accounts. No foreign exchange sales are generally permitted for emigration purposes.

Policy on foreign investment and foreign collaboration has been formulated to attract investment in priority and technologically intensive sectors. Foreign investment and acquisition of technology necessary for India's industrial development, is allowed where investments are in the national interest and on terms determined by the government. As a rule, majority interest in ownership and effective control remains in Indian hands, but exceptions are made in highly export-oriented or sophisticated technology areas, and full foreign ownership has been allowed in the case of 100 percent export oriented industries.

Supportive Efforts

In other areas of intervention, the Indian government is also very active. For example, social justice and equality have been promoted mainly by a mild land reform program, by the establishment of rural cooperatives, and through aid to depressed regions. Concentration of economic power has been attacked through the Monopolies and Restrictive Practices Act of 1970; and through licensing of new industries and encouragement of collective bargaining. Economic opportunities have been expanded through a concerted onslaught on the caste system and preferential educational facilities for the lower social strata. In the area of financial assistance, supervised credit and technical assistance are provided to small farmers under the Community Development Program, rural banks and cooperative credit institutions.[27] Minimum procurement prices have been established for the major

27. Despite these efforts, more than two-thirds of rural credit is still being supplied by traditional village money lenders.

foodgrains, and price support has been offered to a few other agricultural products. The Food for Work Program was started in 1977 to enable state governments to augment their resources for maintenance of public works. The basic objective of this program is to generate additional employment opportunities in the rural areas by utilization of foodgrains for productive purposes and thereby establishing sound infrastructure for rural development. Payment of wages under this program is made in terms of foodgrains. Tax concessions have been extended to favored industries. Tariff protection has been provided on a long list of imports. Technical assistance, including preparation of feasibility studies, and supervisory services have been made available to new industries. The Industrial Development Bank and the Industrial Credit and Investment Corporation of India have extended various types of support (including equity participation) to hundreds of companies in the private sector. Insurance is offered to depositors. Bank credit to exporters is subsidized.

While there is no provision as yet for unemployment insurance in the Western sense for the organized sector,[28] the statutes stipulate workmen's compensation, wage payment regulations, disability insurance for industrial workers, survivors' benefits, safety and health standards, and maternity privileges. State health insurance schemes cover nearly six million workers and their families, totalling about twenty-five million persons. The Social Security (Provident) Fund covers over nine million subscribers.

There is no national minimum wage, but state governments are authorized to establish a minimum rate of pay for workers in certain industries. Basic wage rates are determined through tripartite negotiations. But the other two components of workers' pay, namely, cost of living (dearness) allowances and annual bonuses are determined by law (Payment of Bonus Act of 1965). Government's influence on wages frequently manifests itself in the mediation and adjudication of labor disputes regarding these two elements. More recently, the central government is also actively considering introducing the scheme of workers' participation at the corporate level, plant level and shop floor level. It is generally believed that workers' participation in the decision making process is crucial for achieving better working results in economic and industrial enterprises.

The Market-Oriented Private Sector

The private sector of the Indian economy is the largest and by far the most predominant. It consists of a relatively small modern industrial sector, a large traditional agricultural sector and a trading sector, including household and village handicrafts. Despite the Congress party's official commitment to an Indian-style "socialism," government ownership and operation is mostly concentrated in

28. Organized sector is defined as including all public sector agencies, and the non-farm private establishments employing more than a certain number of individuals.

strategic industries, banking and public transport and utility services. Both in organized and unorganized industry, a not insignificant segment is left to private ownership, and the dominant influence is still private. Even in such "basic" industries as iron and steel, the enterprise is partly in private hands. The private sector which includes the entire agricultural sector accounts for some 75 percent of GNP.

Considering the fact that modern industry (including mining, construction and electricity which are still partially private) constitutes only 26 percent of GDP and accounts for only about 11 percent of the labor force, the scope of the Indian government's entrepreneurial function is clearly rather limited. Agriculture, which supplies more than 40 percent of GDP and accounts for 74 percent of the labor force and 40 percent of export earnings, is private. Road and sea transport, the bulk of commerce, and professional services which roughly claim another 20 percent of the national income are also private, although suffering from a good deal of competitive imperfections.

On the whole, while private business decisions are subject to a honeycomb of government regulations, the prime movers of the Indian private sector are still market prices, the profit motive, and monetary incentives. The modern industrial structure of India's private sector is highly mechanized and quite concentrated. Indian heavy industry is generally dominated by a few firms.

For over two decades, the government's industrial policies were governed by the Industrial Policy Resolution of 1956, which resulted in the growth of per capita national income remaining inadequate, unemployment rising, urban and rural disparities being widened and sharpened, and the rate of real investment stagnating. To remove the distortions, the Janata government announced its new industrial policy on December 23, 1977. The accent of the new policy was placed on effective promotion of cottage and small industries. The list of industries exclusively reserved for the small-scale sector was expanded to cover over eight hundred items. The role of the large-scale private industries was related to a program for meeting the basic needs of the population. Large units engaged in the manufacture of items reserved for the small-scale sector were not allowed to expand their capacity.

Large business houses in the private sector were required to rely on their internal resources for financing new or expansion projects instead of relying on borrowing from public financial institutions and banks. Further, the expansion and diversification of large companies were made subject to the Monopolies and Restrictive Trade Practices Act and no new licenses were issued for giant industrial undertakings.

Intergroup Bargaining

The Indian subcontinent, diversified as it is in geography, ethnic variety, language, religion, politics and customs, is a prime candidate for major reliance on pluralistic decision-making. And yet, due to the less developed nature of its economy (and particularly the dominance of agriculture), countervailing forces in the Indian society are also somewhat underdeveloped. For example, out of an "economically active" population (labor force) of 265 million, less than 10 percent are salaried or wage earners and some less than 5 percent are in organized industry.

Like most other developing societies, India's industrial labor force is relatively weak in self-organization. While trade union rights were recognized in the pre-Independence Trade Union Act of 1926, and the trade union movement was closely identified with the struggle for nationhood, Indian labor unions are not yet economically viable. There are more than 18,000 registered trade unions, which for the most part are seen as financially weak, divided, and having limited bargaining power. Each of the major trade unions is organized along industrial lines and most unions are associated with a political party and active in the political arena. Union leadership is composed mostly of middle-class politicians, lawyers and socially-oriented activists; it leans toward politics, radical ideologies and intellectual pursuits. The unions' strength lie in their being one of the largest organized groups in the country; they form a mass base for political parties, and their militancy can have great impact on the economy. Leadership control over the workers is weak and wildcat strikes are frequent.

Total union membership of roughly about six million is divided among the Indian National Trade Union Congress (2.4 million), the All-Indian Trade Union Congress (1.3 million), the Hind Mazdoor (1.1 million), and Center of Indian Trade Union (0.8 million). The rest belong to many unaffiliated unions of lesser significance. Altogether, no more than one third of the labor force in the wage and salary sector is unionized. Both the absolute and relative low proportion of unionists, however, hide the significant strength of the trade unions in certain strategic economic sectors (railroads, mines, oil, plantations, chemicals, textiles and steel) and certain geographical strongholds (Bombay, Madras, Calcutta).

Industrial relations in India are loosely regulated by the Industrial Employment Act of 1946 and the Industrial Disputes Act of 1947. The first law deals with working conditions, grievance procedures and fringe benefits. The second, permits the government to intervene in case of deadlocks in labor-management negotiations. Since 1956, the tripartite Control Wage Boards (composed of the representatives of the central government, the industry and unions within each state) are in charge of wage recommendations in all major industries plus some other salaried sectors. Wage scales established by the boards may be challenged by the government, but they seldom are.

Paralleling trade unions are employers' organization, of which the Employers' Federation of India (representing over two thousand companies employing near two million working people) and the All-India Organization of Industrial Employers (covering nearly forty-five associations and one hundred fifty firms) are the largest. These organizations represent employer interests before domestic and international bodies, and nominate members of tripartite boards. In addition to lobbying before national and local government agencies, these two organizations (individually and through the Council of Indian Employers) advise and assist their membership in collective bargaining and industrial disputes.

Collective bargaining in the Western sense is not the common practice in India although the unions have acquired considerable bargaining strength over the last few years. Of the major organized groups, it is the government that wields the biggest stick and offers the sweetest carrot. State involvement in labor-management relations is strong and extensive. The reasons are many. First, there is no strict legal requirement for collective bargaining. Second, there is no rigid procedure for designating a particular union as the workers' exclusive bargaining agent, and many rival unions often compete with each other within a single plant. Third, employer-employee relationships are still partly based on traditional values of paternalism and loyalty which preclude strict adversary positions at the bargaining table. Fourth, most unions are no match in financial strength for the management. And, finally, there is no impartial outside arbitration of disputes. As a result, both mediation and arbitration of industrial disputes are mostly in the state's hands.

Collective agreements of relatively medium-term duration—four to five years—are concluded between labor and management. They usually contain provisions for wage adjustments, cost-of-living increases, and bonus payments determined by the government. Delays in effecting these adjustments during the life of the contracts, as well as employment security issues, are the causes of strikes and lockouts, of which there are many each year. In recent years, the loss of industrial production owing to labor unrest has been particularly severe.

Industrial disputes are first handled by the "work committees," composed of labor and management representatives in each organization of more than one hundred employees. In case of failure of such a voluntary machinery of disputes settlement, the state machinery is put into operation. The latter includes Ministry of Labor conciliators, boards of conciliation, and voluntary arbitration. Appeals from these bodies are referred to the labor courts, and industrial tribunals whose decisions are binding.

The Indian Economy: An Overview

India, like other developing countries, but with more intractable problems than most, has been in constant search of an effective way to economic salvation. India's independence from Britain was largely spurred by Mahatma Gandhi who believed in a rural-based economy, with the main emphasis on traditional agriculture and small-scale cottage industries. Jawaharlal Nehru and his successors, on the other hand, put major stock in national planning, heavy industrialization, capital-intensive projects and extensive government involvement in the economy.

The Janata coalition that replaced the Congress party in 1977 sought to reverse some of these policies in favor of rural rehabilitation, labor-intensive undertakings, and greater attention to the plight of the poor. With the collapse of the coalition government, however, the new orientations had little time to succeed. The result was that the targeted rate of planned growth failed to materialize, unemployment and labor unrest continued, and prices began to rise sharply in 1979. The people's mood changed and the electorate chose to return Mrs. Gandhi and her Congress party back to power—with new promises and new directions.

India began independence with political aspirations to be democratic, socialist, and industrialized. The economic counterpart of this national ideology was an emphasis on rapid growth, social equity, and self-reliance. The development strategy adopted to attain these goals stressed centralized planning, public enterprise, and regulation of the private sector. The central objective of public policy and of national endeavor was the promotion of rapid and balanced economic development. The five-year plans were intended as graduated steps in that direction.

India's land and mineral base, even on a per capita basis, is better endowed than many LDCs. Human resources are plentiful, with an abundant stock of technical and managerial skills. And the one invaluable legacy of the colonial era has been the inheritance of modern administrative machinery. On the liability side, there was a shortage of basic infrastructure facilities, including social services (particularly transport and communications); demographic pressures; and the scarcity of savings and foreign exchange. The continuous pressure of population on the largely weather-influenced food supply has been the single largest constraining factor to growth. In all other respects, however, India's economic liabilities were no larger than most LDCs, while its economic assets compared rather favorably with many.

Against this relatively favorable potential for development, India's progress seems to have been both modest and uneven.[29] India's average annual growth rates of GDP in the 1960s and 1970s of 3.6 percent and 3.7 percent have been consistently below the averages for the LDCs (4.9 percent and 4.7 percent); the growth rates have been decidedly lower than those of middle-income LDCs—6 percent and 5.7 percent. Furthermore, there have been increasingly larger shortfalls in the total and sectoral targets of India's five-year plans. The average GNP growth per capita during 1960-78 has been only 1.4 percent.

With respect to social equity, that is, the distribution of wealth, income disparities, and social welfare, the success has also been limited: inequalities of wealth and income persist and do not seem to have been narrowed, and social services seem to have been unequally shared by the urban and rural populous.

29. For a detailed and documented analysis of India's economic development see L. A. Veit, *India's Second Revolution* (New York: McGraw-Hill, 1976), particularly chapters 11 and 12.

Finally, the goal of self-reliance has proved most difficult to attain, due to the ambitiousness of the heavy industrialization strategy in the face of inadequate levels of skills, resources, and markets. India has in fact had to receive credits, technology and management know-how from abroad. Net external assistance provided between 1 to 3 percent of GDP, and nearly 5 percent of total investment outlays. The problems of unemployment, poverty, and precarious food supply still stubbornly persist. In short, despite the growth of the economy and the per capita GNP, India has so far progressed perhaps still too slowly and too erratically to meet either the demands of its urban élite or the needs of its rural masses.

On the favorable side, however, agricultural production has risen, and the production of foodgrains has increased to levels which have made the economy virtually self-sufficient at current low levels of per capita consumption. The country has also built up a grain reserve and discarded its reliance on food imports. At the same time, a stagnant and dependent economy had through the planned process been modernized and made more self-reliant. Despite the growth of population and population pressures, a modest rate of growth per capita income has been maintained.

On the industrial front, over the years the country has been made self-sufficient in most consumer goods and in basic commodities like steel and coal, while the capacity of industries like fertilizer, chemicals, have grown rapidly. The growth of capital goods production has shown impressive increases and the country is now in a position to sustain the growth of most of the industries such as textiles, sugar manufacturing, food processing, metallurgical and engineering industries by domestic production of capital goods supplemented with only marginal imports. The development of productive capacity has been particularly phenomenal in the area of energy resources. Output of coal has expanded threefold. Exploration of oil and gas, both on-shore and off-shore, launched in the 50s, is expected to pay off rich dividends.

On the external trade front, there has been considerable diversification of export trade. Besides exports of primary products, sizeable proportion of exports are comprised of manufactures and mineral ores. In recent years, the export strategy has been to enlarge consistently the value-added exports. Over the planned period, a sizeable measure of import substitution has taken place, but import substitution and export promotion have been achieved at an unduly high cost to the economy.

While Western-oriented analysts are prone to attribute India's lackluster economic performance to its leaders' preoccupation with non-economic issues (military superiority in the region, internal factionalism, feuds with neighbors, etc.), and their doctrinaire concern for socialism, planning and heavy industry[30], other observers find that India's salvation will be only with a mass rebellion and the

30. See L.A. Veit, op.cit., chapter 12; and V. Dagli (ed.) *Twenty-Five Years of Independence: A Survey of Indian Economy* (Bombay: Vora, 1973).

establishment of a Soviet-type economy.[31] Although it is not easy to ascertain the growth-inhibiting influence of socialist ideology in India's economic development, there is perhaps little argument about the major weaknesses of Indian development strategy. Such factors as insufficient emphasis on agriculture, lack of balance between supply of consumer and capital goods, too heavy reliance on an inefficient public sector, excessive tolerance of economic concentration in the private sector, too great a stress on protected import substitution at the expense of competitive export promotion, and finally an excessive trust in comprehensive national planning, for a country as vast and diversified as India, without adequate technical and administrative resources—all these are among India's strategy shortcomings. Given the familiar traditional, cultural, and demographic obstacles to growth, however, there is no certainty that India's overall economic performance would have been much different under a different ideology. The Janata party's brief and unsuccessful move on a non-socialist path may be a fair indication of this uncertainty.

31. See B. Davey, *The Economic Development of India: A Marxist Analysis* (Bristol: Spokesman Books, 1975).

NIGERIA

Nigeria is Africa's most populous country, with more than 85 million people in its 924,000 square kilometers of territory. It is a federated republic with nineteen states. Until September 1979, Nigeria was under a Supreme Military Council, which combined the executive and legislative functions and ruled by decrees. Thereafter, the country returned to civilian rule.

With less than $600 per capita GNP, a high illiteracy rate, and a life expectancy of less than fifty years, Nigeria is among the lowest fifth of the middle-income LDCs. And yet the country's GNP is larger than that of all other black African nations combined. In recent years, oil has been the mainstay of the Nigerian economy. Ninety percent of export earnings, 75 percent of the government revenues, and 25 percent of GDP come from oil. Nigeria now displays many of the main features of an economy under dualistic conditions where the dominant sector—petroleum—dwarfs all others in all economic aspects except employment. And yet the oil industry is structurally segregated from the rest of the economy, having very little real links—forward or backward—with other sectors.

Government's Direct Role in the Economy

Within the framework of the Nigerian government's commitment to building "a free democratic society" and a market economy, the scope of direct public participation in the economy is noteworthy. The government, since independence, has continued to play a dominant role in Nigeria's economic development. With more than 1 million people on its payroll, the federal government is the largest employer of salaried Nigerians. It is also the largest exporter and importer in the country.

Development Planning

In the postwar period, the Nigerian economy has been directed by a series of national development plans.[32] The First National Plan (1962–68) had the modest goals of 4 percent annual growth rate and 1 percent annual increase in per capita consumption; it also had a modest annual investment of only 15 percent of GDP, financed mostly by external aid. The plan was interrupted by the 1966–69 civil war,

---

32. For similar attempts at regional planning, see K. M. Barbour, ed., *Planning for Nigeria* (Ibadan: Ibadan University Press, 1972). See also C. K. Eicher and C. Liedholm (eds.), *Growth and Development of the Nigerian Economy* (East Lansing: Michigan University Press, 1970).

NIGERIA: BASIC DATA

LAND AREA (sq. km.)	924,000
POPULATION (1980 estimate)	85 million
Net annual increase (1970-78 yearly average)	2.5 percent
Urban (percent of total, 1980)	20 percent
Working Age (15–64) (percent of total, 1978)	54 percent
LABOR FORCE (total civilian)	30 million
Agriculture, forestry, fishing (percent of total)	56 percent
Mining, manufacturing, construction (percent of total)	17 percent
Services, etc. (percent of total)	27 percent
GROSS DOMESTIC PRODUCT (market prices, 1978)	$45 billion
Per capita (1978)	$560
Average annual increase (1970–78)	6.2 percent
Public consumption (percent of GDP)	15 percent
Private consumption (percent of GDP)	57 percent
Fixed capital formation (ratio to GDP)	30 percent
Savings (ratio to GDP)	28 percent
GROSS DOMESTIC PRODUCT (market prices, 1978)	$45 billion
Agriculture, forestry, fishing (share in GDP)	34 percent
Mining, manufacturing, construction (share in GDP)	43 percent
Services (share in GDP)	23 percent
(Petroleum)	(15 percent)
FOREIGN TRADE	
Exports (percent of GDP)	33 percent
Imports (percent of GDP)	33 percent

and projected foreign funds were not obtained, yet some major projects were completed: an oil refinery, a paper mill, a sugar mill, the Niger dam and bridge, some trunk roads, and port facilities. Some of the plan's main projects, however, notably the iron and steel plant, were not started.

The Second National Plan (1970–74) was announced in 1970 with broader scope and loftier goals than the previous one. The plan envisaged an annual growth rate of 6.6 percent resulting from a total public investment of some $2.5 billion. Public-sector capital formation was divided equally between the federal and twelve state governments.[33] Priority was given to transportation, manpower training, agriculture, commerce, and water development, in that order. The private sector was expected to invest about $2.3 billion on its own in manufacturing, mining, construction, and distribution.

The Third National Development Plan (1975–80), launched in 1975 and revised in 1977, calls for the expenditure of more than $58 billion, largely by the federal and state governments, local authorities, statutory corporations, and state companies. The private sector is assigned less than 30 percent of the total. The main objective of the plan is the diversification of the economy. As part of this diversification effort, public policy is aimed at eventual self-sufficiency in petroleum products, petrochemicals, pulp, paper, and sugar. Targeted for specific improvements are agriculture, infrastructure, education, health, transport and communications, water, housing, and energy. Emphasis is also placed on the state's role in promoting social and economic equality. In line with the broader objectives of national planning in other LDCs, the Nigerian Third Plan calls for restoring price stability and promoting a more equitable distribution of income. The plan envisions slightly more than 9 percent in annual real growth. Halfway through its course however, the plan, proved too ambitious for available resources and had to be trimmed down.

In none of Nigeria's postwar national plans was employment a primary planning objective. The plans simply defined sectoral investment targets and treated their employment implications as granted. Interestingly enough, the goals of growth and employment were seen as incompatible in the Nigerian case, for planning efforts were directed toward industrialization with capital-intensive technology.

Public Enterprise

Nigerian public entities consist of federal statutory corporations and state-owned companies. The drive toward increased participation of the government in Nigeria's industrial development was signaled by the Second Plan (1970–74), whereby the

33. The number of states was raised to nineteen in 1976.

prevailing policy of aid to the private sector (including foreign investments) was shifted to ensure that the economic destiny of Nigeria would be determined by Nigerians themselves. This policy has been continued and incorporated in the Third Plan. Under the Companies Decree of 1968 and the Nigerian Enterprises Promotion Decree of 1972, as amended, state participation in ownership and operation of business is reserved for strategic industries and for ventures where capital is unavailable or Nigerians unwilling to invest. The federal government owns and operates such activities as radio, TV and telephone service; electric power; rail, sea, and air transportation; water supply; and such other strategic industries as petroleum, iron and steel, and banking. The nineteen state governments, in turn, own large and often majority shares of stock in joint public-private enterprises: petroleum, cement, textiles, food and beverages, consumer products and services, dams and port authorities. Each state government has control over its export crop, such as palm oil, cocoa, peanuts, soybeans, and copra. There are also state companies in construction, banking, insurance, and printing.

There are some twenty-four public corporations under federal government authority. In banking, the state has 60 percent control of all commercial and merchant banks in which there is foreign minority participation. Furthermore, the Nigerian Agricultural Bank, the Nigerian Bank for Commerce and Industry, and the Nigerian Industrial Development Bank, along with the Mortgage Bank and the Savings Bank, are federally controlled. In transportation, Nigeria's rail system is owned by a semiautonomous public enterprise. In power, the lion's share of electricity is supplied by the National Electric Power Authority. Despite all these undertakings, however, the federal, state, and local governments account for no more than 15 percent of the GNP.

Indirect State Intervention

Since its independence in 1960, Nigeria has followed a mixed variety of indirect controls for the management of the economy. Government indirect intervention in the economic life of the country through these controls is officially described as a means of protecting and promoting the public interest.[34] The thrust of these efforts has been directed toward an increase in agricultural productivity, supplying infrastructure facilities, expanding and improving public education, and industrialization via modern technology.[35]

34. See *Second National Development Plan, 1970–74* (Lagos: Federal Ministry of Information, 1970), p. 32.
35. See G. K. Helleiner, *Peasant Agriculture, Government, and Economic Growth in Nigeria* (Homewood: Irwin, 1966).

The Structure of Public Finance

Nigeria's public sector comprises the federal government, nineteen state governments, more than one hundred local authorities, and a number of nonfinancial public industrial and commercial corporations. State and local governments have their own sources of revenue, receive a share of income from the federal government, and can borrow directly in the capital market.

Nigeria's revenue system encompasses three basic taxes: income, capital gains, and oil profits. There are also taxes on international trade, excise duties on a wide range of consumer items, and charges on air travel and toll roads. While tax rates and tax collection have risen in recent years, the federal, state, and local governments have incurred persistent deficits. Most industrial and commercial enterprises in the public sector, with the exception of the National Electric Power Authority and the Nigerian External Telecommunications, Ltd., have been incurring both overall and operational deficits, which are covered by transfers from the federal budget.

Fiscal measures have thus been used for raising public revenues, checking expansion of consumer demand, encouraging growth of private savings and investment, influencing direction and structure of capital formation, safeguarding the national balance-of-payments position, and protecting home industries.

Money and Credit Policy

The banking system in Nigeria comprises the Central Bank, nineteen commercial and five merchant banks, both Nigerian and joint, several development banks, plus a federal mortgage bank and a federal savings bank. The formal credit market, in addition to these banks, includes several finance corporations at the state level, insurance companies, and stock exchanges. All foreign-affiliated banks are 60 percent owned by the federal government.

The Central Bank's credit policy is aimed principally at regulating commercial bank credit to the private sector. Monetary policy is conducted largely through credit guidelines, sectoral credit allocations, maximum ceilings on credit expansion, regulation of loans maturity, compulsory advance deposit obligation for imports, choice of borrowers, a special tax on excess banking profit, a liquidity ratio obligation, cash reserve requirements, and others. The Nigerian Central Bank regulates the interest charged for consumer loans. In recent years, in addition to fixing the minimum and maximum lending rates, the Central Bank has established specific rates for lending to certain sectors. Nigeria's monetary policy has thus been geared toward domestic wage-price stabilization, support for expanding levels of capital formation, provision of private development finance, and the strengthening of balance of payments.

Trade and Exchange Policies

The arsenal of intervention techniques used by the government includes foreign trade and exchange policies, as well as the regulation of business activities and the promotion of private enterprise.

Foreign-trade policy and the administration of trade controls are the responsibility of the Federal Ministry of Trade and the Import Quota Allocation Committee. All imports are subject to a specific or general license. Some imports are banned in order to protect local industries; others are allowed under specific conditions. Imports of invisibles are subject to approval. By LDC standards, Nigerian tariff rates are fairly moderate. The principal objectives are to protect infant industries and to encourage further import substitution. Items imported by the public sector or considered essential to economic development are duty free. Luxury goods and nonessentials are taxed up to 200 percent. Raw materials needed in local industries and construction inputs are taxed as low as 10 percent.

Export policy is under the general direction of the Export Commodity Coordinating Council. Most farm products are subject to export controls. Exports to certain countries are prohibited, as are exports of many food items to ensure adequate domestic supply. Industrial export licenses are required for certain other commodities, such as petroleum. All other goods may be exported without a license. Under the Customs Drawback Regulations, duties paid on raw materials used in exports are refundable. A single tariff schedule exists for certain export items. Petroleum exports are subject to special arrangements.

The Exchange Control Act of 1962, as amended, stipulates the rules governing exchange transactions, repatriation of foreign capital and dividends, negotiation of foreign loans, and dealings in foreign securities. The power is vested in the Federal Ministry of Finance. Under the law, Nigeria follows a flexible exchange-rate policy. The rate for the national currency—the naira—is determined on the basis of a basket of seven currencies and quoted each day by the Central Bank. The exchange-control policy is in the hands of the Federal Ministry of Finance. All exchange transactions by the Central Bank and other authorized banks are for cases approved by the ministry. There are restrictions on nonresident accounts in Nigerian banks. Payments for imported goods, services, and travel are subject to restrictions and limitations. Export proceeds from goods or services must be surrendered to the Central Bank within a short period. Foreign borrowing must have the prior approval of the Federal Ministry of Finance. Equity participation by foreigners in Nigerian businesses is subject to the provision of the indigenization decree of 1972, as amended in 1977.

Quantitative Controls

While the pre-civil-war government of Nigeria showed little inclination toward wage-price control, exchange restrictions, or quantitative prescriptions in the economy, the war and its aftermath made these controls a semipermanent part of public policy. Under the Second National Plan, a Wage and Salaries Review Commission was set up to review individual incomes in the public sector with a view to harmonizing them with remunerations in the private sector. Rent and price controls were also instituted in some areas and for certain activities.

In 1976, in order to curb a high rate of inflation, the government adopted an incomes policy, followed by price guidelines. Price controls were exercised on basic food staples as well as petroleum products. On decontrolled items, the price guidelines allowed price increases only when higher costs could not be painlessly absorbed by company profits. Enterprises were also expected to pass on to consumers the tax concessions granted to them.

A policy of wage restraint was also adopted by the government in 1976–77. The wage guidelines permitted wage and salary increases under specific conditions. Annual merit increases, promotions, and larger fringe benefits were also included in the guidelines. All general increases required the approval of the commissioner of labor. There was also a ceiling on the percentage of dividends that could be paid out of profits. Scrip or bonus shares to stockholders were prohibited.

Regulation of Business Activities

In the area of public regulation, the state control of business activities in Nigeria in recent years has been exercised through a series of decrees dealing with various aspects of the economy. Thus, the Price Control Decree (1977) charges the Price Control Board with: surveillance over the structure of basic prices in the economy, stabilization of general price levels and control of profiteering, and protection of low-income earners. The chief responsibility of the board is to fix a "basic price" for any controlled commodity. The basic price is equal to the cost of production plus normal profits for domestic goods, and the bonded cost plus profits for imports. Offenders are prosecuted by the board before a special Price Control Court.

The Capital Issues Decree (1973), implemented by the Capital Issues Commission, requires companies that intend to sell shares of stock or debentures to the public to seek prior approval of the government on the price of the shares, the timing, and the amount of sale. The Capital Issues Commission, charged with enforcing the law, investigates the financial position of companies seeking public offers and approves or disapproves the issue. Violators are referred to the special Federal Revenue Court.

The Nigerian Enterprises Promotion Decree aims at promoting greater participation by Nigerians in business activities. Working through the Nigerian Enterprises Promotion Board, the law requires the acquisition by Nigerians of certain percentage of shares of business firms owned by foreigners. The board advises the Ministry of Industry on the promotion of Nigerian enterprises and helps the minister in the prompt indigenization of the Nigerian economy. The board also has the power to enforce compliance with the law. As of January 1979, all ventures are placed in one of three schedules: those concerns reserved exclusively for Nigerians; entities that must have at least 60 percent Nigerian control; and firms in which the minimum Nigerian citizen participation is 40 percent. This policy of Nigeriazation is not, however, the same as nationalization.

Promotion of Private Enterprise

The government's promotional activities include a National Accelerated Food Production program to help farmers produce more and higher-quality farm products on a wider range. A related Operation Feed the Nation program is aimed at self-sufficiency in foodstuffs through improved production techniques, greater use of fertilizers, and better seeds. In both programs, the state provides the necessary inputs at subsidized rates. The Third Plan also offers higher producer prices to cash and export crops (cocoa, ground nuts, and palm oil). In industry, the government provides incentives to encourage decentralization and diversification. Tariff and nontariff restrictions are also provided to help infant industries. The Industrial Development (Income Tax Relief) Decree (1971) exempts from income taxes all Nigerian corporations under the "approved status" and engaged in "pioneer industries." Furthermore, the Nigerian tax system allows accelerated depreciation of assets as an additional incentive to fixed capital formation.

The Scope of the Market and Consumer Sovereignty

The Nigerian private sector constitutes the largest sector of the Nigerian economy. It accounts for vital development activities in agriculture, manufacturing, mining, construction, and distribution. Altogether, about 95 percent of the Nigerian labor force is employed in private-sector activities, which constitute nearly 70 percent of GDP.

The agricultural sector, cultivating only about half of the country's arable land, mostly consists of subsistence farmers. Ninety-five percent of farming is done on small farms of two hectares or less. Farming itself, however, contributes less than 20 percent to GDP. Growing at a real annual rate of 1 to 2 percent, a farm output is constantly exceeded by the growth of population. Commerce and manufacturing, including handicrafts are the second largest employer of labor after agriculture.

Intergroup Bargaining

The strongest and most effective bargaining group in Nigeria is the labor union. Nigeria's labor force is roughly estimated to be on the order of 30 million: 56 percent in agriculture and related activities, 17 percent in mining and manufacturing, and 27 percent in services. Wage employment accounts for about 10 percent of the gainfully employed. Others are self-employed, sharecroppers, or otherwise earning their living.

The Nigerian labor movement, concentrated on only about one-third of wage-earners, had its first central organization in 1943, but has since divided into some twenty-five union centers or federations. Five central organizations with nearly six hundred affiliated unions dominated the scene in the early postwar period. In 1977, the more than two hundred existing trade unions were further consolidated into seventy industrial unions. In March 1978, all Nigerian unions were grouped into the Nigerian Labor Congress. The NLC serves as labor spokesman, advises the federal government on matters of interest to workers, and helps resolve intraunion problems as well as trade disputes.

Although the Nigerian trade unions, like those in other LDCs, are politically oriented, they have not yet formed an independent political base. Their influence on the economy has had to do with the promotion of a bargaining environment, the support of politicians, and the "politicization" of the wage bargain itself.

The real impact of collective bargaining on raising the level of wage rates, however, has remained controversial. Because of the inherent financial and organizational weaknesses of trade unions, as well as the greater power of business, collective bargaining has been more often than not formal rather than substantive. Indeed, government actions and policies have played a more important role in the movement of wage levels. State actions have, in turn, been motivated by a response to labor unrest and demonstrations, a precautionary political concern about future labor unrest, and a desire to obtain labor's political support. To these ends, the government has also been instrumental in legislating basic conditions of the work place. Theoretically, labor-management relations have been supposed to be based on free negotiation and collective bargaining. Yet while successive administrations have consistently expressed their commitment to these processes, wages have been "negotiated" in ad hoc semipolitical wage commissions and tribunals set up by the state from time to time, mostly in response to strikes. Industrial bargaining has thus been generally conducted through a process of political actions.

In short, the major elements within the government—politicans, the bureaucracy, and the army—have all vied for the labor unions' friendship and support. The unions, in turn, have used their political appeal in a national bargain for tangible wage hikes and fringe benefits.[36]

36. For a discussion of this process and other aspects of Nigerian trade unionism, see R. Cohen, *Labour and Politics in Nigeria* (London: Heinemann, 1974). See also A. J. Etukudo, *Waging Industrial Peace in Nigeria* (Hicksville: Exposition Press, 1977).

The Nigerian Economy: An Overview

The postindependence governments in Nigeria, both civilian and military, stressed the need to build a dynamic, unified, and self-reliant nation under "free and democratic" institutions where existing inequities in wealth, income, and living standards would be minimized, production efficiency would be enhanced, opportunities for all citizens would be equal, and reasonable economic and price stability maintained.[37]

Available evidence shows that while a reasonably good rate of GNP growth has been obtained (mostly thanks to the development in the petroleum sector), the success in achieving other objectives has fallen short of targets. Nigeria's development strategy emphasizing large-scale, capital-intensive industrialization with the aid of modern technology and foreign industrial investment has caused a great number of problems in other areas. The wage freeze and price control measures intended to combat inflation and attain "social justice" were not very effective. Reliance on private foreign advanced technology aggravated the domestic unemployment and underemployment problems; it also evidently had some adverse effects on the development of indigenous entrepreneurial skills, indigenous domestic industrial development, and adaptive technology.[38] There seems also to have been a steady relative growth of the manufacturing and mining sector at the expense of agriculture. The economic elite who took over from the British the control over international trade, finance, and investment was also in the forefront of cooperation with the multinational corporations in developing Nigeria's resources, particularly petroleum. But multinational investment in Nigeria, in the opinion of a critical observer, seems to have contributed to a net outflow of capital, displaced local artisans, introduced inappropriate products into the domestic market, and created inflationary wage spirals.[39]

Without the continued political instability that plagued Nigeria for most of the postindependence period and with a better management of resources, the situation would have been different. Thanks mostly to growing petroleum revenues, Nigeria is somewhat unique among the LDCs in presenting a capital and land surplus. The major impediment to true economic development is neither foreign exchange shortage nor lack of resources, but essentially one of skilled manpower and managerial talent. For these reasons, overall economic performance in recent years has been uneven. Agricultural output in particular has badly lagged behind most other sectors. The increasing dependence on petroleum as the main source for both foreign-exchange earnings and budgetary income has also become a cause for concern. The future depends on the ability of the new civilian government to cope with existing problems.

37. See V. A. Olorunsola, *Soldiers and Power* (Stanford: Hoover Institution Press, 1977), chapters 2 and 6.
38. See E. W. Nafziger, *African Capitalism: A Case Study in Nigerian Entrepreneurship* (Stanford: Hoover Institution Press, 1977).
39. See T. J. Biersteker, *Distortion or Development* (Cambridge: MIT Press, 1978), chapters 4–8.

Suggestions for Additional Readings

ADEDEJI, A., AND L. ROWLAND, ED. *Management Problems of Rapid Urbanisation in Nigeria*. Nigeria: University of Ife Press, 1973.

AGUIAR, N. *The Structure of Brazilian Development*. New Brunswick: Transaction Books, 1979.

ALEXANDER, R. J. *Organized Labor in Latin America*. New York: Free Press, 1965.

BAER, W. *Industrialization and Economic Development in Brazil*. New Haven: Yale University Press, 1975.

BAER, W., ET AL. "On State Capitalism in Brazil: Some Issues and Questions." *Inter-American Economic Affairs*, Winter 1976.

BHATT, V. V. *Two Decades of Development: The Indian Experiment*. Bombay: Vora, 1973.

BHULESHKAR, A. V., ED. *Growth of Indian Economy in Socialism*. Calcutta: Oxford and IBH Publishing Co., 1975.

CAMPBELL, G. *Brazil Struggles for Development*. London: Charles Knight, 1972.

DALAND, R. T. *Brazilian Planning*. Chapel Hill: University of North Carolina Press, 1967.

DANDEKAR, V. M., AND M. N. RATH. *Poverty in India*. New Delhi: Ford Foundation, 1970.

ELLIS, H. S., ED. *The Economy of Brazil*. Berkeley: University of California Press, 1969.

ERICKSON, K. P. *The Brazilian Corporative State and Working-Class Politics*. Berkeley: University of California Press, 1977.

FRANKEL, F. R. *India's Green Revolution: Economic Gains and Political Costs*. Princeton: Princeton University Press, 1971.

India 2001. New Delhi: Arnold-Heinemann Publishers, 1976.

JHA, P.S. *India: A Political Economy of Stagnation*. Fairlawn: Oxford University Press, 1980.

JOHNSON, B. L. C. *India, Resources and Development*. New York: Harper, 1979.

KILBY, P. *Industrialization in an Open Economy: Nigeria 1945–1966*. Cambridge: Cambridge University Press, 1969.

KOCHANEK, S. A. *Business and Politics in India*. Berkeley: University of California Press, 1974.

KUKLINSKY, A. ED. *Regional Policies in Nigeria, India. and Brazil*. The Hague: Mouton, 1978.

LEWIS, W. A. *Reflections on Nigeria's Economic Growth*. Paris: OECD, 1967.

MALENBAUM, W. *Modern India's Economy: Two Decades of Planned Growth*. Columbus: Charles E. Merrill, 1971.

MALLOY, J. M., ED. *Authoritarianism and Corporatism in Latin America*. Pittsburgh: University of Pittsburgh Press, 1977.

MEHTA, B. *Failures of the Indian Economy*. New Delhi: Chetana Publications, 1974.

MEHTA, F. A. *Economy.* New Delhi: The Macmillan Company of India, 1976.

MESA-LAGO, C. *Social Security in Latin America: Pressure Groups, Stratification, and Inequality.* Pittsburgh: University of Pittsburgh Press, 1978.

MYRDAL, G. *The Challenge of World Poverty.* London: Allen Lane, 1970.

PATTANSHETTI, C. C. *Dimensions of India's Industrial Economy.* Bombay: Somaiya Publications, 1968.

PROEHL, P. O. *Foreign Enterprise in Nigeria.* Chapel Hill: University of North Carolina Press, 1965.

REYNOLDS, L. G. *Image and Reality in Economic Development.* New Haven: Yale University Press, 1977.

ROSENBAUM, H. J., ED. *Contemporary Brazil.* New York: Praeger, 1972.

SCHLAGHECK, J. L. *The Political, Economic and Labor Climate in Brazil.* Philadelphia: The Wharton School, 1977.

SCHNITTER, P. C. *Interest Conflict and Political Change in Brazil.* Stanford: Stanford University Press, 1971.

SCHROEDER, R. C. *Brazil.* Washington: Congressional Quarterly, 1972.

SINGH, J. *The Green Revolution in India—How Green Is It?* Kurukshetra, Haryana: Vishal Publications, 1975.

SINGH, T. *India's Development Experience.* New York: St. Martin's, 1975.

SINHA, R., ET AL. *Income Distribution, Growth, and Basic Needs in India.* London: Croom Helm, 1979.

STEPAN, A., ED. *Authoritarian Brazil.* New Haven: Yale University Press, 1973.

STOLPER, W. F. *Planning Without Facts: Lessons in Resource Allocation from Nigeria's Development.* Cambridge: Harvard University Press, 1966.

THIRLWALL, A. P. *Inflation, Saving and Growth in Developing Economies.* London: Macmillan, 1974.

TURNHAM, D. *The Employment Problem in Less Developed Countries—A Review of Evidence.* Paris: OECD, 1971.

WEIL, T. E., ET AL. *Area Handbook for Brazil.* Washington: GPO, 1975.

WILLIAMS, G., ED. *Nigeria: Economy and Society.* Totowa: Rowman, 1976.

YESUFU, T. M., ED. *Manpower Problems and Economic Development in Nigeria.* Oxford: Oxford University Press, 1969.

Part Five

THE TASK OF
COMPARISON

THE FOREGOING CHAPTERS discussed the relationships between basic national goals and the means of their achievement. Chapter 1 challenged the myth of mutually exclusive systems; it pointed out the actual and potential possibilities of combining the essential elements of the traditional ideologies in an unlimited number of new organizational mixtures. Chapter 2 defined and discussed the type and character of basic economic problems faced by all societies and showed the necessity of an organization or system for the solution of these problems. Chapters 3 and 4 outlined the moral and political nature of a system's objectives, as distinct from the technical character of its economic tools and techniques. Chapters 5 through 9 presented detailed discussions of the five mechanisms of decision making, and chapters 10 through 12 outlined the application of these mechanisms in nine selected world economies. The ground is now laid for a comparison of these economies in terms of their success in achieving the widely accepted objectives of growth, full employment, price stability, and welfare.

13

A World of
Mixed Economies:
An Evaluation

WE BEGAN our study of comparative economics with the propositions that no real-world economy actually represents the old classical prototypes of capitalism, socialism, or communism. We held that all contemporary nation-states are *mixed* economies, with public, private, and regulated sectors operating side by side within a set of national socioeconomic goals; they subscribe, by tradition or by choice, to a set of philosophical beliefs, social values, and socioeconomic organizations. Any meaningful comparison among national economies, then, should center on differences in the national socioeconomic goals as well as in the choice of technoeconomic means for achieving these goals.[1]

A Look at Goals

A natural tendency in any comparison of national objectives may be the temptation for approval or disapproval: Which goals are the worthiest or most rewarding? Which are demeaning or base? Which are universal and which purely parochial? The answers to these questions, however, are not only very difficult, but almost always inconclusive. To judge one set of socioeconomic goals as intrinsically superior or rationally preferable to another, one would need certain philosophical, artistic, or aesthetic standards. Without such transcendental criteria, who can objectively and persuasively argue that growth is superior to choice? Or equity preferable to efficiency? Or technological progress more desirable than security? The people who worry about economic security are not, as a rule, terribly concerned about individual freedoms. Every society, as every individual, seeks something it relatively

1. In the opinion of a seasoned evaluator: "East-West Comparisons of any kind are inherently incapable of providing evidence of the relative economic merit of 'capitalism' and 'socialism.'" See Philip Hanson, "East-West Comparisons and Comparative Economic Systems," *Soviet Studies*, January 1971, p. 327.

lacks. Every society too has its own scale of preference, its own set of socioeconomic values.

To most "conservatives," there is no doubt that individual freedom, consumer choice, the disparity in wealth and income based on individual initiative, skill, and responsibility are good; government meddling in the economy, forced redistribution of income, and welfarism are undesirable and self-defeating. To most modern-day "liberals," on the other hand, it is equally self-evident that private profit and private gadgetry should give place to social equity, environmental quality, cultural and creative endeavors, and genuine social harmony. Modern philosophers of the new right prefer choice to growth. Many leaders in the developing world, by contrast, are proud of their messianic recipe for progress and prosperity through national planning and government direction.

In the absence of transcendental criteria, a judgment in favor or against a set of national goals can thus hardly be defended or attacked rationally and objectively. As many of the philosophical issues that face humanity are not yet resolved, and there are actually no universally accepted standards for evaluating the precedence or priority of social goals, the relative merits of national economic objectives are essentially a political and moral question requiring political and moral judgments. The safest observation that can be made in the comparison of goals is perhaps the simplest: No set of objectives can be better than the results it achieves—the actual performance.

Taking each country's national socioeconomic objectives as politically and independently determined, it may be possible to compare national economies in terms of the success with which they achieve their chosen goals. By this test, the "best" system is the one that fulfills its tasks best. Here the problem is not one of comparison between goals, but only a judgment about means.[2] A comparison of means is certainly easier than an evaluation of goals, but many thorny problems of definition and measurement still remain. Ends and means are not always, or easily, distiguishable. Not only is each end a means to another end; some means or policies, such as industrialization or economic self-sufficiency, may sometimes be ends in themselves. An absolute separation between criteria for evaluating ends and those for evaluating means is also fraught with many other complications.[3]

A judgment on the overall performance of the economy in terms of the four or five universal objectives (growth, full employment, equity, freedom, etc.) would still remain inconclusive, for two reasons. First, a nation must be able to advance on *all* fronts simultaneously or satisfactorily to be number one—an exceedingly difficult task. Second, even if a nation can be found to represent success on all counts, the judgment would still fail to show much about the so-called quality of

2. For a different definition of "performance criteria"—criteria that include both goals as well as means—see Gregory Grossman, *Economic Systems* (Englewood Cliffs, N.J.: Prentice-Hall, 1974).

3. It is, for example, reasonable to argue that if a goal is immoral, antisocial, or worthless, the clumsier and the less suitable the means, the better.

life such as internal peace, social harmony, individual capacity for positive enjoyment, time available for rewarding leisure and so on. A comparison of these achievements would require additional sets of moral and transcendental criteria.

Comparative Economic Performance

Performance may be measured by a variety of "success indicators." The selection of these indicators and their relative priority are to some extent arbitrary and a matter of subjective value judgment.[4] Here we propose to consider five: economic growth, full employment, domestic price stability and external balance, social welfare, and equity. A clearly successful performance would mean some progress on all of these five points; none, by itself can be a sufficient indicator. Higher growth rates, for example, may not qualify as a total indication of success if obtained at the cost of idle labor, rapid exhaustion of resources, or irreparable damages to the environment. By the same token, full employment would not be much of an accomplishment if it were the result of pyramid building or putting everyone in a labor camp. Similar conceptual difficulties exist in regard to the objectives of price stability, welfare, and equity.

Economic Growth

As growth is commonly considered an end in itself and a means of attaining other ends—higher standards of living, economic security, military strength, technological progress, international cooperation—its behavior carries heavier weight in performance comparisons. A comparison of growth rates is also relatively easy, because data can be compared in terms of percentage changes in GNP or GDP in each country. There are, however, three conceptual caveats. First, when the GNP or GDP base is low, as in the case of poor countries, small absolute increments of income may produce comparatively large and somewhat misleading percentage figures. Second, the behavior of growth rates as a measure of success would be meaningful only on a per capita basis, that is, adjusted for changes in population. Third, the same average annual growth rates over a period may invite different value judgments depending on whether or not they have been marred by frequent ups and downs in the intervening years, or achieved smoothly and steadily.

4. For a discussion of some of these criteria, see "Standards for the Performance of our Economic Systems," *American Economic Review, Papers and Proceedings*, May 1960, pp. 1–24. For further discussions of the problems involved in maintaining growth, full employment, price stability, welfare, and international harmony, see pp. 93–298 of the same article.

A WORLD OF MIXED ECONOMIES: AN EVALUATION

Growth among Major Industrial Countries

The rates of growth of MICs, both historically and in more recent years, seem to indicate that richer and economically maturer countries have had a tendency to grow more slowly than the poorer and younger nations; and economies with better government-business cooperation have experienced higher growth rates than others.[5] According to the World Bank figures, the average annual real growth rate of GDP between 1960 and 1970 ranged from 10.5 percent for Japan to 4.3 percent for the United States, and 2.9 percent for the United Kingdom. The rates for 1970–78 were 5 percent, 3 percent, and 2.1 percent, respectively.

Japan's average annual real growth rate in the postwar period has thus been the highest in the industrial world. The reasons for such a significant difference in growth include annual rates of savings and capital formation, the modernity of production facilities; the rate of progress of technology, more disciplined labor and keen labor motivation. A uniquely significant factor has also been Japan's ability to use much less energy per household and per unit of production compared to other rich industrial countries—sometimes as little as one third.

By contrast, Great Britain has had the poorest growth record of any major industrialized nation in the postwar period. Even this low growth rate has been accompanied by wide cyclical swings of as much as 100 percent, giving the annual real growth a range of between zero and 6 percent. The inability of the United Kingdom to achieve a growth rate similar to the other MICs has been partly (but not convincingly) attributed to a relatively low investment-GDP ratio. Gross domestic investment as a percentage of GDP in the United Kingdom has averaged around 18 percent in recent years, as compared to 30 percent for Japan.

The United Kingdom and West Germany are similar in many essential respects: land area, size of population, levels of infrastructure and education, dependence on foreign trade, and even the composition of resources. For this reason, some observers have argued that the differences in economic growth in the two countries (3.4 percent for Germany during 1960–77 compared to 2.5 percent in Britain) are not due in any substantial measure to innate differences in national characteristics but mainly to different national economic postures and policies.

The American growth position has been somewhere in the middle—better than the United Kingdom's, but behind Japan's.[6] The U.S. real growth rate averaged about 3.2 percent a year between 1950 and 1960; it rose by about 4.3 percent between 1960 and 1970, and by 3 percent in 1970–78. This middle-of-the-range

---

5. For the early postwar year comparisons, see Angus Maddison, *Economic Growth in the West* (New York: Norton, 1964). Certain smaller countries (Iran, Brazil, South Korea, and Taiwan) have in some years had growth rates of between 10 percent and 15 percent a year in real terms. But among major countries, none has matched Japan in real growth.

6. In the postwar period, most major European countries have run ahead of the United States in annual growth. But, historically (between 1870 and 1960), the U.S. growth of over 2 percent a year has been better.

position in annual growth can be explained partly by the enormous GDP base of the U.S. economy, and partly by America's traditional priority of choice over growth.[7] The emphasis on maximum individual freedom and a continued hostility to any kind of national planning have been at least partly responsible for America's relatively smaller annual growth rate as well as greater susceptibility to business fluctuations (namely six postwar recessions when GDP declined as much as 5.7 percent in one year).

Of greater overall importance in the comparison of real growth among MICs is perhaps the behavior of labor productivity, or output per worker-hour. Data published by OECD shows that output per person employed in Japan had an average annual growth of over 8.9 percent in 1964–73, and over 3.2 percent in 1974–79. By contrast, the figures for the United States were 1.8 percent for the first period, and near 0.1 percent in the second period. For the United Kingdom, the corresponding figures were 3.2 percent and 0.8 percent. The U.S. business circles attribute the sharp decline in U.S. industrial productivity to increased government spending, higher taxes, stringent safety laws, and other government regulations, but independent observers point to such "culprits" as plant obsolescence,[8] inflation, high energy costs, poorly trained labor, smaller outlays on research and development, a reduction in market competition, and the growing importance of service employment where productivity growth is usually the most laggard.[9]

Growth among Centrally Directed Economies

The centrally directed economies have generally had higher rates of growth compared to both MICs and poorer LDCs (with the notable exceptions of Japan and Brazil in each group). Among the CDEs in our study during the 1960–70 period, Yugoslavia showed an impressive real GDP growth rate of 5.8 percent a year on average; the Soviet Union was second, with 5.2 percent; and China showed 5 percent growth. During 1970–78, China surpassed both with an average real rate of 6 percent compared to 5.6 percent for Yugoslavia, and only 5.3 percent for the Soviet Union.

Yugoslavia's notable growth during the 1960s and 1970s has been attributed to the economy's success in mobilizing a large share of domestic resources (as much as 30 percent of domestic savings for investment); an impressive export performance (18 percent of GNP in some years); and the absorption by the industrial sector of large transfers of labor from private agriculture. Growth performance after the 1965 reforms, however, has experienced certain deterioration.

7. A mere 2 percent annual growth in the United States, for example, is larger than the entire GDP of Nigeria.

8. An average U.S. plant in 1979 was probably ten years older than the equivalent Japanese plant.

9. See E. F. Denison, *Accounting for Slower Economic Growth* (Washington: The Brookings Institution. 1979).

China has published no detailed production figures since 1959. By various accounts, and according to some figures recently revealed, its growth rate, while considerable, has been erratic and uneven.[10] Between 1953 and 1957, with substantial Soviet aid and some soft-pedaling of ideology, economic growth averaged an estimated high rate of 7.5 percent a year in real terms. Under the Great Leap and part of the Cultural Revolution, growth was negative. In years of economic normalcy, the annual rate has hovered between 5 and 9 percent. Between 1952 and 1978, industrial production had the highest growth rate, 11 percent a year, while grain production grew by a mere 2 percent annually. However, Chinese yearly growth during the period exceeded that of the Soviet Union in electricity, crude steel, coal, and even grain output. The major reasons for China's uneven growth performance must be found in its ideological turmoil and experimentation; isolation until recently from world trade and investment; priority given to national self-sufficiency; poor planning; and ideological biases against interest and rent in return calculations. The more basic economic handicaps, however, have been low productivity of agriculture; an immense and rising population which requires increasing economic growth to insure full employment; and shortage of capital and technical resources to exploit investment possibilities.

Soviet economic growth right after World War II presented a formidable challenge to the West and became the subject of admiration and emulation by the newly emerging nations. During the 1950s, the overall rate of growth of GNP averaged 7 percent a year (compared to about 3.2 percent in the United States) and higher than any other industrial country in the world except Japan. In the 1960s and early 1970s, too, annual growth rates still showed a more modest rise in response to changes in leadership, investment policy, foreign commitments, and weather. Toward the end of the 1970s, the rate dwindled to around 1 percent. The 1976–79 growth rate averaged 3.1 percent, against the planned 5 percent. Soviet achievements have been most impressive in industrial production, where both long-term historical and recent trends have shown an impressive rate of between 8 percent and 9 percent (as compared to the American industrial growth of less than 4 percent).[11] By contrast, the long-run growth of Soviet agriculture has averaged no more than 1.5 percent a year. In some poor crop years, there has been an absolute decline. In the current plan, however, almost all industrial outputs are below planned figures.

Russia's moderately respectable annual growth rate of GNP can be attributed to several main factors: abundant reserves of land, labor, and natural resources; a systematic allocation of some 25 percent of GNP on the average to investment, mostly in selective industries with significant growth potentials; large-scale adoption

10. See U.S. Congress, Joint Economic Committee, *People's Republic of China: An Economic Assessment* (Washington: GPO, 1972); and Walter Galenson, *The Chinese Economy under Communism* (Chicago: Aldine, 1970).
11. Figures published for 1979 show that industrial output grew by only 3.4 percent, the lowest rate since World War II and 2.3 percent below the planned target. There are shortfalls in oil, coal, steel, and other key industrial products. Overall labor productivity, at only 2.4 percent, was also below target.

of available Western technology; a well-educated young labor force working with plenty of modern machines; close cooperation between industry and research agencies; and a relatively low industrial and agricultural base.[12]

Growth among Less Developed Countries

Economic progress among emerging nations in the postwar period has been spotty. The poorest developing countries have had a collective average annual growth rate of less than 4 percent in the 1960–70 period and slightly more than 3.5 percent between 1970 and 1978. The middle-income LDCs, on the other hand, have had a credible performance, with growth rates of near 6 percent a year in the entire 1960–78 period. In our own sample, India, with its Western-style parliamentary regime, had a growth rate of only about 3.6 percent a year in 1960–78. Nigeria, compensating for its civil war years with its recently prospering petroleum industry, has achieved a rate of 4.6 percent. And Brazil, under a strong regime after 1964, grew at a rate of 5.3 percent a year in 1960–70, and a stunning 9.2 percent in 1970–78.

Brazil owes its "economic miracle" to a dynamic industrial sector, that has shown a 10.1 percent annual growth in 1970–1978, and an agricultural sector with an uncommonly high growth rate of 5.3 percent a year.[13] By contrast, Nigeria, beset by national strife in the latter part of 1960s, actually had a negative average annual growth rate in agriculture during the 1960–78 period. Its overall 6.2 percent showing in 1970–77 would not have been possible without a sharp upsurge in oil production and prices, giving the manufacturing sector a growth rate of 13.4 percent a year. India's growth has been erratic under varying climatic conditions. During 1960–70, farm production grew by only 1.9 percent a year, while industry had a 5.5 percent growth; but in 1970–78 agriculture had a slightly better showing of 2.6 percent while the average industrial rate fell to 4.5 percent.

Full Employment

A crucial test of economic performance in any country is the ability of its economic system to ensure not only rapid growth but high employment. Indeed, from the

12. For a more detailed examination of Russia's early postwar growth, see Vladimir Treml, ed., *The Development of Soviet Economy: Plan and Performance* (New York: Praeger, 1968); and S. H. Cohn, *Economic Development in the Soviet Union* (Lexington: Heath, 1970).

13. The 1970–80 record of agricultural production has been reportedly closer to 4 percent per year, resulting in the importation of wheat, corn, rice and meat—something of an anomaly for a country of Brazil's size and suitability for year-round farm production.

standpoint of sociopolitical harmony, a high average growth rate without full-employment would not be a viable option.

Unemployment in Major Industrial Countries

Among MICs, the United States has felt the scourge of unemployment longest and with much greater severity than most Europeans.[14] In the postwar period, the United States has had eight years of high unemployment, when between 6 and 8.5 percent of the civilian labor force on an annual average were idle. The peaks of joblessness were reached naturally at the bottoms of the U.S.'s postwar recessions— 1948–49, 1953–54, 1957–58, 1960–61, 1969–71, 1974–75 and 1979–80. During the same period, the United States experienced also eight years of relative high employment when less than 4 percent of the work force were jobless. The near full-employment years were during the Korean War (1953) and the Vietnam escalation (1969). Since 1974, however, unemployment has remained between 5.5 percent and 7.8 at all times (up to June 1980) and has become extremely difficult to bring down to anywhere near the 3–4 percent official target without fueling inflation.

The record of U.S. postwar unemployment has been the subject of an endless controversy between "liberals" and "conservatives." Liberals contend that the national average jobless rate actually understates the true magnitude of the nation's unemployment problem by not accounting for part-time workers who cannot get a full-time job, discouraged workers who have given up looking for a job, and full-timers who are paid less than the "poverty wage."[15] "Conservatives," on the other hand, contend that national unemployment averages always exaggerate the nation's plight by including a large number of irregular workers and non-breadwinners (housewives looking for extra money, teenagers living with parents but seeking additional incomes, etc.); it also allegedly inflates the jobless figure by refusing to pair off the number of unemployed workers with equally significant number of unfilled job vacancies, and by calculating frictional (voluntary) unemployment at too low a rate (3 percent). Thus the estimates of "true" unemployment corresponding to an official figure of 5 percent would range from 30 percent to zero according to the two camps.

By sharp contrast to the United States, unemployment has been no serious problem for Japan in most of the postwar years. While the U.S. unemployment rate at no time fell below 3 percent, Japan seldom had any more than 2 percent of its

14. A comparison of unemployment figures can not be very precise because of differences in the definition of the labor force and the methods of collecting and interpreting unemployed categories.

15. Even without these categories, the national average obviously conceals the much higher rates of unemployment in depressed areas, among women, teenagers, and some minorities. When the national rate was as low as 3.5 percent in 1969, the jobless rate for black teenage girls in Detroit and Los Angeles was upward of 40 percent.

civilian labor force out of a job. Throughout the 1960s and early 1970s, the Japanese unemployment rate was much below 2 percent, with more jobs going unfilled than workers looking for a job.

The Japanese low jobless figures to some extent conceal a good deal of underemployment dormant under Japan's traditional system of "life-time" employment, where men over thirty-five are seldom let go by their large company employers. During periods of uncertainty, businessmen are usually reluctant to hire new workers and assume additional long-term responsibilities, preferring to rely on increased overtime by the existing work force. Consequently, during 1978–79, the jobless rate for the first time exceeded 2 percent by a small amount. But various private estimates put visible and invisible underemployment at 4 to 9 percent of the work force. On the whole, one must conclude that the Japanese "economic miracle" has operated under a condition of what is called high employment. Continued economic expansion resulting in a growing need for labor, the slow rate of growth of population, and the Japanese custom of low labor turnover have been responsible for the tight labor situation and the total success in achieving full employment growth.

The United Kingdom up until 1970 had little or no unemployment problem. In the early 1950s, the percentage of workers out of a job was about 1 percent; in the early 1960s, slightly over 2 percent. The low unemployment rates during the 1950s and 1960s, however, were due to no particular strength in the British economy, but were largely the result of the slow growth of total work force (about 1 percent a year), overmanning in most British industries, and a very restrictive immigration policy. In 1971–72, unemployment approached nearly 4 percent of the work force and triggered some government expansionary policy. The 1974–75 slump and the weak recovery during the 1976–79 period aggravated the problem. After 1975, total British employment dropped continuously, and the jobless rate gradually reached 6.3 percent in 1980. Thus, while the 1963–73 average unemployment rate remained at a modest 2.3 percent, the post 1974–75 depression rate averaged 4.6 percent,[16] and toward the end of the decade the number of workers out of a job approached the previously unthinkable 2 million mark. As can be easily seen, Britain's record in both growth and full employment has been the least enviable of all the MICs.

Unemployment in Centrally Directed Economies

Unemployment is anathema in communist dogma. Article 40 of the 1977 Soviet Constitution guarantees every citizen the right to work. The planned character and

---

16. Owing to differences in definition and methods of calculation of unemployment, Britain's jobless rate of 5.6 percent corresponds to an internationally comparable figure of 7.5 percent.

composition of output also theoretically rule out joblessness, almost by definition, because planners are expected always to provide for the full use of labor. For this reason, Russian party and government leaders as a rule deny the existence of involuntary unemployment within Soviet industries and farms. Since unemployment cannot theoretically exist in a planned economy, the frequently observed and reported pockets of unemployment in the Soviet Union are officially explained away by Soviet authorities as "mismatching" of jobs and workers rather than excess of workers over jobs. They frequently point out acute labor shortages in some industries and localities as the proof of full employment. This is probably true because of increasing demand for labor in the expanding Soviet industries, relatively low birth rate, and the loss of millions of young men during World War II. Data released by the Soviet government show that civilian employment during the 1960s increased by over 20 percent, whereas the civilian labor force had an increase of just over 16 percent.

The apparent paradox of labor shortages along with pockets of unemployment may partly be explained by the growing need for skilled workers. While 2.5 million new workers enter the labor force each year—about 1.5 percent of the total labor force—industrial production grows by a much higher ratio each year, causing some pressure on labor supply. At the same time, the major untapped sources of labor—women and farm workers—are being nearly exhausted. And the current Soviet birthrate is less than 1 percent a year, one-third that in czarist Russia and among the lowest in the world.

A good deal of Soviet unemployment, in the Westerners' view, consists of frictional turnover (about 2 percent) and some large-scale concealed underemployment, overstaffing, and less than efficient use of labor. The reasons frequently advanced for the existence of open unemployment are increased mechanization and automation; small opportunities for industrial work in small cities; long and severe winters; and the increasing sophistication and complexity of the Soviet economy, which is not exactly matched by training of required skills.

Unemployment, hidden or apparent, is thus largely due to a poor use of work force. Many Soviet factories, even those run by shrewd and capable managers, employ several times as many workers as comparable Western plants. It is always safer for a manager to have more workers than less, because he can always fulfill unreasonably high production quotas imposed on him more easily. There are other reasons for padded employment payrolls. A different explanation is that while the MICs chose to take care of their unemployed through unemployment compensation, the Russians prefer to keep them always at work but pay them poorly.

In China, unemployment was denied in the Maoist era, although there were always indications of urban unemployment and rural underemployment. The tradition of guaranteed lifetime job and the socialist promise of right to work gave credence to the existence of a largely full employment—if not very efficient—economy. But with population growing at a rate of 2 to 2.5 percent a year, and the economy in some turbulent years not expanding that fast, surplus labor must have been a problem for the Chinese leaders at some times. In 1979 the Chinese officially admitted that they had 20 million workers "awaiting assignment."[17]

Yugoslavia's record in generating full employment has been mixed. The sharp differences between rural private incomes and urban public-sector earnings have routinely encouraged a large transfer of labor from agriculture to industries and services, thus creating an employment problem for the authorities. After 1965, the rising surplus labor was partly reduced by liberalizing external migration. As a result, by 1973 some 1.1 million Yugoslav workers, 5 percent of the population and 26 percent of the public work force, were employed abroad, mostly in Europe. With the onset of the worldwide recession in 1974, external migration virtually stopped, and many workers began to return, increasing the resident labor force for the first time since 1965. Despite rapid growth in public-sector employment, open unemployment reached 10.4 percent in 1975, as compared to 6.7 percent in 1971. Toward the end of the decade, the rate of joblessness was around 7 percent.

Unemployment in Less Developed Countries

Western-style unemployment is essentially an industrial phenomenon and a problem for a country of wage-earners. It is usually less of a problem in a rural and self-sufficient economy, in an economy of self-employed farmers and shopkeepers, or under traditional land tenure systems where sharecroppers and farm workers are part of the overhead costs. For these reasons, the overt unemployment that exists in less developed countries is mostly urban and mostly among either unskilled farm workers newly arriving in industrial areas or among high school and college graduates with little or no training for specified technical jobs. In the countryside, surplus labor is usually hidden behind low productivity and excessive underemployment.

Hidden or open, however, unemployment is becoming an increasingly serious problem in many rapidly growing developing nations. Some 25 percent of the total labor force in the LDCs are said to be chronically unemployed or underemployed. The clearest source of difficulty is the rapid rate of growth of the population and labor force in the less developed countries—estimated to be 2.3 percent a year during 1970–80, as compared to only 1 percent in the developed nations. The problem is particularly acute in urban centers, which receive considerable inflow of job-seeking young adults from rural areas.[18]

One of the hardest hit countries in our sample is India, with an estimated 30 percent of its rural population unemployed or underemployed. Although it is

17. This figure represents 13 percent of the nonagricultural labor force, with high concentration among young people.

18. See David Turnham, *The Employment Problem in Less Developed Countries—A Review of Evidence* (Paris: OECD, 1971). In the absence of unemployment insurance in most of LDCs, jobless workers are not registered and are therefore difficult to measure.

admittedly difficult to relate Indian unemployment to the Western concept of the term because of the "joint-family" structure of Indian society, where all family members are jointly taken care of, estimates of nonagricultural unemployment vary between 10 to 20 million. For the entire labor force of some 265 million, a figure of near 40 million is the estimate. By official counts, 5.4 million educated young people had registered with employment exchanges in 1977. At the same time, there has been a migration of technical and professional people from India, and a "brain drain," which is causing serious shortages in some occupations and professions.

In Nigeria, there are no comprehensive statistics on the size of employment and unemployment. Since wage employment represents around 10 percent of the total gainfully employed (with the government the largest source of such employment), open joblessness is overshadowed by rural underemployment. Nevertheless, urban unemployment among school leavers and in the young age groups is aggravated by continued rural migration to the cities.

In Brazil, despite a 2.7 percent annual increase in population in the past, there was a near full employment of skilled workers up to 1977. The vexing problem was that of underemployment in the countryside. Since 1977, when the economy's growth rate slackened, urban industrial unemployment has also become a problem. By some estimates, the Brazilian economy must grow by 7 percent a year in order to keep employment steady. For this reason, some private Brazilian analysts estimate the jobless rate in the industrial sector to have been as high as 25 percent in 1979.

In all three countries, rural underemployment is being dealt with through higher producer prices, expansion of infrastructure facilities, social services in the rural areas, and the development of cottage industries.[19]

Price-Level Stability

In combatting postwar inflation, no country has had a perfect record. Some have been able to hold down the pace of price rises better than others, while others have learned to live with inflation as a way of life.

Inflation among Major Industrial Countries

All MICs, even those with a small rate of growth in the postwar period, have been plagued by some degree of inflation. In Europe's ten major economies as a group, prices more than quadrupled between 1950 and 1980. During the 1970s, inflation registered double-digits figures in some industrial countries.

19. See "The Employment in Less Developed Countries," *OECD Observer*, December 1970, pp. 8–9.

For much of the postwar period until 1970, the United States had a better anti-inflation record among the Western democracies than many European countries and Japan.[20] In the 1960–70 period, for example, the U.S. consumer price index rose by less than 3 percent a year on average, while the corresponding figure for the United Kingdom was over 4 percent, and for Japan, nearly 5 percent. Toward the end of the 1960s, however, under the impact of the Vietnam War and the Great Society program at home (guns and butter), prices began to rise. Between 1967 and up until the 1973 energy crunch, the average yearly inflation was still in the politically tolerable range of about 4.5 percent a year. Starting from 1974, a stubborn inflationary spiral began. Average annual increase in consumer prices between 1973–78 reached 8 percent.[21] In 1979, prices rose by more than 13 percent, and in early 1980 they surpassed 18 percent.

The United Kingdom has had the worst inflation record of the three countries in our MIC sample—and one of the worst among all MICs. Between 1950 and 1964 Britain kept cost-of-living increases at about 3 percent a year, at the somewhat obvious expense of economic growth, but once the Labour government began in 1964 to spur production, largely through easy money policy, inflationary pressures mounted. Slowly at first, prices began to rise at about 4 percent a year between 1964 and 1967. After the sterling devaluation, and particularly after the expiration of the wage-price freeze, prices rose by 6 percent a year between 1968 and 1970. The average for the 1960s was still a moderate 4 percent plus. In the early 1970s, while production remained sluggish and unemployment passed the one million mark, there was still no decline in the price level. A virulent and intractable inflation followed the energy crisis and reached an unprecedented peak of 27 percent in 1975. Between 1973 and 1978 the average yearly consumer price rise in Britain was more than 16 percent, twice as much as in the United States; and in early 1980 it hovered around 20 percent.

Japan has occupied a midway position between the United States and Britain. For most of the 1960s, Japanese authorities failed to keep consumer price rises much below 5 percent. In the early 1970s the rate hovered between 7 and 8 percent. Between 1973 and 1978 the average yearly inflation passed 11 percent, partly because of high prices of energy and raw materials. The 11 percent average figure, however, masked two important facts. First, consumer price index reached 24.5 percent in 1974 when Japan followed a stockpiling policy on raw materials and thus partly caused sharp rises in commodity prices. Second, the decline of the price index toward the end of 1970s (to less than 3 percent in 1979) was largely the result of

20. Although milder than the price rise in many other MICs, inflation has been endemic in the United States. Since World War II, prices have fallen only twice, in 1949 and 1955, by a mere 1 percent. In all the seven postwar recessions, prices failed to decline. In the 1973–75—the years of the severest recession since the Great Depression of the 1930s—prices climbed by 21 percent.

21. The percentages are for the whole year; they differ from the average of monthly indexes during each year. They are also somewhat different from the "implicit GNP deflator," which measures price changes in the whole economy and not merely in the consumer area.

continued sharp appreciations in the value of the Japanese yen vis-à-vis the U.S. dollar, which reduced Japan's import costs considerably. The trend was reversed in 1980, and prices began to rise again.

Inflation in Less Developed Countries

Price stability has eluded most of the developing countries in recent years. Increasing population pressures and rising expectations, coupled with limited domestic productive capacity and insufficient foreign assistance and private capital flow, have kept aggregate demand perennially in excess of available supply. In countries with a large and vocal civil service or relatively stronger trade unions, considerable inflation has also resulted from the cost side.

Hardest hit by hyperinflation among LDCs has been Latin America. Latin American inflation has in fact a style and story of its own: it is unusually high by normal American or European standards, and it is endemic. Between 1960 and 1970, average consumer prices increased by 46 percent a year in Brazil. In some years, costs of living rose by more than 150 percent. In the 1970–78 period, Brazil managed to bring the *average* annual rate of inflation down to about 30 percent a year and to minimize undesirable inflationary distortions through its policy of "monetary correction." But toward the end of the decade, inflation climbed again to about 77 percent in 1979, and 100 percent in early 1980.

India, beset by inclement weather and food shortages in part of the postwar period, experienced fluctuating inflationary pressures (as much as 17 percent rise in 1955–56) but an actual cost of living decline in 1967–68. The average for 1960–70, however, was around 7 percent, and for the 1970–78 period, about 8.2 percent.

Nigeria's record is totally mixed. During the 1960s, costs of living rose by a modest 2.6 percent a year, but after the advent of large oil revenues and the start of large-scale planning, inflation surpassed 18 percent a year on average between 1970–78.

Inflation in Centrally Directed Economies

In a centrally directed economy, inflation must be an anomaly. Since all wages and prices are normally determined by central authorities, price levels ought to remain stable in between periodic official price changes.[22] In reality, things do not work that way; almost all CDEs have had their bouts with inflation, both open and concealed. Hidden inflation is evidenced by shortages of consumer goods, long waiting lines, poor quality of daily wares, and black-market operations.[23]

22. By Western estimates, in some CDEs black markets constitute an economy within the economy, where perhaps as much as 20 percent of the GNP may be transacted.
23. Soviet officials routinely deny the existence of inflation in the Soviet Union (except in the war years); they prefer to call it "an adjustment in the state pricing structure."

In the Soviet Union, wage and price inflation was serious before World War II. Between 1928 and 1940, controlled consumer prices in state stores rose by fourteen times; average wages, by nearly six times; and industrial prices, by more than twice. During the same period, uncontrolled farm market prices rose by nearly eighteen times. Russia's wartime inflation was also spectacular. Between 1941 and 1947 the official consumer price index rose to nearly 4,000 from 1,400. The index of free-market produce increased to more than 13,500 from 1,800. Wages rose by less than 75 percent, and prices of industrial goods remained virtually unchanged.

The runaway inflation was brought to a halt by an internal devaluation of the ruble in 1947. In the immediate postwar period, inflation was held in check by keeping increases in money wage rates more or less within labor productivity, substantially increasing the supply of consumer goods, and introducing highly improved credit controls. Thus, for a decade following the war, consumer prices actually declined. But after the introduction of industrial reforms in 1965, some skilled wages rose much faster than productivity, and the excess purchasing power affected prices in the noncontrolled or noncontrollable segments of the economy—collective farm markets and the black markets.[24] Consumer prices as a whole, however, reportedly rose by less than 1 percent a year between 1961 and 1970.

During the 1970s, while Soviet authorities claimed that they had prices in check, creeping inflation seems to have been a fact of Russian life. According to the official retail price index, prices as a whole dropped by 0.5 percent between 1970 and 1979, although there were some sharp "upward adjustments" in prices of individual items (autos, gasoline, restaurant meals).[25] By Western estimates, however, the official figures conceal several important factors: massive state subsidies running at billion of dollars a year; price increases in goods and services not in the "market basket," such as gasoline and coffee beans, whose prices rose by two to six times in the 1974–79 period; numerous disguised increases in the form of "temporary" surcharges, or changes in product's quality and name; shortages in state stores which force people to shop in free markets at prices as high as six times the official level; and "joint sales," where the purchase of a popular item is conditional upon simultaneous purchase of a "reject." Western experts estimate Russia's actual inflation rate to be between 4 and 5 percent a year, double what it was in early 1970s.[26] Even at these rates, however, the Soviet Union can claim a much better record of price stability than the MICs and LDCs.

Yugoslavia's inflation record, under a mixture of planned and market controls, has not been enviable. Despite government efforts toward greater decentralization and emphasis on domestic competition, market forces have not been able to exert a stabilizing influence on domestic prices. As a result of rising wages

24. See F. D. Holzman, "Soviet Inflationary Pressures, 1928–1957," *Quarterly Journal of Economics*, May 1960.
25. In 1979 rents were officially set at the same level as in 1928; bread prices are the same as in 1954; and milk and meat equal to the 1962 levels.
26. See *U.S. News and World Report*, 2 April 1979.

and higher import prices, the rise in domestic cost of living has been steep. Inflation pressures have been particularly strong after the 1965 reforms. Until the early 1960s, prices were fairly tightly controlled by the authorities. With the liberalization of decision making under the reforms, inflation accompanied growth. Thus, while between 1954 and 1964, industrial producer prices rose by an annual average of 1.5 percent, in the 1965–73 period, the annual rate of inflation jumped to 11.1 percent. During 1976–78, consumer prices rose by an average of 18.6 percent a year, worse than all OECD countries except beleaguered Portugal and Turkey. The rate in 1979 was around 22 percent, the highest in Europe.

The major causes of this high inflation are attributed to several factors: higher workers' earnings, market imperfections, cumbersome fiscal policy, ineffective demand management through monetary and credit instruments, and misdirected enterprise autonomy in raising both wages and prices within broad limits. As virtually no Yugoslav enterprise is ever allowed to fail, the green light is given to firms to raise prices in order to stay in the black.

In China, as in the Soviet Union, overt inflation is also somewhat concealed. The existence of rationing for certain consumer staples makes the detection task even more difficult. Capping the difficulties is a Chinese official policy of not publishing price and production data on a systematic basis. Indications are, however, that the Chinese have been more successful in keeping prices in check by tight controls over wages and through rationing. A 33 percent rise in official prices of eight key perishable food items in November 1979 occurred after a long period of stability and was the largest round of inflation since the 1949 communist takeover. By some informal estimates, the average yearly retail price rise from 1950–1979 has been about 1 percent.

Prices and Pay

As can be seen from the foregoing paragraphs, the major causes of worldwide inflation have differed in different groups of countries. Among MICs, several basic factors, such as budget deficits, rapid increases in money supply, lagging productivity, excessive regulations, union-pushed higher wages beyond productivity, decreasing competition in the market, higher energy costs, and floating exchange rates have been responsible. Of these forces, rising labor earnings combined with sluggish productivity and sterling depreciation have been mostly to blame for the British high inflation. In the United States, the main culprits have been inordinate monetary expansion, notable slowdown in productivity, and dollar depreciation against major European and Japanese currencies, partly caused by higher energy costs and balance-of-trade deficits. In the third world, a large part of the blame must be placed on excessive government spendings, the expansion of infrastructural facilities, a small tax base, unfavorable terms of trade, high energy costs, poor weather, and sometimes unrealistic exchange rates. For the CDEs, the reasons for the disguised inflation, or periodic price hikes, have rested with rising costs of raw materials and oil, climatic reverses, lagging technology, bureaucratic inefficiencies, and poor incentives.

By far the most crucial cause of worldwide inflation has been the behavior of wage costs| amidst the slowdown in labor productivity even in the face of rising unemployment. Wage rates in all MICs have shown a distict tendency to overun average labor productivity. While many inflationary wage settlements have no doubt been triggered by continuing price inflation, they themselves have tended to intensify the cost-push pressure upon prices. Many wage contracts not only have tried to catch up with past inflation but, by reflecting past rates of price increases into the future, have triggered an inflationary spiral of their own.

The crucial significance of sluggish labor productivity in accelerating inflationary trends is evident from recent experience of most major industrial countries. In the United Kingdom, manufacturing wage rates between 1960 and 1970 rose by 7.2 percent a year, while industrial productivity went up by only 2.9 percent. During 1972–77, hourly earnings in industry averaged 16.5 percent a year, with labor productivity trailing far behind at about 1 percent. Consumer prices, in turn, kept surprisingly close relations with wages, rising by slightly more than 4 percent a year in the 1960s and 16 percent in the 1970s. In the United States, too, wages rose by 3.7 percent a year on the average between 1960 and 1965, while average productivity was rising by 4.3 percent annually. Thus, a period of relative price stability prevailed. By contrast, in 1972 to 1979, hourly earnings in industry rose by over 8 percent a year, productivity by less than 1 percent, and prices by more than 8 percent. And in Japan, industrial wages rose by about 12 percent a year during the 1960s, slightly higher than labor productivity of 11 percent. Price inflation was thus confined to about 5 percent. In mid-1970s, however, earnings in industry climbed by more than 16 percent, far ahead of labor productivity of around 4 to 5 percent, reflecting an inflationary rate of about 12 percent. In both 1978 and 1979, however, industrial productivity rose by 8–12 percent while wages were kept at 6 percent, and inflation below 3 percent.

Somewhat immune from the effects of increasing wages on production costs have been the Communist bloc countries, where centrally determined wage rates have been deliberately kept below average labor productivity. In China too money wages have been kept low, and workers' real purchasing power has been allowed to improve modestly through low and reduced prices of consumer goods. The possible exception in this group is Yugoslavia, whose workers' councils have not always followed this belt-tightening rule.

External Balance

Closely linked with the maintenance of price stability as a national goal is the achievement of a long-run balance in external accounts. The significance of payments balance as an indication of economic performance depends, for most countries, upon their relative dependence on foreign trade.[27] For the United States and Great Britain, and recently Germany and Japan, the external accounts also depend on their positions as a reserve currency country.[28]

Among the OECD countries, which together account for roughly three-fourths of world trade, the postwar balance-of-payments behavior widely vary. Some members, like Germany and Japan, have usually been surplus countries with strong foreign-exchange reserves and a hard currency. The United States and Great Britain, on the other hand, have experienced persistent deficits.

Among the MICs, the United States is the world's top trading nation, but owing to complex facotrs, it has been singularly unable to bring its external accounts into balance since 1950. Persistent deficits have not only been onerous for the United States, but a major cause of concern in the whole international community because of the leading position of the dollar as a reserve currency (and its convertibility into gold at the fixed price of $35 per ounce up to 1971). Similarly, although foreign trade constitutes a very small portion of U.S. GDP, the U.S. share of world trade is an unusually high 12 percent. Thus, any major imbalance in U.S. external accounts has far-reaching effects on other trading countries.

There are several reasons for continued U.S. deficits. American private business has been investing heavily in foreign production facilities (particularly inside the EEC) as well as in foreign financial assets. American commercial banks have been making substantial loans abroad. The U.S. government has had heavy military and aid commitments all over the world, particularly in Europe and the Far East. Affluent Americans have been travelling abroad in increasing numbers and in more lavish ways. And a large part of U.S. domestic energy consumption—the world's highest per capita—has had to be imported.

Like the United States, Great Britain has for long been a reserve currency country, where part of other countries' reserves are maintained in pound sterling. As in the United States, too, domestic monetary and fiscal policies designed to deal with output fluctuations have often been thwarted by foreign-exchange repercussions. Unlike the United States, however, Great Britain has been heavily dependent on imports of both consumer and capital goods. For these reasons (and in order to offset wartime losses of assets totalling over $20 billion), the pound sterling was twice devalued in 1948 and 1967 and then left floating in the exchange markets after 1972. Nevertheless, between 1960 and 1980, Great Britain had far fewer years of surplus than many years of deficits in its external balance, largely because of its inability to increase its export competitiveness in world markets.

---

27. Among the MICs, for example, exports constitute about 7 percent of GDP in the United States, but over 23 percent for the United Kingdom and 10 percent for Japan. For the Soviet Union and Red China, foreign trade has a smaller share of GDP.

28. A reserve-currency country is one whose money is desired by other countries as a means of storing trade surpluses and international reserves.

In contrast with the United States and Great Britain, Japan provides a success story in international trade and payments. The postwar growth of Japanese exports and imports has been twice the world rate. Japanese external balance has varied both in amount and direction with changes in domestic levels of output and income. Spurred by some overheated domestic economic activities (1957, 1961, 1964, 1967 and 1979), the overall balance of payments recorded a relatively small deficit. In most other years sizable surpluses have been realized. The Japanese success in the trade field can be explained by several factors: modernization of postwar industrial facilities, thus increasing the international competitive strength of Japanese industries; development of superior new technology in transistorized products, optics, and others; abundant, skilled, and relatively cheap labor; continuous aggressive efforts on the part of Japanese exporters to increase sales abroad; net inflow of foreign capital; and an undervalued currency for a long time after the war.

Among the CDEs, only Yugoslavia has significant trade with the non-COMECON nations and is thus subject to balance-of-payments disequilibrium in a real sense. Under its mixture of planned and market operation, Yugoslavia has been singularly vulnerable to balance-of-payments difficulties in recent years. Rapid industrialization without much of an industrial and raw material base, heavy defense expenditures, crop failures, and relatively little access to foreign private capital have put Yugoslav external accounts under persistent stress. The national objective of integration with the world economy has been partly responsible for balance-of-payments vulnerability.[29] For most of the postwar years, Yugoslavia has had significant deficit in its balance of trade, sometimes as high as 50 percent of its total imports. Between 1962 and 1971, moderate deficits also occurred on current accounts, to be followed by further dramatic shortfalls in 1974–75 (mainly owing to a decline in workers' remittances). Despite the post-1975 recovery in the OECD countries that are Yugoslavia's main trading partners, balance-of-payments difficulties have continued unabated. External pressure finally led Yugoslavia to devalue the dinar once again, and to submit to a stabilization program under the supervision of the International Monetary Fund in 1980.

External balance, for the major communist countries like the Soviet Union and Communist China, is not of major significance. Intrabloc trade and foreign transactions with the developing countries usually balance. Occasional surpluses or deficits within the "family" or among "friends" are ordinarily settled in kind with no movement of gold or foreign exchange. The relatively small trade with the West is settled by hard currencies or gold.

Soviet trade with the non-communist countries in recent years has been roughly one-third of the total. Much of the latter trade consists of machinery, equipment, and materials that the Soviet Union needs for its development. In some poor crop years during the 1960s and 1970s wheat was also imported in significant

29. Between 1962 and 1974, the share of exports in GNP rose from 15 percent to nearly 30 percent; that of imports from 18 percent to 28 percent.

amounts. Soviet exports to the West are mostly raw materials and semi-processed items. During 1970–78, Russia had a cumulative trade deficit of some $24 billion, financed mostly by borrowing. Part of Soviet external payments consists of foreign military and economic assistance to more than seventy countries.

China as a rule plans for a balance between exports and imports, as well as between total foreign-exchange receipts and payments. During much of the 1950–72 period, China had a comfortable annual surplus in its trade with the developing non-communist world and an uninterrupted favorable account with Macao and Hong Kong. But trade with OECD countries was in continued deficits; and with the communist bloc, generally in balance. In some poor crop years the large quantities of wheat imports turned the overall balance into a deficit, but in most years China has had a surplus. Deficits and surpluses with non-communist countries are settled in hard currencies (including gold, of which China has a small annual production). Accounts with the communist world are settled by changes in subsequent imports and exports.

In the LDCs, foreign trade is absolutely necessary for both economic growth and a high standard of living. Capital goods have to be imported in order to develop and expand productive capacity and to build up socioeconomic infrastructures. Consumer durables (and even food items) must be brought in to make up deficiencies of domestic production, and exports ought to be increased in order to pay for needed imports.

As a rule, however, goods and services produced in less developed countries (with the exception of raw materials like petroleum) face a protected market in the industrial world, while industrial wares enjoy a virtually limitless demand in the underdeveloped part of the globe. For these reasons, most developing nations are usually faced with chronic and growing deficits in their current external accounts. Of the more than one hundred developing countries in Asia, Africa, and Latin America for which comparative balance-of-payments data are published, only a few major oil-exporting countries have had any appreciable surplus in current accounts during postwar years. Current accounts deficits in the developing countries are usually financed by foreign aid, private long-term investments, foreign loans, and short-term credits, but none of these items has been rising as fast as the countries themselves expect. And the balance-of-payments deficits and foreign debts are on the rise.

Social Welfare

Welfare is an elusive concept. In its ideal sense, it includes a satisfactory measure of consumption, economic security, freedom of choice, and a host of other material and nonmaterial amenities. Because of a number of conceptual and statistical complexities, however, most of these amenities are not quantifiable or internationally comparable. Here we propose to examine only three aspects of consumer welfare: standards of living, socioeconomic security, and individual freedom.

Standards of Living

Living obviously includes much more than mere consumption; it involves leisure, recreation, artistic and cultural enjoyments, and a host of other amenities. Yet even consumption is not easily comparable in different countries because of such factors as differences in climatic requirements for food, clothing, and shelter; cultural and religious habits; and different emphasis on the composition of market baskets. A rough indication of different levels of living is usually obtained by a comparison of per capita GNP or GDP with levels of private consumption.

The per capita GDP may be a fair indication of a country's material well-being and economic strength. That is, if the per capita GDP was possible to measure in physical volumes of goods and services produced or consumed, this yardstick would be by far the easiest means of intercountry comparisons, but the necessity of evaluating different goods and services by a common monetary denominator and, more important, the need to convert different national monies into a comparable currency make the task exceedingly difficult. For this reason, the ranking of countries from richest to poorest may vary depending on market-exchange rates at different times. There are other conceptual and statistical complexities in the comparison of per capitas. The country figures should therefore be interpreted with extreme caution.

The Major Industrial Countries. By World Bank estimates, the U.S. per capita income in 1978 was $9,590 at current prices and prevailing exchange rates. While trailing behind per capita figures for Switzerland, Sweden, and Denmark (as well as some small oil-rich countries in the Persian Gulf), the American level was 2.5 times as much as the Soviet Union's, forty times as high as Communist China's, and fifty times that of India. The relatively lower ranking of the United States—which up to the mid-1970s had the highest living standards in the world—is clearly attributable to the depressed exchange value of the floating U.S. dollar in the world-exchange markets. As indicated before, exchange rates do not accurately measure the real purchasing power of national currencies because, among other things, their fluctuations are often unrelated to their domestic buying power. A more realistic, and perhaps more accurate, measure of per capita income and affluence is offered by a UN International Comparison Project that focuses on actual consumer purchasing power in different countries.[30] By focusing on estimates of how much

30. I. B. Kravis et al, *International Comparisons of Real Product and Purchasing Power* (Baltimore: Johns Hopkins University Press, 1978). World Bank and OECD data based on prevailing exchange values give Britain a 50 or 51 percent ranking compared to the United States. Japan comes out with a 65 to 70 percent rating.

each national currency is worth in terms of purchasing comparable items in other countries (and discarding the notion of exchange rates), this method gives the United States the second highest affluence in the world, second only to the tiny oil-producing Kuwait. By this norm, Britain's per capita GDP was 63.5 percent and Japan's 59.2 percent of the United States' in 1974.

The United Kingdom, once not far behind the United States, has now been overtaken by fourteen major OECD countries. The $5,030 per capita GDP in Britain at current prices and prevailing exchange rates in 1978 was only ahead of New Zealand, Italy and Ireland among MICs. During recent years, the increase in real spending per capita of the British population has been the lowest among industrially advanced nations, despite the fact that the British save proportionally less than most Europeans. British workers also put in less working time during the year than most Europeans (except Germans). The slow growth of the GDP and the diversion of resources into exports through higher sales taxes have been chiefly responsible for the "hard slog."

Japan ranks third in total GDP, behind the United States and the Soviet Union, commanding a figure of $835 billion in 1978, compared to $24 billion in 1955.[31] With the population growing at an unusually low rate of about 1 percent a year, the per capita income and standard of living have also increased to become the highest in Asia, although still behind the United States and many West European countries. The Japanese per capita GDP of $7,280 in 1978 was fourteenth in the world, up from twenty-third in 1960.

The per capita GDP figures, while a good indication of economic success and material progress, are by no means a measure of private consumption or individual level of living. GDP per capita is a simple arithmetic result of dividing the total value of annual goods and services by the existing population. From the standpoint of consumer satisfaction, it masks that portion of GDP used for gross investment and not available for consumption; it fails to show the gaps between incomes of various groups in the economy; and it ignores the nature and composition of goods and services produced (guns or butter). For these reasons, as seen below, while the per capita GDP in country A may be only half that of country B, private consumptions in the two countries may show totally different ratios. This is truer of countries that rely more heavily on the command mechanism than those that take their cues from the market. The need, therefore, is for independent indicators of living standards.

The most common, and perhaps the least controversial, indicators of living standards are those adopted and used by OECD. They include: private consumption per capita; the number of passenger cars, telephones, TV sets, and doctors per 1,000 inhabitants; access to higher education; and infant mortality. Judged by these

---

31. One important reason for this phenomenal economic growth is the Japanese high propensity to save. By saving something over 32 percent of their GNP each year, the Japanese have been by far ahead of all major industrialized countries in this respect—a full 8 percent above frugal Germans and nearly 15 percent ahead of Americans.

indicators, the United States is ahead of the United Kingdom and Japan in the MIC category—and better off than almost all other OECD countries—in every category except infant mortality, where Japan and the Scandinavian countries show a better record. Thanks to its high per capita income, also, more than two-thirds of American families own their homes. More than 25 million individuals own corporate stocks. Individual assets are four times as much as total individual debts. The United States has equally more radios, phonographs, washing and drying machines, refrigerators, dishwashers, freezers, air-conditioners, and other electrical appliances per capita than any nation on earth. In nonmonetary, nonmaterial terms, too, the United States ranks high. In the number of high school diplomas and college degrees conferred, books and magazines published, and other life amenities, the U.S. outranks all other countries.

Among the three countries in our MICs sample, the United Kingdom occupies a middle position between the United States and Japan. British private consumption, at 59 percent, is slightly higher than Japan's 58 percent. Britain is also ahead of Japan in such categories as passenger cars, TV sets, and physicians per 1,000 inhabitants, but it lags in the number of telephones, access to higher education, and infant mortality. (See the next chapter.)

The Centrally Directed Economies. In the late 1970s, Russia had the world's second largest GDP after the United States. In per capita income, however, the Soviet Union still stood far behind the Union States and many Western industrial countries. The Soviet GDP per capita in 1978 was $3700, only better than the figures for Greece, Ireland, Turkey, and Portugal in OECD, and behind those of Czechoslovakia, and East Germany in the Eastern camp.[32] Yugoslavia, with a per capita GDP of $2,380 in 1978 was clearly behind the Soviet Union but far ahead of China, which had an estimated figure of only $230. Other estimates of the Chinese GDP per capita ran as low as $150.

Comparable data of living standards as compiled by the World Bank are available only partly for Yugoslavia among the CDEs. According to published figures, private consumption as a percentage of GDP is only 55 percent. But in terms of the absolute level of goods and services actually consumed, Yugoslavia trails even more behind most Western European countries as well as Japan and the United States. In private automobiles, telephones and TV sets, the OECD figures for Yugoslavia are between 9 percent and 27 percent of the United States; 16 percent and 50 percent of the United Kingdom. And there is also a curious anomaly. While the number of Yugoslav doctors for 1,000 habitants is reportedly higher than six

32. For data regarding Soviet private consumption in the 1960s, see D. W. Bronson and B. S. Severin, "Consumer Welfare," in U.S. Congress, Joint Economic Committee, *Economic Performance and the Military Burden in the Soviet Union* (Washington: GPO, 1970); and their "Recent Trends in Consumption and Disposable Money Income in the U.S.S.R.," in U.S. Congress, Joint Economic Committee, *New Directions in the Soviet Economy* (Washington: GPO, 1966).

OECD countries (including Britain), infant mortality is by far the highest of all (and more than twice that of Britain), reflecting the relatively poor health conditions in the poorer Yugoslav republics.

An assessment of Russia's standard of living can be made by reference to certain details about Soviet private consumption. While the Russian per capita GDP is less than 40 percent of the American level, the same is not true of Russia's private per capita consumption. That is, a larger portion of personal incomes is spent on daily staples, and the average Russian worker must put in far more time on the job than the average U.S. worker in order to buy the same basic items. Soviet daily food still consists of 50 percent starchy materials and absorbs more than half of the family income, but personal services are relatively inexpensive. Rent is still very cheap. In terms of individual ability to obtain a satisfactory level of consumption, an average factory worker in the Soviet Union has to work more than thirty-seven months to earn enough money to buy a small car, as opposed to seven months for an average American. The ratios for a color TV set are 780 hours to 86 hours; for a refrigerator, 168 hours to 47 hours; for a washing machine, 432 hours to 52 hours. An average Russian has to work between two to nine times as much in order to purchase a pound of steak, a half kilogram of sugar, or a dozen eggs. Clothing of much poorer quality costs the Russians four times as much in hours of work as it does in the United States. Only certain items (a loaf of bread, a pound of potatoes, a man's hair cut, a bus ride, some utilities, and rent) cost less in the Soviet Union.

In modern consumer durables, too, the Russian families compare poorly with the Americans, West Europeans, and even some communist nations. Soviet passenger cars are only 1 percent that of the United States. Refrigerators, washing machines, radios, and TV sets are a small fraction of the corresponding units in the United States. In all these categories, the Russian quality does not measure up to U.S. standards. The services expected from many of these items are also limited.

In education, health, culture, and other services, the comparison is more difficult and naturally more controversial. Education at all levels is free for academically qualified Soviet students. Health care is also free for all. Entertainment and cultural events are highly rated and inexpensive. Public transportation is plentiful, reliable, and cheap. Air and rail services are reasonable. Western analysts accept Soviet claims that the Soviet Union has appreciably more doctors and more hospital beds than the United States for the same number of people, more teachers for the same number of high school students, less crowded classrooms for the same type of schools.

It should also be remembered that the Soviet Union's relatively lower standard of living is partly a reflection of traditional low priority given to consumer goods. In the postwar period, less than half of GDP has been earmarked for private consumption.[33] Indeed, substantial improvements in the Soviet consumption level

---

33. See Philip Hanson, *The Consumer in the Soviet Economy* (Evanston: Northwestern University Press, 1969.)

in recent years have been made possible by Soviet economic prowess with seemingly no diminution in military build-up, space exploration and aid to friendly under-developed countries. The characteristic peculiarity of Soviet consumption, however, lies not so much in its low level in relation to Soviet natural wealth and productive capacity as it does in its imbalance between the interminable shortages of certain goods in high demand and surpluses of unwanted items.

China displays the same picture of unbalanced growth witnessed in all communist countries: extraordinary advances in heavy industrialization and marked expansion of public services, accompanied by modest improvements in consumption and level of living. China's living conditions are among the world's lowest. The forty-eight-hour workweek (plus another few hours of political indoctrination) is standard. Leisure is mostly adjunct to labor. But workers and peasants are reportedly adequately fed, clothed, and housed by China's own standards.[34] Medical care is available to all free of charge or at nominal costs. Rent is low, only a fraction of workers' monthly income. Food is adequate, absorbing about 25 to 50 percent of take-home pay, but diet is mostly composed of rice, millet, fish, and vegetables, with fowl and pork as delicacies. There are no beggars in the street, a unique phenomenon in the populated Southeast Asia region. Most people have small savings accounts. Literacy has increased from a mere 10 percent in 1949 to more than 35 percent of the adult population. Health conditions are fast improving. Rationing is limited to a few items in popular demand.[35]

The Less Developed Countries.   An evaluation of standard of living in the developing countries in terms of per capita income is difficult for many reasons. The majority of these countries have a very large nonmonetized and nearly self-sufficient sector where increased food consumption cannot be reflected in comparative incomes and expenditures. In a large number of these countries, economic growth and modernization often favor the small urban population, with the rest of the economy remaining fairly poor over the years. Thus, national averages of consumption or income levels have even more limited significance for comparative purposes in these nations. Despite statistical difficulties, however, two major generalizations can safely be made. First, while LDCs as a whole have a moderately impressive rate of growth of GDP, the growth rate of per capita income has been kept low by the pressure of rising population. Second, the three-quarters of the world's population living in the developing countries generate and consume no more than one-fifth of the world's gross product.

The annual per capita GDP in India in 1978 was still no more than $180. Half of India's population still live on less than $5 a month. Although India has

34. By Western standards, some 35 percent of the urban population live in inadequate housing, with an average of 2.5 square yards of living space per person for some families, and very few houses with toilets or running water.

35. For a survey of recent economic developments in China, see J. S. Prybyla, *The Political Economy of Communist China* (Scranton: Intext, 1970); and *China: A Quarter Century After* (Washington: GPO, 1975).

made genuine efforts to improve the living conditions of its people, and while there is no report of actual famine in normal years, hunger and malnutrition have not been completely wiped out in rural India. The major cause of India's undying poverty is the pressure of population on domestic resources. Other indicators of living standards also reveal India's poverty. Adult literacy rate is only 36 percent; life expectancy, no more than fifty-one years. Although private consumption reaches as high as 70 percent of GDP, per capita energy consumption is only 2 percent of the United States figure and 4 percent of the Soviet Union's. Daily per capita calorie supply is about 90 percent of requirement for health; there is only one physician for 3,620 inhabitants .

Compared to India, Nigeria is much better off, with a per capita GDP of some $560 (in 1978), mostly thanks to increased revenues from petroleum. But life expectancy is lower (forty-eight) and the per capita calorie supply only slightly worse, at 83 percent of requirement. There are nearly 15,800 people for each physician. Part of the reason for Nigeria's poorer food and health conditions may be the much smaller portion of GDP (57 percent) allocated to private consumption.

Brazil has by far the highest per capita GDP of the LDCs in our sample: $1,570. Other indicators also portray Brazil's relative affluence as number ten among all non-oil-producing developing countries. Adult literacy is 76 percent; life expectancy, sixty-two years. Private consumption accounts for some 69 percent of GDP. Energy consumption per capita is three and a half times more than India's. Daily calorie supply equals 107 percent of requirement. There is one doctor for 1,700 inhabitants.

Socioeconomic Security

One of the controversies regarding the performance of an economy is the age-old trade-off between economic security and individual freedom of choice. People generally want to be free in the choice of their work and leisure patterns, type and place of employment, consumption habits, savings plans, and disposition of assets. But they are also vitally interested in the security of their employment and duration of their income and in adequate protection against income losses due to unemployment, illness, disability, old age, or death. As indicated in chapter 3, these two objectives cannot always be obtained simultaneously. As this is an area in which combined quantification is neither easy nor precise, our inquiries will be limited to an examination of each goal separately.

The provision of economic security, long associated with socialist regimes, has now acquired universal acceptance, if not acclaim.[36] There is not a single major country in the world today without a social security program of one kind or another.

36. In the last quarter of the twentieth century all viable national economies are in a sense "welfare states." The differences are in the scope and magnitude of welfare programs. In 1980, for example, more than sixty countries throughout the world had some type of supplementary assistance for the old, the unemployed, the disabled, the sick, and the poor.

An international comparison of social security and welfare systems is exceedingly difficult because of differences in tax schedules, the type of exemptions and deductions, the tax incidence, the extent of compliance, and other factors. A very rough estimate of the scope of social security in each country, however, can be equated with the size of transfer payments by the government out of the public budget. While the size of transfer payments must be judged in the context of the sources (the contributions made by recipients), they still give an indication of the coverage. By this yardstick, the United Kingdom outranks the other two countries in our MICs sample. In the late 1970s, Britain's annual transfer payments accounted for 15.3 percent of its GDP, as compared to 11.6 percent for the United States and 9.2 percent for Japan—although still behind many European nations. In fact, the "cradle to grave" system of social security gives the United Kingdom the highest mark among the MICs in our sample. Total social spending (including income assistance, health and medical programs, and education) reaches as high as 28 percent of British GDP.

The United States occupies a middle position. Total social spending (including income assistance, health and medical program, housing, and education) takes nearly 21 percent of GDP.[37] Due to the enormous number and variety of private charitable organizations, total transfer payments in the U.S. economy must be much larger. In specific terms, however, U.S. transfer payments not only trail Britain's (and most other European countries); they are also indicative of the more limited coverage. For example where the U.S. social security program offers health insurance only to persons over sixty-five or long-term disabled persons, Britain provides medical coverage for persons of all ages. The United States is perhaps the only industrial country that provides child-support payments only to parents who do not work, instead of a general "family allowance" to every family with several children. For most of the U.S. programs, too, a recipient must demonstrate need, while in Europe there is no such means test. At the same time, one should note that U.S. workers pay lower social security taxes, and three-quarters of them are covered by some form of private hospital insurance.

Japanese transfer payments have the weakest redistributive effects of the three countries. Current transfer payments equal only about 9 percent of the GDP, less than one-third of that in Holland and much below Britain and even the United States. By their own admission, qualifications for eligibility and actual benefits under the Japanese social security system are behind other industrial countries. However, a good measure of economic security is provided by large private Japanese firms in the form of "life-time" employment, medical care, pensions, and so forth.

The Soviet Union and the CDEs as a rule provide a comprehensive measure of social and economic security for their citizens, although the absolute amounts of

37. The United States is also the only major industrial country where the social security program itself is totally financed by social security taxes, with no contribution from the general revenues.

benefits in various categories are not usually large by American and West European norms. As was detailed before, sickness, disability, old-age, and survivors' benefits are provided by law for every Soviet citizen. The one difference between CDEs and the West is that unemployment compensation does not exist in the former because they are supposed to always operate at full employment. In both the Soviet Union and Yugoslavia, social spending constitutes about 16 percent of GDP. In both of these countries—and perhaps also in China—the coverage and availability of socioeconomic security compares favorably with the MICs, but the quality of services may not always match.

Socioeconomic security among LDCs is poorest of the three groups, both in quantity and quality. Unemployment compensation is either nonexistent or rudimentary. Pensions are, as a rule, available only to public servants and a small segment of private industrial wage-earners. Health insurance is also limited largely to public employees, although some large industries offer their own private plans. Disability payments and other benefits, too, do not match the coverage either in MICs or CDEs.

Individual Economic Freedoms

Freedom of individual choice in its Western manifestations and free-market implications is not a universal goal. Even among the MICs, it is not always given explicit mention. The primacy of this ideal is generally taken for granted by the free-marketeers. In the CDEs and in a majority of the less developed countries (which put great stock in rapid growth and improvements in living standards), this goal is not usually among the stated national objectives. For these reasons, the significance of comparative performance in this area would primarily apply to the MICs.

Changes in individual economic freedoms obviously are difficult to pin down with statistics. Freedom is not only a reflection of ability to choose among alternatives, but also a function of choices available. A 100 percent freedom in choosing among ten alternatives may not always be better than a 20 percent freedom to choose from among one hundred items. The judgment is even more difficult when comparable international data are unavailable. One possible indicator that may allow some partial comparisons may be the national tax burden. The more heavily a nation is taxed, the less freedom the people may be presumed to have in the disposition of their incomes. But this may be only an indication, and a misleading one at that under different circumstances. For example, people may have near total freedom in the disposition of their incomes between consumption and saving, but little or no freedom in the choice of employment, investment outlays, or professional activity. The conclusions should therefore be drawn with great caution.

Given this caveat, the United States is almost at the very bottom of the list of the most heavily taxed nations. In only one other industrial country—Japan—does the tax burden seem lighter than the United States. According to OECD data for 1977, total public revenues as a share of GDP runs as low as 24.5 percent in Japan and as high as 40.5 percent in Britain—with the U.S. showing a figure of 32 percent.[38] Looked at from a different angle, income and social security taxes together slice away less than 10 percent of the average Japanese factory worker with three dependents. The corresponding figure for the United Kingdom is 26 percent; for the United States, 17 percent.

More important, perhaps, from the standpoint of economic performance, are changes over time in the scope of individual freedoms. Here again, judging by the behavior of the tax burden, both the United States and Great Britain have managed to hold the tax load virtually unchanged in relation to GDP during the 1970s. Japan, however, has outperformed these two countries by holding taxes down more effectively since 1965.

By somewhat less quantifiable but probably more indicative norms, individual dependence on the state and subjugation of individual freedoms to greater state regulations have certainly increased in all these countries in the postwar period. In relative terms, however, the United States still appears to offer greater freedoms of action and opportunities to individuals and private firms than others. The U.S. public sector, in relation to its size and wealth, is still smaller than any major industrialized country. The movement of goods and people within the private sector is least restricted. Public regulation of industry, although intensive and widespread, still trails behind others. Fairly tough antitrust laws, at least in the statutes book, aim at keeping competition healthy and workable. Individuals and private organizations have greater freedom to handle their economic activities and to pursue their own self-interest. Indeed, much of the U.S. economy's major social ills are often attributed to excessive economic freedom on the part of individuals and private groups.

While the performance of the CDEs in the area of individual freedom is not relevant, for reasons mentioned at the outset, a brief glance at the situation in these countries shows that despite some recent progress toward greater economic liberalization, individual economic freedoms have so far received a rather low priority, particularly in China and the Soviet Union. In Russia, which occupies a midposition between China and Yugoslavia, citizens are free to choose their type and place of employment, dispose of their incomes between consumption and saving, and determine the composition of their consumption. Although, the strength and intensity of consumer demand for many goods and services still fail to induce substanial changes in state investment and defense policies, consumers' reluctance to buy unattractive or shoddy goods do influence their further production. Consumers, however, have very little to say about basic priorities in national

38. In the other so-called Western democracies, the 1977 ratios are much higher than the United States. The figure for Austria is 43 percent; for Denmark, nearly 48 percent; for the Netherlands, 54 percent; and for Sweden, almost 61 percent—to mention but a few.

resource allocation or the ex ante composition of national product. Because of the planned nature of jobs, training facilities, and rigid qualifying examinations, even the choice of a career is limited to the state-approved categories.

Restrictions on consumer freedoms among CDEs are severest in China and most relaxed in Yugoslavia. The Chinese Communist party, for example, is reportedly more active in the day-to-day decisions of economic enterprises than either the Soviet or the Yugoslav parties. Furthermore, no link is allowed between enterprise profits and enterprise wages and salaries in China, whereas such connections are prevalent in Russia and routine in Yugoslavia. Finally, China up until now has refrained from allowing relative incomes to encourage movements between jobs; the preference has been for direct job assignments.

Yugoslavia offers a very interesting case in a different way. Annual public expenditures on goods and services in 1977 amounted to only 17.4 percent of GDP, less than the shares in the United States, Great Britain, or Japan. Even the annual public revenue, at 43.1 percent of GDP in 1977, while larger than comparable figures in the three MICs, is still less than such Western European countries as Denmark, Finland, West Germany, Netherlands, Norway, and Sweden. Also, while the share of Yugoslav public consumption in GDP has remained fairly stable between 1966 and 1976, the economic reforms of 1965 have definitely been in the direction of greater enterprise autonomy.

Equity in the Distribution of
Wealth and Income

An expressed goal of almost all nations is to reduce inequities in the distribution of wealth and income through taxes, public outlays, and transfer payments. An important measure of desirable economic performance within this broadly accepted national goal is thus an improvement in distributional equity, i.e., greater equality in wealth and income. Direct country-to-country comparison of equity, however, is most difficult, because comparable data on wealth—or even income—distributions for most countries are hard to come by. Furthermore, any meaningful comparison of income distribution must be net of taxes and transfer payments, for which information is even scantier.

A simple (and, by implication, imperfect) method of income comparison is the percentage of income receivers or households in relation to the percentage of income. In a totally equal income distribution, the lowest or the highest 10 percent of income recipients would each get 10 percent of total national income; the highest or the lowest 20 percent would each get 20 percent of income; and so on. Deviations from this perfectly symmetrical distribution pattern would reflect income inequalities and, by implication, inequities.

The latest World Bank data on the distribution of total disposable household income available for selected countries in the 1970s show a wide variety of inequalities. The figures for the United States (1972), for example, shows that the lowest 20 percent of households received only 4.5 percent of total household income, and the highest 20 percent share about 43 percent.[39] In Britain (1973), the bottom 20 percent of households get 6.3 percent of income; the top 20 percent, nearly 39 percent. For Japan (1969) the corresponding figures are 7.9 percent and 41 percent. The top 20 percent of American households thus receive more than nine times as much income as the bottom 20 percent. The ratio for Japan is nearly six times, and the United Kingdom also about six times.

Among other countries in our study, India (1964–65) had its lowest 20 percent of households receiving 6.7 percent of total income, and the highest 20 percent approximately 49 percent. The most glaring income inequality is attributed to Brazil (1972), where the poorest 20 percent of households receive no more than 2 percent of income, while the richest 20 percent obtain 66.6 percent. Yugoslavia, the only CDE on which data are published for 1973, shows the comparable figures of 6.5 percent and 40 percent respectively. The income ratio of the top 20 percent to the bottom 20 percent in India is almost 7.3, in Yugoslavia, 6.1, and in Brazil, 33.3. An estimated ratio for the Soviet Union (1965) is 6.2.

Further data is even more revealing of the degrees of inequality. In the United States, for example, blacks reportedly earn only 70 percent as much as whites; full-time working women earn only 56 percent as much as men. In terms of physical wealth, the top 20 percent of U.S. households owns 80 percent of all private assets, and the bottom 20 percent owns almost nothing, some of them having debt that exceed their holdings.[40] In Britain, the top 10 percent of the population holds more than 60 percent of the nation's wealth. By these estimates, Britain's wealth appears more unequally distributed than in the United States, but income distribution is less unequal. Existing disparities of income in the Soviet Union, moderate as they are, reflect professional skill, hard work, unpleasant working conditions, and Communist party connections. They are not based on property ownership or large inherited fortunes, the main reasons for income inequalities in the MICs and LDCs.

Western analysts of income distribution in the Soviet Union and Eastern Europe are not unanimous in their assessment of socialist success in the area of income equality. Some flatly believe that the CDEs have done relatively little to reduce economic inequality, and many have not even seriously tried. Others argue that even though the Soviet wage policy has not been guided or constrained by an

39. These pretax figures perhaps slightly exaggerate the gap between the two groups, because they do not include certain benefits in kind, such as food stamps for the poor. On the other hand, some 50 percent of the incomes of the poor are derived from transfer payments, without which the gap would be much wider.

40. L. C. Thurow and R. E. B. Lucas, *The American Distribution of Income: A Structural Problem*, A study for the Joint Economic Committee, Congress of the United States (Washington: GPO, 1972).

egalitarian socialist ideology, income disparities have been reduced as part of the policy of raising national standards of living. In this view, differences in Soviet incomes in 1970 were less than those found in most MICs and less than they had been in 1955,[41] yet it is interesting to note that the concept of need as the basis of income and consumption, the heart of Marx's distribution system, seems to be more seriously observed in the MICs (where the unemployed still get paid) than in the CDEs (where the motto is "He who shall not work, neither shall he eat"). But, then, everybody in the CDEs is guaranteed a job.

Comparable figures for China are not available, but in the opinion of some observers, China has the world's most equal income distribution, because one rarely finds an income differential of more than 4 to 1 there.[42] Since 1956, the sources of property income in the Chinese urban and industrial sectors have been virtually eliminated. While earned income differentials still exist between urban and farm workers, there is much greater emphasis on egalitarianism and spartan life. Equality of social and educational opportunities for the politically faithful are also greater than before, and probably greater than in other communist countries.[43] Outward manifestations of equality, too, are particularly pronounced. University professors and factory workers often wear the same tunic. Factory managers join the rank and file in clean-up jobs in order to show that no job is below anyone's dignity. On the whole, China is probably closest to a classless society than any other major country, communist or otherwise. Yet total equality of income, status, and power is still a distant goal. And there are, reportedly, still a few millionaires in China.

Of equal significance in the measurement of equity are changes over time in income distribution under progressive taxation and transfer payments. In the United States, various studies and analyses have shown that the progressive federal income tax is not a great income leveler. Thus, the richest one-fourth of American households earned some 55.5 percent of total personal income before tax in 1977 and ended up with 53.2 percent after the federal income tax. And this despite the fact that they paid nearly 75 percent of all personal income taxes in that year. Similarly, while the poorest one-fourth had 4.6 percent of pretax and only 5.2 percent of after-tax incomes, they paid less than 0.1 percent of personal income taxes. Taking all those taxes (payroll tax, federal income tax, and state and local taxes of all kinds) into account, the federal tax burden is almost proportional for most

41. See W. D. Connor, *Socialism, Politics and Equality* (New York: Columbia University Press, 1979).

42. See A. McAuley, *Economic Welfare in the Soviet Union* (Madison: University of Wisconsin Press, 1979). A related comparison in terms of pretax income per household shows that in 1970, some 70 percent of U.S. households were below the national average in that year. The figures for the United Kingdom, Japan, and the Soviet Union were 40 percent; but for Yugoslavia it was 15 percent, and for China about 2 percent. See R. L. Carson, *Comparative Economic Systems* (New York: Macmillan, 1973), chapter 6.

43. See Joint Economic Committee, 90th Cong., 1st Sess., *Mainland China in the World Economy* (Washington: GPO, 1967), p. 15.

households. Everyone in the $8,000 to $50,000 categories pay roughly 30 to 32 percent of his income in taxes. The reason is that the mild progressivity of the federal income tax is offset entirely by regressive payroll and other excise taxes. Over the long pull, too, there seem to have been little changes in the overall income distribution. In 1935–1936, for instance, the United States' bottom fifth families got 4.1 percent of income, while the top fifth received 51.7 percent, not very different from the 1972 figure of 4.5 percent for the poorest and 43 percent for the richest.

In Britain, by contrast, the Royal Commission on Income and Wealth has found that the gap between the incomes of the British poor and rich has narrowed dramatically in the postwar period, thanks mostly to steep progressive taxation and generous government benefits. Thus, the top 1 percent of British income receivers, who earned 16.6 percent of total pretax personal income in 1938, had their share clipped to only 5.4 percent in 1976–77; their after-tax share was similarly reduced from 12.17 to a mere 3.5 percent in the same period. In physical affluence, the richest 1 percent, who owned some 55 percent of all personal wealth in 1938, possessed no more than 25 percent in 1976. In the 1966–1976 period, however, welfare measures and public investment in social services did little to change income inequality. By one private estimate, a quarter of the British population still lives in or close to actual poverty.[44]

Income data in our LDCs sample are too scanty to give any fair picture of current income distribution by various classes in each country, much less to reveal any past record. On the whole, extreme income disparities are one of the common characteristics of underdevelopment. The overriding emphasis on growth in the emerging nations also seems to indicate that considerations of equity play a secondary role in ordering national priorities. In some Asian and Latin American nations, the share of the poorest 40 percent of the population in the national economic progress actually declined between 1960 and 1970, whereas the share of richest 5 percent grew considerably.[45]

Even in India, where social justice has been one of the major national goals, there is no evidence of a narrowing of income distribution.[46] Some observers believe

44. For further discussion, see "Britain's Rich and Poor," *The Economist*, 26 February 1966; P. Townsend and N. Bosanquet, eds., *Labour and Equality* (London: Fabian Society, 1972); and J. Pilger, "Thatcherism equals 'Political Iniquity,'" *New York Times*, 18 April 1980.

45. Needless to say, egalitarian progress among individual countries has been varied. In countries that have more or less followed the command model, such as Algeria and Cuba, incomes seem to have been levelled due to reduction of property sources. In others, like Brazil and Mexico, which have given private entrepreneurs greater economic freedoms, egalitarian goals have somewhat suffered. Notable exceptions to this simple generalization have been Taiwan and Israel, which have both achieved greater equality under different regimes.

46. The Indian fiscal system, which gives various states within India some independent tax authority, is blamed for substantial interregional income inequality—unlike the Chinese system, which is marked by greater uniformity in tax effort under which poorer regions get larger federal aid. See *China: A Reassessment of the Economy* (Washington: GPO, 1975).

that rural poverty may actually have increased during the Third Plan, as the percentage of the rural population consuming 25 percent or more below the national standard increased from 35 to 40 percent.[47]

Another indication of economic equity is the percentage of population below the absolute "poverty line."[48] By this criterion, the number of Americans living in actual poverty has decreased dramatically over the last three decades. According to U.S. Census Bureau estimates, there were more than 36 million people below the poverty line in 1964 and only 24.3 million in 1974. The U.S. poor have chiefly been concentrated among the nonwhite, the old, the disabled, the unemployed, the southern farmer, and mothers with no breadwinner in the family.[49] Furthermore, the whole income structure has been steadily moving upward in real terms, so the poor in 1974 are richer than the 1964 poor. At the same time, the number of U.S. millionaires is also on the rise. By last count, there were 520,000 Americans with $1 million dollars or more of net worth as compared to 180,000 in 1972. The rise in the number of millionaires, however, is partly caused by rises in the price levels and not necessarily an indication of reverses in income equality.

More psychologically significant than the differences in the relative and absolute shares of U.S. income is perhaps the absolute differences in certain annual income figures and the huge gap between the well-publicized whims of the rich few and the equally dramatic needs of the poor many. For example, in 1979, while the average annual salary of a U.S. graduating engineer was less than $20,000 and a college professor averaged less than $30,000, some U.S. corporate executives, entertainers, and prize fighters grossed up to 5.1 million in salary and other benefits, and many major league athletes had incomes in the upper six-digit levels.[50]

Glaring income disparities of this sort are not limited to the United States. In Western Europe and some developing countries of Asia and Latin America, similar and probably more eye-catching examples are easy to find. The significance of U.S. poverty is chiefly social and psychological. Even the poorest of the poor Americans are on the average better off by Asian and Latin American standards. What makes U.S. poverty somewhat dramatic is its anachronism in the American context.[51] Whatever shape and form poverty takes is in the United States, it looks much more

47. Wilfred Malenbaum, *Modern India's Economy* (Columbus: Merrill, 1971); see also V. M. Dandekar and M. N. Rath, *Poverty in India* (New Delhi: Ford Foundation, 1970).
48. The poverty line is drawn at about $2,500 annual income for a single person and $5,000 for a nonfarm family of four. The Census Bureau estimates are, however, strongly criticized by those who argue that if all non cash benefits to the poor (food stamps, medicaid, subsidized housing, etc.) were added to individual incomes, the number of Americans below the poverty line would fall to less than 7 million in 1974. See Martin Anderson, *Welfare* (Stanford: The Hoover Institution Press, 1978).
49. R. E. Will, *Poverty in Affluence* (New York: Harcourt Brace, 1970)
50. In some extraordinary cases, the size of individual wealth verges on the incredible. During the stock market declines of April 22 and 23, 1970 a Texas billionaire reportedly lost $600 million in two days as his 81 percent share of an electronic servicing firm lost 60 points.
51. For an interesting view of the American affluent, see G. G. Kirstein, *The Rich: Are they Different?* (Boston: Houghton Mifflin, 1968).

appalling because its eradication seems so easy in the light of American overall affluence.

International comparison of absolute poverty is difficult because of the paucity of data. Among the MICs, the percentage of population below the poverty line (defined as less than 66 percent of per capita disposable income for a one person household) is 12 percent in the Unites States and 16 percent in France. The figure for Britain is about 8 percent. For most of the LDCs, on the other hand, mass poverty is the rule rather than the exception. Income disparities are not only widening among the LDCs themselves, and between them and the MICs, but also within many countries. Despite the noteworthy economic progress achieved in the postwar period, some 800 to 1,000 million LDC people still remain in "absolute poverty." In the three countries in our LDCs sample, the existence of poverty is particularly striking in Brazil. Despite a per capita GDP eight times larger than the average for the low-income countries, and higher even than the average for the middle-income LDCs, some observers believe that 40 percent of Brazilian families are absolutely poor.[52]

Overall Performance: A Composite Index?

As can be surmised from the foregoing discussions, no country in our selection (for that matter, none in the world) has so far been able to achieve total success in all of its national economic goals. Relative progress on one front has usually been accompanied by stagnation or setbacks on others. Front runners in growth and full employment (Japan, Brazil, and the Soviet Union) have not been equally successful in raising consumer welfare, reducing income inequality, or keeping price stability. Those who have avoided high inflation and maintained reasonable growth (the United States) have suffered from unacceptable rates of unemployment and balance-of-payments deficits. Those who have achieved relative income equality (China) have suffered from a low standard of living and restrictions on personal freedoms. Some, like the United Kingdom, have been uniquely laggard in achieving most of their objectives. And the same mixed results go for the rest.

Relatively good economic performance has, in turn, been subject to a number of noneconomic criticisms. U.S. philosophical critics from the right, the left, and the middle have been pointing their fingers at false deities that are supposedly devouring traditional American values. Conservatives point to the excessive paternalism of big governments, to the weakening of faith in individual initiative and self-reliance, to the breakdown of the family as a constructive

---

52. Other estimates indicate that about a third of Brazil lives near the subsistence level, while infant mortality, malnutrition, and income inequality are becoming more severe. See W. H. Overholt, ed., *The Future of Brazil* (Boulder: Westview Press, 1978).

institution; to the permissiveness of social behavior, to the erosion of proverbial American efficiency. The left finds the United States far from being "the last best hope on earth," as Lincoln believed it to be. Critics point to the dichotomy between quantity and quality of life; between "accommodation" and "ideal."[53] The moderates view with alarm the excessive reliance on mechanical gadgetry, the "manipulated" conformity of thoughts and actions, the emphasis on the pursuit of wealth even to the detriment of health and happiness. They point to the almost irreconcilable clash between enormous national defense expenditures and needed appropriations for combating domestic social ills or enhancing the quality of education, artistic endeavors, research, and development.[54]

Japan has been a remarkably good economic performer, but in terms of the quality of life, the story is quite different. Despite its third highest GDP in the world, Japan lacks many modern life amenities and is beset by many social ills. Air pollution is one of the worst in the world. There is high population density, traffic congestion, housing shortage, lack of piped water and sewerage facilities for more than half of urban homes, poor roads, and environmental noise. Public services are inadequate. Water pollution is alarming. The government's export drive has often resulted in forcing the Japanese to pay higher prices for Japanese goods at home than abroad. The average work week is six days, forty-eight hours. Japan may be "number one" in economic and technological progress, but in terms of living comfort, it is not.

The Soviet Union has been still another overachiever in modern science and technology, but the inefficiency of Soviet production is reflected in the failure to narrow the gap between Soviet and Western standards of living despite Soviet endowments with rich natural resources, a young and educated labor force, and almost cost-free adoption of Western technology. Although the Soviet Union has only 20 percent more population than the United States, its civilian labor force is 35 percent larger. While still about 25 million Russians are engaged in farming, the comparable figure for the United States is around 3 million. The time involved in the design, construction, and utilization of Soviet plants is by their own admission much longer than in the West. According to some Western estimates, an average Soviet worker produces only half as much as his American counterpart, and a Russian also evidently suffers from many familiar social ills.

Soviet leaders have often publicly complained about lagging growth rates in many fields of activity, about workers' lack of interest in their jobs, about shirking responsibility and breakdown of discipline in factories, about absenteeism and alcoholism. From other articles and studies published in the Soviet Union itself, it also appears that rapid growth and notable improvement in the living conditions of the Russian people have been accompanied by damages to the environment, by air

53. See R. Segal, *The Americans: A Conflict of Creed and Reality* (New York: Viking, 1969).

54. See Andrew Hacker, *The End of the American Era* (New York: Atheneum, 1971).

and water pollution and deforestation, by parking problems and heavy traffic, (as "all roads lead to Moscow"), and by inadequate service facilities.[55]

The shortage of self-service department stores, the necessity of multiple-store shopping for daily necessities, the limited number of properly packaged goods, supply irregularities, and poor store layouts are responsible for a great deal of time lost by Soviet citizens on their daily errands. According to some estimates, Soviets waste about 30 billion hours a year—the equivalent of 15 million men-years of work, or 70 percent of their leisure time—waiting in long lines for service, in shop-to-shop travel, and in the extra time it takes to purchase an article.

Great Britain, unlike the three foregoing examples, has been an under-achiever in the economic area. It has been plagued by high inflation, high unemployment, balance-of-payments deficits, slow growth, and declining standard of living. And yet the British seem to feel that their relatively low material prosperity is somehow compensated for by a richer quality of life: comparative social peace, political stability, economic security, and individual freedoms. They often point with pride to the fact that most people in the world still find England a good place to live.

Owing to imperfections and distortions embodied in the measurement of economic performance by the conventional criteria outlined above, many socioeconomic analysts have been at work for years trying to find a comparable index of the "quality of life" instead of a mere quantity of goods and services. Professors Nordhaus and Tobin of Yale, for example, have suggested a new concept of "net economic welfare." In their scheme, nonmaterial "disamenities" (social costs of production) are subtracted from the total (private) value of goods and services. In turn, other items of value, such as imputed worth of housewives' services, are added to GDP. The algebraic sum of these adjustments would produce the NEW.

A number of other social indicators have also been suggested for rating countries on a "qualitative" scale. One such composite index combines several positive and negative factors into comparable ratios. The positive factors include early marriage (as a sign of a healthy and prosperous society), number of doctors per population, ratio of cars to people, proportion of students in higher education, number of TVs per population, number of dwellings with bath, ratio of telephones to people, circulation of daily newspapers, and, finally, GDP growth. On the minus side, there are such undesirable factors as population density, incidence of suicides, death from road accidents, murders, and infant mortality. Each country's score is its percentage above or below the average for all countries. A zero mark means that attractive and unattractive features exactly match and balance each other out. A plus mark means a preponderance of attractive features; a minus, the reverse. On this basis, Canada was given the highest score of +301, followed by Sweden at +281;

---

55. Ironically enough, while the strength of the profit motive in the West is usually blamed for decay and erosion of the environment, it is the weakness of the profit motive (disregard for efficiency) that receives the blame in the Soviet Union.

United States, +256; Australia, +198; and United Kingdom, +74. By contrast, Belgium has received the worst score of −269; Italy, −169, Spain, −150; Czechoslovakia, −116, France, −60; and Japan, −32. However, if one were to add such factors as the divorce rate (either as a negative indicator of social tension or a positive sign of a liberal society), the outcome would be vastly different. The United States would gain the lead over all major countries if divorce is a positive indicator, and would fall at the bottom of the positive scale if broken marriages are considered a negative factor. Other marked variations would result if indicators like taxes, calorie intakes, mean temperatures, size of family, legality of abortion, and so on were taken into account.[56]

A private Japanese bank has come up with another series of indicators from which a "happiness index" can be compiled. These indicators include six categories—personal satisfaction, social harmony, working conditions, safety and welfare, absence of irritation, and life worth living—made up from some thirty-three items (comprising such diverse factors as mains water supply, public parks, nursery schools, wages, working hours, leisure facilities, drug addiction, industrial injuries, and suicides). On the basis of these indicators, the United States scores highest with 255; followed by Britain, with 215; Germany, with 190; France, with 185; and Japan, with 100.[57]

Suggestions for Additional Readings

BARKLEY, P. W. *Economic Growth and Environmental Decay.* New York: Harcourt Brace, 1972.

CHEN, E. K. Y. *Hyper-Growth in Asian Economies.* London: Macmillan, 1979.

DE GRAMONT, S. "There are No Superior Societies." *New York Times Magazine.* 28 January 1968.

EHRENREICH, B. AND J. *The American Health Empire: Power, Profits and Politics.* New York: Random House, 1971.

FOXLEY, A. *Income Distribution in Latin America.* Cambridge: Cambridge University Press, 1976.

GALBRAITH, J. K. *The Nature of Mass Poverty.* Cambridge: Harvard University Press, 1979.

GEIGER, T. *Welfare and Efficiency.* Washington: National Planning Association, 1978.

HAY, J. *In Defense of Nature.* Boston: Atlantic-Little, Brown, 1969.

56. For the explanation of the index, method of computation, and the list of countries compared, see "Where the Grass is Greener" and "More Green Grass," *The Economist,* 25 December 1971 and 22 January 1972.

57. See "A Yen for Happiness," *The Economist,* 1 April 1972.

KRISTOL, I. "Taxes, Poverty, and Equality." *The Public Interest*, Fall 1974.

MCCONNELL, C. R. "Social Imbalance: Where Do we Stand?" *Quarterly Review of Business and Economics*, May 1961.

MUNNELL, A. H. *The Future of Social Security*. Washington: The Brookings Institution, 1977.

PASSELL, P., AND L. ROSS. *The Retreat from Riches: Affluence and its Enemies*. New York: Viking Press, 1973.

RICHMAN, B. M. *Soviet Management with Significant American Comparisons*. Englewood Cliffs: Prentice-Hall, 1965.

STEINER, G. Y. *The State of Welfare* Washington: The Brookings Institution, 1971.

TUCKMAN, H. P. *The Economics of the Rich*. New York: Random House, 1973.

Epilogue

No ECONOMIC SYSTEM is perfect. None can be perfect. The dilemma of the competing systems is that none has been able to achieve the ideals of individual freedoms, economic growth, and productive efficiency without jeopardizing the goals of price stability, job security, and income equity. This has been true of the performance of the nine countries in our sample. The accompanying table summarizes individual country performance in six major national objectives. As can be readily seen, none of the countries under discussion has been particularly successful in achieving *all* of its goals unquestionably better than others, either in its own group or in the global sample. Nor does any other country in the world in any ideological camp have a better *overall* record.

The unprecedented occurrence, at present, of common economic woes—high inflation, high unemployment, sluggish productivity, and environmental deterioration—is casting profound doubts on the ability of *any* of the competing economic systems to provide answers. Western analysts of different persuasions grudgingly admit that the acclaimed vitality, flexibility, resilience, and efficiency of free enterprise capitalism in dealing with growth and prosperity are now badly weakened, rigidified and eroded. While not being nearly so candid, the leaders of the market-directed economies are also hard-pressed to explain their economic problems—particularly because they are supposed to be immune to them. Slow economic growth, repressed inflation, sizeable underemployment and supply shortages are among these difficulties. No system, it seems, is capable of delivering what is expected of it today.

The episodic and inconclusive performance of the countries in the MIC group versus the CEDs—and of both these groups vis-à-vis the LDCs—brings us back to the main theme of chapter 1: the role of isms and ideologies in solving modern-day economic problems. We began that chapter with the hypothesis that no ideology or ism has the corner on economic growth, efficiency, or equity; that none holds the secret to full employment, price stability, and environmental sanity. Our discussions in subsequent chapters, culminating in an overall evaluation, showed the plausibility, if not indeed the validity, of that hypothesis.

In the light of our limited and admittedly still tentative findings, the intriguing question that inevitably arises is: What is the exact role of ideology in comparative economics?

Relative Economic Performance, Selected Countries

	MICs		
	USA	UK	Japan
Economic Growth			
Average annual rate, 1970–78	3	2.1	5
GNP per capita, average, 1960–77	2.4	2.1	7.6
Efficiency			
Annual growth of labor productivity 1974–78	0.1	0.8	3.2
Unemployment			
Percent of labor force: annual average 1970–78, minimum and maximum	4.9–8.5	2.9–6.2	1.2–2.3
Inflation			
Consumer prices: average annual increase 1970–78	6.8	14.1	9.6
Standards of Living (latest available data)			
Passenger cars per 1000	505	255	163
Telephones per 1000	718	415	408
Television sets per 1000	571	324	235
Doctors per 1000	1.6	1.3	1.2
Adult literacy (percent of total)	99	99	99
Daily calories intake (percent of requirement)	135	132	126
Equity			
Percentage share of household income:			
Lowest 20 percent	4.5	6.3	7.9
Highest 20 percent	42.8	38.8	41.0
	(1972)	(1973)	(1969)

Sources: For the MICs: World Bank and OECD publications.
For LDCs and CDEs: World Bank, *U.N. Statistical Yearbook,*and
U.S. Statistical Abstract.

CDEs			LDCs		
USSR	China	Yugoslavia	Brazil	India	Nigeria
5.3	6	5.6	9.2	3.7	6.2
4.3	3.7	5.4	4.9	1.4	3.6
. . .	. . .	2.2	. . .	. . .	. . .
. . .	. . .	6.7–10.4	. . .	. . .	. . .
. . .	. . .	17.3	30.3	8.2	18.2
. . .	. . .	80	. . .	7.2	. . .
7	. . .	71	0.9	. . .	0.2
208	1	161	100	14	2
3.3	. . .	1.4	0.6	0.3	0.06
99	. . .	85	76	36	15
135	105	136	107	91	83
. . .	. . .	6.5	2.0	6.7	. . .
. . .	. . .	40.0	66.6	48.9	. . .
		(1973)	(1972)	(1965)	

The Significance of Ideology

In general, no economic system can evolve or be established in an ideological vacuum. Part of any economic system—its socioeconomic objectives—must, by its very nature, reflect an ideology or way of life. But beyond this simple truism, the relationship between political ideology and economic performance is most nebulous. This study has tried to combine "ideology" (national objectives) with the nature of decision making (the choice of mechanism) into a general comparative approach. The choice of objectives and the selection of mechanisms has been shown to be systemically independent of each other. We have specifically seen that the same cluster of objectives among nine countries in different ideological camps has indeed been obtained by a different combination of economic institutions and techniques.

In the face of these stark realities, one can hardly resist the temptation of accepting the fallacy of the false alternative; that is, to conclude that the similarity among ideologically rival nations of many goals, institutions, and techniques must mean that the era of ideological differentiations has passed. Indeed, a number of academic economists, political theorists, and business leaders on both sides of the ideological divide have been supporters of this "end of ideology" thesis. They argue that modern industrial societies have for some time been heading toward politicoeconomic neutralism.[1]

Fortunately for the true believer, however, there is a strong rebuttal to this thesis.[2] Some analysts, for example, argue that the outright repudiation of private property at the Twenty-first Congress of the Communist party of the U.S.S.R., and the emphasis placed on the "absolute superiority" of central planning over the market, are prima facie evidence of a stronger ideological commitment by the Soviet Union and other socialist countries to the Marxist doctrine. Although this particular controversy focuses on ideology, and is not so much concerned with economic systems as such, its implications are of interest here.

Those who believe in the decline of ideology generally interpret the term to mean a comprehensive system of beliefs, orientations, and actions that offers solutions to all problems of human existence and begs almost no question. The dissenters, on the other hand, consider ideology to mean only an "attitude structure," which is secular, culture-bound, institutionalized, and imbued with moral and normative content, but without a "world view" of life and society.[3] In this

1. See, for example, Edward Shils, "The End of Ideology?" *Encounter*, November, 1955; Daniel Bell, *The End of Ideology* (New York: Collier Books, 1961); Raymond Aron, *The Opium of the Intellectuals* (New York: Greenwood House, 1962); S. M. Lipset, *Political Man* (Garden City: Doubleday Anchor Books, 1963). See also "Capitalism: Is It Working?", *Time*, 21 April, 1980.

2. See, for example, Joseph LaPalombara, "Decline of Ideology: A Dissent and an Interpretation," *American Political Science Review*, March 1966.

3. For an illuminating discussion of this and other concepts of ideology, see J. B. Christopher, "Consensus and Cleavage in British Political Ideology," *American Political Science Review* (September 1965.)

view, an ideology may or may not be dogmatic; it may or may not be rational or even believed by all of its supporters. There is also a similar view, according to which people may subscribe to certain abstract ioeologies while seeking to achieve their ideals by concrete, pragmatic means.[4]

Needless to say, if ideology is so defined to encompass *any* particular set of values, policies, programs and practices, then *every* viable nation-state has, almost by definition, an ideology in terms of its national objectives, aspirations, and program of action. By contrast, the ideologies that offer a comprehensive system of beliefs must be regarded as a matter of faith, as are all religions—no matter how much they may claim scientific objectivity. In this study, we have questioned the validity of the abstract ideologies that attempt to present mutually exclusive orientations, institutions, and techniques. We have found them to be only intellectually (and perhaps historically) significant.

What About a Convergence?

The markedly similar responses by modern industrial states in recent years to the challenges of popular expectations, technological innovations, and urban life have led some political economists to another controversial conclusion: an eventual *convergence* of rival politicoeconomic systems.[5] This convergence is supposed to reflect a mixture of the market and command mechanisms toward which capitalism and communism are supposed to approach.

The convergence hypothesis is based partly on the biological phenomenon of gradual assimilation among animals of unrelated lineages as they become accustomed to similar ways of life. It is also based partly on the readily observable pace of worldwide industrialization and urban development under which the imperatives of modern technology lead to certain institutional uniformities in individual attitudes, socioeconomic challenges, and national priorities—uniformities that transcend separatist ideologies.[6]

The arguments in support of the convergence hypothesis take their cue from certain faint aspects of market reorientation in the Soviet Union and China, as well as Yugoslavia's shift from central planning to a socialist market economy. These arguments also point out certain tendencies in many developing economies, and some industrial nations, toward various forms of national planning. A most

4. Cf. N. S. Preston, *Politics, Economics and Power* (New York: Macmillan, 1967), pp. 220–226.

5. The proponents of the convergence hypothesis are not limited to economists. Political pundits (Walter Lippmann and George Kennan), party theoreticians (Norman Thomas), and historians (Arnold Toynbee) also seem to have leaned toward this hypothesis.

6. See J. R. Millar, "On the Merits of the Convergence Hypothesis," *Journal of Economic Ideas*, March 1968; and J. S. Prybyla, "The Convergence of Western and Economic Systems," *The Russian Review*, January 1964.

pertinent "pattern" of convergence is presented by Professor Jan Tinbergen. Tinbergen's thesis is that every society ought to be able to find, within its resource endowment and technological know-how, a social structure that can maximize its welfare. An optimum socioeconomic order for welfare maximization is a mixture of public and private enterprise toward which all welfare maximizers are bound to gravitate. As evidence of his basic thesis in the CDEs, he cites new socialist wage policies based partly on productivity; the role of prices and costs in some aspects of resource allocation; greater emphasis on consumers' preferences; and a trend toward increased foreign trade—all major deviations from original communist dogmas. In the MICs, he points to the increasing size of the public sector; to rising taxes and welfare subsidies; to limitations imposed on free competition and market forces; to increasing attentions paid to centralized guidelines and wage and price control; and to deliberate economic stimulation as indications of movements toward a somewhat "managed" system.[7]

John K. Galbraith also detects some convergent tendencies toward a similar design for organization and planning among industrial societies with different ideological makeups. To Professor Galbraith, modern large-scale production under complex and sophisticated technology leads to an elaborate organization requiring careful planning. Large-scale organization also demands autonomy. Thus, technological progress in the Soviet Union is bound to increase freedom of inquiry, action, and organization. In the United States, on the other hand, large-scale industrialization is bound to override the market and consumers' sovereignty.[8]

The gist of the convergence hypothesis, in short, is that the imperatives of technological progress, industrialization, urbanization, increased international contacts, and affluence will tend to have an assimilating impact on national objectives, socioeconomic institutions, and management techniques of all industrial societies. Yugoslavia is generally regarded as an explicit symbol of such an ultimate convergence of market and command economies. Among the noncommitted developing nations, such as India, one also notes tendencies toward policies designed to combine the best elements of the two systems. The high esteem held for economic planning and the growing size of state ownership and operation in basic industries, alongside the encouragment given to private investment and enterprise, are considered manifestations of this desire for an eclectic management of the economy.

The dissenters from this hypothesis are not few, nor are they limited to one side. Russian leaders, who evidently correlate the emergence of this thesis with the submergence of communist ideology, consider the hybridization of their system with capitalism as sheer capitalist propaganda and a pure heresy. The Soviet

7. Jan Tinbergen, "Do Communist and Free Economies Show a Converging Pattern?" *Soviet Studies*, April 1961, pp. 333–41, and H. Limmemann et al., *Convergence of Economic Systems in East and West* (Rotterdam: Netherlands Economic Institute, 1965).

8. J. K. Galbraith, *The New Industrial State* (Boston: Houghton Mifflin, 1971). For a similar view regarding the influence of technology, see Jaques Ellul, *The Technological Society* (New York: Vintage Books, 1967).

denunciation of the convergence thesis is based on the contention that the basic gaps between capitalism and socialism (Soviet style) are so wide in such key elements as the nature of political ideologies, the role of private property, and the function of profit that no such rapprochement would be possible. Soviet goals, it is contended, favor economic development and interests of "the people," not the selfish interests of "capitalists."[9]

There are also serious doubts in the Western camp regarding an ultimate synthesis of the two systems in the overall levels of advanced technology, higher consumption, parallel scientific achievements, reduction of ideological tension and suspicion, and the expanding role of the government in the economy. There is not as yet a clear-cut trend, and there are formidable basic differences between the two systems with regard, for example, to the place of the individual in society and the nature of the state power.

Other Western social scientists believe that while certain common cultural values and traits may accompany the rise of industrialism among different systems, political differences will remain strong. Economic growth does not necessarily entail political uniformity or tolerance; economic and political changes may in fact precede or succeed each other in influence. Technical specialization among managerial groups in the Soviet Union is not the same thing as Western social pluralism. In short, each political system may use similar economic institutions and techniques, and yet define its own form of government intervention in the economy.[10]

Expectations, Response, and Efficiency: Some Basic Links?

The nature and scope of government intervention in the economy—the "collective involvement"—depends upon a variety of economic and noneconomic factors, such as commitment to a particular ideology, concentration of private economic power, stage of technological advancement, urbanization, range and frequency of economic fluctuations, inequalities of wealth and income, and the pressures of organized vested interests.

The manifestation of collective involvement—indirectly through monetary, fiscal, or incomes policies or directly by public controls, planning, or public enterprise—may thus be categorized as *induced*, or responsive to the people's unavoidable dependence on the community; *contrived*, or imposed from the top without corresponding dependence; or a combination of the two.

The induced involvement resulting from dependence is characteristic of the MICs, where increased industrialization and urbanization, frequent economic ups

9. See L. Leontiev, "Myth About Rapprochement of the Two Systems," in J. S. Prybyla, ed., *Comparative Economic Systems* (New York: Appleton-Century-Crofts, 1969).
10. Cf. B. Ward, *Nationalism and Ideology* (New York: Norton, 1966).

and downs, and international financial interdependence have placed the individual at the mercy of the government. In these highly developed industrial and urban economies of the Western world, despite a history of orientation toward individualism and free enterprise, substantial collective involvement is largely conditioned by the sheer necessity of "modernism." There seems to be a tacit willingness on the part of the majority, as manifested in periodic elections, to sacrifice a certain degree of individual freedom in the hope of obtaining larger benefits from economic growth, job security, and higher standards of living.

The induced involvement resulting from dependence is mostly (but not exclusively) a characteristic of the market-oriented economies. The steady rise of government involvement in Western economies over the past half century is traceable to diverse factors increasingly favoring consumption, security and leisure over parsimony, self-reliance and hard work. The origin of this "cultural revolution" probably goes back to the Great Depression and the popularity of the so-called "stagnation thesis" according to which Western free enterprise countries were running out of new frontiers, and facing a prolonged period of slow growth and high unemployment. The widespread and persistent fear of depressions in the United States and Europe during the 1930s provided the right psychological climate for wholesale embracing of Keynes' accommodating philosophical doctrine of insufficient demand, and the seemingly easy anti-depression remedy offered by state intervention.

Real and imagined fear of protracted depressions due to insufficient market demand has thus served as the turning point in the basic economic policy in the United States and Western Europe. National attention has shifted from expanding productive capacity to stimulating demand, and to promoting a series of economic stabilizers that could guarantee a recession-proof economy. Advertising has been allowed to encourage limitless consumption. Built-in obsolescence has been tolerated as a disguised blessing. State subsidies to the poor have gained greater economic rationale, as have a whole cluster of welfare payments to the needy. Similarly, conviction in the virtue of the equality of opportunity has been gradually redefined to encompass equality of achievement. The popular description of the last quarter of the twentieth century as "the age of anxiety" indicates greater life uncertainty under the threat of a nuclear war, existential consumerism, and hedonism.

Big Power rivalry over the "hearts and minds" of their own people as well as those of the emerging third world nations fit well into this new cultural revolution. The Eastern bloc has referred to its early successes with economic planning as the proof of efficacy of state direction and management. The West in turn has boasted of its higher material standards of living and consumption as the sure indication of the road to economic progress. Increased cross-cultural contacts and more efficient communications have also had significant effects on raising consumption propensities. The so-called "Mediterranean spirit" has gradually changed the American puritanical attitude toward work and leisure. America's push for "democratization" in Japan, Germany and the friendly third world countries, in turn, has encouraged greater participation in politics and, by implication, greater expectations from elected governments. As the developed and developing nations have tried to meet the challenges of rising expectations under various banners of liberalism, welfarism, socialism or communism, a philosophical shift in value has gradually transferred a good part of individual responsibility to the state and society.

Collective involvement among MICs is also induced by the actions and reactions of influential pressure groups. When trade-union power, for example, is allowed to expand in order to counterbalance the bargaining position of business giants, the power of central authority is also enhanced to match the powers of large business enterprises and organized labor groups.

Among the nonindustrial emerging nations with a history of autocracy, colonialism, or tribal rule, the scope of collective involvement may also be induced but for a different reason: rising expectations. In some of the LDCs, the basically agricultural, nonmonetized, technologically backward nature of production and exchange is not such as to allow for a greater degree of individual self-reliance, freedom, and initiative. State intervention, regimentation, and paternalism is thus called for not necessarily as a matter of technoeconomic necessity, but as a means of achieving deliberately promoted sociopolitical objectives. Given the paucity of natural, technological, and human resources in most of these countries, the achievement of economic viability and national identity would often call for stricter care in resource allocation and certain measures of central planning. In the absence of a strong entrepreneurial class, the implementation of national economic plans would thus often necessitate direct government initiative and action. State intervention occurs not only to provide the necessary socioeconomic infrastructures, but also for laying down a strategic industrial base, along with technical assistance and financial credit.

In a substantial number of nations among the LDCs and the CDEs, however, collective involvement may not be induced, but *contrived*—the result of political decision by the elite. Among the LDCs, a group of clever and ambitious leaders often channel pent-up frustrations and popular aspirations into dreams of prosperity and grandeur through promises of state intervention and direction. The more ambitious the national aspirations, the poorer the country, the heavier the population pressure, the stronger the feelings of frustration, and the cleverer the ideological message, the more extensive would be the scope of state ownership, enterprise, and controls. The ruling elite in many of these countries tries to mobilize meager national resources and capabilities in the service of national progress. Whether rightly or wrongly, this minority is often convinced that national development—if not, indeed, the nation's survival—depends on the state taking an active, far-reaching, and well-planned role in channeling development forces into proper paths. The governing elite usually shows itself to be *for* the people; it frequently claims to be *of* the people: and it tries to justify a government that is not necessarily *by* the people, but working in their interest.

In the Soviet Union and some of the relatively more advanced countries among the CDEs, the state's omnipresence is of a third variety. It is largely due to the pressure of ideological indoctrination, and partly a result of urban-industrial exigency. That is, in addition to the ideological primacy of socialist goals, such other factors as rivalry with the West, the urge for greater national prestige, the need for Western technology, and fear of war may all call for increased state intervention and direction.

As a general proposition, a nation's collective involvement may, therefore, reflect any number of different combinations of the key variables discussed above. That is, it may be induced, limited in scope, and fairly efficiently run. Or it may be contrived, unnecessarily big, and badly managed. Each case has to be considered separately and on its own merits. Empirically, however, some basic links can be observed between popular expectations, individual freedoms, and economic efficiency. Collective involvement may be regarded as a positive function of the individuals' dependence on the community. That is, the more the people are dependent upon the society for employment, social security, or welfare, the greater would be their expectations from the state, and the larger would be the government's response, particularly in democratically-run countries. Individual expectations, in turn, are a negative function of desire for direction. That is, the more the people expect from the state to help them in the areas of employment, social security, and welfare, the less they might have to insist on their individual freedoms in the marketplace. Reduction in individual freedoms and initiatives, in their turn, would affect efficiency. Efficiency is frequently a negative function of oversized bureaucracy. That is, the more intricate, complex, and bureaucratized an economy, the less efficient it becomes. At the ultimate extreme, to attempt total state control is to court complete economic disaster.

Toward Greater Pragmatism?

What seems fairly incontestable is that almost all modern complex industrial societies, regardless of their declared politicoeconomic ideologies, are in varying degrees tutelary societies where individual freedoms are necessarily circumscribed by dependence on the community, and the pressure of expectations presents exacting demands for higher economic efficiency. Thus, a tendency toward pragmatism can be detected among them all. This tendency, however, may be neither teleological nor bound toward ideological convergence. It focuses on the likelihood of a long-term trend toward economic rationalism and away from the dead weight of ideological dogmas. It also points to an equally probable rise of demand for collective action on the part of a rapidly rising and gradually democratizing population destined for urban industrial living. To interpret this movement toward similar challenges and similar responses as an ideological rapprochement may thus continue to be too bitter a pill for some ideologues to swallow, and too hard a nut for certain nationalists to crack.[11]

11. Professor Evesy Lieberman's frantic denials of any connection between the Soviet Union's economic reforms of the 1960s and a drift toward capitalism are no less valid

Whether or not the trend toward pragmatic, nonideological solutions to basic economic problems will continue in the years to come is only conjectural at this point. From past indications, it seems that pragmatism will continue to serve as a criterion for judging policy stances under different political banners. This pragmatic attitude exists more or less among all political entities with an instinct for survival. It also manifests itself in the government's increasing acceptance of its social responsibility. In this pragmatic approach, the issues are essentially the same: How much of the responsibility for the happiness, prosperity, and security of the individual is to be borne by society? And how is this responsibility to be met at the lowest social cost?

The answers are not always clear, easy, or painless. The virtues of individual freedom, self-respect, self-responsibility, self-reliance and self-improvement are often counterweighed by imperatives of job security, equality of opportunity, income equity, and material prosperity. Humankind has not found the golden rule as yet—if, in fact, there is one.

Chances are that nations will continue in their experimentation with different combinations of solutions discussed in previous chapters, moving back and forth between command and the market. For the most part, the growing deficiencies and social disamenities of unbridled competition (income inequities, discriminations, abuses of economic power, environmental neglect, and waste) would push peoples and politicians toward greater state intervention, regulation, control, and an ever expanding bureaucracy. An overstretched and overly centralized bureaucracy, in turn, would gradually beget decay. The more monolithic it turns, the more decadent it becomes. At the end, few bureaucracies can escape the erosions of managerial arrogance and administrative self-righteousness. The waste, inefficiencies, and weaknesses of state controls which might have been overlooked or tolerated would gradually become exploitative and overbearing. The setting for the return to a saner economic policy would sooner or later emerge. But as the needs and aspirations of the majority—and the viability of the environment—become neglected once again, the pendulum will start to swing back, and the cycle will repeat itself.

What our comparative analysis has shown is that success in overall economic performance—to the extent that it may be traceable to any given set of factors in state-society relations—is ideologically neutral. That is, a country can make headways in achieving some of its goals most of the time, or most of its objectives some of the time, if it chooses appropriate means based on its own resource base, traditional values, and socioeconomic institutions. However, as resource endowments, ideological orientations, and social and economic institutions vary among nations, there may be no single secret way to economic salvation or prosperity.

---

than Professor Paul Samuelson's insistence that the provision of desirable public services in the United States is not a road to serfdom.

Index